TAX LAW:
AN INTRODUCTION

Tax Law:
An Introduction

Second Edition

by

Thabo Legwaila (Editor)
Bluris (Venda) LLB LLM (Wits) PGDip Tax Law LLM (Cape Town)
LLD (Pretoria)
Professor of Tax Law, University of Johannesburg
Head of Tax (Africa), Citibank

Annet Wanyana Oguttu
LLB (Makerere) LLM Tax Law (UNISA) HDip International Tax Law (UJ)
LLD Tax Law (UNISA)
Professor of Tax Law, University of Pretoria,
Department of Taxation and African Tax Institute

Elzette Muller
BCom Law (Cum Laude) (UP) LLB (Cum Laude) (UP)
LLM Tax Law (UP) LLD (UP)
Advocate of the High Court of South Africa

RC Williams
BA LLB (Cape) LLM (London) H Dip Tax (Wits) PhD (Macquarie)
Emeritus Professor of Law, University of KwaZulu-Natal, Pietermaritzburg

Cornelius Louw SC
BCom (Law) (Cum Laude) (UP) BCom Hon (Econ) (Cum Laude) (UP)
LLB (Cum Laude) (UP) LLM (Tax) (UP)
Senior Advocate of the High Court of South Africa

Peter Surtees
MCom (Rhodes), CA (SA)
Professor Emeritus, Rhodes University
Registered Tax Practitioner

First published 2013
Reprinted 2015
Reprinted 2016
Reprinted 2017
Second edition 2019

First Floor, Sunclare Building, 21 Dreyer Street,
Claremont, 7708, Cape Town
www.jutalaw.co.za

ISBN: 978 1 48512 808 3

Production Co-ordinator: Valencia Wyngaard-Arenz
Editor: Leila Samodien
Indexer: Lexinfo
Cover Design: Drag and Drop
Typesetter: Elinye Ithuba

Foreword

Tax has become increasingly complicated in this country. Every year one, if not two, voluminous bills pass through Parliament and effect vast and complex changes to our tax law. It is probably not inaccurate to observe that due to the unnecessary over-ambition of the drafters of tax legislation, there is hardly anyone within the legal or accounting profession who specialises in tax who can claim to have a comprehensive knowledge of all areas of our tax law.

Teaching tax law has therefore become an increasingly complicated business. Even without this undue complexity, which is a consequence of recent developments, the teaching of tax law to the uninitiated has always posed a problem for the tax teacher. The available literature has consisted of comprehensive treatises, which are not necessarily suitable for a first course in tax, or books which were compiled directly from the notes of lecturers without sufficient consideration for the specific purposes of reliable and coherent teaching material.

Tax Law: An Introduction thus fills an important gap. Written in language which avoids unnecessary jargon and simplifies complex concepts, it will become an important tool for tax teachers who have to explain a vast terrain of tax law to students, many of whom have never had any practical encounter with the field. For these reasons the authors should be congratulated for producing a book that can only enrich the teaching and understanding of this critical area of commercial law.

Dennis Davis
Judge President of the Competition Appeal Court
Honorary Professor of Law at the University of Cape Town
September 2013

Preface

This is the second edition of an introductory textbook that deals with the fundamental principles of income tax and covers the most important tax cases. The first edition came about as a result of Marlinee Chetty, Law Publisher at Juta, identifying a need for an introductory text on tax aimed at law students studying towards the LLB degree. This edition seeks to update and address legislative changes that occurred since the release of the first edition in 2013. It is also an improvement on the first edition, based on, inter alia, the experiences and needs of users of the book, as well as written and verbal reviews and feedback received on the first edition.

The 14 chapters, with the included supplementary materials, will assist lecturers teaching tax to students. As tax laws become increasingly complex and more demanding of taxpayers generally, there is a dire need for more tax practitioners who can serve taxpayers in South Africa. The book aims to simplify (where possible) complex tax concepts and tax law application and thereby encourage law students and other professionals to consider tax consulting as a career.

The legislation referred to is up to date as at 17 January 2019. The book refers to the Income Tax Act 58 of 1962, the Tax Administration Act 28 of 2011 and the Rates and Monetary Amounts and Amendment of Revenue Laws Act 21 of 2018. The following link will provide students with access to an online resource containing all of the above:

https://www.juta.co.za/Tax_Law_An_Introduction

In April 2019, we unfortunately lost Dr Beric J Croome, who was the Managing Editor of the first edition of this book, an accomplished author and an esteemed tax advisor. We remember with sadness and appreciation his leadership in this project. May his soul rest in eternal peace. I would like to extend my thanks to my co-authors: Prof Annet Oguttu, Dr Elzette Muller, Prof Bob Williams, Adv Cornelius Louw and Prof Peter Surtees, as well as the team at Juta. Their contribution was vital in making this book a reality.

Without the support and encouragement of our spouses and families, we would not have been able to finish this book. To them, we express our sincere gratitude.

Thabo Legwaila
Managing Editor
November 2019
Johannesburg, South Africa

Preface

[illegible]

Contents

Table of Statutes

Year	No	Title	Page

Year	No	Title	Page

Year	No	Title	Page

Year	No	Title	Page
		s 13*bis*(6)	264, 265
		s 13*quat*	260, 265, 267, 268, 298, 299, 300, 450
		s 13*quat*(1)	265, 266, 267
		s 13*quat*(2)	266, 268
		s 13*quat*(2A)	268
		s 13*quat*(3)	266
		s 13*quat*(3)*(a)*	266, 268
		s 13*quat*(3)*(b)*	266, 268
		s 13*quat*(3A)	266
		s 13*quat*(3A)*(a)*	267, 268
		s 13*quat*(3A)*(b)*	266, 267, 268
		s 13*quat*(3B)	268
		s 13*quat*(4), (5)	268
		s 13*quat*(8)	265
		s 13*quin*	225, 260, 269, 283, 300, 444, 450
		s 13*quin*(1)	268, 269
		s 13*quin*(3)	269, 282
		s 13*quin*(4), (5), (6), (7)	269
		s 13*sex*	260, 271, 300, 450
		s 13*sex*(1)	270, 271
		s 13*sex*(2)	270
		s 13*sex*(3), (4), (5), (6), (7), (8)	271
		s 13*sept*	260, 272
		s 13*sept(1)*, (2), (3), (4)	272
		s 13*ter*	260, 300, 450
		s 13*ter*(6A)	282
		s 14	253, 357
		s 14(1)*(a), (b)*	250
		s 14(2)	247, 255
		s 14*bis*	250, 253, 279, 357
		s 15	224
		s 15*(a)*	119, 445
		s 15*(b)*	445
		s 15A*(a)*	445
		s 17A	225
		s 17A(1)	120
		s 18	219, 224, 581
		s 18A	221, 225, 580, 581
		s 20	225, 226, 448
		s 20(1)	42, 226, 532
		s 20(1)*(a)*	226
		s 20(1)*(a)*(i)	379
		s 20(1)*(a)*(ii)	226
		s 20(2)	291
		s 20(2A)(*b*)	226
		s 20A	226
		s 20A(3)	227–228
		s 20B	228, 256, 259
		s 20B(1)	258
		s 20B(2)	258
		s 20B(3)	258
		s 20C	228, 565
		s 20C(2)	565, 566
		s 20C(2A), (3)	566
		s 21	51, 101, 228, 370

Year	No	Title	Page

Year	No	Title	Page

Table of Cases

A

B

C

D

E

F

G

H

I

J

K

L

M

N

O

P

R

S

T

U

V

W

Z

Chapter 1

The origin and historical development of taxation

1.1 INTRODUCTION

As a point of departure, this chapter briefly describes the historical development of taxation in general, emphasising the development of modern income tax. An outline of the contemporary South African tax system is also provided. In view of the importance of underlying policy considerations, the objectives and essential principles of taxation are explained, with special reference to the South African context. This is followed by a brief discussion of South African constitutional considerations in the realm of taxation. A few comments are also made on the process involved in the collection of taxation, as well as the interpretation of fiscal legislation.

1.2 THE ORIGIN AND HISTORICAL DEVELOPMENT OF TAXATION

The idea of taxation developed closely with the idea of an orderly society and the institution of a government with authority.[1] In ancient times the mere power of the sovereign was the foundation of its entitlement to commit acts of aggression against its subjects, including its claim against their resources.[2] Apparently, the first known system of taxation can be found in Ancient Egypt around 3000 BCE–2800 BCE, where the pharaoh conducted a biennial tour of the kingdom, collecting contributions from the people. The tax was at some point calculated by measuring the rise and fall of the Nile River.[3] In the ancient Roman and Greek Empires, contributions were initially collected in indirect ways, such as through spoils of war, harbour dues, tolls and customs on trade and commerce.[4] During the reign of the Roman Emperor Diocletian (284–305 CE), the first extensive direct[5] taxes were imposed on Roman citizens based on heads (*capita*) and land (*iuga*) to provide funding for the increasing expenditure needs of the empire. After the decline and fall of the Western

[1] Piek JN & Franzsen RCD 'Belastingreg' in SR Van Jaarsveld & MJ Oosthuizen (eds) *Suid-Afrikaanse Handelsreg* vol II 3 ed (Lex Patria 1988) 903; Brautigam DA 'Introduction: Taxation and State-Building in Developing Countries' in D Brautigam, O Fjeldstad & M Moore (eds) *Introduction: Taxation and State-Building in Developing Countries: Capacity and Consent* (Cambridge University Press 2008) 1.

[2] Adriani PJA & Van Hoorn J *Het Belastingrecht* vol 1 (LJ Veen's Uitgeversmij NV 1954) 184–186.

[3] Croome BJ *Taxpayers' Rights in South Africa: An Analysis and Evaluation of the Extent to which the Powers of the South African Revenue Service Comply with the Constitutional Rights to Property, Privacy, Administrative Justice, Access to Information and Access to Courts* (unpublished PhD Thesis, University of Cape Town 2008) 1 n 2 and accompanying text; Croome BJ *Taxpayers' Rights in South Africa* (Juta & Co Ltd 2010) 1.

[4] Seligman ERA *The Income Tax: A Study of the History, Theory and Practice of Income Taxation, at Home and Abroad* (The MacMillan Company 1921) 4; Sabine BEV *A Short History of Taxation* (Butterworths 1980); Piek & Franzsen in Van Jaarsveld & Oosthuizen (eds) *SA Handelsreg* 904.

[5] A direct tax is imposed on a specific person, whereas an indirect tax is generally transaction-based.

Roman Empire (circa 476 CE), these taxes, being symbols of oppression, became unenforceable and disappeared completely.[6]

With the subsequent rise of various empires and kingships, for example, the empire of Charlemagne in Europe and the Saxon kings in England, contributions to the sovereign were initially voluntary. It was unacceptable for a sovereign to impose taxation on his or her subjects, unless in times of war or in exchange for a specific benefit.[7] Indirect collection of revenue through excise taxation on, for example, salt, beer, soap, candles, leather and meat became the principal way of filling the ruler's coffers.[8] These voluntary contributions were based on the principles of the social contract, the so-called 'contractual taxation'.[9] However, the difficulty with contractual taxation is that it requires a consensual undertaking by the citizen.[10]

During the Middle Ages, the idea developed that taxation is actually an inherent and indispensable power of the government to coerce its subjects to surrender their property without their consent, a process of 'forced exchange' or 'coercive taxation'.[11] This ideology was reinforced with the development of nation-states and an increased need for public revenue. Initially, fixed head taxes (or 'poll taxes') were levied on individuals. The development of private property and the differentiation of economic classes led to the introduction of taxes on property. A further development was the notion of tax on expenditure. The fact that a tax on expenditure became an increasingly heavy burden on the least wealthy classes contributed to the development of the next stage, namely the notion of taxing the produce of property, irrespective of who owned the property. This development was a forerunner of the taxation of net profits, or income (the universally preferred tax base in modern tax systems today).[12]

---

[6] Klein-Wassink HJW 'De Ideologie van het Belastingrecht' in AKP Jongsma & J Verburg (eds) *Cyns en Dyns: Opstellen Aangeboden aan Prof HJ Hofstra* (Deventer, Kluwer 1975) 93–94.

[7] Seligman ERA *Essays in Taxation* (Augustus M Kelly Publishers 1969) 2; Klein-Wassink in Jongsma & Verburg (eds) *Cyns en Dyns* 94; Piek & Franzsen in Van Jaarsveld & Oosthuizen (eds) *SA Handelsreg* 903–904; Sabine BEV *A History of Income Tax* (Routledge 2006) 11; Brautigam in Brautigam, Fjeldstad & Moore (eds) *Taxation and State-Building* 7.

[8] Smith A *An Inquiry into the Nature and Causes of the Wealth of Nations* (1776) book v chapter ii part ii article iv, available at http://www.adamsmith.org; Klein-Wassink in Jongsma & Verburg (eds) *Cyns en Dyns* 94.

[9] Adriani & Van Hoorn *Het Belastingrecht* 186–188; Epstein RA 'Taxation in a Lockean World' (1986) 4 *Social Philosophy & Policy* 49 n 1; Klein-Wassink in Jongsma & Verburg (eds) *Cyns en Dyns* 96; Brautigam in Brautigam, Fjeldstad & Moore (eds) *Taxation and State-Building* 12–15.

[10] Epstein (1986) *Social Philosophy & Policy* 49; Franzsen RCD *'n Regskritiese Ondersoek na Hereregte in Suid-Afrika* (unpublished LLD Thesis, University of Stellenbosch 1990) 10; Theron L *'n Regsteoretiese Ondersoek na 'n Landbougrondbelasting in Suid-Afrika* (unpublished LLD Thesis, RAU 1994) 16; Mack E 'Self-Ownership, Taxation and Democracy: A Philosophical-Constitutional Perspective' in DP Racheter & RE Wagner (eds) *Politics, Taxation, and the Rule of Law: The Power to Tax in Constitutional Perspective* (Kluwer 2002) 9–26 and Steenekamp T 'Introduction to Taxation and Tax Equity' in P Black, E Calitz & T Steenekamp (eds) *Public Economics* (Oxford University Press 2008) 116.

[11] Adriani & Van Hoorn *Het Belastingrecht* 190; Klein-Wassink in Jongsma & Verburg (eds) *Cyns en Dyns* 95; Epstein (1986) *Social Philosophy & Policy* 51–54; Piek & Franzsen in Van Jaarsveld & Oosthuizen (eds) *SA Handelsreg* 904, 906–912; Franzsen LLD Thesis 10; Theron LLD Thesis 12, 17; Mack in Racheter & Wagner (eds) *The Power to Tax* 11.

[12] Seligman *The Income Tax* 5–18; Seligman *Essays in Taxation* 10–18; Piek & Franzsen in Van Jaarsveld & Oosthuizen (eds) *SA Handelsreg* 904–905.

1.3 THE DEVELOPMENT OF INCOME TAX (AND CAPITAL GAINS TAX)

Broad-based income taxation is a relatively modern innovation. Apparently, the first true progressive direct income tax was introduced in Britain by William Pitt the Younger in 1799, to pay for weapons and equipment in preparation for the Napoleonic wars.[13] It developed in the early nineteenth century principally in England, Sweden and some of the German and American states. Many industrialised countries imposed an income tax only towards the end of the nineteenth century or early in the twentieth century.[14]

Historically, two distinctly different notions of legal income developed, namely the English source-based concept (influenced by the trust concept) and the American accretion-based concept. According to the *source concept*, which originated in an English agricultural economy, income is described as the fruits produced by capital. According to this approach a receipt is considered to be income only if it is periodic in nature and derived from personal exertion, activities or capital. The capital itself, namely the source of the income, is excluded from the tax base. Under this approach, income includes salaries, wages, interest, rent, trade profits, royalties and dividends. This source-based concept of income was adopted in Canada, Australia and most of the continental European countries. The dramatically different accretion-based concept originated in the United States. This notion of income does not contain the sharp distinction between income and capital that originated in England and Europe. Apparently this is attributable to the fact that wealth accumulation in England and Europe was traditionally retained through rental or farming income, whereas in America gains from the sale of capital assets often constituted the profit contemplated from a transaction. Capital gains have thus been taxed under the United States income tax system since 1913.[15]

Although capital gains taxation[16] barely existed in source-based income tax systems prior to 1950, most OECD countries introduced this type of taxation between 1958 and 2000 to improve the equity, neutrality and redistributive

[13] Sabine *A Short History of Taxation* 115–117; Holmes K *The Concept of Income: A Multidisciplinary Analysis* (IBFD Publications 2000) 154.

[14] Thuronyi V *Comparative Tax Law* (The Hague, Kluwer 2003) 231. For example, the first US income tax was imposed in July 1862. See also Vivian RW 'Equality and Personal Income Tax – the Classical Economists and the Katz Commission' (2006) *SA Journal of Economics* 79 82.

[15] See Holmes *Concept of Income* chapter 5 and Thuronyi *Comparative Tax Law* 235–240 for a comprehensive discussion.

[16] A capital gains tax is usually imposed on a realisation basis, whereby only the gains that have accrued to a taxpayer on the disposal (usually by way of a sale or exchange) of his or her capital assets during the year of assessment are taxed. A capital gain is generally assessed as the difference between the (1) original acquisition price (or value) plus value enhancement expenditures and (2) the consideration received for the asset on disposal. It is therefore a tax levied on the 'profit' made by the taxpayer on the disposal of his or her capital assets. See Steenekamp T 'Income Taxation' in Black, Calitz & Steenekamp (eds) *Public Economics* 180.

justice of their tax systems.[17] Some countries provided for it within the existing income tax legislative framework,[18] whereas other countries elected to introduce separate legislation.[19]

1.4 THE POWER TO TAX

An express provision conferring the power to tax on a government is not essential. Hyatali CJ in *Attorney-General of Trinidad and Tobago v Ramesh Dipraj Kumar Mootoo*[20] explained that:

> The power to tax rests upon necessity, and it is inherent in any sovereignty. The legislature of every free State will possess it under the general grant of legislative power, whether particularly specified in the Constitution among the powers to be exercised or not. No constitutional government can exist without it.

However, in modern times a government does not have unlimited powers as far as taxation is concerned in view of the notion that a government should be accountable to its citizens, requiring fiscal legislation to comply with the relevant country's constitutional restrictions.[21] The constitutional principles relevant for the South African context are discussed in para 1.9 below.

1.5 A MODERN DESCRIPTION OF TAXATION

Providing a comprehensive definition of taxation is challenging. It can best be described as a monetary-based compulsory contribution payable by the public as a whole or a substantial sector thereof to a government (at a national or sub-national level). Its primary purpose is to defray government expenditures, but it can also serve as an instrument to attain socio-economic and political objectives. Taxes are levied in terms of legislation, which should comply with the constitutional law of the relevant jurisdiction. They are not levied as a *quid pro quo* for specific, defined benefits provided by the government, but should rather be utilised for public benefit.[22]

---

[17] Messere KC, De Kam F & Heady C *Tax Policy, Theory and Practice in OECD Countries* (Oxford University Press 2003) 23. It was introduced in the UK in 1965 (following the recommendations of a Royal Commission Report in 1955), Canada in 1971 (following a political process) and Australia in 1985 (following the recommendations of the Asprey Report). See Arnold BJ & Edgar T 'Selected Aspects of Capital Gains Taxation in Australia, New Zealand, the United Kingdom and the United States' (1995) 21 *Canadian Public Policy* 58 60.

[18] Such as Australia, Canada, France, Japan, Sweden and Spain. See Arnold & Edgar (1995) *Can Publ Pol* 61 and Messere, De Kam & Heady *Tax Policy in OECD Countries* 177.

[19] Such as the UK, Italy and Ireland. See Arnold & Edgar (1995) *Can Publ Pol* 61 and Messere, De Kam & Heady *Tax Policy in OECD Countries* 177.

[20] (1976) 28 WIR 304 326.

[21] Epstein (1986) *Social Philosophy & Policy* 50; Steenekamp 'Introduction' in Black, Calitz & Steenekamp (eds) *Public Economics* 116.

[22] See *Maize Board v Epol (Pty) Ltd* 2009 (3) SA 110 (D) 120G–H; Adriani & Van Hoorn *Het Belastingrecht* 101; Franzsen LLD Thesis 12–13; Theron LLD Thesis 25–26; Thuronyi *Comparative Tax Law* 4; Croome PhD Thesis 30; Muller E *A Framework for Wealth Transfer Taxation in South Africa* (unpublished LLD Thesis UP 2010) 14–15.

1.6 THE SOUTH AFRICAN TAX SYSTEM

The current South African tax system (like any other modern tax system) comprises a mix of various taxes levied in terms of various statutes. Most of these taxes can be classified under three broad tax bases, namely the taxation of income, consumption and wealth (or capital).

1.6.1 The taxation of income

Nearly 60% of national revenue is currently derived from a direct income tax,[23] currently levied in terms of the Income Tax Act.[24] In view of the fact that the first income tax enacted for the South African Union in 1914 was based on the Land and Income Tax Assessment Act of 1895 from New South Wales, which was in turn based on English income tax legislation, the South African concept of income was formulated on the English source-based concept of income.[25] Capital gains taxation was, however, introduced into the income tax system by virtue of the Eighth Schedule to the Income Tax Act in 2001.

1.6.2 The taxation of consumption

The taxation of goods and services is accomplished by a variety of indirect taxes. Customs duties, which constitute a levy on the importation and exportation of goods, are levied on a variety of products in terms of the Customs and Excise Act.[26] This statute imposes excise duties (or 'sin taxes')[27] on, for example, wine, spirits, beer, tobacco, other fermented beverages, fuel, diesel, plastic bags, international air travel and various other products.[28] A diamond export levy is also levied under a separate statute.[29] In 1978 a general sales tax (GST) was introduced on the sale of goods and services in the Republic. This tax, with its single-stage collection system, was replaced by a value-added tax[30] in

---

[23] See the statistics available at http://www.treasury.gov.za.

[24] 58 of 1962.

[25] See para 1.3 above.

[26] Act 91 of 1964.

[27] Excise duties are levies charged on specific goods and services produced, sold or delivered within a country and on licences granted for certain activities. These duties are typically based on the physical characteristic of a product – for example, the weight of salt or tobacco, the strength of alcohol and the volume of fuel or oils. See Thuronyi *Comparative Tax Law* 328–329.

[28] See in general Cnossen S *Excise Tax Policy and Administration in Southern African Countries* (Unisa Press 2006) for a comparative overview of excise taxation in Southern African countries.

[29] Diamond Export Levy Act 15 of 2007.

[30] VAT was invented by the French economist Maurice Laure in 1954 and has been adopted in the member states of the European Union, the Nordic countries, New Zealand, Australia, Canada and Japan. The only member of the OECD that continues to resist the introduction of VAT is the United States. VAT has also been adopted by the majority of countries in Africa. See Krever R *VAT in Africa* (Pretoria University Law Press 2008) 1–7.

1991, when the Value-Added Tax Act[31] was implemented. Besides the income tax, value-added tax is currently the second largest revenue raiser in South Africa.[32]

1.6.3 The taxation of wealth (capital or property)

Wealth (or property) is taxed by virtue of 'rates', property transfer taxes, wealth transfer taxes and capital gains tax.

Rates, which embrace a periodic tax charged upon the owner (or in some instances the occupier) of immovable property, are levied in the local government sphere in terms of the recently introduced Local Government: Municipal Property Rates Act.[33] This form of taxation is a major source of revenue for municipalities.

Property transfer taxes apply in general to the gross value of assets transferred, without taking any liabilities into account. In South Africa, a tax ('transfer duty') is levied on the transfer of immovable property in terms of the Transfer Duty Act.[34] The transfer of listed and unlisted securities is taxed under the Securities Transfer Tax Act.[35]

Wealth transfer taxes are taxes on inheritances, gifts and estates. South Africa currently levies an estate duty on deceased estates in terms of the Estate Duty Act[36] as well as a donations tax on *inter vivos* transfers (provided for in part V of the Income Tax Act).

The taxation of capital gains was introduced into the South African tax system by means of the inclusion of the Eighth Schedule to the Income Tax Act, which applied with effect from 1 October 2001.[37] It was decided that capital gains tax would be incorporated as an integral part of the income tax system, because a tax on capital gains 'is regarded as a tax on income'.[38] On the practical side, it was stated that such an approach has administrative advantages, as the existing procedures and provisions of the Income Tax Act relating to matters such as returns, assessments, payment and recovery of the tax and objection and appeals could be utilised for purposes of capital gains tax.[39]

---

[31] Act 89 of 1991.

[32] See the statistics available at http://www.treasury.gov.za.

[33] Act 6 of 2004.

[34] Act 40 of 1949. See in general Franzsen LLD Thesis for a comprehensive and critical discussion on transfer duty in South Africa.

[35] Act 25 of 2007.

[36] Act 45 of 1955.

[37] The Minister of Finance announced in his budget speech of 23 February 2000 that a tax on capital gains was to be introduced into the South African tax system, thereby bringing the system more into line with the international position. The design of the Eighth Schedule was influenced by the tax legislation of especially Australia and the UK, and to a lesser extent, the US and Canada. See Williams RC *Capital Gains Tax* 2 ed (Juta & Co Ltd 2005) 1.

[38] Explanatory Memorandum on the Taxation Laws Amendment Bill, 2001 7.

[39] Explanatory Memorandum on the Taxation Laws Amendment Bill, 2001 7.

1.6.4 Miscellaneous taxes

The system also provides for a number of social security contributions such as a skills development levy[40] and an unemployment insurance contribution.[41]

1.7 OBJECTIVES OF TAXATION

The objectives of taxation can be categorised into two main parts. Firstly, taxation is an important fiscal tool to provide for the financing of public expenditure. Secondly, taxation can be utilised to accomplish numerous socio-economic and political objectives. Taxation is therefore a central component of state-building.[42]

1.7.1 Revenue

Almost all social policy efforts require expenditure, which can be financed through loan capital, user charges, administrative fees, government-induced inflation or taxation.[43] An important purpose of taxation is therefore to generate sufficient revenue to assist in the financing of government activities. In South Africa, more than 90% of government expenditure is in general financed through tax revenue.[44]

1.7.2 Socio-economic objectives

Taxation can also be used as an instrument of social and economic policy. Taxes can for instance assist socio-economic objectives such as the redistribution of resources, economic growth and reprising, that is, the encouragement or discouragement of certain activities by means of taxation. Each of these is dealt with below.

1.7.2.1 Redistribution of resources

According to liberal thought, a legal system should value political liberty, equality of opportunity and fairness in distribution so that all people may have an equal opportunity to pursue their economic dreams.[45] The redistribution of resources can assist these values by reducing the economic and political power that is concentrated in the hands of the wealthy and by raising the socio-economic standards of the poor. Confiscatory taxation could, however,

---

[40] Levied in terms of the Skills Development Levies Act 9 of 1999.

[41] Levied in terms of the Unemployment Insurance Contributions Act 4 of 2002.

[42] See collection of essays in Brautigam, Fjeldstad & Moore (eds) *Taxation and State-Building in Developing Countries: Capacity and Consent* (Cambridge University Press 2008) on this topic (with special reference to developing countries).

[43] See Steenekamp 'Introduction' in Black, Calitz & Steenekamp (eds) *Public Economics* 115–116 for further discussion.

[44] See the statistics available at http://www.treasury.gov.za.

[45] See in general Rawls JA *A Theory of Justice* (Harvard University Press 1971).

violate constitutionally protected property rights, increase tax avoidance and evasion, and have a negative impact on the economy. The extent to which the redistribution of resources should be an objective of a jurisdiction's tax system is therefore likely to depend on political considerations. Nonetheless, in developing countries such as in South Africa, where poverty and inequality are extreme problems, the redistribution of income is a common goal of tax policy.[46]

1.7.2.2 Economic growth

Adequate levels of investment and saving are essential for economic growth. Tax policy can be formulated to act as an incentive for economic growth and development, the avoidance of inflation and unemployment and the promotion of saving and investment. Both the Margo Report and the Katz Report[47] considered the effect of tax incentives on the levels of saving and investment in the South African economy.[48]

1.7.2.3 Reprising

The encouragement or discouragement of certain types of activities (referred to as 'reprising') can be addressed by means of taxation. The so-called 'sin taxes', levied on products such as alcohol and tobacco, were initially implemented to discourage people from consuming these products.[49] The criticism against reprising through taxation flows from the principle of non-discrimination, which requires the government to be neutral towards all kinds of activities. However, the counter-argument is that these taxes can assist in the raising of revenue towards the social cost associated with the misuse or abuse of these products, which justifies discriminatory taxation. As mentioned above, South Africa levies excise duties on a variety of products.[50]

1.8 TAX POLICY: THE 'CANONS OF TAXATION'

In his 1776 treatise, *An Inquiry into the Nature and Causes of the Wealth of Nations*, the Scottish classical economist Adam Smith outlined four criteria of a good tax system, commonly referred to as the 'canons of taxation'. The principles of equity, certainty, convenience and cost efficiency have become the most enduring and widely acknowledged principles for tax policy. These principles provide (ideal) rational, non-political guidelines to policy-makers,

46 See Third Interim Katz Report (1995) para 7.1.4.

47 See para 1.11 below.

48 See Margo Report (1986) paras 4.6, 4.24, 4.40; Interim Katz Report (1994) para 15.6.1 (see also paras 15.6.2–15.6.16 for further discussion), endorsed by Third Interim Katz Report (1995) para 17.1.4.

49 Smith (1776) book v chapter ii part ii article iv, available at http://www.adamsmith.org.

50 See para 1.6.2.

although fiscal legislation need not conform to these 'canons' in order to be enforceable.[51]

1.8.1 The first canon: Equity

Smith stated that the principle of equity demands that taxpayers ought to contribute towards the state's coffers in proportion to the revenue that they respectively enjoy under the protection of the state.[52] The most widely accepted measure for equity is the criterion of ability-to-pay; the underlying idea is that taxation is a sacrifice levied upon some kind of 'personal economic well-being'. It has become customary to define the two dimensions of ability-to-pay, namely horizontal equity, requiring taxpayers with equal capacity to contribute in equal proportions, and vertical equity, requiring taxpayers with greater capacity to pay more taxes (which is accomplished through progressive taxation). Appropriate measures of taxable capacity include income, consumption, wealth and utility.[53]

1.8.2 The second canon: Certainty and simplicity

Smith's second maxim dictates that the tax that a person is bound to pay ought to be certain, and not arbitrary, which implies that the time, manner and amount of payment should be clear and ascertainable to the taxpayer.[54] Certainty also involves simplicity, requiring that taxes should be simple in concept, collection and administration.[55] It is, for example, desirable that the taxpayer should ascertain his or her tax liability according to operations and records that he or she needs to perform and preserve anyway. Certainty of law is closely linked to legality, both principles of adherence to the rule of law, and is an essential quality of a true democracy where the taxing authorities are accountable to the electorate.

1.8.3 The third canon: Convenience

Smith's third maxim provides that every tax ought to be levied at a time, or in a way, most convenient to the taxpayer.[56] This principle touches upon the proposition that taxes should preferably be levied in cash rather than in kind. Furthermore, taxes should ideally be levied in a way that takes cognisance of a taxpayer's liquidity. If a tax is levied on the value of unrealised assets, the

---

[51] In *Partington v Attorney-General* (1869) LR 4 HL 100, 21 LT 370 it was stated that: '[I] f a person sought to be taxed comes within the letter of the law, he must be taxed, however great the hardship may appear to the judicial mind to be, even though the so-called "canons of taxation" as propounded by Adam Smith in *The Wealth of Nations*, namely equity, neutrality, certainty and administrative efficiency, have not been observed.'

[52] Smith (1776) book v chapter ii part ii, available at http://www.adamsmith.org.

[53] Seligman *The Income Tax* 4, 25–29; Margo Report (1986) para 4.43–4.44; Third Interim Katz Report (1995) para 7.1.4; Thuronyi *Comparative Tax Law* 15; Steenekamp 'Introduction' in Black, Calitz & Steenekamp (eds) *Public Economics* 122.

[54] Smith (1776) book v chapter ii part ii, available at http://www.adamsmith.org. See also Margo Report (1986) para 4.47.

[55] Margo Report (1986) para 4.47.

[56] Smith (1776) book v chapter ii part ii, available at http://www.adamsmith.org.

assets need to be valued, which opens the door for inconsistencies and tax avoidance through discretionary valuations.

1.8.4 The fourth canon: Cost-effectiveness and efficiency

The economic function of a tax in a market economy is to transfer resources from the private sector to the public sector. Smith's fourth maxim requires that the costs of a tax should not be a disproportionately high percentage of the revenue yield.[57] There are three major components of costs, namely collection costs, 'dead-weight' market costs and unproductive costs.

1.8.4.1 Collection costs

The first component is the collection costs of the system, which consist of (1) administrative costs, namely the cost of establishing and maintaining a tax collection system, and (2) compliance costs, namely the cost for taxpayers to comply with their tax liabilities (in terms of time, money and effort).[58] An efficient collection system requires that the resources available for public use be as nearly as possible equal to the resources withdrawn from the private sector: that is, that the process by which resources are transferred involve minimal waste.[59] Both costs will be less if the taxpayers' tax liability can be easily established. Efficiency will therefore be enhanced by a certain and simple tax system.

1.8.4.2 Dead-weight market costs and neutrality

A tax has an efficiency cost in that it influences the economic decisions of taxpayers. Taxation perceived as being unfair and a penalty to the economically active may discourage work effort and savings and may encourage tax avoidance. This involves the cost to society of the misallocation of resources (referred to as 'dead-weight losses'), resulting in the underlying economic activity being distorted or even destroyed.[60] This underlines the criterion that the tax system should be neutral: a taxpayer should not be influenced by the tax system to choose one course of action above another predominantly because its tax position is better. It is, however, inevitable that taxation distorts economic decision-making to some extent. The criterion of efficiency therefore requires that taxes should be designed to redistribute purchasing power with the least distortion or disruption to the market economy.[61]

---

[57] Smith (1776) book v chapter ii part ii, available at http://www.adamsmith.org. See also Margo Report (1986) para 4.49.

[58] Margo Report (1986) para 4.48; Steenekamp 'Tax Efficiency and Tax Reform' in Black, Calitz & Steenekamp (eds) *Public Economics* 142.

[59] Steenekamp 'Tax Efficiency' in Black, Calitz & Steenekamp (eds) *Public Economics* 142. As stated by Jean-Baptiste Colbert: 'The art of taxation consists in so plucking the goose as to obtain the largest amount of feathers with the least amount of hissing.'

[60] A classic example of a tax that destroyed economic activity is the French 'gabelle', an excise duty on salt that destroyed the salt trade and yielded no income. See Margo Report (1986) para 4.49.

[61] Margo Report (1986) paras 4.41–4.42; Steenekamp 'Tax Efficiency' in Black, Calitz & Steenekamp (eds) *Public Economics* (2008) 137.

1.8.4.3 Unproductive costs

A third component is the costs of tax planning and tax advisors, resulting in resources being employed in the unproductive activity of finding loopholes and tax-free alternatives, which may even further distort the allocation of resources.[62] An efficient tax system therefore dictates that tax avoidance and evasion be kept to a minimum, which requires simple tax laws.[63]

1.9 CONSTITUTIONAL CONSIDERATIONS: A SOUTH AFRICAN PERSPECTIVE

In a South African context, coercive taxation has certainly evolved to a level that is accountable, especially with the constitutional transformation and democratisation that has taken place since 1994.[64] The introduction of the interim Constitution,[65] which was replaced by the final Constitution in 1996,[66] brought about a new era.[67] In the realm of taxation, the importance of the Constitution lies especially in the fact that certain fundamental rights (such as the right to equality, privacy, property, access to information and access to justice) are enshrined in the Bill of Rights (contained in chapter 2 of the final Constitution).[68] In addition, fiscal legislation should conform to certain procedural requirements.

---

[62] Margo Report (1986) para 4.50; Steenekamp 'Tax Efficiency' in Black, Calitz & Steenekamp (eds) *Public Economics* 142.

[63] Steenekamp 'Tax Efficiency' in Black, Calitz & Steenekamp (eds) *Public Economics* 143.

[64] Although members of the coloured races were generally not permitted to participate in elections, they were still required to pay taxes in the era prior to 1994. Various poll and 'hut taxes' were levied on so-called 'natives' in the colonial era by the colonial governments. To consolidate and amend the law relating to the taxation of natives, the Natives Taxation and Development Act 41 of 1925 was enacted. It provided for the levying of an annual general poll tax on every adult male native domiciled in the Union of South Africa (s 2(1)). An additional local tax was payable by the native occupier of every hut or dwelling in a native location within the Union (s 2(2)). This Act was repealed by the Bantu Taxation Act 92 of 1969, which provided for the levying of an annual graduated income tax on the taxable income of any Black person as well as a fixed poll tax, payable by any Black male who had attained the age of 18 years in the year of assessment. This Act also imposed a local ('hut') tax on the occupier of every hut or dwelling. The Act was repealed in 1984. See in general Trevor D 'South African Native Taxation' (1936) 3 *Rev of Econ Studies* 217 *et seq* and Redding S *Sorcery and Sovereignty* (Ohio University Press 2006) for an extensive historic discussion on the taxation of non-white South Africans for the period 1880–1963.

[65] Constitution of the Republic of South Africa, Act 200 of 1993.

[66] Constitution of the Republic of South Africa, 1996.

[67] Following the enactment of the interim Constitution and the subsequent recommendations by the Katz Commission in chapter 6 of its report titled *'Implications of the Constitution of the Republic of South Africa'*, some of the discriminatory provisions in fiscal statutes were deleted or amended. See summary and discussion by Croome BJ 'Constitutional Law and Taxpayers' Rights in South Africa – An Overview' (2002) 17(1) *Acta Juridica* 1 3–6 and Croome PhD Thesis 11–14.

[68] For further reading on taxpayers' rights in general, see Croome BJ *Taxpayers' Rights in South Africa* (Juta & Co Ltd 2010).

1.9.1 The power to pass fiscal legislation

The national legislative authority, as vested in Parliament, confers on the National Assembly the power to amend the Constitution and to pass legislation in respect of any matter, including a matter listed within the functional areas of concurrent national and provincial legislative competence listed in Schedule 4, but excluding any matter within the functional areas of exclusive provincial competence listed in Schedule 5.[69] However, the National Assembly has the power to assign any of its general legislative powers, except the power to amend the Constitution, to any legislative body in another sphere of government.[70] The area of taxation is not listed in either Schedule 4 or 5, which means that the National Assembly primarily has the exclusive authority to pass tax legislation, unless such authority has been assigned to a sub-national sphere of government, or unless the Constitution expressly confers some power on another sphere of government. Section 228 provides that a provincial legislature may impose (a) taxes, levies and duties other than income tax, value-added tax, general sales tax, rates on property or customs duties and (b) flat-rate surcharges on any tax, levy or duty that is imposed by national legislation, other than corporate income tax, value-added tax, rates on property or customs duties. However, no province in South Africa has yet exercised the right to introduce a new provincial tax.[71] Section 229 confers on a municipality the right to impose (a) rates on property and surcharges on fees for services provided by or on behalf of the municipality, and (b) other taxes, levies and duties appropriate to local government, but only if sanctioned by national legislation and excluding income tax, value-added tax, general sales tax and customs duty.

1.9.2 Substantive limitations: The Bill of Rights

The most important substantive limitation to the government's taxing power is the Bill of Rights contained in chapter 2 of the Constitution, which is applicable to all laws and binds the legislature, the executive, the judiciary and all organs of state.[72] However, the fundamental rights are not absolute and may be restricted in terms of s 36, which provides that a right may only be limited in terms of—

> law of general application to the extent that the limitation is reasonable and justifiable in an open and democratic society based on human dignity, equality and freedom, taking into account all relevant factors, including (a) the nature of the right, (b) the importance of the purpose of the limitation, (c) the nature and extent of the limitation, (d) the relation between the limitation and its purpose and (e) less restrictive means to achieve such purpose.

---

[69] Constitution chapter 4 s 44(1)*(a)*(i) and (ii).

[70] Constitution chapter 4 s 44(1)*(a)*(iii).

[71] Croome PhD Thesis 15–16. The Western Cape has mentioned the possible introduction of a provincial fuel levy.

[72] Constitution chapter 2 s 8(1).

In the realm of taxation, and especially the imposition of a tax, the fundamental rights enshrined in s 9 (equality) and s 25 (property) deserve consideration.

1.9.2.1 Right to property

Section 25(1) provides that '[n]o one may be deprived of property except in terms of law of general application, and no law may permit arbitrary deprivation of property'. Although a comprehensive description of 'property' is difficult to achieve for purposes of s 25, the term has a wide meaning.[73] The levying of a tax on a taxpayer's 'entitlement to certain benefits or rights' would generally constitute a deprivation of property as envisaged in s 25 of the Constitution.[74]

In *First National Bank of SA Ltd t/a Wesbank v CSARS*[75] Conradie J (at 449) commented:

> Taxation does not amount [in principle] to a deprivation of property. Nor is there anything which is expropriated. No one would think of claiming compensation for having been taxed. Freedom from taxation is not a fundamental right. Nothing protects the subject against taxation. Not even death ... It may be different where the impugned tax is oppressive or partial and unequal in its operations ... If its reach seems broader than it need be, that is no ground for a constitutional challenge.

This line of thinking is also in accordance with the internationally accepted viewpoint.[76] Thus, where a taxing measure applies equally to all citizens of South Africa, a taxpayer will generally fail to challenge its constitutionality merely because it constitutes a violation of the right to property.[77]

1.9.2.2 Right to equality

Section 9 provides that '[e]veryone is equal before the law and has the right to equal protection and benefit of the law'.[78] It furthermore directs that the state may not unfairly discriminate against anyone on grounds such as race, gender, sex, pregnancy, marital status, ethnic or social origin, colour, sexual orientation, age, disability, religion, conscience, belief, culture, language or

---

[73] In *First National Bank of SA Ltd t/a Wesbank v CSARS* 2002 (4) SA 768 (CC), 2002 (7) BCLR 702 (CC), 64 SATC 471 the court stated (at para [51]) that 'at this stage of our constitutional jurisprudence it is ... practically impossible to furnish – and judicially unwise to attempt – a comprehensive definition of property for purposes of s 25. Such difficulties do not, however, arise in the present case. Here it is sufficient to hold that ownership of corporeal movable property must – as must ownership of land – lie at the heart of our constitutional concept of property'.

[74] Croome PhD Thesis 28.

[75] 2001 (3) SA 310 (C), 2001 (7) BCLR 715 (C), 63 SATC 432.

[76] Croome PhD Thesis 32–36 discusses the approaches of the European Convention on Human Rights and the constitutional law of Australia, Switzerland, Trinidad and Tobago, India, the US, Ireland and Canada.

[77] Croome PhD Thesis 36.

[78] Constitution chapter 2 s 9(1).

birth,[79] unless it is established that the discrimination is fair.[80] It is therefore not lawful, for example, to impose a tax that applies exclusively to a section of the community.[81] Because the fiscal statutes that levy taxes in South Africa constitute laws of general application, they do not currently discriminate unfairly on the grounds set out in s 9 of the Constitution.[82]

1.9.3 Procedural limitations

The Constitution provides that a national bill that imposes a tax is defined as a 'money bill'.[83] Money bills must be considered in accordance with a special detailed procedure, which enhances the level of parliamentary scrutiny.[84]

The power of a provincial legislature or a municipality to impose a tax or levy may not be exercised in a way that materially and unreasonably prejudices national economic policies, economic activities across provincial borders and the mobility of services, goods, capital or labour.[85] Any provincial tax must comply with the provisions of the Provincial Tax Regulation Process Act[86] and any municipal tax with the Municipal Fiscal Powers and Functions Act.[87]

1.10 THE SOUTH AFRICAN REVENUE SERVICE

In 1997, the South African Revenue Service Act[88] ('SARS Act') established the South African Revenue Service ('SARS') as an organ of state within the public administration, but as an institution outside the public service.[89] The Commissioner of SARS is primarily responsible for the administration of fiscal legislation, as well as the efficient and effective collection of revenue, customs and excise duties at the national sphere of government.[90] Under fiscal legislation the Commissioner has extensive powers to collect taxes effectively and efficiently.[91] These powers should comply with constitutional standards,

[79] Constitution chapter 2 s 9(3).

[80] Constitution chapter 2 s 9(5).

[81] Croome PhD Thesis 17.

[82] Croome PhD Thesis 31.

[83] Constitution chapter 4 s 77(1). See also Steenekamp 'Introduction' in Black, Calitz and Steenekamp (eds) *Public Economics* 116.

[84] Constitution chapter 4 s 77(3). The special procedure is set out in s 75. See also Steenekamp 'Introduction' in Black, Calitz and Steenekamp (eds) *Public Economics* 116.

[85] Constitution chapter 13 ss 228(2)*(a)*, 229(2)*(a)*.

[86] Act 53 of 2001. See Croome PhD Thesis 15 n 53 and accompanying text.

[87] Act 12 of 2007 (to be read with Constitution chapter 13 s 229(2)*(b)*).

[88] Act 34 of 1997.

[89] SARS Act s 2 (the Act became effective on 1 October 1997).

[90] SARS Act ss 3, 4. Previously, revenue was primarily collected and administered by the Commissioner for Inland Revenue (CIR) and the Controller of Customs and Excise. See Croome PhD Thesis 17.

[91] These powers have been the subject of constitutional attack. See *Metcash Trading Ltd v CSARS and Another* 2001 (1) SA 1109 (CC), 2001 (1) BCLR (1) CC, 63 SATC 13 (the case dealt with some powers of SARS in terms of the Value-Added Tax Act 89 of 1991).

as they could violate the taxpayer's fundamental rights, such as the right to property, privacy, access to information, administrative justice and access to the courts.

1.11 TAX REFORM IN SOUTH AFRICA

In South Africa, fiscal statutes (tax legislation) are revised on a regular basis. Each year the Minister of Finance presents an annual budget in February, in which the following year's government expenditure and proposed amendments to tax legislation are announced. Subsequent to the budget speech, one or more 'money bills'[92] are prepared by National Treasury. Each bill is usually accompanied by an explanatory memorandum providing explanatory notes to the proposed amendments. Upon acceptance by Parliament, a bill becomes an amendment Act. The amendments (some of which are merely annual adjustments to rates or threshold amounts, whereas others constitute reformative amendments to the substantive tax law) come into effect either on a date determined in the relevant amendment Act or on the date of its promulgation.

From time to time, the government appoints commissions of enquiry to report extensively on aspects of the tax structure for purposes of identifying areas in need of reform. Historically, three commissions have been appointed since the country's inception as a republic, namely:

- the Commission of Enquiry into Fiscal and Monetary Policy in South Africa, chaired by DG Franzsen ('Franzsen Commission'), which issued two reports under the title *Taxation in South Africa* in 1968 and 1970;
- the Commission of Inquiry into the Tax Structure of the Republic of South Africa, chaired by CS Margo ('Margo Commission'), which issued a single, wide-ranging report in 1986;
- the Commission of Inquiry into Certain Aspects of the Tax Structure of South Africa, chaired by MM Katz ('Katz Commission'), which issued nine interim reports during the period 1994–1999; and
- the tax advisory committee to inquire into the role of the tax system in the promotion of inclusive economic growth, employment creation, development and fiscal sustainability, chaired by Judge D Davis (Davis Tax Committee), which issued wide-ranging reports during the periods 2013–2018.

1.12 TAX COLLECTION: A GENERAL OVERVIEW

Taxes are usually collected by virtue of an assessment system. For purposes of South African income tax the taxpayer is (at the outset) required to complete and submit to SARS an annual tax return. From the information furnished on the

[92] See para 1.9.3 above.

tax return, SARS then issues an assessment reflecting the amount of tax due (or to be refunded). Should the taxpayer feel aggrieved by the Commissioner's decision, he or she may lodge an objection against the assessment (as more fully explained in chapter 12).

Income tax is collected through a system of employees' tax and provisional tax payments. Employers are required to withhold tax from their employees' salaries and to pay it over to SARS on a monthly basis under either the 'Pay as You Earn' (PAYE) or the 'Standard Income Tax on Employees' (SITE) system. The payments made by the employer are then credited against the relevant employee's liability for income tax (for a specific year of assessment). Provisional taxpayers, on the other hand, make bi-annual payments to SARS (six months after the end of the year of assessment and at the end of it). Although the payments are made on an estimation basis, a provisional taxpayer's final tax liability is determined upon assessment.

1.13 INTERPRETATION OF FISCAL LEGISLATION

As in the case of any other statute, fiscal legislation should be interpreted by ascertaining what the legislature intended in using the words it chose to use.[93] Of cardinal importance are the scope and purpose of the legislation and the context in which the words and phrases are used.[94] Furthermore, s 39(2) of the Constitution requires that the spirit, purport and objects of the Bill of Rights should be promoted in the interpretation of any legislation. However, a purposive approach to legislation cannot be used, even in a post-constitutional era, when it is at odds with the ordinary meaning of the words used by the legislature. The disregard of words used by the legislature on a basis of general 'fairness' leads not only to uncertainty, but also to a failure to observe the separation of powers.[95] In general, it is only where the text is ambiguous or unclear, or if a strict literal meaning will be absurd, that the literal meaning of the words may be departed from. In, for example, *CSARS v Airworld CC and Another*[96] the Supreme Court of Appeal followed a purposive and contextual approach in the interpretation of a word contained in the Income Tax Act in circumstances where more than one meaning could be accorded to the relevant word. Where the enactment is ambiguous, the taxpayer may also rely on the *contra fiscum* rule, requiring the court (in interpreting the enactment) to follow the interpretation that favours the taxpayer.[97]

[93] *Glen Anil Development Corporation Ltd v SIR* 1975 (4) SA 715 (A) 727G–H.

[94] *Standard General Insurance Co Ltd v Commissioner for Customs and Excise* 2005 (2) SA 166 (SCA) para [25].

[95] *South African Airways (Pty) Ltd v Aviation Union of South Africa and Others* 2011 (3) SA 148 (SCA) paras [19], [28] and [32].

[96] 2008 (3) SA 335 (SCA), 70 SATC 48.

[97] See, for example, *Welch's Estate v CSARS* 2005 (4) SA 173 (SCA), 66 SATC 303 para [35]; *Kommissaris, Suid-Afrikaanse Inkomstediens v Boedel Wyle De Beer* 2002 (1) SA 526 (SCA), 63 SATC 467 para [8]; *Shell's Annandale Farm (Pty) Ltd v CSARS* 2000 (3) SA 564 (C) 575F–H, 62 SATC 97 108.

Chapter 2

Structure of income tax

2.1 INTRODUCTION

The purpose of this chapter is to explain to the reader the entire tax system so as to contextualise the different attributes contained in income tax. The starting point in taxation is that each person should carry the tax burden allocated to him or her in terms of the taxing statute. The piece of legislation imposing income tax is the Income Tax Act 58 of 1962 ('the Act'). Ancillary to imposing the tax, the bulk of the Act is dedicated to determining the tax burden allocable to taxpayers.

Income tax is essentially a tax levied on a person's income. It is generally levied on the occurrence of the earning of income. For tax purposes, the earning of income takes place at the earlier of the person becoming entitled to the income and the person receiving the income. Generally, there will be no income tax unless a taxpayer earns income, unless the person is deemed to have earned the income.

The charging provision contained in s 5 of the Act provides for the annual levying of income tax on a taxpayer's taxable income for the year of assessment at rates that are fixed annually. Income tax is calculated and levied annually.

2.2 TAXABLE PERSONS

The Act imposes a tax on individuals, companies and other entities including trusts, clubs and deceased and insolvent estates.

2.3 RESIDENCE AND SOURCE BASES OF TAXATION

Tax is levied on residents on their worldwide income, and on non-residents on income sourced in South Africa. This is to ensure that South African residents together contribute to the fiscus as well as to ensure that non-residents who utilise South African resources to earn income contribute to the creation and maintenance of such resources proportionate to their South African sourced income.

2.4 CALCULATING TAXABLE INCOME

Income tax is levied on the taxable income of a taxpayer. The taxable income is the amount to which the tax rate, ie the tax percentage applicable to the taxpayer, or the amount of tax, is applied. With regard to individuals, the tax amount and percentage are progressive, ie the higher the taxable amount, the higher the percentage. With regard to companies and trusts, the percentage is fixed.

Taxable income is the amount that remains after exempt income and allowable deductions are subtracted from gross income. Thus, in calculating taxable income, the starting point is gross income. The formula is as follows:

Gross income

Minus:	Exemptions
Equals:	Income
Minus:	Allowable deductions
Equals:	Taxable income

Gross income generally refers to the total of all amounts, in cash or otherwise, received by or accrued in the taxpayer's favour in a tax year. This amount does not necessarily have to be received by the taxpayer. It suffices that the amount accrues (in other words that the taxpayer is entitled to the amount) to the taxpayer, provided there are no conditions attaching to the payment of such amounts which suspend the payment thereof until the conditions are fulfilled.

Gross income includes only income that is of a revenue nature. In this regard, income of a revenue nature is contrasted with income that is of a capital nature. The capital or revenue nature of income is determined by the nature of the asset in relation to which the income is received. For example, if a taxpayer sells an asset that is of a revenue nature, the income arising from that sale will be of a revenue nature.

Capital assets generate income of a revenue nature, for example, a bakery store and all the bread-making machinery in it produce bread. The bakery store building and the machinery in it are capital assets, the sale of which will generate income of a capital nature. The turnover derived by the bakery from the sale of bread constitutes income of a revenue nature, which forms part of gross income. In addition to amounts that form part of gross income in terms of the general definition, there are amounts that are specifically included in gross income that might ordinarily not form part of gross income.

2.5 EXEMPTIONS

From gross income, certain amounts are exempt and are excluded in calculating the taxpayer's taxable income. Exemptions thus reduce a taxpayer's taxable income. Exemptions are generally the result of tax breaks or concessions granted by the government. In other jurisdictions, the structure of the tax system excludes these amounts from gross income. In South Africa, these amounts form part of gross income, which the Act specifically excludes from the determination of income, and are therefore not subject to income tax. Amounts are exempt either due to the nature of the amount or the identity of the person or institution paying or receiving that amount, and for a variety of reasons. The amount of gross income remaining after the exclusion of exempt income is referred to as 'income'.

2.6 DEDUCTIONS

Deductions also reduce a taxpayer's taxable income. However, this reduction generally arises as a result of a taxpayer's expenses associated with the income-earning activity conducted by the taxpayer. The general rule allows a deduction for expenses to the extent that they are incurred in deriving amounts included in gross income. The rationale is that the taxpayer should not be taxed on amounts that the taxpayer spent in producing taxable income.

Allowable deductions can be divided into two groups: general deductions as described above and specific deductions. Paramount amongst specific deductions are those deductions allowed in relation to the depreciation of assets used in the trade of the taxpayer producing the income. These deductions are premised on the decline in the value of all assets used in the business and take account of all obligations incurred in producing the income generated by the business, thereby taking into account accumulated gains and losses of the undertaking at the end of every tax period. Thus, for example, if a taxpayer uses a vehicle in its business undertaking and the value of the vehicle depreciates by 20% each year, a corresponding tax deduction should account for that reduction, as this represents a real loss of value to the taxpayer in relation to the business undertaking. The amount remaining after claiming those amounts qualifying as a deduction against income is referred to as 'taxable income'.

2.7 ASSESSED LOSSES

From the calculation of taxable income, one can determine that a positive amount of taxable income would arise if the income (ie the amount remaining after excluding exempt income from gross income) exceeded the amount of allowable deductions. In this case, the tax payable is calculated on the amount of taxable income remaining. If the amount of allowable deductions exceeds the amount of income, the result would be a negative taxable income. This is referred to as a tax loss. Tax losses (also referred to as assessed losses) are carried forward to the next tax year to reduce the taxable income in that following year.

Note that only allowable deductions exceeding the income generated by a taxpayer can result in an assessed loss. Exemptions cannot result in a tax loss as the exempt amounts cannot exceed gross income. At most, exemptions could match gross income resulting in zero income and therefore no taxable income.

2.8 CAPITAL GAINS

As stated above, income of a capital nature is excluded from gross income. However, capital gains are taxable in terms of a separate dispensation. Although capital gains do not form part of gross income, they are calculated separately and are included in taxable income. These amounts are included in taxable income at varying inclusion rates depending on the nature of the taxpayer. The inclusion rate for individuals is 40% and for companies and trusts it is 80%. A capital gain is an amount arising from the disposal of a capital asset. The amount incurred in acquiring, producing or establishing the asset is deducted from the proceeds of the disposal in order to arrive at the amount of the taxable capital gain. Following the example above, any gain made from the sale of the bakery store by the baker will yield a capital gain, as the store is held as a capital asset.

2.9 DIVIDENDS

In order for a company to transfer after-tax profits to its shareholders, the company declares and pays those profits to shareholders as dividends. Dividends are strictly and generally income in the hands of the shareholders. However, because these dividends arise out of amounts that would have been taxed in full in the hands of the company, they are not fully taxed as income in the hands of the taxpayers. They are subject to a lower rate of tax, and in terms of a special regime applicable to dividends. Dividends are subject to dividends tax in the hands of the beneficial owner of the dividends.

2.10 TAX AVOIDANCE

Often taxpayers attempt to avoid or evade tax that is leviable on their circumstances or transactions. They do so by postponing, reducing or eliminating the tax liability. This is undesirable as it disproportionately shifts the burden of the tax to other taxpayers. There are common-law and statutory methods of combating the evasion and avoidance of tax. Tax evasion comprises a fraud on the fiscus and exposes a taxpayer to criminal sanction. Tax avoidance can be described as schemes used by a taxpayer in an attempt to fall outside the strict provisions of the tax laws, which are combated by the legislature introducing either a general anti-avoidance provision or targeted specific anti-avoidance measures. At an international level, taxpayers may prefer to move their business operations from South Africa, or relocate income so that it is taxed in a different jurisdiction where the tax rate is lower than the South African tax rate. These attempts are combated by international anti-avoidance measures such as controlled foreign company legislation, and thin capitalisation and transfer pricing provisions.

2.11 ADMINISTRATION

The Act is administered by the South African Revenue Service ('SARS'). SARS also has the responsibility to collect the tax and pay it over to the National Revenue Fund. At the end of each tax year, taxpayers complete and submit tax returns reporting their income and deductions for the tax year. Taxpayers also calculate the tax due to SARS, or, where there has been overpayment, the refund due from SARS. SARS then calculates the tax to ensure that the appropriate amount is payable. If SARS disagrees with the amount as calculated by the taxpayer, SARS reassesses the tax payable. The taxpayer can either pay the amount as assessed by SARS or object to that amount. If SARS rejects the objection, the taxpayer can appeal to the Tax Court, and if dissatisfied with that court's judgment, can further appeal to the High Court and finally to the Supreme Court of Appeal.

2.12 SPECIAL KINDS OF TAXES

Alongside income tax, there are other taxes imposed in South Africa. The most prevalent of these include the following:

- Donations tax is a tax levied on gratuitous gifts made by a taxpayer, subject to certain exemptions. The tax is payable by the donor as opposed to the recipient.
- Value-added tax is levied on the purchase of goods and services. This tax is levied on the transaction and is not dependent on the identity of the persons transacting.
- Estate duty is levied on the transfer of the assets previously owned by a deceased to his or her heirs.

- Securities transfer tax is a tax that is levied on the transfer of ownership of shares from one person to another.
- Note that 'Pay As You Earn' (PAYE) or employees' tax is a component of income tax that is also a mechanism that ensures the collection of the tax payable by individual taxpayers on the remuneration derived by them.
- There are also special tax provisions that apply to taxpayers depending on their nature and circumstances. These include special tax provisions for partnerships, small businesses, film owners, ships and aircraft operators, co-operatives, insurance, farming and mining.

Chapter 3

Jurisdiction to tax

3.1 INTRODUCTION

For any country to levy a tax on income, a connection or tax nexus (tax basis) must be established between itself and that income.[1] The two main connecting factors underlying the taxation of income are the 'source' and the 'residence' principles of taxation. Under the source principle, persons are taxed on income that originates within the territorial jurisdiction or geographical confines of the country, despite the taxpayer's country of residence.[2] The justification for the source basis of taxation is that a taxpayer can be expected to share the costs of running the country that makes it possible for the taxpayer to produce an income.[3] Under the residence principle of taxation, residents are taxed on their worldwide income regardless of the source of the income.[4] The justification for the residence basis of taxation is that as a resident enjoys the protection of the state, he or she should contribute towards the cost of the government of the country in which he or she resides, even if income is earned outside that country. This basis of taxation is also justified by the fact that residents know that they can always return to their country of residence whenever they want and that they will have the protection of their government whenever they are abroad.[5] Most jurisdictions, including South Africa, have adopted a combination (hybrid system) of these two taxation principles.[6]

The first income tax laws in South Africa were based on the principle that taxes would be levied only on income that was sourced in South Africa.[7] The predominant use of the source basis of taxation opened up numerous loopholes for tax abuse, since income was taxed only when it was generated in South Africa.[8] Over the years, a number of commissions of inquiry were set up to recommend, amongst other issues, a proper basis of taxation in South Africa.[9] Consequently, from the years of assessment commencing 1 January 2001, the residence-based system of taxation was introduced in South Africa, by way of the Revenue Laws Amendment Act 59 of 2000 (the Amendment Act) which

---

[1] Olivier L & Honiball M *International Tax: A South African Perspective* 5 ed (Siber Ink CC 2011) 50; Oguttu AW *Curbing Offshore Tax Avoidance: The Case of South African Companies and Trusts* (LLD Dissertation UNISA 2007) 70.

[2] Meyerowitz D *Meyerowitz on Income Tax* (Taxpayer CC 2008) para 7.1.

[3] *Kergeulen Sealing & Whaling Co Ltd v CIR* 1939 AD 487 507.

[4] Meyerowitz *Income Tax* para 7.1.

[5] Ibid.

[6] Olivier L 'Residence Based Taxation' (2000) 1 *TSAR* 20; Oguttu AW & Van der Merwe B 'Electronic Commerce: Challenging the Income Tax Base?' (2005) 17 *SA Merc LJ* 306.

[7] Income Tax Act 58 of 1962 as amended by the Revenue Laws Amendment Act 59 of 2000. See also Meyerowitz *Income Tax* para 7.3.

[8] Oguttu *Curbing Offshore Tax Avoidance* 71.

[9] Steyn R (Chairman) *First Interim Report of the Committee of Inquiry into the Income Tax Act* UG No 75–1951; Franszen DG (Chairman) *Commission of Inquiry into the Fiscal and Monetary Policy in South Africa: Taxation in South Africa, Second Report* RP 86/1970; Margo CS (Chairman) *Report of the Commission of Inquiry into the Tax Structure of the Republic of South Africa* (Margo Commission Report) RP 34/1987 paras 26–30; MM Katz (Chairman) *Fifth Interim Report of the Commission of Inquiry into Certain Aspects of the Tax Structure of South Africa* (1997).

amended the Income Tax Act[10] ('the Act'). In terms of the Amendment Act, the basis of taxation of income that is applied in South Africa rests on the definition of 'gross income' in s 1 of the Act.

3.2 GROSS INCOME

Determining a person's 'gross income' is the point of departure for determining his or her taxable income. If a person does not have gross income, no normal tax can be levied on that person. In terms of s 1 of the Act:

Gross income, in relation to any year or period of assessment, means:

(a) in the case of any resident, the total amount, in cash or otherwise, received by or accrued to or in favour of such resident; or

(b) in the case of any person other than a resident, the total amount, in cash or otherwise, received by or accrued to or in favour of such person from a source within or deemed to be within the Republic,

during such year or period of assessment, excluding receipts or accruals of a capital nature. The definition contains various specific inclusions.[11]

The definition of gross income makes a distinction between the basis of taxation applied to tax residents and that applied to non-residents.[12] Residents are taxed on a residence basis. This implies that the worldwide income of South African residents is taxable in South Africa, irrespective of where it is earned.[13] The source basis of taxation was, however, not discarded. It is used to tax the income of non-residents which is derived from a South African source.[14]

3.3 'GROSS INCOME' WITH REGARD TO RESIDENTS

For a resident, gross income, in relation to any year or period of assessment, means the total amount, in cash or otherwise, received by or accrued to or in favour of such resident excluding receipts or accruals of a capital nature. Thus, residents are taxed on their worldwide income. The term 'resident' as defined in s 1 of the Act distinguishes between natural persons and persons other than natural persons (for instance companies and trusts).

---

[10] Act 58 of 1962.

[11] See chapter 4 below.

[12] The definition of 'gross income' in s 1 of the Act.

[13] Section 1 of the Act.

[14] Meyerowitz *Income Tax* para 7.3; Olivier & Honiball *International Tax* 52; Huxham K & Haupt P *Notes on South African Income Tax* (Hedron Tax Consulting and Publishing CC 2011) 294.

3.3.1 Determining the residence of natural persons

A natural person is resident in South Africa when the person is 'ordinarily resident' in South Africa or when the person meets the requirements of the physical presence test.

3.3.1.1 Ordinary residence

The phrase 'ordinary residence' is not defined in the Act and consequently case law has to be relied on to determine its parameters. In the English case *Shah v Barnet London Borough Council and Other Appeals*[15] it was held that to be ordinarily resident in a specific country 'a person must be habitually and normally resident there, apart from temporary or occasional absences of long or short duration'. In *Levene v IRC*,[16] it was held that the term 'ordinary residence' connotes residence in a place with some degree of continuity, apart from accidental or temporary absences. In *Cohen v CIR*,[17] the court proposed in an *obiter dictum* that a person's ordinary residence 'would be the country to which he would naturally and as a matter of course return from his wanderings'. This would be the country a taxpayer might call his or her 'usual or principal residence and would be described ... as his real home'. In *CIR v Kuttel*[18] the court adopted this formulation and acknowledged that, even though the taxpayer was still substantially connected to South Africa through business activities, visits and the retention of a house in Cape Town, his activities and mode of life in the USA (he rented a house, his family lived and worked with him, he joined a church, opened banking accounts, acquired an office, bought a car and registered with social security) and the purpose of his remaining connections with South Africa (his initial visits were primarily business-orientated and the Cape Town house was retained for financial reasons and not to retain a 'home') indicated that his 'real home' was in fact not in South Africa, but in the USA. In *ITC 11253*[19] the court dealt with the issue of a person who moved from the United Kingdom to South Africa temporarily for the purposes of a two-year work assignment. The court looked at the question of ordinary residence. It recognised the importance of *Cohen's* case and *Kuttel's* case and in looking at the meaning of 'usual place of residence' in the Seventh Schedule to the Act, stated that phrase meant 'ordinary residence'. The court held that as the taxpayer was 'ordinarily resident' in the United Kingdom, he was away from his 'usual place of residence' while he worked in South Africa. In the Canadian case of *Thompson v Minister of National Revenue*,[20] it was held that a person is ordinarily resident in the place 'where in the settled routine of his life he regularly, normally or customarily lives' or 'at which he in mind and in fact settles into or maintains or centralises his ordinary mode of living with its accessories in social relations, interest and conveniences'.

---

15 [1983] 1 All ER 226 (HL) 234*b–c*.
16 1928 AC 217.
17 1946 AD 174, 13 SATC 362 371.
18 1992 (3) SA 242 (A), 54 SATC 298.
19 Unreported, ITC case no 11253 (Cape Town), 9 February 2006.
20 2 DTC 812 (SCC).

It is important to note that the ordinarily resident test in the definition of resident applies regardless of how many days in the tax year the person is in the Republic. In other words, ordinary residence is not determined by physical presence. It is in effect a state of mind. A person who is ordinarily resident in South Africa in terms of the principles set out above is a resident as defined even though he or she may not be in the Republic for the required number of days.[21] In terms of South African Revenue Services (SARS) Interpretation Note 3,[22] the following two requirements need to be present for a person to be 'ordinarily resident' in South Africa:

- an intention to become ordinarily resident in a country; and
- steps indicative of this intention having been or being carried out.

Interpretation Note 3 further provides that SARS considers the following factors in determining the above two requirements, but that the list is not intended to be exhaustive or specific, merely a guideline:

- most fixed and settled place of residence;
- habitual abode, ie present habits and mode of life;
- place of business and personal interest;
- status of individual in country, ie immigrant, work permit periods and conditions, etc;
- location of personal belongings;
- nationality;
- family and social relations (involvement in schools, church, etc);
- political, cultural or other activities;
- application for permanent residence;
- period abroad; purpose and nature of visits; and
- frequency of and reasons (for) visits.

3.3.1.2 Physical presence

In terms of the definition of 'resident' in s 1*(a)*(ii) of the Act, a natural person who is not ordinarily resident in South Africa will be resident if he or she is physically present in South Africa for a period or periods:

- exceeding 91 days in aggregate during the current year of assessment;
- exceeding 91 days in aggregate during each of the five years of assessment preceding the current year of assessment; and
- exceeding 915 days in aggregate during the five years of assessment preceding the current year of assessment.

[21] Huxham & Haupt *South African Income Tax* 25.

[22] SARS Interpretation Note 3 'Resident: Definition in Relation to a Natural Person – Ordinarily Resident' 4 February 2002.

The 91-day and 915-day periods of physical presence in the Republic need not be continuous. If a person is present for several intermittent periods, which in aggregate exceed 91 or 915 days in the preceding five years of assessment, and 91 days in the current year of assessment, residence will be established.

When a person is not ordinarily resident, for example, because his or her usual or principal residence is not in the Republic and he or she becomes a resident by virtue of the physical presence test, he or she will be treated as a resident from the beginning of the current year of assessment (that is, 1 March). In these circumstances, he or she will become liable for income tax on a worldwide basis.

There are two provisos to the above criteria for determining physical presence:

> Proviso (A) to para *(a)*(ii) of the definition of resident states that for the purposes of determining the number of days during which a person is physically present in South Africa, a part of a day is included as a day.

A day spent in transit through South Africa is not included as a day, provided that the person does not formally enter South Africa through a port of entry. A day does not include any day that a person is passing through the Republic (through a 'port of entry' as contemplated in s 9(1) of the Immigration Act 13 of 2002, or at any other place as may be permitted by the Director-General of the Department of Home Affairs or the Minister of Home Affairs in terms of that Act).

SARS Interpretation Note 4[23] states that a day begins at 00:00 and ends at 24:00. Therefore, a person who arrives in the Republic through a port of entry at 23:55 and departs at 00:05 would be regarded as being physically present in the Republic for two days.

SARS Interpretation Note 25,[24] which deals with the way the physical presence test applies in the year a person dies or becomes insolvent, provides that the day that a person dies is included in that period of assessment. In the case of insolvency of the individual, the period of assessment ends on the day before the sequestration order is granted.

In terms of proviso (B) to para *(a)*(ii) of the definition of 'resident', a person who is a resident because of physical presence ceases to be such from the day he or she ceases to be physically present in the Republic, if he or she remains outside the Republic for a continuous period of at least 330 days. The period of 330 full days required to terminate his or her residence must be continuous and will extend over two years of assessment. In order to be a resident the person must have been physically present in the Republic for more than 91 days in the year that he or she ceases to be resident, and because the period of 330 days commences only after that, it will span two tax years. SARS Interpretation Note 4 (Issue 4) clearly explains that the continuous period of 330 full days cannot be observed over a single year of assessment because the person must have

[23] (Issue 3) dated 8 February 2006.

[24] (Issue 3) dated 12 March 2014.

been physically present in South Africa for at least 92 days during that year in order to qualify as a resident during that year of assessment. De Koker[25] explains that if, for example, a person departs South Africa on 1 October in year 3 and remains outside for a continuous period of at least 330 days, he or she will be taxed as a resident until the day he or she ceases to be such. From 1 October, he or she will be regarded as a non-resident if he or she indicates that he or she will not return within a period of 330 days immediately after departure. It needs mentioning that it cannot be known with certainty until year 4 whether in fact he or she will have been physically absent for at least 330 days. If he or she subsequently returns within the 330-day period, he or she will be regarded as a resident for the whole of tax year 3. In practice, SARS agrees with this interpretation.

3.3.2 Determining the residence of persons other than natural persons

In terms of the definition of 'resident' in s 1 of the Act, a person other than a natural person is resident if incorporated, established or formed in the Republic or if his or her place of effective management is located in the Republic.

3.3.2.1 Meaning of 'incorporated, established or formed in the Republic'

The term 'incorporated' as used in the definition of residents that are persons other than natural persons refers to companies. In terms of s 13 of the Companies Act 71 of 2008, a company comes into existence when the founder of the company files a Notice of Incorporation, accompanied by a Memorandum of Incorporation, with the Companies and Intellectual Property Commission. If all the registration requirements of the Companies Act (as set out in s 14) have been complied with, the company is deemed to be a South African resident and is liable to tax in South Africa on its worldwide income.

The terms 'established or formed' as used in the definition of residents that are persons other than natural persons are particularly relevant to trusts. In terms of s 1 of the Act, a trust is formed or established by the founder, who is usually the original owner of the property being placed in the trust. The founder appoints the trustees by way of a trust deed and specifies the beneficiaries to the trust property. Section 4 of the Trust Property Control Act 57 of 1988 requires that the trust should be registered with the Master of the High Court. A trust that is registered with the Master is deemed to be resident in South Africa, which means that in terms of s 1 of the Act, its worldwide income is liable to tax in South Africa.

[25] Example adopted from De Koker AP *Silke on South African Income Tax* (LexisNexis 2011) para 5.2B.

3.3.2.2 Meaning of 'place of effective management'

The Act does not provide a definition for the concept 'place of effective management'. It should, however, be noted that the term 'place of effective management' is used in a tax treaty context as a tie-breaker rule in the case of dual or multiple resident entities (for details on the treaty aspects in this regard, see chapter 13).[26] In *SIR v Downing*,[27] the court held that South Africa is bound to take cognisance of the guidelines for interpretation issued by the Organisation for Economic Co-operation and Development (OECD) in its commentaries on the concepts used in the OECD Model Tax Convention. Article 4 of the OECD Model Tax convention defines the place of effective management as—

> the place where the key management and commercial decisions that are necessary for the conduct of the entity's business are in substance made. All relevant facts and circumstances must be examined to determine the place of effective management. An entity may have more than one place of management, but it can have only one place of effective management at any one time.[28]

This interpretation of the term can be applied in South Africa. Most of South Africa's treaties largely follow the OECD Model Tax Convention on Income and on Capital,[29] although South Africa is not a member of the OECD.[30] It is also notable that s 231 of the Constitution of the Republic of South Africa provides that courts are bound to apply customary international rules and practices, such as the commentaries on the concepts used in the OECD Model Tax Convention.

It is, however, notable that the OECD's interpretation of the concept differed from SARS' first Interpretation Note 6,[31] which referred to the place of 'effective management' as the 'regular, day-to-day management by directors or senior managers of the entity through implementation of the policy and strategic decisions of its board of directors'.

Some clarity on the meaning of the term 'place of effective management' was provided in the Western Cape High Court decision of, *Oceanic Trust Co Ltd NO v CSARS*.[32] Oceanic Trust Co Ltd, a company incorporated in Mauritius, was the trustee of a Mauritian trust (SISM) which carried on business as a captive reinsurer. The premiums of the reinsurance policies were transferred to SISM, which invested in South African assets and for which it had a South African asset manager. SARS issued assessments to SISM, on the basis that it was a South African resident by virtue of having its place of effective management in

[26] Article 4(3) of the OECD Model Tax Convention on Income and on Capital (2008).

[27] 1975 (4) SA 518 (A), 37 SATC 249.

[28] Paragraph 24(1) of Commentary on Article 4 of the OECD Model Tax Convention (2008 condensed version).

[29] Olivier & Honiball *International Tax* 7; Huxham & Haupt *South African Income Tax* 341.

[30] Olivier & Honiball *International Tax* 10; Huxham & Haupt *South African Income Tax* 341.

[31] SARS Interpretation Note 6 of 26 March 2002; see also Van der Merwe BA 'The Phrase "Place of Effective Management" Effectively Explained?' (2006) 18 *SA Merc LJ* 124–125.

[32] Unreported, case no 22556/09 (WCC), 13 June 2011.

South Africa. SARS appointed SISM's South African bank as an agent in terms of s 99 of the Act and required the bank to pay SISM's taxes due in the amount of R1 billion. SISM approached the High Court to issue an order that it was, inter alia, not a resident of South Africa. SARS argued that SISM was required to pay the tax due in terms of the 'pay now argue later' principle, even as the merits of its objection were being considered.

With regard to whether SISM was effectively managed in South Africa, the High Court relied on a UK decision, *Commissioner for Her Majesty's Revenue and Customs v Smallwood and Another*,[33] pointing out that the place of effective management is the place where 'key management and commercial decisions that are necessary for the conduct of the entity's business are in substance made'. Noting inter alia that:

- the place of effective management will ordinarily be the place where the most senior group of persons (eg a board of directors) makes its decision, where the actions to be taken by the entity as a whole are determined;
- no definite rule can be given and all relevant facts and circumstances must be considered to determine the place of effective management of an entity; and
- although there may be more than one place of management, there may only be one place of effective management at any one time.

Although the High Court only had jurisdiction to hear the matter on questions of law and not the facts, the judge dismissed SISM's request for an order that it was not a resident of South Africa, ruling that—

> the place where key management and commercial decisions that were necessary for the conduct of SISM's business, were in substance made, has in my view not been established to be outside South Africa ... Therefore, applying the *Smallwood* test, the facts to the extent that they have been established, does not, in my view, establish that the place of effective management of SISM was in Mauritius, and not in South Africa.

This case clarified the position in South Africa that the place of effective management of a person other than a natural person is the place where key management and commercial decisions that are necessary for the conduct of a person's business are in substance made. The court's decision is in line with the OECD interpretation of the term, which is contrary to SARS's interpretation, which focuses on the place where the day-to-day decisions of an entity are implemented.[34]

In 2011 SARS came up with a discussion paper on Interpretation Note 6 in which SARS proposed to revise the meaning of 'place of effective management',

[33] [2010] EWCA Civ 778.

[34] Pearson B & Gounden N 'Place of Effective Management – Foreign Entities to Take Heed of a Recent Court Case' *Deloitte Tax News* No 3 of 2011 at 15.

so as to reduce the uncertainties that conflict with international views on the interpretation of the term. SARS proposed to place the primary emphasis on 'top' personnel who 'call the shots' and exercise 'realistic positive management'.

Following up on these developments, in 2012, the Supreme Court of Appeal made a ruling on the meaning of 'place of effective management' in the case of *CSARS v Tradehold Ltd.*[35] This case, which dealt with the capital gains tax consequences of ceasing to be a resident (and is discussed in 3.5.1 below), made it clear that the position in South Africa is that the 'place of effective management' is where the highest level of management of an entity is situated with regard to decision-making. This is in line with the position in the commentary on article 4(3) of the OECD Model Tax Convention.

On 3 November 2015 SARS issued Interpretation Note 6 (Issue 2).[36] The new Interpretation Note provides that the place of effective management of a company is the place where key management and commercial decisions that are necessary for the conduct of business as a whole are in substance made. The new Interpretation Note confirms that the place of effective management is the place where strategic decisions are taken or adopted, as opposed to the place where strategic decisions and policies are executed and implemented. SARS states that definitive rules cannot be laid down in determining the place of effective management and all relevant facts and circumstances must be examined on a case by-case basis. The place of effective management test is one of substance over form. It therefore requires a determination of those persons in a company who actually 'call the shots' and exercise 'realistic positive management'. This approach is consistent with the OECD Model Tax Convention and its accompanying commentary.

It should, however, be noted that SARS's Interpretation Notes are not law.[37] In *ITC 1675*,[38] it was stated that SARS is not bound by its own Practice Notes and Interpretation Notes. This implies that South Africa's local courts are not bound to follow SARS's Interpretation Notes.[39]

It should also be noted that the meaning of 'residence' with regard to persons other than natural persons applies not only to companies but also to entities such as deceased estates, trusts, clubs and associations, which are also capable of having a residence and being resident.[40] Such entities are deemed resident if established or formed or if they have their place of effective management in the Republic.[41] The actual place where the entity is established or formed is

---

35 [2012] 3 All SA 15 (SCA).

36 SARS issued Interpretation Note: No.6 (Issue 2) "Section 1(1): Resident – Place of Effective Management (Companies)" (3 November 2015).

37 Oguttu AW 'Resolving Double Taxation: The Concept "Place of Effective Management" Analysed from a South African Perspective' (2008) XLI *Comparative & International Law Journal of South Africa* 80 at 102.

38 62 SATC 219, Income Tax Case no 10230 2000 (6) JTLR 219 (TvlSpCrt).

39 This also applies to Practice Notes.

40 *Nathan's Estate v CIR* 1948 (3) SA 866 (N), 15 SATC 328; *CIR v Jagger & Co (Pty) Ltd* 1945 CPD 331, 13 SATC 430.

41 Definition of 'resident' in s 1 of the Act.

a matter of fact and each case must be decided on its own merits. The place where the assets of the entity are effectively managed will be also crucial. In the case of trusts, if the trustees (managers) of the trust are resident in the Republic or if the trust fund is administered from the Republic (for example, if the trustees meet to attend to the affairs of trust in the Republic), then the trust would be resident in the Republic.[42] For details on determining the place of effective management of a trust, see chapter 10.

3.3.2.3 Capital gains tax and residence

There is a capital gains tax implication when a person becomes resident in South Africa, and when a person becomes non-resident. On becoming resident, the person is deemed to have disposed of and reacquired his or her worldwide assets at their market value on that day.[43]

On becoming non-resident, that person is deemed to have disposed of all his or her assets (worldwide) for their market value on the day he or she becomes non-resident.[44] Paragraph 12(2)*(a)* of the Eighth Schedule to the Act provides that when a South African tax resident ceases to be a tax resident by virtue of the application of the provisions of a tax treaty entered into by South Africa with another jurisdiction, the resident must, subject to certain exclusions, be treated as having disposed of all his or her assets. The provision would for instance apply if a company moves its place of effective management out of South Africa. These deeming provisions do not apply to:

- immovable property that the person owns, directly or indirectly, which is situated in South Africa; and
- to the assets that are attributable to a permanent establishment of the resident through which a trade is carried on in the Republic, because these are subject to the normal capital gains tax rules.

3.4 DEEMED RESIDENCE

Certain types of income are deemed to be the income of a South African resident, notwithstanding the fact that the actual income is received by or accrues to a foreign entity:

3.4.1 Section 9D

South African residents are taxed on imputed income, namely a proportional portion of the net income accruing to controlled foreign companies (as defined) in certain circumstances. For details on the effect of the controlled foreign company provisions, see chapter 14.

[42] Oguttu *Curbing Offshore Tax Avoidance* 347.
[43] Huxham & Haupt *South African Income Tax* 28.
[44] Ibid.

3.4.2 Section 25B(2A)

If a resident's income is accumulated in a non-resident trust, s 25B(2A) provides:

> Where during any year of assessment any resident acquires any vested right to any amount representing capital of any trust which is not a resident, that amount must be included in the income of that resident in that year, if—
>
> *(a)* that capital arose from any receipt and accruals of such trust which would have constituted income if such trust had been a resident, in any previous year of assessment during which that resident had a contingent right to that income; and
>
> *(b)* that amount has not been subject to tax in the Republic in terms of this Act.

Note though that only residents who have acquired *vested rights* to such capital will be taxable in terms of this provision. For details on the operation of s 25B(2A), see chapter 10.

3.4.3 Section 7(8)

South African residents are taxed on income received by or accruing to non-residents (other than a controlled foreign company) to the extent that such income resulted by reason of or in consequence of any donation, settlement or other disposition made by the resident. For details on the working of s 7(8), see chapter 10.

3.5 CEASING TO BE A RESIDENT

3.5.1 Capital gains tax implications of ceasing to be a resident

There is a capital gains tax implication when a person becomes resident in South Africa, and when a person becomes non-resident. On becoming resident, the person is deemed to have disposed of and acquired his or her worldwide assets at their market value on that day he or she becomes non-resident. See 3.3.2.3 above for full discussion.[45]

On becoming non-resident, that person is deemed to have disposed of all his or her assets (worldwide) for their market value on the day he or she becomes non-resident.[46] Paragraph 12(2)*(a)* of the Eighth Schedule to the Act provides that when a South African tax resident ceases to be a tax resident by virtue of the application of the provisions of a tax treaty entered into by South Africa with another jurisdiction, the resident must, subject to certain exclusions, be treated as having disposed of all his or her assets. The provision would, for instance, apply if a company moved its place of effective management out of South Africa. These deeming provisions do not apply to:

---

[45] Huxham & Haupt *South African Income Tax* 28.

[46] Ibid.

- immovable property that the person owns, directly or indirectly, which is situated in South Africa; and
- to the assets that are attributable to a permanent establishment of the resident through which a trade is carried on in the Republic, because these are subject to the normal capital gains tax rules.

The 2012 Supreme Court of Appeal case of *CSARS v Tradehold Ltd*[47] dealt with the capital gains tax implications of para 12(2)*(a)* of the Eighth Schedule to the Act. The facts related to Tradehold Ltd, an investment holding company incorporated in South Africa and listed on the Johannesburg Stock Exchange. During the tax year that ended on 28 February 2003, Tradehold Ltd's only relevant asset was its 100% shareholding in Tradegro Holdings which, in turn, owned 100% of the shares in Tradegro Limited, a company incorporated in Guernsey which owned approximately 65% of the issued share capital in a United Kingdom-based company, Brown & Jackson Plc. On 2 July 2002, at a meeting of Tradehold Ltd's board of directors in Luxembourg, it was resolved that all further board meetings would be held in Luxembourg. This meant that Tradehold Ltd effectively became managed in Luxembourg as from 2 July 2002. Even though Tradehold Ltd had relocated its place of effective management to Luxembourg, it remained a 'resident' of South Africa by reason of the definition of the term 'resident' in s 1 of the Act, which provides that a company is resident in South Africa if it is incorporated, established or formed in the Republic or if his or her place of effective management is located in the Republic.

Relying on para 12 of the Eighth Schedule to the Act, the Commissioner contended that when Tradehold Ltd relocated its place of effective management to Luxembourg on 2 July 2002, or when it ceased to be a resident of South Africa on 26 February 2003, it was deemed to have disposed of all its assets which comprised its 100% shareholding in Tradegro Holdings, resulting in a capital gain in the 2003 year of assessment in an amount of R405 039 083. This tax is colloquially referred to as an 'exit tax'.

Tradehold Ltd appealed to the Tax Court against the assessment raised by the Commissioner, relying on article 13(4) of the double taxation agreement between South Africa and Luxembourg which provides that 'gains from the alienation of property other than that referred to in paras 1, 2 and 3, shall be taxable only in the contracting state of which the alienator is resident'. The Tax Court held that, since none of the exceptions in article 13 were applicable, the gains from the alienation of property were only taxable in Luxembourg where Tradehold Ltd was resident. The Commissioner argued that a deemed disposal of property should not be treated as an alienation of property for purposes of article 13(4). Nevertheless, the Tax Court upheld Tradehold's appeal.

On Appeal to the Supreme Court of Appeal, the issue was, inter alia, whether a deemed disposal as contemplated in para 12 of the Eighth Schedule to the Act constitutes an 'alienation' as contemplated in article 13(4) of the double

[47] [2012] 3 All SA 15 (SCA).

taxation agreement. The Supreme Court of Appeal upheld the decision of the Tax Court. In considering whether the term 'alienation' as used in the double taxation agreement includes gains arising from a deemed (as opposed to actual) disposal of assets, the Supreme Court of Appeal held that the term 'alienation' as used in the double taxation agreement is not restricted to an actual alienation, but is rather a neutral term having a broader meaning, including deemed disposals of assets giving rise to taxable capital gains. On this basis, the Supreme Court of Appeal held that from 2 July 2002, when Tradehold Ltd relocated its seat of effective management, the provisions of the double taxation agreement became applicable and Luxembourg accordingly had exclusive taxing rights to Tradehold Ltd's capital gains.

Following up on this decision, the definition of 'resident' in the Act was amended by the Revenue Laws Amendment Act 45 of 2003, effective from 1 June 2004, to the effect that the meaning of the term resident (for a natural person or a person other than a natural person) does not include any person who is deemed to be exclusively a resident of another country for purposes of the application of any double tax treaty. Provided that where any person who is a resident ceases to be resident during a year of assessment, that person must be regarded as not being resident from the day on which the person ceases to be resident.[48]

3.5.2 Ceasing to be a resident; becoming a headquarter company; or ceasing to be a controlled foreign company

Section 9H of the Act, introduced by the Taxation Laws Amendment Act 24 of 2011 and amended by the Taxation Laws Amendment Act 22 of 2012, included provisions in respect of any person that:

- ceases to be a resident;
- becomes a headquarter company; or
- ceases to be a controlled foreign company in relation to a resident, on or after that date.

These provisions (discussed below) came into operation on 8 May 2012.

In terms of s 9H(2) of the Act, as amended by the Taxation Laws Amendment Act 22 of 2015, where a person (other than a company) that is a resident ceases, during any year of assessment of that person, to be a resident—

(a) that person must be treated as having—

(i) disposed of each of that person's assets to a person that is a resident on the date immediately before the day on which that person so ceases to be a resident for an amount received or accrued equal to the market value of the asset on that date; and

[48] Definition of 'resident' in s 1 of the Act.

(ii) reacquired each of those assets on the day on which that person so ceases to be a resident at an expenditure equal to the market value contemplated in subparagraph (i);

(b) that year of assessment must be deemed to have ended on the date immediately before the day on which that person so ceases to be a resident; and

(c) the next succeeding year of assessment of that person must be deemed to have commenced on the day on which that person so ceases to be a resident.

In terms of s 9H(3)*(a)*: where a company that is a resident ceases during any year of assessment of that company to be a resident or where a company that is a resident becomes a headquarter company in respect of a year of assessment, that company must be treated as having—

(i) disposed of each of that company's assets to a person that is a resident on the date immediately before the day on which that company so ceased to be a resident or became a headquarter company; and

(ii) reacquired each of those assets on the day on which that company so ceased to be a resident or became a headquarter company,

for an amount equal to the market value of each of those assets.

In terms s 9(H)(3)*(c)*, where a company that is a resident ceases to be a resident or becomes a headquarter company during any year of assessment of that company as contemplated in s 9H(3)*(c)*(i)—

(i) that year of assessment must be deemed to have ended on the date immediately before the day on which that company so ceased to be a resident or became a headquarter company;

(ii) the next succeeding year of assessment of that company must be deemed to have commenced on the day on which that company so ceased to be a resident or became a headquarter company; and

(iii) that company must, on the date immediately before the day on which the company so ceased to be a resident or became a headquarter company and for the purposes of section 64EA*(b)*, be deemed to have declared and paid a dividend that consists solely of a distribution of an asset *in specie*—

(aa) the amount of which must be deemed to be equal to the sum of the market values of all the shares in that company on that date less the sum of the contributed tax capital of all the classes of shares in the company as at that date; and

(bb) to the person or persons holding shares in that company in accordance with the effective interest of that person or those persons in the shares in the company as at that date.

In terms s 9(H)(3)*(d)*, where a controlled foreign company ceases to be a controlled foreign company during any foreign tax year of that controlled foreign company as contemplated in s 9H(3)*(a)*(ii)—

(i) that foreign tax year must be deemed to have ended on the date immediately before the day on which that controlled foreign company so ceased to be a controlled foreign company; and

(ii) the next succeeding foreign tax year of that controlled foreign company must be deemed to have commenced on the day on which that controlled foreign company so ceased to be a controlled foreign company.

It should, however, be noted that in terms of s 9H(4), the provisions of s 9H(2) and (3) (set out above) do not apply in respect of an asset of a person where that asset constitutes—

(a) immovable property situated in the Republic that is held by that person;

(b) ......

[para. (b) deleted by s. 21 (1) of Act 31 of 2013.]

(c) any asset which is, after the person ceases to be a resident or a controlled foreign company as contemplated in subsection (2) or (3), attributable to a permanent establishment of that person in the Republic;

(d) any qualifying equity share contemplated in section 8B that was granted to that person less than five years before the date on which that person ceases to be a resident as contemplated in subsection (2) or (3);

(e) any equity instrument contemplated in section 8C that had not yet vested as contemplated in that section at the time that the person ceases to be a resident as contemplated in subsection (2) or (3); or

(f) any right of that person to acquire any marketable security contemplated in section 8A.

In terms of s 9H(5), the provisions in s 9H(2) and (3) do not apply if—

(a) a person disposes of an equity share in a foreign company that is a controlled foreign company;

(b) the capital gain or capital loss determined in respect of a disposal contemplated in paragraph *(a)* is disregarded in terms of paragraph 64B of the Eighth Schedule; and

(c) as a direct or indirect result of a disposal contemplated in paragraph *(a)*, a foreign company ceases to be a controlled foreign company, subsection (3) must not apply to any foreign company contemplated in paragraph *(c)*.

However, s 9H(6) provides that s 9H(5) does not apply in respect of—

(a) any company that ceases to be a controlled foreign company as a result of:

  (i) an amalgamation transaction as defined in section 44(1) to which section 44 applies; or

  (ii) a liquidation distribution as defined in section 47(1) to which section 47 applies; or

(b) any person that is a resident and that ceases to be a resident by reason of the coming into operation of section 2(1)*(w)* of the Taxation Laws Amendment Act, 2012.

3.6 RESIDENCE AND THE IMPLICATIONS FOR DOUBLE TAX TREATIES

The application of the residence basis of taxation is subject to the various double tax agreements South Africa has with other countries. Section 108(1) of the Act empowers the National Executive 'to enter into an agreement with the government of any other country, whereby arrangements are made with such government with a view to the prevention, mitigation or discontinuance of the levying, under the laws of the Republic and of such other country, of tax in respect of the same income, profits or gains ... under the said laws of the Republic and of such other country'.

Tax treaties provide a separate set of rules for determining whether a person is a resident of a country. Under most of these tax treaties a person is a resident of a country if that person is liable to tax in that country by reason of that person's domicile or residence. If a person is a resident of two countries by virtue of the criteria described in the tax treaty, that person's residence is determined by the various tie-breaker rules in the tax treaty (for details on tie-breaker rules, see chapter 14).

Note that in terms of the proviso to the definition of 'resident' in s 1 of the Act, this term does not include any person who is deemed to be exclusively a resident of another country for purposes of the application of any agreement entered into between the governments of the Republic and that other country for the avoidance of double taxation. The other provision is that where any person that is a resident ceases to be a resident during a year of assessment, that person must be regarded as not being a resident from the day on which that person ceases to be a resident.

Note that in a treaty context:

- Residents are entitled to the rebate or deduction for foreign taxes under s 6*quat* if an amount is taxable both in South Africa and in another country. (For details, see chapter 14.)
- Residents are entitled to claim deductions and allowances against their income derived from outside South Africa, when determining taxable income. However, in terms of s 20(1), an assessed loss arising from a trade outside South Africa may not be set off against the South African income of a resident.

3.7 'GROSS INCOME' WITH REGARD TO NON-RESIDENTS

As stated at para 3.2 above, when the residence basis of taxation was introduced from the years of assessment commencing 1 January 2001,[49] the source basis of taxation, which was predominately applied before then, was not discarded. The source basis of taxation is relevant for two reasons.

[49] Section 1 of the Act.

Firstly, persons who are not resident in South Africa are only subject to tax (in South Africa) on income from a South African source. The definition of 'gross income' in s 1 of the Act, which distinguishes between the basis of taxation applied to residents and that applied to non-residents, clarifies that for non-residents, 'gross income' in relation to a year or period of assessment is the total amount, in cash or otherwise, received by or accrued to or in favour of such non-resident from a source within or deemed to be within the Republic, excluding receipts or accruals of a capital nature. This general rule applies to both companies and persons other than companies. With the exception of non-resident companies, which are currently taxed at the rate of 28%, non-residents that derive South African source income are taxed at the rates that apply to residents and they are entitled to the deductions that apply to residents. Non-residents could also be subject to withholding taxes, which are discussed below.

Secondly, the source basis of taxation is relevant with regard to its use in the double tax treaties South Africa has entered into with other countries. The principal objective of tax treaties is to prevent double taxation of income. In resolving conflicts regarding the identification of the source of income, double tax treaties make reference to the concept of 'permanent establishment'. In general, if a non-resident company wishes to do business in South Africa, it could open up either a subsidiary or a branch. It could also have an agent to transact business on its behalf in South Africa. If a non-resident company incorporates a subsidiary company in another jurisdiction, the subsidiary is considered a separate legal entity that is liable to tax as a resident of that jurisdiction. But if a non-resident company opens a branch, or acts through a dependent agent, such branch or dependent agent is not considered a resident of the jurisdiction in which it is situated and it has to be taxed on a source basis of taxation.[50] In a treaty context, such a branch or dependent agent is referred to as a permanent establishment.

For South African income tax purposes a 'permanent establishment' is defined in s 1 of the Act, with reference to the definition of the concept in article 5 of the OECD Model Convention, in terms of which a permanent establishment is defined as 'a fixed place of business through which the business of an enterprise is wholly or partly carried on'. This would include a place of management; a branch; an office; a factory; a workshop; and a mine, an oil or gas well, a quarry or any place of extraction of natural resources.[51] In *Transvaal Associated Hide and Skin Merchants v Collector of Income Tax Botswana*,[52] a South African company purchased hides from abattoirs in Botswana and processed/cured them at a shed in Botswana in preparation for sale, which was executed at the head office in Pretoria. It was held that the company's occupation of a shed at an annual rental was permanent and not temporary or occasional, and that it had created a permanent establishment in Botswana. In *AB LLC and BD Holdings Tax*,[53] an American company provided strategic and financial

[50] Oguttu AW & Tladi S 'E-commerce: A Critique on the Determination of a "Permanent Establishment" for Income Tax Purposes from a South African Perspective' (2009) 20(1) *Stell LR* 74.

[51] Article 5(2) of the OECD Model Tax Convention.

[52] 29 SATC 97.

[53] [2015] ZATC 2 (15 May 2015).

services in South Africa whereby its employees occupied the boardroom at the recipient's premises in South Africa for a period exceeding 183 days to conduct those services. The court ruled that since the company provided consulting services through its employees in South Africa for a period exceeding 183 days, a permanent establishment had been created. The court also ruled that that boardroom where the services were performed constituted a fixed place of business and therefore a permanent establishment. Therefore, the income earned by the company that was attributable to that permanent establishment was taxable in South Africa.[54]

The definition of a permanent establishment also covers a dependent agent (article 5(5)) who has authority to conclude contracts on behalf of the enterprise and habitually exercises this authority in the source country.[55] In *SIR v Downing*,[56] the dependent agent article in South Africa's treaty with Switzerland was interpreted. In this case, Downing immigrated to Switzerland in 1960 and ceased to be a South African resident. However, part of his share portfolio remained in South Africa due to exchange control regulations. Downing authorised a stock broker to take care of his share portfolio and the proceeds therefrom were included in Downing's gross income. The court had to deal with the issue of whether the stock broker was Downing's dependent agent, which would imply that he had created a permanent establishment in South Africa and that the income from the share portfolio would be taxed in South Africa. It was held that the income was not taxable in South Africa as the stock broker was an independent agent, acting in the ordinary course of his business.

The permanent establishment definition excludes activities of an auxiliary or preparatory nature.[57] Article 7(1) of the OECD Model Tax Convention provides:

> The profits of an enterprise of a contracting state shall be taxable only in that state unless the enterprise carries on business in the other contracting state through a permanent establishment situated therein. If the enterprise carries on business as aforesaid, the profits of the enterprise may be taxed in the state but only so much of them as is attributable to that permanent establishment.

Thus, the significance of the permanent establishment concept is that it gives the country in which the permanent establishment is situated (the source country) the right to tax the permanent establishment's income, notwithstanding the fact that the permanent establishment has no separate legal existence.[58] For a detailed discussion on the permanent establishment concept, see chapter 14.

---

[54] See Legwaila T 'Permanent establishment on the furnishing of services: *AB LLC and BD Holdings LLC v Commissioner of the South African Revenue Services* (13276) 2015 ZATC 2' (2016) 4 *TSAR* 822.

[55] Article 5(5) of the OECD Model Tax Convention. See also Danziger L *International Tax Law* (1991) 334; Rohatgi R *Basic International Taxation* (Kluwer Law International 2002) 77

[56] 1975 (4) SA 518 (A).

[57] Article 5(4) of the OECD Model Tax Convention.

[58] Skaar AA *Permanent Establishment: Erosion of a Tax Treaty Principle* (Kluwer 1991) 1; Oguttu AW 'The Challenges of Taxing Profits Attributed to Permanent Establishments: A South African Perspective' (2010) 64(3) *Bulletin for International Taxation* 172–200.

3.7.1 The meaning of 'source'

The Taxation Laws Amendment Act 24 of 2011 changed the rules regarding the determination of the source of income from the years of assessment commencing 1 January 2012. Although non-residents are taxed on income from a 'source' in the Republic, the term 'source' is not defined in the Act. The meaning of 'source' has been determined with reference to the common law, which entails deducting the meaning of 'source' from case law. In *Rhodesia Metals Ltd (in Liquidation) v COT*[59] it was held that source means, not a legal concept, but something which the practical man would regard as the 'real source of income' and that the ascertaining of the actual source is a practical, hard matter of fact. The principle that was established in this case is found in the following quote from the judgment of Watermeyer CJ:[60]

> The source of receipts, received as income, is not the quarter whence they come, but the originating cause of their being received as income and that this originating cause is the work which the taxpayer does to earn them, the *quid pro quo* which he gives in return for which he receives them. The work which he does may be a business which he carries on, or an enterprise which he undertakes, or an in activity in which he engages and it may take the form of personal exertion, mental or physical, or it may take the form of employment of capital either by using it to earn income or by letting its use to someone else.

This was confirmed in *CIR v Lever Bros and Another*[61] where it was decided that the source of income is established by first determining the originating cause (that is what the taxpayer does to produce the income) and then by locating the originating cause.

In determining whether the originating cause is located in the Republic of South Africa, it is important to note that since South Africa is a coastal country, the portion of the ocean along its coastline constitutes part of the Republic of South Africa. In terms of the Revenue Laws Second Amendment Act 36 of 2007, the definition of the Republic of South Africa, when used in a geographical sense, includes the territorial sea thereof as well as any area outside the territorial sea which has been or may be designated, under international law and the laws of South Africa, as areas within which South Africa may exercise sovereign rights or jurisdiction with regard to the exploration or exploitation of natural resources.

3.7.2 Determining source in the case of multiple sources

Before the amendments to the Act, ushered in by the Taxation Laws Amendment Act 24 of 2011, common-law principles were also relied on in the case of multiple sources of income, which made it difficult to determine the location of the source of income if the activities that result in the income being received

---

[59] 1938 AD 282.

[60] *CIR v Lever Bros and Another* 1946 AD 441 at 450.

[61] 1946 AD 441 442, 14 SATC 1.

are performed partly in South Africa and partly in one or more countries. Since the Act did not provide for the apportionment of the source of income, common law had to be relied on to determine the 'main, real, dominant or substantial source'. These principles still apply in determining the source of income from years of assessment before 1 January 2012. In *CIR v Black*,[62] a stockbroker who carried on the business of buying and selling shares in Johannesburg had a similar but clearly separate business in London. The authorisation or confirmation of the transactions was mostly given telephonically by the stockbroker in Johannesburg to his agents in London, who bought and sold the shares for him. Only the capital and certain overdraft facilities which he held in London were used to finance the London transactions. The Appellate Division held that it was reasonable to conclude that the main, real, dominant and substantial source of the income was the use of the stockbroker's capital in London and the conclusion and execution of the contracts in London.

In the case of profits resulting from the combined transactions of 'buying and selling', there is no clear-cut answer, but the 'activities test' has been applied in some cases to determine the source of income. In *Essential Sterolin Products (Pty) Ltd v CIR*[63] the taxpayer developed a medicine in South Africa, but registered it in West Germany. The active substance of the medicine was manufactured in South Africa and then exported to Germany where fillers were added, packed and marketed. The medicine had to be properly registered and patented in Germany before it could be sold in Germany. The dispute was about the right to a lump sum paid to the company for the right to be able to manufacture the medicine in the event that the company was unable to. It was held that the dominant cause of the income was the selling of the medicine, as the medicine could only be sold in Germany since that is where it was registered. As a result, Germany was held to be the source of the income.

3.8 THE SOURCE OF DIFFERENT TYPES OF INCOME

From years of assessment commencing 1 January 2012, the Taxation Laws Amendment Act 24 of 2011 amended the Act to provide for new rules for determining the source of different types of income. Before dealing with the new source rules, let us consider the working of the old source rules, which applied to years of assessment before 1 January 2012.

For years of assessment before 1 January 2012, case law sets out the different rules for determining the 'true' source of different types of income, and there are some 'deeming' source rules in respect of some categories of income, such as interest, royalties and capital gains (amongst others). In effect, the deeming rules create deemed South African source income in addition to South African source income under the common law. If the true source of a receipt is outside the Republic but a deemed source provision deemed the source to be within

62 1957 (3) SA 536 (A), 21 SATC 226.
63 1993 (4) SA 859 (A), 55 SATC 357.

South Africa, the deemed source rule prevailed over the true source rule. Foreign source income existed only once it was determined that the income was neither actual South African source under common-law principles nor deemed South African source under income tax legislation.

3.8.1 Old source rules

3.8.1.1 True source: The sale of immovable property

The true source of income from the sale of immovable property is the location of the immovable property. In *Rhodesia Metals Ltd (in Liquidation) v COT*,[64] a company was located and registered in England, but it had its main asset and mining claims in Rhodesia. When the claims were sold to another English company, the court held that the proceeds from the sale had their originating case from the employment of the capital in Rhodesia and that is where the source of income was located.

3.8.1.2 True source: The sale of movable goods

Common law provides that the true source of income from the sale of movable goods can be determined by considering the place of conclusion of the contract, the performance by the seller, the payment by the buyer or a combination of the abovementioned possibilities. The decision will depend on which is the dominant cause. In *CIR v Epstein*[65] goods were bought in the Republic and sold elsewhere under a joint venture. Schreiner JA, in his dissenting judgment, was of the opinion that the country in which the goods are sold is the country in which the profits originate. However, the majority judges ignored this aspect completely. They held that all the activities of the taxpayer, who was responsible for buying the goods, were carried on in the Republic. His share of the partnership/joint venture income was his *quid pro quo* (reward) for the services rendered to the partnership, which in this instance took place in the Republic.

3.8.1.3 True source: Services

Common law provides that the originating cause of income from services rendered is the service or the work and it is located where the service is performed or rendered or where the work is done. In *COT v Shein*[66] the court held that accepting responsibility constituted the rendering of a service and that the service was provided where the responsibility was exercised.

---

64 1938 AD 282, 9 SATC 363.
65 1954 (3) SA 689 (A), 19 SATC 221.
66 1958 (3) SA 14 (FC), 22 SATC 12.

3.8.1.4 True source: Interest

In terms of the old source rules, the source of interest income was where the credit was made available (normal source rules) or where the capital was employed (deemed source rules).

One of the earliest cases on determining the source of interest is *COT v William Dunn & Co Ltd*,[67] in which the court held that the source of interest is the place where the capital is employed and that this need not necessarily be the place where the debt is located or the debtor resides. For years, however, the leading authority on the source of interest was *CIR v Lever Bros and Another*[68] in which the court held that the source of interest was not the debt but rather the granting of the credit, which is normally where the credit is made available, ie where the creditor's business is located (this case sets up the position for determining the source of interest under the normal source rules).

However, in *First National Bank of Southern Africa Ltd v CSARS*[69] the taxpayer relied on *Lever Bros,* arguing that the source of interest was in New York where the credit was made available. The court found that the principles used in *Lever Bros* would not be appropriate in the situation where the taxpayer carried on the business of banking. The court held in *First National Bank of Southern Africa Ltd* that the source of interest earned was the bank's business activities and operations in South Africa, even though the loans were denominated in a foreign currency and were lent to customers outside South Africa. The court ruled that, apart from the fact that contractually the foreign currency was availed to the borrowers in New York and had to be repaid there, all the other dominant and important factors which caused the interest to arise had their origin in South Africa and flowed from the banks' business activities and operations in South Africa. The court overlooked the narrow view in the *Lever Bros* case of considering only where funds were made available and considered the whole transaction that generated the interest with a view to determining the location of its source.

To ensure clarity on the source of interest income in light of the above cases, two deeming source provisions (the previous s 9(6) and 9(7) – now amended in terms of the rules) were added to the Act in 1998.

(a) Deemed source: Interest

Section 9(6) deemed any interest (as defined in s 24J) to be received or accrued from a South African source where such interest was derived from the utilisation or application in the Republic by any person of any funds or credit obtained in terms of any interest-bearing arrangement.

Section 9(7) clarified what was meant by 'utilised or applied' in the Republic. Until the contrary was proved, these terms meant:

---

[67] 1918 AD 607, 32 SATC 33.

[68] 1946 AD 441, 14 SATC 1.

[69] 2002 (3) SA 375 (SCA), 64 SATC 245.

- where the funds or credit are utilised by a natural person, the place where such person is ordinarily resident; and
- where the funds or credit are utilised or applied by a person other than a natural person, its place of effective management.

3.8.1.5 True source: Rent

The true source of rent is where the asset is situated. In *COT v British United Shoe Machinery (SA) (Pty) Ltd*[70] a company had its place of business in South Africa and it dealt in machinery used in the manufacture of footwear. The company leased machinery to a trader in Rhodesia; the court held that the rental income had its source in Rhodesia where the machines were located. Based on the authority in the *British United Shoe Machinery* case, in *ITC 1087*[71] the court held that 'where income is derived from the use of immovable property, its source is where the property is used'.

3.8.1.6 True source: Dividends

In terms of the old source rules, the source of dividends was determined by reference to location of the share register. In *Boyd v CIR*[72] it was held that the originating cause of income from dividends was the shares that gave rise to the dividends. The shares are situated where the share register is located. In terms of the South African Companies Act 71 of 2008, which came into force on 1 May 2011, all companies registered in South Africa must keep their register of shareholders in South Africa. Thus in terms of the old source rules, the shares of a company registered in a foreign country were regarded as being located in that foreign country. In applying these principles, regard was given to the fact that, with certain exceptions, all dividends from a South African source are exempt from tax in terms of s 10(1)*(k)*(i).

3.8.1.7 True source: Royalties

In terms of the old source rules, the source of royalty income arising from created work or personal effort was where the work was done. The main case that was relied on to determine the source royalty was *Millin v CIR*,[73] in which an author of novels who resided in South Africa received royalties from an English publisher in terms of a contract negotiated in England. It was held that it was the exercise of her wits and labour that produced the royalties and this was done in the Union (as the Republic was then known). As her faculties were employed in the Union, both in writing the book and in dealing with her publishers, the source of her whole income was in the Union.

---

70 1964 (3) SA 193 (FC), 26 SATC 163.
71 (1966) 28 SATC 196 (R).
72 1951 (3) SA 525 (A), 17 SATC 366.
73 1928 AD 207, 3 SATC 170.

Where the royalties were derived by a person who is not the original author or inventor, other considerations are applied, depending on the facts of each case. This is often the case where a person acquires royalties on a copyright from the original author or patent rights from the original inventor. Such royalties are not derived from that person's wits or labour, but from the ownership of the copyright or patent rights. The source of the royalties in such cases was determined by considering factors such as: the business of the owner of the rights, the employment of the capital invested in the acquisition of the rights, or the contract providing for the earning of the royalties from the exploitation of the rights. In *ITC 1491*,[74] it was held that the exploitation in the United Kingdom of a patented process and know-how for resurfacing bathtubs gave rise to non-South African source income. The development of the process in South Africa was irrelevant because the rights to the process had been acquired in South Africa by purchase and not developed by the taxpayer personally, as was the case in *Millin*.

In a treaty context, the provisions of the double tax treaty that relate to the taxation of royalties derived by South African residents from sources in other countries and the royalties derived by non-residents from sources in the Republic were taken into consideration. For example (subject to the provisions of an applicable tax treaty) s 10(1)*(m)* of the Act provides for an exemption from tax on royalties received by an author (not a company) in respect of the grant of an interest in a copyright, of which the author is the first owner, if the amount is taxed in another country.[75]

(a) Deemed source: Royalties

The old source rules also had a deeming provision regarding royalty income, in that royalty income was deemed to be from a South African source if intellectual property was used in South Africa. The then s 9(1)*(b)* (now amended in terms of the new rules) provided that an amount was deemed to be from a South African source if it was received by or accrued to a non-resident by virtue of the use or right of use (or permission to use) in the Republic of:

- any patent, design, trademark, copyright, model, pattern, plan, formula or process (or any property of similar nature); or
- any motion picture film, video tape or disc or any sound recording or advertising matter.

Section 9(1)*(bA)* (now amended in terms of the new rules) deemed any amount to be from a South African source if it was received by or accrued to a non-resident in respect of imparting or undertaking to impart scientific, technical, industrial or commercial knowledge or information for use in the Republic. In taxing income from royalties, consideration was given to the then s 35 withholding tax on royalties of the Act (now repealed in terms of the Taxation Laws Amendment Act 22 of 2012). The withholding tax on royalties is now contained in ss 49A–D in part IVA in chapter II of the Act.

[74] 53 SATC 115.

[75] De Koker *South African Income Tax* para 5.13.

3.8.1.8 True source: Shares

In *CIR v Black*[76] a South African stockbroker carried on a secondary business in London. Certain profits accrued from the sale of shares in London. The court found that the income had accrued as a result of the employment of capital and the carrying on of a separate business in London and was, therefore, non-South African source income.

3.8.1.9 Deemed source: Mining leases

Section 9(1)*(cA)* (now repealed in terms of the new source rules) provided that an amount was deemed to be derived from a source in the Republic if it had been received by or had accrued to or in favour of a taxpayer by virtue of a contract made by him or her for the disposal of any mineral won by him or her in the course of mining operations carried on in terms of the Minerals Act 50 of 1991 and the Mineral and Petroleum Resources Development Act 28 of 2002, no matter where the contract was made or where the mining operations were carried on.

3.8.1.10 True source: Government employees

Section 9(1)*(e)* (now repealed in terms of the new source rules) deemed an amount to be from a South African source if it was received by a person:

- by virtue of any services rendered or work or labour done for or on behalf of any employer in the national or provincial sphere of government or any municipality or any national or provincial public entity;
- if not less than 80% of the expenditure of such entity was defrayed from funds voted by Parliament; and
- if the work done was in accordance with a contract of employment entered into with the government or local authority.

(a) Deemed source: Government pensions

Section 9(1)*(g)*(i) (now repealed in terms of the new source rules) provided that an amount was deemed to be from a source in the Republic if it had been received or had accrued to or in favour of a taxpayer by virtue of any pension or annuity granted to him or her by the government of the Republic, no matter where payment was made or where the funds from which payment was made are situated.

3.8.1.11 Deemed source: Divorce

In terms of s 21 of the Act, alimony paid by a spouse as a result of a divorce before 21 March 1962 is allowed as a deduction. Section 9(1)*(h)* (now repealed in terms of the new source rules) deemed such income in the hands of the receiving spouse to be from a South African source irrespective of where the amount was paid.

[76] 1957 (3) SA 536 (A), 21 SATC 226.

3.8.1.12 Deemed source: Capital gains and losses in respect of immovable property situated in South Africa

A capital gain or capital loss was deemed to be from a source in the Republic if it was, in respect of the disposal of immovable property (or any right in immovable property), situated in the Republic. This included equity shares in a company where more than 80% of the market value of those shares was attributable to fixed property held (directly or indirectly) by the company as *a capital asset* and the taxpayer (or both the taxpayer and anyone connected to him) held at least 20% of the equity shares of that company (directly or indirectly).

3.8.1.13 Deemed source: Capital gains and losses in respect of assets other than immovable property

A capital gain or capital loss in respect of any asset, other than immovable (or any interest or right to or in immovable), was deemed to be from a Republic source if:

- the person who disposed of the asset was a resident and the asset was not attributable to a permanent establishment situated outside the Republic and the proceeds were subject to tax on income in another country; or
- the person who disposed of the asset was not a resident and the asset was attributable to a permanent establishment of that person which was situated in the Republic.

3.8.1.14 Other deemed source provisions in the 'gross income' definition

The definition of gross income in s 1 of the Act also covered the deemed source of certain types of income to be derived from a source located in South Africa.

Paragraph *(e)* of the definition of gross income (which includes retirement fund lump sum benefits in gross income), read together with the Second Schedule (which deals with the taxability of lump sums), was subject to the apportionment rule in s 9(1)*(g)*. In terms of this rule, no portion of a pension, lump sum benefit or annuity was deemed to be derived from a source in the Republic when the person who earned it worked both in and outside the Republic during a certain period.

Paragraph *(n)* of the definition of gross income provides that the recoupment of expenditure allowed as a deduction must be included in a taxpayer's income in terms of s 8(4). Such recouped amounts were deemed to have been derived from a source in the Republic, even though they might have been recouped outside the Republic.

Section 8E deems dividends declared by a company on a 'hybrid equity instrument' as defined to be interest received by the recipient from a source within the Republic.

3.8.2 New source rules from years of assessment commencing 1 January 2012

As noted above, in terms of the Taxation Laws Amendment Act 24 of 2011, the source rules have been amended to ensure a uniform system of these rules under s 9(1) of the Act. The Explanatory Memorandum on the Taxation Laws Amendment Bill, 2011 states that the previous source rules gave rise to uncertainty, thereby imposing additional costs in respect of cross-border activities with little or no benefit for the fiscus. Part of this uncertainty stemmed from differing interpretations about the application of common law.[77] The new system represents an amalgamation of the common law, pre-existing statutory law and tax treaty principles.[78] The uniform source rules reflect international tax treaty principles (with a few added, built-in protections) to ensure that the South African system is in line with international practices. The common-law source rules largely remain as a residual method for certain categories of income, but the deemed source concept has been eliminated.

3.8.2.1 Source of dividend income

In terms of the old source rules discussed above, the source of dividends depended on the common law, which mainly focuses on the share register. This view was not in line with international practices such as the OECD model treaty principles, which focus on residence. A dividend is locally sourced (subject to the 'tie-breaker' rules) if the distributing company is a resident (residence is based on the country where that company was formed or established or where that company's effective management resides).

In order to bring the dividend source rules in line with international trends, the source of dividend income has been amended. The new source of dividend rules is now designed to ensure roughly the same outcome as the OECD principles. The new source rules of dividends now provide that dividends from domestic resident companies will be sourced in South Africa, whereas 'foreign dividends' are sourced from the relevant foreign country. The 'share register' concept of common law is no longer relevant.[79]

The new s 9(2)*(a)* provides that an amount is received by or accrues to a person from a source within the Republic if that amount constitutes a dividend received by or accrued to that person.

Section 9(4)*(a)* provides that an amount is received by or accrues to a person from a source outside the Republic if that amount constitutes a foreign dividend received by or accrued to that person.

---

[77] Paragraph 4.2 (II) of the Explanatory Memorandum on the Draft Taxation Laws Amendment Bill, 2011.

[78] Paragraph 4.2 (III) of the Explanatory Memorandum on the Draft Taxation Laws Amendment Bill, 2011.

[79] Explanatory Memorandum on the Taxation Laws Amendment Bill, 2011 97.

3.8.2.2 Source of interest income

The old source rules for interest were determined through a combination of common law and deeming legislation. The common-law rules follow the doctrine of originating cause. The originating cause for interest was viewed as the supply of credit and the location of the originating cause was the place where that credit was supplied. Therefore, interest was sourced in South Africa if the credit was provided by a South African credit provider. In addition, legislative rules deemed interest to be sourced in South Africa if the interest was derived from the utilisation or application of funds within South Africa. South African residents paying interest were presumed to be utilising or applying funds within South Africa.[80]

The old source rules were not in line with international practices. For instance, the OECD model tax treaty principles focus on the tax residence of the payor (ie the debtor incurring the interest). However, if the payment of interest arises from a permanent establishment located in the source country, the focus shifts to the source country.

The source of interest rule was thus amended to fall in line with the OECD principles. The determination of source of interest is now based on a two-part test:

(a) the residence of the debtor paying/incurring the interest; or

(b) the place in which the loan funds are utilised or applied.

Therefore, interest will be sourced in South Africa if:

(a) paid by a South African resident; or

(b) the interest is derived from use or application in South Africa (eg from a South African permanent establishment). The new rules remove the focus on the credit provider.[81]

Section 9(2)*(b)* provides that an amount is received by or accrues to a person from a source within the Republic if that amount constitutes interest as defined in s 24J or deemed interest as contemplated in s 8E(2) where that interest—

> (i) is attributable to an amount incurred by a person that is a resident, unless the interest is attributable to a permanent establishment which is situated outside the Republic; or
>
> (ii) is received or accrues in respect of the utilisation or application in the Republic by any person of any funds or credit obtained in terms of any form of interest-bearing arrangement …

Section 9(4)*(b)* provides that an amount is received by or accrues to a person from a source outside the Republic if that amount constitutes interest as defined in s 24J(1) or deemed interest as contemplated in s 8E(2) received by or accrued to that person that is not from a source within the Republic in terms of s 9(2)*(b)*.

---

80 Explanatory Memorandum on the Taxation Laws Amendment Bill, 2011 at 97.

81 Ibid.

3.8.2.3 Source of royalty income

The source of royalties under the old rules was determined through a combination of common law and deeming legislation. The common-law doctrine of originating cause for determining the source of royalties focused on where the intellectual property producing the royalty was created, devised or developed. In addition, legislation deemed royalties to be South African sourced if the royalties related to the use, right of use or the grant of permission to use the intellectual property within South Africa.

These rules were not in line with international practices. In terms of the OECD model tax treaty principles the source of royalties is based on the tax residence of the party paying the royalties or on royalties having an economic link with a permanent establishment. To bring the source rules in line with international practices, the determination of the source of royalties is now based on the residence of the party paying the royalties. In addition, royalties are sourced in South Africa if they relate to the use, right of use or grant of permission to use intellectual property within South Africa. The new rules remove any focus on the party creating, devising or developing intellectual property (thereby removing the current disincentive to generate intellectual property within South Africa).[82]

Section 9(1) provides that for the purposes of this section, 'royalty' means any amount that is received or accrues in respect of the use, right of use or permission to use any intellectual property as defined in s 23I.

Section 9(2)*(c)* and *(d)* provides that an amount is received by or accrues to a person from a source within the Republic if that amount—

> *(c)* constitutes a royalty that is attributable to an amount incurred by a person that is a resident, unless that royalty is attributable to a permanent establishment which is situated outside the Republic;
>
> *(d)* constitutes a royalty that is received or accrues in respect of the use or right of use of or permission to use in the Republic any intellectual property as defined in section 23I ...

Section 9(4)*(c)* provides that an amount is received by or accrues to a person from a source outside the Republic if that amount constitutes a royalty received by or accrued to that person that is not from a source within the Republic in terms of s 9(2)*(c)* or 9(2)*(d)*.

3.8.2.4 Source of scientific, industrial or commercial knowledge or information

Section 9(2)*(e)* and *(f)* provides that an amount is received by or accrues to a person from a source within the Republic—

[82] Ibid.

(e) if that amount is attributable to an amount incurred by a person that is a resident and is received or accrues in respect of the imparting of or the undertaking to impart any scientific, technical, industrial or commercial knowledge or information, or the rendering of or the undertaking to render, any assistance or service in connection with the application or utilisation of such knowledge or information, unless the amount so received or accrued is attributable to a permanent establishment which is situated outside the Republic;

(f) if that amount is received or accrues in respect of the imparting of or the undertaking to impart any scientific, technical, industrial or commercial knowledge or information for use in the Republic, or the rendering of or the undertaking to render, any assistance or service in connection with the application or utilisation of such knowledge or information.

3.8.2.5 Source of income from services rendered

The old rules for determining the source of income from services rendered were based solely on the common law. The focus was on the place where the services are rendered (with some minority arguments in favour of the dominant activity giving rise to those services). If services are rendered partly within and partly outside South Africa, the allocation of source is based entirely on the facts and circumstances (eg time and value addition). The basic common-law source rules for services have not been changed.[83]

3.8.2.6 Source of public office income

As is the case with the old source rules, the source of services for (or on behalf of) the various tiers of government are considered to be from a South African source. No regard is given to where those services were rendered.[84]

Section 9(2)*(g)* provides that an amount is received by or accrues to a person from a source within the Republic if that amount is received or accrues in respect of the holding of a public office to which that person has been appointed or is deemed to have been appointed in terms of an Act of Parliament.

3.8.2.7 Source of income from services rendered in the public sector

Section 9(2)*(h)* provides that an amount is received by or accrues to a person from a source within the Republic if that amount is received or accrues in respect of services rendered to or work or labour performed for or on behalf of any employer—

(i) in the national, provincial or local sphere of government of the Republic;

83 Explanatory Memorandum on the Taxation Laws Amendment Bill, 2011 at 99.

84 Ibid.

(ii) that is a constitutional institution listed in Schedule 1 to the Public Finance Management Act, 1999 (Act 1 of 1999);

(iii) that is a public entity listed in Schedule 2 or 3 to that Act; or

(iv) that is a municipal entity as defined in section 1 of the Local Government: Municipal Systems Act, 2000 (Act 32 of 2000).

3.8.2.8 Source of pensions and annuities

The rules for determining the source of income from pensions and annuities follow the same principles as the source determination for service income (the rules have not been changed). The source of annuity and pension payments is thus based on the source of the underlying services giving rise to those payments. If the underlying services are rendered within South Africa, the associated annuities and pensions will be viewed as a South African source. If the annuities and pensions relate to mixed services (ie services rendered within and without South Africa), the allocation will be based on time spent.[85]

Section 9(2)*(i)* provides that an amount is received by or accrues to a person from a source within the Republic if that amount constitutes a pension or an annuity and the services in respect of which that amount is so received or accrues were rendered within the Republic:

> Provided that if the amount is received or accrues in respect of services which were rendered partly within and partly outside the Republic, only so much of that amount as bears to the total of that amount the same ratio as the period during which the services were rendered in the Republic bears to the total period during which the services were rendered must be regarded as having been received by or accrued to the person from a source within the Republic.

Section 9(3) provides that for the purposes of s 9(2)*(i)*, any amount granted to a person by way of pension or annuity must be deemed to have been received by or to have accrued to that person in respect of services rendered by that person.

3.8.2.9 Source of capital gains from immovable property located in South Africa

As is the case with the old source rules, gains in respect of immovable property are sourced in South Africa if the immovable property is situated in South Africa. However, the new source rules contain special look-through rules, which apply if ownership exists through company shares and 80% or more of the market value of the company shares stems from the immovable property.[86]

Section 9(2)*(j)* provides that an amount is received by or accrues to a person from a source within the Republic if it constitutes an amount received or accrued in respect of the disposal of an asset that constitutes immovable property held

85 Ibid.

86 Ibid.

by that person or any interest or right of whatever nature of that person to or in immovable property and that property is situated in the Republic.

Section 9(3) provides that for the purposes of s 9(2)*(j)*, an interest in immovable property held by a person includes any equity shares in a company or ownership or the right to ownership of any other entity or a vested interest in any assets of any trust, if—

> (i) 80 per cent or more of the market value of those equity shares, ownership or right to ownership or vested interest, as the case may be, at the time of disposal thereof, is attributable directly or indirectly to immovable property held otherwise than as trading stock; and
>
> (ii) in the case of a company or other entity, that person (whether alone or together with any connected person in relation to that person) directly or indirectly holds at least 20 per cent of the equity shares in that company or ownership or right to ownership of that other entity.

Section 9(4)*(d)* provides that an amount is received by or accrues to a person from a source outside the Republic if that amount constitutes an amount received or accrued to that person in respect of the disposal of an asset that is not from a source within the Republic in terms of s 9(2)*(j)*.

3.8.2.10 Source of capital gains from movable property

As is the case with the old source rules, the source of gains from movable property is based on the residence of the person disposing of the movable property (ie if the party disposing of the property is a South African resident, the disposal will be considered to be from a South African source). The notion of deemed source has been eliminated.[87]

Section 9(2)*(k)* provides that an amount is received by or accrues to a person from a source within the Republic if it constitutes an amount received or accrued in respect of the disposal of an asset other than an asset contemplated in para *(j)* if—

> (i) that person is a resident and—
>
> *(aa)* that asset is not attributable to a permanent establishment of that person which is situated outside the Republic; and
>
> *(bb)* the proceeds from the disposal of that asset are not subject to any taxes on income payable to any sphere of government of any country other than the Republic; or
>
> (ii) that person is not a resident and that asset is attributable to a permanent establishment of that person which is situated in the Republic …;

Section 9(4)*(d)* provides that an amount is received by or accrues to a person from a source outside the Republic if that amount constitutes an amount received or accrued to that person in respect of the disposal of an asset that is not from a source within the Republic in terms of s 9(2)*(k)*.

[87] Ibid.

3.8.2.11 Source of income from exchange differences

Section 9(2)*(l)* provides that that an amount is received by or accrues to a person from a source within the Republic if it is attributable to any exchange difference determined in terms of s 24I in respect of any exchange item as defined in that section to which that person is a party if—

(i) that person is a resident and—

(aa) that exchange item is not attributable to a permanent establishment of that person which is situated outside the Republic; and

(bb) that amount is not subject to any taxes on income payable to any sphere of government of any country other than the Republic; or

(ii) that person is not a resident and that exchange item is attributable to a permanent establishment of that person which is situated in the Republic.

Section 9(4)*(e)* provides that an amount is received by or accrues to a person from a source outside the Republic if that amount is attributable to any exchange difference determined in terms of s 24I in respect of any exchange item as defined in that section to which that person is a party and is not from a source within the Republic in terms of s 9(2)*(l)*.

3.9 WITHHOLDING TAXES ON NON-RESIDENTS

To enable the collection of taxes from non-residents, governments often impose a withholding tax on payments to non-residents. Taxes are collected via a withholding tax by appointing a resident as the non-resident's agent and imposing an obligation on the resident agent to withhold a certain percentage of tax from specified payments made to the non-resident. If the resident agent does not comply with this duty or if he or she withholds an incorrect amount of tax, personal liability can be imposed on the resident agent.[88]

3.9.1 The withholding tax on royalty income

The provisions dealing with withholding tax on royalties were previously found in s 35 of the Act. However, s 65 of the Taxation Laws Amendment Act 22 of 2012 repealed s 35 of the Act with effect from 1 July 2013. In terms of the Taxation Laws Amendment Act 22 of 2012, the provisions that relate to the withholding tax on royalties are now contained in ss 49A–D in part IVA in chapter II of the Act. Section 49A defines 'royalty' to mean any amount that is received or accrues in respect of—

(a) the use or right of use of or permission to use any intellectual property as defined in section 23I; or

(b) the imparting of or the undertaking to impart any scientific, technical, industrial or commercial knowledge or information, or the rendering of or the undertaking to render any assistance or service in connection with the application or utilisation of such knowledge or information.

[88] Olivier & Honiball *International Tax* 362–363.

Section 49B provides for the levying of withholding tax on royalties. In terms of s 49B(1), the withholding tax on royalties is calculated at the rate of 15% of the amount of any royalty that is paid by any person to or for the benefit of any foreign person to the extent that the amount is regarded as having been received by or accrued to that foreign person from a source within the Republic in terms of s 9(2)*(c)*, *(d)*, *(e)* or *(f)*. In terms of s 49B(2), a royalty is deemed to be paid on the earlier of the date on which the royalty is paid or becomes due and payable.

Section 49B(3) provides that the withholding tax on royalties is a final tax. In addition, s 49B(4) provides that a person who makes a payment of a royalty to or for the benefit of a foreign person and has withheld an amount as contemplated in s 49E(1) must be deemed to have paid the amount so withheld to that foreign person.

Section 49C identifies the person who is liable for the payment of the royalty withholding tax. The section provides that a foreign person to which a royalty is paid is liable for the withholding tax on royalties to the extent that the royalty is regarded as having been received by or accrued to that foreign person from a source within the Republic in terms of s 9(2)*(c)*, *(d)*, *(e)* or *(f)*. Thus, any amount of withholding tax on royalties that is withheld and paid is a payment made on behalf of the foreign person to which the royalty is paid in respect of that foreign person's liability.

There are, however, certain exemptions from withholding tax on royalties. Section 49D provides that a foreign person is exempt from the withholding tax on royalties if—

(a) that foreign person—

(i) is a natural person who was physically present in the Republic for a period exceeding 183 days in aggregate during the twelve-month period preceding the date on which the royalty is paid; or

(ii) at any time during the twelve-month period preceding the date on which the royalty is paid carried on business through a permanent establishment in the Republic; or

(b) that royalty is paid by a headquarter company in respect of the granting of the use, right of use or permission to use intellectual property as defined in section 23I to which section 31 does not apply as a result of the exclusions contained in section 31(5)*(c)* or *(d)*.

3.9.2 The withholding tax on the disposal of immovable property

In terms of s 35A of the Act, amounts paid for the disposal of the immovable property of a non-resident are subject to a withholding tax. In terms of s 35A(1) the withholding tax is equal to:

- 5% if the non-resident is an individual;
- 7,5% if the non-resident is a company; and
- 10% if the non-resident is a trust.

In terms of s 35A(2), the seller may apply to the Commissioner for a directive that no amount or a reduced amount be withheld. The Commissioner may have regard to the following factors in deciding whether to grant the directive sought by the seller:

- any security furnished for the payment of any tax due on the disposal of the immovable property by the seller;
- the extent of the seller's assets in the Republic;
- whether that seller is subject to tax in respect of the disposal of the immovable property; and
- whether the actual liability of that seller for tax in respect of the immovable property is less than the amount required to be withheld.

3.9.3 The withholding tax in respect of foreign entertainers and sportspersons

In the Explanatory Memorandum to the 2005 Revenue Laws Amendment Bill, SARS recognised that it is difficult to collect income tax on the earnings received by foreign entertainers and sportspersons from activities that they perform in South Africa since they are present in South Africa for a short period of time, which impacts on SARS's ability to collect tax. In terms of ss 47A–47K, a final withholding tax at a flat rate of 15% is levied on the amount received by or accrued to a non-resident entertainer or sportsperson.

In terms of s 47A the definition of 'entertainer or sportsperson' broadly includes any person who:

- performs any activity as a theatre, motion picture, radio or television artiste or a musician;
- takes part in any type of sport; or
- takes part in any other activity which is usually regarded as of an entertainment character.

Section 47B(1) provides that this withholding tax does not apply to a non-resident person who is employed by a resident employer and is physically present in South Africa for more than 183 days in aggregate during any 12-month period in which the activity is exercised.

3.9.4 Withholding tax on dividends

From years of assessment commencing 1 April 2012, a dividend withholding tax was introduced in South Africa levied at a rate of 15%. In terms of s 64D to 64N of the Act, the withholding tax on dividends is levied on shareholders in respect of dividends paid by any company other than a headquarter company. The shareholder is referred to in the dividends tax provisions as the 'beneficial owner' – the person entitled to the benefit of the dividend attaching to a share.

The dividends tax is payable by South African resident companies or by non-resident companies listed on a South African exchange. The withholding tax on dividends replaces 'Secondary Tax on Companies' which was levied at company level. In terms of s 64K(1), the liability for the dividends tax falls upon the beneficial owner (shareholder) who must pay the tax by the last day of the month following the month during which the dividend is paid by the company. The duty to withhold dividends tax is, however, imposed at the corporate level. Where the company distributes an asset *in specie*, the amount of dividends withheld is the market value of the asset distributed.

Although the obligation to withhold dividends tax falls on the company declaring the dividend, the company paying the dividend is exempted from withholding the tax under three circumstances:

- The person to whom the dividend payment is made has furnished the distributing company with a declaration from the beneficial owner that the dividend is exempt from the dividends tax or is subject to a lower rate in terms of the applicable double tax treaty. The declaration must be made by a date determined by the company or, if the company did not determine a date, by the date of payment of the dividend. The declaration must be accompanied by a written undertaking to forthwith inform the company in writing should the person cease to be the beneficial owner. Both the declaration and the written undertaking must be in the prescribed form (s 64G(2)*(a)*).
- The beneficial owner forms part of the same group of companies as the company paying the dividend (s 64G(2)*(b)*).
- The payment is made to a regulated intermediary. Normally the dividend would be paid to a regulated intermediary, in the case of uncertificated shares (paperless shares of a listed company), whereby the intermediary distributes it to the ultimate beneficial owner. In that case, the obligation on the company paying the dividend to withhold tax is effectively eliminated and, instead, the intermediary assumes the liability to withhold the dividends tax on dividends received and distributed to the beneficial owner. An intermediary could, for example, be a stockbroker, a nominee company, an insurer or a fund manager (s 64G(2)*(c)*).

A regulated intermediary is exempted from withholding the tax under the following circumstances:

- where the payment of the dividend is made to another regulated intermediary; or
- if the regulated intermediary is also exempted from withholding dividends tax upon timely receipt of a written declaration that the beneficial owner is entitled to exemption or tax treaty relief.

In terms of s 64K(2)*(a)* a company declaring a dividend or a regulated intermediary who is obliged to withhold the tax must pay it over to SARS by the last day of the month following the month during which the dividend is paid. Section 64K(3) provides that where a company or intermediary fails to withhold the tax, or withholds the tax but fails to pay it to SARS, it becomes liable for payment of the tax as if it were a tax due by that company or intermediary. Such company or intermediary will be relieved of this liability only if the tax is paid by another person (for example, the beneficial owner).

The following recipient entities are exempted from dividends withholding tax:

- a company which is a resident;
- the government, a provincial administration or a municipality;
- a public benefit organisation approved by the Commissioner in terms of s 30(3) (it may be local or foreign, but must be approved);
- a trust contemplated in s 37A (ie rehabilitation trust);
- an institution, board or body contemplated in s 10(1)*(cA)* (eg Water Board, Tribal Authority etc);
- a fund contemplated in s 10(1)*(d)*(i) or (ii) (ie pension/provident/retirement annuity/benefit fund);
- a person contemplated in s 10(1)*(t)* (ie CSIR, SANRAL, ARMSCOR, Development Bank of SA etc);
- a shareholder in a registered micro business (as defined in the Sixth Schedule) paying that dividend, to the extent that the aggregate amount of dividends paid by that registered micro business to its shareholders during the year of assessment in which that dividend is paid does not exceed the amount of R200 000; and
- a non-resident beneficial owner, where the dividend was declared by a non-resident company in respect of shares listed on the JSE (s 64F*(j)*).

3.9.5 Withholding tax on interest

The withholding tax on interest ('WHTI') is levied on interest paid to a non-resident or that is due and payable to a non-resident. A non-resident is a person that is not a tax resident of South Africa. Resident is defined in s 1 of the Act as a natural person that is ordinarily resident in South Africa or that satisfies the physical presence test in South Africa. In relation to persons other than natural persons, a person is resident if it is established, formed or incorporated in South Africa or has its place of effective management in South Africa. A person that does not fall under this definition is a non-resident and therefore liable to the withholding tax.

The liability for the tax on interest falls on the recipient or payee of the interest (s 50C). However, South Africa does not have jurisdiction over non-residents; therefore, it would be administratively burdensome for SA to collect the tax on interest due by non-residents. The administrative solution to this problem is in the form of a withholding tax. While the liability for the tax is on the recipient of the interest, the Act placed the administrative burden, in terms of calculation and collection, on the resident paying the interest (s 50E).

The WHTI is leviable on any interest paid to a non-resident at the rate of 15% (s 50B(1)*(a)*(i)). This rate is lower than the 28% flat corporate income tax rate. While the 15% rate may at first sight seem low and favourable, it should be noted that the 15% rate is applied to the gross amount of the interest paid, and not the net amount of exemptions and deductions attributable to normal income subject to the 28% corporate income tax. The WHTI is a final tax on the non-resident (s 50B(3)).

The following categories of interest are exempt from WHTI:

- interest paid by the government, bank, South African Reserve Bank, Development Bank of Southern Africa, the Industrial Development Corporation or headquarter company (s 50D*(a)*(i));
- interest paid in respect of a listed debt (s 50D(1)*(a)*(ii));
- interest payable as contemplated in s 21(6) of the Financial Markets Act 19 of 2012 to any foreign person that is a client as defined in s 1 of that Act (s 50D(1)*(b)*);
- interest paid by a foreign person in respect of a debt owed by another foreign person in specific circumstances (s 50D(1)*(c)*);
- interest paid to:
  - the African Development Bank established on 10 September 1964;
  - the World Bank established on 27 December 1945, including the International Bank for Reconstruction and Development and the International Development Association;
  - the International Monetary Fund established on 27 December 1945;
  - the African Import and Export Bank established on 8 May 1993;
  - the European Investment Bank established on 1 January 1958 under the Treaty of Rome; or
  - the New Development Bank established on 15 July 2014 (s 50D(1) *(d)*); or
- interest included in the income of a resident as is attributable to a donation, settlement or other disposition made by a resident as contemplated in s 7(8)*(a)* of the Act (s 50D(1)*(e)*).

Chapter 4

Gross income

4.1 INTRODUCTION

The concept of 'gross income' is central to the Income Tax Act[1] ('the Act'). This chapter provides a broad discussion of the definition of this foundational concept as well as its respective requirements.

[1] 58 of 1962.

4.2 DEFINITION OF 'GROSS INCOME'

'Gross income' is defined in s 1 of the Act. Apart from a general description of the concept at the outset, the definition also expressly includes under gross income a number of items listed under paras *(a)* to *(n)*.[2] The idea is to establish for a certain period of assessment a global amount totalling all the various accruals or receipts that comprise gross income for a particular person.[3] The period of assessment is usually a year.[4] For natural persons the period commences on the first day of March and ends on the last day of February of the subsequent calendar year. For corporate entities the year of assessment runs concurrently with their financial years.[5]

Principally, gross income (for a person) comprises:

- the total amount in cash or otherwise (see para 4.3 below);
- received by or accrued to or in favour of such person (see para 4.4 below);
- excluding receipts or accruals of a capital nature (see para 4.5 below).

A distinction is made between a 'resident' (of the Republic of South Africa) and 'any person other than a resident' (colloquially referred to as a 'non-resident'). In the case of a resident, gross income includes *all amounts* that meet the requirements of the concept whether or not they originated from South Africa. In the case of a non-resident, gross income is limited to amounts from a source within the Republic.[6] Although the worldwide income of a resident is (in principle) subject to South African income tax, tax treaties and s 6*quat* of the Act provide for relief to counteract any double taxation. The concepts of a resident, South African source and tax treaties are more fully canvassed in the chapter on international taxation below.[7]

---

[2] See para 4.6 below.

[3] A 'person' for purposes of income tax includes a natural person, a juristic person (such as a company and a close corporation) as well as an insolvent estate, a deceased estate, any trust and a collective investment scheme. A foreign partnership is specifically excluded. See definition of 'person' in s 1.

[4] The period can also be shorter than a year. For example, in the case where a person passed away on 1 September 2010, his period of assessment will extend from 1 March 2010 to 1 September 2010. His deceased estate would have to account for an assessment for the period 2 September 2010 to 28 February 2011 (unless the deceased estate is finalised at a date earlier than the last day of February, in which case the end of the period of assessment would be that earlier date).

[5] Definition of 'year of assessment' in s 1.

[6] In levying income taxation, it is common practice for countries to adopt a combination of connecting factors such as residency, nationality, domicile and source. Resident-based taxation can be justified on the basis that a resident enjoys the protection of the state and should therefore contribute towards the cost of the government. Source-based taxation, on the other hand, ignores a person's place of residence (nationality or domicile) and levies a tax on a country's national resources or income derived from the national resources. Although South African income tax was traditionally levied on a source basis only, the tax basis was reformed to provide for a combination of residency and source as the primary connecting factors in respect of years of assessment ending on or after 1 January 2000. See Olivier L 'Residence Based Taxation' (2001) *TSAR* 20 et seq for a comprehensive discussion on the change in the basis of charge.

[7] See chapter 14.

4.3 THE TOTAL AMOUNT IN CASH OR OTHERWISE

Gross income, although expressed as an 'amount' in the definition, need not be an actual amount in money but may constitute 'every form of property earned by the taxpayer, whether corporeal or incorporeal, which has a money value ... including debts and rights of action'.[8] In *CIR v Delfos*[9] Wessels CJ confirmed the principle that '[income] tax is to be assessed in money on all receipts and accruals having a money value. If it is something which is not money's worth or cannot be turned into money, it is not to be regarded as income'.[10] In some cases (and especially where the *quid pro quo* given to the taxpayer consisted of a benefit other than money) this principle was interpreted to mean that, where a benefit could not be turned into money, such a benefit could not constitute an 'amount in cash or otherwise'.[11] However, the Supreme Court of Appeal laid any uncertainty to rest in the seminal case of *CSARS v Brummeria Renaissance (Pty) Ltd*,[12] where Cloete JA explained that:

> [T]he question whether a receipt or accrual in a form other than money has a money value is the primary question and the question whether such receipt or accrual can be turned into money is but one of the ways in which it can be determined whether or not this is the case; in other words, it does not follow that if a receipt or an accrual cannot be turned into money, it has no money value. The test is objective, not subjective.[13]

In the *Brummeria* case the taxpayer was a developer of retirement villages. Instead of selling occupancy rights (so-called 'life rights'), the taxpayer (instead) obtained an interest-free loan from a potential occupant, and in return granted such a lender the right of lifelong occupation of a unit. The taxpayer was obliged to pay back the loan to the occupant upon cancellation of the agreement or upon the occupant's death. The court had to decide whether the taxpayer's right to use the loan capital free of any interest constituted an 'amount' for purposes of gross income. It was held that the right to retain and use the borrowed funds interest-free was a valuable right with a money value and the fact that such a right could not be ceded or alienated (and therefore not turned into money) did not negate such value. As a consequence, the court held that the Commissioner was correct in valuing the benefit acquired by the taxpayer (the interest-free loans) and including such amount in the taxpayer's gross income. The *Brummeria* decision elicited positive and negative criticism from commentators (see discussion in para 4.4.12 below).

The Commissioner, however, bears the burden of proof to show on a balance of probabilities that some 'amount' has accrued to or has been received by a taxpayer.[14]

---

[8] *WH Lategan v CIR* 1926 CPD 203 at 209, 2 SATC 16.

[9] 1933 AD 242, 6 SATC 92.

[10] 1933 AD 242 at 251, 6 SATC 92 at 99.

[11] See eg *Stander v CIR* 1997 (3) SA 617 (C), 59 SATC 212.

[12] 2007 (6) SA 601 (SCA), 69 SATC 205.

[13] 2007 (6) SA 601 (SCA), 69 SATC 205 para [15].

[14] *CIR v Butcher Bros (Pty) Ltd* 1945 AD 301 at 322, 13 SATC 21 at 39; *ITC 1545* 54 SATC 464 at 470.

4.4 RECEIVED BY OR ACCRUED TO

4.4.1 General

In general, no liability for income tax can arise unless there is a receipt or an accrual.[15] This rule is, however, subject to a number of exceptions provided for in the Act (deeming an amount taxable in a person's hands whether or not the amount was received by or accrued to that person in terms of the general rules).[16]

It is noteworthy that the Act requires either a receipt *'or'* an accrual. It may often happen that an amount accrues to a taxpayer in the same tax period that he or she receives it, in which case the amount would only be included in the taxpayer's gross income once. However, where an amount accrues in one tax period, but is received in another, it could never have been intended that income tax should be paid twice over.[17] The question that arises is in which year of assessment the amount should be so included.[18]

It was established in *SIR v Silverglen Investments (Pty) Ltd*[19] that, in the event where a taxpayer disclosed an amount that accrued to him in a period of assessment, the Commissioner cannot elect to rather tax the amount in a subsequent tax period (during which it had been received by the taxpayer).

4.4.2 Meaning of 'received by'

In *Geldenhuys v CIR*[20] it was held (in 1947) that the words 'received by' indicate that the taxpayer should have received the amount 'on his own behalf and for his own benefit'. In that case, the taxpayer was the usufructuary of a flock of sheep, which she sold with the permission of the *bare dominium* owner. The court held that, although the taxpayer physically received the proceeds of the sale, she received it on behalf of the *bare dominium* owner and not on behalf of herself. It follows that, where a person receives an amount as an agent or trustee, such an amount would not form part of the gross income of that agent or trustee.[21]

---

[15] The 'accrued to' or 'received by' requirements flow from the well-established (international) principle in income tax law that, in order to constitute gross income, some or other form of realisation must first take place.

[16] For example, the deeming provisions provided for in s 7.

[17] See *CIR v People's Stores (Walvis Bay) (Pty) Ltd* 1990 (2) SA 353 (A), 52 SATC 9.

[18] This is important to establish in view of the fact that different tax rates, rebates and statutory principles apply to different years of assessment.

[19] 1969 (1) SA 365 (A), 30 SATC 199.

[20] 1947 (3) SA 256 (C), 14 SATC 419.

[21] However, it seems as though the position of an agent acting on behalf of an undisclosed principal is problematic. One view is that it is likely that there will be an accrual of benefits for the agent upon entering into an agreement in his own name for the benefit of the principal (mainly because the agent would be entitled to litigate on the agreement without the assistance of the principal). See Taljaard C 'Die Toevallingsbeginsel in Belastingreg in die Konteks van die *Undisclosed Principal*-leerstuk' (2005) 16 *Stell LR* 313 at 313–323.

What should be noted is that the courts have applied various approaches in determining whether a person has received an amount for his or her own benefit. In cases dealing with receipts other than receipts derived in an illegal manner, the courts have invariably adopted an objective approach by enquiring whether a person was objectively entitled to receive an amount for own benefit. In other cases (and especially in cases concerning the receipt of income derived from illegal activities) the courts predominantly (but not exclusively) applied a subjective approach.

4.4.2.1 Receipts derived from legal activities: Objective approach

In *Brookes Lemos Ltd v CIR*[22] and *Greases (SA) Ltd v CIR*[23] (the so-called 'deposit cases') the taxpayer required a customer to pay a deposit on a container, to be refunded when the empty container was returned to the taxpayer. In both cases the courts held that the deposits were beneficially received for purposes of gross income, because there was no absolute obligation on a customer to return a container.

Following this reasoning, the court noted in *CIR v Genn & Co (Pty) Ltd*[24] that the borrower of a sum of money does not 'receive' the money for his or her own benefit, in view of the fact that he or she is obliged to repay it to the lender.

In some instances the application of the objective approach has caused hardship. In *CIR v Witwatersrand Association of Racing Clubs*[25] the taxpayer held a horse-racing event in aid of charity. Notwithstanding the fact that the taxpayer was not contractually obliged to pay over the proceeds to the charities, it effected payment to such charities as publicly advertised. The Commissioner nonetheless included the amount in the gross income of the taxpayer. Counsel for the taxpayer argued that an amount should only be regarded as beneficially received when the receiver's right to it 'is absolute and under no restriction, contractually or otherwise, as to its disposition, use or enjoyment'. However, the Appellate Division held that a mere moral restriction as to the disposition, use and enjoyment of an amount received, does not destroy the beneficial character of the receipt. The fact that the taxpayer received the money with the explicit intention of paying it over to the charities was regarded as irrelevant. In the premises the taxpayer's appeal was dismissed and the amount was included in the taxpayer's gross income.

The outcome of the *Witwatersrand* case seemed to fly in the face of equity and justice. Critics argued that, although the taxpayer was not strictly speaking an agent or trustee, it received (for all practical purposes) the money as a mere conduit.[26] However, the result could (in all probability) have been prevented if

[22] 1947 (2) SA 976 (A), 14 SATC 295.

[23] 1951 (3) SA 518 (A), 17 SATC 358.

[24] 1955 (3) SA 293 (A), 20 SATC 113.

[25] 1960 (3) SA 291 (A), 23 SATC 380.

[26] See eg Williams RC 'Two Recent Cases Reconsider the Concept of "Beneficial" Receipt or Accrual for Income Tax Purposes' (2000) 117 *SALJ* 40 at 44.

(prior to the race) a contract had been concluded between the taxpayer and the charities providing that either (a) the taxpayer ceded all its rights to the proceeds of the race to the charities (as supported by the outcome of the *Smant* judgment as discussed below) or (b) the taxpayer acted as agent on behalf of the charities.

In *SIR v Smant*[27] the taxpayer disposed of shares and ceded all his rights to receive future payments in respect of the shares to the purchaser thereof. Subsequent to this transaction, the taxpayer received certain payments in respect of the shares, which he then duly paid over to the purchaser. The question was whether the taxpayer received the money for his own benefit. The majority of the judges in the Appellate Division held that the cession divested the taxpayer of his right to receive future income in respect of the shares and he was in fact obliged to pay it over to the new owner. As a consequence, it was decided that the taxpayer did not receive the amount for his own benefit. (It is evident from this judgment that the cession of rights may have significant consequences for the tax position of the cedent and the cessionary, and it will more fully be addressed in para 4.4.10 below.)

In *CSARS v Cape Consumers (Pty) Ltd*[28] (a Cape Provincial Division case) the taxpayer, a buy-aid organisation, assisted its customers (buyers) in arranging collective discounts for them with certain suppliers. The taxpayer was obliged to credit any discount received to a buyers' reserve fund (where the money was invested for the benefit of all the buyers). Interestingly, the court was hesitant to find that the taxpayer was *strictu sensu* an agent of the buyers, although counsel for the taxpayer relied heavily on this point. It was nonetheless decided that the money so held was not received for the benefit of the taxpayer, because it was obliged to credit the income to the mutual fund to be kept on behalf of all the buyers. According to Williams, this judgment had a laudable objective (namely to provide relief for taxpayers who are not agents *strictu sensu*, but who receive money merely en route to an ultimate beneficiary), although he emphasised that it would probably have been overturned by the Appellate Division (had the Commissioner appealed against the judgment) in the view of the narrow approach followed in the *Witwatersrand* case.[29]

4.4.2.2 Receipts derived from illegal activities: Subjective approach

Historically the judiciary has been inconsistent in its approach towards the treatment of income derived from illegal activities. Some courts followed an objective approach by determining whether the taxpayer was (objectively speaking) *entitled* to receive the amount in question. Under this approach, the conclusion was invariably that the receiver of ill-gotten gains could not be said to have 'received' the money because such person (upon receipt thereof) fell

27 1973 (1) SA 754 (A), 35 SATC 1.
28 1999 (4) SA 1213 (C), 61 SATC 91.
29 Williams (2000) 117 *SALJ* 40 at 46.

under an immediate obligation to repay the money.[30] In following an earlier Zimbabwean case,[31] other courts interpreted the meaning of 'an amount received for own benefit' in the context of illegal earnings to mean any amount which a person received with the *intention* to benefit therefrom.[32]

In the case of *MP Finance Group CC (in liquidation) v CSARS*[33] the Supreme Court of Appeal finally laid any uncertainty to rest in 2007. In this case the taxpayer had operated an illegal pyramid investment scheme and appropriated substantial amounts of money for itself. The court decided that the taxpayer received the money for purposes of gross income in view of the fact that it *intended* to benefit therefrom, thereby clearly favouring the subjective approach in the context of illegal earnings. This development evoked mixed reactions from commentators.[34] What seems to be an unsatisfactory result from a policy perspective is that SARS would now be in a position (in circumstances where the perpetrator becomes insolvent) to collect tax from the insolvent estate at the expense of and to the detriment of the people who had been defrauded by the taxpayer (as a consequence of the preference awarded to the South African Revenue Service in terms of insolvency legislation). One commentator is of the opinion that the judgment may even be susceptible to constitutional attack by defrauded investors on the basis that they are being unlawfully deprived of their property by the state (a violation of s 25 of the Constitution).[35]

4.4.3 Meaning of 'accrued to'

For more than sixty years there was uncertainty in South African law on the fundamental meaning of the concept 'accrued to' for purposes of gross income. Two distinctly different interpretations were developed.

In the (1926) case of *WH Lategan v CIR*[36] a wine farmer sold and delivered wine to a customer. Although part of the purchase price was payable in the year of assessment in which the transaction was concluded (and in which delivery was effected), the balance was only payable in a subsequent tax year. The taxpayer's contention that the outstanding balance had not yet accrued to him at the end of year in which the wine was sold was rejected by the court (*per* Watermeyer J). The Cape Provincial Division (as it then was) held that an amount accrues to a taxpayer in the year of assessment when he or she becomes 'entitled' to it, notwithstanding the fact that it may be payable in a future year of assessment.

---

30 See eg *ITC 1792* 67 SATC 236; *ITC 1810* 68 SATC 189.

31 *COT v G* 1981 (4) SA 167 (ZA).

32 See eg *ITC 1545* 54 SATC 464; *ITC 1624* 59 SATC 373.

33 2007 (5) SA 521 (SCA), 69 SATC 141.

34 See eg Muller E 'The Taxation of Illegal Receipts: A Pyramid of Problems!' (2007) *Obiter* 166; Classen L 'Legality and Income Tax – Is SARS "Entitled to" Levy Income Tax on Illegal Amounts "Received by" a Taxpayer?' (2007) *SA Merc LJ* 534.

35 Goldswain G 'Illegal Activities: Taxability of Proceeds' (2008) 22 *Tax Planning* 143 at 146.

36 1926 CPD 203, 2 SATC 16.

In the case of *CIR v Delfos*[37] five members of the Appellate Division expressed divergent views (as *obiter dicta*) on the principle laid down in the *Lategan* case (notwithstanding the fact that it was unnecessary for that court to determine whether the latter case was correctly decided).[38] Wessels CJ, with whose judgment Curlewis JA mainly agreed, supported the interpretation in *Lategan*;[39] whereas De Villiers JA[40] and Stratford JA[41] were of the opposing view that an amount will only accrue to a person once that amount becomes due and payable. Since Beyers JA did not express an opinion, the court was equally divided on the issue.

Although later decisions confirmed that a *spes* or a conditional right to claim an amount does not give rise to an accrual,[42] the more difficult question that remained unanswered was whether an unconditional right to claim payment of an amount in future (at a date following the last day of the year of assessment) would give rise to an accrual. In 1990 the Appellate Division had the opportunity to clarify the murky waters in the landmark decision of *CIR v People's Stores (Walvis Bay) (Pty) Ltd.*[43] In this case the taxpayer (a subsidiary in the Edgars group of companies) was a retailer that sold clothing and related goods to its customers either for cash or under a credit scheme in terms of which amounts charged to a customer's account were payable in six equal monthly instalments. During the 1983 year of assessment the taxpayer sold goods under the scheme totalling about R1,3 million, of which about R341 281 (representing instalments not yet due and payable) was still outstanding at the end of the tax period. The Commissioner included the latter amount in the gross income of the taxpayer. Having unsuccessfully objected to the assessment, the taxpayer appealed to the Income Tax Special Court on (inter alia)[44] the grounds that the amount of R341 218 did not accrue to the taxpayer in the particular year of assessment. The Special Court applied the principle laid down in the *Lategan* case and gave judgment in favour of the Commissioner, against which decision the taxpayer appealed. Taking into consideration that a right to which a monetary value can be attached may indeed constitute an 'amount' for purposes of gross income, the court (*per* Hefer JA with all the other judges concurring) upheld the Special Court's judgment and endorsed the *Lategan* principle that an amount accrues to a taxpayer once such person becomes entitled thereto (whether or not yet due and payable).

---

37 1933 AD 242, 6 SATC 92.

38 This was the position because the taxpayer became entitled to the amount in dispute in the same year of assessment in which it became due and payable to him.

39 1933 AD 242 at 251.

40 1933 AD 242 at 260.

41 1933 AD 242 at 262.

42 See *Ochberg v CIR* 1933 CPD 256 at 263–264, 6 SATC 1; *Mooi v SIR* 1972 (1) SA 675 (A) 683, 34 SATC 1.

43 1990 (2) SA 353 (A), 52 SATC 9. See Swart GJ 'The Accrual of Income – Some Answers' (1990) 97 *SA Merc LJ* 97 et seq for a case discussion.

44 In addition to the issue of the correct meaning of the concept accrual, the court also dealt with the valuation of an amount (due and payable in the future) in the gross income of a taxpayer. See para 4.4.4 below.

The *Lategan* principle was recently applied by the Tax Court in *ITC 1900*.[45] The court reiterated that one has to distinguish between the date when a person becomes entitled to an amount, and the date when the amount becomes payable.

In *Commissioner for South African Revenue Service v Reunert*[46] the Supreme Court of Appeal confirmed that should the taxpayer not be *unconditionally* entitled to an amount in a specific year of assessment, the amount cannot accrue in that year of assessment.

Examples

1. On 1 April X (an estate agent) assisted the parties to a sale agreement of immovable property. The sale is subject to the purchaser obtaining a bond for the full purchase price on or before 1 June. In terms of the agreement, X is entitled to commission of R100 000, subject to the property being successfully transferred in the deeds office. The purchaser obtained a bond on 15 May and the property was transferred on 15 July. The commission payable to X accrued to him on registration of transfer (on 15 July).

   Should the agreement have provided that X would become unconditionally entitled to the commission on signature of the agreement, then the commission would have accrued to X on 15 May (on fulfilment of all the suspensive conditions).
2. X concluded a building contract with Y in terms of which he undertook to attend to construction work at a price of R100 000. In terms of the agreement, 10% of the contract price constitutes 'retention moneys' and will only be payable to X after the lapse of a period of six months from the completion date, provided that an engineering certificate has been issued. X will only become entitled to the R10 000 retention moneys once the six months have elapsed and provided a certificate has been issued.

According to Williams (in reaction to the *People's Stores* judgment) controversies arose because our courts have been far too literal in their approach. Instead of seeking an interpretation that is meaningful in conceptual terms (by asking the question 'at what point in time have the proceeds of a transaction ripened into and attained the quality of income?'), the courts have been fixated by the *ipsissima verba* used in the Act.[47] Broomberg also advocates a concept of income (and application of the principles) based on the 'profits theory' (in contrast to the 'artificial theory'), by taking cognisance of the commercial reality of a transaction.[48]

---

[45] 79 SATC 341.

[46] 80 SATC 113.

[47] Williams RC 'Amount "Accrued to" a Taxpayer during a Year of Assessment' (1990) 107 *SALJ* 400 at 403–405.

[48] Broomberg EB 'The Basis of Income Taxation in South Africa' (1972) 89 *SALJ* 179 et seq.

4.4.4 Date and valuation of receipt or accrual

The gross income of a taxpayer is calculated at the end of a year or period of assessment. Since gross income includes receipts and accruals, an 'accrual' by implication does not cover an amount that had already been received by the taxpayer during the period of assessment.

The valuation of a receipt is usually straightforward, being simply the value of whatever the taxpayer received during the year of assessment. Where X (for example) rendered services to Y for R10 000 and Y paid X R10 000 in cash, then the value of X's receipt is R10 000. Also, where Y delivered a computer with a market value of R10 000 to X as *quid pro quo* for the services rendered, the value of X's receipt is R10 000. Although the principle seems simple, difficulties may arise where the consideration agreed upon differs from the value of the benefit eventually received. Say, for example, that the market value of the computer (in the latter example) is actually R12 000. Should an amount of R10 000 (being the consideration agreed upon) or R12 000 (being the actual market value of the computer) be included in X's gross income? This problematic issue was addressed in *Lace Proprietary Mines Ltd v CIR*,[49] where a company disposed of trading stock to another company for a consideration expressed as 'P250 000'. The purchase price was payable by the allotment of 1 000 000 fully paid-up shares with a nominal value of 5 shillings in the purchasing company, the market value of which amounted to P120 000. The court held that the amount received had to be determined with reference to the actual value of the shares (the P120 000) and not with reference to the amount expressed in the agreement. In the computer example illustrated above, X would therefore have to include an amount of R12 000 in his gross income (and not the R10 000 expressed in the agreement).

In the case of an accrual, two scenarios should be distinguished. Where the amount that accrued to the taxpayer (during the year of assessment) became both due and payable during the year (but is still outstanding at the end of the year), the value of the accrual is simply the value of the amount (or benefit) outstanding.

Where, however, the amount is only due and payable (and therefore enforceable) at a date following the end of the year of assessment, the actual (market) value of such a future claim would strictly speaking be worth less than its face value (on the last day of the year of assessment). The question of what value, for such an accrual, ought to be included in the gross income of the taxpayer was the second issue adjudicated on in the *People's Stores* case (discussed in the paragraph above). The court (*per* Hefer JA) remarked that it is the right to receive payment in the future that accrues to the taxpayer, the value of which is obviously affected by its lack of immediate enforceability. As a consequence, it was held that the present (discounted) value of the right should be included (and not the face value thereof).[50] However, the Act was amended following

49 1938 AD 267, 9 SATC 349.

50 1990 (2) SA 353 (A) 367, 52 SATC 9 at 24.

this decision by the inclusion of a proviso to the definition of gross income, the effect of which is that an accrual (payable on a date falling after the last day of the year of assessment) must be included in gross income at its face value.

Example

A taxpayer sold and delivered trading stock during the 2019 year of assessment for R200 000. The purchase price is only payable on 31 December 2020. On 28 February 2019 (the last day of the 2019 year of assessment) the present value of the outstanding purchase price is R190 000. The outstanding purchase price constitutes an accrual for the taxpayer in the 2019 year of assessment. According to the proviso to the definition of gross income, an amount of R200 000 should be included in the taxpayer's gross income for that period (and not the present value of the claim).

Where the object of the accrual is something other than cash, it has to be valued on the date of the accrual. In a case where the benefit constitutes a right to an interest-free loan (such as in the *Brummeria* case) the benefit should be valued in accordance with the guidelines published by SARS in General Binding Ruling no 8 (Issue 2) (read with Interpretation Note 58 (Issue 2)).

4.4.5 Unquantified amount

Where a person disposes of an asset for a consideration which consists of or includes an amount that cannot be quantified in the year of assessment in which it is disposed of, the unquantified amount is deemed not to have accrued in that year. Instead, the unquantified amount is deemed to have accrued to the disposer and to have been incurred by the acquirer in any subsequent year when it can be quantified by virtue of s 24M.

4.4.6 The accrual of foreign income

The general principles described above are equally applicable to income of a foreign source, except to point out that s 9A provides that, in the instance where such income cannot be remitted to the Republic of South Africa, the income is only deemed to accrue in the year of assessment in which it may be remitted to the Republic.

4.4.7 Reciprocal agreements

An interesting scenario arises in the case of reciprocal agreements. It is an established principle of our law that a party to such an agreement would only become entitled to enforce in terms thereof once he or she has rendered performance as agreed, failing which the other party may raise a defence known as the *exceptio non adimpleti contractus* (the '*exceptio*').[51] In some instances, the reciprocity is bilateral in the sense that the performances represent concurrent

[51] See the seminal case of *BK Tooling (Pty) Ltd v Scope Precision Engineering (Pty) Ltd* 1979 (1) SA 391 (A).

duties, which entail that each reciprocal duty is dependent upon the other; for example, the delivery of the *res vendita* and payment of the purchase price under a cash sale. In other instances, the reciprocity may be one-sided in that it is a pre-requisite that the performances should be performed consecutively. An example of this would be a *locatio conductio operis* where the *conductor operis* is normally obliged to carry out the work that he or she is engaged to do before the consideration can be claimed. In such a case the obligation to pay the money is dependent on the pre-performance of the obligation to carry out the work, but of course the converse does not apply.[52] The principle of reciprocity entails that the performance of a reciprocal duty is conditional upon the performance (or tender of performance) of another (reciprocal duty). In essence, the person with the *duty to perform* has a conditional right to withhold his or her own performance until the other party has performed in terms of the agreement. It is this 'right to withhold' that is conditional, and not the other party's right to claim performance.

In the realm of taxation, however, there is precedent in our case law for treating an entitlement to claim as 'conditional' (for tax purposes), if the enforcement of that right can be defeated with the *exceptio*. As a consequence, an amount would in general only be regarded as having accrued to a party under a reciprocal agreement once that person has performed himself.[53] The converse has also been accepted, namely that an item of expenditure arising from a reciprocal contract is 'conditional' upon performance of the other obligation.[54] Some commentators have acknowledged that tax principles in this regard deviate from contractual principles.[55]

In the case where a merchant sells goods, the purchase price would therefore only accrue to the merchant once the goods have been delivered.[56] It must be noted, however, that date of delivery is not necessarily the date of the accrual. Where there are unfulfilled conditions on date of delivery, then the performance will only accrue once those conditions have also been fulfilled.[57]

In the case of an employment agreement the employee would only be entitled to remuneration once his or her services have been rendered, which agreement is usually effected on a month-to-month basis.[58] However, if the employee is pre-paid for his or her services, any such amount received will be included in his or her gross income in terms of para *(c)* to the definition of gross income.[59]

---

[52] *ESE Financial Services (Pty) Ltd v Cramer* 1973 (2) SA 805 (C) 808.

[53] *Ochberg v CIR* 1933 CPD 256 at 264, 6 SATC 1; *ITC 316* 8 SATC 166.

[54] See *ITC 1444* 51 SATC 35; *ITC 1485* 52 SATC 337.

[55] Van der Merwe BA 'Die Onvoorwaardelikheidsvereiste in die Suid-Afrikaanse Inkomstebelastingreg' (1995) 8 *De Jure* 279 at 288–291; Swart GJ '*Cactus Investments (Pty) Ltd v CIR*: Some Thorny Issues, and the New Dispensation under Section 24H of the Income Tax Act' (2000) *SA Merc LJ* 465 at 476.

[56] See *ITC 424* 10 SATC 338; *ITC 1609* 59 SATC 72.

[57] *ITC 1847* 73 SATC 126.

[58] See *ITC 1415* 48 SATC 179.

[59] See para 4.6.3 below.

Example

X (a retailer) sold and delivered 1 000 bottles of wine to Y for R10 000 on 5 February 2019. The contract between X and Y does not contain any suspensive conditions. The purchase price is payable by Y on or before 5 March 2019. The amount of R10 000 accrued to X on 5 February 2019 and will be included in his gross income for that year, notwithstanding the fact that the purchase price is only payable at a date in a subsequent year of assessment (*Lategan* principle).

However, if X had not delivered the wine to Y by 28 February 2019 (the end of the 2019 year of assessment) then the amount would not have accrued to him in that particular year (because of the reciprocity principle).

4.4.8 Interest

Prior to the case of *Cactus Investments (Pty) Ltd v CIR*,[60] the judiciary's approach was to treat interest as accruing on the date on which it becomes payable.[61] It seems as though this practice was, at least in part, based on the reciprocity principle. In the *Cactus* case, the taxpayer advanced a substantial sum of capital to various financial institutions for a fixed period (which extended over more than one tax year) at a fixed rate of interest. The interest as well as the capital was, however, only repayable at the end of the loan period. Counsel for the taxpayer argued that the lender's entitlement to the interest was conditional upon his willingness and ability to make the money available to the borrower for the whole of the fixed period (based on the principles of reciprocity). However, the Supreme Court of Appeal agreed with counsel for the Commissioner that the lender's only obligation was to make the money available to the borrower and that there was no other continuing (reciprocal) obligation. As a consequence, the right to the interest accrued to the lender on the day when the investment was made.

To provide some form of relief for taxpayers, the legislature subsequently introduced special timing rules for the accrual (and incurral) of interest by the introduction of s 24J to the Act. Simply put, it is provided that the accrual (and incurral) of interest is evenly spread over the period of the loan or the financial arrangement by compounding the interest over fixed accrual periods using a predetermined rate referred to as the 'yield to maturity'. The practical result is that interest accrues on a day-to-day basis. However, it is submitted that the principles laid down in the *Cactus* case will still apply in instances falling outside the scope of s 24J.

4.4.9 Discounts

Where a taxpayer sells goods or renders services and (for purposes of marketing or to ensure prompt payment) it is often agreed with the customer that, should he or she pay the invoice on or before a certain date, he or she will be

60 1999 (1) SA 315 (SCA), 61 SATC 43.

61 *ITC 268* 7 SATC 159.

unconditionally entitled to a discount (usually expressed as a percentage of the outstanding invoice). The issue that arises is whether the full amount accrues to the taxpayer (once he or she has performed in terms of the agreement and accepting that there are no suspensive conditions to be fulfilled), or whether only the lesser (discounted) amount accrues to him or her with the balance of the invoice only accruing should the customer fail to pay in time. The issue becomes significant where the rebate period extends over two or more years of assessment. For example, A sells and delivers a chair to B for R1 000 on 25 February 2009 and in terms of the agreement B is entitled to a discount of 10% should he pay on or before 25 March 2009 (which date falls in the 2010 tax year). Does an amount of R1 000 accrue to A on 25 February (for purposes of the 2009 tax year) or does R900 accrue on 25 February (for purposes of the 2009 tax year) and a further amount of R100 on 25 March (for purposes of the 2010 tax year), in the event of B not paying on or before 25 March?

In *ITC 1645*,[62] a case that was heard by the Transvaal Income Tax Special Court in 1995, it was customary for the taxpayer to send out invoices to his customers on the last day of every month under an agreement that, should a customer pay the invoice within thirty days, the customer would be entitled to a rebate. If payment was received within the agreed rebate period, the customer would become unconditionally entitled to the rebate and the taxpayer was contractually obliged to make such payment (which payment then usually occurred in the month following the month in which the invoice was due). The court emphasised that, in this particular case, the taxpayer was entitled to the *full amount* of an invoice and a customer was not entitled to withhold any part of the amount reflected in the invoice. It was then the duty of the taxpayer to reimburse a customer with the amount of the rebate. The court held that it was untenable to contend that the taxpayer received the rebate portion of the invoiced amount as trustee or agent for the customer, having to repay that amount unless the customer failed to pay the invoice within the rebate period. As a consequence, it was decided (*per* Southwood J) that the full amount accrued to the taxpayer.

In *Gud Holdings (Pty) Ltd v CSARS*,[63] a Full Bench decision of the Natal Provincial Division of the Supreme Court (as it then was) had to consider a similar issue. The taxpayer in this case (a manufacturer and distributor of automotive parts) operated a discount scheme in terms of which a customer was entitled to an early settlement discount if he or she made payment (in respect of a sale) on or before the 25th day of the month following the month in which the relevant invoice was issued by the taxpayer. The customer would deduct the settlement discount himself and pay the *net amount* over to the taxpayer.[64] Although the taxpayer only included the lesser (discounted) amount

---

62 61 SATC 31.

63 69 SATC 115.

64 The exact wording of the clause in the contract that provided for these discounts was as follows:

> Should payment be made by the PURCHASER to SELLER not later than the 25th day (or earlier full business day) of the month following the month during which delivery

in its gross income, the Commissioner contended that the full amount should have been included. In delivering the judgment (in an appeal by the taxpayer), Hurt J made the following comment:[65]

> I think that this is one of the fairly rare cases where the maxim *'plus valet quod agitur quam quod simulation (sic) concipitur'* [the so-called substance over form doctrine] applies in favour of the Taxpayer and against the Commissioner. What is aimed at by the Taxpayer and its customers, alike, is that the customer will purchase the goods for the net price, after deducting the ... discount. The prescription that this price must be paid within the stipulated time is an incentive, to the customer, to take advantage of the lower price. The customer only becomes indebted for the full invoice price if his payment is tardy. Judged from this viewpoint, the 'settlement discount'... is not so much a 'discount' as it is a penalty which will be added for late payment. From this viewpoint, also, the concept that an amount equivalent to the discount 'accrues' to the Taxpayer for the purpose of determining the gross income is as illogical as saying that, where a contract of sale provides for the payment of interest if payment is made after a certain date, such interest 'accrues' to the seller at the time of the sale.

In the premises, it was held (*per* Hurt J, with Van der Reyden J and Gyanda J concurring) that the lesser (discounted) amount was the only amount that a customer was obliged, and likely, to pay and it was erroneous to suggest that the full, invoiced price had accrued to the taxpayer at the close of the tax year.

The conflicting decisions described above lead to the conclusion that the question whether the full amount or the discounted amount should be included in gross income of the taxpayer depends to a large extent on the terms of the underlying agreement. Where a discount is structured in such a way that the full amount becomes payable (unless payment is made before a certain date, whereupon a discounted amount becomes due), the full amount would seem to be regarded as gross income. On the other hand, where the discount is structured in the form of a penalty which becomes payable by a certain date, the penalty amount would not accrue until the date so determined.[66]

4.4.10 The cession of income

Cession is a particular method of transferring rights in a movable corporeal thing in the same manner in which delivery (*traditio*) transfers rights in a movable corporeal thing. It is in substance an act of transfer (*'oordragshandeling'*) by means of which the transfer of a right from the cedent to the cessionary is achieved. Although the actual cession is accomplished by a transfer agreement, it usually coincides with or is preceded by an obligationary

---

takes place, the PURCHASER shall be entitled to deduct a settlement discount from his payment, in accordance with the SELLER's discount scheme, which may be revised by the SELLER from time to time.

65 69 SATC 115 at 119.

66 Olivier L 'Negotiating the Murky Waters of Settlement Discounts' (2008) 71 *THRHR* 689 at 689–692.

agreement (providing the *justa causa* for the transfer), such as a contract of sale or donation. Not only vested (unconditional) rights may be ceded, but also contingent (or conditional) rights.[67]

For income tax purposes, it is essential to determine whether or not the object of the cession (the right) accrued to the cedent prior to the cession. Where the right had already accrued to the cedent, the subsequent cession (or transfer) of the right would not alter the tax liability for the cedent. On the other hand, where the object of the cession is a conditional right, the moment of accrual will arise in the hands of the cessionary.[68]

In the *Witwatersrand* case (discussed in para 4.4.2*(a)* above), the proceeds of the race were included in the horse-racing association's hands notwithstanding the fact that they were subsequently donated to a charitable organisation. The tax liability could probably have been avoided had the association ceded its right to the proceeds antecedently, that is, prior to its accrual, to the charitable organisation.

On the other hand, *Hiddingh v CIR*[69] provides an example of a case where the future income accrued in the hands of the cessionary. In this case a fiduciary heir ceded his (conditional) right to enjoy all future income of the immovable property (subject to the *fideicommissum*) as and when it accrued (in future) to certain beneficiaries. The court held that the fiduciary heir had validly ceded his right and that the income had subsequently accrued in the hands of the cessionaries. In *ITC 1378*,[70] a shareholder donated and ceded his rights to future dividends to a certain fund (for a specific period of time). Melamet J was of the view that conditional rights (to the future dividends) had been ceded and that the dividends subsequently distributed by the company were taxable in the hands of the cessionary.

Confusion may, however, arise where a cedent physically receives income subsequent to a valid cession. Where the income had actually accrued in the hands of the cessionary, the cedent would receive the income on behalf of the cessionary. The income should not be included in the cedent's gross income merely because he or she has physically received the money.[71]

Care must also be exercised where the right is not ceded outright (in terms of an out-and-out cession), but where it forms merely the object of a cession *in securitatem debiti*. In the latter instance, the *dominium* of the right remains with the cedent. As a consequence, any resultant income would accrue in the hands of the cedent.[72]

---

[67] See *First National Bank v Lynn NO and Others* 1996 (2) SA 339 (A). See Scott S 'Cession of Future Rights' (1996) 59 *THRHR* 689 et seq for a case note.

[68] See Van der Merwe BA 'Cession of a Right to Future Income – Income Tax Implications' (1998) 10 *SA Merc LJ* 354 et seq for further reading on this topic.

[69] 1941 AD 111, 11 SATC 205.

[70] 45 SATC 230.

[71] *SIR v Smant* 1973 (1) SA 754 (A), 35 SATC 1.

[72] See *Moodie v CIR, Transkei and Another* 1993 (2) SA 501 (TkA).

In view of the fact that cession may be used as a handy tool to effectively avoid a potential tax liability, the Act contains numerous anti-avoidance provisions to counteract such avoidance. See, for example, para *(c)* to the definition of gross income and s 7.[73]

4.4.11 Erroneously included in gross income

In the event where a taxpayer mistakenly includes an amount in a certain year of assessment and where it subsequently transpires that he or she was not entitled to such an amount, the question arises whether the taxpayer (having himself to blame for having paid more tax than was due to the *fiscus*), is entitled to any relief. Where the error is detected within three years of the date of assessment, the taxpayer would ordinarily rely on the statutory *condictio indebiti* provided for in s 102 of the Act and s 190 of the Tax Administration Act 28 of 2011. However, where the taxpayer cannot rely on s 102, the Tax Court has held that a taxpayer can even rely on his or her own mistake to object to the assessment as an 'aggrieved taxpayer' as provided for in s 104 of the Tax Administration Act.[74]

4.4.12 Notional income

A well-accepted principle in income tax law is that any unrealised appreciation in the value of assets or notional income (meaning 'income' that a taxpayer could have earned, but did not) does not 'accrue' and consequently cannot qualify as gross income.[75]

Examples

1. A property developer purchased a vacant stand for R1 000 000 for purposes of property development. At the end of the year of assessment, the market value of the stand is R1 100 000. The unrealised appreciation in the value of the asset of R100 000 does not constitute an accrual for purposes of gross income.
2. X owns R50 000 in cash, which he stores in a strongbox beneath his bed. Although X could have deposited the money in an interest-bearing bank account, in which event he could have earned interest of, say, R5 000 for the year of assessment, he chose not to do so. The R5 000 constitutes notional income and cannot be included in X's gross income for the relevant year of assessment.

The above flows from the basic principle in income tax law that, in order to constitute gross income, some or other form of realisation must first take place. Put differently, there must be either a receipt or an accrual (of an amount).

73 See chapter 10.

74 *ITC 1785* 67 SATC 98 at 102–103; *ITC 1824* 70 SATC 27 at 38.

75 See *Land Dealing Co v COT* 1959 (3) SA 485 (SR), 22 SATC 310.

A number of commentators have expressed concern that the *Brummeria* case (discussed in para 4.3 above) has trampled this principle by including in the gross income of a borrower a value attached to the benefit of the enjoyment of an interest-free loan, notwithstanding the fact that the borrower (in that case the property developer) did not *acquire* any proprietary 'right' (to income).[76] The argument is that the judgment negated the realisation principle of income tax law. Other commentators, however, applauded the court's recognition of an 'economic benefit'.[77]

4.4.13 Waiver of income before accrual

In general terms, where a taxpayer unconditionally waives (future) income before its accrual, then such taxpayer would not have to include that amount in his or her gross income (unless some or other deeming provision ensures that it should be so included).

In *Van Heerden and Others v The State*[78] the Western Cape High Court was, inter alia, confronted with the question whether commission waived by a close corporation that conducted an estate agency (under the name 'MCC') 'accrued' to the corporation prior to the waiver thereof. This issue had to be decided for purposes of determining whether or not MCC (and other persons involved) were guilty of fraud and contravention of certain provisions of the Income Tax Act. In this case MCC effected various sale agreements for a seller (one 'Plattner') against the payment of commission. The relevant commission clause (under the mandate agreement entered into between Plattner and MCC) read as follows: 'The Consultancy (MCC) shall be entitled to receive commission of 5 percent on all its sales ... effected and concluded by the Consultancy.'

Before the transfer of the properties was effected in the Deeds Registry, MCC (under one of several transactions) waived commission in the amount of R500 000 in favour of Plattner. In return, Plattner agreed to sell a property to a company called 'Lodge 816' (mainly controlled by the members of MCC) at a reduced purchase price of R1 million (instead of R1,5 million). MCC did not include the amount of the waived commission in its tax return. The main issue in dispute was whether MCC's right to payment of the commission was conditional on the transfer of the properties and whether MCC divested itself of the commission prior to its accrual. The court preferred the view that the use of the word 'concluded' (in the commission clause quoted above) indicated that any commission was subject to (and therefore conditional upon) the successful

[76] See, for example, Cilliers C '*Brummeria Renaissance*: The Interest Free Cat Among the Carrier Pigeons' (2007) 56 *The Taxpayer* 184; Jansen van Rensburg E '*CSARS v Brummeria Renaissance (Pty) Ltd and Others*: Does the Judgment Benefit an Understanding of the Concept "Amount"?' (2008) 19 *Stell LR* 34; Editorial '*SARS v Brummeria*: An Economic Disaster' (2008) 56 *The Taxpayer* 161.

[77] See, for example, Olivier L 'Taxability of Interest-free Loans: A Storm in a Teacup' (2008) 10 *TSAR* 155–156; Cohen SB 'Does *Brummeria* Sweep Clean? A US Tax-law Perspective' (2009) 126 *SALJ* 489.

[78] 73 SATC 7.

transfer of the relevant property. This view was also supported by the way the parties understood and implemented the agreement. As a consequence, MCC divested itself of the commission before its accrual and did not have to include it as part of its gross income in its tax return. The benefit of the reduced purchase price (R500 000) also did not constitute gross income in the hands of Lodge 816 (in view of the fact that the company did not receive the benefit in exchange for the sale of goods, services or some other benefit granted, in contrast to the position under the *Brummeria* case[79]). On the facts, the court then came to the conclusion that (even if the amount was to be deemed to be gross income in the hands of MCC in terms of para *(c)* of the definition of gross income),[80] the state had not discharged the onus of proving that the accused persons knew or foresaw or ought to have known that the waived commission did form part of or must be deemed to form part of MCC's gross income. As a consequence, the accused persons were acquitted of the charges against them. Although this case illustrates the basic principles (and especially the importance of the terms of the underlying contract), it should be borne in mind that SARS may in principle attack any scheme entered into for purposes of tax avoidance under the provisions of s 80A–80L.[81]

4.5 RECEIPTS OF CAPITAL NATURE

4.5.1 Introduction

The general definition of gross income excludes receipts and accruals of a capital nature.[82] However, this does not mean that all capital receipts/accruals are excluded from constituting gross income, in that certain receipts (whether of a capital nature or not) are specifically included in the concept of gross income, such as an amount received by a natural person as compensation for the imposition of a restraint of trade (see para 4.6.4 below).

Although capital accruals have been subjected to income tax since 2001 (albeit under the provisions of the Eighth Schedule to the Income Tax Act, which provides for the levying of capital gains tax), the distinction between income and capital is still of significance because capital gains are taxed at a lower effective rate. Also, the capital gains tax provisions are only applicable on the disposal of certain specific assets, and certain receipts of a capital nature will therefore fall outside the scope of the Eighth Schedule.

Generally speaking, when an amount qualifies as a receipt or an accrual of a capital nature (and is therefore excluded from the gross income of the taxpayer), then the next step would be to establish whether any capital gains tax implications would ensue. Should the amount, however, fall within the

[79] See paras 4.3 and 4.4.12 above.

[80] See para 4.6.3 below.

[81] See chapter 13.

[82] As explained in chapter 1 para 1.3 read with para 1.6.1, the notion of excluding capital from the income tax base was inherited from the English tradition.

taxpayer's gross income (and therefore be classified as an amount of a revenue nature), then capital gains tax would not also be payable in respect thereof.

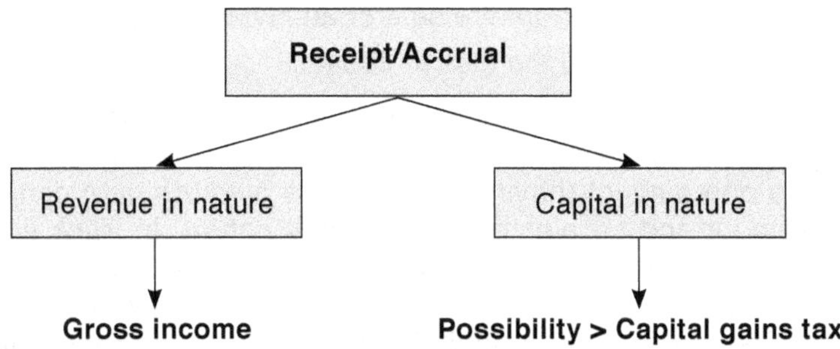

4.5.2 Income versus capital

The definition of 'gross income' excludes receipts and accruals 'of a capital nature', which concept is not defined in the Act. As a consequence, the judiciary has developed certain guidelines over the years in an attempt to provide clarity as to the distinction between what constitutes an amount of an 'income' (or 'revenue') nature on the one hand, and an amount of a 'capital' nature on the other. There is, unfortunately, no single infallible test to apply.[83]

A guideline often used to illustrate the difference between income and capital was eloquently captured by Maritz J in the judgment handed down in 1937 in *CIR v Visser*,[84] where the learned judge said that 'income is what "capital" produces, or is something in the nature of fruit as opposed to principal or tree'. According to this approach, income is produced as a result of the employment of capital such as interest (income) derived from money in the bank (capital). This tree-and-fruit test, however, cannot always be used to characterise an amount as revenue or capital.

Nevertheless, the following receipts/accruals are generally regarded as being of an income nature:

- compensation received for services rendered (such as a salary);[85]
- an amount received or accrued for the employment of capital (such as interest or royalties);
- the proceeds derived from the sale of trading stock; and
- damages that relate to the loss of revenue.

On the other hand, the following receipts/accruals are generally of a capital nature:

- an inheritance;
- a donation;

---

[83] *CIR v Pick 'n Pay Employee Share Purchase Trust* 1992 (4) SA 39 (A) 56H, 54 SATC 271 at 279.

[84] 1937 TPD 77, 8 SATC 271 at 276.

[85] These amounts are also specifically included under gross income. See para 4.6.3 below.

- gambling or betting profits (unless systematically undertaken);[86]
- an amount received or accrued in terms of a restraint of trade;[87]
- the proceeds derived from the sale of an investment; and
- damages that relate to the loss of capital.

In general, an amount should be classified as either income or capital in nature (there being no 'half-way house' in between).[88] Apportionment is, however, possible where one amount (having regard to its *quid pro quo*) contains both an income element and an element of a capital nature. In *Tuck v CIR*[89] the taxpayer was the managing director of a pharmaceutical company who had received certain shares in terms of a management incentive plan. The court held that the shares were partly attributable to a restraint of trade term (and therefore capital in nature) and partly attributable to services rendered (and therefore income in nature). In delivering the judgment, Corbett JA remarked that '[i]t could hardly have been the intention of the legislature that in such circumstances the receipt be regarded wholly as an income receipt, to the disadvantage of the taxpayer, or wholly as a capital receipt, to the detriment of the *fiscus*.' As to the basis of apportionment, the court considered (in the absence of any other basis) that a 50/50 apportionment would be fair and reasonable in the circumstances.[90]

What needs to be emphasised is that, should a capital/revenue dispute between a taxpayer and SARS end up in court, the taxpayer bears the onus to prove on a balance of probabilities that the amount is not of an income nature (see s 102 of the Tax Administration Act 28 of 2011, previously s 82 of the Act).[91] The principles of the law of evidence are therefore of vital importance.

4.5.3 Proceeds received on the disposal of assets

4.5.3.1 General

When a taxpayer disposes of an asset, two possibilities arise. The first is where such a taxpayer is merely realising an asset that is held in an unproductive form or as an investment (for purposes of deriving income therefrom). The proceeds of such a sale would constitute a receipt or an accrual of a capital nature. The alternative possibility is where a taxpayer realises an asset as part of a scheme of profit-making. A scheme of profit-making basically entails

---

[86] See *ITC 1377* 45 SATC 221 228; *Morrison v CIR* 1950 (2) SA 449 (A), 16 SATC 377.

[87] In certain instances, a restraint of trade payment is specifically included under gross income. See para 4.6.4 below.

[88] *Pyott Ltd v CIR* 1945 AD 128, 13 SATC 121.

[89] 1988 (3) SA 819 (A), 50 SATC 98.

[90] According to Emslie T & Jooste R 'Causation and the Concomitant Issue of Apportionment with reference to Gross Income in South African Income Tax Law' (1989) 106 *SALJ* 292 at 304, the outcome of the *Tuck* case (and the confirmation of the apportionment principle) was unassailable in the light of the general principles of causation.

[91] Where the probabilities are evenly balanced, the taxpayer has not discharged the onus. See *Reliance Land & Investments Co Pty Ltd v CIR* 1946 WLD 171 at 181–182, 14 SATC 47 at 57.

a project where the taxpayer acquires an asset with the idea to resell it, at an opportune time, at a profit, which is then the result of the productive turnover of capital represented by the asset. Under such a scenario, the asset disposed of constitutes trading stock and the proceeds thereof would be of a revenue nature.[92] In some instances (and especially in the context of a business), the courts have referred to the distinction between 'fixed capital' and 'floating capital'.[93] Floating capital constitutes assets that are frequently disposed of and basically comprises trading stock.

The issue whether the proceeds constitute a receipt of a revenue or a capital nature is especially problematic because the mere realisation of a profit by the taxpayer does not cause the proceeds to be classified as revenue in nature. The principle is that a taxpayer has the right to realise a capital asset to his or her best advantage.[94]

The test employed by the judiciary to establish whether the proceeds are revenue or capital in nature is the test of *'intention'*. What has to be established is whether the taxpayer intended to resell the asset at a profit through a scheme of profit-making or whether he or she merely intended to realise an investment.

Examples

1. X (Pty) Ltd, a property developing company, sold a unit in a residential sectional title scheme developed by it to Y for R1,5 million. The sectional title unit constitutes trading stock for X and the proceeds of R1,5 million would have to be included in X's gross income. Y (who used the property for residential purposes and who required a larger house) sold it five years later to Z for R2 million. The proceeds of R2 million are of a capital nature in Y's hands and do not constitute gross income. The mere fact that Y derived a profit from the sale does not cause the proceeds to be classified as revenue in nature.
2. McX's Cars (Pty) Ltd operates a motor dealership in Cape Town. McX sold a motor car to Y for R200 000. The R200 000 constitutes gross income for McX (being revenue in nature). If Y sold the car a few years later to Z (to acquire a new car for himself), the proceeds would be of a capital nature.

4.5.3.2 Intention: The golden rule

The starting point of an enquiry into the intention of a taxpayer at the time of the realisation of an asset is to determine what the intention of that taxpayer was at the time of the initial acquisition of that particular asset.[95] Secondly, it

---

[92] *Californian Copper Syndicate v Inland Revenue* 1904 41 ScLR 691; *Overseas Trust Corporation Ltd v CIR* 1926 AD 444, 2 SATC 71 at 75.

[93] See eg *CIR v George Forest Timber Co Ltd* 1924 AD 516 at 524, 1 SATC 20 at 23–24; *Elandsheuwel Farming (Edms) Bpk v SBI* 1978 (1) SA 101 (A), 39 SATC 163 at 101.

[94] See eg *CIR v Stott* 1928 AD 252, 3 SATC 253; *John Bell & Co (Pty) Ltd v SIR* 1976 (4) SA 415 (A), 38 SATC 87.

[95] Urquhart G 'Capital v Revenue: Some Light in the Darkness' (1979) *Acta Juridica* 299 at 319 proposes that the intention test should be jettisoned in favour of a purely objective decision on the facts of the particular case.

has to be established whether the taxpayer has changed his or her intention (with respect to that asset) during the whole period that the asset was held. Lastly, it has to be established what the intention of the taxpayer was at the time of the disposal of the asset.

In view of the fact that the intention of a taxpayer established through his or her own evidence (his *ipse dixit*) would be subjective (and could be manipulated), the courts will test his or her subjective thoughts against the background of objective factors. Significant factors include:

- the activities of the taxpayer in relation to the asset in question;
- the reason why the asset was sold and circumstances under which it was sold;
- the manner of its realisation;
- the length of time the asset was held;
- the other activities conducted by the taxpayer (eg his or her occupation);
- the frequency of similar transactions; and
- documentary evidence (such as correspondence, minutes of meetings etc).[96]

In the event where a taxpayer has alternative intentions (to deal with an asset), effect will generally be given to the taxpayer's dominant intention, but only if the alternative intention is entirely secondary.[97] However, where a taxpayer envisages making a profit with regard to an asset in one of two ways (and the one is not secondary to the other), then the preferred manner will not constitute a dominant intention. The court will consider the proceeds to be of a revenue nature.[98]

4.5.3.3 Intention of company

As a general rule the intention of a company is determined with reference to the intention of its directors, the idea being that the directors are in control of the affairs of the company.[99] This may be derived from the formal acts of the directors (for example, resolutions and minutes of meetings) and those of the company (for example, the objects clause in its memorandum of association or the memorandum of incorporation), the oral evidence of the directors or other objective factors. Apart from the directors, the judiciary has also acknowledged the importance of the activities and intention of other persons effectively in

---

[96] See Griessel R 'The Nature of the Proceeds Derived from the Sale of an Asset for the Purposes of Income Tax' (1997) 9 *SA Merc LJ* 138 at 144–150 for a discussion of objective criteria as manifested in the case law.

[97] *COT v Levy* 1952 (2) SA 413 (A) 420–421, 18 SATC 127 at 135–136; *Malan v KBI* 1981 (2) SA 91 (C) 94, 43 SATC 1 at 5. But cf the position of secondary intention of dealing in shares discussed in para 4.5.3.7 below.

[98] *Overseas Trust Corporation Ltd v CIR* 1926 AD 444 at 457, 2 SATC 71 at 78–79.

[99] *CIR v Richmond Estates (Pty) Ltd* 1956 (1) SA 602 (A) 606, 20 SATC 355 at 361; *SIR v Trust Bank of Africa Ltd* 1975 (2) SA 652 (A) 668, 37 SATC 87 at 105.

control of the company, such as a management committee[100] and an investment committee.[101]

The role of the shareholders in establishing the intention of a company is a controversial issue. Traditionally the activities of the shareholders (except in their capacity as directors) are irrelevant to the enquiry.[102] However, in the case of *Elandsheuwel Farming (Edms) Bpk v SBI*[103] the Appellate Division (as it then was) clearly acknowledged that the activities (and historic activities) of shareholders effectively in control of a company may be significant. In this case, the taxpayer company owned a piece of agricultural land in the vicinity of the Krugersdorp municipal area. For a number of years, the land was leased to individuals for purposes of farming operations. At some stage, all the shares in the company were acquired by a group of persons (with a history of speculating with properties). Soon after the change in shareholding, the company sold the land (virtually its only asset) to the Krugersdorp Municipality (for purposes of township development) and derived a substantial profit from it. The Commissioner included the proceeds of the sale in the gross income of the company, against which decision the company appealed. The majority of the judges sitting on the bench in the Appellate Division (Wessels, Hofmeyr and Trollip JJA) concluded that the company had changed its intention following upon the change of its shareholders. As a consequence, the proceeds of the land were indeed of a revenue nature and therefore taxable in the hands of the company. The fact that the new shareholders of the company were speculators in land played a significant role in their decision. In a dissenting minority judgment, Corbett JA, as he then was, (with Kotze JA concurring) held that it would be inappropriate for the court to fail to distinguish between the intentions of the shareholders in acquiring their shares in the company and the intentions manifested by them as directors in the conduct of the affairs of the company. On the facts, the minority's view was that the evidence did not support an inference of a change of the company's intention and as a consequence it held that the proceeds were of a capital nature. What should be kept in mind, it is submitted, is that the new shareholders (of the private company) were also the new directors of the company (following the change in shareholding). It is therefore arguable that it was rather the intention of the shareholders (in their capacity as directors in control of the company) that was imputed to the company. Viewed from this perspective, the approach followed by the majority in *Elandsheuwel* did not in essence deviate from the traditional approach. The division in opinion was merely a consequence of different interpretations on the evidence of the case. However, and notwithstanding any criticism one may level against the majority's approach, the *Elandsheuwel* case has established that a change in shareholding may certainly be relevant to the enquiry of a company's intention.

[100] *SIR v Trust Bank of Africa Ltd* 1975 (2) SA 652 (A), 37 SATC 87.

[101] *African Life Investment Corporation (Pty) Ltd v SIR* 1969 (4) SA 259 (A), 31 SATC 163; *Barnato Holdings Ltd v SIR* 1978 (2) SA 440 (A), 40 SATC 75.

[102] See eg *Tati Company Ltd v COT* 37 SATC 68 at 77–80.

[103] 1978 (1) SA 101 (A), 39 SATC 163.

4.5.3.4 Change of intention

It is entirely possible that a taxpayer could have acquired or created an asset with the intention to trade with that asset, but subsequently changed his or her intention and decided to keep the asset for private purposes or as an investment as part of the capital structure. The proceeds derived on the disposal of that asset should then be classified as a receipt or accrual of a capital nature.

Example

X is a property developer. X purchased a vacant stand in Hatfield, Pretoria, and subsequently established an office block on the property in the form of a sectional title scheme. The scheme comprises 100 offices (in the form of sectional title units). X sold 99 of the office units, but retained one unit for himself to use as his own office in future. If X sells his own unit after 40 years the proceeds would in all probability be classified as a receipt of a capital nature. Although X developed the office as part of a scheme of profit-making, he changed his intention when he kept the office to form part of his own capital structure.

Conversely, a taxpayer may change his or her original intention of keeping an asset as part of his or her capital structure, to trade with the asset instead (and to realise the asset as part of a scheme of profit-making as a landjobber). Very often the taxpayer would deny that he or she was in fact disposing of the asset as part of a scheme of profit-making, especially if one considers that a taxpayer is entitled to realise a capital asset to his or her best advantage (and indeed to derive a profit from it). In many instances, the answer is borderline and depends to a large extent on the totality of the circumstances, as illustrated by three prominent cases discussed below.

(a) CIR v Stott

In *CIR v Stott*[104] the taxpayer, an architect and land surveyor, purchased a 54-acre piece of coastal land with the intention of building a seaside residence on it. A year later, he purchased a small fruit farm which was subject to a seven-year lease. Stott also owned one or two town properties from which he received rent. He later subdivided the coastal property in two parts, retaining the part on which the house was situated. After having subdivided the other part of the property into a number of lots, he sold the lots at a profit over the next few years. When the fruit farm's lease was cancelled as a result of breach of contract by the lessee, Stott re-let the farm to another lessee, but subject to the right to subdivide the land and to sell the portions off, which he subsequently did at a profit over the next three to four years. The Commissioner was of the view that the proceeds in respect of the coastal lots as well as the subdivided pieces of farmland constituted gross income in the hands of the taxpayer.

The Income Tax Special Court held that the proceeds were indeed of a revenue nature because the taxpayer changed his intention and embarked on a scheme

[104] 1928 AD 252, 3 SATC 253.

of profit-making. The fact that Stott surveyed and subdivided the land was an important consideration taken into account by the court. This decision was, however, reversed by the High Court (Natal Provincial Division, as it then was), holding that the accruals were of a capital nature.

On appeal, it was explained that the mere fact that the land was cut up into lots, rather than sold as a whole, could not by itself alter the character of the proceeds derived from the land from capital to gross income. In addition, it was held that the fact that Stott as a surveyor knew somewhat more than the ordinary public about the value of land made no material difference. It was stressed that every person who invests surplus funds in an asset is entitled to realise that asset to the best advantage and to accommodate the asset to the exigencies of the market. The court held that, to convert an ordinary investment into a profit-making business, 'there must be proof of some special acts which in the ordinary experience of men shows that the taxpayer has conceived some scheme for profit-making and has made it his business to carry it out'. On the facts, the court was not satisfied that these acts were indeed present and found in favour of the taxpayer.

(b) Natal Estates v SIR

In *Natal Estates Ltd v SIR*[105] the taxpayer was a public company that had carried on business as a grower and miller of sugar cane and a manufacturer of sugar since 1921. The company owned vast areas of land in Natal, a large part of which was under cane. For the period 1965 to 1970, the company sold various pieces of land. The Secretary for Inland Revenue (as it then was) included the proceeds of these sales in the company's gross income, against which decision it objected and appealed. The Special Court for hearing Income Tax Appeals ruled in favour of the Secretary in respect of certain sales, and in favour of the taxpayer company in respect of others. The taxpayer noted an appeal and the Secretary a cross-appeal against this decision. The Appellate Division dismissed both the appeal and the cross-appeal after having analysed the individual sales as set out below.

(b)(i) *La Lucia and Umhlanga Rocks*

The coastal land owned by the company was increasingly encroaching on the expansion of Durban as a city. In 1962 the taxpayer's board of directors decided to proceed with the township development of La Lucia and Umhlanga Rocks. Town planners, estate agents, surveyors, consulting engineers, architects and financial advisors were appointed to assist in the development. The taxpayer sold individual lots directly to members of the public as well as bulk areas to property developing companies. The taxpayer's main contention was that it was merely realising capital assets to its best advantage. Holmes JA (with the rest of the bench in the Appellate Division concurring) agreed with the Special Court and decided that the taxpayer had changed its intention and embarked on a scheme of profit-making. It was stated that the taxpayer had 'crossed the

[105] 1975 (4) SA 177 (A), 37 SATC 193.

Rubicon'[106] by doing much more (than realising capital assets) in that it had committed itself on a large scale to the course and business of selling land for profit. As a consequence, the proceeds were held to be of a revenue nature.

(b)(ii) *Ottawa*

A small area of land owned by the taxpayer in the Ottawa district was subdivided and sold to members of the Indian community, a number of purchasers being employees of the taxpayer. The Special Court decided that there was not sufficient material before it to enable it to come to a firm conclusion. As a consequence, the taxpayer had not discharged the onus of showing that the Secretary was wrong in treating the receipt as revenue. The Appellate Division agreed with this conclusion. As a consequence, the proceeds of these sales constituted a receipt of a revenue nature.

(b)(iii) *Effingham, KwaMashu and other inland areas*

To avoid expropriation under the Group Areas legislation, the taxpayer sold land at Effingham. It also disposed of various pieces of land situated at KwaMashu and other inland areas, after receipt of notices of expropriation. Counsel for the Secretary argued that the proceeds of these disposals were of a revenue nature, viewed from the context of the taxpayer's general change of intention (to deal in land as a land-jobber). The Special Court, however, pointed out that the taxpayer's land-dealing scheme at La Lucia and Umhlanga Rocks could not automatically be extended to every sale of the taxpayer elsewhere. Every sale had to be considered on its own merits. The court was satisfied that the taxpayer initially acquired these pieces of land for purposes of its sugar business and that it was basically obliged to dispose of them. As a consequence, the proceeds were held to be of a capital nature. The Appellate Division agreed with this reasoning.

(b)(iv) *Newlands*

Lastly, the taxpayer sold a piece of land near Newlands, basically because it had become isolated and redundant (following the expropriation of KwaMashu). The Special Court (confirmed by the Appellate Division) held that the proceeds were clearly of a capital nature.

(c) John Bell & Co (Pty) Ltd v SIR

In *John Bell Co (Pty) Ltd v SIR*[107] the taxpayer (a company that operated a flower-selling business and was involved in the exportation and importation of textiles) owned an industrial site in Johannesburg. The taxpayer had conducted its business from the premises since 1922. During 1957 the taxpayer's board of directors decided to transfer the textile business to another company, as a result of which the business was relocated. After discontinuing its business as

[106] The 'crossing of the Rubicon' is a metaphor that refers to the historic event when Julius Caesar crossed the Rubicon River in North Italy in 49 BC, prompting the outbreak of a war.

[107] 1976 (4) SA 415 (A), 38 SATC 87.

a flower-seller and transferring its textile business, the taxpayer's property was no longer required for its erstwhile business operations. The directors, however, intended to retain the property for the purpose of selling it at a good profit when the market for property in the area had risen sufficiently. The property was subsequently leased to another company for a period of 10 years (for purposes of operating a cinema from the property). A few months before the expiry of the lease agreement, one of the shareholders of the lessee company made an offer to purchase the property from the taxpayer, which offer was duly accepted by the directors. The proceeds of the sale were included in the taxpayer's gross income. On appeal to the Special Court, it was decided that the taxpayer had changed its intention or purpose in holding the property in 1957 when the directors decided to realise the property at some point in the future (at a profit). This decision was, however, overturned by the Appellate Division. According to the court the mere fact that a person deliberately delays the disposal of a capital asset because of an undervalued property market (at the relevant time) does not result in the change in the character of the asset from a capital asset to stock in trade. As a result, the proceeds were held to be of a capital nature and the taxpayer succeeded with its appeal.

4.5.3.5 Unsuccessful projects and forced sales

The judiciary has often stated that the fact that a sale occurred under forced circumstances is a neutral fact and does not in itself render the proceeds of the sale of a capital (or a revenue) nature.[108] The forced circumstances would, however, be a relevant factor in the enquiry of whether the taxpayer was carrying on a scheme of profit-making. The reasoning is that where a person sells only or mainly to make the best of a bad situation (albeit under forced circumstances), he or she does so to protect his or her own investment, rather than to embark on a scheme of profit-making.[109]

An interesting scenario arose in the case of *CSARS v Heron Heights CC*,[110] which was heard by a Full Bench of the High Court (Eastern Cape Division) in 2002. The taxpayer, a close corporation, acquired two pieces of land for purposes of developing a group housing scheme. The plan was to build eight units on the property, of which three were earmarked for the private use of the three members of the close corporation. The idea was to sell the remaining five units for a profit. Subdivision plans were prepared and submitted and an engineer was appointed for the project. The project was, however, slowed down when the developer of a neighbouring property (Group Five) intervened and threatened legal action to stop the development. This resulted in the close corporation deciding, instead, to settle the dispute with Group Five by selling the whole piece of undeveloped property to it. The close corporation made a profit on this sale and the Commissioner included the proceeds in its gross

[108] *ITC 1239* 37 SATC 289 at 293–294; *ITC 1507* 53 SATC 425 at 438; *ITC 1547* 55 SATC 19 at 24–25.
[109] *Wyner v CSARS* 64 SATC 254.
[110] 64 SATC 433.

income. The Tax Court was of the view that, although the taxpayer initially acquired the properties for purposes of a scheme of profit-making, a change of intention occurred and that the taxpayer was merely disposing of a capital asset. The court came to this conclusion because (1) what was sold (a whole piece of undeveloped land) differed markedly from what was intended to be sold (eight developed subdivisions); (2) very little had been done for purposes of the group housing scheme and a lot of effort and expenditure was still to be incurred; and (3) the circumstances under which the sale occurred differed markedly from what had been intended. The Commissioner appealed against the decision to the High Court, where a Full Bench agreed with the court *a quo* that the taxpayer had (on the acquisition of the two properties) the intention to embark on a scheme of profit-making. Kroon J stressed that the mere fact that the success of the scheme was conditional upon certain events (such as approval of the plans) could never mean that an intention to embark on a profit-making scheme would only be ascribed to a taxpayer once these conditions were fulfilled. The court, however, upheld the Commissioner's appeal on the basis that it was not satisfied that a change of intention had occurred (from profit-making scheme to capital asset), although it conceded that such a change could (in principle) supervene. The court was of the view that the replacement of an intention to sell developed property at a profit with an intention to sell a whole piece of undeveloped land, also at a profit, could not on the facts justify an inference that a change of intention had occurred (to merely realise an unproductive asset). The mere fact that the manner of realisation differed from what had been intended and the fact that there was an element of compulsion did not make any material difference.

4.5.3.6 Realisation companies

The realisation of an asset by a company or trust, the sole purpose of which is to facilitate the realisation, has often been viewed as a mere realisation of a capital asset (in contrast to the carrying out of a scheme of profit-making). Authority for this proposition is inter alia the cases of *Berea West Estates (Pty) Ltd v SIR*[111] and *JM Malone Trust v SIR.*[112]

In the *Berea West* case a testator (one Konigkramer) bequeathed his estate (which included a large farm, Berea West, near Durban) to his 13 children upon his death in 1927. The administration of the estate proved to be difficult and the liabilities were considerable. Eventually, an agreement was concluded in 1950 between the beneficiaries (who by then included grandchildren who inherited their parents' share by representation) and the executors of the estate, to transfer the land to a 'realisation company', the main purpose of which was to realise the land (worth P120 000 at that stage) on behalf of the beneficiaries of the estate in their capacity as shareholders of the company. Subsequent to the incorporation of the company and the eventual transfer of the land into its name, the company proceeded to develop several townships on the land.

[111] 1976 (2) SA 614 (A), 38 SATC 43.
[112] 1977 (2) SA 819 (A), 39 SATC 83.

In 1950 there was no obvious buyer for the whole of its land at a price of P120 000. Nearly all the (subdivided) lots of land were subsequently sold over a period of about 20 years, of which a large number of lots were disposed of in the fiscal year ending 30 June 1967. The Commissioner included the proceeds of these lots in the gross income of the company for the 1967 year of assessment. The Special Court upheld the Commissioner's assessment and decided that a change of intention had taken place when the land was transferred to the company. This judgment was, however, overruled by the Appellate Division where it was held that, on the totality of the evidence, the company never deviated from its intention of being a mere realisation company. As a consequence, the proceeds were held to be of a capital nature.

The idea of a realisation entity was further developed in the *Malone* case. In this case one Malone resided until his death on a farm (situated near East London) that he had inherited from his mother. Because Malone's savings were rapidly dissipated, he decided to proceed with the piecemeal realisation of the farm (through the establishment of a township on the land). In view of his deteriorating health and the financial irresponsibility of his wife, Malone (on the advice of his attorney) set up a trust for the protection of his three minor children. Shortly after Malone's death, his attorney transferred the property to the trust (the main object of which was to realise the farm to the best advantage of the three children). The general plan of the township was finally approved about a year after Malone's death and most of the stands were sold during the 1970 and 1971 tax years. The Commissioner included the proceeds in the trust's gross income. The Income Tax Special Court dismissed the taxpayer's appeal against the assessments, but the Appellate Division overruled this decision. The court held that the deceased's intention to realise his only property to its best advantage through the township scheme did not cease when he established the trust. On the contrary, the trust was charged with carrying it out on his behalf, with the additional safeguard concerning the interests of the children. The proceeds were therefore held to be of a capital nature.

However, the Supreme Court of Appeal (*per* Lewis JA, with the remainder of the bench concurring) reiterated in the recent case of *CSARS v Founders Hill (Pty) Ltd*[113] that merely calling an entity a 'realisation company' (or 'trust') is not in itself a magical act that inevitably classifies the proceeds from the sale of an asset as those of a capital nature. In this case the taxpayer (Founders Hill Pty Ltd) was a 'realisation company' and wholly owned subsidiary of AECI Ltd. Apparently it was formed for the purpose of realising a vast tract of surplus land initially owned by AECI. Although the taxpayer contended that, on the transfer of the properties, AECI held the land as a capital asset, the court found that AECI had at that point already embarked on a scheme of developing and reselling the land for profit (and that the land actually constituted trading stock in the hands of AECI). It was held that the mere interposition of Founders Hill as a 'realisation company' could not alter the nature of the proceeds to a capital nature. The court held that Founders Hill was formed solely for the

[113] 2011 (5) SA 112 (SCA), 73 SATC 183.

purpose of acquiring the land and then developing and selling it at a profit. The proceeds were therefore held to be of an income nature. With reference to the *Berea West* and *Malone* cases the court explained that in each of them there was a real justification for the formation of the company or trust in addition to the purpose of realising the assets. A so-called realisation company (or trust) would merely stand in the shoes of the entity that has transferred the assets to it, and hold them in turn as capital assets only in exceptional circumstances.

4.5.3.7 The sale of shares

Where a taxpayer is involved in share-dealing, namely the buying and selling of shares at a profit, then the shares constitute trading stock and the proceeds thereof would be of an income nature. Even where the taxpayer holds a portfolio of shares as investment with a *secondary* intention of dealing in shares, the judiciary has taken the view that the proceeds would be income in nature.[114] However, if the taxpayer realises gains merely incidental to his or her investment activities and not as a result of having a secondary purpose of dealing in shares, then the proceeds of the sales would in principle be of a capital nature.[115]

The majority of the judges in the case of *CIR v Pick 'n Pay Employee Share Purchase Trust*[116] held that the proceeds realised on the sale of shares sold by an employees' share purchase trust (in the carrying out of an incentive scheme for the benefit of the employees) were not of an income nature. Although profits were 'contemplated' by the trust, it was clear on the evidence that it was not the 'purpose' of the trust to operate a scheme of profit making.[117]

4.5.4 Employment of capital

Where a taxpayer employs or uses his or her capital to derive a benefit, the resultant benefit is generally treated as income in nature. The principle is that the capital (the tree) produces the income (the fruit); for example, rent for the use of property; interest for the employment of money; royalties for the use of patents or other immaterial property rights; dividends for the investment in shares; and compensation for the excavation of sand[118] or other mineral rights.

---

[114] *African Life Investment Corporation (Pty) Ltd v SIR* 1969 (4) SA 259 (A), 31 SATC 163; *Barnato Holdings Ltd v SIR* 1978 (2) SA 440 (A), 40 SATC 75; *CIR v Nussbaum* 1996 (4) SA 1156 (A), 58 SATC 283.

[115] See eg *CIR v Middelman* 1991 (1) SA 200 (C), 52 SATC 323.

[116] 1992 (4) SA 39 (A), 54 SATC 271.

[117] See Jooste RD 'The Role of Profit Motive in the Capital/Revenue Inquiry' (1993) 110 *SALJ* 212 et seq for a case note.

[118] See *Samril Investments Pty Ltd v CSARS* 2003 (1) SA 658 (SCA), 65 SATC 1; *Ernst Bester Trust v CSARS* 2008 (5) SA 279 (SCA), 70 SATC 151. For a case note on the *Samril Investment* case, see Badenhorst PJ & Skelton LN 'Sale of Unsevered Sand: The Sandman and the Tax(wo)man' (2003) *Obiter* 253 et seq.

4.5.5 Damages or compensation

Where a taxpayer receives an amount as compensation for a loss suffered in relation to his or her trade, the question arises whether such an award constitutes an amount of an income or a capital nature. The basic test that is usually applied is to ask whether the compensation was designed to fill a hole in the taxpayer's profits (in which case the compensation would be of an income nature) or whether it was intended to fill a hole in his or her assets (in which case the compensation could be of either an income nature *or* a capital nature, depending on the nature of the asset(s) in the taxpayer's hands).[119] Where the asset constituted floating capital prior to its destruction (such as trading stock or standing crops) the compensation would be of an income nature. Conversely, if the payment was received as compensation for a capital asset, it would not constitute gross income.[120]

Although the test may seem simple, it can be difficult to apply in practice.[121] Where the taxpayer receives compensation for the cancellation of a contract, the enquiry seems to be especially problematic. As a general rule, an award for the termination of a contract constituting a substantial part of the taxpayer's business would be classified as capital in nature (because an important limb of the fruit-bearing tree would be cut off), whereas compensation for the loss of future profits would be income in nature.[122] In *WJ Fourie Beleggings v CSARS*[123] the Supreme Court of Appeal reiterated that there is a fundamental distinction between a contract that is a means of producing income and a contract directed by its performance towards making a profit. In this case the taxpayer (an hotelier) concluded an agreement with a company in terms of which it agreed to accommodate and provide meals to a substantial number of guests for the period April 2001 to May 2003 and the majority of the hotel's rooms had to be set aside for that purpose. The taxpayer anticipated earning about R8,7 million from the contract. However, the company repudiated the agreement at a stage where the balance of the cancelled contract was worth an estimated R4,7 million. The taxpayer entered into a settlement agreement with the company and accepted an offer of R1,2 million in full and final settlement of all claims arising from the early cancellation of the contract. The court held that the contract was merely a product of the taxpayer's income-earning activities and not the means by which it earned income. The taxpayer traded as an hotelier before the contract and continued to do so, both once it had

---

119 *Burmah Steam Ship Ltd v IRC* [1931] SC 156.

120 *Bourke's Estate v CIR* 1991 (1) SA 661 (A) 672, 53 SATC 86 at 94. For case notes, see Editorial 'Income tax – Capital or Revenue Nature of Compensation Received for Damage Caused by Fire to Pine Plantation' (1991) *Taxpayer* 31 et seq and Jooste R 'Capital, Revenue and Trading Stock – Foundations Shaken' (1991) 108 *SALJ* 414 et seq.

121 See Clegg DJM 'Compensation and Damages: A Fiscal Pot-pourri' (2002) *Acta Juridica* 173 et seq.

122 See *Taeuber and Corssen (Pty) Ltd v SIR* 1975 (3) SA 649 (A), 37 SATC 129; *ITC 1259* 39 SATC 65; *ITC 1279* 40 SATC 254; *ITC 1341* 43 SATC 215; *KBI v Transvaalse Suikerkorporasie Bpk* 1987 (2) SA 123 (A), 49 SATC 11.

123 2009 (5) SA 238 (SCA), 71 SATC 125. See Silke J 'A Case of Common Sense' 2009 23 *Tax Planning* 137 et seq for a case note.

commenced and after it had been cancelled. In the event it was decided that the compensation received for the early termination was of an income nature.

The case of *Stellenbosch Farmers' Winery Ltd v CSARS*[124] provides another example of the difficulties that can arise when the nature of compensation received on the termination of a contract is required to be classified as either income or capital. In this case a long-term liquor distribution agreement, providing the taxpayer with the exclusive right to distribute a certain brand of whiskey in Southern Africa, was cancelled three years in advance. In terms of the termination agreement, the taxpayer agreed to compensation of R67 million for the early termination. The court was satisfied that a substantial part of the income-producing structure of the taxpayer had been sterilised by the transaction in question (roughly 18–25%). The difficulty was that the compensation was calculated with reference to the profits flowing from the contract. The court then recognised that in the valuation of a capital asset it is an acceptable principle to use the profits expected to be earned from the utilisation of the asset as a basis. Also, it was emphasised that the termination agreement referred to payment of full compensation for the closure of the taxpayer's business and there was no reference to a payment for loss of profits. As a result, the compensation was held to be capital in nature.

What needs to be kept in mind (in general), is that damages payable in the form of an annuity are taxable in terms of para *(a)* of the definition of 'gross income'.[125] Also, where the damages relate to the relinquishment, termination, loss, repudiation, cancellation or variation of any office or employment, the amount so received would be included in gross income under para *(d)* of the definition.[126] Damages may furthermore be included under para *(n)* of the definition if it represents a recoupment of (for example) expenditure previously allowed as a deduction against taxable income.[127]

4.5.6 Government grants

Where a person receives a government grant from the state in the operation of his or her business, the question arises whether the amount received is of a capital or a revenue nature. The answer depends on the circumstances. In *Volkswagen South Africa (Pty) Ltd v Commissioner for South African Revenue Service*,[128] the Supreme Court of Appeal held that the test is two-fold. First, what was the real and basic cause of the accrual (put differently, why or in respect of what conduct or activity was the grant made). Secondly, was the cause more closely associated with the taxpayer's income-producing machinery (in which

124 2012 (5) SA 363 (SCA), 74 SATC 235.

125 See para 4.6.1 below. Dendy M 'Damages for Loss of Earning Capacity – the Income Tax Ramifications I: Compensation by Annuity' (1995) 112 *SALJ* 643 et seq provides an insightful discussion of the practical ramifications. See also Editorial 'Income – Gross Income – Third Party Damages – Annuity – Employees Tax' (1993) *Taxpayer* 215 et seq.

126 See para 4.6.4 below.

127 See para 4.6.18 below.

128 80 SATC 179.

event it should be regarded as capital) or with its income-earning operations (in which event it should be regarded as revenue). In that case the taxpayer received a government grant in the form of a certificate which was redeemable against customs duties paid. The grant was calculated with reference to the taxpayer's capital expenditure. The SCA held that the grant reimbursed a taxpayer in respect of a percentage of its capital expenditure. Thus, the grant was held to be capital in nature.

4.6 SPECIFIC INCLUSIONS IN DEFINITION OF GROSS INCOME

Paragraphs *(a)* to *(n)* of the definition of gross income in s 1 of the Act specifically include certain amounts in a taxpayer's gross income. These inclusions are discussed in the paragraphs below.

4.6.1 Annuities – para *(a)*

In terms of para *(a)* of the definition of gross income, any amount received by or accrued to the taxpayer by way of an *annuity* or *living annuity* is included in that person's gross income. An amount contemplated in the definition of 'annuity amount' in s 10A(1) of the Act is also expressly included.

The term 'annuity' is not defined in the Act, but the courts have traditionally attributed the following characteristics to the concept: it is a fixed periodic payment; the payment is repetitive and the amount is chargeable against property or is an obligation of someone and not merely a payment at will.[129] In addition, true annuities differ from other investments in that the capital sum invested is not returnable when the annuity ceases to be payable (the so-called 'disappearance of capital test').[130]

An annuity can arise in various ways. Often, an annuity is granted in terms of a will. Where, for example, A is entitled to a monthly payment of R5 000 for a period of 10 years from the deceased estate of his father B, the R5 000 monthly payments would constitute an annuity in the hands of A.

Example

X, who was employed as a driver at Fast Movers Pty Ltd, was fatally injured in a collision during April 2016. Fast Movers decided to pay X's widow an *ex gratia* amount of R10 000 per month for the period May 2017 to May 2019. These payments constitute individual donations and not annuities. Voluntary payments, even where made regularly, do not constitute annuities.

---

[129] See *ITC 761* 19 SATC 103 and *Secretary for Inland Revenue v Watermeyer* 1965 (4) SA 431 (A).

[130] *KBI v Hogan* 1993 (4) SA 150 (A) 159.

Annuities are also often bought from insurance companies. An 'annuity amount' as defined in s 10A means an amount payable by way of an annuity under an annuity contract and any amount payable in consequence of the commutation or termination of any such annuity contract. Broadly speaking, these are annuities acquired from insurers in return for a lump sum cash consideration. These annuities have a capital and an income element, which is calculated in accordance with a formula provided for in s 10A. The capital element of the annuity is excluded from the recipient's gross income. Only the income element is specifically included in gross income under this paragraph.

The reference to 'living annuity' in para *(a)* (and its corresponding definition in s 1 of the Act) was introduced as a consequence of the decision *CSARS v Higgo*[131] handed down by the Cape of Good Hope Provincial Division in 2006, where the 'disappearance of capital test' (referred to above) came under scrutiny. In this case, the taxpayer entered into a contract with Momentum in terms of which he invested an amount just in excess of R6 million in a 'life annuity' which would give him an initial guaranteed income of more or less R40 000 per month (to be revised from time to time in accordance with certain guidelines). The taxpayer was not allowed to make withdrawals from his investment save for certain specified amounts. On the taxpayer's death, Momentum was to pay the balance of the investment to the taxpayer's nominee or deceased estate. The main issue before the court was whether the monthly payments made by Momentum to the taxpayer constituted annuities or not. The linchpin that had to be decided was whether or not the capital of the taxpayer had disappeared. Foxcroft J dealt with the 'disappearance of capital test' and concluded that, on the facts, the capital could not be said to have 'disappeared' (in view of the fact that the balance of the fund was payable to the taxpayer's beneficiaries on his death). As a result, the payments did not constitute annuities. This judgment prompted the legislature to intervene in order to capture certain repetitive payments payable under retirement annuity plans bought from life insurance companies. As a consequence of the introduction of the concept 'living annuity' in the Act, these payments would presently be included in the recipient's gross income.

Annuities should be distinguished from instalments payable in respect of the sale of capital assets.

Example

X sells his property for R500 000 to Y, the purchase price to be payable in 25 monthly instalments of R20 000 each. The instalments would not constitute annuities, but merely the paying off of the purchase price, a contractual obligation.

---

[131] 68 SATC 278. See Williams RC 'When is an Annuity not an Annuity?' (2007) *Obiter* 352 for a case note.

4.6.2 Alimony – para *(b)*

Although any alimony or maintenance payable to a taxpayer by a former spouse under an order of divorce (as well as any amount payable for the maintenance of a child under a maintenance order) is included in that taxpayer's gross income (in terms of para *(b)*), the amount so included is currently exempt from tax in the taxpayer's hands in terms of s 10(1)*(u)* of the Act, provided that the order was granted after 21 March 1962.[132] In essence, the payer-spouse would be liable for the payment of any income tax on such amount (and not the recipient-spouse).

4.6.3 Services – para *(c)*

Paragraph *(c)* includes in gross income any amount, including a voluntary award, received or accrued in respect of services rendered or to be rendered (as well as any amount received or accrued in respect of any employment or the holding of an office), excluding amounts contemplated in ss 8(1), 8B or 8C. According to a proviso to the paragraph, the amount would be included in the gross income of the person who rendered the services (or the employee or the office-holder), irrespective of the fact that it may have been paid to another person.[133] This provision therefore prevents the employee or office-holder from avoiding tax by ceding his or her right to the benefits to another person in advance.

Although a salary or any award for services rendered would ordinarily constitute gross income in accordance with the general definition, the specific inclusion provided for in para *(c)* has wider application. In particular, it extends to ex gratia (voluntary) payments as well as payments received for future services. In addition, it would (for example) include a salary received in lieu of leave, a prize won by an employee for excellent services, bonuses and 'tips'.

It is essential that the amount received or accrued must be causally linked to the services rendered. In *Stevens v CSARS*[134] it was decided that an ex gratia payment by a company to the taxpayer for the loss of a share option held in terms of a share incentive scheme (when the company was voluntarily wound up) was in fact a payment made as employer *vis-à-vis* an employee for services rendered.

The mere fact that a benefit received by a person is not convertible into cash would not preclude its inclusion in the recipient's gross income, provided that a monetary value can be placed on the benefit. This principle was confirmed in *CSARS v Brummeria Renaissance (Pty) Ltd*[135] (discussed in para 4.3 above),

---

[132] Where the order was granted on or before 21 March 1962, the position is reversed. The payer-spouse will be entitled to a deduction in terms of s 21 and the amount will not be exempt from tax in the recipient-spouse's hands (in terms of s 10(1)*(u)*).

[133] In terms of Practice Note 4 SARS will not invoke the proviso in the case where a natural person is nominated by his or her employer to act as a nominee director of a company in which the employer is a shareholder.

[134] 69 SATC 1.

[135] 69 SATC 205.

where the Supreme Court of Appeal overturned an earlier decision handed down in the case of *Stander v CIR*,[136] where it was held that a prize (an overseas trip) awarded to a car salesman did not constitute an inclusion under para *(c)* in view of the fact that the prize was not convertible into cash.

4.6.4 Restraint of trade – paras *(cA)* and *(cB)*

A payment received as consideration for the imposition of a restraint of trade[137] would ordinarily be classified as an amount of a capital nature (and would therefore fall outside the scope of gross income in accordance with the general definition). In certain instances, an amount received for a restraint of trade is, however, specifically included in the recipient's gross income in terms of the provisions of paras *(c*A*)* and *(c*B*)* to the definition of gross income.[138]

In terms of para *(c*A*)* a restraint of trade payment is so included where the restraint is imposed on a labour broker, a personal service provider, or a personal service trust or personal service company as defined in the Fourth Schedule to the Act.[139] A labour broker means a natural person who, for reward, provides a client of his or her business with other persons to render a service or perform work for such client.[140] A personal service provider (as defined in the Fourth Schedule) basically embraces a company or trust used as a vehicle by a natural person mainly for the rendering of services performed by that person.[141]

Where the restraint is imposed on a company or trust (other than a personal service provider constituted as a company or trust), any payment received as a result thereof would not fall within the scope of para *(c*A*)*.

In terms of para *(c*B*)* a restraint of trade payment is included in the gross income of a natural person where that payment was received or accrued to that person in respect of employment or the holding of an office (or any past or future employment of the holding of an office).

4.6.5 Compensation for loss of office – para *(d)*

Paragraph *(d)* includes in gross income any amount (including a voluntary award) received or accrued in respect of the relinquishment, termination, loss, repudiation, cancellation or variation of any office or employment. Specifically

---

136 1997 (3) SA 617 (C), 59 SATC 212.

137 In terms of a restraint of trade, a person is contractually prohibited from engaging in a certain business or employment in a defined area for a specified period of time.

138 Where the amount is so included in the recipient's gross income, the payer would be entitled to a deduction under s 11*(c*A*)*. See chapter 6.

139 The provisions of para *(c*A*)* also apply to personal service companies and personal service trusts prior to s 66 of the Revenue Laws Amendment Act 60 of 2008 coming into operation. See para *(c*A*)*(iv).

140 Definition of 'labour broker' para 1 Fourth Schedule to the Act.

141 The definition of a 'personal service provider' in the Fourth Schedule contains a number of requirements. See chapter 8.

excluded from the scope of this paragraph is any lump sum award from a pension fund, pension preservation fund, provident fund, provident preservation fund or retirement annuity fund (in view of the fact that these amounts are included in gross income under para *(e)* of the definition of gross income).[142]

Also included (from 1 March 2012) are the proceeds of a so-called key-man insurance policy where the person insured was an employee or director of the policyholder and where the proceeds are intended to benefit the employee (or nominee). The proceeds are included in the gross income of the employee (or nominee). Should the proceeds be paid out for the benefit of the employer, the proceeds would be included in the latter's gross income in terms of para *(m)* if such employer elected to deduct the premiums in terms of s 11*(w)*.[143]

Where any such compensation (falling within the scope of para *(d)*) is payable in consequence of or following upon the death of a person, such amount shall be deemed to have accrued to the person immediately prior to his or her death.[144] This deeming provision ensures that the amount is taxable in the deceased's hands (and not in the deceased estate or in the hands of any heir).

4.6.6 Fund benefits – paras *(e)* and *(eA)*

Paragraph *(e)* includes in gross income a 'retirement fund lump sum benefit' or a 'retirement fund lump sum withdrawal benefit'. These concepts are defined and calculated in accordance with the provisions of the Second Schedule to the Act. In essence, the Second Schedule provides for a formula to calculate the taxable portion of the amount and it is only this taxable portion that is included in gross income under para *(e)*, and not the gross lump sum benefit received.

Although pension benefits received by a member of a public sector pension fund were historically excluded from the income tax base, the Act was amended (with effect from 1 March 1998) to ensure that these benefits are also included in the gross income of the beneficiary. Paragraph *(eA)* was introduced simultaneously with these amendments to provide for the situation where such a member remains in the employment of the public sector employer. Two-thirds of the benefits so received are included in the beneficiary's gross income.

4.6.7 Services: Commutation of amounts due – para *(f)*

According to para *(f)* any amount received or accrued in commutation of amounts due under any contract of employment or service should be included as gross income.

---

142 Proviso *(aa)* para *(d)*.
143 See para 4.6.18 below.
144 Proviso *(bb)* para *(d)*.

4.6.8 Lease premiums – para *(g)*

Paragraph *(g)* provides for the inclusion of lease premiums.[145] Any amount received or accrued as a premium or consideration in the nature of a premium for the use or occupation (or the right of use or occupation) of (a) land or buildings; (b) plant or machinery; (c) films, video tapes, discs, sound recordings or advertising matter in connection therewith or (d) any patent, design, trade mark, copyright or other similar rights would constitute gross income in the hands of the recipient.[146] A lease premium is any amount payable *in addition* to the rent or royalties.

Example

On 1 June 2018 X entered into a contract with Y in terms of which Y rented an industrial property from X for a period of five years for an amount of R10 000 per month. In terms of the contract Y is also liable for the payment of R100 000 on signature thereof (for procuring the lease with X). The R100 000 constitutes a lease premium and would be included in X's gross income for the tax year ending 28 February 2019 (the 2019 tax year). In view of the reciprocity principle discussed in para 4.4.7 above, X would only have to include the rent for the period 1 June 2018 to 28 February 2019 (9 x R10 000) in his gross income for the 2019 tax year.

4.6.9 Compensation for know-how – para *(gA)*

Included in gross income (in terms of para *(g*A*)*) is any amount received or accrued from another person as consideration for the imparting of or the undertaking to impart any scientific, technical, industrial or commercial knowledge or information. Also included is any amount for rendering or undertaking to render any assistance or service in connection with the application or utilisation of such knowledge or information. In essence, this paragraph includes in gross income any amount received for 'know-how'.[147]

4.6.10 Leasehold improvements – para *(h)*

Paragraph *(h)* caters for the inclusion of the value of improvements in the lessor's gross income where the lessee (in terms of the lease agreement) is obliged to effect certain improvements to the leased land (or buildings). The inclusion would occur in the year or period in which the right to have the improvements effected has accrued to the lessor. The amount that would be included is the amount stipulated in the agreement as the value of the improvements or the amount to be expended on such improvements. Where,

[145] See Brownlie SP & Jooste RD 'The Lease Premium Concept in South African Tax Law' (1995) *Acta Juridica* 241 et seq for a discussion of the concept of a 'lease premium' in South African income tax law.

[146] Where the premium is so included, the lessee would be entitled to a deduction spread over the period of the lease (in terms of s 11*(f)* of the Act). See chapter 7.

[147] Where the amount is so included, the payer would be entitled to a deduction spread over a period (in terms of s 11*(f)* of the Act). See chapter 7.

however, no such amount is stipulated it would be the amount representing the fair market value of the improvements.

Example

In terms of a lease agreement between X (the lessor) and Y (the lessee), Y agreed to erect an additional garage on the premises (to be built according to certain specifications). It is agreed between the parties that the value of the improvements would constitute R400 000. In effecting the improvements, Y expended an amount of R450 000. The amount included in X's gross income would be R400 000.

4.6.11 Fringe benefits – para *(i)*

Paragraph *(i)* provides for the inclusion of so-called 'fringe benefits' in the gross income of an employee, which basically comprise certain benefits granted to such employee (by the employer) generally in a form other than cash. The amount included is the cash equivalent (as determined under the Seventh Schedule to the Act) of the value of any 'taxable benefit' (as defined in para 2 of the said schedule). Also included is any amount required to be included under s 8A.

In essence, the benefit should be granted because of or in consequence of the employee's employment with the employer or as a reward for services rendered or to be rendered to the employer. Thus, a benefit granted by an employer to an employee would only constitute a 'fringe benefit' if there was a causal connection between the employee's employment and the granting of the advantage.[148]

The taxable benefits are listed in para 2 and are valued in accordance with specific paragraphs of the Seventh Schedule. The paragraphs below provide a brief description of the various benefits (and their valuation rules).

4.6.11.1 Assets acquired for no consideration (or a consideration less than market value)

A taxable benefit arises where an employee acquires an asset (other than money) from the employer (or any associated institution) for no consideration or for a consideration that is less than the value of the asset (but excluding meal and refreshment benefits as well as securities or shares contemplated in s 8A, 8B or 8C).[149]

[148] See, for example, *ITC 1626* 60 SATC 17, where an interest-free loan to a director (and shareholder), who was also an employee of the company, was not held to be a taxable benefit. In this case the company's bankers required the director (and shareholder) to take out a life insurance policy as security for a loan made by the company. The director was unable to finance the premiums. As a result, the premiums were advanced by the company and debited against the director's loan account (without provision for any interest). The court held that the loan was not granted as a consequence of the employer-employee relationship and decided that the loan did not constitute a taxable ('fringe') benefit.

[149] Paragraph 2*(a)* Seventh Schedule.

The cash equivalent of the benefit is so much of the value of the asset (upon its acquisition by the employee) as exceeds the value of any consideration given.[150] Subject to certain special rules (discussed below), the 'value' of an asset would be its market value.[151]

However, where the asset constitutes *movable property that was acquired by the employer for the purpose of disposing of it to the employee*, the value to be placed on it would be the cost price to the employer, unless the asset was a marketable security or the asset had been used by the employer prior to acquiring ownership (such as an asset acquired subsequent to the lapse of a financial lease), in which case the market value would be used.

In the event of the asset being held as *trading stock* by the employer, the value of the benefit to the employee would be the lower of the market value and the cost price to the employer, except in the case of a marketable security, in which case the market value would be used.

Where an award was granted to an employee for bravery or long service,[152] the first R5 000 of the value of the asset awarded is exempt from tax (if the cost exceeds R5 000).[153] It must be noted that if cash is awarded, the full amount is taxable.

Examples

A computer, which was purchased by the employer for use in the business five years ago at a price of R10 000, was sold to an employee for R2 000. The market value of the computer on the date of its acquisition by the employee was R3 000. The cash equivalent of the fringe benefit is R1 000 (market value less R2 000).

A computer was acquired by an employer (for R4 000) to sell to an employee. The employee paid R2 500 for the computer. The market value of the computer on the date of its acquisition by the employee was R5 000. The cash equivalent of the fringe benefit is R1 500 (cost price of R 4 000 less R2 500).

4.6.11.2 Private use of assets (other than residential accommodation) – para 2(b)

Where an employee has been granted the right to use any asset (other than residential accommodation or household goods supplied therewith) for his or her private purposes free of charge or for a consideration that is less than the value of such use, such private use would be regarded as a taxable benefit.[154] Where the asset constitutes a motor vehicle, the travelling between the employee's place of residence and place of work would be regarded as private use. For purposes of valuation, a distinction is made between the use of a motor vehicle and the use of all other assets.

150 Paragraph 5(1).

151 Paragraph 5(2).

152 'Long service' means an initial unbroken period of service of not less than 15 years or any subsequent unbroken period of service of not less than 10 years.

153 Paragraph 5(2)*(a)* and *(b)*.

154 Paragraph 2*(b)*.

(a) Use of motor vehicle

Where an employee has been granted the right to use a motor vehicle, the cash equivalent of the benefit would be so much of the value of the private use of the vehicle as exceeds any consideration given by the employee for the use of such vehicle, other than consideration in respect of the cost of the licence, insurance, maintenance or fuel in respect of such vehicle.[155]

The value to be placed on the private use of the vehicle shall be determined for each month or part of a month during which the employee was entitled to use the vehicle for private purposes and shall be calculated as follows:[156] 3,5% multiplied by the *'determined value'* of a vehicle (not subject to a 'maintenance plan')[157] or 3,25% multiplied by the *'determined value'* of a vehicle (subject to a 'maintenance plan').

(a)(i) *Determined value*

The 'determined value' of a motor vehicle is one of the following:

- where such vehicle was acquired by the employer (other than on the termination of a lease), the *retail market value* thereof as determined by the Minister by regulation, excluding any finance charges or interest;
- its *retail market value* at the time the employer first obtained the right of use of the vehicle, where such motor vehicle was held by the employer under a lease or where it was held under a lease and the ownership thereof was acquired by the employer on the termination of the lease;
- its *'cash value'* (as defined in s 1 of the Value-Added Tax Act 89 of 1991) in the case of an instalment credit lease agreement (as provided for in para *(b)* of the definition of 'instalment credit agreement' in the same section); or
- its *retail market value*, as determined by the Minister by regulation, at the time when the employer first obtained the vehicle or the right of use thereof, in any other case.[158]

A deduction is allowed against the 'determined value' of a *depreciation allowance* where an employer acquired the motor vehicle (or the right of use of the vehicle) not less than 12 months before the employee was granted the right of use. The depreciation allowance is calculated according to the reducing balance method at the rate of 15% for each completed period of 12 months (from the date on which the employer obtained the vehicle or the right of use

---

155 Paragraph 7(2).

156 Paragraph 7(4)*(a)*. Where the employee was only entitled to the right of use for a period shorter than a month, then the value of the monthly benefit would be apportioned accordingly (eg monthly value × $\frac{6}{31}$, where the motor vehicle was used for six days during January). However, no reduction would be made where the employee temporarily did not use the vehicle for private purposes during any period for any reason. Paragraph 7(4)*(b)* read with para 7(5).

157 For definition of 'maintenance plan', see para 7(11).

158 Paragraph 7(1).

of the vehicle to the date on which the employee was granted the right of use for the first time).[159]

Where the motor vehicle was acquired by the employer from an associated institution in relation to the employer and the employee concerned had, prior to the acquisition, enjoyed the right of use of such motor vehicle, the determined value shall be determined as at the date on which the employee was granted the use of the vehicle for the first time.[160]

(a)(ii) *Transferring of rights under lease agreement*

Where an employer's rights and obligations under a lease agreement (in respect of a motor vehicle) are transferred to the employee, the employer shall be deemed to have granted the employee the right to use of the vehicle for the remainder of the period of the lease. In such a case, the 'determined value' would be determined as at the date on which the employee was granted the use of the vehicle for the first time. Any rentals becoming payable by the employee under the lease shall be deemed to be consideration payable for such right (and therefore deductible against the determined value for purposes of calculating the value of the benefit).[161]

(a)(iii) *Reduction allowed where vehicle also used for business purposes*

Where it is proved to the satisfaction of the Commissioner that accurate records of distances travelled for business purposes in such vehicle are kept, there are three 'annual' deductions available to the employee *against the value of the right of use of the vehicle* (as calculated above):

- First, the value of private use must be reduced by an amount that bears to that calculated value the same ratio as the number of kilometres travelled for business purposes bears to the total amount of kilometres travelled in such vehicle during that year of assessment (thus, where the value of the private use is R100 000 and the employee used the vehicle 40% for business purposes, the R100 000 will be reduced by R40 000 and the taxable benefit would be R60 000).[162]
- Secondly, where the employee bears the *full cost* of the licence, insurance or maintenance of such vehicle, then the value of use must be reduced by that part of the costs attributable to the kilometres travelled for *private* purposes (the 'private element' of the respective expenses).[163]
- Thirdly, where the employee bears the full cost of fuel for private use of such vehicle, then the value of use must also be reduced by a 'fuel cost' corresponding to the total number of kilometres travelled for *private* purposes. The reduction is calculated by multiplying the fuel cost rate

159 Paragraph 7(1) proviso *(a)*.
160 Paragraph 7(1) proviso *(b)*.
161 Paragraph 7(3).
162 Paragraph 7(7).
163 Paragraph 7(8).

per kilometre (published by the Minister in the *Government Gazette*) by the total number of private kilometres travelled). The intention is to allow a deduction for the 'private element' of the fuel costs.

(a)(iv) *More than one vehicle*

Where more than one vehicle was made available for the employee for private use (at the same time) and the Commissioner is satisfied that each vehicle was used by the employee during the year of assessment primarily for business purposes, then the value of the private use (of both vehicles) will only be the value of the private use of the vehicle having the highest value of private use (or such other value as the Commissioner may direct). This concession will, however, not apply where the employee seeks a reduction of the value of the private use for any of the three annual deductions discussed above.[164]

(a)(v) *No value in certain instances*

The private use by an employee of a motor vehicle shall have no value if:

- the vehicle is available to and is in fact used by employees of the employer in general;
- the private use of the vehicle is infrequent or is merely incidental to its business use; and
- the vehicle is not normally kept at or near the residence of the respective employee when not in use outside of business hours; *or*
- the nature of the employee's duties are such that he or she is regularly required to use the vehicle for the performance of those duties outside his or her normal business hours of work, and he or she is not permitted to use the vehicle for private purposes other than travelling between his or her place of residence and place of work, or for private use that is infrequent or is merely incidental to its business use.[165]

[164] Paragraph 7(6).
[165] Paragraph 7(10).

Example

On 1 March 2019 an employer granted his employee the right of use of a motor vehicle, which was purchased by the employer at a cost of R250 000 (inclusive of VAT). The vehicle is not subject to a maintenance plan. The employee kept a log book which reflects that he travelled a total of 24 000 kilometres during the year of assessment, of which 18 000 kilometres are attributable to business purposes (and thus 6 000 to private purposes). The employee, in terms of his employment contract, is responsible for the maintenance, insurance costs and fuel (for private purposes) in respect of the vehicle. For the 2020 year of assessment, the employee bore the following costs in respect of such expenses: maintenance R9 000 and insurance R12 000. The relevant 'fuel cost' published in the *Government Gazette* is 102,7 cents per kilometre. Calculate the cash equivalent to be included in the employee's gross income for the 2020 year of assessment.

Value of private use R250 000 × 3,5% × 12 months	R 105 000
Less: Reduction for business kilometres (R105 000 × $\frac{18\,000}{24\,000}$)	R(78 750)
Maintenance – private element (R9 000 × $\frac{6\,000}{24\,000}$)	R (2 250)
Insurance – private element (R12 000 × $\frac{6\,000}{24\,000}$)	R (3 000)
Fuel cost – private (6 000 × R1,027 cents)	R (6 162)
Value of private use to be included in gross income	R 14 838

(b) Use of sundry assets

In all other cases (other than residential accommodation and any motor vehicle), the cash equivalent of the right to the private use of an asset would be the value of such private use less any consideration given by the employee as well as any amount expended by the employee on the maintenance or repair of the relevant asset.[166]

For purposes of determining the value of the private use of the asset, it depends upon whether the asset is owned or leased by the employer. Where the asset is leased, the value is the amount of rent payable by the employer (for the period of use by the employee).[167] Where the asset is owned by the employer, the value of use is calculated (*for the period of use*) at the rate of 15% per year on the lesser of the market value at the date of the commencement of the use *or* the cost price of the asset to the employer. However, where an employee is granted the sole right of the use of the asset for a period extending over the useful life of the asset or over a major portion thereof, the value of the benefit would be the cost thereof to the employer.[168]

It is specifically provided, however, that no value shall be placed on the private use of an asset by an employee if:

---

166 Paragraph 6(1).

167 Paragraph 6(2)*(a)*.

168 Paragraph 6(2)*(b)*. In the latter case the benefit shall be deemed to have accrued to the employee on the date on which he or she was first granted the right of use of such asset (para 6(2)*(b)* proviso).

- such use is incidental to the employer's business or the asset is provided by the employer as an amenity to be enjoyed by the employee at his or her place of work or for recreational purposes at that place or a place of recreation provided by the employer for the use of his or her employees in general (the item does not apply to clothing);
- the asset consists of any equipment or machine that the employer concerned allows his or her employees in general to use from time to time for short periods (and the value thereof does not exceed an amount determined on a basis as set out by public notice issued by the Commisisoner;
- the asset consists of telephone or computer equipment which the employee uses mainly for the purposes of the employer's business; or
- the asset consists of books, literature, recordings or works of art.[169]

4.6.11.3 The provision of meals and refreshments – para 2(c)

A taxable benefit arises where an employee has been provided with any meal, refreshment or voucher entitling him to any meal or refreshment (other than any board or meals provided for in item *(d)*, discussed below), either free of charge or for a consideration that is less than the value of such meal, refreshment or voucher.[170]

The cash equivalent of the benefit would be so much of the value of such meal, refreshment or voucher as exceeds any consideration given by the employee. The value of such meal, refreshment or voucher would be its cost to the employer, provided that no value shall be placed on:

- any meal or refreshment supplied by an employer to his or her employees in any canteen, cafeteria or dining room operated by or on behalf of the employer and patronised wholly or mainly by his or her employees or on the business premises of the employer;
- any meal or refreshment supplied by an employer to an employee during business hours or extended working hours or on a special occasion; or
- any meal or refreshment enjoyed by an employee in the course of providing a meal or refreshment to any person whom the employee is required to entertain on behalf of the employer.[171]

4.6.11.4 Residential accommodation – para 2(d)

The provision of residential accommodation (whether furnished or unfurnished and with or without board, meals, fuel, power or water), either free of charge or for rental consideration that is less than the rental value of such accommodation, constitutes a taxable benefit.[172]

169 Paragraph 6(4).
170 Paragraph 2*(c)*.
171 Paragraph 8.
172 Paragraph 2*(d)*.

The cash equivalent of the benefit would be the rental value of such accommodation (in respect of the year of assessment) calculated in terms of a formula specified in para 9(3), (3C), (4) or (5) less any rental consideration given by the employee for such accommodation in respect of such year, any rental consideration given by him in respect of household goods supplied with such accommodation and any charge made to the employee by the employer in respect of power or fuel provided with the accommodation.[173]

4.6.11.5 Free and cheap services

A taxable benefit arises where a service (other than a service relating to residential accommodation or a service under item *(j)* discussed in 4.6.11.10 below) is rendered to the employee at the expense of the employer in circumstances where that service has been utilised by the employee for his or her private purposes, either for no consideration or a consideration that is less than the value of the benefit.[174]

In valuing the benefit, a distinction is made between the granting of a travel facility and any other service.

(a) Travel facility

Where the benefit constitutes a travel facility granted by an employer who is engaged in the business of conveying passengers for reward by *sea* or by *air* to enable an employee (or any relative) to travel to any destination *outside the Republic* for his or her private purposes, the value of the benefit would be an amount equal to the *lowest fare* payable by a passenger utilising such facility. For any other travel facility, the value of the benefit would be the *cost* to the employer. To calculate the value of the cash equivalent (to be included in the employee's gross income) the value of the benefit (calculated on either the lowest fare or cost basis) would be reduced by any consideration given by the employee (or his or her relative) for such travel facility.[175]

However, no value shall be placed on any travel facility granted by an employer who is engaged in the business of conveying passengers for reward by *land*, *sea* or *air* to enable any employee (or such employee's spouse or minor child) to travel:

- to any destination *in* the Republic;
- overland to any destination *outside* the Republic; or
- to any destination *outside* the Republic if such travel was undertaken on a flight or voyage made in the ordinary course of the employer's business and such employee (spouse or minor child) was not permitted to make a firm advance reservation of the seat or berth occupied by him or her.[176]

---

173 Paragraph 9(2).
174 Paragraph 2*(e)*. The service can be rendered by either the employer or someone else.
175 Paragraph 10(1)*(a)* read with para 10(1)*(b)*. A forward journey and a return journey will be regarded as a single journey.
176 Paragraph 10(2)*(a)*.

In addition, no value shall be placed on any travel facility granted by an employer to the spouse or minor child of an employee, if:

- that employee is for the duration of the term of his or her employment stationed further than 250 kilometres away from his or her usual place of residence in the Republic;
- that employee is required to spend more than 183 days during the relevant year of assessment at that place; and
- the facility is granted in respect of travel between that employee's usual place of residence in the Republic and that specific place where the employee is stationed.[177]

Example

X (who lives in Pretoria, South Africa) is employed as a pilot at International Air Ltd, an airline company that is engaged in the business of conveying passengers by airline from airports in the Republic to destinations outside the Republic (and *vice versa*). X's wife booked a seat on a flight, administered by International Air, from Johannesburg to Rome (for purposes of a private visit to family) free of charge. The lowest fare payable by a passenger for such flight is R6 000. The cash equivalent to be included in X's gross income is an amount of R6 000.

Where, however, X's wife did not pre-book the seat in advance, but merely travelled on the flight as a 'stand-by passenger', no value would be included in X's gross income for the particular year of assessment.

(b) Any other service

Where the benefit constitutes the enjoyment of any other service, the value of the benefit is the *cost* to the employer. To calculate the value of the cash equivalent (to be included in the employee's gross income) the value of the benefit is reduced by any consideration given by the employee (or his or her relative) for such service.[178]

However, no value shall be placed on the following types of services:

- any transport service rendered by an employer to his or her employees in general for the conveyance of such employees to and from their homes, from and to the place of their employment;
- any communication service provided to an employee if the service is used mainly for the purpose of the employer's business; or
- any services rendered by an employer to his or her employees at their place of work for the better performance of their duties or as a benefit enjoyed by them at that place or for recreational purposes at that place or a place of recreation provided by the employer for the use of his or her employees in general.[179]

---

[177] Paragraph 10(2)*(d)*.
[178] Paragraph 10(1)*(b)*.
[179] Paragraph 10(2)*(b)*, *(b*A*)* and *(c)*.

Example

- An employer grants an employee the use of a cellular phone for private purposes at R200 per month. For the 2019 year of assessment, the employer incurred a cost of R10 000 in respect of that phone. The cash equivalent to be included in the employee's gross income is R7 600 (R10 000 less (R200 x 12)).
- Where, however, the use of the phone was granted to the employee mainly for business purposes, no value would be included in his gross income.

4.6.11.6 Low-interest loans

Where a loan has been granted to the employee free of interest or against payment of interest at a rate lower than the official rate of interest, a taxable benefit arises in the hands of the employee. Loans to enable employees to purchase qualifying equity shares in terms of s 8B (or to pay uncertified securities transfer tax on such shares) and loans in respect of which subsidies are payable as contemplated under item *(g*A*)* discussed in 4.6.11.7 below, are excluded as taxable benefits.[180]

The cash equivalent of such a benefit shall be the amount of interest that would have been payable by the employee on such a loan (in respect of the year of assessment) at the official rate of interest *less* the amount of interest (if any) actually incurred by the employee in respect of the loan for such year.[181]

The 'official rate of interest' may be adjusted from time to time by the Minister by way of publication in the *Government Gazette*.

No value shall, however, be placed on the taxable benefit derived from an employer granting his or her employee any casual loan or loans if such loan or the aggregate of such loans does not exceed the sum of R3 000 at any relevant time.[182] In practice SARS regards a 'casual loan' as a short-term loan granted at irregular intervals and requires the limit of R3 000 not to be exceeded at any time. It does not cover loans made to employees on a regular basis.

In addition, no value shall be placed on any loan for the purpose of enabling that employee to further his or her own studies.[183] In its Practice Note 17 SARS has expressed the view that a scholarship or bursary awarded to an employee subject to repayment on non-fulfilment of conditions may be treated as a loan (and as such a taxable benefit under para *(g)*) in the year of assessment

[180] Paragraph 2*(f)*. The paragraph applies where the loan was granted by the employer or by any other person by arrangement with the employer or any associated institution in relation to the employer.

[181] Paragraph 11(1). Special rules are provided for when the cash equivalent is deemed to accrue to the employee. See para 11(2). Paragraph 11(3) provides that, with the consent of the Commissioner, a different method of calculating the cash equivalent or portions thereof may be employed if the Commissioner is satisfied that the method achieves substantially the same result as the methods provided for in paras 11(1) and (2).

[182] Paragraph 11(4)*(a)*.

[183] Paragraph 11(4)*(b)*.

in which such conditions are invoked and the employee becomes liable to repay the scholarship or bursary.[184] According to De Koker this view seems extraordinary and could very well be wrong.[185]

Where the employee uses the loan in the production of income, the cash equivalent of the benefit is also allowed as a deemed s 11*(a)* deduction.[186] The effect is that the employee is effectively not taxed on this benefit in these circumstances.

Example

The following loans were made by an employer to some of his employees during the 2019 year of assessment:

- a loan of R100 000 made to employee A on 1 September 2018 to assist him with bond payments on his home (at an interest rate of 10% per annum);
- an interest-free *ad hoc* loan of R2 000 made to employee B on 1 January 2019 to assist her with the payment of some outstanding debts; and
- a loan of R30 000 made to employee C on 1 December 2018 (at an interest rate of 5% per annum) to assist him in paying university tuition fees

The official rate of interest was 12% throughout the year. All loans were still outstanding at 28 February 2019. The cash equivalent of the loans to be included in the respective employees' gross income for the 2019 year of assessment would be:

- Employee A: $(\frac{12}{100} \times \text{R}100\ 000) - (\frac{10}{100} \times \text{R}100\ 000) \times \frac{6}{12}$ (for only 6 months) = R1 000;
- Employee B: no value (casual loan); and
- Employee C: no value (purpose of loan is the further studies)

4.6.11.7 Subsidies

Where an employer has paid any subsidy in respect of any amount of interest or capital repayments payable by the employee in terms of any loan, the subsidy so paid shall constitute a taxable benefit.[187] In addition, a taxable benefit arises where the employer has in respect of any loan granted to the employee by any lender, paid to such lender any subsidy, being an amount which (together with any interest payable by the employee on such loan) exceeds the amount of interest which, if calculated at the official rate of interest, would have been payable on such loan.[188] In both these instances the cash equivalent of the benefit shall simply be the amount of the subsidy.[189]

---

[184] Practice Note 17.

[185] *Silke on SA Income Tax* para 4.50.

[186] Paragraph 11(5).

[187] Paragraph 2*(g)*.

[188] Paragraph 2*(gA)*. Where the amount is less than what would have been payable on the loan had the official rate of interest applied, SARS would probably treat the benefit as a low-interest loan for purposes of para 2*(f)*.

[189] Paragraph 12.

4.6.11.8 Discharging of obligations

A taxable benefit arises where an employer has, directly or indirectly, paid any amount owing by the employee to any third person (other than an amount falling within the ambit of items *(i)* and *(j)* of para 2), without requiring the employee to reimburse the employer for the amount paid. A benefit will also arise where the employer has released the employee from an obligation to pay any amount owing by the employee to the employer or has allowed any such debt to prescribe under circumstances where the employer could have recovered the amount owing or caused the prescription to be interrupted (unless, in the latter instance, the Commissioner is satisfied that the failure of the employer was not due to any intention of the employer to confer a benefit on the employee).[190]

The cash equivalent of any such benefit would be an amount paid by the employer or the amount owing to such employer (as the case may be).[191]

No value shall, however, be placed on any benefit derived by reason of the fact that the employer has paid:

- subscriptions due by his or her employee to a professional body, if membership of such body is a condition of the employee's employment;
- insurance premiums indemnifying an employee solely against claims arising from negligent acts or omissions on the part of the employee in rendering services to the employer;
- any portion of the value of a benefit which is payable to the Government Employees' Pension Fund (on behalf of a member of such fund); or
- a bursary obligation owing to a former employer arising from non-compliance with the terms of the bursary (which was granted by the former employer) under circumstances where the employee undertook to render services to the present employer (in consideration for such payment made to the former employer).[192]

---

[190] Paragraph 2*(h)*.

[191] Paragraph 13(1).

[192] Paragraphs 13(2) and 13(3).

Example

X is employed as an attorney at the firm A&A Inc. During the 2019 year of assessment, A&A paid the following amounts for the benefit of X (in addition to his salary):

- an amount of R5 000 to X's former spouse for maintenance owed by A to such spouse
- an amount of R1 600 in respect of X's annual subscription to the relevant Law Society (X's subscription to the Law Society is compulsory)
- an amount of R3 000 in respect of premiums on a professional indemnity insurance policy

The cash equivalent to be included in A's gross income for the 2019 year of assessment is:

- for the maintenance, an amount of R5 000
- for the subscription payable to the Law Society, zero (no value)
- for the insurance premiums, zero (no value)

4.6.11.9 Medical aid contributions

Any contribution made by an employer (whether directly or indirectly) to any medical scheme registered under the Medical Schemes Act 131 of 1998 (or any fund which is registered under a similar provision contained in the laws of any other country where the medical scheme is registered) for the benefit of any employee or dependants, will constitute a taxable benefit in the hands of the employee.[193] The cash equivalent of the benefit is the total amount of such contributions so made for the relevant year of assessment.[194]

No value shall be placed on a benefit derived from an employer by:

- a person who has retired from the employment of the employer by reason of superannuation, ill-health or other infirmity;
- the dependants of a deceased employee (who was in the employment of the employer at his or her date of death); or
- the dependants of a deceased former employee, if that employee had earlier retired from the employment of the employer as a result of superannuation, ill-health or other infirmity.[195]

Example

An employer made a contribution of R500 per month to a medical scheme for the benefit of an employee. The employee himself also made a contribution of R500 per month. The cash equivalent to be included in the employee's gross income for the relevant year of assessment is R500 x 12 = R6 000.

---

193 Paragraph 2*(i)*.

194 Paragraph 12A(1). Subparagraphs (2), (3) and (4) provide for special rules where the contributions made by the employer cannot be attributed to a specific employee.

195 Paragraph 12A(5).

4.6.11.10 Costs relating to medical services

A taxable benefit arises where the employer has, directly or indirectly, incurred any amount (other than a contribution contemplated in item *(i)* discussed in 4.6.11.9 above) in respect of any medical, dental and similar services, hospital services, nursing services or medicines provided to the employee or his or her spouse, child, relative or dependant.[196] The cash equivalent of the benefit would be the amount incurred by the employer in respect of such expenses.[197]

No value shall, however, be placed on:

- any treatment listed by the Minister of Health under the category of prescribed minimum benefits provided to the employee, his or her spouse or children in terms of a scheme or programme of that employer (subject to certain conditions);
- services rendered on medicines supplied for purposes of complying with any law of the Republic;
- services rendered by the employer to its employees in general at their place of work for the better performance of their duties; or
- any benefit derived from an employer by:
  - a person who has retired from the employment of the employer by reason of superannuation, ill-health or other infirmity;
  - the dependants of a deceased employee (who was in the employment of the employer at his or her date of death);
  - the dependants of a deceased former employee, if that employee had earlier retired from the employment of the employer as a result of superannuation, ill-health or other infirmity; or
  - a person who is entitled to a secondary rebate (being 65 or older) during the year of assessment.[198]

4.6.11.11 Contributions to insurance policies

A taxable benefit arises where the employer makes a payment to an insurer under an insurance policy directly or indirectly for the benefit of an employee, his spouse, child or nominee: provided that it does not apply where the insurance policy relates to an event arising solely out of and in the course of the employment of the employee.[199]

The cash equivalent of the benefit is the expenditure incurred by the employer during the year of assessment in respect of any premiums payable under the insurance policy. [200]

---

[196] Paragraph 2*(j)*.

[197] Paragraph 12B(1). Subparagraph (2) provides for special rules where the payments made by the employer cannot be attributed to a specific employee.

[198] Paragraph 12B(3).

[199] Paragraph 2*(k)*.

[200] Paragraph 12C(1). Subparagraph (3) provides for special rules where the payments made by the employer cannot be attributed to a specific employee.

4.6.11.12 Contributions to pension funds or provident funds

A taxable benefit arises where the employer makes a contribution to a pension fund or provident fund.[201]

4.6.12 Proceeds from disposal of assets by mines – para *(j)*

There are numerous special provisions contained in the Act relating to mines. Paragraph *(j)* includes in the gross income of a mine a certain part of the proceeds that accrued on the disposal of an asset by such mine. The amount is determined with reference to the amount of 'capital expenditure' (relating to the asset) allowed as a deduction under s 15*(a)* of the Act. The intention is to recoup any expenditure claimed by the mine in a previous year of assessment.

4.6.13 Proceeds from disposal of certain assets – para *(jA)*

As discussed above, the proceeds of capital assets are ordinarily excluded from gross income. In view of the fact that it would be relatively easy for a manufacturer of an asset to initially use such an asset as part of its own capital structure, only to dispose of it at a later event (at a profit), para *(jA)* provides for a special inclusion catering for such circumstances. According to this provision, any amount received or accrued to a person (during the year of assessment) in respect of the disposal of any asset manufactured, produced, constructed or assembled by that person, which is similar to any other asset manufactured, produced, constructed or assembled by that person for purposes of manufacture, sale or exchange by that person (or on his or her behalf), will constitute gross income.

Example

ABC Pty Ltd is a manufacturer of certain motor vehicles. ABC regularly uses some of the motor vehicles manufactured by them as demonstration models. After a few months, these demo models are usually sold to traders at a discounted price. Although these motor vehicles have been used as capital assets by ABC, their proceeds would be included in ABC's gross income in terms of the provisions of para *(jA)*.

4.6.14 Dividends – para *(k)*

Paragraph *(k)* includes in the gross income of a shareholder any amount received or accrued by way of dividend or a foreign dividend.

[201] Paragraph 2(l). The taxable benefit is calculated in terms of para 12D.

4.6.15 Subsidies and grants – para *(l)*

Any amount received or accrued by way of a grant or subsidy in respect of any 'soil erosion works'[202] (or any related matters) is included in the gross income of the recipient in terms of para *(l)*.

4.6.16 Transfer to sporting body – para *(lA)*

Paragraph *(lA)* includes in the gross income of a sporting body (involved in the development and promotion of certain sporting activities) any amount received by or accrued to the body from a similar body (where the latter body would be entitled to a corresponding deduction in terms of s 11E).

4.6.17 Government grants – para *(lC)*

Paragraph *(lC)* includes any amount received or accrued to a person by way of a government grant defined in s 12P.

4.6.18 Key-man policies – para *(m)*

Subject to certain requirements, para *(m)* caters for the inclusion of life insurance benefits payable under a so-called 'key-man insurance policy'. A key-man policy is effected by a person or company in respect of the life of an employee (or a director) who is a key-person in the relevant business operated by such person or company. The idea underlying such a policy is that the benefits payable on the death of the key-person would enable the insured person or company to overcome difficulties that may arise as a consequence of the death of the key-person. The owner of a key-man policy (namely the employer or the company) is generally entitled to deduct the premiums paid under the policy under the provisions of s 11*(w)*. As a corollary, the benefits paid out under the policy would be included in the insured employer or company's gross income in terms of this paragraph. Note, however, that since 1 March 2012, the proceeds would be included in the gross income of the employee if the proceeds are intended to benefit the employee (and not the employer).[203]

4.6.19 Amounts to be included in terms of other provisions of the Act – para *(n)*

Paragraph *(n)* includes in gross income any amount that is specifically required by the Act to be included in the taxpayer's income (for example, an amount recouped or recovered in terms of s 8(4)).[204]

---

[202] As referred to in s 17A(1) of the Act.

[203] See para 4.6.5 above.

[204] See *Silke on SA Income Tax* para 4.2 for a comprehensive list of these items.

Chapter 5

Exempt income

5.1 INTRODUCTION

After a taxpayer's gross income has been determined, the next step is to determine if any of it is exempt from tax. General exemptions are contained in ss 10 and 10A of the Income Tax Act 58 of 1962 ('the Act') and can be broadly divided into two groups: absolute exemptions and partial exemptions. These two broad categories could relate to either income that is exempt from tax or persons that are exempt from tax.

With regard to income exempt from tax, certain types of income are totally exempt from tax, including South African dividends, South African interest earned by non-residents and foreign pensions. There is also income that is partially exempt, such as interest earned by natural persons, or certain lump sums from employers.

With regard to persons that are exempt from tax, some entities are totally exempt from tax, including pension and provident funds, the government and municipalities. Other entities are partially exempt from tax, depending on the income they earn (this would apply to public benefit organisations, recreational clubs, share block companies and sectional title bodies corporate).

Some of the legislature's reasons for exempting certain receipts or accruals from tax would be, for example, to encourage courtesy between states, or to encourage investment in state securities, while some of them would be rooted in the nature and reasons for the accrual or receipt, or to avoid double or multiple layers of taxation.

5.2 ABSOLUTE EXEMPTIONS

In the case of absolute exemptions, all amounts received by or accruing to a specific person or institution are exempt from tax irrespective of the nature of the income. A few general examples of institutions or persons are discussed below.

5.2.1 Government and municipalities

- Section 10(1)*(a)* exempts from tax receipts and accruals of the government or any provincial administration.
- Section 10(1)*(b)* exempts from tax receipts and accruals of municipalities.
- Section 10(1)*(b*A*)* exempts from tax receipts and accruals of the government of any other country, and any foreign government agency appointed by that government.

5.2.2 Institutions, boards, bodies or companies

Section 10(1)*(c*A*)* exempts institutions (such as universities), boards, bodies or companies from tax, provided that:

- the institution, board, body or company has been approved by the Commissioner and that its activities are wholly or mainly directed to the furtherance of its sole or principal object;
- the constitution of the institution, board, body or company does not permit the distribution of any of its profits or gains to any person (other than, in the case of a company, to its shareholders) and it is required to utilise its funds solely for investment or the object for which it has been established; and
- the institution, board, body or company is required, where it is established under any law, to transfer its assets on dissolution to another institution, board or body which is also granted exemption from tax in terms of s 10(1)*(c*A*)* and where it fails to transfer, or to take reasonable steps to transfer, its assets to that other institution, board or body, the accumulated net revenue which has not been distributed will be deemed to be an amount of taxable income which accrued to it during the year of assessment.

If the Commissioner is satisfied that an institution, board, body or company has failed to comply with the provisions of s 10(1)*(c*A*)* during the year of assessment, the Commissioner may withdraw his approval of the institution, board, body or company to be exempt from tax with effect from the commencement of that year of assessment. A decision made by the Commissioner in the exercise of his or her discretion under s 10(1)*(c*A*)* is, however, subject to objection and appeal.

5.2.3 Public benefit organisations

Section 10(1)*(cN)* exempts from tax the receipts and accruals of public benefit organisations approved in terms of s 30(3) of the Act if:

- those receipts and accruals are not derived from business and trading activities; and
- they are so derived they are integral, occasional or approved business or trading activities.

5.2.4 Bodies corporate

Section 10(1)*(e)* exempts the levies received by sectional title bodies corporate, share block companies and other associations of persons. The 'other associations of persons' must be formed solely for purposes of managing the collective interest common to all their members, including the collection of levies and administration of the expenditure in respect of the common property. The following rules apply:

- Such other associations can be s 21 companies, but cannot be ordinary companies, close corporations, co-operatives or trusts.
- Other associations are not permitted to distribute their funds to any person, other than a similar association.
- Other associations lose the 'levy' exemption if they knowingly become party to a tax avoidance scheme.

In addition, any *other receipts and accruals* derived by sectional title bodies corporate, share block *companies* and other associations of persons are exempt up to R50 000 per annum.

5.2.5 Recreational clubs

Section 10(1)*(cO)* exempts from tax receipts and accruals of any recreational club (approved by the Commissioner in terms of s 30A) in respect of membership or subscription fees, members' payments for social or recreational services, and receipts from occasional and voluntary fundraising activities – if they do not exceed 5% of membership fees or R120 000. The taxable portion of the clubs' trading income is taxed at a rate of 28%.

5.2.6 Benefit, pension, provident and retirement annuity funds

Section 10(1)*(d)*(i) exempts from tax the receipts and accruals of any pension fund, pension preservation fund, provident fund, provident preservation fund, beneficiary fund and retirement annuity fund (under the Pension Funds Act 24 of 1956). The exemption also applies to any trade union, chamber of commerce, local publicity association, mutual loan assistance, fidelity or indemnity fund approved by the Commissioner. Also exempt are societies or associations established to promote the common interests of their members.

5.2.7 Disability and war pensions

Section 10(1)*(g)* exempts any amount received as a war pension and any award or benefit under any law relating to the payment of compensation in respect of diseases contracted by persons employed in mining operations.

Section 10(1)*(gA)* exempts any disability pension paid under s 2 of the Social Assistance Act 13 of 2004.

5.2.8 Workmen's compensation and death benefits

Section 10(1)*(gB)* exempts workmen's compensation and death benefits paid by an employer in terms of the Workmen's Compensation Act 30 of 1941 or the Compensation for Occupational Injuries and Diseases Act 130 of 1993.

5.3 PARTIAL EXEMPTIONS

Partial exemptions exempt a taxpayer from tax either with regard to a certain kind of income or with regard to a certain portion of a specific type of income. A few examples are discussed below.

5.3.1 Foreign governments and assistance agreements

Section 10(1)*(bA)* exempts from tax receipts and accruals of:

- the government of any other country (10(1)*(bA)*(i);
- any foreign government agency appointed by that government to administer its responsibilities and functions in terms of an official development assistance agreement 10(1)*(bA)*(ii); and
- any multinational organisation providing foreign donor funding in terms of an official development assistance agreement.[1] The Minister must announce the exemption in terms of a notice in the *Government Gazette*.

5.3.2 Salaries of foreign government officials and their staff

- Section 10(1)*(c)*(ii) exempts from tax any pension payable to any former State President or Vice President or his or her surviving spouse.
- Section 10(1)*(c)*(iii) exempts from tax the salary or remuneration paid to foreign state officials (such as diplomats, consuls and ambassadors) if they are not ordinarily resident in the Republic.
- Section 10(1)*(c)*(iv) exempts from tax amounts paid to a domestic or private servant of a foreign diplomat for domestic or private services rendered to the foreign diplomat, if the servant is not a South African citizen and if the servant is not ordinarily resident in the Republic.

---

[1] Section 231(3) of the Constitution of the Republic of South Africa, 1996.

5.3.3 Special inter-government agreements

Section 10(1)*(c)*(v) exempts from tax the salary of a foreign subject temporarily employed in the Republic, provided the exemption is authorised by an agreement entered into by the government of the foreign state in South Africa.

5.3.4 Foreign social security and pension payments

- Section 10(1)*(gC)*(i) provides an exemption for any amount received by or accrued to any resident under the social security system of any other country.
- Section 10(1)*(gC)*(ii) (amended by Taxation laws Amendment Act 17 of 2017) provides an exemption for a lump sum, pension or annuity received by or accrued to any resident from a source outside the Republic as consideration for past employment outside the Republic other than from any pension fund, pension preservation fund, provident fund, provident preservation fund or retirement annuity fund as defined in s 1(1) or a company that is a resident and that is registered in terms of the Long-term Insurance Act as a person carrying on long-term insurance business excluding any amount transferred to that fund or that insurer from a source outside the Republic in respect of that member. The commencement date of this provision was 1 March 2018.

5.3.5 Funeral benefits

Section 10(1)*(gD)* exempts from tax any funeral benefit payable in terms of s 6F of the Special Pensions Act 69 of 1996.

5.3.6 Awards from pension funds

Section 10(1)*(gE)* exempts from tax any amount awarded to a person by a beneficiary fund as defined in the Pension Funds Act.

5.3.7 Policies with no cash value or surrender value

Section 10(1)*(gG)* exempts from tax any amount received by or accrued to a person:

- in the case of a risk policy with no cash value or surrender value, if the amount of premiums paid in respect of that policy by the employer of the person has been deemed to be a taxable benefit of the person in terms of the Seventh Schedule; and
- in the case of any other policy, if an amount equal to the aggregate of the amount of any premiums has been included in the income of the person as a taxable benefit in terms of the Seventh Schedule since the date on which the policy was entered into.

5.3.8 Insurance policies relating to death, disablement or illness of an employee or director, or former employee

Section 10(1)*(gH)* exempts from tax any amount received or accrued in respect of a policy of insurance where:

- the policy relates to death, disablement or illness of an employee or director, or a former employee or director, of the person that is the policyholder; and
- no amount of premiums payable in respect of that policy on or after 1 March 2012 is deductible from the income of that person for the purposes of determining the taxable income derived by the person from carrying on any trade.

5.3.9 Insurance policy relating to death, disablement, illness or unemployment

Section 10(1)*(gI)* exempts from tax any amount received or accrued in respect of an insurance policy relating to the death, disablement, illness or unemployment of any person, including the policyholder or an employee of the policyholder, to the extent to which the benefits in terms of that policy are paid as a result of death, disablement, illness or unemployment, other than any policy of which the benefits are paid or payable by a retirement fund.

5.3.10 Amounts received by or accrued to a member of a bargaining council

Section 10(1)*(gJ)* exempts from tax any amount received by or accrued to a person who is a member of a bargaining council that is established in terms of s 27 of the Labour Relations Act 66 of 1995.

5.3.11 Exemption for interest received by or accruing to a non-resident

Section 10(1)*(h)* exempts from tax any amount of interest which is received or accrues by or to any person that is not a resident, unless:

- that person is a natural person who was physically present in the Republic for a period exceeding 183 days in aggregate during the twelve-month period preceding the date on which the interest is received or accrues by or to that person; or
- the debt from which the interest arises is effectively connected to a permanent establishment of that person in the Republic.

5.3.12 Amounts received by or accrued to the holder of a debt, if the holder is a company that forms part of the same group of companies

Section 10(1)*(h*A*)* exempts from tax any amount received by or accrued to the holder of a debt, if the holder is a company that forms part of the same group of companies, as defined in s 41, as the issuer of that debt, to the extent that the amount is attributable to any amount of interest as defined in s 23K(1) that is not deductible as a result of the application of s 23K.

5.3.13 Amounts received by or accrued to a holder of a participatory interest in a portfolio of a collective investment scheme in securities

Section 10(1)*(i*B*)* exempts from tax any amount received by or accrued to a holder of a participatory interest in a portfolio of a collective investment scheme in securities by way of a distribution from that portfolio if that amount is deemed to have accrued to that portfolio in terms of s 25BA(1)*(b)* and that amount was subject to normal tax in the hands of that portfolio.

5.3.14 Foreign banks

Under s 10(1)*(j)*, receipts and accruals of foreign banks are exempt from tax if all the following requirements are met:

- The bank is not resident in South Africa.
- The bank is entrusted by the government of a territory outside the Republic with the custody of the principle foreign exchange reserves of that territory.
- The Minister of Finance must have granted this exemption to the specific bank for the particular year of assessment. The exemption is granted annually.

5.3.15 Ship crews

Section 10(1)*(o)*(i) exempts from tax any remuneration (as defined in the Fourth Schedule to the Act) derived by any person as an officer or crew member of a ship engaged in international transportation of passengers or goods if:

- such person was outside the Republic for a period or period exceeding 183 full days in aggregate during the year of assessment; and
- the crew of the ship is used in the prospecting, exploration, mining or production (including surveys and other work of a similar nature) for any minerals (including natural oils) from the seabed outside the Republic. Such officer or crew members may also have their remuneration exempted under this provision where such officer or crew member is employed on board such ship solely for purposes of the 'passage' of such ship, as defined in the Marine Traffic Act 2 of 1981, and the 'days' requirement is met. A full day runs from 00:00 to 24:00.

According to SARS Interpretation Note 34 of 12 January 2006, s 10(1)*(o)*(i) was inserted into the South African Income Tax in 1993 in order to bring the provisions of the Act in line with those of the major maritime nations, which exempt their seamen from income tax if they are absent from their home countries for a period exceeding 183 days in aggregate during the tax year. For the purpose of this exemption, weekends, public holidays, vacation and sick leave spent outside South Africa are considered to form part of the 183-day period.

- Section 10(1)*(o)*(i) applies to any person, whether a South African tax resident or not, as long as such person is engaged in the international transportation for reward of passengers or goods. This will include passenger lines and cargo ships travelling in international waters.
- The transportation must be for reward, which means there must be a *quo pro quo* for the conveyance of passengers or goods.
- According to Interpretation Note 34, the requirement that the ship must be engaged in the business of transportation means that the transport of fish from the fishing ground to the port by a fishing trawler will not constitute transportation.
- Applying the same reasoning, the crew of a luxury yacht owned by a wealthy businessman for private use would not be able to utilise this exemption.

5.3.16 South African dividends

Section 10(1)*(k)*(i) totally exempts from tax South African dividends received by or accrued to or in favour of any person except dividends distributed by a real estate investment trust or by a controlled property company as defined in s 25BB of the Act. This exemption excludes those distributed out of profits of a capital nature and those received by or accrued to or in favour of any person who is neither a resident nor carrying on business in the Republic.

5.3.17 Foreign dividends and dividends paid or declared by a headquarter may qualify for the following exemptions

Paragraph *(k)* of the definition of the term 'gross income' in s 1 includes in gross income any amount received or accrued by way of local dividends or foreign dividends. A foreign dividend is defined in s 1 as an amount paid by a foreign company in respect of a share in that foreign dividend. A foreign company is defined in s 1 as a non-resident company. However, s 10B exempts the following foreign dividends from tax (subject to the following exceptions):

- *The participation exemption in s 10B(2)*(a)*:* Subject to certain exceptions, if the person receiving the foreign dividend holds at least 10% of the total equity shares and voting rights in the company declaring the foreign dividend, the foreign dividend will be exempt. If the recipient of the foreign dividend is a company, the interest that any other company forming part of the same group of companies as the recipient has in the company declaring the dividend is added to the recipient's interest when determining whether the 10% threshold is exceeded.

- *Country-to-country exemption in s 10B(2)*(b)*:* Subject to certain exceptions, if the foreign dividend is received by a foreign company, which is a resident in the same country as the person paying the dividend, the dividend is exempt. This exemption applies irrespective of the interest that the recipient company has in the equity shares and voting interest in the company declaring the foreign dividend. Since foreign dividends received by foreign companies are normally not included in such foreign companies' gross income for South African income tax purposes (since such dividend will not be from a South African source), the country-to-country exemption will only have practical application where the recipient foreign entity is a controlled foreign company. The foreign dividend received by a controlled foreign company will, if it is not exempt in terms of s 10B(2)*(b)*, be included in the controlled foreign company's net income in terms of s 9D(2A) and consequently in the resident shareholder's income in terms of s 9D(2).
- *The controlled foreign company exemption in s 10b(2)*(c)*:* If a foreign dividend is received by a resident, it will be exempt in the resident's hands to the extent that the foreign dividend does not exceed the aggregate of all amounts that are included in the resident's income in any year of assessment in terms of s 9D. Section 9D(2) includes a proportionate amount of a controlled foreign company's net income in the income of a resident shareholder. This rule prevents the double taxation of the same profits both in terms of s 9D and again when the profits are distributed as a dividend.
- *The exemption for dividends declared in respect of JSE listed shares (ss 10B(2)*(d) *and 10B(2)*(e)*):* If a foreign dividend is received in respect of a listed share, it will be exempt if it does not consist of a distribution of an asset *in specie.* A listed share is a share that is listed on the JSE.[2] This exemption will not apply to any payment out a foreign dividend received by or accrued to any person.[3] Where a foreign dividend in the form of an *in specie* distribution is received in respect of a JSE listed share by a resident company on or after 1 March 2014, the foreign dividend will be exempt.[4]
- *The ratio exemption (s 10B(3)):* A foreign dividend may qualify for the ratio exemption to the extent that it does not qualify for the exemptions above (participation exemption, country-to-country exemption, controlled foreign company exemption or JSE listed share exemption). This exemption is calculated in terms of a certain formula.

---

2 Definition of 'listed share' in s 1 of the Act.

3 Section 10B(5).

4 Section 10B(2)*(e)*.

5.3.18 Exemption for royalties (as defined in s 49A) received by or accrued to a non-resident

Section 49A of the Income Tax Act defines 'royalty' to mean any amount that is received or accrues in respect of—

- the use or right of use of or permission to use any intellectual property as defined in s 23I; or
- the imparting of or the undertaking to impart any scientific, technical, industrial or commercial knowledge or information, or the rendering of or the undertaking to render any assistance or service in connection with the application or utilisation of such knowledge or information.

Section 10(1)*(l)* exempts the amount of any royalty, as defined in s 49A, which is received by or accrues to any person that is not a resident, unless:

- that person is a natural person who was physically present in the Republic for a period exceeding 183 days in aggregate during the twelve-month period preceding the date on which the amount is received by or accrues to that person; or
- the intellectual property or the knowledge or information in respect of which that royalty is paid is effectively connected with a permanent establishment of that person in the Republic.

5.3.19 Exemption for amounts subjected to withholding tax on foreign entertainers or sportsmen

In terms of ss 47A–47K, a final withholding tax at a flat rate of 15% is levied on an amount received by or accrued to a non-resident entertainer or sportsperson. Section 10(1)*(l*A*)* exempts amounts amount received by or accrued to foreign entertainer or sportsmen if that amount is subjected to withholding tax on foreign entertainers or sportsmen under ss 47A–47K.

5.3.20 Benefit or allowances payable under the Unemployment Insurance Act

Section 10(1)*(m*B*)* exempts from tax any benefit or allowance payable in terms of the Unemployment Insurance Act 63 of 2001.

5.3.21 Employment outside the Republic

Section 10(1)*(o)*(ii) exempts from tax, under certain circumstances, any form of remuneration derived by an employee in respect of service rendered outside South Africa.

This exemption applies in a year of assessment for amounts received or accrued by way of any salary, leave pay, wage, overtime pay, bonus, gratuity, commission, fee emolument or allowance, including any fringe benefit and amounts under ss 8, 8B and 8C, but only if:

- the employee was outside South Africa for more than 183 full days in total during any period of 12 months;
- the period outside South Africa includes a continuous period of absence of more than 60 full days during that period of 12 months; and
- ·the service was rendered for or on behalf of an employer, who can be situated in or outside South Africa.

In the calculation of the number of days during which a person is outside of South Africa, Interpretation Note 16 of 27 March 2003 provides that weekends, public holidays, vacation leave and sick leave spent outside South Africa are considered to be part of the days during which services are rendered and should therefore be included in the calculation of the 183-day and 60-day period of absence.

The 183-day test is a formalistic time test in that the reason for the physical absence or physical presence (other than for services rendered) is relevant. Consequently, even if the 60-day period is interrupted by the fact that the taxpayer had to return to South Africa during the 60-day period, say, due to family illness, the exemption will not apply. SARS issued Interpretation Note 16 of 27 March 2003 on s 10(10)*(o)*(ii), 'Exemption from Income Tax: Foreign Employment Income', regarding the application of this exemption. Section 1 of the Act defines 'Republic' as follows:

> 'Republic' means the Republic of South Africa and, when used in a geographical sense, includes the territorial sea thereof as well as any area outside the territorial sea which has been or may be designated, under international law and the laws of South Africa, as areas within which South Africa may exercise sovereign rights or jurisdiction with regard to the exploration or exploitation of natural resources.

Consequently, remuneration for services performed on the continental shelf but outside the territorial waters relating to, for example, the exploitation of oil and natural gas, will not qualify for the exemption.

According to SARS Interpretation Note 16, each month in the 12-month period is a 'month' as defined in the Interpretation Act 33 of 1957, ie a calendar month. The 183-day period mentioned above must fall within a period of 12 consecutive calendar months. The 12-month period is not necessarily a year of assessment, a financial year or a calendar year; it is any 12-month period that commences or ends in the year of assessment in which the remuneration in question must be taxed or exempted.

According to SARS Interpretation Note 16, as is the case with the s 10(1)*(o)*(i) exemption, weekends, public holidays, vacation and sick leave spent outside the Republic are considered to be part of the days during which services were rendered during the 183-day and 60-day periods of absence.

For the purpose of this exemption, a person is deemed to be outside of South Africa if that person is in transit through South Africa between two places outside of South Africa and does not formally enter South Africa through a designated port of entry. If remuneration is received by an employee during a year of assessment in respect of service rendered by that employee over a period of longer than one year, the remuneration is deemed to have accrued evenly over the period for which the service was rendered. The amount received can thus be apportioned and the exemption under s 10(1)*(o)*(ii) can be claimed in all of the relevant years of assessment. This provision ensures that income from, for example, a share incentive scheme, that relates back to services rendered outside South Africa over a period of longer than a year, will be deemed to have accrued over such longer period. This exemption will be available during every year of assessment falling within such period and is not only limited to the year of assessment during which the requirements of s 10(1)*(o)*(ii) were met.

This exemption applies only to the normal tax on the person's remuneration. It does not extend to other income earned by the taxpayer during his or her absence, nor does it extend to other taxes (for example the skills development levy payable on remuneration).

In terms of proviso (B) to s 10(1)*(o)*(ii), this exemption is not applicable to remuneration:

- derived from the holding of any public office as contemplated in s 9(2)*(g)*, which refers to a public office to which the person was appointed in terms of an Act of Parliament; or
- received in respect of service rendered or work or labour performed on behalf of an employer in the national, provincial or local sphere of government of the Republic, that is, a constitutional institution listed in Schedule 2 of the Public Finance Management Act 1 of 1999 or that is a public entity in Schedule 1 of the Local Government: Municipal Systems Act 32 of 2000.

The remuneration that is covered by the exemption relates to remuneration received or accrued in the year of assessment in which the 12-month period commences or ends. In terms of SARS Interpretation Note 16, payments in respect of the relinquishment, termination, loss, repudiation, cancellation or variation of any office or employment, or of any appointment (or right to be appointed) to any office or employment, are not covered by this exemption.

An amendment of s 10(1)(o)(ii) is envisaged, with effect from 1 March 2020. In terms of the Taxation Laws Amendment Bill, 2017, s 10(1)*(o)*(ii) will be amended to the following:

> Exempt from normal tax any form of remuneration to the extent to which that remuneration does not exceed one million Rand in respect of a year of assessment and is received by or accrues to any employee during any year of assessment by way of any salary, leave pay, wage, overtime pay, bonus, gratuity, commission, fee, emolument or allowance, including any amount referred to in paragraph *(i)* of the definition of gross income in s 1 or an amount referred to in ss 8, 8B or 8C, in respect of services rendered outside the Republic by that employee for or on behalf of any employer, if that employee was outside the Republic—

(aa) for a period or periods exceeding 183 full days in aggregate during any period of 12 months;

(bb) for a continuous period exceeding 60 full days during that period of 12 months ...

Provided that—

(A) for purposes of this subparagraph, a person who is in transit through the Republic between two places outside the Republic and who does not formally enter the Republic through a port of entry as contemplated in section 9 (1) of the Immigration Act, 2002 (Act 13 of 2002), or at any other place as may be permitted by the Director-General of the Department of Home Affairs or the Minister of Home Affairs in terms of that Act, shall be deemed to be outside the Republic;

(B) the provisions of this subparagraph shall not apply in respect of any remuneration—

(AA) derived in respect of the holding of a public office contemplated in section 9(2)*(g)*; or

(BB) received by or accrued to any person in respect of services rendered or work or labour performed as contemplated in section 9(2)*(h)*; and

(C) for the purposes of this subparagraph, where remuneration is received by or accrues to any employee during any year of assessment in respect of services rendered by that employee in more than one year of assessment, the remuneration is deemed to have accrued evenly over the period that those services were rendered ...;

The Explanatory Memorandum to the Taxation Laws Amendment Bill, 2017 explains that the purpose of introducing the exemption was to prevent double taxation of an individual's income between South Africa and the host country. Unfortunately, the exemption instead creates opportunities for double non-taxation in instances where the host country imposes little or no tax on employment income. This is contrary to the policy intent expressed when the foreign employment income tax exemption was introduced. The Explanatory Memorandum on the Revenue Laws Amendment Act, 2000 cautioned against the undue exploitation of this exemption by stating that 'the effect of this relief measure will be monitored to determine whether certain categories of employees abuse it to earn foreign employment income without foreign taxation'.

The Explanatory Memorandum to Taxation Laws Amendment Bill, 2017 notes that it is required of policy-makers to continuously ensure that the tax system espouses the principle of fairness and progressivity. Therefore, considerable attention should be given to the principle of equity which ensures that taxpayers in an equal position should be taxed in an equal manner as they have the same ability to bear the tax burden (horizontal equity), and that taxpayers with better circumstances should bear a larger part of the tax burden as a proportion of their income (vertical equity).

For this reason, it was proposed that foreign employment income earned by a resident should no longer be fully exempt as is currently provided. Tax residents who spend more than 183 days outside of South Africa rendering employment services will now only be exempted up to the first R1 million of their employment income earned abroad.

The R1 million exemption will provide relief for lower to middle income South Africans working abroad. Any foreign employment income earned over and above this amount will be taxed in South Africa, applying the normal tax tables for that particular year of assessment. Residents will still be required to have spent a continuous period of at least 60 full days rendering employment services outside South Africa, during any 12-month period, in order to qualify for the exemption. The proposed amendment will come into effect on 1 March 2020 and applies in respect of years of assessment commencing on or after that date.

5.3.22 Amounts received by non-resident for services on behalf of government

Section 10(1)*(p)* exempts from normal tax any amount received by or accrued to:

- any person who is not a resident;
- for services rendered by him or her outside South Africa; and
- for or on behalf of any qualifying employer in the national or provincial sphere of government or municipality in South Africa or similar qualifying entities (if 80% or more of the expenditure of such entity is defrayed directly or indirectly from funds allocated by Parliament).

In order to qualify for this exemption, the amount should be chargeable with income tax in the country in which the person is ordinarily resident. The tax should be borne by the taxpayer himself or herself and may not be paid on the taxpayer's behalf by the government, municipality or public body entity.

5.3.23 International shipping income

In terms of s 12Q, international shipping income received by an international shipping company in respect of years of assessment that commence on or after 1 April 2014 will be exempt from normal tax. The purpose of the exemption is for this industry to remain competitive internationally. The international trend has been to reduce the taxation of international shipping transport due to the highly mobile nature of this activity.

In order to qualify for this exemption, the international shipping company must be a South African resident that holds a share or shares in one or more South African ships that are used in international shipping. International shipping is defined in s 12Q as the conveyance for compensation of passenger or goods by means of the operation of a South African ship mainly engaged in international traffic. A South African ship is a ship which is registered in the Republic in accordance with s 15 of the Ship Registration Act 58 of 1998.

The tax regime for qualifying international shipping companies includes exemptions from normal tax, capital gains, dividends tax as well as cross-border withholding tax on interest.

5.3.24 Ships and aircraft: Foreign owners or characters

Section 33 imposes what is known as a 'lifting's tax' on owners or charterers of ships or aircraft who are not residents but embark on the transportation of passengers or load livestock, mail or goods in South Africa. However, s 10(1) *(cG)* provides that receipts and accruals of non-resident ship or aircraft owners or charterers are exempt if 'a similar exemption or equivalent relief' is granted to South African residents by the country in which that person is resident.

5.3.25 Interest earned by resident individuals

Section 10(1)*(i)* exempts from tax interest received by or accruing to a natural person up to a specified amount. For the 2018/2019 tax year, for persons above the age of 65 the maximum is R34 500, and for persons below the age of 65 the maximum is R23 800. These amounts are subject to annual review by the Minister of Finance.

5.3.26 Uniform allowance

Section 10(1)*(nA)* provides that where an employee must, as a condition of his or her employment, wear a special uniform while on duty, the uniform provided to the employee by the employer, or any allowance for the uniform given to the employee by the employer, is exempt from tax if the uniform is clearly distinguishable from ordinary clothing.

5.3.27 Relocation or transfer costs

Section 10(1)*(nB)* provides that where an employee is appointed, transferred or dismissed, and moves at the insistence of his or her employer and the employer bears the cost of the move, the amount expended will not be taxed in the employee's hands. The costs dealt with are transportation costs, settling-in costs and the cost of hiring temporary accommodation for less than 183 days. The employee will also not be taxed on any costs borne by the employer in respect of the sale of the employee's previous residence. The amount allowed in respect of expenditure relating to the sale of the employee's previous residence and settling into permanent residential accommodation at his or her new place of residence is at the discretion of the Commissioner.

5.3.28 Employee share schemes

Section 10(1)*(nC)*, *(nD)* and *(nE)* exempts the following from tax:

- the receipt of qualifying equity shares in terms of s 8B;[5]
- the receipt of an equity instrument contemplated in s 8C if it has not yet vested in the employee;[6]

[5] Section 10(1)*(nC)*.
[6] Section 10(1)*(nD)*.

- the receipt of proceeds on the disposal of a s 8C equity instrument which has not yet vested in the employee;[7] and
- an amount received on the cancellation of a share scheme purchase transaction or on the repurchase of shares acquired under that scheme, provided that the employee is only refunded what he or she actually paid for the shares or options (excluding transactions conducted in terms of s 8C or the cancellation of such transactions).[8]

5.3.29 Bursaries and scholarships

Section 10(1)*(q)* exempts from tax any *bona fide* scholarship or bursary granted to assist or enable any person to study at a recognised education or research institution.

In the case of a bursary or scholarship granted to an employee, the exemption does not apply unless the employee agrees to reimburse the employer if the employee fails to complete his or her studies other than for reasons of death, ill-health or injury.

If the scholarship or bursary is granted to a relative of the employee, the exemption is limited to R10 000 per year if the employee's remuneration exceeds R100 000 per annum. If the remuneration does not exceed that amount, there is no limit.

5.3.30 Alimony and maintenance

Section 10(1)*(u)* exempts from tax alimony and maintenance granted under a judicial order of divorce or separation in the hands of the recipient spouse if the divorce or separation proceedings took place after 21 March 1962.

Note: After all the amounts which, in terms of the Act, are *exempt* from taxation have been deducted from the taxpayer's gross income, what remains is the taxpayer's *'income'* for income tax purposes. Thus, the term 'income', as defined in s 1 of the Act, means the amount of 'gross income' remaining of any person for any year or period of assessment after the deduction therefrom of all amounts exempt from normal tax in terms of the Act.

[7] Ibid.

[8] Section 10(1)*(n*E*)*.

Chapter 6

Deductions

6.1 INTRODUCTION

This chapter deals with the provisions contained in the Income Tax Act 58 of 1962, as amended ('the Act'), which regulate the deduction of expenditure incurred by the taxpayer. Once a taxpayer has determined his or her income, the Act requires that the taxpayer establishes what expenditure has been incurred and which may be deducted for tax purposes in order to arrive at the taxpayer's taxable income on which tax, at the applicable rate, must be paid.

The Act contains the general deduction formula in s 11*(a)* which deals with general principles of deductibility of expenditure. Furthermore, s 23 of the Act sets out those items of expenditure that may not be claimed for tax purposes. In addition, the Act comprises various sections allowing for the deduction of certain specific types of expenditure, each of which is dealt with below, to encourage certain economic activities in the country, thereby achieving government's policy objectives.

6.2 THE GENERAL DEDUCTION FORMULA (S 11*(a)*)

The preamble to s 11 states as follows:

> 11 General deductions allowed in determination of taxable income
>
> For the purpose of determining the taxable income derived by any person from carrying on any trade, there shall be allowed as deductions from the income of such person so derived ...

Taking account of the above wording, it is necessary that a taxpayer is conducting a trade to successfully claim a deduction against income for tax purposes. Section 1 of the Act defines a trade as including:

> [E]very profession, trade, business, employment, calling, occupation, or venture, including the letting of any property and the use of or the grant of permission to use any patent as defined in the Patents Act, 1978 (Act 57 of 1978), or any design as defined in the Designs Act, 1993 (Act 195 of 1993), or any trade mark as defined in the Trade Marks Act, 1993 (Act 194 of 1993), or any copyright as defined in the Copyright Act, 1978 (Act 98 of 1978), or any other property which is of a similar nature ...

A taxpayer will fail in claiming expenditure that is unrelated to the carrying on of a trade as defined or where the expenditure is personal in nature. The term 'trade' is widely defined but does not include certain activities which may generate income in the form of interest or dividends.[1] Thus, expenditure incurred in generating interest income is typically not allowed by the Commissioner for the South African Revenue Service on the basis that interest income is passive in nature and does not result from an activity which constitutes the carrying on of a trade.

If a taxpayer incurs expenditure prior to commencing the carrying on of a trade, that expenditure will not qualify as a deduction under s 11 of the Act.[2] This is on the basis that the expenditure was not incurred in carrying on a trade, but rather in preparing for the carrying on of the trade. So-called pre-trade expenditure may be deductible if it falls within the provisions of s 11A of the Act.

Section 11*(a)* of the Act allows the following to be claimed for tax purposes: '[E]xpenditure and losses actually incurred in the production of the income, provided such expenditure and losses are not of a capital nature'.

For a taxpayer to succeed in claiming a deduction under s 11*(a)* of the Act, each of the requirements of the section must be complied with. These will be dealt with below.

---

[1] De Koker AP *Silke on South African Income Tax* 11 ed (LexisNexis) para 7.2 at 7–6.

[2] See SARS Interpretation Note 33 (Issue 2) 'Assessed losses: Companies: The "trade" and "income from trade" requirements' (30 June 2010) 4 and 7.

6.2.1 Expenditure and losses

The section refers to both 'expenditure and losses' and it is necessary to establish what the legislature meant by using these two terms. Watermeyer AJP, as he then was, in *Port Elizabeth Electric Tramway Co Ltd v CIR*[3] indicated that the term 'losses' meant losses of floating capital utilised in a business which generates the income. Subsequently, Watermeyer CJ in *Joffe & Co Ltd v CIR*[4] stated the following:

> The word 'loss' has several meanings and its meaning in Section 11(2)*(a)* is somewhat obscure. In relation to trading operations the word is sometimes used to signify a deprivation suffered by the loser, usually an involuntary deprivation, whereas expenditure usually means a voluntary payment of money. When trading operations cause damage to third parties and this damage has to be made good, then the payment which is made in satisfaction of such damage (and possibly even the pre-existing liability to make such payment) may properly be called a loss, but when the payment has been made then it can also properly be called an expenditure. Consequently, it is not clear to me that the word 'losses', if used in this sense ... means anything different from 'expenditure'.[5]

In the case of a moneylender, the funds advanced to a debtor who is unable to repay the loan will give rise to the business suffering a loss as opposed to constituting expenditure incurred by the taxpayer.[6]

In *ITC 1783*[7] it was necessary for the Tax Court to determine if the issue of shares by a company constituted expenditure incurred by it. Goldblatt J decided that the taxpayer had not incurred any expenditure for the purposes of s 11*(gA)* of the Act. Support for this view can be found in *Silke on South African Income Tax* at para 7.4, where it is stated that no expenditure is incurred if a company issues its own shares for services rendered to it or for trading stock acquired by it. Later, in *ITC 1801*,[8] Jooste J reached the opposite conclusion in a very similar case. SARS was dissatisfied with his decision and appealed to the North Gauteng High Court where Sapire J, for the full bench of that court, ruled in favour of Labat.[9] SARS remained unhappy with the decision and noted an appeal to the Supreme Court of Appeal. In the case of *CSARS v Labat Africa Ltd*,[10] Harms AP decided that the issue of shares by the company in satisfaction of the debt due for the intellectual property acquired by the company did not comprise expenditure incurred by it. The judge analysed the meaning of the term 'expenditure' and expressed the view that the ordinary

---

3 1936 CPD 241, 8 SATC 13.

4 1946 AD 157, 13 SATC 354.

5 At 360.

6 *Stone v SIR* 1974 (3) SA 584 (A), 36 SATC 117.

7 66 SATC 373.

8 68 SATC 57.

9 *Commissioner for the South African Revenue Service v Labat Africa Limited* 72 SATC 75. See Legwaila T 'The Issue of Shares is not "Expenditure" for Purposes of the Income Tax Act: *Commissioner, South African Revenue Service v Labat Africa Ltd*' (2013) 130 *SALJ* 318.

10 2013 (2) SA 33 (SCA), 74 SATC 1.

meaning of the term refers to the 'action of spending funds, disbursement or consumption.'[11] The court stated that expenditure requires a reduction in the assets of the taxpayer or, at the very least, a movement of the assets of the person who expends an amount.

In *ITC 1783*[12] Goldblatt J indicated that an allotment or issue of shares does not reduce the assets of a company and it therefore cannot qualify as 'expenditure' for purposes of the Act. Harms AP agreed with the conclusion reached by Goldblatt J and thus Labat failed in claiming the deduction under s 11*(gA)* of the Act. Based on the decision of the Supreme Court of Appeal, a company cannot claim the value of shares issued by it for goods or services acquired by it. Certain exceptions to the above rule exist under ss 24BA and 40CA where a company issues shares for assets acquired by it or where shares are issued under a qualifying broad-based employee share scheme envisaged in s 8B of the Act. (See chapters 7 and 11 for further detail.)

6.2.2 Actually incurred

Expenditure must be 'actually incurred' for a taxpayer to fall into s 11*(a)*. It is necessary to establish what is meant by the term 'actually incurred'. This refers to the timing of a deduction, as a taxpayer cannot anticipate expenditure or provide for it; expenditure can only be claimed in the year of assessment in which it is incurred.

Where a taxpayer pays for goods or services in the same year of assessment there is little doubt that the taxpayer has incurred expenditure as required under s 11*(a)*. Where, however, the taxpayer has not yet paid for the expenditure it must be established if the taxpayer has an unconditional liability for the expenditure as at the end of the year of assessment.

A taxpayer cannot deduct amounts set aside as a reserve for future expenditure, as such amounts do not comprise expenditure actually incurred in the year of assessment. This is supported by the judgment of the court in *ITC 169*,[13] where the amounts allocated to a staff benefit fund were held not to have been incurred by the company in the tax year in question. Davis KC, President of the court, stated as follows:

> Now the deduction can only be allowed if it is 'expenditure actually incurred in the Union' in the production of income and the question which we will have to direct our minds to is whether this book entry can be described as 'expenditure actually incurred in the Union' in the production of income. In order that there may be such 'expenditure' it seems to me that there must be a sum of money or money's worth going out from the company to the payee, but there is no evidence of any such act having taken place in this case.[14]

---

[11] Paragraph 12.
[12] 66 SATC 373.
[13] 5 SATC 162.
[14] At 163.

Thus, the court dismissed the appeal on the basis that the company had not incurred any expenditure in the tax year in dispute.

In *ITC 183*[15] the proprietor of a motor garage sought to claim a deduction for amounts set aside as a reserve for servicing cars. The court disallowed the deduction in terms of the equivalent of s 23*(e)* of the Act, which specifically precludes the deduction of amounts transferred to a reserve fund. Clearly, the amount claimed in *ITC 183*[16] did not represent an amount of expenditure actually incurred and could also have been disallowed on the basis that the expenditure did not meet the requirements of s 11*(a)* of the Act.

In *Port Elizabeth Electric Tramway Company Ltd v Commissioner for Inland Revenue*[17] Watermeyer AJP explained the meaning of the term 'actually incurred' as follows:

> But expenses 'actually incurred' cannot mean 'actually paid.' So long as the liability to pay them actually has been incurred they may be deductible. For instance, a trader may at the end of the income tax year owe money for stocks purchased in the course of the year or for services rendered to him. He has not paid such liabilities but they are deductible.[18]

Based on the above it is clear that 'actually incurred' does not mean that the taxpayer has paid the liability in question. So long as the taxpayer has an unconditional liability to incur the expenditure it will be deductible for tax purposes.

Where a company pays commissions to agents on the sale of land and a portion thereof is retained until the sale of the land is completed, the retained portion is not actually incurred until the purchaser of the land pays the last instalment due.[19] The court stated that even though the expenditure may be reflected in the accounting records, it does not mean that it is actually incurred for tax purposes.[20]

In *ITC 674*[21] the taxpayer had claimed leave pay due to its employees as a deduction for tax purposes. The Commissioner had disallowed the deduction on the basis that the expenditure had not been incurred by the end of the taxpayer's year of assessment. The leave pay due to the taxpayer's employees arose under an industrial agreement concluded by the taxpayer. The employer was obliged by 24 December of each year to grant three weeks holiday leave on full pay to each of his employees who had been in his employ from any date prior to the first day of February of the same year. Employees who commenced employment after February or terminated employment before 1 December

15 5 SATC 262.
16 Ibid.
17 8 SATC 13.
18 At 15.
19 See *ITC 380* 9 SATC 347.
20 At 347.
21 16 SATC 235.

were entitled to holiday pay on a proportionate basis, taking account of the employee's period of service.

The court concluded as follows:

> Under that agreement the right of the employee to holiday pay proportionate to his period of service is absolute. There is no contingency upon which it can be withheld... . It is only the payment thereof that is postponed. Hence as at the 30th of June a liability attached to the partnership to pay *in futuro* to its employees the amounts so accruing up to that date.[22]

Thus, in *ITC 674*[23] the court decided that the taxpayer had incurred an absolute liability to pay the leave pay and allowed the deduction claimed by it.[24]

Subsequently in *Nasionale Pers Bpk v Kommissaris van Binnelandse Inkomste*[25] the former Appellate Division had to determine whether the staff bonuses claimed by the taxpayer had been incurred by the end of the company's year of assessment. Nasionale Pers had a year end of 31 March of each year and claimed amounts in respect of bonuses to be paid on the following 30 September.

The company's policy was that bonuses would only be paid to employees in the company's employ on 31 October. The bonus was paid on 30 September and if an employee left the company's employ in October the company would reclaim the full amount of the bonus. The payment of the bonus was conditional upon the employee being in the company's employ on 31 October. The company claimed a deduction of half of the bonus payable in the case of employees who already had six months' service as at 31 March. The company made a pro rata adjustment for those employees who had less than six months' service with the company as at 31 March. The Commissioner disallowed the deduction on the basis that the payment of the bonus was conditional upon the employee being in the employ of the company on 31 October.

The court agreed with the views expressed by Friedman J in the court *a quo* that it did not matter whether the conditions attached to the bonus are suspensive or resolutive in nature.[26] The fact of the matter was that the liability to pay the bonus could only be determined on 30 September as a result of the conditions attached thereto, and as a result the expenditure had not been incurred by 31 March and could not be allowed under s 11*(a)* of the Act.[27] The court distinguished the facts before it from those in *ITC 674*[28] on the basis that in the earlier case the taxpayer had incurred an unconditional liability by the

[22] At 237.
[23] 16 SATC 235.
[24] At 238.
[25] 1986 (3) SA 549 (A), 48 SATC 55.
[26] *Kommissaris van Binnelandse Inkomste v Nasionale Pers Bpk* 1984 (4) SA 551 (C) 556B–D, 46 SATC 83.
[27] Ibid.
[28] 16 SATC 235.

end of the year of assessment, even though actual payment of the amounts due would take place after the end of the year.[29]

Based on the decision in *ITC 542,*[30] where the legal obligation to pay an expense only arises in a subsequent year of assessment, that expense cannot be claimed for tax purposes in the earlier year. In *ITC 542*[31] the company's directors passed a resolution on 17 September 1941 approving the payment of interest on the directors' loan accounts as at 30 June 1941. The company claimed the interest in question on the basis that it was incurred in the production of the company's income in 1941. However, the legal obligation to pay interest only arose after the end of the tax year, that is, the date on which the resolution was passed by the directors, and the court held that the interest was not incurred in the 1941 financial year.[32]

In a case similar to that of *ITC 542,*[33] a company attempted to claim ten years' interest on a loan in one tax year in *ITC 1094*[34] in accordance with a resolution passed in 1962 for the payment of interest on the loan for a period of ten years to 1961. The court held that the company had failed to demonstrate that it had incurred a legal liability to pay interest at all, or to establish that the interest had been incurred to produce income or for the purposes of its trade in the tax years concerned.[35]

Caution must thus be exercised when parties agree on the manner in which interest is to be paid on a loan. This is borne out when reference is made to *ITC 1117,*[36] where the company and its shareholders agreed that interest on loans granted by the shareholders to the company would be paid at a rate of not less than 5% per annum. The company had a tax year of 31 March and in May 1966 the decision was made to pay interest at the rate of 12,75% per annum. Interest on the shareholders' loans was accounted for at the rate of 12,75% and claimed for tax purposes. The Commissioner allowed interest up to the rate of 5% and disallowed the excess on the basis that such excess was not incurred in the 1966 tax year. The court expressed the view that there was no legal liability on the company to pay interest at the rate of 12,75% as that rate was only determined after the end of the 1966 tax year.[37] Thus, the taxpayer's appeal was dismissed and the court allowed interest up to the rate of 5%, which was the amount actually incurred during the 1966 year of assessment.[38]

Where a business sells goods in returnable containers for which a deposit is refunded to the customer on the return of the container, the question arose

---

29 *Nasionale Pers Bpk v Kommissaris van Binnelandse Inkomste* 1986 (3) SA 549 (A), 48 SATC 55 at 68.

30 13 SATC 116.

31 Ibid.

32 At 117.

33 13 SATC 116.

34 28 SATC 275.

35 *ITC 1094* 28 SATC 275 at 284.

36 30 SATC 130.

37 At 131.

38 At 133.

as to whether the taxpayer could exclude those amounts from its income.[39] The taxpayer alternatively sought to claim the likely amount to be refunded to customers for the deposits on the containers as a deduction for tax purposes.[40] The difficulty the taxpayer faced was that there was no certainty that a customer would return the containers in question. Thus, Pyott had no legal liability as at the end of its tax year which qualified as a deduction under s 11*(a)*, as the amount would only be incurred when the container was in fact returned to Pyott.[41] As a result the provision created by Pyott was disallowed as a deduction for tax purposes.[42]

The court referred to the manner in which Pyott accounted for the provision it created for the containers to be returned to it and Davis AJA stated the following:

> Reliance was, however, placed, for the making of this provision, generally upon the principles of sound accountancy and upon English cases. While, no doubt, it is in accordance with those principles to make this provision in the Balance Sheet, the answer is that our Income Tax Act has laid down what is to be taxed, even if in so doing it may be said to disregard those principles... . But since 1917 we have had in South Africa an artificial and purely statutory definition of 'taxable income', derived ultimately from the definition of 'gross income' as set out above ...[43]

Thus, in establishing whether an expense has been incurred for tax purposes, no regard must be had to the manner in which a taxpayer has prepared its annual financial statements. Consequently, what may be prudent from an accounting point of view has no impact on the determination of the taxpayer's taxable income. What is critical in determining the deductibility of an expense is whether the taxpayer has actually incurred the expenditure in accordance with the provisions of the Act and in compliance with the principles laid down by the cases referred to.

It must be noted that a taxpayer cannot trade with itself, pass accounting entries relating to different businesses owned by one legal entity, and claim the amounts relating thereto as expenditure actually incurred by the taxpayer. This is what happened in *Afrikaanse Verbond Begrafnis Onderneming Beperk v Commissioner for Inland Revenue*.[44] In this case, the company carried on business as an insurer and as a funeral undertaker. The Act required that the taxable income derived from the insurance business be calculated in a particular way. The company chose to claim deductions of interest purportedly paid by its undertaker business to the insurance business.[45] Clearly, if the different businesses had been operated by two separate legal entities the

---

[39] See *Pyott Ltd v Commissioner for Inland Revenue* 1945 AD 128, 13 SATC 121.

[40] Ibid 125.

[41] At 127.

[42] At 125.

[43] At 126. See further *Joffe & Co Ltd v Commissioner for Inland Revenue* 1946 AD 157 at 165, 13 SATC 354.

[44] 1950 (3) SA 209 (A), 16 SATC 401.

[45] At 408.

deduction would have been allowed on the grounds that the interest was incurred. However, the company conducted the two businesses itself and constituted one taxpayer. The Act did not treat the two departments as distinct taxpayers and the court decided that a taxpayer cannot trade with itself, and thus disallowed the interest claimed as no amount had been incurred by it.[46]

The Act requires that the expenditure is 'actually incurred' and does not restrict the deduction to expenditure necessarily incurred by the taxpayer. The comments made by Watermeyer AJP in *Port Elizabeth Electric Tramway Co Ltd v Commissioner for Inland Revenue*[47] are useful:

> Taking these in turn, the words of the statute are 'actually incurred' not 'necessarily incurred.' The use of the word 'actually' as contrasted with the word 'necessarily' may widen the field of deductible expenditure. For instance, one man may conduct his business inefficiently or extravagantly actually incurring expenses which another man does not incur; such expenses therefore are not 'necessary' but they are actually incurred and therefore deductible.[48]

So long as the expenditure is incurred by the taxpayer and the taxpayer complies with the other requirements for deductibility, the expense will qualify as a deduction for tax purposes, even if the expenditure is unnecessary or extravagant.

A difficulty arises in quantifying the expenditure to be allowed under s 11*(a)* when the legal obligation is incurred in foreign currency on one date and that liability remains unpaid at the end of the tax year, or when it is settled and the exchange rate has changed. In *Caltex Oil (SA) Ltd v Secretary for Inland Revenue*[49] the court had to ascertain the quantum of the deduction to be allowed to the taxpayer where the foreign debt incurred for the purchase of trading stock remained unpaid at the end of the year of assessment. Caltex had incurred an unconditional liability as at the end of the tax year; the only issue in dispute was the quantification of the deduction to be allowed for tax purposes.

Caltex Oil (SA) Limited acquired crude oil and other petroleum products from Caltex (UK) Ltd in an amount of P4 659 486 and other supplies necessary to process crude oil from Caltex Services Ltd for P48 925. When the crude oil was acquired, the rand equivalent of the foreign debt amounted to R9 353 920 and by the end of the tax year, as a result of the devaluation of the foreign currency, the rand amount was reduced to an amount of R8 017 647, a reduction in rand terms of R1 336 271. The Secretary for Inland Revenue allowed a deduction of the lesser amount of R8 017 647 on the basis that this was the amount actually

[46] At 410. See also *Anglo American Corporation of SA Ltd v Commissioner of Taxes* 1975 (1) SA 973 (RA), 37 SATC 45 where the court refused the deduction of charges levied by one branch of a company on another branch of the same company on the basis that no amount was incurred.

[47] 1936 CPD 241, 8 SATC 13.

[48] At 15.

[49] 1975 (1) SA 665 (A), 37 SATC 1.

incurred by the taxpayer. Caltex argued that the amount incurred was the rand equivalent of the foreign debt converted into rand when the debt was incurred and that it was unnecessary to reduce the amount for the devaluation of the foreign currency. Insofar as the amount of P48 925 is concerned, the rand equivalent on the date of the transaction was R98 217 and by the time the debt was paid, within the same tax year, it was R84 186, that is an amount of R14 031 less than the amount recorded in the books of account. The Secretary only allowed the amount of R84 186 as a deduction. The taxpayer was dissatisfied with the disallowance and the appeal proceeded to the Income Tax Special Court, which held in favour of the Secretary. The case was then heard by the Appellate Division, as it was then known, and that court decided that it is only at the end of the year of assessment that it is possible to establish the amount of expenditure incurred by the taxpayer.[50]

Botha JA pointed out that it would be incorrect for a taxpayer to claim a deduction in an amount that is greater than the amount actually expended by the taxpayer in the particular year of assessment.[51] He stated:

> I agree with counsel for the respondent that it would be doing violence to language to suggest that, where a trader has incurred a liability to pay a fixed amount for trading stock during any tax year, and that amount is for any reason reduced during that year and before it is paid, the amount of the expenditure actually incurred by that trader was the original amount and not the reduced amount.[52]

The court thus decided that Caltex was only entitled to claim the amount of R8 017 647 for the crude oil acquired by it as that was the rand equivalent of the foreign debt as at the end of the tax year.[53] Regarding the other items purchased, the court held that the taxpayer could only claim the amount actually paid by it in the tax year in question, that is, the amount of R84 186 and not the amount of R98 217.[54] After the *Caltex* decision[55] the Act was amended specifically to deal with the conversion of amounts expressed in foreign currency into rand and to regulate the treatment of gains and losses arising out of transactions concluded in foreign currency.[56]

The complication of quantifying the deduction to be allowed to a taxpayer also arises where a loss on a bad debt is incurred during one tax year but the quantum of the loss cannot be established with total accuracy until a future date. This was the dilemma faced by the court in *Commissioner of Taxes v 'A' Company.*[57] In this case, the taxpayer conducted business as a merchant

---

[50] At 11. See also *Port Elizabeth Electric Tramway Co Ltd v Commissioner for Inland Revenue* 1936 CPD 241 244, 8 SATC 13.

[51] *Caltex* supra 13.

[52] At 13.

[53] At 16.

[54] At 16.

[55] *Caltex Oil (SA) Limited v Secretary for Inland Revenue* 1975 (1) SA 665 (A), 37 SATC 1.

[56] Section 25D of the Act deals with the determination of taxable income in foreign currency and s 24I regulates the tax treatment of gains or losses on foreign exchange transactions.

[57] 1979 (2) SA 409 (RA), 41 SATC 59.

banker and claimed an amount of $72 000 for the tax year ended 31 March 1976, being an estimate of the loss suffered as a result of a loan advanced to the borrower. The court had to decide whether the fact that the precise amount of the loss had not been quantified by 31 March 1976 resulted in the taxpayer being unable to claim the loss in that tax year. Lewis JP was satisfied that the company had suffered a loss and that it was entitled to the deduction in the 1976 tax year, even though the final decision to write off the loss of $72 000 was only made after 31 March 1976.[58] The fact that the amount of $72 000 was an estimate of the loss to be suffered by the taxpayer did not preclude it from claiming that amount as a loss actually incurred in the 1976 tax year.[59] The High Court of what was then Rhodesia (Appellate Division) thus endorsed the decision made by the court *a quo.*[60] That court held that 'a bad debt is deductible notwithstanding that the precise amount of the loss is not quantifiable'.[61]

Where the expenditure claimed by the taxpayer is subject to some form of contingency, that amount cannot be claimed until the liability to pay is no longer contingent. In *Commissioner for Inland Revenue v Edgars Stores Ltd*[62] the taxpayer claimed a deduction of rentals payable by it which were determined on the turnover derived by the company. In terms of the lease agreements concluded by Edgars with its landlords, it was liable to pay a basic rental and in addition, depending on the level of turnover generated at each store, it would become liable for additional rental referred to as 'turnover rental'. The leases concluded by the company were entered into on different dates and the turnover rental was calculated by taking account of Edgars's turnover for the period of twelve months from the date on which the lease was concluded. As a result this period of twelve months did not necessarily coincide with the company's tax year, which ended on 30 June of each year.

Edgars claimed an amount of R123 560 in respect of its 1978 year of assessment and an amount of R322 203, being the turnover rental it believed would become payable. Where the lease year coincided with Edgars's tax year, no dispute arose as the turnover was quantified and no contingency existed regarding the payment of the turnover rental for such leases. The Commissioner took the view that the amounts claimed by Edgars were not deductible as they had not been actually incurred as required under s 11*(a)* of the Act. Edgars's appeal was first heard by Nestadt J in the Transvaal Income Tax Special Court, who allowed the appeal. The Commissioner was unhappy with this decision and the case proceeded to the former Supreme Court where Ackermann J ruled in favour of the Commissioner.[63] Ackermann J referred to the following principle

[58] At 65.

[59] At 72.

[60] *ITC 1284* 41 SATC 45 at 52.

[61] At 52.

[62] 1986 (4) SA 312 (T), 48 SATC 89.

[63] *Commissioner for Inland Revenue v Edgars Stores Limited* 1986 (4) SA 312 (T), 48 SATC 89.

to be adhered to in establishing if expenditure has been 'actually incurred' as required under s 11 *(a)* of the Act:

- the case where the existence of the liability itself is conditional and dependent upon the happening of an event after the tax year in question, in which event the liability is not incurred in the tax year in question; and
- the case where the existence of the liability is certain and established within the tax year in question, but the amount of the liability cannot be accurately determined at the year-end, in which event the liability is nevertheless regarded as having been incurred in the tax year in question.[64]

The court reached the conclusion that the obligation to pay the turnover rental was conditional and dependent on the fulfilment of a condition only after the end of Edgars's tax year.[65] Ackermann J confirmed that the basic rental was incurred in the respective tax years and was deductible.[66] As a result, the Commissioner's appeal was upheld and the turnover rental was disallowed as a deduction for tax purposes.

Edgars was dissatisfied with the decision and appealed to the then Appellate Division of the Supreme Court.[67] Corbett JA pointed out that the basic rental accrued and was paid monthly in advance but that the liability to pay the turnover rental could only be ascertained when the lease year in question was completed.[68] Corbett JA held that the obligation to pay the turnover rental was contingent until the turnover for the lease year was quantified at the end of the lease year, which was after the end of Edgars's tax year.[69] Thus, the turnover rental was disallowed as a deduction on the basis that it was contingent and did not represent expenditure actually incurred as required under s 11 *(a)* of the Act in the tax year in question.[70]

The question as to when a deduction should be allowed where the expenditure is the subject of a dispute arose in *ITC 1499*.[71] In this case, the company claimed a deduction of R3 081 750 in its 1985 year of assessment. The Commissioner disallowed the deduction on the basis that the amount had been incurred in the 1981 tax year, alternatively that the expenditure was capital in nature and was not wholly or exclusively laid out for the purposes of trade. The taxpayer company employed an employee and during 1980 the company offered the employee shares in the company if he performed under the contract in question. The employee contended that he had fulfilled his obligations and claimed the shares offered by the company. The company took legal advice and refused

[64] At 94.
[65] At 103.
[66] Ibid.
[67] *Edgars Stores Ltd v commissioner for Inland Revenue* 1988 (3) SA 876 (A), 50 SATC 81.
[68] At 93.
[69] Ibid.
[70] Ibid.
[71] 53 SATC 266.

to deliver the shares to the employee and the dispute proceeded to litigation. Initially the court dismissed the employee's claim, but in a subsequent appeal finalised in 1985, the then Appellate Division upheld the employee's appeal.

The company claimed the cost of the shares delivered to the employee in its 1985 tax return and the Commissioner disallowed that amount on the grounds that the deduction should have been claimed in 1981 when the company first offered the shares to the employee. Goldstein J agreed with the arguments raised by the taxpayer's counsel that the expenditure was not incurred in 1981 as it was the subject of a bona fide dispute.[72] The court accepted that the amount was only incurred once the legal dispute had been settled by the Appellate Division in 1985, and thus the expenditure could only be claimed in that tax year.[73] The court dismissed the Commissioner's argument that the expenditure was capital in nature and that it was not wholly or exclusively laid out for the purposes of the company's trade.[74] The company also sought to deduct certain legal expenses relating to the dispute that had been incurred in earlier tax years. The court held that those costs could not be deducted in 1985 as those amounts were not incurred in that year of assessment.[75]

The Commissioner was unhappy with the decision of the court *a quo*[76] and the case was heard by the Appellate Division.[77] Corbett CJ stated:

> A liability is contingent in that sense in a case where there is a claim which is disputed, at any rate genuinely disputed and not vexatiously or frivolously for the purpose of delay. In such a case the ultimate outcome of the situation will be confirmed only if the claim is admitted or if it is finally upheld by the decision of a court or arbitrator. Where at the end of the tax year in which a deduction is claimed the outcome of the dispute is undetermined, it cannot be said that a liability has been actually incurred. The taxpayer could not, in the light of the *onus* provision of s 82 of the Act, properly allow it.[78]

Thus, based on the above case, a taxpayer cannot claim a deduction where the amount is in dispute until that dispute is resolved. The Act requires that the expenditure must have been actually incurred and that there is no contingency or uncertainty attaching to the expense, in which case the deduction will only be available once the uncertainty has been removed.

The fact that the amount may be difficult to quantify does not prevent the taxpayer from claiming the expense as a deduction, so long as the amount has been unconditionally incurred.[79]

---

[72] At 270.

[73] Ibid.

[74] At 271.

[75] Ibid.

[76] *ITC 1499* 53 SATC 266.

[77] *Commissioner for Inland Revenue v Golden Dumps (Pty) Ltd* 1993 (4) SA 110 (A), 55 SATC 198.

[78] At 206.

[79] *Commissioner of Taxes v 'A' Company* 1979 (2) SA 409 (RA), 41 SATC 59 and *Edgars Stores Ltd v Commissioner for Inland Revenue* 1988 (3) SA 876 (A), 50 SATC 81 95.

6.2.3 In the production of income

For a taxpayer successfully to claim a deduction for tax purposes, the expenditure must be incurred in the production of the taxpayer's income. It must be remembered that the term 'income' is defined in s 1 in the Act as comprising the amount of gross income derived by the taxpayer after deducting from it those amounts that are exempt from income tax. Thus, where a taxpayer incurs expenditure which relates to the generation of domestic dividends which are exempt from tax under s 10(1)*(k)*(i) of the Act, such expenditure will not be allowed as a deduction as it relates to amounts that are not taxable.

In *ITC 224*[80] the taxpayer company borrowed money at interest to lend to the purchaser of shares in the company so that the purchaser could pay the seller for the shares acquired by it. The company carried on business as a hotelkeeper and derived income in the form of rentals from the letting out of the hotel property. The company claimed the interest paid on the borrowings against the rental income derived by it and the Commissioner disallowed the interest on the basis that it was not incurred in the production of the company's income and was not incurred for the purpose of the company's business. The court decided that the interest was not incurred for purposes of facilitating the company's business, but rather to assist the purchaser in financing the purchase price due to the seller for the shares in the company. Nathan KC, President of the Tax Court, said:

> [T]he intention of the company has to be looked at, and in this case the intention of the parties was not to effect the earning of profit but to effect a change in the shareholding of the company.[81]

As a result, the court reached the conclusion that the interest was not legally deductible as it was not incurred by the company to produce income and the court confirmed the assessments issued by the Commissioner.[82]

The legislature chose to use the word 'the' before the word 'income' and in *Sub-Nigel Ltd v Commissioner for Inland Revenue*[83] the Commissioner sought to argue that if the expenditure does not actually produce income, it does not qualify as a deduction for tax purposes.[84] The Commissioner relied on the fact that the legislature used the word 'the' before the word 'income' and contended that there must be a direct link between the expenditure incurred and the income derived by the taxpayer.[85]

Sub-Nigel carried on business as a gold mining company and paid insurance premiums against the loss of profits and the cost of standing charges during the suspension of mining operations as a result of a fire. The company claimed

80 6 SATC 156.
81 At 156.
82 Ibid.
83 1948 (4) SA 580 (A), 15 SATC 381.
84 At 390.
85 Ibid.

the insurance premiums as a deduction for tax purposes. The Commissioner disallowed the deduction on the basis that the expenditure was not wholly and exclusively laid out for the purposes of trade and that the insurance premiums did not produce any income.[86] The Special Court for hearing Income Tax Appeals dismissed Sub-Nigel's appeal,[87] agreeing with the assessments issued by the Commissioner to disallow the deduction of the insurance premiums. Sub-Nigel was dissatisfied with the outcome of its appeal and the matter proceeded to the Appellate Division. At 393 Centlivres JA said:

> The conclusion at which I arrive on this part of the case is that there is no reason to think that the Legislature, in using the definite article 'the' before 'income' in sec 11(2)*(a)*, intended the result contended for by Mr *Ettlinger*. It seems to me clear on the authorities that the Court is not concerned whether a particular item of expenditure produced any part of *the* income: what it is concerned with is whether that item of expenditure was incurred for the purpose of earning income. The reason why the Legislature used the definite article 'the' before 'income' in sec 11(2)*(a)* is probably because it had previously used it in the immediately preceding sub-section.
>
> ... Now was the act entailing the expenditure of the amounts paid by way of premium performed for the purpose of earning income? In my opinion the answer to this question is in the affirmative. The mere fact that no income has actually resulted is, in my view, irrelevant: the purpose was to obtain income on the happening of a fire which would prevent the carrying on of income-producing operations.[88]

The court thus decided that the insurance premiums were incurred to produce income even though no income had actually been received in the year in question.[89] In determining whether expenditure is deductible, regard must be had to the purpose for which the expenditure is incurred.[90] *Sub-Nigel* does not require that the expenditure produces income in the year in which the expense is incurred or in fact in any subsequent year.

It was also decided that the expenditure was not capital in nature[91] and held that the expenditure was wholly and exclusively laid out for the purposes of trade as required under the wording of the Act at that time.[92] In the result the court allowed the insurance premiums claimed by Sub-Nigel on the basis that the expenditure met the criteria contained in the forerunner to s 11*(a)*, which is substantially the same as s 11*(a)* of the Act.

Watermeyer J, as he then was, evaluated the meaning of the term 'in the production of income' in *Port Elizabeth Electric Tramway Co Ltd v Commissioner for Inland Revenue.*[93] In that case, the taxpayer carried on business as a

86 Ibid.
87 At 387.
88 At 394.
89 Ibid.
90 Ibid.
91 At 397.
92 At 402.
93 1936 CPD 241, 8 SATC 13 at 16.

tramway operator and it claimed the compensation paid to a driver for injuries sustained whilst on duty as a deduction for tax purposes. The Commissioner disallowed the deduction on a number of grounds, one of them being that the expenditure claimed was not incurred in the production of the company's income as required under the Act. Watermeyer J stated:

> Now, as pointed out above, income is produced by the performance of a series of acts, and attendant upon them are expenses. Such expenses are deductible expenses, provided they are so closely linked to such acts as to be regarded as part of the cost of performing them.
>
> A little reflection will show that two questions arise, *(a)* whether the act, to which the expenditure is attached, is performed in the production of income and (b) whether the expenditure is linked to it closely enough. Now, at first sight, it would appear that only acts *necessary* to earn the income and expenditure *necessarily* attendant upon such acts should be deducted; but this is not so... . The purpose of the act entailing expenditure must be looked to. If it is performed for the purpose of earning income, then the expenditure attendant upon it is deductible.[94]

Watermeyer also made the point that where the act entailing the expenditure is bona fide undertaken for purposes of carrying on the trade which generates the income, that expenditure should be deductible.[95] Where, however, the act in question is unlawful or negligent, he expressed the view *obiter* that the resulting expenditure would probably not be deductible.[96] Insofar as unlawful payments are concerned, the legislature belatedly removed the uncertainty when it amended the Act in 2005 by inserting s 23*(o)* in the Act to make it clear that fines and other payments arising from unlawful acts will not be allowed as a deduction for tax purposes.

The court made the point that the company needed to employ drivers to carry on its business as a tramway operator and by doing so the company accepted the risk that its drivers could be injured whilst employed by the company.[97] There was a risk that drivers could be injured whilst driving the trams owned by the company and this was directly related to the production of income by the company. Thus, the compensation paid by the company to a driver for injuries sustained whilst in the company's employment was held to deductible as having been incurred in the production of the company's income in conformity with the requirements contained in the equivalent of s 11*(a)* of the Act.[98]

In *Commissioner for Inland Revenue v Hickson*[99] the taxpayer was unable to travel without someone accompanying him because of his physical disability. Hickson travelled on business to New York and the United Kingdom and claimed his wife's travelling costs as a deduction for tax purposes. The Commissioner

94 At 16.
95 At 17.
96 Ibid.
97 At 18.
98 At 19.
99 1960 (1) SA 746 (A), 23 SATC 243.

disallowed the deduction on the basis that the expenditure was not incurred in the production of income nor was it laid out wholly for the purposes of trade and, in addition, constituted domestic expenditure, which is specifically excluded as qualifying as a deduction for tax purposes.

The Special Court upheld the taxpayer's appeal and the Commissioner, being unhappy with the decision of that court, noted an appeal to the Appellate Division. Beyers JA referred to the decision of the court in *Port Elizabeth Electric Tramway Co Ltd v Commissioner for Inland Revenue,*[100] which made it clear that the taxpayer does not need to show that the expenditure was necessarily incurred.[101] Where the taxpayer can show the expenditure was incurred bona fide and incurred in the production of income it is allowable for tax purposes.[102] The Commissioner argued that the wife's travelling expenses were not sufficiently closely connected to the income produced by the taxpayer.[103] Beyers JA commented that the expenses incurred by the taxpayer may have been extravagant but decided that they were directly related to the business conducted by Hickson and that they were incurred in the production of his income.[104] The taxpayer travelled abroad to meet business associates and his income increased after the trip and it would not have been possible for Hickson to travel on his own as a result of his health. Hickson's circumstances were unusual but the court was satisfied that the expenditure was incurred in the production of his income.[105]

In *ITC 247*[106] a jockey claimed travelling and hotel expenses, the replacement of riding gear and the costs of Turkish baths for purposes of reducing his weight so that he could take part in horse races, as deductions for tax purposes. The Commissioner disallowed the expenditure on the basis that it was not incurred in the production of the jockey's income and the appeal was heard by Nathan KC, President of the Tax Court. Nathan decided that the expenditure claimed by the jockey was allowable as the items in dispute were incurred in order to earn his income.[107] The court recognised that a jockey needs to travel from one race to another to derive his income and thus the court decided that the cost of travelling from the jockey's home to a race meeting in another place was deductible for tax purposes.[108]

A question that arises is whether unexpected or fortuitous expenditure can be successfully claimed as a deduction for tax purposes. This is what the court had to decide in the case of *Commissioner of Taxes v Rendle.*[109] Rendle was an accountant who suffered a loss as a result of the misappropriation of

[100] 1936 CPD 241, 8 SATC 13.
[101] At 248.
[102] Ibid.
[103] At 250.
[104] At 251.
[105] Ibid.
[106] 6 SATC 379.
[107] At 380.
[108] At 382.
[109] 1965 (1) SA 59 (SRA), 26 SATC 326.

client moneys and theft of money belonging to the accounting practice itself. Costs were incurred in conducting an investigation to establish the precise quantum of the funds misappropriated by the accountant's employee. The Commissioner disallowed the deductions claimed by the taxpayer on the basis that the expenditure was not incurred in the production of income nor for the purposes of the taxpayer's trade or, alternatively, that the amounts were capital in nature.[110]

Beadle CJ pointed out that the expenditure was fortuitous in nature in that the amounts did not comprise amounts willingly laid out by the taxpayer.[111] In considering the issue before him he said:

> All the cases dealing with this subject indicate that before fortuitous expenditure can be deducted, it must be so closely connected with the business operation concerned as to be inseparable from it or necessarily incidental to the carrying on of that business. See, for example, *Ash v Federal Commissioner of Taxation*, AITR at 453, where Rich J said:
>
> > 'There is no difficulty in understanding the view that involuntary outgoings and unforeseen or unavoidable losses should be allowed as deductions, where they represent that kind of casualty, mischance or misfortune which is a natural or recognized incident of a particular trade or business, the profits of which are in question.'[112]

Where losses arising from misappropriation by employees are an inherent risk attached to the business conducted by the taxpayer, those losses should qualify as a deduction for tax purposes under s 11*(a)* of the Act, on the grounds that those losses were incurred in the production of income and are not amounts of a capital nature.

Beadle CJ paraphrased what Roper J had said in *ITC 815*[113] as follows:

> Before fortuitous expenditure can be deducted, the taxpayer must show that the risk of the mishap which gives rise to the expenditure happening, must be inseparable from or a necessary incident of the carrying on of the particular business.[114]

The court reached the conclusion that the risk of embezzlement by employees of funds from the accountant's clients and the accountant's own firm was incidental to the business in question. Beadle CJ thus allowed the deductions claimed by Rendle.[115] The court made the obiter point that where a proprietor embezzles funds, such loss cannot be allowed for tax purposes.[116]

---

110 At 328.
111 At 333.
112 Ibid.
113 20 SATC 487.
114 At 333.
115 At 335.
116 At 335 and see further *Lockie Bros Ltd v Commissioner for Inland Revenue* 1922 TPD 42, 32 SATC 150.

In *Lockie Bros Ltd v Commissioner for Inland Revenue*[117] the company suffered a loss as a result of the manager having misappropriated funds belonging to the company. The company claimed the losses as a deduction for tax purposes on the basis that the amount was incurred in the production of income and did not constitute an expense of a capital nature. The Commissioner disallowed the deduction and the Special Court dismissed the taxpayer's appeal. Mason J accepted that the losses were incurred during the course of the company's business operations.[118] He indicated that it was important to establish if the losses were due to the operations conducted by the company.[119] The court decided that the losses incurred as a result of the manager's embezzlement of funds were not deductible for tax purposes.[120] Mason J drew a distinction between the negligent handling of goods by employees, which is closely related to the carrying on of a company's business and the embezzlement of funds, which is not undertaken for the purpose of the business.[121]

De Waal J made the point that the question that had to be answered was whether the defalcations were incidental to the production of the company's income.[122] The manager was appointed to manage the business of the company and not to steal its funds and the court decided that the loss was not incurred in the production of income.[123] De Waal J expressed the view that the expenditure claimed by the company constituted a loss of a capital nature and was not deductible for tax purposes.[124] This was on the basis that once the company sold its goods and received cash from those sales, the cash formed part of the company's capital and any loss of that cash would constitute a loss of the company's capital.[125]

If a taxpayer suffers losses as a result of theft or embezzlement, those losses should be deductible for tax purposes where the losses are incidental to the business carried on by the taxpayer and the acts giving rise to the losses are perpetrated by employees and not by the management of the business.[126] Thus, the risk of theft must be closely linked to the business operations conducted by the taxpayer.

In *ITC 815*[127] the taxpayer, a partner in a firm of attorneys, claimed losses incurred in respect of trust moneys held by the partnership for investment of client funds and losses suffered as a result of the embezzlement of funds belonging to the partnership by employees of the partnership. Roper J concluded that the loss in

117 1922 TPD 42, 32 SATC 150.
118 At 152.
119 Ibid.
120 At 153.
121 At 152.
122 At 155.
123 Ibid.
124 Ibid.
125 Ibid.
126 See *Lockie Bros Ltd v Commissioner for Inland Revenue* 1922 TPD 42, 32 SATC 150 and *Commissioner of Taxes v Rendle* 1965 (1) SA 59 (SRA), 26 SATC 326.
127 20 SATC 487.

respect of trust moneys was incidental to the business of attorneys conducted by the partnership.[128] The business derived income from the investment of funds for its clients and the loss was incurred in the production of income as required and was thus deductible.[129]

The court considered the funds embezzled by the partnership's employees and made the point that those funds did not constitute trust moneys.[130] The taxpayer's counsel argued that the losses should be allowed on the basis that the funds were embezzled by employees and that such loss was a risk which faced attorneys and was thus incurred in the production of income.[131] Roper J held that the losses were not deductible as it was not possible to establish whether the funds stolen were trust moneys or funds belonging to the partnership, having been earned by the firm from services rendered to its clients.[132] It is submitted that this part of the decision of the court, with respect, is incorrect. When reference is made to the decision of the court in *Rendle's*[133] case, it is contended that the risk of theft and embezzlement is incidental to the business conducted by an attorney or an accountant.[134]

In *Commissioner for Inland Revenue v Genn & Co (Pty) Ltd*[135] the company incurred interest and raising fees on funds borrowed by it to use in its business. The Commissioner allowed the interest claimed but chose to disallow the raising fees claimed on the basis that those fees were capital in nature. Schreiner JA stated that interest paid on funds borrowed to use in the business 'would appear to be expenditure actually incurred in the production of the income of the business'.[136] It did not matter to the court whether the loan was used to acquire fixed or floating capital. The court pointed out that the funds received by Genn did not constitute the receipt of gross income in its hands.[137] The Commissioner sought to argue that the expenditure incurred in connection with the loans should not be allowed for tax purposes as the amounts received by way of loans did not constitute 'income' as defined.[138] The court decided that the raising fees should not be treated differently from the interest incurred on the loans and accordingly ruled that the fees were incurred in the production of income and were deductible for tax purposes.[139]

The expenditure incurred by a taxpayer must in some way be connected or linked to the income generated by the taxpayer. Where, for example, a taxpayer incurs expenditure to generate domestic dividends that are exempt from income

128 At 493.
129 Ibid.
130 At 495.
131 Ibid.
132 At 496.
133 1965 (1) SA 59 (SRA), 26 SATC 326.
134 At 335.
135 1955 (3) SA 293 (A), 20 SATC 113.
136 At 121.
137 At 122.
138 Ibid.
139 At 119 and 121.

tax under s 10(1)*(k)* of the Act, such expenditure cannot be claimed for tax purposes as it is related to amounts which do not constitute income as defined.

In *Commissioner for Inland Revenue v Rand Selections Corporation Ltd*[140] the company acquired shares in a company about to be liquidated. The company received a payment from the liquidator of the company which comprised two parts. The first comprised the return of share capital and constituted income in the hands of the company, as it was a share dealer for tax purposes. The second part of the payment constituted a dividend which was not liable to tax. The company claimed the full costs of the shares as a deduction for tax purposes on the basis that it was incurred in generating the payment received from the liquidator, which constituted income in its hands, and that the receipt of the dividend did not preclude the company from claiming the cost incurred by it.

The Commissioner sought to disallow a portion of the cost of the shares on the grounds that part of that cost related to the production of the dividend, which did not constitute income for tax purposes. Centlivres CJ decided that the amount expended by the taxpayer generated 'income' as defined, as well as a dividend which was exempt from tax.[141] The company argued that the Act did not specify the manner in which the cost of the shares should be apportioned as to the 'income' and as to the dividend received.[142] The court pointed out that the allocation of the expenditure cannot be arbitrary but should be determined by allocating the expenditure to that which relates to the 'income' expressed as a proportion of the sum of the dividend and 'income' derived by the company from the shares in question.[143] The company spent P367 859 in acquiring the shares and received P124 123 as a dividend and P212 311 as 'income'. The Commissioner originally allowed an amount of P212 311 as a deduction for tax purposes and disallowed the balance of the cost of the shares of P155 548. This amount was arbitrarily determined and was not calculated in an attempt to ascertain what part of the cost of the shares of P367 859 related directly to the dividend received by the company. Applying the formula adopted by the court, the allowable deduction, that is, that part of the cost of the shares which was attributable to the 'income' derived by the company, amounted to P232 142. The balance of the cost of the shares amounting to P135 717 would, under the formula prescribed by the court, not have been deductible as this related to the dividend received by the taxpayer and was thus not incurred in the production of 'income'. The Act did not specifically allow for the apportionment of expenditure to take account of the nature of the amounts received by the taxpayer, but the court did not see this as a hurdle in arriving at what it believed was an appropriate apportionment of expenditure to take account of the fact that the company received 'income' and an exempt dividend.[144]

CHAPTER 6

140 1956 (3) SA 124 (A), 20 SATC 390.
141 At 399.
142 At 400.
143 Ibid.
144 Ibid.

However, in *ITC 1274*[145] the court decided not to follow the decision handed down in the *Rand Selections* case.[146] In *ITC 1274*[147] the taxpayer company carried on business as a share dealer and acquired shares in a company at a cost of R680 521. The taxpayer subsequently received a dividend of R338 100 and resold the shares for R551 250 and thus realised a loss on the disposal of the shares of R129 721. The Commissioner reduced the cost of the shares allowed to the taxpayer by taking account of the dividend received by the taxpayer on the grounds that the full cost of the shares was not incurred in the production of income. The court reviewed the circumstances regarding the purchase and sale of the shares and decided that the transaction in question did not constitute a classic dividend-stripping operation whereby a taxpayer buys shares in a company pregnant with reserves, receives a substantial dividend and then sells the shares for a nominal consideration and seeks to claim the cost of the shares as a deduction for tax purposes.[148]

The court reached the conclusion that the taxpayer acquired the shares to realise a profit from them and would have been satisfied in concluding a commercial transaction whereby it would generate a substantial commercial profit.[149] In the case at hand there was no certainty that a substantial dividend would be received at the time the shares were acquired, as was the case in *Rand Selections.*[150] The Commissioner's representative argued that the court should apportion the cost of the shares in accordance with the decision in *Rand Selections*[151] on the basis that the cost of the shares was not incurred to produce income only. Trengove J stated that there was no justification for apportioning the cost of the shares in the present case based on the *Rand Selections*[152] decision.[153] Thus, the court decided that the amount received as a dividend on the shares was exempt from tax under s 10(1)*(k)* of the Act and that the cost of acquiring the shares of R680 521 was fully deductible for tax purposes on the basis that the amount had been incurred in the production of income as required under the Act.[154]

Subsequently, in *Commissioner for Inland Revenue v Nemojim (Pty) Ltd,*[155] the Appellate Division had to decide whether Nemojim was entitled to claim the costs incurred in acquiring shares in other companies as part of a so-called 'dividend stripping' operation for tax purposes. Nemojim acquired shares in various dormant companies which held cash and had reserves available for

---

145 40 SATC 185.

146 *Commissioner for Inland Revenue v Rand Selections Corporation Ltd* 1956 (3) SA 124 (A), 20 SATC 390.

147 40 SATC 185.

148 At 195.

149 Ibid.

150 *Commissioner for Inland Revenue v Rand Selections Corporation Ltd* 1956 (3) SA 124 (A), 20 SATC 390.

151 Ibid.

152 Ibid.

153 *ITC 1274* 40 SATC 185 at 196.

154 At 197.

155 1983 (4) SA 935 (A), 45 SATC 241.

distribution to their shareholders as a dividend. The sellers of these shares did not wish to declare the distributable reserves as a dividend as that would have caused an adverse tax consequence in their hands. Thus, Nemojim would buy the shares in dormant companies, declare the reserves as a dividend and would then sell the shares in the cleaned-up company. Commercially, Nemojim realised a profit from its business activities as the dividends received together with the proceeds received from the sale of the shares exceeded the cost of buying the shares in the dormant company.

However, for tax purposes, Nemojim sought to claim a loss on the basis that the cost of purchasing the shares was fully deductible for tax purposes, whereas the dividends received were exempt from tax under s 10(1)*(k)* of the Act. Initially, the Commissioner allowed the losses claimed by Nemojim and accepted that the cost price of the shares acquired was fully deductible for tax purposes. Later, the Commissioner issued additional assessments disallowing part of the cost of the shares on the grounds that such cost was not incurred in the production of income. The court *a quo* decided in favour of Nemojim and directed the Commissioner to allow the full cost of the shares claimed by the company on the basis that the company was a dealer in shares and was entitled to claim the cost of purchasing shares in full. The Commissioner was dissatisfied with the court's decision and appealed directly to the Appellate Division.

The court accepted that Nemojim was conducting a trade as a share dealer.[156] Corbett JA, as he then was, referred to the submission made by the Commissioner's counsel that in order to determine whether the amounts incurred by Nemojim in acquiring the shares in the dormant companies were deductible, it was necessary to establish the purpose for which the expenditure was incurred.[157] In addition, Nemojim had to discharge the onus of showing that the cost of acquiring the shares in the dormant companies was intended to produce income as defined in the Act.[158] If the expenditure was incurred to produce income from the sale of the shares, the costs would rank as a deduction under s 11*(a)*.[159] If, however, the costs were incurred with the purpose of producing dividends, which are exempt from tax, the company would not be entitled to a deduction under s 11*(a)* of the Act on the basis that the expenditure was not incurred in the production of income.[160]

Corbett JA referred with approval to the views expressed by Schreiner JA in *Commissioner for Inland Revenue v Genn & Co (Pty) Ltd*[161] regarding the purpose for which expenditure is incurred and the closeness of the connection

156 At 254.
157 Ibid.
158 Ibid.
159 Ibid.
160 Ibid.
161 1955 (3) SA 293 (A), 20 SATC 113.

between the expenditure and the taxpayer's income-earning operations.[162] Corbett JA commented as follows:

> It seems to me, too, that when considering whether moneys outlaid by the taxpayer constitute expenses incurred in respect of amounts received or accrued which do not constitute 'income' as defined (for the sake of brevity I shall call this 'exempt income'), the court must assess the closeness of the connection between the expenses incurred and the exempt income received or accrued, having regard to the purpose of the expenses and what the expending thereof actually effects.[163]

The court reached the conclusion that Nemojim had a dual purpose in incurring the expenditure in dispute.[164] The first purpose was to generate proceeds on the sale of shares, which amounts constituted 'income' as defined in the Act.[165] The second purpose was to receive the dividends from the companies once Nemojim had taken control of those companies.[166] The court referred to the fact that in *Commissioner for Inland Revenue v Rand Selections Ltd*[167] the court correctly pointed out that the Act does not make provision for the apportionment of expenditure, but such approach may yield an equitable result where expenditure is incurred with a dual purpose.[168] Corbett JA decided that it was appropriate to apportion the cost of the shares acquired by Nemojim, as the shares were acquired to produce 'income' and exempt income.[169] The court referred to the formula proposed in the *Rand Selections*[170] case and decided it was appropriate to modify that formula in the *Nemojim* case.[171] In essence the formula adopted by the court apportioned the cost of acquiring the shares in the dormant companies and other costs related to share dealing into two parts, that is, the part related to the earning of dividends, which is not deductible for tax purposes, and the balance, which was linked to the generation of proceeds on the sale of shares, which was deductible for tax purposes.[172] In the result the court allowed the Commissioner's appeal and Nemojim was not entitled to deduct the full amount of the purchase price paid in acquiring the shares in the dormant companies as that amount was not incurred in the production of income.[173]

---

162 At 256.

163 Ibid.

164 Ibid.

165 Ibid.

166 Ibid.

167 1956 (3) SA 124 (A), 20 SATC 390.

168 *Commissioner for Inland Revenue v Nemojim (Pty) Ltd* 1983 (4) SA 935 (A), 45 SATC 241 at 259.

169 At 261.

170 1956 (3) SA 124 (A), 20 SATC 390.

171 *Commissioner for Inland Revenue v Nemojim (Pty) Ltd* 1983 (4) SA 935 (A), 45 SATC 241 at 267.

172 At 267.

173 Ibid.

Nemojim's counsel sought to rely on the decision of the court in *Umtali Finance (Pvt) Ltd v Commissioner of Taxes*[174] where the court allowed the taxpayer's deduction of costs incurred in acquiring shares in a 'dividend-stripping' operation.[175] Umtali acquired shares and received dividends and claimed the cost of the shares acquired by it.[176] The Commissioner refused the deduction of the cost of the shares and Clayden CJ for the court decided 'that the loss incurred on the purchase price of the shares was expenditure wholly incurred for the purposes of that trade' and was deductible for tax purposes.[177] However, Corbett JA in the *Nemojim*[178] case indicated that he had considered the decision of the Federal court in Umtali[179] and disagreed with that decision.[180] Corbett JA did not accept that the cost of acquiring shares with the express purpose of stripping the company of its reserves in the form of a dividend meant that the cost of the shares was deductible in full.[181] Nemojim's counsel contended that share dealers generally would have to apportion their costs of acquiring shares to take account of the exempt dividends received if the court were to decide that the apportionment of the expenditure incurred in acquiring shares is necessary.[182] However, in the case of a share dealer engaged in 'dividend-stripping' the majority of the shares in dormant companies are acquired in anticipation of the receipt of significant dividends, which are exempt from tax.[183] The court did not accept this submission on the basis that share dealers in general purchase shares to sell at a profit and do not normally acquire shares to receive dividends, and where dividends are received they are incidental to the proceeds received on the sale of shares.[184] Thus, it is clear that where a taxpayer incurs expenditure with a dual purpose, that is, to produce 'income' and exempt income, the expenditure relating thereto must be apportioned in an appropriate manner to determine what expenditure should be allowed under s 11 *(a)* of the Act.

In the case of *Commissioner for Inland Revenue v De Beers Holdings (Pty) Ltd*[185] the share dealing company had acquired shares in a private company to obtain access to that company's revenue and capital reserves. Once De Beers had received the reserves from the private company in question it sold those shares for a nominal consideration and claimed the resulting loss for tax purposes. The Commissioner disallowed the loss claimed of R4 158

[174] 1962 (3) SA 281 (FC), 24 SATC 680.

[175] *Commissioner for Inland Revenue v Nemojim (Pty) Ltd* 1983 (4) SA 935 (A), 45 SATC 241 at 260.

[176] *Umtali Finance (Pvt) Ltd v Commissioner of Taxes* 1962 (3) SA 281 (FC), 24 SATC 680.

[177] At 691.

[178] *Commissioner for Inland Revenue v Nemojim (Pty) Ltd* 1983 (4) SA 935 (A), 45 SATC 241 at 264.

[179] *Umtali Finance (Pvt) Ltd v Commissioner of Taxes* 1962 (3) SA 281 (FC), 24 SATC 680.

[180] *Commissioner for Inland Revenue v Nemojim (Pty) Ltd* 1983 (4) SA 935 (A), 45 SATC 241 at 264.

[181] At 264.

[182] Ibid.

[183] Ibid.

[184] Ibid.

[185] 1984 (3) SA 286 (T), 46 SATC 47.

936. The Special Court ruled in favour of De Beers and the Commissioner, being dissatisfied with that decision, appealed to the erstwhile Transvaal Provincial Division of the Supreme Court. The Special Court had agreed with De Beers' submission that the loss arose out of a normal share dealing transaction and that when the shares were purchased in the private company there was no purchase of the dividends to be declared on those shares.[186] The court *a quo* took the view that 'there is a single purchase of the shares "with their potentialities"'.[187] Goldstone J referred to the judgment of the court in *Nemojim*[188] and reached the conclusion that the principles laid down in that case must be applied to De Beers.[189] In *De Beers* the purpose of incurring the expenditure was to receive a taxable distribution in the course of liquidation and the effect of the expenditure was a receipt of a non-taxable amount as a result of the company's liquidation.[190] The court thus decided that no part of the expenditure incurred by De Beers in acquiring the shares had the effect of producing income and thus the expenditure could not be claimed, as it did not meet the 'incurred in the production of the income' requirement contained in s 11*(a)* of the Act.[191]

De Beers also sought to argue that, under s 22 of the Act, the Commissioner was precluded from disallowing the deduction of expenditure which is properly carried forward from one tax year to the next.[192] Goldstone J rejected this argument on the grounds that s 22 must be adapted for dividend stripping operations as laid down in *Nemojim.*[193] As a result the Commissioner's appeal was upheld and the expenditure incurred in acquiring the shares in the private company was held to be non-deductible for tax purposes.[194]

De Beers was dissatisfied with Goldstone J's decision and the case proceeded to the Appellate Division.[195] That court reached the conclusion that the expenditure was not allowable for different reasons than those relied on by the court *a quo.*[196] Corbett JA ruled that the shares acquired by De Beers did not constitute trading stock as envisaged in s 22 of the Act.[197] The court made the point that, even though the shares in question did not constitute trading stock, that did not conclude the enquiry as to whether the expenditure was deductible for tax purposes.[198] The deductibility of the expenditure had to be

---

[186] At 53.
[187] Ibid.
[188] *Commissioner for Inland Revenue v Nemojim (Pty) Ltd* 1983 (4) SA 935 (A), 45 SATC 241.
[189] *De Beers* supra 55.
[190] At 56.
[191] Ibid.
[192] At 57.
[193] At 57 and see further *Commissioner for Inland Revenue v Nemojim (Pty) Ltd* 1983 (4) SA 935 (A), 45 SATC 241.
[194] At 57.
[195] *De Beers Holdings (Pty) Ltd v Commissioner for Inland Revenue* 1986 (1) SA 8 (A), 47 SATC 229.
[196] At 261.
[197] At 257.
[198] Ibid.

determined by taking account of ss 11*(a)* and 23*(g)* of the Act.[199] The court reviewed the requirement contained in s 23*(g)* of the Act that expenditure must be laid out or expended for purposes of trade.[200] Corbett JA accepted that the absence of a profit does not mean that a transaction does not form part of the taxpayer's trade.[201] De Beers' purchase of the shares in the private company was distinguishable from the normal share dealing transactions undertaken by the company and was not undertaken to generate a profit.[202] The court held that the expenditure incurred in acquiring the shares was not laid out for purposes of trade as required under s 23*(g)* of the Act and the cost of the shares was disallowed.[203] Corbett JA thus agreed with the conclusion reached by the court *a quo*, albeit for different reasons.[204]

Where an investment holding company receives both dividends and interest income it faces a difficulty in satisfying the Commissioner that all of the expenditure incurred by it is deductible for tax purposes. In *Mobile Telephone Networks Holdings (Pty) Limited v Commissioner for the South African Revenue Service*,[205] the South Gauteng High Court was required to determine whether the Commissioner was correct in disallowing MTN's deduction of audit fees for the 2001 to 2004 years of assessment and the expenditure incurred by the company in respect of professional fees charged for the training of staff on a new accounting package.

The company initially appealed the Commissioner's finding to the Tax Court. In *ITC 1842*[206] MTN succeeded partially on the deductibility of audit fees by securing a deduction of 50% on the audit fees claimed for the 2001 to 2004 years of assessment.[207] The Tax Court agreed with the Commissioner that the cost incurred in the training of staff for the new accounting package was not deductible for tax purposes.[208]

The Commissioner was dissatisfied with the Tax Court's decision and cross-appealed in respect of the decision on the audit fees, and contended that the deduction of 50% of the audit fees was incorrect. In deciding whether the audit fees, or the fees paid for professional services, were deductible, the Tax Court was required to consider the provisions of s 11*(a)* of the Act, and also to take account of ss 23*(f)* and *(g)*, which preclude the deduction of expenses incurred in relation to amounts which do not constitute income, or which are not expended for the purposes of the taxpayer's trade.

199 Ibid.
200 Ibid.
201 At 260.
202 Ibid.
203 Ibid.
204 At 261.
205 73 SATC 315.
206 72 SATC 118.
207 At 129.
208 At 132.

MTN is a wholly-owned subsidiary of the MTN Group Limited ('MTN Group') and has five wholly-owned subsidiaries. MTN Group conducts business by providing mobile telecommunication networks and related services. Victor J pointed out that it was agreed in a pre-trial meeting that MTN carries on a trade.[209] SARS disallowed the audit fees, which were incurred for purposes of complying with the company's statutory obligation to have its accounts audited, as well as for the purpose of trading. Professional fees relating to the second issue, which SARS disallowed in full, comprised services provided in order to train the company's staff on a computer accounting system.

The judgment stated that it was common cause between the parties that the company traded during the tax years in dispute.[210] The audit required the input and consideration of an auditor regarding the dividends received by the company, and income in the form of interest. The court pointed out that the dividend income represented the largest portion of MTN's income, ranging between 89% and 99%, during the tax years in dispute.[211]

The Tax Court decided that the audit fees were incurred for a dual purpose and thus reached the conclusion that it was appropriate to apportion the expenditure and decided that 50% was deductible and the balance was not.[212]

The High Court indicated that the taxpayer contended that, on average, only 6% of the entries in its books of account related to dividends, which was not disputed by SARS, and that this was an important factor.[213] SARS argued that the audit fees did not advance the trade of the company and were not directly related to the production of its income and, thus, all audit fees claimed by the company should be disallowed.[214]

SARS contended that the audit fees were incurred by the company to comply with its statutory obligations, and relied on Australian tax authority where expenditure was disallowed for undertaking a statutory task, *FCT v The Swan Brewery Company Limited.*[215]

The court pointed out that it was common cause that the amount of work undertaken by the auditors extended beyond the verification of interest income and receipt of dividends, but that those additional tasks did not detract from the appellant's contention that the audit fees related to its income-earning activities.[216]

It would appear that only 6% of the audit time was spent on the dividend section of the audit. The court decided that the expenditure incurred by the company

[209] *Mobile Telephone Networks Holdings (Pty) Limited v the Commissioner for the South African Revenue Service* 73 SATC 315 at 319.

[210] At 319.

[211] At 320.

[212] *ITC 1842* supra 129 and 132.

[213] *Mobile Telephone Networks Holdings (Pty) Limited* supra 321

[214] At 321.

[215] (1991) 22 ATR 295.

[216] *Mobile Telephone Networks Holdings (Pty) Limited* supra 321.

on the audit fees was incurred to directly facilitate the carrying on of its trade, not only in a legally compliant manner, but also to generate income.

The court decided that the only fair basis on which the audit fees should be apportioned was that 94% of those costs should be allowed as a deduction for tax purposes.[217] The court thus decided that it was appropriate to take account of the time spent on auditing the interest income, as opposed to the fact that a substantial part of the income derived by the company comprised dividends.[218]

When dealing with SARS's cross-appeal, the court indicated that SARS sought to argue that the audit fees did not attach to the company's operations and even where trading is conducted through the company, the taxpayer should accept that there are additional expenses for audit fees and the legal obligation relating thereto is unrelated to the earning of the taxpayer's income.[219] The court pointed out that SARS's approach would provide an enormous obstacle to the world of commerce and trade if the deduction of audit fees was to be denied on this basis.[220]

In reaching its apportionment ratio, SARS took account of the values of income derived and did not take account of the amount of work involved in the audit process. The court rejected SARS's method of apportionment as being factually and legally incorrect. The court held that the bulk of the audit fees related to the earning of interest and not dividends based on the time spent by the auditors on the different tasks required to complete their audit.

In addition, SARS disallowed the professional fees paid for services rendered regarding the implementation of the computerised accounting system. The court pointed out that the majority of transactions in MTN's financial records related to the interest income derived and that the accounting system was not used in relation to the dividend income received by the company.[221] The expenditure claimed by MTN related to its business only and was not used for the benefit of its subsidiary companies. The court expressed the view that the professional fees were closely connected to the earning of the interest income received by the company and that the professional fees were directly related to the company's trading activities.[222]

SARS argued that MTN had not provided sufficient information and decided that the company had not discharged the onus placed on it in relation to the accounting system.[223] The court was critical of SARS and pointed out that SARS had failed to consider the relevant information before disallowing the professional fees relating to the accounting system.[224]

---

217 At 322.
218 Ibid.
219 Ibid.
220 Ibid.
221 At 323.
222 At 325.
223 At 324.
224 Ibid.

Thus, the unanimous decision of the court was that 94% of the audit fees were deductible and that the expenditure relating to the training on the accounting system must be allowed. SARS was, accordingly, ordered to pay the costs of the company's appeal.[225]

Dissatisfied with the decision of the High Court, SARS appealed to the Supreme Court of Appeal on both issues.[226] The SCA considered the well-settled principle that, in deciding whether expenditure has been incurred in the production of income, as required by the Act, 'important, sometimes overriding, factors are the purpose of the expenditure and what the expenditure actually effects'.[227] The court has to assess the closeness of the connection between the expenditure and the income-earning operations. Accordingly, the audit fees were a part of the general overhead expenditure enabling it to carry out all its activities. Thus, the audit of financial records is 'necessarily attached' to the performance of the income-earning operations.

The question was the extent to which those income-earning operations generated taxable revenue. The court acknowledged the principle of apportionment where expenditure meets the 'necessarily incurred' test but relates to both taxable and exempt income. The problem was establishing an acceptable basis of apportionment. Previously the courts had applied formulae, as in *CIR v Nemojim (Pty) Ltd*[228] and *CIR v Rand Selections Corporation Ltd*,[229] or a basis that the court deemed to be fair in the circumstances, as in *Tuck v CIR*.[230] The court recoiled from basing the apportionment on a formula which might not reflect the actual situation, or on the respective number of entries, or even on a narrow comparison of the sources of revenue. It was not possible to lay down general rules as to how to apply apportionment. The court acknowledged that 'an auditor has to undertake a wide range of general tasks which do not relate to specific income items'.[231]

The MTN audit function involved far more than the time spent on the book entries, which may well have made up a relatively small component of the overall audit time. For example, the group consolidation would necessarily have taken considerable time. It was clear that the interest-earning operations made up a modest part of the operations, and the apportionment would have to reflect this reality. SARS's approach was too narrow, and that of the taxpayer was too generous. In all the circumstances, the court considered it fair and reasonable to allow 10% of the audit fees.

---

[225] At 325.

[226] *Commissioner for South African Revenue Service v Mobile Telephone Networks Holdings (Pty) Ltd* 76 SATC 205.

[227] *Commissioner for Inland Revenue v Standard Bank of SA Ltd* 1985 (4) SA 485 (A) 498F–G.

[228] 45 SATC 291.

[229] 20 SATC 390.

[230] 50 SATC 98.

[231] At 213.

Where does this leave taxpayers in relation to audit fees and similar expenses? In their favour is the fact that the court has confirmed that audit fees are 'necessarily attached' to operations. In SARS's favour is the finding that audit fees are subject to apportionment. And both parties are on notice that consideration of the specific circumstances and not formulaic approaches is necessary in apportioning expenditure.

Turning to the expenses attached to the implementation of the computerised accounting system, the taxpayer alleged that the fee was in respect of the 'implementation, adjustment, fine tuning and user operation of the system'.[232] Unfortunately for the taxpayer, both witnesses it chose to provide evidence in support of its submission had joined the taxpayer after the system had been implemented and their only contribution was to display their ignorance of the circumstances surrounding the implementation. As a result, 'given the inadequacy of the evidence adduced by [the taxpayer], it was well-nigh impossible to determine whether the ... fee fell legitimately to be deducted by [the taxpayer]'.[233] It followed that the SCA reversed the High Court's decision and confirmed SARS's decision to disallow the fee in its entirety.

6.2.4 Not of a capital nature

For a taxpayer to succeed in claiming a deduction for tax purposes, the expenditure must meet the further requirement in s 11*(a)* that the expenditure does not constitute an item of a capital nature. Unfortunately, the Act does not define what is meant by the term 'capital'. As a result one of the most frequent disputes between taxpayers and the Commissioner which reaches the courts relates to whether an amount of income or expenditure constitutes an amount of a revenue or capital nature. It is necessary to refer to the judgments handed down by various courts in an attempt to distil from those decisions what tests should be used to determine whether an item of expenditure is revenue or capital in nature.

In determining whether an item of expenditure is deductible for tax purposes it is necessary to establish the purpose for which the amount was expended. In *Commissioner for Inland Revenue v Genn & Co (Pty) Ltd*[234] the court had to decide whether the raising fees paid on the loans used in the business were of a capital nature for tax purposes and thus not deductible.

Genn procured loans from another company to finance the purchase of its trading stock and became liable to pay interest and raising fees on those loans. The Commissioner allowed the deduction of the interest but disallowed the claim of the raising fees on the basis that those fees constituted expenditure of a capital nature.

232 At 214.
233 At 216.
234 1955 (3) SA 293 (A), 20 SATC 113.

Schreiner JA referred to the decision of the court in *Port Elizabeth Electric Tramway Co Ltd v Commissioner for Inland Revenue1936 CPD 241*[235] and made the point that in determining whether expenditure is deductible, regard must be had to the closeness of the link between the expenditure and the production of income.[236] The court took the view that it was not possible to treat the interest and the raising fees differently as both items were expended to secure the purchase of the company's stock-in-trade, which constituted floating capital and qualified as a deduction for tax purposes.[237]

To determine whether expenditure is deductible Schreiner JA said:

> In deciding how the expenditure should properly be regarded the Court clearly has to assess the closeness of the connection between the expenditure and the income-earning operations, having regard both to the purpose of the expenditure and to what it actually effects.[238]

Thus, where the expense is directly related to the business operations carried on by the taxpayer and that expense is incurred to generate income, it will rank as a deduction for tax purposes. If, however, the expenditure seeks to expand the business operations it will be regarded as being an item of a capital nature and will not be deductible even though it may be incurred in order to generate income.

The court made the point that interest incurred to purchase trading stock or fixed assets constitutes expenditure incurred in the production of income.[239] The court indicated that where interest is incurred for the acquisition of fixed capital a question arises whether such interest constitutes expenditure of a capital nature.[240] The court was not required to consider this issue as the interest in *Genn's* case[241] related only to the financing of the purchase of trading stock and not the acquisition of fixed assets.[242] Taking account of the nature of the raising fees and the fact that they were incurred to purchase stock-in-trade, the court held that the raising fees were incurred in the production of income and did not constitute expenditure of a capital nature.[243]

In *Plate Glass & Shatterprufe Industries Finance Company (Pty) Ltd v Secretary for Inland Revenue*[244] the court had to determine if the losses on foreign exchange suffered by the company were actually incurred as required by s 11*(a)* of the Act and also whether the losses were incurred on revenue or

---

[235] 1936 CPD 241, 8 SATC 13.

[236] At 17 and see *Commissioner for Inland Revenue v Genn & Co (Pty) Ltd* 1955 (3) SA 293 (A), 20 SATC 113 at 120.

[237] *Genn* supra 119.

[238] At 121.

[239] Ibid.

[240] Ibid.

[241] Supra.

[242] At 122.

[243] Ibid.

[244] 1979 (3) SA 1124 (T), 41 SATC 103.

capital account. The court did not need to consider s 24B, a special provision which dealt with exchange gains and losses as the losses in question arose before that section took effect. Currently, s 24I of the Act regulates the tax treatment of foreign exchange gains and losses.

The company claimed losses suffered by it as a result of adverse movements in exchange rates on the basis that the losses were incurred on revenue account, as part of its trading activities and were thus deductible under the provisions of the Act.[245] The Secretary disallowed the deductions claimed by the company on the grounds that no losses were actually incurred and that the losses were capital in nature.[246] The company was created as the finance company for a large group of trading companies, with operations within and outside South Africa. It was contended that the company carried on the business of banking and money-lending and acted as the financial and banking company to the various members of the group.[247] The company borrowed funds from banks, fellow subsidiaries and its holding company, Plate Glass and Shatterprufe Industries Limited ('PGSI'), and in turn lent those funds to its fellow subsidiaries. PGSI arranged for a loan to be made available by a foreign bank to an overseas company in the group, namely Solaglass International Establishment ('SIE').

Subsequently, the South African Reserve Bank granted approval that the funds received by SIE from the foreign bank could be advanced to the appellant. That company in turn made the funds available to other companies in the group. At the end of 1974 and 1975 the company reflected losses on foreign exchange of R74 137 and R431 231, respectively. The Special Court held that the company had failed to prove that the losses had actually been incurred in 1974 and 1975.[248] Margo J accepted that there was merit in relying on accounting to determine if losses has actually arisen in those tax years.[249] The court indicated that for an expense to have been incurred under s 11*(a)* it does not mean that the taxpayer must have paid the amount in question.[250] The court referred to the case of *Caltex Oil (SA) Ltd v Secretary for Inland Revenue*,[251] where Botha JA dealt with the fact that expenditure must be allowed in the year in which the liability arises and not when the taxpayer settles the liability in question.[252] Margo J concluded that the company had incurred the losses as required in 1974 and 1975.[253] A further question that the court had to decide was whether the company was the entity in the group which was liable for the full amount of exchange losses suffered.[254] The court was of the view that the appellant should have been entitled to recover the losses reflected by it from

245 At 106.
246 Ibid.
247 Ibid.
248 At 107.
249 At 108.
250 Ibid.
251 1975 (1) SA 665 (A), 37 SATC 1.
252 *Plate Glass* case supra 108.
253 At 108.
254 At 109.

its related group companies, as those companies used the funds received by the appellant from SIE.[255] The court did not rule on this aspect of the case as further evidence would need to be led and that would depend on the taxpayer succeeding in showing that the losses were revenue in nature.[256]

The court then weighed up whether the exchange losses claimed by the taxpayer were capital or revenue in nature.[257] In reaching a decision, Margo J reviewed the nature of the business conducted by the appellant, which argued that it acted as a financial and banking company to the PGSI group.[258] The taxpayer sought to rely on *Stone v Secretary for Inland Revenue*,[259] in which it was decided that losses suffered by a money-lender are revenue in nature and thus deductible for tax purposes.

Margo J referred to the business conducted by the appellant as follows:

> The Special Court found that, on the evidence, the appellant's sole function was that of controlling and channelling funds available to the group. In the judgment the learned President drew attention to the following features *inter alia*: The appellant did not lend money to outside borrowers or to the public in general. It was a wholly owned subsidiary of PGSI. Its issued share capital was a mere R200. It 'borrowed' and 'lent' vast amounts, running into millions of rands, within the group, without giving or obtaining any security. The evidence of Mr Reid, the group accountant of the PGSI group, on whether the appellant was concerned to make profits out of its loan transactions was equivocal and unsatisfactory.[260]

The court also referred to the fact that the interest received by the appellant was only slightly greater than the interest paid by the company.[261] Taking all of the above factors into account the court found that the business operations conducted by the company were not aimed at promoting trading operations to its own best advantage, but were rather intended to redistribute the capital of the group to address the needs of the group and not of the company itself.[262] The court held that the funds received by it from SIE did not constitute floating capital and thus the foreign exchange losses suffered by it were capital in nature.[263] In light of the court's decision on the nature of loans received from SIE being fixed capital, the court was not required to determine whether the losses were in fact suffered by the company or whether those losses were recoverable from its fellow subsidiaries.[264]

255 Ibid.
256 Ibid.
257 At 110.
258 Ibid.
259 1974 (3) SA 584 (A), 36 SATC 117.
260 At 111.
261 Ibid.
262 Ibid.
263 At 112.
264 At 113.

In the case of *New State Areas Ltd v Commissioner for Inland Revenue*[265] the court had to adjudicate whether the cost incurred by a mining company relating to the installation of water-borne sewerage was capital or revenue in nature. The company was liable to pay the local authority two basic charges, the first referred to as basic charge 'A', which represented the cost of the sewers and connections on the company's own property. The second charge, referred to as basic charge 'B', represented the cost of connecting the sewers between the company's own property and the local authority's main sewerage system. The company claimed the costs of basic charges 'A' and 'B' as a deduction for tax purposes. The Commissioner disallowed the deduction and the company noted an appeal to the Special Court which dismissed the company's appeal. The case proceeded to the Supreme Court, which held that both payments constituted expenditure of a capital nature.[266]

The taxpayer remained dissatisfied with the outcome and the appeal was heard by the Appellate Division.[267] Counsel for the Commissioner contended that the payments made for both basic charge 'A' and basic charge 'B' were payments of a capital nature and were also not incurred in the production of income.[268] Watermeyer CJ analysed the types of expenditure incurred by a taxpayer and commented:

> Expenditure may also occur in the acquisition by the taxpayer of the means of production, i.e. the property plant, tools, etc., which he uses in the performance of his income-earning operations and not only for their acquisition but for their expansion and improvement. Both these forms of expenditure can be described as expenditure in the production of the income but the former is, as a rule, current or revenue expenditure and the latter is, as a rule, expenditure of a capital nature. As to the latter the distinction must be remembered between floating or circulating and fixed capital.[269]

Clearly, based on the above, the cost of acquiring plant and machinery for a business constitutes expenditure of a capital nature. However, the cost of maintaining and insuring the plant and machinery is revenue in nature.

In determining whether expenditure is capital or revenue in nature the following statement by Watermeyer CJ is useful:

> The problem which arises when deductions are claimed is therefore usually whether the expenditure in question should properly be regarded as part of the cost of performing the income-earning operations or as part of the cost of establishing or improving or adding to the income-earning plant or machinery.[270]

---

265 1946 AD 610, 14 SATC 155.

266 *New State Areas Ltd v Commissioner for Inland Revenue* 13 SATC 400 1945 TPD.

267 *New State Areas Ltd v Commissioner for Inland Revenue* 1946 AD 610, 14 SATC 155.

268 At 163.

269 Ibid.

270 At 164.

Those costs incurred in operating the business are revenue in nature and thus deductible under s 11*(a)* of the Act. Where costs are incurred to create or expand the business operation, those costs are capital in nature and cannot be claimed for tax purposes under s 11*(a)*. A taxpayer may obtain tax relief if the capital expenditure qualifies as a deduction under another part of the Act.

The court referred to the test suggested by Lord Dunedin in *Vallambrosa Rubber Co v Farmer*[271] which specified that 'a payment made once for all is capital expenditure and a recurrent expenditure is revenue expenditure'[272] which may assist in some cases in deciding whether an item of expenditure is revenue or capital in nature. Where a payment is made in instalments this test may not be appropriate on the basis that even though an amount may be paid regularly it may still constitute an expense of a capital nature.[273]

Watermeyer CJ made the point that where expenditure is incurred to acquire a capital asset, such expenditure constitutes capital.[274] However, where the cost is incidental to the performance of the income-earning operations it is revenue in nature and deductible for tax purposes.[275] The court held that the costs incurred in respect of the basic charge 'A' was capital in nature as it related to the internal sewers which were located on the taxpayer's property and thus became part of its fixed capital.[276] This was despite the fact that the company was obliged to pay the local authority the cost of these sewers in instalments on a regular basis.[277]

The court drew a distinction between the internal and external sewers on the basis that the internal sewers became part of the taxpayer's mine, whereas the external sewers always remained the property of the local authority.[278] The expenditure incurred for the external sewers was more in the nature of a payment for the use of those sewers as those sewers never became the property of the taxpayer.[279] Watermeyer CJ concluded that expenditure comprising basic charge 'B' was revenue in nature and deductible for tax purposes.[280]

In *Palabora Mining Company Limited v Secretary for Inland Revenue*[281] the court had to decide whether the loss of R1 816 149 incurred by the company to ensure the supply of water to commence the earlier production of copper was deductible under s 11*(a)* of the Act. The company claimed the loss against its profits and the Secretary disallowed the deduction. On appeal to the Special Court, that court ruled that the expenditure was incurred to equip the structure of the mine by securing a permanent supply of water and was a cost incurred

---

271 1910 SC 519.
272 *New State Areas v Commissioner for Inland Revenue* 1946 AD 610, 14 SATC 155 at 165.
273 At 165.
274 At 170.
275 Ibid.
276 Ibid.
277 Ibid.
278 At 171.
279 At 172.
280 At 173.
281 1973 (3) SA 819 (A), 35 SATC 159.

in creating the mine and not operating it.[282] The company was dissatisfied with the decision of the Special Court and the case proceeded to the Appellate Division.

Palabora Mining was formed in 1956 to exploit mineral deposits at Phalaborwa. Up to the end of 1962 the company was engaged in exploratory work and in 1963 it had identified the existence of large deposits of copper ore and other minerals. It took almost three years to construct the mine and the company wished to commence milling of copper during 1966. To do so it needed to secure an adequate supply of water, which the company expected to be supplied by a statutory water board. Because of delays, the company decided to incur the costs of building a barrage to dam up water from the rain that fell in 1965 and 1966, thereby enabling it to generate profits from its operations earlier than originally expected.

The company tendered for part of the water board's work to build the barrage and was awarded those tenders. As a result the company incurred expenditure of R1 816 149, net of fees received from the Water Board for the Phalaborwa area. The Water Board was always going to construct the barrage but the company wanted to make certain that it would be completed in time to catch the rains that fell in the 1965–6 season. The completion of the dam in March 1966 allowed the company to earn profits eight months earlier than it had originally scheduled.[283]

Once the barrage was completed it became an asset belonging to the water board and at no time did it become the property of the company.[284] The company did not acquire any preferential rights from the water board to the use of the water from the dam as a result of having built the barrage.[285] By incurring the loss in question the company gained net revenue of approximately R3 million for each month that the production of anode copper was brought forward.[286]

Ogilvie Thompson CJ pointed out that the dam was always going to be built by the water board and that the expenditure incurred by the company did not secure the supply of water for the long term, but rather accelerated the supply of water to allow the company to start generating profits earlier than originally planned.[287] The court stated that the advantage which the company derived from building the barrage was short-lived and adapted to a short-term purpose, namely the acceleration of the supply of water, and once the eight-month period had passed, the purpose of the expenditure had been exhausted.[288]

The court reached the decision that there was a direct relationship between the expenditure incurred in building the barrage and the company's

[282] At 170.
[283] At 169.
[284] Ibid.
[285] Ibid.
[286] Ibid.
[287] At 174.
[288] Ibid.

income-earning operations and as a result allowed the deduction claimed.[289] This was despite the fact that when the expenditure was incurred the company had not yet derived profits from the sale of anode copper.[290] The court was satisfied that the company was conducting a 'trade' as defined in s 1 of the Act when the expenditure was incurred and thus the cost of the barrage did not constitute pre-production expenditure that would not have been allowed as a deduction.[291] Ogilvie Thompson CJ allowed the expenditure on the basis that the cost of the barrage was revenue in nature and qualified as a deduction under s 11*(a)* of the Act.

Where a company pays a consideration for its release from an onerous contract, the question that arises is whether such consideration is capital or revenue in nature under s 11*(a)* of the Act. In *Secretary for Inland Revenue v John Cullum Construction Co (Pty) Ltd*[292] the Appellate Division of the Supreme Court was called on to decide whether the consideration of R16 000 paid for the release of the company from its obligations under a contract concluded with another company was deductible for tax purposes. The Secretary disallowed the amount claimed on the basis that the expenditure was linked to the company's income-producing machine and thus constituted an amount of a capital nature and did not rank as a deduction for tax purposes.[293]

John Cullum Construction ('Cullum') carried on business as a building contractor and concluded a contract with a finance corporation which undertook to provide guarantees to a financial institution to assist prospective purchasers in financing the purchase of homes built by the company. This contract proved profitable for both parties at the outset but as the building industry became more competitive the contract proved to be onerous for Cullum, as it tied up a significant part of the company's funding. As a result, Cullum approached the finance corporation to be released from its obligations and paid it the amount of R16 000, which amount was based on the income the corporation would have received over the next two years from Cullum. The payment made by Cullum brought to an end an onerous contract and allowed the company to conclude financing arrangements with any other business, while claiming the amount paid as a deduction for tax purposes.

The Secretary disallowed the expenditure on the basis that it did not meet the requirements of s 11*(a)* and the dispute was heard by the Special Court. That court allowed Cullum's appeal on the basis that the expenditure was part of the income-producing activities conducted by the company, as it was aimed at generating income for Cullum and met the requirements of s 11*(a)*.The Secretary appealed to the Appellate Division where Steyn CJ concluded that the findings reached by the Special Court were findings of fact and not findings

[289] At 177.
[290] At 176.
[291] Ibid.
[292] 1965 (4) SA 697 (A), 27 SATC 155.
[293] At 156.

of law, and for this reason the court could not interfere with the decision made by the Special Court.[294]

Williamson JA summarised the facts of the dispute and interrogated whether the amount paid by Cullum was a payment of a capital nature or not. He referred to the fact that the Commissioner contended that expenditure to get rid of an onerous agreement was not an income-producing operation as required under s 11*(a)*.[295] The Secretary also argued that the expenditure was of a capital nature on the grounds that the cancelled contract was capital in nature, and that the main reason for cancelling the contract with the finance corporation was to reduce the amount of capital used by Cullum in financing the guarantees issued by it.[296]

Williamson JA referred to the English case of *Anglo-Persian Oil Co Ltd v Dale*,[297] where Anglo-Persian paid an amount of P300 000 to terminate an onerous agreement with certain commission agents. The Special Income Tax Commissioners refused to allow the consideration paid as a deduction for tax purposes, which decision was reversed by Rowlatt J on appeal on the basis that the amount was revenue in nature. That decision was upheld by Romer LJ on appeal, who held as follows:

> If a contract be onerous simply and solely because it entails a heavy drain upon the annual revenue of the company, the company will not secure an 'enduring' benefit for its trade by getting rid of it. Yet looking at the special case, it would appear that the Commissioners thought that it necessarily would. For there is nothing in it from beginning to end to suggest that the Company in fact secured an enduring benefit such as was referred to by Lord Cave.[298]

In deciding whether the consideration is deductible it is important to understand the true nature of the contract being cancelled.[299] Where a contract is cancelled and at the same time a party is restrained from competing with the entity paying the settlement consideration, that amount is likely to regarded as capital in nature as it secures an enduring benefit for the party paying the settlement.[300] Williamson JA decided that the amount paid by Cullum did not result in it acquiring or creating any asset and did not preserve any asset, but rather—

> received the temporary benefit of being free to attempt to obtain better terms upon which it could arrange finance for customers requiring assistance in the purchase of houses built by the company.[301]

294 At 167.
295 At 170.
296 Ibid.
297 [1932] 1 KB 124, 16 TC 253.
298 At 275.
299 *Secretary for Inland Revenue v John Cullum Construction Co (Pty) Ltd* 1965 (4) SA 697 (A) 714, 27 SATC 155 at 173.
300 At 174.
301 Ibid.

The payment made by Cullum allowed the company to conduct its business more economically and the purpose was to extricate the company from the onerous contract.[302] Thus, the court decided that the expenditure was revenue in nature and was wholly and exclusively laid out for purposes of its trade and was deductible for tax purposes under s 11*(a)*.[303]

The Act does not define the phrase contained in s 11*(a)* 'not of a capital nature' and in deciding whether a particular item of expenditure is revenue or capital in nature it is necessary to draw on the tests laid down in the judgments handed down by the courts in deciding whether a particular expense is deductible or not.

Steyn CJ in the *Cullum* case[304] stated:

> The Act does not speak of costs incidental to the performance of the income-producing operations or of costs incurred in the equipment of the income-producing machine or structure. It speaks of expenditure 'not of a capital nature'. The former phrases emanate from our courts, where they have been used in describing the *indicia* which would in the appropriate category of cases lead to a conclusion as to whether or not the expenditure is of a capital nature, i. e. whether or not it falls within the language of the Act. It may be said that these *indicia* have, in a sense, been arrived at by way of interpretation of the language of the Act. They have, however, not been arrived at in an attempt to define what Parliament has refrained from defining, with the same effect, for present purposes, as a definition in the Act itself would have had.[305]

Steyn CJ referred to the statement by Centlivres JA in *Sub-Nigel Ltd v Commissioner for Inland Revenue*[306] in interpreting the phrase 'not of a capital nature', which is instructive:

> It is, in my view, impossible to give a definition of what is expenditure of a non-capital nature which will act as a touchstone in deciding all possible cases and it would be impracticable to attempt such a definition.[307]

Thus, in deciding whether expenditure is revenue or capital in nature, regard must be had to the *indicia* relied on by the courts in adjudicating the nature of expenditure incurred by a taxpayer.

In *Commissioner for Inland Revenue v African Oxygen Ltd*[308] the company concluded an agreement with a Swedish competitor, with the result that a new company was to be formed. The new company was appointed the exclusive

---

302 Ibid.

303 Ibid.

304 *Secretary for Inland Revenue v John Cullum Construction Co (Pty) Ltd* 1965 (4) SA 697 (A), 27 SATC 155 at 164.

305 At 164.

306 1948 (4) SA 580 (A), 15 SATC 381.

307 At 396.

308 1963 (1) SA 681 (A), 25 SATC 67.

representative of the Swedish company and the parties agreed that the new company would not compete with the Swedish company or with African Oxygen. The agreement was to last for five years and African Oxygen undertook to make good any losses incurred by the joint venture company created with the Swedish company. In 1956 and 1957 losses of R2 424 and R1 520 were incurred respectively and African Oxygen claimed those losses as a deduction for tax purposes. The Commissioner disallowed the deductions claimed on the grounds that the expenditure was capital in nature.[309] The taxpayer's appeal was upheld by the Special Court, against which decision the Commissioner appealed.[310]

Steyn CJ indicated that the Commissioner raised two contentions in the Special Court.[311] The first was that even though the taxpayer had concluded the agreement with the Swedish company with the motive of protecting its own market, the making good of the losses was meant to ensure that the joint venture company was viable and thus the expenditure was not wholly or exclusively laid out for purposes of African Oxygen's trade.[312] The second was that the expenditure was capital in nature as it related to the elimination of competition by the Swedish company, with the result that African Oxygen obtained a right or advantage of an enduring nature for the benefit of its trade.[313]

The court accepted that the expenditure was incurred in the production of income.[314] The dispute thus related to whether the expenditure was revenue in nature and also if the expenditure was laid out wholly or exclusively for purposes of trade.[315] Steyn CJ made the point that the assets constituting the company's income-producing concern included its goodwill and that the joint venture agreement was entered into in order to preserve the company's asset.[316] African Oxygen, as a result of concluding the agreement with its Swedish competitor, secured the right, enforceable in a court, to prevent the foreign company from competing with it.[317] Thus, the payments made by African Oxygen were to be regarded as capital in nature as they related to the elimination of a competitor, which was directly associated with the protection of the company's income-earning machine and was not a cost of performing its income-earning operations.[318]

In *Commissioner for Inland Revenue v George Forest Timber Co Ltd*[319] the company had acquired land on which a forest of trees was located. The company carried on business as timber merchants and sawyers and felled

[309] At 73.
[310] At 68.
[311] At 73.
[312] Ibid.
[313] At 74.
[314] Ibid.
[315] Ibid.
[316] At 76.
[317] Ibid.
[318] At 77.
[319] 1924 AD 516, 1 SATC 20.

trees to process and sell in the course of its business. In submitting its 1919 tax return the company claimed an amount of P1 000 as representing the proportion of the cost of the forest relative to the timber felled in 1919. The Commissioner disallowed the deduction on the basis that the amount was capital in nature. The court had to decide if the company was entitled to claim a deduction for the wasting asset comprising the forest of trees located on the land acquired by the taxpayer, which trees were not renewable and required new trees to be planted to take their place.

Innes CJ pointed out that the dispute between the taxpayer and the Commissioner revolved around the question as to whether the proportionate cost of the land with the trees thereon constituted an expense actually incurred in the production of income and whether such amount was of a capital nature.[320] The company bought the land with the forest on it so that it could fell the trees, process the timber and sell it to customers.[321] The greater portion of the value of the land was attributable to the trees located thereon, and without the trees the land would have had a negligible value.[322] Innes CJ said:

> No doubt the trees constituted the chief value of the property and formed the inducement for its acquisition. But the same might be said of the stone or the clay in land purchased for the purpose of a quarry or a brick-field. They formed part of the realty to which they acceded, and they passed with it. Money spent in creating or acquiring an income-producing concern must be capital expenditure. It was invested to yield future profit and while the outlay did not recur, the income did. There was a great difference between money spent in creating or acquiring a source of profit, and money spent in working it. The one was capital expenditure, the other not.[323]

The court reached the decision that the taxpayer was not entitled to the deduction claimed as it constituted an expense of a capital nature.[324] The court expressed the opinion that the amount claimed represented the cost of the revenue-producing asset from which income would be derived over a period of time.[325]

The reference to a United Kingdom decision by Innes CJ is useful:

> The remarks of Channell, J, in *Alianza Co. v Bell* (1904, 2 K. B. at p.673) are instructive upon the question of capital expenditure: 'If it is merely a manufacturing business,' he said, 'then the procuring of raw material would not be a capital expenditure. But if it is like the working of a particular mine, or bed of brick earth, and converting the stuff worked into a marketable commodity, then the money paid for the prime cost of the stuff so dealt with is just as much capital as the money sunk in machinery or building.'[326]

---

320 At 25.
321 Ibid.
322 Ibid.
323 Ibid.
324 At 26.
325 Ibid.
326 At 27.

Innes CJ held that the expenditure claimed by the company was capital in nature, even though it related to a wasting asset, and disallowed the deduction claimed by the company.[327] De Villiers JA concurred with the decision reached by Innes CJ and agreed that the cost of acquiring the land on which the trees stood was capital in nature.[328] He pointed out that the land with the trees thereon constituted the fixed capital of the company and would be used for the purpose of producing income.[329]

In another case dealing with a taxpayer involved in the timber business the court had to decide whether the cost of constructing access roads to facilitate the removal of timber was deductible for tax purposes.[330] In *Commissioner of Taxes v Rhodesia Congo Border Timber Co Ltd*[331] the company procured a concession whereby it was entitled to fell and remove timber from land owned by the Government of Northern Rhodesia. It could not decide which trees to fell but had to work in specific blocks designated by the Conservator of Forests.[332] It took approximately three years to remove all the timber from a specified block and it could only start working on a new block once the previous block had been fully worked out.[333]

To remove the timber from the blocks it worked the company constructed, at a cost of P4 890, a rough roadway which would last for the dry season.[334] It was anticipated that such roads would last for approximately six weeks. Once the block had been worked the access roads were abandoned and allowed to be taken over by nature.[335] The company also spent P15 778 in constructing a hard road which was planned to last for a period of three years.[336] It must be noted that the roads were constructed on land owned by the government and the company would not derive any benefit from the roads constructed, other than secure access to the forest from which it was entitled to remove the timber.[337] The court had to decide whether the cost of constructing the roads was deductible on the basis that the expenditure was not of a capital nature. The court *a quo* held that the company was entitled to claim the cost of the roads built for tax purposes.[338]

The Commissioner was dissatisfied with the decision and appealed to the Federal Supreme Court. Clayden CJ expressed the opinion that the fact that the roads had no residual value to the company was an important factor to

327 At 28.
328 Ibid.
329 Ibid.
330 *Commissioner of Taxes v Rhodesia Congo Border Timber Co, Ltd* 24 SATC 602, 1961 (FC).
331 Supra.
332 At 604.
333 Ibid.
334 Ibid.
335 At 605.
336 Ibid.
337 Ibid.
338 Ibid.

consider in deciding if the expenditure was capital in nature.[339] Furthermore, the fact that the cost of building access roads was recurrent was relevant in determining the nature of the expense for tax purposes.[340] Clayden CJ referred to the finding made by the court *a quo* that the cost of the roads was spent 'in working the timber-taking-source-of-profit' and stated that it was not an afterthought but was a conclusion reached on other grounds.[341]

Briggs FJ, in a concurring judgment, made the point that it was appropriate for the court *a quo* to take account of the fact that the roads were not built on the taxpayer's land and that they were expected to have a short life, without any residual value to the company.[342] The court unanimously decided that the costs of the roads constructed by the company were not of a capital nature for the reasons stated above and were thus deductible for tax purposes.[343]

Where one company pays a consideration to another company for it agreeing to abandon its production, the question arises if such payment is capital or revenue in nature for tax purposes. In *Commissioner of Taxes v N'Changa Consolidated Copper Mines Ltd*[344] N'Changa paid an amount of P1 384 569 in 1959 to a group company to abandon its production of copper for a year and claimed the amount as a deduction for tax purposes. The price of copper fell in 1957 and the various producers agreed to reduce production in order to stabilise the price.[345] The Anglo American group owned three copper mines owned by separate companies, namely N'Changa Copper Mines Ltd, Rhokana Corporation Ltd and Bancroft Mines Ltd.[346] Bancroft was a new mine which had a high cost of production and it was decided that N'Changa and Rhokana would pay it an amount of P2 165 000 for not producing copper for one year.[347] This allowed the two companies to produce a greater amount of copper, which resulted in their being able to increase their profitability.

The Commissioner disallowed the deduction claimed by N'Changa on the ground that the amount was capital in nature and the High Court of Southern Rhodesia dismissed the company's appeal on the basis that the expenditure was aimed at preserving N'Changa's organisation and conferring on it an enduring advantage.[348] The Federal Supreme Court of the Federation of Rhodesia and Nyasaland decided that the company was entitled to the deduction and the matter proceeded to the Privy Council to hear the appeal lodged by the Commissioner against the decision of that court.[349]

339 At 608.
340 Ibid.
341 Ibid.
342 At 612.
343 At 609, 613 and 616.
344 1964 (2) SA 472 (PC), 26 SATC 37.
345 At 39.
346 Ibid.
347 At 40.
348 At 42.
349 At 39.

The Privy Council decided that the effect of the agreement concluded by N'Changa with Bancroft was to acquire the right to have Bancroft out of production for twelve months.[350] The Commissioner contended that the expenditure was not incurred wholly and exclusively by N'Changa for the purposes of its trade or in the production of its income on the basis that the payment was made in the interests of Bancroft's trade. Young J in the Supreme Court rejected this argument. Viscount Radcliffe referred to the distinction made by the courts between—

> the cost of creating, acquiring or enlarging the permanent (which does not mean perpetual) structure of which the income is to be the produce or fruit and the cost of earning that income itself or performing the income-earning operations.[351]

Clearly, the costs that fall into the first category are capital in nature, whereas those items falling into the second category are revenue in nature. The Privy Council concluded that N'Changa acquired one right as a result of compensating Bancroft and that was the right to have Bancroft desist from production for twelve months.[352] N'Changa did not acquire Bancroft's business or seek to close down its business for good.[353] What N'Changa obtained was a temporary right or advantage whereby Bancroft would not produce copper for twelve months only.[354] The Privy Council decided that the amount paid to Bancroft was revenue in nature as it was an expense incurred in the carrying on of its business and to generate a profit as a result of having incurred the expense.[355] N'Changa would have increased its profits as a result of the fact that it was able to produce and sell more copper than if it had chosen not to compensate Bancroft. As a result the deduction was allowed under the provisions equivalent to s 11*(a)*.

6.2.5 In the year of assessment

It is clear from the above analysis of the provisions of s 11*(a)* that a taxpayer must have incurred the item of expenditure for that amount to qualify as a deduction for tax purposes. In addition, the amount must have been incurred in the production of income and not constitute an amount of a capital nature.

Section 11*(a)* does not specifically provide that the expenditure incurred in one year of assessment must be claimed in that year of assessment. The question that arises is what happens if a taxpayer incurs expenditure in its 2011 year of assessment and for some reason fails to claim it in that year: can the expenditure be claimed in a subsequent year of assessment, for example, in 2012 or even later, in 2015?

350 At 41.
351 At 43.
352 Ibid.
353 At 44.
354 Ibid.
355 At 46.

This principle was first considered by the Special Court in *ITC 47.*[356] In this case the taxpayer claimed the cost of a building completed on 28 April 1922 in its tax return for 30 June 1923 as a result of the death of the life tenant in that tax year, and the fact that the building had to be knocked down to meet the requirements of the local authority.[357] Sutton, Acting President, said the following:

> Now, after the life tenant has died they claim it in respect of the year ended 30th June 1923, and that is not right. If it is a loss or outgoing deductible it ought to be deducted in respect of the particular year in which it was incurred and it was really incurred as soon as the property was completed in April, 1922. On this simple point, the appeal must fail.[358]

Subsequently, in *Baxter v Commissioner of Taxes, Southern Rhodesia*[359] the court had to decide whether the interest incurred in various tax years could be claimed in a later tax year. The taxpayer had failed to claim the interest in each tax year in which it was incurred.[360] The court accepted that the interest was incurred in the production of income but it had a difficulty in allowing the interest accumulated from 1923 to 1935 on the basis that the accumulated amount was not incurred in 1935.[361]

Hudson J commented on the issue as follows:

> The Income Tax Ordinance contemplates that, subject to specific exceptions, each tax year must stand by itself. In each year the whole of the taxpayer's income and expenditure must be taken into account and dealt with. That, I think, is the clear implication arising from the definition of income and, indeed, from the whole frame of the statute. And while it is true that the words 'during the year of assessment' which appear in other clauses of sub-sec 14(1) are not present in clause *(a)* I do not think that the implication I have referred to is thereby negative. If any authority is needed for this conclusion it is to be found in *Income Tax Case No 47* (2 SATC 47).[362]

The court thus disallowed the deduction of the accumulated interest on the basis that those amounts were incurred in tax years other than the tax year under consideration.[363] In *Commissioner for Inland Revenue v Delfos*[364] the court emphasised the following principle: 'But it is important to note that the tax is an annual one and is to be levied on the "taxable income" received by or accrued to any person during the year of assessment.'[365]

---

356 2 SATC 120.
357 At 120.
358 Ibid.
359 1937 SR 48, 9 SATC 1.
360 At 4.
361 Ibid.
362 Ibid.
363 At 5.
364 1933 AD 242, 6 SATC 92.
365 At 105.

Thus, even though s 11 *(a)* may not refer to the requirement that the expenditure must be incurred in the correct year of assessment, it is clear from the cases and the scheme of the Act that this is indeed a requirement that must be met for expenditure to rank as a deduction.

The case of *Concentra v Commissioner for Inland Revenue*[366] also dealt with the question of expenditure incurred in previous tax years and whether such amounts could be claimed by a taxpayer in a later tax year. In this case expenditure was incurred between April 1937 and August 1940 and was only claimed in the 1940 tax year.[367] Howes J pointed out that the one difficulty that the taxpayer faced was whether it is possible for a taxpayer to postpone the payment of its liabilities and thereby place it in another tax year.[368] In addition, the further question which arises is 'whether the expenditure must be in connection with the production of the income of that particular year only'.[369] The court made the point that the basis of the Act is the assessment of tax on an annual basis and that it is necessary to take account of the income and expenditure on an annual basis.[370] Howes J concluded as follows:

> The 'expenditure and losses incurred' referred to in sec 11(2)*(a)* of Act 40 of 1925 are expenditure and losses incurred in the year of assessment and it is quite unnecessary for the decision of this case to decide whether or not they were incurred for the production of income of that year only or merely for the production of income generally.[371]

The court made it clear that a taxpayer cannot delay the claiming of qualifying expenditure to a tax year that suits the taxpayer.[372] If the taxpayer chooses, for whatever reason, not to claim expenditure actually incurred in a particular tax year, it cannot seek to claim that expenditure in a subsequent tax year.[373]

6.3 DEDUCTIONS SPECIFICALLY PROHIBITED (S 23)

Section 23 of the Act sets out in negative terms those deductions that taxpayers may not claim as a deduction for tax purposes, whereas s 11 *(a)* of the Act sets out in positive terms the tests a taxpayer must meet for expenditure to qualify as a deduction for tax purposes. The various deductions prohibited by s 23 will now be considered.

366 1942 CPD 509, 12 SATC 95.
367 At 97.
368 At 98.
369 Ibid.
370 Ibid.
371 Ibid.
372 Ibid.
373 Ibid.

6.3.1 Maintenance of taxpayer

Section 23*(a)* of the Act precludes any deduction being claimed by a taxpayer regarding their maintenance or that of their family or establishment. In *CIR v Hickson*[374] Beyers JA stated:

> I take 'maintenance of the taxpayer, his family or establishment' to mean feeding and clothing himself and his family, providing them with the necessities of life, and comforts, and, as it were, maintaining a certain standard of living, and keeping up his establishment.

Thus, those personal expenses incurred by a taxpayer and his or her family to enable them to live cannot be claimed for tax purposes.[375]

6.3.2 Domestic or private expenses

Section 23*(b)* of the Act prohibits a taxpayer claiming any private or domestic expenses as a deduction for tax purposes in the following terms—

> domestic or private expenses, including the rent of or cost of repairs of or expenses in connection with any premises not occupied for the purposes of trade or of any dwelling-house or domestic premises except in respect of such part as may be occupied for the purposes of trade: Provided that—
>
> *(a)* such part shall not be deemed to have been occupied for the purposes of trade, unless such part is specifically equipped for purposes of the taxpayer's trade and regularly and exclusively used for such purposes; and
>
> *(b)* no deduction shall in any event be granted where the taxpayer's trade constitutes any employment or office unless—
>
> (i) his income from such employment or office is derived mainly from commission or other variable payments which are based on the taxpayer's work performance and his duties are mainly performed otherwise than in an office which is provided to him by his employer; or
>
> (ii) his duties are mainly performed in such part ...

Since the Commissioner lost the case of *Kommissaris van Binnelandse Inkomste v Van der Walt*[376] where the taxpayer, a university lecturer, succeeded in claiming the costs attributable to the use of his study at home, the law has been repeatedly amended to prevent taxpayers from being able to claim the cost of a study against remuneration. Eloff DJP decided that the maxim *generalia specialibus non derogant* applied and this meant that the specific provision, namely s 23*(b)*, operates to the exclusion of the general provision contained in s 23*(g)*.[377]

374 1960 (1) SA 746 (A), 23 SATC 243 at 249.
375 *Silke on SA Income Tax* para 7.10 at 7–34.
376 48 SATC 104.
377 48 SATC 104 at 111.

Thus, in accordance with s 23*(b)* taxpayers are precluded from claiming those expenses that are domestic in nature, including the rental paid for their home and repairs and maintenance relating thereto. Where taxpayers conduct their trade or profession from a part of their home, the costs relating thereto will qualify as a deduction for tax purposes. An example is where a doctor has consulting rooms attached to his home which are used only for seeing his patients, and those rooms are not used at any time for private purposes. The rent and other running costs attributable to the consulting rooms would rank as a deduction for tax purposes.

The section requires that that part of the home for which the taxpayer seeks to claim expenses must be specifically equipped for the purposes of the taxpayer's trade and be used for those purposes only. It is not sufficient that the taxpayer occasionally uses the dining room table for work purposes or meets with his or her clients in his or her lounge.

Where the taxpayer derives a salary from employment no deduction of expenses relating to a home study, for example, is available. The section requires that the taxpayer must derive income mainly in the form of commission or other variable payments, such as performance bonuses. The use of the word 'mainly' in the section means that the bulk or most of the income is derived by the taxpayer in the form of commission income for him or her to successfully claim expenses relating to that part of the home used for work purposes. Furthermore, if the employer supplies the taxpayer with an office, no deduction is available as the Act requires that the duties performed by the taxpayer are mainly performed from his or her home and not from an office supplied to him or her.

Where the taxpayer is not supplied with an office by his or her employer, which is becoming more common as employers seek to reduce their overheads, and the employee uses part of the home for the business of his or her employer, the expenditure related to that part of the home used exclusively for work purposes will qualify as a deduction for tax purposes.

A question that arises in practice is whether the salary paid to a domestic worker to care for the taxpayer's children, thereby enabling the taxpayer to go to work and derive an income, can be claimed for tax purposes. Unfortunately, the salary paid to the domestic worker constitutes private expenditure and cannot be claimed for tax purposes when reference is made to the prohibition contained in s 23*(b)* of the Act.

6.3.3 Losses recoverable under insurance

Section 23*(c)* of the Act provides that no deductions shall be made in respect of 'any loss or expense, the deduction of which would otherwise be allowable, to the extent to which it is recoverable under any contract of insurance, guarantee, security or indemnity'.

Where, for example, a taxpayer suffers a loss of income and incurs expenses as a result of a fire or a natural disaster, those expenses may not be claimed for tax purposes to the extent to which the expenses are recoverable under an insurance policy. The section uses the word 'recoverable' and thus the taxpayer need not actually recover the amounts in question for the section to apply.[378] It is sufficient that if the expenses are recoverable under a contract of insurance, guarantee, security or indemnity, the taxpayer is unable to claim those expenses for tax purposes.

In addition, if a taxpayer incurs expenses for faulty goods supplied to its customers and the taxpayer can recover those expenses under an insurance policy or a guarantee issued by the manufacturer of the goods, those expenses cannot be claimed for tax purposes as result of the prohibition contained in s 23*(c)* of the Act.

6.3.4 Taxes paid

Section 23*(d)* of the Act provides that a taxpayer is unable to claim any tax, duty, levy, interest or penalty imposed under the Act or the Tax Administration Act 28 of 2011 or any additional tax payable under the Value-Added Tax Act 89 of 1991 for tax purposes. Furthermore, the section provides that any interest or penalty incurred by a taxpayer as a result of the late payment of any tax, duty, levy or contribution payable under any Act administered by the Commissioner, the Skills Development Levies Act 9 of 1999 and the Unemployment Insurance Contributions Act 4 of 2002 may not be claimed as a deduction for tax purposes.

6.3.5 Income transferred to a reserve fund

The transfer of income to a reserve fund may not be claimed as a deduction under s 23*(e)* of the Act. Thus, the transfer of funds to a provision to meet future liabilities or obligations of the business may not be claimed as a deduction for tax purposes under this section. It was pointed out above that, under the general deduction formula contained in s 11*(a)* of the Act, a taxpayer may only claim expenses that have been actually incurred. This section reinforces the requirement that the expenditure must be incurred by the taxpayer; it is not sufficient to merely appropriate profits by transferring those to a provision for the future, as such transfers to a reserve fund are specifically precluded from being claimed as a deduction for tax purposes.

6.3.6 Expenses relating to exempt income

Expenditure incurred by a taxpayer in generating any amounts which do not constitute income as defined as such in s 1 of the Act may not be claimed as a deduction for tax purposes under s 23*(f)* of the Act. It must be remembered that income comprises the gross income received by or accrued in favour of the taxpayer after deducting those amounts that are exempt from tax in terms of s 10 of the Act. Thus, expenses incurred in generating, for example, domestic dividends, which are not liable to income tax, may not be claimed as a deduction for tax purposes under s 23*(f)* of the Act.

[378] *Silke on SA Income Tax* para 7.10 at 7–36.

This section provides in negative terms what is stated positively in s 11*(a)*, which requires that expenditure must be incurred in the production of income to qualify as a deduction for tax purposes.

In *CIR v Standard Bank of SA Ltd*[379] the taxpayer received deposits from its clients, was liable to pay interest on those amounts and those funds were placed into the general pool of funds held by the bank for its use in its business as a bank. Certain of the funds were lent to other clients of the bank at interest and a portion of the funds was invested by the bank in preference shares which generated tax-free dividends. The Commissioner sought to disallow a part of the interest incurred by the bank on the basis that that interest was incurred to generate exempt income. The bank argued that the purpose of paying interest to its clients was to enable the bank to use those funds in order to generate income and that it was incidental that a portion of the funds received was used to invest in preference shares which could only generate exempt income. The court decided that all of the interest incurred by the bank and claimed by it for tax purposes was deductible and that it was unnecessary to apportion the interest incurred to take account of the types of income generated by the bank.

More recently, in *Mobile Telephone Networks Holdings (Pty) Limited v Commissioner for the South African Revenue Service*,[380] as discussed more fully in 6.2.3 above, the Supreme Court of appeal found that audit fees (and, by implication, similar professional fees) could be apportioned between income earning activities and those generating exempt income or for capital purposes.

6.3.7 Expenses not incurred for purposes of trade

Section 23*(g)* of the Act prohibits a taxpayer from claiming for tax purposes 'any moneys, claimed as a deduction from income derived from trade, to the extent to which such moneys were not laid out or expended for the purposes of trade'.

The section now allows a taxpayer to deduct expenditure to the extent to which such expenditure relates to the trade conducted by the taxpayer. This is an improvement on what the position was when the section required that the expenditure must be incurred 'wholly or exclusively for the purposes of trade'.

In *CIR v Pick 'n Pay Wholesalers (Pty) Ltd*[381] the court had to determine whether the donation of R100 000 made by Pick 'n Pay to the Urban Foundation was deductible for tax purposes. The donation was made with two objects in mind, namely a philanthropic objective of assisting a deserving charity, on whose main board the founder of Pick 'n Pay served, and, in addition, the objective of gaining advertising and marketing exposure from its donation and thereby attracting customers to its stores.

379 1985 (4) SA 485 (A), 47 SATC 179.

380 76 SATC 205.

381 1987 (3) SA 453 (A), 49 SATC 132.

Nicholas AJA held:

> In all the circumstances I am of the opinion that Pick 'n Pay did not show, on the probabilities, that in making the donation it did not have a philanthropic purpose as well as a business purpose.[382]

Thus, the deduction claimed by Pick 'n Pay was disallowed on the basis that the donation had been made to the Urban Foundation with two purposes in mind. As the section required that the expenditure had to be incurred 'wholly or exclusively' for purposes of the taxpayer's trade, it was not possible for the court to apportion the expenditure into two parts, that is, that which could be allowed and that which had to be disallowed.

The court referred to the decision of the House of Lords in *Mallalieu v Drummond*[383] with approval and quoted from the speech by Lord Brightman who, in his judgment, indicated that 'the distinction between the object of the expenditure and its effect was basic':[384]

> The object of the taxpayer in making the expenditure must be distinguished from the effect of the expenditure. An expenditure may be made exclusively to serve the purposes of the business, but it may have a private advantage. The existence of that private advantage does not necessarily preclude the exclusivity of the business purpose.[385]

In *Mallalieu* the taxpayer was a barrister and claimed the costs of her clothing used for court appearances as a deduction for tax purposes. The House of Lords decided that the expenditure on clothing was incurred with a dual purpose, that is, to comply with the rules of the court and to be properly clothed.[386] The court therefore disallowed the expenditure as it was not incurred wholly and exclusively for the purposes of conducting her profession.

Fortunately for taxpayers, the strict provisions contained in s 23*(g)* of the Act were relaxed by way of s 20*(b)* of the Income Tax Act 141 of 1992, with the result that taxpayers can now claim expenditure to the extent to which it is incurred for the purposes of their trade. Thus, if the Pick 'n Pay case were to come before a court today the court would be entitled to apportion the donation made of R100 000 to that relating to the business purpose and that relating to the philanthropic intent of the company.

In applying s 23*(g)* the taxpayer must seek to establish what portion of expenditure incurred with a dual purpose can be shown to relate to the carrying of the taxpayer's trade. That part of the expenditure will be deductible for tax purposes, whereas the balance will not be deductible.

---

382 At 468F, 151.

383 [1983] 2 All ER 1095 (HL).

384 *CIR v Pick 'n Pay Wholesalers (Pty) Ltd* 1987 (3) SA 453 (A), 49 SATC 132 at 148.

385 *Mallalieu v Drummond* [1983] 2 All ER 1095 (HL) 1100.

386 At 1100.

6.3.8 Notional interest

A taxpayer is unable to claim as a deduction any 'interest which might have been made on capital employed in trade' in terms of s 23*(h)* of the Act. Thus, taxpayers cannot claim notional interest, that is, interest which may have been derived on capital employed by them in their trade.

6.3.9 Certain deductions from retirement lump sums

Section 23*(i)* prohibits a taxpayer from claiming any expenditure, loss or allowance to the extent to which it is claimed as a deduction from any retirement fund lump sum benefit or retirement fund lump sum withdrawal benefit.

It must be noted that persons in receipt of a lump sum benefit from a retirement fund as a result of death, retirement or withdrawal are subject to tax in a particular manner and according to a special table of tax rates. It is for this reason that a taxpayer is unable to claim any deductions against such lump sums.

6.3.10 Expenses incurred by labour brokers and personal service providers

Section 23*(k)* of the Act precludes a labour broker and personal service provider as defined in the Act from claiming any expenditure which is not related to the remuneration of employees or expenses relating to premises or assets used wholly and exclusively for the purposes of the taxpayer's trade in the following terms—

> any expense incurred by—
>
> (i) a labour broker as defined in the Fourth Schedule, other than a labour broker in respect of which a certificate of exemption has been issued in terms of paragraph 2(5) of the said Schedule; or
>
> (ii) a personal service provider as defined in the said Schedule,
>
> other than any expense which constitutes an amount paid or payable to any employee of such labour broker or personal service provider for services rendered by such employee, which is or will be taken into account in the determination of the taxable income of such employee and, in the case of such personal service provider, any expense, deduction or contribution contemplated in paragraphs *(c)*, *(i)*, *(l)*, *(n*A*)* or *(n*B*)* of section 11, expenses in respect of premises, finance charges, insurance, repairs and fuel and maintenance in respect of assets, if such premises or assets are used wholly and exclusively for purposes of trade ...

The purpose of the prohibition contained in s 23*(k)* is to prevent labour brokers and personal service providers from claiming expenses that do not relate wholly and exclusively to their trade. Some years ago it was popular for employees to resign from employment and to render their services to their erstwhile employer via labour brokers or personal service providers in the mistaken belief that substantial expenditure, primarily of a personal nature, could be claimed for tax purposes. This section makes it clear that a labour broker or personal service provider will only be entitled to claim remuneration paid to its employees and certain other specified expenditure which must be directly related to the trade carried on by it.

6.3.11 Restraint of trade payments

Section 23*(l)* of the Act precludes a taxpayer from claiming any expense in respect of the payment of any restraint of trade, except to the extent allowed under s 11*(c*A*)* of the Act, which is deal with below. Thus, in principle, any restraint of trade payments incurred by a taxpayer do not qualify as a deduction for tax purposes.

6.3.12 Deductions relating to persons in employment

Over the years the Act has been repeatedly amended to prevent taxpayers in employment from being able to claim expenses, which would normally be regarded as personal in nature, as a deduction for tax purposes. Section 23*(m)* generally provides that persons in employment may not claim any expenditure for tax purposes. However, s 23*(m)*(i) to (iv) sets out what deductions an employee may claim for tax purposes. The section provides as follows—

> subject to paragraph *(k)*, any expenditure, loss or allowance, contemplated in section 11, which relates to any employment of, or office held by, any person (other than an agent or representative whose remuneration is normally derived mainly in the form of commissions based on his or her sales or the turnover attributable to him or her) in respect of which he or she derives any remuneration, as defined in paragraph 1 of the Fourth Schedule, other than—
>
> (i) any contributions to a pension or retirement annuity fund as may be deducted from the income of that person in terms of section 11*(k)* or *(n)*;
>
> (ii) any allowance or expense which may be deducted from the income of that person in terms of section 11*(c)*, *(e)*, *(i)* or *(j)*;
>
> (iiA) any deduction which is allowable under section 11*(n*A*)* or *(n*B*)*; and
>
> (iii) ......
>
> (iv) any deduction which is allowable under section 11*(a)* or *(d)* in respect of any rent of, cost of repairs of or expenses in connection with any dwelling house or domestic premises, to the extent that the deduction is not prohibited under paragraph *(b)* ...

The prohibition of expenditure applicable to employees earning a salary is similar to that applicable to labour brokers and personal service providers. An employee is entitled to claim legal expenses incurred in recovering any salary due to him or her as well as contributions to a pension fund or a retirement annuity fund. The strict rules found in s 23*(k)* of the Act do not apply to those persons who derive their income mainly in the form of commissions based on turnover generated by them. Commission earners are able to deduct those costs that are incurred in producing their commission income, such as entertainment, marketing and office expenses related to their trade as a commission earner.

Where an employee takes out an income protection insurance policy, the premiums are not deductible for tax purposes, in terms of s 23*(r)*, which is discussed below. An employee who acquires textbooks or a computer to use for work purposes can claim wear and tear on those assets under s 11*(e)* of the Act.

Should an employee be required to refund an employer an amount of salary or restraint of trade consideration, those amounts can be claimed as a deduction under ss 11*(n*A*)* and *(n*B*)*, respectively, despite the provisions of s 23*(k)*.

In those cases where a member of a professional body derives a salary and is liable to pay annual subscription fees to that body, those subscriptions are not deductible for tax purposes as a result of the restrictive wording contained in s 23*(k)* of the Act. It would be far preferable if the employee's employer required the employee to belong to a professional body and settled the subscription fees under the contract of employment concluded with the employee. In such a case the employee would not face fringe benefits tax in terms of the exemption provided for in para 13(2)*(b)* of the Seventh Schedule to the Act.

Travelling expenses incurred by employees in travelling from their home to their place of work constitute private expenditure and cannot be claimed for tax purposes as a result of s 23*(k)* read together with s 23*(b)* of the Act.

When reference is made to s 23*(k)* of the Act, it is apparent that persons in employment have very limited scope in terms of what expenditure can be claimed for tax purposes. These rules have been tightened over the years by the legislature to ensure that personal and private expenses cannot be claimed for tax purposes.

6.3.13 Deductions and allowances relating to exempt amounts

Section 23*(n)* of the Act prohibits a taxpayer from claiming—

> any deduction or allowance in respect of any asset or expenditure to the extent that amount—
>
> (i) is granted or paid to the taxpayer and is exempt from tax in terms of 10(1)*(y*A*)*; and
>
> (ii) is so granted or paid for purposes of the acquisition of that asset or funding of that expenditure.

The purpose of the above provision is to deny a taxpayer a deduction or allowance where the taxpayer has received a grant from the state which is exempt from tax under s 10(1)*(y*A*)* of the Act. This seeks to prevent the taxpayer receiving amounts that are exempt from tax and then using those amounts to incur expenditure that would otherwise be deductible for tax purposes, or to acquire fixed assets that would be written off over a period of time for tax purposes.

6.3.14 Fines and corrupt payments

Section 23*(o)* of the Act prevents a taxpayer from claiming any expenditure relating to bribery and corruption as well as fines and penalties incurred as a result of unlawful activities conducted by a taxpayer in South Africa or elsewhere. The section provides that no deductions shall be made in respect of any expenditure incurred—

(i) where the payment of that expenditure or the agreement or offer to make that payment constitutes an activity contemplated in Chapter 2 of the Prevention and Combating of Corrupt Activities Act, 2004 (Act 12 of 2004);

(ii) which constitutes a fine charged or penalty imposed as a result of an unlawful activity carried out in the Republic or in any other country if that activity would be unlawful had it been carried out in the Republic; or

(iii) any expenditure incurred constituting fruitless and wasteful expenditure as defined in section 1 of the Public Finance Management Act, determined in accordance with that Act.

The legislature intended that taxpayers falling foul of the Prevention and Combating of Corrupt Activities Act 12 of 2004 should not qualify for tax relief for any corrupt payments made by them in the form of bribes. It was arguable whether such payments could ever have ranked as a deduction for tax purposes but the legislature chose to place the matter beyond doubt. Paragraph (iii) was added in 2018, with effect from 1 April 2019, and applies to public entities. Fruitless and wasteful expenditure is defined in the Public Finance Management Act 1 of 1999 as expenditure that was made in vain and would have been avoided had reasonable care been exercised.

A further question arose in the past and that was whether a cartage contractor fined for overloading his trucks should be entitled to claim that fine as a deduction for tax purposes. In *ITC 1490*[387] the court had to determine if the traffic fines claimed by the taxpayer should be allowed under s 11*(a)* of the Act. The courts have held that to allow the traffic fines as a deduction for tax purposes would have been contrary to public policy and that the fines did not assist the taxpayer in the earning of income and were not an inevitable concomitant of the taxpayer's business.[388]

From a policy perspective the legislature takes the view that a taxpayer liable to any fine or similar financial sanction for violating the laws of the country should not enjoy tax relief on such fines.[389] SARS indicates that s 23*(o)* should not affect the deductibility or otherwise of damages and compensation incurred under a contract concluded by a taxpayer with another person.[390] In such cases the deductibility of the damages and/or compensation will be determined by reference to the general deduction formula contained in s 11*(a)* of the Act.

---

[387] 53 SATC 108.

[388] Ibid. See also SARS Interpretation Note 54 'Deductions – corrupt activities, fines and penalties' 26 February 2010 3.

[389] SARS Interpretation Note 54 'Deductions – corrupt activities, fines and penalties' 26 February 2010 3.

[390] Ibid 9.

6.3.15 Value of certain insurance policies ceded

Section 23*(p)* of the Act denies a taxpayer claiming as a deduction the value in respect of any cession of a policy of insurance ceded by the taxpayer to any employee (or former employee), director (or former director), or dependant or nominee of the employee or director of the taxpayer. The section also applies where the insurance policy is ceded by a taxpayer to any 'retirement fund'[391] for the benefit of any employee, director or dependant or nominee of the employee or director of the taxpayer.

6.3.16 Expenditure relating to foreign dividends

Section 23*(q)* of the Act prohibits a taxpayer from deducting any expenditure incurred in the production of income in the form of foreign dividends.

The rationale for this change is based on the fact that under the dividends tax regime foreign dividends are either exempt from tax or will be subject to income tax, but at a maximum rate of 20%.

6.3.17 Premiums on certain policies

Section 23*(r)* prohibits the deduction of premiums on policies that cover the person against illness, injury, disability, unemployment or death.

6.4 SPECIFIC DEDUCTIONS ALLOWED UNDER S 11

6.4.1 Legal expenses

A taxpayer who incurs legal costs needs to be mindful of s 11*(c)* of the Act, which provides that—

> any legal expenses (being fees for the services of legal practitioners, expenses incurred in procuring evidence or expert advice, court fees, witness fees and expenses, taxing fees, the fees and expenses of sheriffs or messengers of court and other expenses of litigation which are of an essentially similar nature to any of the said fees or expenses) actually incurred by the taxpayer during the year of assessment in respect of any claim, dispute or action at law arising in the course of or by reason of the ordinary operations undertaken by him in the carrying on of his trade: Provided that the amount to be allowed under this paragraph in respect of any such expenses shall be limited to so much thereof as—
>
> (i) is not of a capital nature; and
>
> (ii) is not incurred in respect of any claim made against the taxpayer for the payment of damages or compensation if by reason of the nature of the claim or the circumstances any payment which is or might be made in satisfaction or settlement of the claim does not or would not rank for deduction from his income under paragraph *(a)*; and

[391] 'Retirement fund' in this context includes a pension fund, pension preservation fund, provident fund, provident preservation fund or retirement annuity fund.

(iii) is not incurred in respect of any claim made by the taxpayer for the payment to him of any amount which does not or would not constitute income of the taxpayer; and

(iv) is not incurred in respect of any dispute or action at law relating to any such claim as is referred to in paragraph (ii) or (iii) of this proviso ...

A taxpayer who incurs legal expenses must meet all of the criteria contained in s 11*(c)* to successfully claim those costs as a deduction for tax purposes. The legal expenses must be related to the operations conducted by the taxpayer and the carrying on of the taxpayer's trade. Where the legal expenses are of a capital nature they are not deductible for tax purposes.

A leading case which deals with the deductibility of legal expenditure for tax purposes is *Port Elizabeth Electric Tramway Co Ltd v Commissioner for Inland Revenue*,[392] which decided that the compensation paid for the injuries sustained by a bus driver was deductible for tax purposes as that amount was so closely connected with the operations conducted by the taxpayer.[393] However, the court decided that the legal costs incurred in resisting the claim for damages could not be deducted for the following reasons:

> Legal costs can sometimes be deducted, as was done in the case of *Usher's Wiltshire Brewery Ltd. v Bruce* (1915, A.C. 433); but they must be so closely connected with the earning of the income as to be regarded as part of the costs of earning it. In the present case they were expended in resisting a demand for compensation; this is not an operation entered upon for the purpose of earning income.[394]

The legal costs had been claimed under s 11(2)*(a)* of the Income Tax Act 40 of 1925, that is, the predecessor of s 11*(a)*, and before the existence of a section similar to s 11*(c)*. In *Port Elizabeth Electric Tramway Co Ltd v Commissioner for Inland Revenue*[395] the taxpayer had claimed the legal costs on the basis that if the compensation was deductible the legal costs should also be allowed. This illustrates why it was necessary to introduce a specific section dealing with the deduction of legal costs. In terms of s 11*(c)* the general rule is that the deductibility or otherwise of legal expenses follows the nature of the underlying action.

In *African Greyhound Racing Association (Pty) Ltd v Commissioner for Inland Revenue*[396] the taxpayer incurred legal costs relating to a commission appointed to consider whether dog-racing should be abolished or restricted. The court held that the legal fees incurred by the taxpayer were not deductible on the basis that the fees were not incurred in the production of income but rather to prevent the total or partial extinction of the activities conducted by the company.[397]

---

392 1936 CPD 241, 8 SATC 13.

393 At 17.

394 At 20.

395 1936 CPD 241, 8 SATC 13.

396 13 SATC 259.

397 *African Greyhound Racing Association (Pty) Ltd v Commissioner for Inland Revenue*, 13 SATC 259 at 263.

The court, in *Joffe & Co Ltd v Commissioner for Inland Revenue,*[398] disallowed the deduction of damages paid by construction engineers relating to an accident caused by faulty construction and denied the deduction of the legal costs incurred in resisting the claim for damages. This was on the basis that the taxpayer had failed to show that negligent construction was a necessary concomitant of the trading operations conducted by the taxpayer and the expenditure had not been incurred for the purposes of the taxpayer's trade.[399] Watermeyer CJ pointed out that the taxpayer's counsel admitted that he could not succeed in claiming the legal costs unless he succeeded with the deductibility of the damages paid by the taxpayer.[400]

In *Commissioner for Inland Revenue v Stellenbosch Farmers' Winery*[401] the taxpayer sought to deduct legal expenses incurred in opposing the registration of a trade mark that may have adversely affected the taxpayer's turnover of a particular type of sherry. The Commissioner disallowed the deduction on the basis that the expenditure was not incurred in the production of income and was of a capital nature. Sutton J decided that the legal expenses were deductible on the grounds that they had been incurred in the production of the taxpayer's income.[402] The court reached the conclusion that the expenses were incurred 'to preserve the dividend earning capacity of the taxpayer, and was therefore a purpose which was well within the ordinary purposes of the trade of the taxpayer.'[403] Furthermore, the court held that the legal costs were a 'business necessity'[404] and that the costs were not capital in nature. The taxpayer faced stiff competition from competitors seeking to sell sherry under the same name used by the taxpayer and had successfully initiated legal action against those competitors. Thus, the court held that the taxpayer was not enhancing its income-producing infrastructure but was rather seeking to preserve and maintain its business, which is not capital in nature.[405] For this reason the legal expenses claimed in opposing the competitor's trade mark registration were deductible for tax purposes.

However, in *Secretary for Inland Revenue v Cadac Engineering Works (Pty) Ltd*[406] the court decided that the legal expenses incurred to interdict the manufacture and sale of a similar product by a competitor were capital in nature. In the *Cadac* case, the taxpayer was of the opinion that Homegas, a competitor, had infringed its design and sought an interdict preventing Homegas from manufacturing its products. The court concluded that Cadac was seeking to eliminate Homegas as a competitor and that the legal costs were incurred to augment Cadac's income-earning structure and were not

CHAPTER 6

398 1946 AD 157, 13 SATC 354.
399 At 358.
400 At 361.
401 13 SATC 381.
402 At 392.
403 At 394.
404 Ibid.
405 Ibid.
406 1965 (2) SA 511 (A), 27 SATC 61.

incidental to its income-earning operations.[407] Ogilvie Thompson JA referred to *Commissioner for Inland Revenue v Stellenbosch Farmers' Winery* supra and recognised that the decision was in conflict with the views expressed by him in the *Cadac* case.[408] He stated that the judges had paid 'insufficient regard to the necessity for linking such costs with the taxpayer's income-producing operations.'[409] When comparing the outcome of the *Cadac* case[410] with that of the *Stellenbosch Farmers' Winery* case[411] it does appear that the legal costs were more closely related to the taxpayers' income-earning structures than their ongoing income-earning operations.

The Tax Court in *ITC 1370*[412] applied the decision reached in the *Cadac* case.[413] In *ITC 1370*[414] the taxpayer applied for and was granted an interdict against a competitor from passing off hacksaw blades manufactured by it as having been manufactured by the taxpayer. The court decided that the legal expenses incurred in obtaining the interdict were capital in nature and were not deductible for tax purposes.[415] This was on the basis that the legal expenses were not closely connected to the taxpayer's income-earning operations but were incurred to enhance the profits of the business by eliminating a competitor, which was capital in nature.[416]

In yet another case dealing with legal expenses incurred in unsuccessfully opposing an application for an interdict relating to the alleged infringement of a copyright, the court in *ITC 1528,*[417] with Melamet J presiding, decided that based on the particular facts the legal expenses were deductible in the taxpayer's hands. The taxpayer initially carried on business as a manufacturer of components of valves and undertook certain repair work. Later it commenced the manufacture of diaphragm valves by copying the valves made by another company. The copying of the valves was done by utilising a process referred to as 'reverse engineering.' The patent previously owned by the other company had expired but that company contended that the drawings used by the taxpayer to produce the valves infringed its copyright. The taxpayer incurred legal costs in unsuccessfully defending the action against the other company and claimed those costs for tax purposes. Melamet J reached the conclusion that the costs did not enhance the income-earning structure of the taxpayer; all that it was seeking to achieve was to be entitled to continue manufacturing and selling the valves as it had done previously.[418] The court decided that the legal costs were incurred to enable the taxpayer to continue with its existing

407 At 76.
408 27 SATC 61 at 76.
409 At 77.
410 27 SATC 61.
411 13 SATC 381.
412 45 SATC 55.
413 27 SATC 61.
414 45 SATC 55.
415 At 57.
416 Ibid.
417 54 SATC 243.
418 251.

income-producing operations and were not aimed at creating an asset belonging to the taxpayer.[419]

In *ITC 1076*[420] the taxpayer, a manufacturer, instituted proceedings against a competitor and claimed damages for alleged false advertising. The costs were incurred by the taxpayer to recover the income lost as a result of the alleged unlawful conduct by the competing manufacturer. The court held that the legal costs were deductible as they were incurred to recover profits lost by the taxpayer.[421] James J stated as follows:

> In our view that intention was to obtain recompense from the competitor for the unlawful erosion of its profits and to prevent the erosion continuing in the future. If the appellant had been successful in recovering damages then it seems to the Court that those damages, which related quite clearly to loss of profits, would have attracted income tax.[422]

Thus, if the damages which may be recovered are taxable, the attendant legal costs would rank as a deduction for tax purposes under s 11*(c)*. The court thus decided that the legal costs were incurred to recover income and were therefore directly related to the income-earning operations conducted by the taxpayer.[423]

There have been a few tax cases dealing with the deductibility of legal expenses incurred by public accountants. In *ITC 992*[424] the taxpayer was a registered public accountant and acted as auditor, secretary, director and public officer of various companies and derived remuneration for the services rendered to those companies. The taxpayer was indicted on charges of fraud and contravention of the Insolvency Act 24 of 1936. He incurred legal costs in defending the charges and was subsequently acquitted. The court decided that the legal expenses were capital in nature and were not deductible for tax purposes.[425] This was on the basis that the costs were incurred to protect the capital of the taxpayer's practice, which is the means by which he derived his income.

Subsequently, on appeal directly to the Appellate Division, in *Smith v Secretary for Inland Revenue*,[426] the court reversed the decision of the Tax Court and decided that legal costs incurred in defending criminal proceedings flowing from the carrying on of a professional practice were not capital in nature.[427] Steyn CJ reached the conclusion that the freedom from imprisonment did not

419 At 252.
420 28 SATC 31.
421 At 32.
422 Ibid.
423 At 33.
424 25 SATC 129.
425 At 130.
426 1968 (2) SA 480 (A), 30 SATC 35.
427 At 42.

constitute a capital asset in the ordinary sense and thus the legal costs incurred in defending the action were not of a capital nature.[428]

For legal expenses to qualify as a deduction under s 11*(c)* those costs must relate to a 'dispute or action at law'. The meaning of 'action at law' was considered by the court in *ITC 1419*.[429] In this case the taxpayer incurred legal expenses in attending a commission of enquiry conducted in terms of s 417 of the Companies Act 61 of 1973. The Commissioner disallowed the expenses on the basis that they had not been incurred as a result of a 'dispute or action at law.' The court reviewed the manner in which a s 417 enquiry is established and conducted and it concluded that the s 417 enquiry constituted an 'action at law' and that the legal expenses met the requirements contained in s 11*(c)* of the Act.[430]

Where a taxpayer incurs legal costs in applying for a trade licence, those legal costs are not deductible on the grounds that the costs are capital in nature, as the licence must be secured before the taxpayer can lawfully commence trading.[431] However, the costs incurred in renewing a trade licence are deductible for tax purposes.[432] The fact that the taxpayer in *ITC 1224*[433] was a large chain store with a significant number of trade licences being applied for each year did not mean that those costs were revenue in nature. The court indicated that the true nature of the costs must be established and where those costs are incurred to secure a trade licence, the costs are capital in nature and not deductible for tax purposes.[434]

Subsequently, in *ITC 1772*,[435] the court had to decide if the licence fees paid by a taxpayer who had been granted a licence to provide a national cellular telephony service was deductible. In addition, the taxpayer claimed legal costs regarding the preparation of various agreements. The basic licence fee payable by the taxpayer amounted to R100 million and the taxpayer sought to claim this over the term of the licence in terms of s 11*(gA)* of the Act. The court decided that the nature of the licence fee did not fall into the provisions contained in s 11*(gA)* of the Act.[436] The taxpayer incurred legal fees relating to an 'infrastructure sharing agreement', an 'interim roaming agreement' and an interconnection agreement. The court reviewed the purpose of the various agreements and concluded that the agreements were aimed at reducing the capital expenditure required by the taxpayer, were closely related to the income-earning structure of the taxpayer, and were not deductible as the expenses were capital in nature.[437] In 2012, s 11*(g*D*)*, discussed in chapter 7,

[428] At 41.
[429] 49 SATC 45.
[430] At 49.
[431] *ITC 1224* 37 SATC 30.
[432] At 31.
[433] 37 SATC 30.
[434] At 32.
[435] 66 SATC 211.
[436] At 217.
[437] At 218.

was introduced into the Act. Had it been in operation when *ITC 1772* was decided, the result might have been different.

Where a Premier of a province incurs legal fees defending an action for defamation resulting from statements made by him in the course of a press conference, those costs are deductible in the light of *ITC 1837*.[438] The court decided that the legal fees arose in the scope of the Premier's employment, which constituted the carrying on of a trade, and that the legal fees were thus deductible under s 11*(c)* of the Act and were not precluded from being claimed under s 23*(m)* of the Act.[439] The Commissioner's counsel seemed to suggest that the Premier had acted unlawfully or negligently and on this basis the legal fees could not be allowed for tax purposes.[440] The court rejected this argument in light of the decision of the court in *Commissioner for South African Revenue Service v Thor Chemicals SA (Pty) Ltd*.[441] The court also decided that the damages paid by the Premier pursuant to the defamation action were deductible under s 11*(a)* of the Act as the damages arose from the inadvertent statements made by the Premier, which were an inherent risk of performing the duties of Premier.[442]

In the *Thor* case[443] the taxpayer incurred legal costs relating to an enquiry into an industrial accident which resulted in certain of its employees suffering from mercury poisoning. Subsequently, two of the affected employees died. The Commissioner argued that the dominant purpose in Thor incurring the legal costs was to protect its goodwill and to retain its clients as a chemical manufacturer. Furthermore, the Commissioner's counsel contended that the legal expenses can only be allowed where it is shown that the taxpayer was not negligent and based this approach on the decision in *Joffe & Co Ltd v Commissioner for InlandRevenue*.[444] Booysen J decided that *Joffe's* case[445] supra was no authority for contending that legal expenses may only be deducted under the Act if the taxpayer is not negligent.[446] The court allowed the legal expenses incurred by Thor on the basis that the risk of negligence resulting in mercury poisoning was closely related to the trade conducted by the company; that the costs were not incurred primarily to protect the company's goodwill; and that the company had met the requirements contained in s 11*(c)* of the Act.[447]

In *ITC 1310*[448] the taxpayer deducted damages paid pursuant to an arbitration award and the related legal costs. The Commissioner disallowed the deductions claimed on the basis that the amounts were capital in nature. The taxpayer,

438 71 SATC 177.
439 At 186.
440 Ibid.
441 62 SATC 308.
442 71 SATC 177 at 185.
443 1946 AD 157, 62 SATC 308.
444 13 SATC 354.
445 Ibid.
446 62 SATC 308 316.
447 At 315.
448 42 SATC 177.

an accountant, had been in practice with two others and chose to leave the partnership. As part of the dissolution of the partnership he was bound by a restraint that prevented him from servicing certain clients for a period of two years. He took advice and rendered services to certain clients in breach of the restraint and the arbitrator appointed to deal with the matter ruled that the taxpayer had to pay his former partners an amount of damages for the fees that had been received by him for the two-year period of the restraint. The taxpayer claimed the damages of R10 758 for tax purposes as well as the legal costs relating to the arbitration. The Commissioner disallowed the expenses on the basis that the amounts were capital in nature. The court decided that the amount of R10 758 was linked to the taxpayer's income-earning operations as an accountant and was deductible for tax purposes.[449] In addition, the court ruled that 95% of the legal expenses qualified as a deduction for tax purposes in terms of s 11*(c)* of the Act.[450]

The decision in *ITC 1710*[451] once again illustrates the principle that where a taxpayer pays damages and those damages are deductible under s 11*(a)* of the Act the concomitant legal expenses are deductible under s 11*(c)* of the Act. In this case the taxpayer, a farmer producing table grapes, employed an employee who went into the bush to relieve himself and at the same time lit a cigarette, which caused a fire to start on another famer's property and which later spread to other neighbouring farms. In the resulting litigation the taxpayer was found legally liable for the damage suffered by the other farmers and was required to pay compensation of R750 000. He also incurred legal costs in resisting the claim for damages. The farmer claimed both the damages and the legal costs for tax purposes and the Commissioner denied the deductions claimed. The matter proceeded on appeal to the Tax Court. Hodes J decided that the risk of an employee causing a fire was sufficiently closely connected to the income-generating operations conducted by the farmer and that the damages were deductible under s 11*(a)* of the Act, that is, the risk or chance of such an event occurring were high in the case of the farmer employing staff who smoked.[452] As a direct consequence of the decision that the damages were deductible the court held that the legal expenses were also deductible under s 11*(c)* of the Act.[453]

Legal expenses incurred by a taxpayer to terminate an agency agreement where the agent did not perform satisfactorily were held to be deductible in *ITC 1154*.[454] The court decided that the legal costs incurred in terminating the agency arrangement did not constitute expenditure of a capital nature and arose from a dispute or action at law directly related to the ordinary operations of the taxpayer and thus met the requirements of s 11*(c)* of the Act.[455] Watermeyer J

449 At 182.
450 Ibid.
451 63 SATC 403.
452 At 409.
453 At 410.
454 33 SATC 159.
455 At 163.

indicated that the taxpayer changed agents from time to time and that the expenses incurred were not capital in nature, but were part and parcel of the ordinary operations conducted by the taxpayer. He accordingly upheld the taxpayer's appeal.[456]

It is appropriate to refer to the decision of the court in *ITC 1677*[457] as that related to legal expenses incurred by a taxpayer involved in the publishing of tax books. A dispute arose between the taxpayer and a competing publisher. As a result legal costs were incurred by the taxpayer and the Commissioner disallowed the legal costs claimed by the taxpayer. The taxpayer incurred legal costs in opposing an interdict sought by the competitor on the grounds that the new tax book constituted an infringement of its copyright. The court held that the legal costs attributable thereto were capital in nature and could not be claimed.[458] Legal expenses were also incurred in relation to the competitor's claim of unlawful competition and whether its advertising had been misleading, and the court held that those costs were related to the taxpayer's income-earning operations.[459] In addition, part of the legal costs related to the interdict against the new tax work and the history and origins of the affected work. It was decided that those costs were capital in nature.[460] Furthermore, it was held that the costs incurred regarding the undertaking given by the taxpayer to withdraw the affected work were not of a capital nature on the grounds that the taxpayer did not seek to protect its copyright in the affected work, and those costs were related to its income-earning operations and thus deductible for tax purposes.[461] This case is significant as it decided that some of the legal expenses were deductible for tax purposes, and that some were not, and directed the Commissioner to review the matter, to apportion the legal costs in accordance with the judgment handed down by the court.[462]

In deciding whether legal expenses incurred by a taxpayer are deductible for tax purposes reference must be made to the specific provisions contained in s 11 *(c)* of the Act and the various decisions of the court which have considered the deductibility of legal costs.

6.4.2 Restraint of trade payments

Despite the fact that restraint of trade payments are usually capital in nature, because they result in the sterilisation of a taxpayer's means of earning income, s 11 *(c*A*)* regulates the manner in which these payments are deducted by persons who pay them to natural persons, labour brokers or personal service providers. On the other side of the tax coin, the recipients are fully taxable on them in the year of accrual.

456 Ibid.
457 62 SATC 276.
458 At 285.
459 At 286.
460 At 286 and 287.
461 At 287.
462 At 288.

The person paying a restraint of trade is allowed to claim a deduction of the payment where the recipient is taxed on it. The deduction in any one year of assessment is limited to an amount which is the lesser of one-third of the restraint of trade payment and an amount equal to the restraint consideration divided by the number of years the restraint applies.

Thus, if a restraint payment of R1 500 000 is made to restrain a person for two years, the person paying the restraint will be entitled to claim an amount of R500 000 for each year of assessment over a period of three years. If the restraint period were five years, the person paying the restraint would be entitled to claim an amount of R300 000 per year for five years. This is despite the fact that the recipient would, under para *(cA)* of the gross income definition, be liable to tax in the year in which the amount is received or accrues.

6.4.3 Repairs and maintenance

Section 11*(d)* regulates the deduction of costs incurred by a taxpayer in repairing or maintaining property used for the purposes of trade. The section provides that deductions will be allowed in respect of—

> expenditure actually incurred during the year of assessment on repairs of property occupied for the purpose of trade or in respect of which income is receivable, including any expenditure so incurred on the treatment against attack by beetles of any timber forming part of such property and sums expended for the repair of machinery, implements, utensils and other articles employed by the taxpayer for the purposes of his trade ...

The determination of whether a particular expense is a repair and thus deductible for tax purposes is difficult, as the distinction between a repair and an improvement to an asset is not always apparent. The courts have over the years considered the matter and have laid down tests which may assist a taxpayer in concluding whether an expense is a repair or an improvement.

In an early case decided in 1930, namely *ITC 163*,[463] the taxpayer had previously occupied the residence and undertook certain expenditure in the form of repairs to suit the requirements of the lessee. The Commissioner disallowed the expenditure claimed by the taxpayer. The court decided that it made no difference whether the repairs were concluded prior to the lessee taking occupation of the premises or were undertaken during the currency of the lease.[464] It was pointed out that the premises were fit for occupation and the court concluded that the expenditure was deductible on the basis that the amount constituted repairs incurred on property from which income was receivable by the taxpayer.[465]

[463] 5 SATC 77.
[464] At 79.
[465] At 79.

The taxpayer in *Rhodesia Railways Ltd v Collector of Income Tax Bechuanaland*[466] conducted a railway operation and claimed the cost of renewing certain parts of the railway track as a deduction for tax purposes. The Privy Council decided that the periodical renewal of tracks which had become worn out constituted a repair and not a reconstruction of the whole railway and ruled that the expenditure was deductible for tax purposes.[467] The court confirmed that the taxpayer did not create a new asset by merely replacing the tracks which had become worn out.[468] The taxpayer had placed additional steel sleepers into certain sections of the railway line and had correctly treated these items as capital in nature.

For an expense to constitute a repair it requires that the taxpayer is replacing something that has become worn out and is not adding something new to the building. This was the difficulty faced by the taxpayer in *ITC 491*.[469] In this case the taxpayer carried on business as a butcher and was required by the municipality to tile the premises that he leased from a landlord. The court decided that the cost of the tiles was not deductible as the tiles were new and did not constitute a repair of any part of the premises which had become worn out.[470] The tiles were required under the municipal bye-laws and not for any other reason, and the tenant derived no financial benefit from undertaking the tiling as he did not own the premises; but it did ensure that he could trade as a butcher.[471] The court concluded that the tiling amounted to a fixture to the property and that the expenditure was capital in nature and could not be claimed for tax purposes.[472]

In *ITC 617*[473] the taxpayer was a club engaged in horse racing and sought to deduct various items of expenditure on the grounds that those items were repairs to the facilities operated by the club. Ingram KC, President of the court, referred to various cases which dealt with the nature of repairs and summarised the following principles to be considered in determining whether an item is in the nature of a repair or not:

- Repair is restoration by renewal or replacement of subsidiary parts of the whole. Renewal as distinguished from repair is reconstruction of the entirety, meaning by the entirety not necessarily the whole but substantially the whole subject matter under discussion.
- In the case of repairs effected by renewal it is not necessary that the materials used should be identical with the materials replaced.

466 6 SATC 225.
467 At 229.
468 Ibid.
469 12 SATC 77.
470 At 78.
471 Ibid.
472 At 79.
473 14 SATC 474.

- Repairs are to be distinguished from improvements. The test for this purpose is: has a new asset been created resulting in an increase in the income-earning capacity or does the work undertaken merely represent the cost of restoring the asset to a state in which it will continue to earn income as before?[474]

The court then reviewed the various items of expenditure claimed by the taxpayer and sought to apply the above tests in determining which items constituted repairs and which were to be regarded as improvements and were therefore not deductible for tax purposes.[475] Thus, where the taxpayer incurs costs in improving the property or adding something to the property which was not there before, that will not constitute a repair. Where, however, the cost relates to fixing or repairing something that has become worn out, that will be regarded as a repair, even if different materials are used to repair the item concerned.[476]

Where a taxpayer incurs expenditure in strengthening the retaining and supporting walls, that cost will probably be treated as capital in nature in light of the decision of the court in *ITC 626*.[477] The taxpayer was obliged by the local council to improve the retaining walls to reduce the risk of damage to his property. The walls needed to be improved and could not merely be repaired as they could not serve the purpose for which they were originally intended. Thus, the work undertaken was not considered a repair and the taxpayer's appeal was dismissed.[478]

In *ITC 637*[479] the taxpayer owned a building which was used as a cold storage facility and which had become dilapidated and dangerous. As a result the building was reconstructed with concrete to replace the cork and wooden structure that was previously in use.

Ingram KC, President of the court, referred to the criterion laid down by Buckley LJ in *Lurcott v Wakely & Wheeler*[480] to determine what is a repair and what is not, which is as follows:

> 'Repair' and 'renewal' are not words expressive of a clear contrast. Repair always involves renewal; renewal of a part; of a subordinate part. A sky-light leaks; repair is effected by hacking out the putties, putting in a new one, and renewing the paint. A roof falls out of repair; the necessary work is to replace the decayed timbers by sound wood; to substitute sound tiles or slates for those which were cracked, broken or missing; to make good the flashings, and the like. Part of a garden wall tumbles down; repair is effected by building it up again with new mortar, and so far as necessary, new bricks or stone. Repair is restoration by renewal or replacement of

---

474 At 476.
475 Ibid.
476 At 479.
477 14 SATC 530.
478 At 535.
479 15 SATC 126.
480 [1911] 1 KB 905.

> subsidiary parts of a whole. Renewal, as distinguished from repair, is reconstruction of the entirety, meaning by the entirety not necessarily the whole, but substantially the whole subject-matter under discussion ... . It follows that the question of repair is in every case one of degree, and the test is whether the act to be done is one which in substance is the renewal or replacement of defective parts or replacements of substantially the whole.[481]

Using the above as a guide the court reached the conclusion that the work undertaken by the taxpayer did not constitute a repair and accordingly dismissed the taxpayer's appeal.[482]

A further case, namely *ITC 651,*[483] was similar to *ITC 637*[484] and the taxpayer failed in claiming the costs incurred on the basis that they were capital in nature. In *ITC 651*[485] the taxpayer reinstated the store which was destroyed as a result of subsidence. New materials were used and thicker walls were built and a concrete roof was erected in place of the original iron roof. The court dismissed the taxpayer's appeal on the basis that the expenditure did not constitute a repair.[486] The taxpayer's argument that the amount that would have constituted repairs should be allowed for tax purposes was also turned down, as no actual repairs were undertaken and the court cannot allow what may be termed 'notional repairs'.[487]

In *ITC 1264,*[488] the taxpayer conducting business as a hotel was required to convert the septic tank system to the municipal sewerage system. The Commissioner disallowed the deduction claimed by the taxpayer on the basis that the expenditure constituted a reconstruction or improvement and did not qualify as a deduction under s 11*(d)* of the Act. Grosskopf J pointed out that the sewerage system was a subsidiary part of the property and that the pipes used in the septic tank system had become worn out and needed to be replaced.[489] The court accordingly allowed the costs incurred by the taxpayer as a repair falling within s 11*(d)* of the Act.[490] This case is an example of the court considering whether the utility of the asset had been improved by the expenditure. The most celebrated example of this approach is *Commissioner for Inland Revenue v African Products Manufacturing Company Ltd,*[491] which was heard in the High Court in 1944. The taxpayer manufactured starch from maize in a process that required the application of great heat to the raw materials in kilns whose roofs were constructed from Baltic pine. In time, the

CHAPTER 6

---

481 At 129.
482 At 130.
483 15 SATC 369.
484 15 SATC 126.
485 15 SATC 369.
486 At 372.
487 Ibid.
488 39 SATC 133.
489 At 137.
490 Ibid.
491 13 SATC 164.

heat caused the pine to deteriorate to the point where it needed to be replaced. Wartime shipping restrictions prevented the taxpayer from procuring Baltic pine, and local pine was unsuitable, so it resorted to using a new technique using concrete to replace the timber roofs. The Commissioner disallowed the cost on the grounds that the new roof was a different and better asset than its predecessor. The court found that the utility of the kiln had not been affected, but that a subsidiary part of the whole had been replaced.

A question that arises in the case of renting out property is when can it be said that the trade commences by the taxpayer? Is it only once the first rental is actually received from the tenant or is it when the property is capable of being let out? This question was considered in *ITC 1475*,[492] where the taxpayer incurred repair costs on property and claimed those costs in the tax year before any rental was received. Section 11*(d)* of the Act requires that 'income is receivable' from the property and the court had to decide what this means. Is it necessary to take account of the fact that no rental is received, not because the repairs were being undertaken, but rather as a result of the fact that the taxpayer was unsuccessful in finding a lessee? Leveson J decided that even though a lessee is not found, despite the fact that the taxpayer had advertised the property seeking a tenant, it does not mean that the property was not lettable and held that the requirements in s 11*(d)* had been met.[493] As a result the taxpayer's appeal was upheld.

Where a taxpayer owns a building and undertakes significant work on that building it is important to retain detailed records of the nature of the work undertaken so that the costs are correctly dealt with from a tax point of view. Where it can be shown that part of the expenditure constitutes repairs to the building, that portion will rank as an immediate deduction under s 11*(d)* of the Act. Where the taxpayer incurs expenditure on fixtures, fittings and plant, those items will be capable of being written off over a period of time in terms of s 11*(e)* of the Act (see chapter 7 for more details in this regard). Those items of expenditure constituting improvements will not be capable of being claimed as an expense immediately for tax purposes but, depending on the particular circumstances, may qualify for one of the capital allowances granted under Act, which are dealt with in chapter 7.

6.4.4 Wear and tear

Section 11*(e)* of the Act allows a taxpayer to claim wear and tear on certain assets and this is dealt with fully in chapter 7.

6.4.5 Lease premiums

Section 11*(f)* of the Act contains provisions whereby a taxpayer may claim lease premiums for tax purposes. These rules are considered in chapter 7.

492 52 SATC 135.
493 At 141.

6.4.6 Leasehold improvements

Section 11*(g)* of the Act permits taxpayers to claim improvements to leasehold property in particular circumstances. These provisions are analysed in chapter 7.

6.4.7 Costs relating to intellectual property

Sections 11*(g*A*)*, *(g*B*)*, *(g*C*)* and *(g*D*)* regulates the deduction of costs relating to intellectual property, which are dealt with in chapter 7.

6.4.8 Relief for leasehold improvements included in income

Section 11*(h)* confers an allowance on a landlord who becomes entitled to leasehold improvements and is considered in chapter 7.

6.4.9 Deduction of rehabilitation costs

Section 11*(h*A*)* of the Act used to regulate the deduction of certain costs incurred in rehabilitating property and was repealed with effect from 1 January 2012. The repeal applies in respect of years of assessment commencing on or after that date.

6.4.10 Deduction of certain mining-related royalties

Section 11*(h*B*)* of the Act deals with the deduction of particular mining-related royalties and is not dealt with further in this text.

6.4.11 Bad debts

Section 11*(i)* of the Act allows a taxpayer to claim qualifying bad debts for tax purposes. The section provides that deductions will be allowed in respect of—

> the amount of any debt due to the taxpayer which [has] during the year of assessment become bad, provided such amount is included in the current year of assessment or was included in previous years of assessment in the taxpayer's income ...

In order to successfully claim a debt for tax purposes it must have become bad and most importantly the amount claimed must have previously been included in the taxpayer's income. It is thus not possible to claim a deduction under s 11*(i)* where a taxpayer advances a loan to another person and is unable to recover the debt, because the loan was never included in the taxpayer's income. The taxpayer would then have to show that the irrecoverable loan falls within the scope of s 11*(a)* of the Act and is not prohibited from being claimed under the provisions of s 23. See further the decisions of the court in *Stone v Secretary for Inland Revenue,*[494] *ITC 1284*[495] and *Commissioner of Taxes v 'A' Company.*[496]

---

494 1974 (3) SA 584 (A), 36 SATC 117.

495 41 SATC 45.

496 1979 (2) SA 409 (RA), 41 SATC 59.

Where a taxpayer sells goods and the customer fails to pay the consideration due, and the taxpayer is unable to recover the debt due, the debt can be written off and claimed for tax purposes under s 11*(i)*. The taxpayer must be able to satisfy the Commissioner that the debt is bad and steps to recover the debt have been exhausted. Thus, the taxpayer would need to show, if called on to do so, that letters of demand have been issued and possibly a summons in an attempt to recover the debt. Clearly where the debtor has been placed into liquidation or has been sequestrated this should satisfy the Commissioner that the debt is bad. It is preferable that the amounts claimed as bad are reflected as such in the annual financial statements and not merely provided for on the basis that the debts are doubtful. If the debts are only doubtful and not bad the Commissioner will only allow the allowance available in s 11*(j)* of the Act and not 100% of the debt written off.

A question arises as to when the taxpayer must establish that the debt is bad. According to the *Income Tax Practice Manual*[497] the determination must be made 'by the knowledge existing as to the debts at the time when the accounts of a taxpayer are prepared and cannot be corrected or influenced in the light of subsequent events'.

Thus, a taxpayer cannot take account of events that occur after the finalisation of the taxpayer's annual financial statements. The decision as to whether a debt is bad must be adjudicated at the time the financial statements are being compiled and the fact that a debtor subsequently goes insolvent will not assist the taxpayer in satisfying the Commissioner that the debt was bad in the previous year of assessment.

The taxpayer needs to retain details of the debts written off as the Commissioner may call for a detailed schedule setting out the debts written off and details of the debtor and the steps taken by the taxpayer before the debts were written off.

Difficulties arise where a business is sold and the purchaser takes over the debts previously due to the seller. In such a case the purchaser cannot claim for tax purposes any purchased debts that may go bad, on the basis that those amounts were never included in the income of the purchaser. The income giving rise to the debt would have been accounted for by the seller but by the time the debt goes bad the seller no longer owns the debt and cannot claim the bad debt for tax purposes.

The above is what faced the seller of a business in *ITC 451*.[498] In this case the seller sold his business to a purchaser 'lock stock and barrel' comprising all of the seller's assets, including the debts. The seller sought to deduct as a bad debt an amount relating to a debt sold to the purchaser. Nathan KC pointed out that the bad debts had become the property of the purchaser and thus the debt was no longer due to the seller and could not be claimed as a bad debt by him.[499] The court stated:

497 Preiss M (ed) *Income Tax Practice Manual* (LexisNexis) para [A:B5] at A-86(1).
498 11 SATC 103.
499 At 108.

> These debts are no longer due to the taxpayer. He has parted with them. He has ceded them in terms of the agreement. The person entitled to sue for them is the new company. The appellant company no longer has any claim to the bad debts. It is impossible to see, therefore, how the appellant can claim to set off as against his income the amount of the bad debts which are no longer his bad debts.[500]

In the result the taxpayer's appeal was dismissed and the claim under the provisions regulating the deduction of the bad debt was refused as the debt no longer belonged to the taxpayer. A similar decision was reached in *Cooper v Commissioner of Taxes*[501] where the seller also attempted to claim a bad debt deduction in respect of debts sold to the seller.

However, in *Secretary for Inland Revenue v Kempton Park Furnishers (Pty) Ltd*[502] the seller was more fortunate as a result of the manner in which the business was sold to the purchaser. The seller sold the assets of the business subject to a resolutive condition that if the purchaser was unable to recover any of the book debts due within a stipulated time period, the seller, as a result of the debts being re-ceded to it, was required to reimburse the purchaser the face value of those debts.

The seller claimed the write-off of the book debts re-ceded to it and the Commissioner disallowed that claim on the basis that the debts no longer belonged to the seller. The court held that by virtue of the book debts being re-ceded to the seller, the seller was the owner of the debts and was entitled to claim the deduction as the amounts had previously been included in its income.[503] Thus, where a seller sells a business to a purchaser it is practice that the debts that go bad are re-ceded to the seller, thereby enabling the seller to claim the bad debt deduction. Clearly, the purchaser would not be entitled to claim the bad debt as a deduction, as the amount written off would never had been included in the purchaser's income.

In *Commissioner for Inland Revenue v Delfos*[504] the court had to determine when certain amounts due to the taxpayer should be taxed. Delfos was a director of a company which was in financial difficulty and was unable to pay him the full amount of the salary and fees due to him for the period 1924 to 1929. However, in 1930 the company paid the accumulated amount due to him. In each of the 1924 to 1929 years of assessment, Delfos had included in his income only the amount actually received by him. The Commissioner taxed the amount received in 1930 in that year and Delfos contended that the Commissioner should amend each of the previous years of assessment to tax the proportionate amount in each of 1924 to 1929, and that it was incorrect to tax the full amount received in 1930.

Wessels CJ decided that the gross amount due by the company to Delfos in each year had accrued in his favour in each tax year but that the Commissioner

---

500 Ibid.
501 18 SATC 259.
502 36 SATC 67.
503 At 71.
504 1933 AD 242, 6 SATC 92.

had allowed the amount not actually received as a bad debt, as there was no certainty that it would ever be recovered.[505] The court considered the position of the amount received in 1930 and held that that fell to be taxed in 1930 as it represented the recovery of the amounts allowed as bad debts in the previous years and that it was not possible for the Commissioner to apportion the amount received in 1930 into that relating to 1924 to 1929 and tax the respective portion in each of those earlier years.[506]

6.4.12 Doubtful debts allowance

Where a debt is not actually bad but doubt exists whether the debt will be recovered, the taxpayer may claim the allowance available in s 11*(j)* of the Act. Before 2019 the section provided for the deduction of—

> an allowance as may be made each year by the Commissioner in respect of so much of any debt due to the taxpayer as the Commissioner considers to be doubtful, if that debt would have been allowed as a deduction under any other provisions of this Part had they become bad: Provided that such allowance shall be included in the income of the taxpayer in the following year of assessment ...

This required the Commissioner to make an annual evaluation of the reasonable amount of the deduction, and in time a practice developed in terms of which the taxpayer would be permitted an allowance equivalent to 25% of the doubtful debts determined in the course of compiling the annual financial statements. From 1 January 2019 the allowance is determined as follows (in all instances excluding leases):

(a) where the taxpayer applies IFRS 9 for financial reporting purposes, the sum of:
  - (i) 40% of the aggregate of: the loss allowance relating to impairment measured at an amount equal to the lifetime expected credit loss; and bad debts written off and not allowed under s 11*(i)*; and
  - (ii) 25% of the loss allowance relating to impairment in respect of other debt; or

(b) if the taxpayer does not apply IFRS 9, the sum of:
  - (i) 40% of any debt older than 120 days; and
  - (ii) 25% of any debt older than 60 days.

In both instances the Commissioner may issue a directive increasing the 40% to 85% after taking into account: the history of the debt, enforcement steps taken, the likelihood of recovery, any security available, the criteria the taxpayer applied in classifying the debt as bad, and such other considerations as the Commissioner may deem relevant.

Any allowance for doubtful debts claimed in one year of assessment must be added to income in the subsequent year of assessment. The taxpayer would then be entitled to determine a new allowance for that new year of assessment.

---

[505] At 100.
[506] At 103.

6.4.13 Additional doubtful debts allowance

Section 11*(j*A*)* of the Act provides for an additional doubtful debts allowance of 25% of the loss allowance relating to impairment as contemplated in IFRS 9, other than for lease receivables, if the person is a 'covered person' as defined in s 24JB(1). The allowance must be increased to 85% of a default as defined in regulation 67 of the regulations issued in terms of the Banks Act, and to 40% of so much of that allowance as is equal to the difference between the amount of the loss allowance relating to impairment measured at an amount equal to the lifetime expected credit losses and the 85% allowance.

6.4.14 Lump sums paid by an employer to a retirement fund

Employers are, in terms of s 11*(l)* of the Act, entitled to deduct contributions made to any pension fund, provident fund or retirement annuity fund for the benefit or on behalf of their employees or for the nominees or beneficiaries of deceased employees.

6.4.15 Deemed deduction for s 8B share schemes

Section 11*(l*A*)* of the Act provides that, where an employer implements a broad-based share scheme in compliance with the provisions of s 8B of the Act, the employer may deduct the cost of the shares awarded to an employee limited to an amount of R10 000 per year of assessment up to a maximum of R50 000 over a period of five years. This section is the only provision in the Act whereby a taxpayer can deduct the market value of shares awarded to an employee as a deduction for tax purposes. Where an employer awards shares to an employee which fall within the parameters of s 8C, the employee is liable to tax on the value received when the equity instrument vests and can be disposed of, but no deduction is available to the employer in such circumstances.

6.4.16 Annuities paid to former employees

Section 11*(m)* of the Act allows an employer to claim as a deduction—

> any amount paid by way of annuity during the year of assessment by any taxpayer—
>
> (i) to a former employee who has retired from the taxpayer's employ on grounds of old age, ill health or infirmity; or
>
> (ii) to a person who was for a period of at least five years a partner in an undertaking carried on by the taxpayer and who retired from the partnership in respect of that undertaking on grounds of old age, ill health or infirmity, provided that the amount so paid to such person is reasonable, having regard to the services rendered by such person as a partner in such undertaking prior to his retirement and the profits made in such undertaking, and that the said amount does not represent consideration payable to such person in respect of his interest in the partnership; or

(iii) to any person who is dependent for his maintenance upon a former employee or a former partner in an undertaking carried on by the taxpayer or (where such former employee or former partner is deceased) was so dependent immediately prior to his death ...

To qualify for the deduction in s 11*(m)* the payment must constitute an annuity. Where an employer makes a voluntary payment to a former employee or a dependant of that employee, that payment will not fall within the scope of the section. Such a payment may, depending on the facts, be deductible under s 11*(a)*. Based on the decision of the court in *Provider v Commissioner of Taxes,*[507] where the employer can show that the payments can be said to induce the employees to enter and remain in the taxpayer's service and the payments are made in terms of the company's settled terms and conditions of employment, they may be deducted in terms of the general deduction formula.

However, in *W F Johnstone & Co Ltd v Commissioner for Inland Revenue*[508] the court decided that the payments made to employees in respect of past services were not deductible for tax purposes on the basis that the amounts were not incurred in the production of income. It appeared that the company did not have a history of making such payments in the past and that the payments were made *ex gratia,* and thus it could not be said that the payments were incurred in the production of income.[509] Thus, the taxpayer should be able to show that making payments to former employees for past services is a policy adopted by the employer and that this contributes to a content and happy work force, which therefore benefits the business conducted by the employer.

The Act does not itself define the term 'annuity' and reference must be made to the cases to establish what constitutes an annuity. In *ITC 768*[510] De Wet J referred to *ITC 761,*[511] where Price J set out the main characteristics of an annuity:

- It is an annual payment. (This would probably not be defeated if it were divided into instalments.)
- It is repetitive – payable from year to year for, at any rate, some period.
- It is chargeable against some person.[512]

Thus, where the amount paid by an employer does not constitute an annuity it cannot be claimed under s 11*(m)* of the Act. Based on the above analysis, the payment must be annual, regular and chargeable against some person. That is, there must be an obligation that the payment will, for example, be made by the employer so long as the employee is alive. Where an employer makes a voluntary payment to an employee, it cannot constitute an annuity and would fall outside of the scope of s 11*(m)* of the Act.[513]

507 1950 (4) SA 289 (SR), 17 SATC 40.
508 1951 (2) SA 283 (A), 17 SATC 235.
509 At 246.
510 19 SATC 211.
511 19 SATC 103.
512 19 SATC 211 at 213.
513 See *Secretary for Inland Revenue v Watermeyer* 1965 (4) SA 431 (A), 27 SATC 117.

6.4.17 Refunds of remuneration and restraint of trade payments

Section 11*(nA)* of the Act provides for a deduction in respect of–

> so much of any amount, including any voluntary award, received or accrued in respect of services rendered or to be rendered or any amount received or accrued in respect of or by virtue of any employment or the holding of any office as was included in the taxable income of that person and is refunded by that person ...

The rationale for this provision is to grant tax relief to those persons who may receive remuneration from an employer and subsequently are obliged to refund to their employer part or all of the remuneration that was received from their employer as a result of a breach of their contract of employment. Prior to the enactment of this section there was no legal basis on which a taxpayer could deduct remuneration or similar payments refunded to an employer or former employer. An example of where this section would apply is where an employee receives a salary from his or her employer whilst studying for a degree and upon completion of his or her studies, chooses not to return to employment and must then refund the remuneration received whilst studying. The remuneration refunded would qualify as a deduction for tax purposes under this section.

Section 11*(nB)* makes a similar provision to allow a deduction where a taxpayer received a restraint of trade payment which was included in gross income under para *(c*A*)* of the gross income definition and is required to refund all or part of that consideration to the employer.

Thus, where an employee receives a restraint of trade payment in one year and later breaches its conditions and is obliged to refund a part of that consideration to the employer or former employer, the refund will rank as a deduction for tax purposes under s 11*(nB)*.

6.4.18 Scrapping allowance 2018 amendment

Section 11*(o)* of the Act deals with the allowance available when a taxpayer scraps certain assets used in trade and is considered in detail in chapter 7.

6.4.19 Premiums on insurance policies

Section 11*(w)* of the Act allows a taxpayer to deduct premiums paid on certain types of insurance policies. The section allows as a deduction–

> expenditure incurred by a taxpayer in respect of any premiums payable under a policy of insurance (other than a policy of insurance that relates to the death, disablement or severe illness of an employee or director of the taxpayer arising solely out of and in the course of employment of such employee or director) of which the taxpayer is the policyholder, where–
>
> (i) *(aa)* the policy relates to the death, disablement or severe illness of an employee or director of the taxpayer; and

(bb) the amount of expenditure incurred by the taxpayer in respect of the premiums payable under the policy is deemed to be a taxable benefit granted to an employee or director of the taxpayer in terms of paragraph 2*(k)* of the Seventh Schedule; or

(ii) (aa) the taxpayer is insured against any loss by reason of the death, disablement or severe illness of an employee or director of the taxpayer;

(bb) the policy is a risk policy with no cash value or surrender value;

(cc) the policy is not the property of any person other than the taxpayer at the time of the payment of the premium; and

(dd) in respect of any policy entered into—

(A) on or after 1 March 2012, the policy agreement states that this paragraph applies in respect of premiums payable under that policy; or

(B) before 1 March 2012, it is stated in an addendum to the policy agreement by no later than 31 August 2012 that this paragraph applies in respect of premiums payable under that policy ...

The section requires that the taxpayer is the policyholder and it excludes premiums paid in respect of an insurance policy taken out solely against an accident as defined in s 1 of the Compensation for Occupational Injuries and Diseases Act 130 of 1993. The premium will rank as a deduction where the policy covers the death, disablement or severe illness of an employee or director of the taxpayer and the employee or director is liable to tax on the premiums paid on the basis that those amounts are treated as a fringe benefit as envisaged in the Seventh Schedule to the Act.

The section also seeks to allow the deduction of premiums paid on so-called 'key-man' policies where the policy insures the taxpayer against any loss flowing from the death, disablement or severe illness of a person employed by the taxpayer. The policy must constitute a risk policy that has no cash value or surrender value and thus the section excludes investment-type policies from its ambit. In addition, at the time the premiums are paid on the policy, it must belong to the taxpayer. It is possible to cede the policy for security over the taxpayer's debts. The cession will not prevent the premiums from being deductible for tax purposes.

6.4.20 Section 11*(x)*

Section 11*(x)* of the Act allows as a deduction 'any amounts which in terms of any other provision in this Part, are allowed to be deducted from the income of the taxpayer'.

The purpose of s 11*(x)* is to ensure that deductions available under other provisions of the Act, that is, other than those found in s 11, such as, for example, an assessed loss brought forward and available for set-off under s 20 or other allowances and deductions not found in s 11 itself, are taken into account in determining the taxpayer's taxable income.[514] In *Sekretaris van Binnelandse Inkomste v Die Olifantsrivierse Ko-operatiewe Wynkelders Bpk*[515] Rumpff CJ expressed the view that s 11*(x)* is an inclusionary provision aimed at allowing deductions against the income derived by the taxpayer and not necessarily from the carrying on of a particular trade as is required under, for example, s 11*(a)* of the Act.[516]

6.5 SPECIALISED DEDUCTIONS AND ALLOWANCES

The Act contains a number of specialised deductions aimed at, inter alia, achieving various policy objectives of the government and conferring relief on taxpayers for some or other reason. These various specialised provisions will be dealt with in this part of the chapter.

6.5.1 Medical scheme fees tax credit – ss 6A and 6B

Historically, s 18 of the Act allowed taxpayers meeting specific criteria and certain thresholds to claim a deduction of contributions to a medical aid scheme as well as qualifying medical expenditure. This was later changed to a system whereby taxpayers may receive a specified tax credit, that is, a reduction in tax payable in respect of contributions to a medical aid scheme, which is similar to a tax rebate.

The credit depends on the number of dependants who belong to the taxpayer's medical aid scheme. The tax credit available for a taxpayer is published every year in the Annual Budget papers.

S6B provides for an additional medical expenses credit in respect of expenses incurred above those taken into account under s6A and for disabled persons and those older than 65. The formula is subject to periodical amendments, so it is advisable to consult the current Budget announcements each year.

6.5.2 Timing of accrual and incurral of variable remuneration – s 7B

Section 7B regulates the timing of the deduction of variable remuneration. It provides that the meaning of 'employee' and 'employer' is as defined in para 1 of the Fourth Schedule to the Act.

'Variable remuneration' is defined in s 7B as including overtime pay, bonus, or commission as envisaged in the definition of 'remuneration' in para 1 of the Fourth

514 *Income Tax in South Africa* (LexisNexis) para 10.1 at 10–3.

515 1976 (3) SA 261 (A), 38 SATC 79. In this case the court allowed the deduction of the building allowance against the interest income derived by the taxpayer. All of its other income was exempt from tax and even though the deriving of interest is not strictly regarded as carrying on of a trade, the deduction claimed was allowed by virtue of s 11*(x)* of the Act. See *Income Tax in South Africa,* footnote 4, para 10.1 at 10–3.

516 38 SATC 79 85; *Income Tax in South Africa* para 10.1 at 10–3.

Schedule. It also includes any allowance or advance paid in respect of travelling expenses, which is dealt with in s 8(1)*(b)*(ii) of the Act. In addition, the definition of 'variable remuneration' includes any leave pay payable by an employer to an employee in respect of leave due to but not taken by the employee.

The section provides that the employer will only be entitled to deduct the amount of 'variable remuneration' when it is actually paid to the employee. Thus, the section seeks to ensure that the timing of the deduction of the expense is only available to the employer when the employee is liable to income tax on the 'variable remuneration' in question. This should ensure the matching of deductions to the employee and taxability in the hands of the employee.

6.5.3 Pre-trade expenditure – s 11A

Without a specific provision to allow a taxpayer to claim expenses incurred prior to the commencement of trade, such expenditure would constitute a sunk cost which cannot be claimed for tax purposes. This interpretation was confirmed by the court in *Borstlap v Sekretaris van Binnelandse Inkomste.*[517]

Prior to the insertion of s 11A into the Act a taxpayer was entitled to deduct certain so-called pre-production interest which fell within the parameters of the since repealed s 11*(bA)* of the Act. Section 11A is wider than the repealed section in that it is not restricted to interest.

Section 11A allows as a deduction any expenditure that has been actually incurred by the taxpayer prior to the commencement of and in preparation of the taxpayer's trade. In order to qualify for the deduction, the expenditure incurred would otherwise have been deductible by the taxpayer. Thus, where a taxpayer incurs expenditure of a capital nature, it will remain non-deductible as the expenditure would not have ranked as a deduction under s 11*(a)* of the Act.

Furthermore, the section will not allow a taxpayer to claim a deduction under s 11A if the amount was allowed under some other provision of the Act.

The section provides that the expenditure and losses incurred by the taxpayer can only be deducted against income derived by the taxpayer from carrying on of a trade. The earning of interest is typically not regarded as income derived from the carrying on of a trade. Thus, where the taxpayer has funds on deposit earning interest, that interest will fall to be taxed and the expenses incurred before the commencement of trade or incurred in preparing for the carrying on of the taxpayer's trade will be carried forward and allowed only when the trade conducted by the taxpayer commences.

In summary, the pre-production expenses incurred by the taxpayer are not lost as a deduction but may only be claimed against income derived by the taxpayer from carrying on a trade and will not reduce income derived in the form of interest or other income which cannot be said to derived from the carrying on of a trade. The pre-production expenses will become deductible once the taxpayer derives income from the carrying on of the trade.

[517] 1981 (4) SA 836 (A), 43 SATC 195.

6.5.4 Research and development

The government introduced s 11D into the Act to encourage innovation and invention in South Africa and sought to create a framework that allows taxpayers to claim enhanced allowances where they undertake qualifying research and development.

The section defines what constitutes 'research and development' and where the taxpayer incurs expenditure directly relating to research and development as defined, the expenditure is deductible under s 11D(2) of the Act. Where the taxpayer meets the strict requirements set out in s 11D(3) or (4), the taxpayer qualifies for a further deduction of 50% of the qualifying research and development expenditure. Thus, if a taxpayer incurs R250 000 on qualifying research and development and complies with the provisions of the Act, the taxpayer secures a deduction of R375 000.

The section confers a significant benefit on qualifying taxpayers and thus contains strict rules to ensure that the expenditure meets the strict criteria of the section. The section sets out in detail the administrative provisions whereby a committee must be established to evaluate the research and development undertaken by the taxpayer to determine whether the taxpayer should receive the additional 50% deduction referred to above. The committee comprises persons appointed by the National Treasury and the Minister of Science and Technology.

The taxpayer can claim relief on plant, and machinery and buildings used for research and development. The allowances available are dealt with in chapter 7.

Taxpayers qualifying for the enhanced relief contained in s 11D must file a report on the progress of the research and development with the committee established under the section. This is to ensure that those taxpayers qualifying for the 150% deduction of research and development expenditure are complying with the strict rules contained in the section. The committee may, in appropriate cases, withdraw the approval granted for the 50% enhanced deduction.

6.5.5 Section 11E and sporting bodies

Section 11E of the Act allows for qualifying sporting bodies, controlled by a national federation, to claim as a deduction certain amounts paid over to an amateur sporting body where that amount will be spent on the development and promotion of sporting activities contemplated in para 9 of Part I of the Ninth Schedule to the Act.

6.5.6 Contributions to retirement funds

Section 11F of the Act provides for the deduction by natural persons of contributions to retirement funds, limited to the lesser of R350 000 and 27,5% of the higher of remuneration or taxable income. For this purpose, retirement lump sum and severance benefits, deductions for qualifying donations under s 18A and deductions in respect of foreign taxes paid under s 6*quat*(1C) are excluded from the calculations of remuneration and taxable income.

6.5.7 Deduction of railway operating losses

Section 11*sex* of the Act allows a taxpayer deriving taxable income from the carrying on of a trade to deduct any compensation paid to Transnet Limited for the losses suffered by it on the operating of a railway line where the taxpayer's liability to Transnet was incurred in connection with the taxpayer's trade.

6.5.8 Deduction for learnership agreements

Section 12H, the so-called learnership allowance, was introduced to encourage employment and the training of employees by their employers. The section operates by conferring an additional deduction on employers who meet the requirements contained in the section.[518]

There are two levels of allowance: where a learner, as defined in s 1 of the Skills Development Act 97 of 1998, holds a qualification of between levels 1 and 6 in terms of the National Qualifications Framework, and where the learner's NQF qualification lies between levels 7 and 10. Where a learner concludes a registered learnership agreement with an employer, and that agreement is concluded pursuant to a trade carried on by the taxpayer, the employer may claim an annual allowance.

In respect of levels 1 to 6 learners, the annual allowance is R40 000, and for levels 7 to 10 learners it is R20 000. In respect of learners with disabilities, the allowances are R60 000 and R50 000 respectively.

In addition, there is an allowance on completion of the agreement. There are two categories of completion allowance. Where the period of the agreement is less than 24 months, the allowances are R40 000 for levels 1 to 6 and R20 000 for level 7 to 10 learners. Where the period of the agreement is for 24 months or longer, the completion allowance is R40 000 for each consecutive 12 month period in the agreement for levels 1 to 6 learners. For levels 7 to 10 learners the corresponding amount is R20 000.

If a learner abandons his or her learnership agreement, the deduction may only be claimed up to the date on which the agreement was abandoned. Clearly, the employer will not be able to deduct the completion deduction, as the learner failed to complete the learnership agreement.

6.5.9 Deduction for cost of shares in venture capital companies

Section 12J of the Act was introduced to encourage investment in so-called venture capital companies. The section allows a taxpayer to claim a deduction of the cost of acquiring shares in a venture capital company as defined in s 12J.

The venture capital company must be a tax resident and its tax affairs must be in order. It must acquire shares either in a junior mining company as

---

518 See SARS Interpretation Note 20 (Issue 4) 'Additional deduction for learnership allowance' 10 June 2011.

defined in the section, or in a qualifying company which does not conduct an impermissible trade. The section defines an impermissible trade as a trade conducted by a bank, insurer, most financial services or any trade involved in advisory services, gambling, or any trade related to liquor, tobacco, arms or ammunition.

The section requires the venture capital company to invest not more than R500 million into junior mining companies or R50 million for other qualifying companies.

The venture capital company is required to provide a certificate to its investors confirming that the Commissioner has approved the company as a venture capital company under s 12J(5) of the Act. This will enable the investors to claim the deduction available under s 12J of the Act.

The section contains a number of definitions and the requirements to be complied with by the taxpayer and the venture capital company in order that the taxpayer may claim the deduction envisaged in s 12J. It also deals with the position where the venture capital company fails to comply with the requirements of the section.

6.5.10 Allowance for energy savings

The Act is being amended more and more to encourage the use of so-called clean energy and to encourage taxpayers to reduce the energy they consume. Section 12L of the Act was introduced to confer on taxpayers an allowance that takes account of the energy saved by the taxpayer.

Section 12L(1) Act provides that in determining the taxable income derived by any person from carrying on any trade in respect of any year of assessment ending before 1 January 2020, there must be allowed as a deduction from that person's income an amount in respect of energy efficiency savings by that person as calculated in sub-s (2) and subject to the provisions of sub-s (3).

Section 12L(2) provides that the deduction contemplated in sub-s (3) must be calculated at 45 cents per kilowatt hour or kilowatt hour equivalent of energy efficiency savings.

In terms of s 12L(3) the taxpayer must procure an energy efficiency certificate from the duly accredited institution. Section 12L(3) prescribes the formula to be used in determining the quantum of the allowance available to the taxpayer. The allowance is not available where the taxpayer receives any concurrent benefit in respect of energy efficiency savings in accordance with s 12L(4).

Section 12L(5) requires the Minister of Finance, in consultation with the Minister of Energy and the Minister of Trade and Industry, to make regulations to deal with certain aspects dealt with in s 12L. The deduction is based on the number of kilowatt hours of energy savings.

6.5.11 Deduction of medical lump sum payments

Section 12M was introduced into the Act to allow employers to deduct certain lump sums paid in respect of medical aid contributions for the benefit of former employees. That part of the section dealing with the deduction provides as follows:

> (2) In determining the taxable income derived by any taxpayer in any year of assessment from carrying on any trade, there must be allowed as a deduction from the income of that taxpayer so derived any amount paid by way of a lump sum during the year of assessment by that taxpayer—
>
> *(a)* to any former employee of the taxpayer who has retired from the taxpayer's employ on grounds of old age, ill health or infirmity or to any dependant of that former employee; or
>
> *(b)* under any policy of insurance taken out with an insurer solely in respect of one or more former employees or dependants contemplated in paragraph *(a)*,

but only to the extent that the amount is paid for the purposes of making any contribution, in respect of any former employee or dependant contemplated in para *(a)*, to any medical scheme or fund contemplated in section 6A(2)*(a)*(i) or (ii): Provided that no deduction may be allowed in terms of this section if the taxpayer making the payment, or a connected person in relation to that taxpayer, retains any further obligation, whether actual or contingent, relating to the mortality risk of any former employee or dependant contemplated in para *(a)*.

The section only deals with lump sum medical payments in respect of former employees or dependants of employees. It does not apply to persons who are currently in the employ of the employer.

The section requires that the amount be paid to the former employee or to an insurer for purposes of securing cover for a former employee or dependants. The expense must be aimed at financing contributions to a medical scheme as envisaged in s 18 of the Act for former employees or their dependants.

Many companies entered into employment contracts on the basis that where an employee retired from the employer's employment, the company's contributions to the medical aid scheme would continue until the person passed away. This resulted in a significant liability for employers and it was previously exceptionally difficult for employers to crystallise that liability and secure a deduction for tax purposes.

Thus, s 12M was introduced to allow employers which meet the requirements of the section to be able to claim the cost incurred for tax purposes.

6.5.12 Deductions from income derived from mining operations

Section 15 of the Act contains specific deductions available to those taxpayers conducting mining operations. The section provides that the allowance available to other taxpayers under ss 11*(e)*, *(f)*, *(gA)*, *(gC)*, *(o)*, 12D, 12DA, 12F and 13*quin* is replaced by the deduction available to mining taxpayers in terms of s 36 of the Act.

In addition, the section allows taxpayers engaged in prospecting for minerals to deduct the expenditure they incur in such operations against the income they derive from mining.

6.5.13 Soil erosion expenditure

Section 17A of the Act allows a taxpayer who leases out land to a person who conducts farming operations on the land to deduct expenditure incurred in respect of the construction of soil erosion works. The expenditure is limited to the taxable income derived from the letting of land for farming purposes. Where the expenditure exceeds the taxable income so derived, the excess must be carried forward and is deemed to constitute an item of expenditure incurred in that subsequent year.

6.5.14 Qualifying donations

Where a taxpayer makes a donation, it may attract donations tax at the rate of 20% in terms of ss 54 and 64 of the Act where the donation is not otherwise exempt from donations tax under s 56 of the Act. However, where a taxpayer makes a donation to a public benefit organisation ('PBO') approved by the Commissioner under s 30 of the Act, no donations tax is payable. In addition, certain PBOs qualify under s 18A of the Act to issue certificates confirming the donation, in which event the taxpayer may claim a deduction of that donation, up to a maximum of 10% of the taxpayer's taxable income, determined before the deduction available under s 18A and lump sum benefits from funds. The taxpayer should receive a s 18A certificate from the recipient of the donation confirming that the donation is deductible for tax purposes.

The section sets out the administrative procedures to be adhered to by those taxpayers which are approved under s 18A, which enables taxpayers to claim the donation made for tax purposes. The deduction under s 18A is specific to a particular tax year and any deduction not utilised in one tax year cannot be carried forward to another year.

If the taxpayer incurs a tax loss in the current tax year or an assessed loss is brought forward, no deduction is available under s 18A as the relief only applies to the taxable income of the taxpayer.

6.5.15 Assessed losses

Where a taxpayer's expenditure exceeds income, the taxpayer has no taxable income and reflects a loss for tax purposes. Under the provisions contained in s 20 of the Act the loss incurred is carried forward and goes to reduce any taxable income derived by the taxpayer in the following year of assessment.

In the case of a company, the company must trade during a tax year to keep the assessed loss alive.[519] If the company suffers a loss in year 1, trades in year 2 and does not trade in any way at all in year 3, the assessed loss brought forward is lost and is forfeit.[520]

The above rule does not apply in the case of a natural person.[521] If a natural person incurs a loss in one tax year and derives no income in the next year, the loss remains available to be carried forward until it is used.

When the tax system moved to the so-called world-wide basis or resident basis of tax, the authorities were concerned that taxpayers might incur substantial losses from trading overseas, which could denude the domestic tax base. As a result, s 20 of the Act does not allow foreign losses to reduce the taxable income derived from South Africa.[522] Unused losses from foreign trading are carried forward and may bet set off against future foreign trading profits. A trading loss derived in South Africa can reduce the tax payable on foreign taxable income.

Should a taxpayer enter into a compromise with creditors, the benefit so derived must go to reduce the assessed loss of the taxpayer where those debts were used to finance the taxpayer's expenditure or an asset and the taxpayer claimed that expense or purchase of that asset under s 11 of the Act.[523]

Retirement lump sums are now subject to a specific set of tax rules. Where a taxpayer to whom such a lump sum accrues has an assessed loss, that loss is disregarded and the tax payable according to the tax table applicable to retirement lump sums will apply.[524]

6.5.16 Ring-fencing of assessed losses of certain trades

Section 20A of the Act was introduced to prevent individual taxpayers at the maximum marginal tax rate from embarking on secondary trades, the losses from which could be set off against the income from the taxpayer's main activity. Certain secondary trades, so-called suspect trades, are treated more strictly than other secondary trades. The first test is if the person incurs losses in three out of any five years. Unless the taxpayer can make a good case for having a reasonable prospect of making profits in the near future, but never for more than six years out of ten, at that point the loss is ring-fenced and may only be set off against future profits from that trade. Suspect trades, on the other hand, are ring-fenced immediately. These are—

(i) any sport practised by that person or any relative;

(ii) any dealing in collectibles by that person or any relative;

---

519 Section 20(1) requires that the taxpayer must conduct a trade for the assessed loss to be set off against taxable income.

520 *SA Bazaars (Pty) Ltd v Commissioner for Inland Revenue* 1952 (4) SA 505 (A), 18 SATC 240.

521 Section 20(2A)*(b)*.

522 Proviso *(b)* to s 20(1)*(a)*.

523 Section 20(1)*(a)*(ii).

524 Proviso *(c)* to s 20(1)*(a)*.

(iii) the rental of residential accommodation, unless at least 80 per cent of the residential accommodation is used by persons who are not relatives of that person for at least half of the year of assessment;

(iv) the rental of vehicles, aircraft or boats as defined in the Eighth Schedule, unless at least 80 per cent of the vehicles, aircraft or boats are used by persons who are not relatives of that person for at least half of the year of assessment;

(v) animal showing by that person or any relative;

(vi) farming or animal breeding, unless that person carries on farming, animal breeding or activities of a similar nature on a full-time basis;

(vii) any form of performing or creative arts practised by that person or any relative; or

(viii) any form of gambling or betting practised by that person or any relative.

Section 20A(3) sets out the objective criteria that must be complied with to satisfy the Commissioner that the taxpayer has a reasonable prospect of deriving taxable income from the trade in question within a reasonable period and that the ring-fencing provisions should not apply. The factors are as follows—

(a) the proportion of the gross income derived from that trade in that year of assessment in relation to the amount of the allowable deductions incurred in carrying on that trade during that year;

(b) the level of activities carried on by that person or the amount of expenses incurred by that person in respect of advertising, promoting or selling in carrying on that trade;

(c) whether that trade is carried on in a commercial manner, taking into account—

(i) the number of full-time employees appointed for purposes of that trade (other than persons partly or wholly employed to provide services of a domestic or private nature);

(ii) the commercial setting of the premises where the trade is carried on;

(iii) the extent of the equipment used exclusively for purposes of carrying on that trade; and

(iv) the time that the person spends at the premises conducting that business;

(d) the number of years of assessment during which assessed losses were incurred in carrying on that trade in relation to the period from the date when that person commenced carrying on that trade and taking into account—

(i) any unexpected events giving rise to any of those assessed losses; and

(ii) the nature of the business involved;

(e) the business plans of that person and any changes thereto to ensure that taxable income is derived in future from carrying on that trade; and

(f) the extent to which any asset attributable to that trade is used, or is available for use, by that person or any relative of that person for recreational purposes or personal consumption.

Taxpayers would have to analyse their particular circumstances with a view to satisfying the Commissioner that, based on the objective facts set out in answer to s 20A(3), the loss should not be ring-fenced.

6.5.17 Limitation of losses on sale of certain assets

Section 20B of the Act regulates the above matter and is dealt with in chapter 7.

6.5.18 Headquarter companies and ring-fencing of interest

Section 20C of the Act contains provisions dealing with the ring-fencing of interest incurred by headquarter companies and is considered in chapter 14.

6.5.19 Deduction of alimony or maintenance

Section 21 of the Act provides that alimony and maintenance payable in terms of divorce orders made after 21 March 1962 are neither taxable in the hands of the recipient nor deductible by the payer.

6.5.20 Limitation of allowance granted to lessors of certain assets

Section 23A limits the deduction of allowances to lessors of assets in certain circumstances and is dealt with in chapter 7.

6.5.21 Prohibition of double deductions

The Act prohibits a taxpayer from deducting an item of expenditure on more than one occasion in terms of s 23B. The section makes it clear that where expenditure may fall into two separate provisions regulating deductions, the taxpayer shall only be entitled to deduct the expense on one occasion, unless the Act confers an incentive, such as the deduction for research and development expenditure in s 11D(8) of the Act, s 23B does not apply. In addition, if a specific provision restricts the quantum of a deduction that would otherwise fall into s 11*(a)*, that specific provision will prevail. Should, for example, a taxpayer qualify for the learnership allowance under s 12H, s 23B will not seek to neutralise such an incentive.

Furthermore, the section makes it clear that no deduction shall be allowed under s 11*(a)* in respect of any expenditure incurred by a person in respect of a premium paid under a policy of insurance, where that policy relates to the death, disablement or severe illness of an employee or director or former employee or director, of the person that is the policyholder, other than a policy that relates to death, disablement or severe illness arising solely out of and in the course of employment of the employee or director. The section also seeks to ensure that if an amount of taxable income is included in the Act under more than one provision it will only be liable to tax on one occasion.

6.5.22 Reduction of cost of certain assets

Section 23C requires a taxpayer to reduce the cost of assets for tax purposes in certain circumstances. This is referred to briefly in chapter 7.

6.5.23 Limitation of allowances on certain assets

Section 23D of the Act restricts the deduction of allowances on assets in certain circumstances and this is dealt with in chapter 7.

6.5.24 Provisions relating to leave pay

Section 23E was introduced to determine when a taxpayer may deduct amounts of leave pay due by an employer to its employees.

The section defined 'leave pay' as—

> any amount which a taxpayer has during any year of assessment become liable to pay to his employee in consequence of the employee having during such year become entitled to any period of leave which had not been taken by him during that year ...

Thus, leave pay comprises the amount payable to an employee by an employer in respect of leave that has accrued in the employee's favour but has not been taken as leave.

Section 23E was introduced to clarify the position and an employer may now only deduct leave pay as and when it is paid to the employee or becomes due and payable to the employee.

6.5.25 Acquisition or disposal of trading stock

A taxpayer is required to account for trading stock for tax purposes in accordance with the provisions of s 22 of the Act. Section 1 of the Act contains a comprehensive definition of what items constitute trading stock for tax purposes.

In essence, anything acquired or manufactured or held by the taxpayer for sale or use in his or her business constitutes trading stock. Section 22 contains detailed rules setting out the costs which a taxpayer must take into account to determine the value of trading stock for purposes of the Act.

The cost of goods and materials acquired by a taxpayer for his or her business qualifies as expenditure which is deductible under s 11*(a)* of the Act. At the end of the year of assessment the taxpayer must establish the value of closing trading stock, which then constitutes income for tax purposes. In the subsequent tax year the value of closing stock is treated as the taxpayer's opening stock and is effectively deductible for tax purposes.

Section 23F of the Act was introduced to ensure that where a taxpayer purchases material for his or her business and may not hold those goods at the end of the tax year, the deduction for that purchase will only be available when the goods are received and are actually held by the taxpayer and disposed of.[525] The section is an anti-avoidance provision inserted into the Act to ensure that taxpayers are unable to claim the deduction of the liability incurred to purchase trading stock without having to include such trading stock in their income.

The section also seeks to prevent the deduction of the cost of trading stock where that stock is disposed of and the proceeds do not accrue in that tax year, but only in a subsequent tax year. Furthermore, the cost of the stock will in these cases only be deductible to the extent that proceeds are received or accrue in favour of the taxpayer.

6.5.26 Sale and leaseback transactions

Section 23G seeks to regulate the deductions and allowances available in respect of assets subject to a sale and leaseback arrangement and is considered in chapter 7.

6.5.27 Limitation of certain deductions

Historically taxpayers entered into arrangements whereby an unconditional obligation was incurred for expenditure and the economic benefit would only be derived over a period of time, possibly a few tax years. In terms of s 11*(a)* the expenditure was deductible as long as it was actually incurred for tax purposes, despite the fact that the services procured may only be received over a few years. This did not prevent the deduction of the expense for tax purposes. Section 23H was inserted into the Act to ensure that so-called prepaid expenditure can only be claimed as and when the taxpayer derives a benefit from having incurred the expenditure in question. The section seeks to match the timing of the deduction of expenditure with when the taxpayer will derive an economic benefit from it.

Section 23H applies to expenditure which is allowable under the provisions of s 11*(a)*, *(c)*, *(d)*, or *(w)*, s 11A, or s 11D(1). In addition, the section will apply where the expenditure incurred relates to goods or service, all of which will not be supplied to the taxpayer during that tax year, or where any other benefit to be derived by the taxpayer for expenditure incurred by him or her extends beyond the tax year in which the expenditure is incurred.

Where the expenditure relates to goods to be supplied the taxpayer may only deduct the expenditure to the extent to which goods are received in the tax year in question. In those cases where the expenditure relates to services to be rendered to the taxpayer, reference must be had to the anticipated period over which the services will be rendered. The taxpayer may only deduct the cost incurred by taking the number of months for which services were rendered over the total period. Thus, where a taxpayer concludes a consultancy agreement

[525] *Income Tax in South Africa* para 11.9.1 at 11–121.

and incurs, say, a cost of R1 million for a period of five years and only three months of services are rendered in the first tax year, the taxpayer will only be entitled to claim an amount of R50 000 in year one, being 3/60 x R1 million.

The taxpayer will then claim amounts of R200 000 in years 2, 3, 4 and 5 and the balance of R150 000 in year 6.

Should the expenditure give rise to any other benefit, the taxpayer will have to apportion the cost incurred by taking account of the benefit received in the first tax year and divide that over the anticipated period over which the benefit will be derived, and the resulting amount will be deductible in the first year with the balance being claimable over the future tax years.

The restriction found in the section will not apply where all the goods or services will be supplied or rendered, as the case may be, within a period of six months after the end of the taxpayer's year of assessment, or the taxpayer will derive the full benefit from such expenditure within that period, unless the expenditure falls into s 11D(1). In addition, the limitation contained in s 23H will not apply where the aggregate of the affected expenditure does not exceed R100 000. Furthermore, the provisions of s 23H will not apply to expenditure governed by s 24K or s 24L. Finally, the section cannot apply where the expenditure was actually paid in respect of any unconditional liability to pay an amount under legislation.

The Commissioner is authorised under the section to challenge the basis used by the taxpayer in apportioning the expenditure between the year in which the amount was incurred and the period over which the benefit will be derived.[526]

Where the taxpayer can show that the anticipated benefit will never be derived the remaining, unclaimed amount can be deducted immediately. [527]

6.5.28 Prohibition of deductions in respect of intellectual property

Section 23I restricts the deduction allowable in the case of affected intellectual property and is dealt with in chapter 7.

6.5.29 Limitation of allowances on assets previously held by connected persons

Section 23J regulates the allowances available to a taxpayer where the asset was previously held by a connected person and is referred to in chapter 7.

526 Section 23H(2).
527 Section 23H(3).

6.5.30 Limitation of deductions regarding reorganisation transactions

Section 23K of the Act seeks to restrict the deduction of interest in certain specific reorganisation transactions and is considered in chapter 11.

6.5.31 Investment policies disguised as short-term insurance policies – s 23L

Section 12L provides that no deduction is available in respect of premiums incurred by taxpayers in terms of an investment policy as defined in s 23L(1) of the Act. An 'investment policy' means a policy which is not an insurance contract as defined in International Financial Reporting Standard 4 of IFRS.

Where policy benefits are received by or accrued to a person in terms of an investment policy, such amounts must be included in that person's gross income. At the same time the premiums paid on that policy which were not deductible under s 23L(2) of the Act must then be allowed as a deduction against the benefits received.

6.5.32 Credit agreement and allowance for debtors

Section 24 was inserted into the Act to grant relief to those taxpayers who conclude credit agreements and comply with the requirements of the section. Section 24(1) of the Act has the result that where a taxpayer enters into a credit agreement by which ownership of movable property or transfer of immovable property is delayed until the consideration has been paid either in part of in full, the full consideration is deemed to accrue in the seller's hands on the date the agreement is concluded.

It must be noted that s 24 is subject to the provisions contained in s 24J, which section regulates the timing of the accrual of interest for tax purposes. Thus, s 24 can only apply to the capital amount due under the credit agreement and not to the interest payable thereunder.

Section 24(2) sets out the conditions a taxpayer must comply with to secure the relief available under the section. If a taxpayer concluded credit agreements which fall outside the scope of s 24(2) of the Act, the taxpayer will be liable to tax on the total consideration payable under the credit agreement with no relief available on the unpaid balance due to him or her.

Where the taxpayer meets the strict criteria of s 24(2), the taxpayer may claim what is referred to as the 'debtor's allowance'. Any allowance granted in one year must be added to the taxpayer's income in the following tax year and a new allowance determined in that year.

The allowance is calculated by taking account of the taxpayer's gross profit, excluding the interest payable under the agreement, and the remaining balance due as at the end of the tax year.[528]

In *Secretary for Inland Revenue v Silverglen Investments (Pty) Ltd*[529] an issue arose as to whether the arrangement concluded with the purchaser fell within the ambit of s 24. Steyn CJ decided that s 24 applied to the agreement for the sale of land concluded by the taxpayer with the purchaser and held as follows:

> There is no substance to this. The meaning of 'amount payable ... under the agreement' is not limited to an amount payable before transfer, and in the case of immovable property it is inappropriate to speak, as in the case of movable property delivered under a hire-purchase agreement, of the suspension of the passing of ownership, as ownership could in any case not pass under an agreement before transfer.[530]

Thus, the taxpayer was entitled to the relief available in the section.[531]

Taxpayers engaged in selling goods in terms of a credit agreement need to ensure that the terms and conditions of those agreements fall into the provisions of s 24, failing which the full consideration may be taxable on the date the agreement is concluded without the relief under the section being available.

6.5.33 Allowance for future expenditure on contracts

Section 24C was introduced primarily to grant relief to those taxpayers deriving income from contracts that may span a number of years. In such cases the taxpayer is placed in funds by his or her client to fund the purchase of goods and services needed to render the services in terms of the contract in place. Prior to the introduction of the section, the taxpayer would have received an amount for tax purposes which was taxable in the first year, even though substantial expenditure would be incurred in future tax years. The taxpayer faced paying tax in the first year and possibly incurring losses in the later years, which was a serious cash flow problem for the taxpayer.

Section 24C was thus introduced to allow a taxpayer who receives an amount in one tax year but under the contract with his or her client is required to use those funds to finance expenditure to render the services to be rendered to claim an allowance for future expenditure.

The section provides as follows:

> (1) For the purposes of this section, 'future expenditure' in relation to any year of assessment means an amount of expenditure which the Commissioner is satisfied will be incurred after the end of such year—

[528] SARS Interpretation Note 48 'Instalment credit agreement and debtors' allowance' 28 July 2009.

[529] 1969 (1) SA 365 (A), 30 SATC 199.

[530] At 205.

[531] Ibid.

(a) in such manner that such amount will be allowed as a deduction from income in a subsequent year of assessment; or

(b) in respect of the acquisition of any asset in respect of which any deduction will be admissible under the provisions of this Act.

(2) If the income of any taxpayer in any year of assessment includes or consists of an amount received by or accrued to him in terms of any contract and the Commissioner is satisfied that such amount will be utilised in whole or in part to finance future expenditure which will be incurred by the taxpayer in the performance of his obligations under such contract, there shall be deducted in the determination of the taxpayer's taxable income for such year such allowance (not exceeding the said amount) as the Commissioner may determine, in respect of so much of such future expenditure as in his opinion relates to the said amount.

For a taxpayer to fall into the section, the Commissioner must be satisfied that the expenditure will be incurred in a future year of assessment.[532] If there is a high degree of uncertainty that the taxpayer will in fact incur the expenditure in question, the section cannot apply.

Furthermore, the taxpayer's income must include an amount received under a contract and either the whole or a part of that amount must be used by the taxpayer to perform under that contract. Thus, where subscribers pay their subscription for a magazine a year in advance and the supplier has a contractual obligation to supply the subscribers with a copy of the magazine on, say, a monthly basis, the section should apply. The taxpayer would have to show the amount received as income and then claim an allowance under s 24C.

The allowance is normally determined by taking account of the taxpayer's anticipated gross profit to be derived under the contract. Where a taxpayer receives amounts in advance of rendering services to clients it cannot be assumed that the allowance equates the amount received. The Commissioner will require the taxpayer to submit a calculation of how the allowance was arrived at and may call for copies of the contract to ensure that the taxpayer falls into the strict confines found in s 24C.

In *ITC 1527,* the taxpayer conducted business as a retailer of furniture. It sold goods to its customers on the basis that customers purchased goods subject to a two-year guarantee. The taxpayer argued that s 24C was applicable to the contracts with its customers but the court decided that there was no certainty that the taxpayer would incur expenditure pursuant to the contracts concluded by it with its customers and the deduction was refused.[533]

The application of the section is best illustrated by way of an example. Assume a taxpayer concludes a contract with a client for the construction of a building which will cost R2 million. The client pays an amount of R500 000 in year 1. The taxpayer expects a gross margin of 5% on the contract, that is, total revenue amounts to

[532] See *ITC 1527* 54 SATC 227.

[533] At 240. See also *ITC 1601* 58 SATC 172 and *ITC 1739* 65 SATC 43.

R2 million and total costs to R1,9 million. The taxpayer incurs costs amounting to R30 000 in year 1. Calculate the s 24C allowance available in year 1:

Gross income		R500 000
Less expenditure incurred		R30 000
		R470 000
Less s 24C allowance		
$\frac{1\,900\,000}{2\,000\,000} \times 500\,000$	R475 000	
Less actual costs	R30 000	R445 000
Taxable income		R25 000

The allowance claimed in year 1 must be added back in year 2.

The section affords relief to those taxpayers in the construction industry and other sectors where amounts are received in advance of incurring expenditure in terms of the contract concluded by the taxpayer with its clients.

The Commissioner has a discretion as to whether the taxpayer will incur expenditure in the future and whether the amount received by the taxpayer will be utilised to finance such expenditure and regarding the quantum of the allowance. The exercise of the Commissioner's discretion is subject to objection and appeal.

6.5.34 Deductions regarding National Key Points

Section 24D grants a deduction in respect of expenditure incurred on so-called National Key Points and is dealt with in chapter 7.

6.5.35 Allowance in respect of future expenditure by sporting bodies

Section 24E is a special allowance for future expenditure available to sporting bodies contemplated in s 11E of the Act which receive an amount of income for an event that will not recur in the following year of assessment.

Any allowance granted in one year of assessment must be included in the taxpayer's income in the following year of assessment.

6.5.36 Toll road operators

The legislature introduced s 24G to regulate the deductions available to toll road operators. The section contains a number of definitions which are relevant to the business conducted by a toll road operator. A toll road operator may only claim the deductions available under the section and not under any other section of the Act.

The section allows the operator to claim an annual allowance of either 4% or 12,5% per year on the assets specified in s 24G(3). The section also contains a ring-fencing rule that allowances and deductions from one toll road cannot go to reduce the income derived from administering another toll road.

6.5.37 Partnerships

Section 24H contains certain rules regulating the manner in which persons conducting business in the form of a partnership are liable to tax and is considered in chapter 10.

6.5.38 Gains and losses on foreign exchange transactions

Section 24I of the Act prescribes the manner in which taxpayers must deal with gains and losses arising on foreign exchange transactions and is analysed in chapter 14.

6.5.39 Incurral of interest in terms of certain debts deemed to be in the production of income – s 24O

Generally, a taxpayer is unable to deduct interest incurred on a loan to finance the purchase of shares as the shares will only generate income which is exempt from income tax. The legislature chose to introduce s 24O into the Act to allow the deduction of interest on the purchase of shares in limited circumstances.

The section applies in respect of an 'acquisition transaction' as defined in s 24O(1) of the Act. An 'acquisition transaction' is a transaction whereby a company acquires an equity share in an operating company and the purchasing company becomes a controlling group company, as envisaged in s 1 of the Act, in relation to that operating company.

An 'operating company' is defined in s 24O(1) of the Act as a company which carries on business continuously and in conducting that business provides goods or services for consideration. It also includes a controlling group company in relation to a company which carries on business continuously.

Section 24O(2) of the Act prescribes the criteria that need to be met for the taxpayer to qualify in claiming the interest relating to an instrument which is incurred on acquiring the shares in the operating company. The instrument as defined in s 24J(1) of the Act must be issued, assumed or used by the company for the purpose of funding the purchase by the company of an equity share in an operating company in terms of an acquisition transaction. The section will also apply where the company issues an instrument in substitution for an instrument which has been issued, assumed or used as required in s 24O(2) of the Act.

Where the company incurring the interest meets the requirements set out in s 24O(2) of the Act, the interest incurred in respect of the instrument in question is deemed to have been incurred in the production of the company's income, laid out for the purposes of its trade, and incurred in respect of an amount received by or accrued to that company that constitutes income. This ensures that the interest is deductible for tax purposes and effectively overrides the provisions contained in ss 11*(a)*, 23*(g)* and 23*(f)* of the Act.

Section 24O(3) of the Act provides that no interest may be deducted if the company referred to in s 24O(2) is not a controlling company in relation to the operating company referred to in that subsection. The section also requires that the controlling group company and the operating company form part of a group of companies as defined in s 41(1) of the Act. In addition, should the operating company cease to be an operating company, the interest deduction will come to an end when the company ceases to be an operating company.

Section 24O came into operation on 1 January 2013 and applies in respect of acquisitions transactions entered into on or after that date.

The section therefore grants tax relief on interest incurred on the acquisition of shares in an operating company. The company acquiring the shares in the operating company needs to have taxable income to fully enjoy the benefit of the provisions of the section. If the company acquiring the equity shares in the operating company is a pure holding company, which does not generate taxable income, the deduction will have no practical value to the holding company.

6.5.40 Redemption allowance and unredeemed balance of capital expenditure for mining operations

Section 36 of the Act contains provisions regulating the deduction of capital expenditure incurred by a taxpayer conducting mining operations. A taxpayer conducting mining operations is entitled to deduct mining capital expenditure as defined in s 36(11) from income derived from mining operations as opposed to only being able to claim an allowance on such assets. The section also recognises that there is a long lead time before a new mining venture will generate income and accordingly allows a so-called redemption allowance to certain mining taxpayers, effectively increasing the value of the capital expenditure incurred by a taxpayer.

6.5.41 Closure rehabilitation company or trust

Section 37A of the Act allows a taxpayer conducting any trade to deduct any amount paid to a company or trust where the trust or company must utilise its funds for the sole purpose of rehabilitating the environment as a result of the premature closure, decommissioning and final closure of a mining operation.

6.5.42 Deductions for environmental expenditure

Section 37B provides for the deduction of qualifying environmental expenditure and is referred to in chapter 7.

6.5.43 Deductions in respect of environmental conservation and maintenance

Section 37C allows a deduction to be claimed for expenditure actually incurred by a taxpayer to conserve or maintain land by deeming such expenditure to have been incurred in the production of income and for purposes of the taxpayer's trade in certain circumstances.

The conservation or maintenance must be undertaken in accordance with a biodiversity management agreement that has a duration of at least five years and is concluded in terms of s 44 of the National Environmental Management: Biodiversity Act 10 of 2004. In addition, the land must be utilised by the taxpayer in the production of income and for purposes of his trade.

The section contains provisions setting out the tax consequences where the land is declared a national park or nature reserve and where the taxpayer does not adhere to the management agreement referred to above.

Chapter 7

Deductions and capital allowances

7.1 INTRODUCTION

Expenditure that is capital in nature does not qualify for deduction in terms of the general deduction formula in s 11*(a)* read with s 23, in calculating taxable income. The Act does, however, recognise that taxpayers should be entitled to relief for normal tax purposes for certain capital expenditure, for example, for assets that diminish in value as they are used in a taxpayer's trade. This relief is granted by way of so-called 'capital allowances' that are available for a wide variety of capital assets used for trade purposes, ranging from computer equipment to vehicles to commercial buildings. Capital allowances are also used as incentives to encourage taxpayers to invest in particular types of assets; for example, the allowance available in terms of s 12C for new and unused assets brought into use by a taxpayer in a process of manufacture is 40% in the first year of use, whereas for a previously used (ie second-hand) asset the allowance is only 20% in that year.

Many of the capital allowances are calculated as a percentage of the cost or market value of the relevant asset. It is important to remember the provisions of s 23C: if the taxpayer concerned is a vendor for purposes of the Value-Added

Tax Act 89 of 1991 (the 'VAT Act') and is entitled to an input tax deduction on the acquisition of an asset, the amount of the input tax deduction must be excluded from the cost or market value of the asset when calculating a capital allowance in respect of that asset.

7.2 WEAR AND TEAR OR DEPRECIATION ALLOWANCE

When determining the taxable income derived by a person from carrying on any trade, a deduction may be claimed of 'such sum as the Commissioner may think just and reasonable' as representing the amount by which the value of any machinery, plant, implements, utensils and articles owned by the taxpayer and used by the taxpayer for the purpose of his or her trade has been 'diminished by reason of wear and tear or depreciation' during the year of assessment (s 11*(e)*).

A wear and tear or depreciation allowance is also available for any machinery, plant, implements, utensils and articles that are not owned by a taxpayer but are acquired by him or her as the *purchaser* in terms of an instalment credit agreement contemplated in para *(a)* of the definition of 'instalment credit agreement' in s 1 of the VAT Act (s 11*(e)*). No allowance is, however, available in respect of these assets for the *seller* (who retains ownership of the assets) in terms of one of these instalment credit agreements (proviso (iA) to s 11*(e)*).

There is a wide range of assets for which a wear and tear or depreciation allowance is *not* available, as indicated in the following list:

- machinery, plant, implements, utensils and articles in respect of which a deduction may be granted under another provision of the Act:
  - para 12(2) of the First Schedule (farming assets);
  - s 12B (assets used in farming or in the production of renewable energy);
  - s 12C (assets used by manufacturers, for the storage and packing of agricultural products, and by hotelkeepers; ships and aircraft and assets used for research and development);
  - s 12DA (rolling stock);
  - s 12E(1) (assets used in a process of manufacture by a small business corporation); and
  - s 37B (environmental expenditure);

  (Section 11*(e)*)
- buildings or other structures or works of a permanent nature (proviso (ii) to s 11*(e)*); and
- any machinery, implement, utensil or article, the cost of which has been allowed as a deduction from the taxpayer's income under the provisions of s 24D (so-called National Key Points) (proviso (iiiA) to s 11*(e)*).

Although s 11*(e)* refers to an amount by which the 'value' of a qualifying asset has been diminished, in most situations the allowance is based on the cost of the asset. The cost is deemed to be the cost which, in the opinion of the Commissioner, a person would, if he or she had acquired the qualifying asset in a cash transaction concluded at arm's length on the date on which the transaction for the acquisition of the asset was in fact concluded, have incurred in respect of the direct cost of the acquisition of the asset, including the direct cost of the installation or erection thereof (proviso (vii) to s 11*(e)*).

Whilst the Act does not specify how a wear and tear or depreciation allowance must be calculated, it is usually calculated by writing off the value of the asset over a number of years of assessment. The Commissioner has published a list of acceptable write-off periods,[1] for example, three years for personal computers and five years for passenger cars.

The amount of any expenditure (other than expenditure referred to in s 11*(a)*) which is incurred by a taxpayer in moving an asset that qualifies for a wear and tear or depreciation allowance from one location to another must be added to the value of the asset (proviso (v) to s 11*(e)*). Effectively, the amount of the moving cost is written off over the remaining period for which the wear and tear or depreciation allowance on the asset is claimed.

Where any asset qualifying for a wear and tear or depreciation allowance is mounted on or affixed to any concrete or other foundation or supporting structure and:

(a) the foundation or supporting structure is designed for the asset and is constructed in such manner that it is or should be regarded as being integrated with the asset; and

(b) the useful life of the foundation or supporting structure is or will be limited to the useful life of the asset mounted thereon or affixed thereto,

the foundation or supporting structure must for the purposes of the wear and tear or depreciation allowance not be deemed to be a structure or work of a permanent nature, but must be deemed to be a part of the asset mounted thereon or affixed thereto (proviso (iiA) to s 11*(e)*).

If a taxpayer used a qualifying asset during any previous year or years of assessment for the purposes of any trade carried on by him or her and the receipts and accruals of the trade were not included in his or her income during those years, the Commissioner must take into account the period of use of the asset during those previous years in determining the amount by which the value of the asset has been diminished (proviso (ix) to s 11*(e)*). This could arise where an organisation, for example, a public benefit organisation, is exempt from paying normal tax but then loses the exemption and becomes a taxpayer.

[1] SARS Interpretation Note 47 'Wear-and-tear or depreciation allowance' 11 November 2009.

7.3 DEDUCTION IN RESPECT OF CERTAIN MACHINERY, PLANT, IMPLEMENTS, UTENSILS AND ARTICLES USED IN FARMING AND IN THE PRODUCTION OF RENEWABLE ENERGY

Section 12B provides a deduction for certain assets used in farming or in the production of renewable energy.

7.3.1 Farming assets

The farming assets that qualify for the s 12B deduction are machinery, implements, utensils or articles (other than livestock) which meet all of the following requirements:

- The machinery, implements, utensils or articles are owned by the taxpayer. They may also be acquired by the taxpayer as *purchaser* in terms of an instalment credit agreement as defined in para *(a)* of the definition of 'instalment credit agreement' in s 1 of the Value-Added Tax Act.
- They are brought into use for the first time by that taxpayer.
- They are used by him or her in the carrying on of his or her farming operations.

The deduction in s 12B is, however, *not allowed* for:

- any motor vehicle the sole or primary function of which is the conveyance of persons;
- any caravan;
- any aircraft (other than an aircraft used solely or mainly for the purpose of crop-spraying); or
- any office furniture or equipment.

(Section 12B(1)*(f)*)

The deduction is also available for improvements (other than repairs) to any farming machinery, plant, implement, utensil or article that meets the requirements of s 12B(1)*(f)* (s 12B(1)*(i)*).

7.3.2 Assets used to produce bio-diesel or bio-ethanol

A deduction in terms of s 12B is allowed for machinery, plant, implements, utensils or articles that meet all of the following requirements:

- The machinery, plant, implements, utensils or articles are owned by the taxpayer. They may also be acquired by the taxpayer as *purchaser* in terms of an instalment credit agreement as defined in para *(a)* of the definition of 'instalment credit agreement' in s 1 of the Value-Added Tax Act.

- They were or are brought into use for the first time by the taxpayer for the purpose of his or her trade.
- They are used for the production of bio-diesel or bio-ethanol.

(Section 12B(1)*(g)*)

The deduction is also available for improvements (other than repairs) to any machinery, plant, implement, utensil or article used for the production of bio-diesel or bio-ethanol that meet the requirements of s 12B(1)*(g)* (s 12B(1)*(i)*).

7.3.3 Assets used to generate electricity

The electricity-generating assets that qualify for the s 12B deduction are machinery, plant, implements, utensils or articles that meet all of the following requirements:

- The machinery, plant, implements, utensils or articles are owned by the taxpayer. They may also be acquired by the taxpayer as *purchaser* in terms of an instalment credit agreement as defined in para *(a)* of the definition of 'instalment credit agreement' in s 1 of the Value-Added Tax Act.
- They were or are brought into use for the first time by the taxpayer for the purpose of his or her trade.
- They are used by the taxpayer in the generation of electricity from:
  - wind power;
  - photovoltaic solar energy of more than 1 megawatt;
  - photovoltaic solar energy not exceeding 1 megawatt;
  - concentrated solar energy;
  - hydropower to produce electricity of not more than 30 megawatts; or
  - biomass comprising organic wastes, landfill gas or plant material.

(Section 12B(1)*(h)*)

Where any machinery, plant, implement, utensil, article or improvement that qualifies for a deduction under s 12B(1)*(h)* (referred to here as a 'qualifying asset') is mounted on or affixed to any concrete or other foundation or supporting structure, the foundation or supporting structure is deemed to be part of the qualifying asset mounted on or affixed to it, if:

- the foundation or supporting structure is designed for the qualifying asset and is constructed in such a manner that it is (or should be regarded as being) integrated with the qualifying asset;
- the useful life of the foundation or supporting structure is or will be limited to the useful life of the qualifying asset mounted on or affixed to it; and
- the foundation or supporting structure was brought into use on or after 1 January 2013 (proviso to s 12B(1)).

The deduction is also available for improvements (other than repairs) to:

- any machinery, plant, implement, utensil or article; or
- any foundation or supporting structure that is deemed to be part of the machinery, plant, implement, utensil or article,

used for the generation of electricity that meet the requirements of s 12B(1)*(h)* (s 12B(1)*(i)*).

7.3.4 Amount of the deduction

The deduction is calculated on the cost to the taxpayer of the asset at the following rates:

- in respect of the year of assessment during which the asset is brought into use, 50% of the cost;
- in respect of the second year, 30% of the cost; and
- in respect of the third year, 20% of the cost (s 12B(2)).

The deduction is granted in the year of assessment in which the asset is brought into use and in each of the two succeeding years.

The deductions allowed in terms of s 12B in respect of any asset may not in the aggregate exceed its cost to the taxpayer (s 12B(5)).

Where any asset in respect of which a deduction is claimed in terms of s 12B was used by the taxpayer during any previous year of assessment for the purposes of any trade carried on by him or her, the receipts and accruals of which were not included in his or her income during that year, any deduction which could have been allowed in terms of s 12B during that previous year or any subsequent year that the asset was used by the taxpayer shall for the purposes of s 12B be deemed to have been allowed during that previous year or years as if the receipts and accruals of that trade had been included in the income of the taxpayer. (Section 12B(4B))

Any expenditure (other than that referred to in s 11*(a)*) incurred by a taxpayer during any year of assessment in moving an asset from one location to another and in respect of which a deduction was allowed or is allowable under s 12B, shall be allowed to be deducted from his or her income in that year (s 12C(6)*(b)*).

7.3.5 Cost of an asset

For the purposes of calculating the s 12B deduction, the cost to a taxpayer of any asset acquired by him or her is deemed to be the lesser of:

- the actual cost to him or her; or
- the cost which a person would, if he or she had acquired the asset under a cash transaction concluded at arm's length on the date on which the transaction for the acquisition of the asset was in fact concluded, have incurred in respect of the direct cost of acquisition of the asset.

The cost includes the direct cost of the installation or erection of the asset.

Where the asset has been acquired to replace an asset that has been damaged or destroyed, the cost must be reduced by any amount which has been recovered or recouped in respect of the damaged or destroyed asset and has been excluded from the taxpayer's income in terms of s 8(4)*(e)*, whether in the current or any previous year of assessment.

(Section 12B(3))

7.3.6 Excluded assets

No deduction is allowed under s 12B in respect of any asset which has been let by the taxpayer under a lease other than an operating lease as defined in s 23A(1), unless:

- the lessee under the lease derives, in the carrying on of his or her trade, amounts constituting income for the purposes of the Act; and
- the period for which the asset is let under the lease is at least five years or a shorter period that is shown by the taxpayer to be the useful life of the asset (s 12B(4)*(a)*).

If a qualifying asset is let by a taxpayer under a finance lease to a lessee that is a taxpayer that derives income, for example, from operating a business, the s 12B deduction is available to the lessor. If, however, the lessee in respect of that asset does not derive income, for example, because it is an exempt public benefit organisation, the lessor may not claim a deduction in terms of s 12B.

Where a lessor of any asset under a lease contemplated in s 12B(4)*(a)* has, within the five-year or shorter period, reckoned from the commencement of the period for which the asset is let under that lease, disposed of the whole or a portion of his or her interest in the lease or of his or her right to receive rent under the lease, there must be included in his or her income for the year of assessment during which the disposal is made a sum equal to the aggregate of any deductions allowed to him or her under s 12B, less a proportionate amount in respect of the expired portion of the lease or any portion of that interest or right which has not been disposed of by him or her (s 12B(6)).

Further, no deduction is allowed under s 12B in respect of the following assets:

- any asset contained in, or forming part of, any ship, if the cost of the asset has been included in the adjustable cost of the ship as defined in s 14(2) (s 12B(4)*(b)*);
- any asset brought into use by a company during a year of assessment if the asset was previously brought into use by any other company during that year and both the companies are managed, controlled or owned by substantially the same persons, and a deduction under s 12B was previously granted to the other company (s 12B(4)*(c)*);
- any asset which has been disposed of by the taxpayer during any previous year of assessment (s 12B(4)*(d)*);
- any asset in respect of which an allowance has been granted to the taxpayer under s 12E (an asset of a small business corporation) (s 12B(4)*(f)*); and
- any asset the ownership of which is retained by the taxpayer as a *seller* in terms of an agreement contemplated in para *(a)* of an 'instalment credit agreement' as defined in s 1 of the Value-Added Tax Act (s 12B(4)*(g)*).

7.4 DEDUCTION FOR ASSETS USED: BY MANUFACTURERS, FOR THE STORAGE AND PACKING OF AGRICULTURAL PRODUCTS, BY HOTEL KEEPERS, FOR SHIPS AND AIRCRAFT, AND FOR RESEARCH AND DEVELOPMENT

Certain assets used by manufacturers, by agricultural co-operatives, by hotel-keepers, ships and aircraft, and assets used for research and development qualify for a deduction in terms of s 12C rather than for a wear and tear or depreciation allowance in terms of s 11*(e)*.

7.4.1 Qualifying assets

7.4.1.1 Manufacturing assets

Machinery or plant qualifies for the s 12C deduction if the following requirements are all met:

- The machinery or plant is owned by the taxpayer. It can also be acquired by the taxpayer as the purchaser in terms of an instalment credit agreement (as defined in para *(a)* of the definition of 'instalment credit agreement' in s 1 of the Value-Added Tax Act).
- The machinery or plant was or is brought into use for the first time by the taxpayer for the purposes of his or her trade (other than mining or farming).
- The machinery or plant is used by him or her directly in a process of manufacture carried on by him or her or any other process carried on by him or her which in the opinion of the Commissioner is of a similar nature. (Section 12C(1)*(a)*)

The deduction is also available for machinery and plant that meet the first requirement above but that are let by the taxpayer and that:

- were or are brought into use for the first time by the lessee for the purposes of the lessee's trade (other than mining or farming); and
- are used by the lessee directly in a process of manufacture carried on by him or her or any other process carried on by him or her which in the opinion of the Commissioner is of a similar nature. (Section 12C(1)*(b)*)

7.4.1.2 Assets used by an agricultural co-operative

Machinery or plant used by an agricultural co-operative that is registered or deemed to be incorporated under the Co-operatives Act 91 of 1981, or registered under the Co-operatives Act 14 of 2005, qualifies for the s 12C deduction if the following requirements are all met:

- The machinery or plant is owned by the taxpayer. It can also be acquired by the taxpayer as the purchaser in terms of an instalment credit agreement (as defined in para *(a)* of the definition of 'instalment credit agreement' in s 1 of the Value-Added Tax Act).

- The machinery or plant was or is brought into use for the first time by the agricultural co-operative.
- The machinery or plant is used by the agricultural co-operative directly for storing or packing pastoral, agricultural or other farm products of its members (including any person who is a member of another agricultural co-operative which is itself a member of that agricultural co-operative) or for subjecting the products to a primary process as defined in s 27(9). (Section 12C(1)*(c)*)

7.4.1.3 Equipment used by hotel keepers

Machinery, implements, utensils or articles ('hotel equipment') used by hotel keepers qualify for the s 12C deduction if the following requirements are both met:

- The hotel equipment is owned by the taxpayer. It can also be acquired by the taxpayer as the purchaser in terms of an instalment credit agreement (as defined in para *(a)* of the definition of 'instalment credit agreement' in s 1 of the Value-Added Tax Act).
- The hotel equipment was or is brought into use for the first time by the taxpayer for the purposes of his or her trade as hotel keeper and is used by him or her in a hotel.

A hotel keeper is any person carrying on the business of hotel keeper or boarding or lodging house keeper where meals and sleeping accommodation are supplied to others for money or its equivalent (definition of 'hotel keeper' in s 1).

The deduction is not, however, available for any vehicle or equipment for offices or managers' or servants' rooms.

(Section 12C(1)*(d)*)

The allowance is also available for hotel equipment that meets the first requirement above but that is let by the taxpayer and that:

- was or is brought into use for the first time by the lessee for the purposes of the lessee's trade as hotel keeper; and
- is used by the lessee in a hotel.

The deduction for leased hotel equipment used by a hotel keeper is also not available for any vehicle or equipment for offices or managers' or servants' rooms.

(Section 12C(1)*(e)*)

7.4.1.4 Aircraft

A deduction under s 12C is available for an aircraft if the following requirements are both met:

- The aircraft is owned by the taxpayer. It can also be acquired by the taxpayer as the purchaser in terms of an instalment credit agreement (as defined in para *(a)* of the definition of 'instalment credit agreement' in s 1 of the Value-Added Tax Act).
- The aircraft was or is brought into use for the first time by the taxpayer for the purposes of the taxpayer's trade.

A deduction under s 12C is, however, not available for an aircraft in respect of which an allowance has been granted to the taxpayer under s 12B (for example, an aircraft used in farming operations) or s 14*bis* (which provided for a now obsolete allowance for aircraft).

(Section 12C(1)*(f)*)

7.4.1.5 Ships

A deduction under s 12C is available for a ship if the following requirements are both met:

- The ship is owned by the taxpayer. It can also be acquired by the taxpayer as the purchaser in terms of an instalment credit agreement (as defined in para *(a)* of the definition of 'instalment credit agreement' in s 1 of the Value-Added Tax Act).
- The ship was or is brought into use for the first time by the taxpayer for the purposes of his or her trade.

A deduction under s 12C is, however, not available for a ship in respect of which an allowance has been granted to the taxpayer under s 14(1)*(a)* or *(b)* (which provided for a now obsolete allowance for ships).

(Section 12C(1)*(g)*)

7.4.1.6 Assets used for research and development

Machinery or plant used for purposes of research and development qualifies for the s 12C deduction if the following requirements are all met:

- The machinery or plant is owned by the taxpayer. It can also be acquired by the taxpayer as the purchaser in terms of an instalment credit agreement (as defined in para *(a)* of the definition of 'instalment credit agreement' in s 1 of the Value-Added Tax Act).
- The machinery or plant is new or unused.
- The machinery or plant is first brought into use by the taxpayer for the purposes of research and development as defined in s 11D. (Section 12C(1)*(gA)*)

The proviso *(d)* to s 12C(1) sets out additional requirements for plant or machinery (or improvements to plant and machinery (see below)) that is used for research and development:

- The machinery, plant or improvement is or was acquired by the taxpayer under an agreement formally and finally signed by every party to the agreement on or after 1 January 2012.
- The machinery, plant or improvement is or was brought into use by the taxpayer on or after 1 January 2012 for the purpose of research and development.

The s 12C deduction is available for expenditure incurred in respect of research and development on or after 1 April 2012 or a later date determined by the Minister of Finance by notice in the *Gazette,* but before 1 April 2022.

7.4.1.7 Improvements

A deduction in terms of s 12C can be claimed on improvements (other than repairs) to any machinery, plant, implement, utensil or article referred to in s 12C(1)*(a)*, *(b)*, *(c)*, *(d)*, *(e)* or *(g*A*)*, which are acquired and brought into use during the relevant year of assessment for the purposes contemplated in those paragraphs (s 12C(1)*(h)*).

7.4.1.8 Foundations and supporting structures

Where any asset qualifying for a s 12C allowance is mounted on or affixed to any concrete or other foundation or supporting structure and:

(a) the foundation or supporting structure is designed for the asset and is constructed in such manner that it is or should be regarded as being integrated with the asset; and

(b) the useful life of the foundation or supporting structure is or will be limited to the useful life of the asset mounted thereon or affixed thereto,

the foundation or supporting structure must be deemed to be a part of the asset mounted thereon or affixed thereto (further proviso to s 12C(1)).

7.4.1.9 Machinery, plant, implements, utensils and articles

The Act does not define what is meant by the words 'machinery', 'plant', 'implements', 'utensils' and 'articles'. It is therefore necessary to refer to case law for guidance.

When determining whether an asset qualifies as an asset of the types listed, a useful test is the functional test: ask the question 'in what way is the asset used by the taxpayer in his business?'[2]

[2] *Blue Circle Cement Ltd v CIR* 1984 (2) SA 764 (A), 46 SATC 21 at 32.

Another helpful test is the durability test. To qualify as an asset of the type listed, the asset must display some degree of durability: it must be used by the taxpayer for a period of time.[3]

Examples of assets that passed these tests are:

- a railway line 41 km in length from a quarry to a processing plant (this was held to be plant);[4]
- movable partitions used in a building (these were held to be articles);[5] and
- cutting knives and lasts used by a manufacturer of shoes for a minimum period of two to three years (these were held to be plant).[6]

7.4.1.10 Process of manufacture and similar processes

The term 'process of manufacture' is not defined in the Act: the courts have therefore, on a number of occasions, considered whether an asset is used directly in a process of manufacture. The decisions handed down in these cases provide useful principles that can be used in determining whether a particular process is one of manufacture or not, and whether the relevant asset is used directly in the process of manufacture.

In *SIR v Safranmark (Pty) Ltd*[7] Galgut JA agreed with the statements of Miller J in *ITC 1247*:[8]

> That the ordinary connotation of the term 'process of manufacture' is an action or series of actions directed to the production of an object or thing which is different from the materials or components which went into its making, appears to have been generally accepted. The emphasis has been laid on the difference between the original material and the finished product ... Invariably, in cases in which plant or machinery has been found to have been used in a process of manufacture, the result of such process has been the creation of a substance or an article which, although it might have contained all the various components from which it evolved in the process of manufacture, became upon completion an essentially different entity in its own right.

In *Safranmark* the process undertaken by the taxpayer in producing Kentucky Fried Chicken was held[9] to be a process of manufacture.

In *COT v Processing Enterprises (Pvt) Ltd*[10] it was stated:[11]

> A manufacturing process need not necessarily produce the end product provided it is an essential stage in the final production of that end product, or an important stage in the final production of that end product.

---

3 *ITC 1234* 37 SATC 188 at 191.

4 *Blue Circle Cement Ltd v CIR* (see above) 32.

5 *SIR v Charkay Properties (Pty) Ltd* 1976 (4) SA 872 (A), 38 SATC 159 at 166.

6 *ITC 1468* 52 SATC 32 at 40.

7 1982 (1) SA 113 (A), 43 SATC 235 at 246.

8 38 SATC 27 at 31 and 32.

9 At 248.

10 1975 (2) SA 213 (RA), 37 SATC 109.

11 At 113.

In *CIR v Stellenbosch Farmers' Winery Ltd*[12] Tebbutt J considered whether tankers used to transport wine from the taxpayer's suppliers to its own premises were used 'directly' in a process of manufacture. He stated[13] that the process of manufacture—

> clearly starts at the supplier's tanks when the wine is mixed in the latter's 'dispatch tank', or in the process of filling the tankers or in the tankers themselves ... [the tankers] are used directly in the process of manufacture.

In contrast, the taxpayer in *National Co-operative Dairies Limited v CIR*[14] was not successful in showing that its tankers that were used to transport milk to its depots, were used directly in a process of manufacture (the pasteurisation of milk). It was held[15] that the process of manufacture started only at the taxpayer's depots.

Practice Note 42 lists those processes that the Commissioner considers to be processes of a similar nature to manufacture. Examples of similar processes include the drying of biltong; the filming and processing of motion pictures; panel beating and spray painting; and dry cleaning.

7.4.1.11 Amount of the deduction

The s 12C deduction is equal to 20% of the cost to the taxpayer to acquire the qualifying asset (machinery, plant, implement, utensil, article, ship, aircraft or improvement) in the year of assessment during which the asset is brought into use and in each of the four succeeding years of assessment (s 12C(1)).

If the asset is a ship or aircraft, the deduction is calculated on the adjustable cost as determined in terms of s 14 or s 14*bis* (proviso *(a)* to s 12C(1)). The adjustable cost means the cost to the taxpayer of the ship or aircraft or, in respect of a replacement ship or aircraft, the cost less any recovery or recoupment in respect of the replaced ship or aircraft that was deferred.

The deduction for any new or unused qualifying machinery or plant used by a taxpayer in his or her process of manufacture or similar process or any improvement to qualifying plant or machinery that:

(a) is or was acquired by the taxpayer under an agreement formally and finally signed by every party to the agreement on or after 1 March 2002; and

(b) is brought into use by the taxpayer on or after that date in that process of manufacture or similar process, carried on by him or her in the course of his or her business other than banking, financial services, insurance or rental business,

[12] 1989 (4) SA 772 (C), (1988) 51 SATC 81.
[13] At 782, 92.
[14] 1992 (1) SA 694 (A), 54 SATC 1 (A).
[15] At 6.

is increased to 40% of the cost to that taxpayer of that machinery, plant or improvement in respect of the year of assessment during which the plant, machinery or improvement was or is so brought into use for the first time and is 20% in each of the three subsequent years of assessment (proviso *(c)* to s 12C(1)). The s 12C deduction may be claimed in full for a particular year of assessment even if the relevant asset is used for only one month or one day during that year and the deduction need not be apportioned, as is the case with the wear and tear or depreciation allowance.

The deductions allowed in terms of s 12C and s 11*(o)* in respect of any asset shall not in the aggregate exceed the cost to the taxpayer of the asset.

(Section 12C(5))

Where any asset in respect of which a deduction is claimed in terms of s 12C was during any previous year of assessment used by the taxpayer for the purposes of any trade carried on by him or her, the receipts and accruals of which were not included in his or her income during that year, any deduction which could have been allowed in terms of s 12C during that previous year or any subsequent year that the asset was used by the taxpayer shall for the purposes of s 12C be deemed to have been allowed during that previous year or years as if the receipts and accruals of that trade had been included in his or her income (s 12C(4A)).

Any expenditure (other than that referred to in s 11*(a)*) incurred by a taxpayer during any year of assessment in *moving an asset* from one location to another and in respect of which a deduction was allowed or is allowable under s 12C shall:

- where the taxpayer is entitled to a deduction in respect of the asset under s 12C(1) in that year and one or more succeeding years, be allowed to be deducted from his or her income in equal instalments in each year in which the deduction is allowable; and
- in any other case, be allowed to be deducted from his or her income in that year (s 12C(6)).

7.4.1.12 Brought into use for the first time

The requirement that an asset must be brought into use by the relevant taxpayer for the first time means that second-hand assets acquired by a taxpayer and brought into use by him or her for the second time do not qualify for the s 12C deduction. An example of this situation is when a previously leased and used asset is acquired by a taxpayer on the termination of the lease.

7.4.1.13 Cost of an asset

For the purposes of calculating the s 12C deduction, the cost to a taxpayer of any asset shall be deemed to be the lesser of:

- the actual cost to the taxpayer to acquire that asset; or

- the cost that a person would, if he or she had acquired that asset under a cash transaction concluded at arm's length on the date on which the transaction for the acquisition of that asset was in fact concluded, have incurred in respect of the direct cost of acquisition of the asset.

The cost of the asset includes the direct cost of the installation or erection thereof.

Where the asset has been acquired to replace an asset that has been damaged or destroyed, the cost must be reduced by any amount which has been recovered or recouped in respect of the damaged or destroyed asset and has been excluded from the taxpayer's income in terms of s 8(4)*(e)*, whether in the current or any previous year of assessment.

(Section 12C(2))

7.4.1.14 Excluded assets

No deduction is allowed under s 12C in respect of the following assets:

- any asset contained in, or forming part of, any ship, if the cost of the asset has been included in the adjustable cost of the ship as defined in s 14(2) (s 12C(3)*(b)*);
- any asset which has been disposed of by the taxpayer during any previous year of assessment (s 12C(3)*(c)*);
- any asset in respect of which an allowance has been granted to the taxpayer under s 12E (an asset of a small business corporation) (s 12C(3)*(d)*);
- any asset the ownership of which is retained by the taxpayer as a *seller* in terms of an agreement contemplated in para *(a)* of an 'instalment credit agreement' as defined in s 1 of the Value-Added Tax Act (s 12C(3)*(e)*); or
- any asset which has been let by the taxpayer under a lease other than an operating lease as defined in s 23A(1), unless the lessee under the lease derives, in the carrying on of his or her trade, amounts constituting income for the purposes of the Act (s 12C(3)*(a)*). If a qualifying asset is let by a taxpayer under a finance lease to a lessee, that is, a taxpayer that derives income, for example, from operating a business, the s 12C deduction is available to the lessor. If, however, the lessee in respect of that asset does not derive income, for example, because it is an exempt public benefit organisation, the lessor may not claim a deduction in terms of s 12C.

CHAPTER 7

Example

MNO Ltd acquired a new and unused machine on 1 July 2014 and brought it into use on that date in a process of manufacture. The cost of the machine was R1 140 000 (including VAT of R140 000) and the cost of installing the machine on the factory floor was R57 000 (including VAT of R7 000). MNO Ltd is a registered VAT vendor.

Calculate the amount of the s 12C deduction that MNO Ltd may claim in respect of the new machine for its years of assessment ending 31 December 2014, 2015, 2016, 2017 and 2018, assuming that the machine continues to be used by it during each of those years.

Solution

The cost of the machine for the purposes of claiming the s 12C allowance is R1 050 000 (cost of R1 140 000 × 100/115 + installation cost of R57 000 × 100/115).

Year of assessment ending 31 December	Section 12C deduction	Comment
2014	R420 000	In the year that the machine is brought into use the deduction is 40% × R1 050 000. The deduction is claimed in full and is not apportioned even though the machine was not used for a full year.
2015	R210 000	In subsequent years the deduction is 20% × R1 050 000
2016	R210 000	In subsequent years the deduction is 20% × R1 050
2017	R210 000	In subsequent years the deduction is 20% × R1 050 000
2018	RNil	The aggregate deduction in terms of s 12C is limited to the amount of the original cost.

7.5 DISPOSALS OF ASSETS

When a taxpayer disposes of a capital asset, the provisions of ss 11*(o)*, 20B and 24M(1) may apply to the disposal.

7.5.1 Section 11*(o)* deduction

When an amount is received by or accrues to a taxpayer from the alienation, loss or destruction (referred to here as a disposal) of a depreciable asset that qualified for certain allowances or deductions in the year of assessment of the disposal or a previous year of assessment, the taxpayer may elect to claim a deduction in terms of s 11*(o)*, provided that the following requirements are both met:

- The asset must be a depreciable asset which qualified for an allowance or deduction in terms of the following sections:
  - 11*(e)* (wear and tear allowance);
  - 11D (scientific or technological research and development);
  - 12B (assets used in farming operations and in generating renewable energy);
  - 12C (assets used by manufacturers; for the storage and packing of agricultural products; by hotel keepers; ships and aircraft; and assets used for research and development);
  - 12DA (rolling stock);
  - 12E (small business corporation assets); or
  - 37B(2)*(a)* (environmental expenditure). (Section 11*(o)*(i))

  A depreciable asset is an asset as defined in para 1 of the Eighth Schedule, other than any trading stock and any debt, in respect of which a deduction or allowance determined wholly or partly with reference to the cost or value of that asset is allowable in terms of the Act for purposes other than the determination of any capital gain or capital loss (definition of 'depreciable asset' in s 1).
- The expected useful life of the asset for tax purposes did not exceed ten years as determined on the date of original acquisition (s 11*(o)*(ii)).

  No election may be made by a taxpayer if the amount received or accrued from the alienation, loss or destruction of the asset was received or accrued from a person that is a connected person in relation to him or her (further proviso to s 11*(o)*).

  The allowance is the amount by which the cost to the taxpayer of the depreciable asset exceeds the sum of:
  - the amount received or accrued from the disposal of that asset; and
  - the amount of any allowance or deduction allowed in respect of that asset in the year of disposal or any previous year of assessment and any allowance or deduction deemed to have been allowed in terms of s 12B(4B), s 12C(4A), s 12DA(4) or 37B(4) or taken into account in terms of s 11*(e)*(ix).

The cost of any plant, machinery, implements, utensils or articles is deemed to be the actual cost plus the amount by which the value of the asset has been increased in respect of moving costs in terms of proviso (v) to s 11*(e)* (proviso *(aa)* to s 11*(o)*).

The actual cost of any plant, machinery, implement, utensil or article acquired by the taxpayer is deemed to be the cost of that asset as determined under proviso (vii) to s 11*(e)* (proviso *(bb)* to s 11*(o)*).

CHAPTER 7

7.5.2 Section 20B limitation on losses from the disposal of assets

If a person has disposed of an asset in any year of assessment and the full consideration from that disposal will not accrue to him or her during that year, any deduction which is allowable in that year of assessment under s 11*(o)* in respect of that disposal by him or her must be disregarded in that year (s 20B(1)).

In any subsequent year of assessment, so much of any amount disregarded in terms of s 20B(1) which has not otherwise been allowed as a deduction, may be deducted from the income of that person to the extent that any consideration which is received by or accrued to him or her in that subsequent year from that disposal is included in his or her income (s 20B(2)).

If during any year of assessment a person who has had to disregard a s 11*(o)* deduction in terms of s 20B(1) proves that no further consideration will accrue to him or her in that year and any subsequent year, so much of the amount which was disregarded in terms of s 20B(1) as has not been allowed as a deduction in any year, must be allowed as a deduction from his or her income in that year of assessment (s 20B(3)).

7.5.3 Section 24M – assets acquired or disposed of for unquantifiable amounts

If an asset has been disposed of by a person for consideration which consists of or includes an amount which cannot be quantified in that year of assessment, then the accrual of the unquantifiable amount is deferred. The portion of the consideration that:

- cannot be quantified in the year of disposal must be deemed not to have accrued to him or her in that year; and
- becomes quantifiable during any subsequent year of assessment must be deemed to have accrued to him or her from that disposal in that subsequent year. (Section 24M(1))

A similar provision in s 24M(2) defers the incurral of unquantifiable expenditure in the hands of the person who acquires an asset.

These provisions are often referred to as the 'open transaction' method.

The deferred accruals and incurrals must be taken into consideration when determining the amount of any deduction in respect of the asset (s 24M(4)) or any recovery or recoupment of any deductions in respect of the asset (s 24M(3)).[16]

[16] This example is based on an example in the Explanatory Memorandum on the Revenue Laws Amendment Bill 2004.

Example (ss 11(o), 20B and 24M)[16]

ABC Ltd acquired and brought into use a manufacturing machine in July 2015 at a cost of R500 000, excluding VAT. After claiming a s 12C deduction for the machine of R200 000 (R500 000 × 40%) in its year of assessment ending 31 December 2015, it sold the machine to DEF Ltd on 1 January 2016. In terms of the contract of sale, DEF Ltd must pay 10% of the value of the products produced by the machine for five years subsequent to the sale of the machine. Assume that the amounts eventually received are R190 000, R40 000, R250 000, R280 000 and R240 000, starting in 2016.

Calculate the tax consequences of the disposal of the machine and the subsequent receipts in the hands of ABC Ltd for its years of assessment ending on 31 December 2016, 2017, 2018, 2019 and 2020.

Solution

The open transaction rules of s 24M apply because unquantified payments are involved.

In the 2016 year of assessment a R110 000 s 11*(o)* loss will be triggered for ABC Ltd but will be suspended in terms of s 20B(1) as the full consideration does not accrue in that year. The suspended s 11*(o)* loss is calculated as follows:

Cost of machine		R500 000
Less: sum of		
Amount received	R190 000	
Section 12C deduction	R200 000	R390 000
Suspended s 11*(o)* loss		R110 000

This suspended loss will be offset against income in subsequent years (s 20B(2)).

In the 2017 year of assessment, ABC Ltd receives a further R40 000: this is offset against the suspended loss of R110 000 brought forward, resulting in no inclusion in its taxable income for that year and a reduced suspended loss of R70 000 to be carried forward.

In the 2018 year of assessment, ABC Ltd receives a further R250 000: this is offset against the suspended loss of R70 000 brought forward, resulting in an inclusion of R180 000 in its taxable income for that year of a recoupment in respect of the machine (s 8(4)*(a)*). The suspended loss is reduced to RNil as it has been fully offset.

In the 2019 year of assessment, ABC Ltd receives a further R280 000: there is no longer any suspended loss to be brought forward against which the amount can be offset, resulting in the inclusion of R20 000 in its taxable income for that year for a further recoupment in respect of the machine. The cumulative recoupments in respect of the machine are R200 000 (R180 000 in 2018 and R20 000 in 2019) and are equal to the amount of the s 12C deduction claimed on the machine. The balance of R260 000 received in 2019 is a capital receipt that must be taken into account in calculating the capital gain in respect of the disposal of the machine.

In the 2020 year of assessment, ABC Ltd receives a further R240 000: this full amount is a capital receipt that must be taken into account in calculating the capital gain in respect of the disposal of the machine. The cumulative amount to be taken into account in calculating the capital gain is R500 000 (R260 000 in 2019 and R240 000 in 2020), that is, equal to the excess of the total proceeds on disposal of the machine (R1 000 000 over the five-year period) over its original cost (R500 000).

7.6 BUILDING ALLOWANCES

Although the wear and tear or depreciation allowance in s 11*(e)* is not available for buildings, structures and works of a permanent nature (proviso (ii) to s 11*(e)*), there are various other allowances available for the following buildings:

- buildings used in a process of manufacture or for research and development (s 13);
- buildings used by hotel keepers (s 13*bis*);
- buildings in urban development zones (s 13*quat*);
- certain commercial buildings (s 13*quin*); and
- certain residential units (s 13*sex*).

There was also an allowance available for certain residential buildings (in s 13*ter*) that is effectively obsolete as it applies only to buildings the erection of which commenced before 21 October 2008.

In addition, although not a building allowance per se, an allowance is available when a taxpayer advances a qualifying loan for the sale of low-cost residential units (s 13*sept*).

Meaning of the word 'building'

A taxpayer seeking to claim one of the building allowances must be able to show that the relevant structure qualifies as a building. There is no definition of a 'building' in the Act but the concept has been considered by the courts in a number of cases.

In *CIR v Le Sueur*[17] Botha AJA stated[18] that 'a building is a substantial structure, more or less of a permanent nature, consisting of walls, a roof and the necessary appurtenances thereto' and that the question of what appurtenances form part of a building is a question of fact that must be dealt with objectively. He considered[19] the 'purely objective test' of whether—

> the movable has by actual physical incorporation in the immovable been deprived of its separate identity, or been so securely attached to the immovable that separation would involve substantial injury to the immovable or to the accessory.

In *SIR v Charkay Properties (Pty) Ltd*[20] the issue before the court was whether demountable partitions that were used in the taxpayer's building instead of interior walls were so integrated with the building as to form part of it. Trollip JA stated[21] that the partitions were not part of the building, but he recognised that it was not an easy problem to resolve.

---

[17] 1960 (2) SA 708 (A), 23 SATC 261.
[18] At 273.
[19] At 273–4.
[20] 1976 (4) SA 872 (A), 38 SATC 159.
[21] At 171.

In *ITC 1007*[22] James J stated[23] that the word 'building' should be understood in a non-technical sense as it would be used in everyday speech and he did not accept that the word 'building' is synonymous with the word 'structure'. He stated:[24]

> In our view when one speaks of a building in ordinary conversation one has in mind only things such as houses, store-rooms and offices and does not have in mind things such as memorial statues, retaining and boundary walls and similar structures. These have undoubtedly been built but in common parlance they are not buildings.

When claiming an allowance for a qualifying building, an important issue is the timing of when exactly the 'erection' of the building commences. In *ITC 1137*[25] the issue between the parties was whether, upon a proper construction of the words 'any building the erection of which was commenced not later than [a certain date]', the erection of the store in question had commenced when excavations were made preparatory to the laying of the foundations or when the laying of the foundations themselves was started. Van Winsen J stated[26] that while the digging of trenches to take foundations is a necessary preliminary to the raising of the foundations themselves, he did not think that it could be said to be the commencement of the erection of the building which is to stand in those trenches. Excavation is preparatory to, but not part of, the process of erection.

7.6.1 Buildings used in a process of manufacture or for research and development

Section 13 has for many years provided for an allowance for buildings used in a process of manufacture, but has been amended also to provide an allowance for buildings used for research and development on or after 1 April 2012.

The allowance for buildings used in a process of manufacture has undergone a number of amendments over the years, with different rates applying for buildings erected at different times. The focus below is on the allowance as it applies to buildings erected in recent times, although there are older buildings that may still qualify for earlier versions of the allowance. The legislation needs to be checked carefully to establish the rate of the allowance for which a particular building may qualify.

7.6.1.1 Qualifying buildings

A building qualifies for the s 13 allowance if it was erected by the taxpayer and was wholly or mainly used by the taxpayer during the year of assessment for the purpose of carrying on therein, in the course of his or her trade, any process

22 (1962) 25 SATC 251 (N).
23 At 253.
24 Ibid.
25 (1969) 32 SATC 1 (C).
26 At 2–3.

of manufacture, research and development or any other process which in the opinion of the Commissioner is of a similar nature. A building that was let by the taxpayer and was wholly or mainly used by a tenant or subtenant for the purpose of carrying on therein any process of manufacture, research and development or similar process in the course of any trade also qualifies for the allowance. Buildings used for mining or farming do not qualify. (Section 13(1)*(b)*)

The allowance is available for a building used for manufacturing or research and development, meeting similar requirements to those of s 13(1)*(b)*, if the building:

- was acquired by the taxpayer by purchase from any other person who was entitled to an allowance in respect of it under s 13(1)*(b)* or s 13(1)*(d)* rather than having been erected by the taxpayer (s 13(1)*(d)*); or
- has never been used, if the building has been acquired by the taxpayer by purchase from any other person (s 13(1)*(d*A*)*).

Improvements (other than repairs) to a building qualify for the allowance, if the building was wholly or mainly used by the taxpayer during the year of assessment for the purpose of carrying on therein, in the course of his or her trade, any process of manufacture or any other similar process, or the building was let by the taxpayer and was wholly or mainly used by a tenant or subtenant for the purpose of carrying on therein any process of manufacture or similar process in the course of any trade. Improvements to buildings used for mining or farming do not qualify for the allowance. (Section 13(1)*(f)*) Improvements to a building used for research and development do not qualify for the allowance.

'Improvements' means any extension, addition or improvements (other than repairs) to a building which is or are effected for the purpose of increasing or improving the industrial capacity of the building (definition of 'improvements' in s 13(9)).

7.6.1.2 Calculation of the allowance

The allowance is calculated on the cost of the building or improvements to the taxpayer (s 13(1)). If, however, the taxpayer has elected that an amount which has been recovered or recouped in terms of s 8(4)*(a)* in respect of any allowance made under s 13(1) in respect of any building or improvements was to be set off against the cost of a qualifying replacement building, then the cost of the replacement building must be reduced by the amount set off (s 13(3)). To qualify for the set-off, the replacement building must be purchased or erected by the taxpayer within twelve months (or a further period allowed by the Commissioner) from the date on which the event giving rise to the recovery or recoupment occurred (s 13(3)).

In calculating the s 13 allowance for a manufacturing or research and development building used by a taxpayer, the cost of the building or the improvements effected to it must be reduced by the amount that has been taken into account in the calculation of any allowance to that taxpayer under s 11*(g)* (leasehold improvements), whether in the current or any previous year of assessment (proviso *(a)* to s 13(1)).

Where any building in respect of which any deduction of an allowance is claimed in terms of s 13 was during any previous financial year or years used by the taxpayer for the purposes of any trade carried on by him or her, the receipts and accruals of which were not included in his or her income during those years, any deduction which could have been allowed during those previous years in terms of s 13 shall for the purposes of the section be deemed to have been allowed during those previous years as if the receipts and accruals of that trade had been included in the income of that taxpayer (s 13(1A)).

The aggregate of the allowances allowed under s 13(1), or deemed to have been allowed in terms of s 13(1A), in respect of any building or improvements shall not exceed the cost (after the deduction of any set off referred to in s 13(3)), less the aggregate of any allowances made to the taxpayer in respect of the building or improvements, under s 11*(g)* (leasehold improvements) (s 13(2)).

7.6.1.3 Rate of the allowance

The rate of the allowance depends on the date on which the erection of the building or the improvements to the building commenced, as set out in the table below.

Date of commencement of erection of building or improvements	**Rate of allowance**
On or after 1 July 1996 until 30 September 1999 (must have been brought into use on or before 31 March 2000) (proviso (c) to s 13(1))	10%
On or after 1 January 1989 (but see above for increased rate between 1 July 1996 and 30 September 1999) (proviso (b) to s 13(1))	5%

In the case of an improvement completed by a taxpayer as contemplated in s 12N (which deals with, for example, improvements effected to land or buildings in terms of a public private partnership), the expenditure incurred by the taxpayer to complete the improvement shall for the purposes of s 13(1) be deemed to be the cost to the taxpayer of a building or improvement (proviso *(d)* to s 13(1)).

7.6.2 Buildings used by hotel keepers

The allowance for buildings used by hotel keepers has undergone a number of amendments over many years, with different rates applying for buildings erected at different times. The focus below is on the allowance as it applies to buildings erected in recent times, although there are older buildings that may still qualify for earlier versions of the allowance. The legislation needs to be checked carefully to establish the rate of the allowance for which a particular building may qualify.

7.6.2.1 Qualifying buildings

To qualify for the s 13*bis* allowance, the building (or portion of the building) must have been erected by the taxpayer and used by him or her during the year of assessment for the purpose of carrying on therein his or her trade of hotel keeper, or must have been let by him or her during that year and been used by the lessee for the purpose of carrying on the lessee's trade of hotel keeper (s 13*bis*(1)*(d)*). (A building used by a hotel keeper in his or her trade as hotel keeper will be referred to below simply as a 'hotel building'.) The allowance is also available for improvements to a hotel building (but not for repairs) (s 13*bis*(1)*(d)*).

7.6.2.2 Calculation of the allowance

The allowance is equal to 5% of the cost of the hotel building (after the set-off of any recoupment as provided in s 13*bis*(6)) to the taxpayer (further proviso to s 13*bis*(1)). (For hotel buildings the erection of which started before 4 June 1988, the allowance was 2%.)

To the extent to which the portion of any improvements to a hotel building does not extend the existing exterior framework of the building, the allowance under s 13*bis* is increased to 20% of the cost of that portion (second, further proviso to s 13*bis*(1)). This increased allowance applies to improvements which have been or are commenced on or after 17 March 1993.

Where any building, in respect of which a deduction of an allowance is claimed in terms of s 13*bis*, was during any previous financial year or years used by the taxpayer for the purposes of any trade carried on by him or her, the receipts and accruals of which were not included in his or her income during those years, any deduction that could have been allowed during those previous years in terms of s 13*bis* shall, for the purposes of s 13*bis,* be deemed to have been allowed during those previous years as if the receipts and accruals of that trade had been included in the income of that taxpayer (s 13*bis*(3A)).

The aggregate of the allowances under s 13*bis* or any amount deemed to have been allowed in terms of s 13*bis*(3A), in respect of the cost of any building or portion thereof or any improvements or portion thereof, may not exceed that cost or, if the allowances have been calculated on a portion of that cost, that portion (s 13*bis*(5)).

7.6.2.3 Cost of the building

In calculating the s 13*bis* allowance for a hotel building, the cost of the building or the improvements effected to it must be reduced by an amount that has been taken into account in the calculation of any allowance to that taxpayer under s 11*(g)* (leasehold improvements), whether in the current or any previous year of assessment (proviso to s 13*bis*(1)).

The hotel building allowance is normally calculated on the cost of the building or improvements to the taxpayer (s 13*bis*(1)). If, however, the taxpayer has elected that an amount which has been recovered or recouped in terms of s 8(4)*(a)* in respect of any allowance made under s 13*bis*(1) in respect of any building or improvements was to be set off against the cost of a qualifying replacement building, then the cost of the replacement building must be reduced by the amount set off (s 13*bis*(6)). To qualify for the set-off the replacement building must be erected by the taxpayer within twelve months (or a further period allowed by the Commissioner) from the date on which the event giving rise to the recovery or recoupment occurred (s 13*bis*(6)).

7.6.3 Buildings in urban development zones

The s 13*quat* allowance for certain buildings and improvements in urban development zones was introduced in 2003 as an incentive allowance aimed at urban regeneration. An 'urban development zone' is an area demarcated by a municipality in terms of s 13(6), the particulars of which were published in the *Government Gazette* in terms of s 13(8) (definition of 'urban development zone' in s 13*quat*(1)). For example, the details of designated urban development zones for Johannesburg and Cape Town were published in *Government Gazette* 26866 dated 14 October 2004 and those for eThekwini (and six other cities) were published in *Government Gazette* 27077 dated 10 December 2004. There are a range of administrative and reporting requirements for the Commissioner, municipalities, developers and qualifying taxpayers in respect of the allowance, which are beyond the scope of this text but that must be borne in mind when dealing with the allowance in practice.

7.6.3.1 Qualifying buildings

The allowance is available for any commercial or residential building or part of a building that is owned by a taxpayer and is used solely for purposes of his or her trade, if the following requirements are all met:

- The building is situated within an urban development zone.
- The erection, extension, addition or improvement was commenced by the taxpayer or the developer, as the case may be, on or after the date of publication of the notice contemplated in s 13*quat*(8) in respect of that urban development zone, in terms of a contract formally and finally signed by all parties thereto on or after that date.
- The erection, extension, addition or improvement by the taxpayer or the developer covers either the entire building or a floor area of at least 1 000 square metres of that building.
- In the case where the taxpayer purchased the building or part of the building from a developer:
  - the agreement to purchase was concluded on or after 8 November 2005;
  - the developer has not claimed any allowance under s 13*quat* in respect of that building or part; and

- if the developer improved the building or part as contemplated in s 13*quat*(3)*(b)* or s 13*quat*(3A)*(b)*, that developer has incurred expenditure in respect of those improvements which is equal to at least 20% of the purchase price paid by the taxpayer in respect of that building or part (s 13*quat*(2)).

A 'developer' is a person who:

- erects, extends, adds to or improves a building or part of a building with the purpose of disposing of that building or part thereof immediately after completion of that erection, extension, addition or improvement; and
- disposes of the building or part of a building within three years after completion of that erection, extension, addition or improvement (definition of 'developer' in s 13*quat*(1)).

The 'purchase price' in relation to any building or part of a building purchased by a taxpayer means the lesser of:

- the actual cost to him or her to purchase that building or part; or
- the cost which a person would have incurred had that person purchased that building or part under a cash transaction concluded at arm's length on the date on which that taxpayer purchased that building or part (definition of 'purchase price' in s 13*quat*(1)).

7.6.3.2 Calculation of the allowance

The allowance that may be deducted from the income of a taxpayer in respect of the cost of the erection, extension, addition or improvement of a qualifying commercial or residential building or part of a building is determined in terms of s 13*quat*(3) or s 13*quat*(3A) (s 13*quat*(2)).

The amount of the allowance in the case of the erection of any new building or the extension of or addition to any building (other than a building referred to in the next paragraph) is equal to:

- 20% of the cost to the taxpayer of the erection or extension of or addition to that building, which is deductible in the year of assessment during which that building is brought into use by him or her solely for the purposes of his or her trade; and
- 8% of that cost in each of the 10 succeeding years of assessment (s 13*quat*(3)*(a)*).

The amount of the allowance in the case of the improvement of any existing building or part of a building (including any extension or addition which is incidental to that improvement) where its existing structural or exterior framework is preserved, is equal to:

- 20% of the cost to the taxpayer of the improvement, extension or addition which is deductible in the year of assessment during which the part of the building so improved, extended or added is brought into use by him or her solely for the purposes of his or her trade; and
- 20% of that cost in each of the four succeeding years of assessment (s 13*quat*(3)*(b)*).

The amount of the allowance in the case of the erection of any new building or the extension of or addition to any building, to the extent that it relates to a low-cost residential unit (other than any improvement as referred to above) is equal to:

- 25% of the cost to the taxpayer of the erection or extension of or addition to that building, which is deductible in the year of assessment during which that building is brought into use by him or her;
- 13% of that cost in each of the five succeeding years of assessment; and
- 10% of that cost in the year of assessment following the last year for which the allowance was 13% (s 13*quat*(3A)*(a)*).

The amount of the allowance in the case of the improvement of any existing building or part of a building, to the extent that it relates to a low-cost residential unit (including any extension or addition which is incidental to that improvement) where the existing structural or exterior framework thereof is preserved, is equal to:

- 25% of the cost to the taxpayer of the improvement, which is deductible in the year of assessment during which the part of the building so improved is brought into use by him or her; and
- 25% of that cost in each of the three succeeding years of assessment (s 13*quat*(3A)*(b)*).

For a discussion on the meaning of the term 'low-cost residential unit' please refer to 7.7.5.

7.6.3.3 Cost for purposes of the allowance

For the purposes of the s 13*quat* allowance, the 'cost' of a qualifying building means the costs (other than borrowing or finance costs) actually incurred in erecting or extending, adding to or improving a building or part of it and includes any costs incurred:

- in demolishing any existing building or part of it;
- in excavating the land for purposes of that erection, extension, addition or improvement; and
- in respect of structures or works directly adjoining the building or part so erected, extended, added to or improved, for purposes of providing:
  - water, power or parking with respect to that building or part;
  - drainage or security for that building or part;
  - means of waste disposal for that building or part; or
  - access to that building or part, including the frontage thereof.

(Definition of 'cost' in s 13*quat*(1))

Where the taxpayer purchased a building or part of a building from a developer, the cost incurred by that taxpayer in respect of the erection, extension, addition to or improvement of that building or part of a building is deemed to be as follows:

- 55% of the purchase price of that building or part of a building, in the case of a new building erected, extended or added to by that developer as contemplated in s 13*quat*(3)*(a)* or s 13*quat*(3A)*(a)*; and
- 30% of the purchase price of that building or part of a building, in the case of a building improved by that developer as contemplated in s 13*quat*(3)*(b)* or s 13*quat*(3A)*(b)*.

(Section 13*quat*(3B))

If a taxpayer completes an improvement as contemplated in s 12N (which deals with, for example, improvements effected to land or buildings in terms of a public private partnership), the expenditure incurred by him or her to complete the improvement is deemed to be the cost of the erection, extension, addition or improvement contemplated in s 13*quat*(2) (s 13*quat*(2A)).

No deduction is allowed under s 13*quat* in respect of any building or part of a building:

- where the taxpayer ceased to use that building or part solely for purposes of his or her trade during any previous year of assessment in or prior to which an allowance was claimed;
- which has been disposed of by the taxpayer during any previous year of assessment; or
- which is brought into use by the taxpayer after 31 March 2014 (this date is to be extended to 31 March 2020) (s 13*quat*(5)).

No deduction is allowed under s 13*quat*, unless the taxpayer has complied with the requirements of s 13*quat*(4) in respect of the submission of certain information to the Commissioner.

7.6.4 Commercial buildings

The tax allowance for commercial buildings applies to buildings and improvements that were contracted for on or after 1 April 2007 and for which the construction or erection commenced on or after that date. It is also available for the acquisition of a part of a building or improvement on or after 21 October 2008.

7.6.4.1 Qualifying buildings

The allowance is available for:

(a) any new and unused building owned by a taxpayer; or

(b) any new and unused improvement to any building owned by him or her,

if that building or improvement is wholly or mainly used by him or her during the year of assessment for purposes of producing income in the course of his or her trade, other than the provision of residential accommodation (s 13*quin*(1)). An office building used by a taxpayer for his or her own business or which is let out by him or her to be used in the tenant's business would both qualify, as they are both used in the taxpayer's trade for the purpose of earning income.

7.6.4.2 Calculation of the allowance

The allowance is equal to 5% of the cost to the taxpayer of a qualifying building (s 13*quin*(1)).

The cost to the taxpayer of any building or improvement is deemed to be the lesser of:

- the actual cost to him or her; or
- the cost which a person would, if he or she had acquired, erected or improved the building under a cash transaction concluded at arm's length on the date on which the transaction for the acquisition, erection or improvement of the building was in fact concluded, have incurred in respect of the direct cost of the acquisition, erection or improvement of the building (s 13(2)).

The deductions which may be allowed (or may be deemed to have been allowed) in terms of s 13*quin* and any other provision of the Act in respect of the cost of any building or improvement shall not in the aggregate exceed the amount of its cost (s 13*quin*(6)).

In the case of an improvement completed by a taxpayer as contemplated in s 12N (which deals with, for example, improvements effected to land or buildings in terms of a public private partnership), the expenditure incurred by the taxpayer to complete the improvement shall be deemed to be the cost to the taxpayer of a new and unused building or any new and unused improvement to a building (s 13*bis*(1A)).

Where any building or improvement in respect of which any deduction is claimed in terms of s 13*quin* was during any previous financial year brought into use for the first time by the taxpayer for the purposes of any trade carried on by him or her, the receipts and accruals of which were not included in his or her income during that year, any deduction which could have been allowed during that or any subsequent year in terms of s 13*quin* shall for the purposes of s 13*quin* be deemed to have been allowed during those years as if the receipts and accruals of that trade had been included in the income of that taxpayer (s 13*quin*(3)).

No deduction is allowed under s 13*quin* in respect of any building that has been disposed of by the taxpayer during any previous year of assessment (s 13*quin*(4)).

No deduction is allowed under s 13*quin* in respect of the cost of a building or improvement if any of that cost has qualified or will qualify for deduction from the taxpayer's income as a deduction of expenditure or an allowance in respect of expenditure under any other section of the Act (s 13*quin*(5)).

To the extent that a taxpayer acquires a part of a building without erecting or constructing that part:

(a) 55% of the acquisition price, in the case of a part being acquired; and

(b) 30% of the acquisition price, in the case of an improvement being acquired,

is deemed to be the cost incurred by him or her in respect of that part of the building or improvement (s 13*quin*(7)).

7.6.5 Residential units

The allowance currently available for qualifying residential units came into operation on 21 October 2008 and applies to any residential unit or improvement to a residential unit acquired, or the erection of which commenced, on or after that date.

7.6.5.1 Qualifying residential units

The allowance is available for any new and unused residential unit (or any new and unused improvement to a residential unit) owned by the taxpayer if:

- that unit or improvement is used by him or her solely for the purposes of a trade carried on by him or her;
- that unit is situated within the Republic; and
- he or she owns at least five residential units within the Republic, which are used by him or her for the purposes of his or her trade (s 13*sex*(1)).

7.6.5.2 Calculation of the allowance

The allowance is equal to 5% of the cost to the taxpayer of a qualifying residential unit (s 13*sex*(1)).

An additional allowance of 5% of the cost of a *low-cost* residential unit of a taxpayer may be claimed for a year of assessment if deductions are allowable to him or her in respect of that unit in terms of s 13*sex*(1) in that year of assessment (s 13*sex*(2)).

A low-cost residential unit is defined as:

- an apartment qualifying as a residential unit in a building located within the Republic, where:
  - the cost of the apartment does not exceed R250 000; and
  - the owner of the apartment does not charge a monthly rental in respect of that apartment that exceeds 1% of the cost; or
- a building qualifying as a residential unit located within the Republic, where:
  - the cost of the building does not exceed R200 000; and
  - the owner of the building does not charge a monthly rental in respect of that building that exceeds 1% of the cost plus a proportionate share of the cost of the land and the bulk infrastructure.

For the purposes of calculating the rental limit of 1% of the cost, the cost is deemed to be increased by 10% in each year succeeding the year in which the apartment or building is first brought into use. (Definition of 'low-cost residential unit' in s 1.)

The cost to the taxpayer of a residential unit (or an improvement to a residential unit) is deemed to be the lesser of:

- the actual cost to him or her; or

- the cost which a person would, if that person had acquired or improved the residential unit under a cash transaction concluded at arm's length on the date on which the transaction for the acquisition of the new and unused residential unit (or of the new and unused improvement to the residential unit) was in fact concluded, have incurred in respect of the direct cost of the acquisition or erection of the residential unit or improvement (s 13*sex*(3)).

In the case of an improvement completed by a taxpayer as contemplated in s 12N (which deals with, for example, improvements effected to land or buildings in terms of a public private partnership), the expenditure incurred by the taxpayer to complete the improvement shall be deemed to be the cost to the taxpayer of a new and unused residential unit or any new and unused improvement to a residential unit (proviso to s 13*sex*(1)).

Where any residential unit (or an improvement to the residential unit) in respect of which any deduction is claimed in terms of s 13*sex* was during any year of assessment used by the taxpayer for the purpose of any trade carried on by him or her, the receipt and accruals of which were not included in his or her income during that year, any deduction which could have been allowed in terms of s 13*sex* during that year or any subsequent year in which that residential unit (or an improvement to the residential unit) was used by him or her shall for the purposes of s 13*sex* be deemed to have been allowed during that previous year or those years as if the receipts and accruals of that trade had been included in his or her income (s 13*sex*(4)).

No deduction is allowed under s 13*sex* in respect of the cost of any residential unit (or an improvement to a residential unit) that has been disposed of by the taxpayer during any previous year of assessment (s 13*sex*(5)).

No deduction is allowed under s 13*sex* in respect of the cost of a residential unit (or an improvement to a residential unit) if any of the cost has qualified or will qualify for deduction from the taxpayer's income as a deduction of expenditure or an allowance in respect of expenditure under any other section of the Act (s 13*sex*(6)).

The deductions which may be allowed (or may be deemed to have been allowed) in terms of s 13*sex* and any other provision of the Act in respect of the cost of any residential unit (or any improvement to a residential unit) shall not in the aggregate exceed the amount of that cost (s 13*sex*(7)).

To the extent that a taxpayer acquires a residential unit (or improvement to a residential unit) representing only a part of a building without erecting or constructing that unit or improvement:

- 55% of the acquisition price, in the case of the unit being acquired; and
- 30% of the acquisition price, in the case of the improvement being acquired

is deemed to be the cost incurred by him or her in respect of that unit or improvement (s 13*sex*(8)).

7.6.6 Sales of low-cost residential units on loan account

If a taxpayer disposes of a low-cost residential unit to his or her employee (or an employee of an associated institution as defined in the Seventh Schedule in relation to him or her), he or she is allowed a deduction from his or her income (s 13*sept*(1)). The deduction is available for a sale of a low-cost residential unit, as defined in s 1 (see 7.7.5). To qualify for the deduction the sale must be on loan account and certain requirements must be met. The deduction came into operation on 21 October 2008 and it applies to disposals of qualifying low-cost residential units on or after that date.

7.6.6.1 Calculation of deduction

The deduction is an amount equal to 10% of *any amount owing* to the taxpayer by the employee in respect of the unit at the end of his or her year of assessment (s 13*sept*(2)). No deduction is allowed in the eleventh and subsequent years of assessment after the disposal of that low-cost residential unit (proviso to s 13*sept*(2)). The deduction may therefore be claimed for a maximum of ten years.

No deduction is allowed in terms of this section in respect of a disposal by the taxpayer if any of the following apply:

- The disposal is subject to any condition, other than a condition in terms of which the employee is required:
  - on termination of employment; or
  - in the case of consistent failure for a period of three months on the part of the employee to pay an amount owing to the taxpayer (or an associated institution, as defined in the Seventh Schedule, in relation to the taxpayer) in respect of the low-cost residential unit,

  to dispose of the low-cost residential unit to the taxpayer (or an associated institution, as defined in the Seventh Schedule, in relation to the taxpayer) for an amount equal to the actual cost (other than borrowing or finance costs) to the employee of the unit and the land on which the unit is erected.
- The employee must pay interest to the taxpayer in respect of the amount owing to him or her by the employee in respect of the unit.
- The disposal is for an amount that exceeds the actual cost (other than borrowing or finance costs) to the taxpayer of the unit and the land on which the unit is erected. (Section 13*sept*(3))

7.6.6.2 Recoupment

If the amount owing by the employee or any part thereof is paid to the taxpayer, the taxpayer is deemed to have recovered or recouped an amount equal to the lesser of:

- the amount so paid; or
- the amount allowed as a deduction in terms of s 13*sept* in the current and any previous year of assessment (s 13*sept*(4)).

7.7 LEASED ASSETS

7.7.1 Lease premiums

A premium paid by a taxpayer for the right of use or occupation of, for example, land or buildings, is an amount paid by a lessee to a lessor distinct from and in addition to or instead of the normal rental payable (*CIR v Butcher Bros (Pty) Ltd*).[27] The payment of a premium is usually made to secure the right of use of the leased asset. It is therefore capital in nature and is not deductible in the hands of the taxpayer (the lessee) in terms of the general deduction formula in s 11*(a)*. A special allowance may, however, be available to the taxpayer in terms of s 11*(f)* if the requirements of the section are met.

7.7.1.1 Qualifying expenditure

The s 11*(f)* allowance is available in determining the taxable income of a taxpayer from carrying on a trade, in respect of any premium, or consideration in the nature of a premium, paid by him or her for any of the following:

- the right of use or occupation of land or buildings that are used or occupied for the production of income or from which income is derived;
- the right of use of any plant or machinery that is used for the production of income or from which income is derived;
- the right of use of any motion picture film or any sound recording or advertising matter connected with the film, if the film, sound recording or advertising matter is used for the production of income or income is derived from it;
- the right of use of any patent as defined in the Patents Act 57 of 1978, or any design as defined in the Designs Act 195 of 1993, or any trade mark as defined in the Trade Marks Act 194 of 1993, or any copyright as defined in the Copyright Act 98 of 1978, or of any other property which is of a similar nature, if the patent, design, trade mark, copyright or other property is used for the production of income or income is derived from it;
- the imparting of or the undertaking to impart any knowledge directly or indirectly connected with the use of the film, sound recording, advertising matter, patent, design, trade mark, copyright or other property referred to above;
- the right of use of any pipeline, transmission line or cable or railway line contemplated in the definition of 'affected asset' in s 12D; or
- the right of use of any line or cable used for transmission of electronic communications contemplated in para *(c)* of the definition of 'affected asset' in s 12D. (Section 11*(f)*)

[27] 1945 AD 301, 13 SATC 21 at 34.

Any premium or consideration paid by a taxpayer which is not income of the person to whom it is paid does not qualify for the allowance (proviso *(dd)* to s 11*(f)*). A premium paid to a tax-exempt body, for example a public benefit organisation, will not qualify. Any premium or consideration that is paid in respect of a right of use of a line or cable used for the transmission of electronic communications, substantially the whole of which is located outside the territorial waters of the Republic, where the term of the right of use is 20 years or more, will, however, qualify for the allowance (proviso *(dd)* to s 11*(f)*).

7.7.1.2 Calculation of the allowance

The allowance under s 11*(f)* may not exceed for any one year the amount of the premium or consideration paid divided by the number of years for which the taxpayer is entitled to the use or occupation, or one twenty-fifth of the premium or consideration paid, whichever is the greater (proviso *(aa)* to s 11*(f)*). The allowance for the imparting of or the undertaking to impart any knowledge directly or indirectly connected with the use of a film, sound recording, advertising matter, patent, design, trade mark, copyright or other property is, however, the amount as may be determined, having regard to the period during which the taxpayer will enjoy the right to use the relevant asset and any other circumstances which, in his opinion, are relevant, but not less than one twenty-fifth of the amount of the premium or consideration paid (proviso *(cc)* to s 11*(f)*).

If the taxpayer is entitled to the use or occupation for an indefinite period, or he or she or the person by whom the right of use or occupation was granted holds a right or option to extend or renew the original period of the use or occupation, he or she shall be deemed, for the purposes of the allowance, to be entitled to the use or occupation for the probable duration of the use or occupation (proviso *(bb)* to s 11*(f)*).

Example

JKL Ltd entered into a lease agreement with a lessor who is a taxpayer, for the use of a factory building from 1 April 2016. In terms of the lease, JKL Ltd paid a premium of R100 000 (excluding VAT) on signing the lease. Calculate the s 11*(f)* allowance to which JKL Ltd is entitled in its year of assessment ended 31 December 2016 and 2017 if:

- the period of the lease is twenty years; and
- the period of the lease is thirty years.

Solution

Period of lease is 20 years:

Section 11*(f)* allowance for 2016	R100 000 × 1/20 × 9/12	R3 750
Section 11*(f)* allowance for 2017	R100 000 × 1/20	R5 000

The allowance must be apportioned for the period that the building was used by the taxpayer to produce income (nine months in the 2016 year of assessment).

Period of lease is 30 years:

Section 11*(f)* allowance for 2016	R100 000 × 1/25 × 9/12	R3 000
Section 11*(f)* allowance for 2017	R100 000 × 1/25	R4 000

The allowance must be apportioned for the period that the building was used by the taxpayer to produce income (nine months in the 2016 year of assessment).

7.7.2 Leasehold improvements

Any expenditure incurred by a taxpayer in respect of improvements to land or buildings leased by him or her is capital in nature and therefore not deductible in terms of the general deduction formula in s 11*(a)*. A special deduction may, however, be available to the taxpayer in terms of s 11*(g)* if the requirements of the section are met.

7.7.2.1 Qualifying expenditure

The s 11*(g)* allowance is available in determining the taxable income of a taxpayer from carrying on a trade in respect of any expenditure actually incurred by him or her:

- in pursuance of an *obligation* to effect improvements on land or to buildings;
- under an agreement whereby the right of use or occupation of the land or buildings is granted by any other person; and
- where the land or buildings are used or occupied for the production of income or income is derived from them (s 11*(g)*).

If the improvements are not an obligation in terms of the agreement of lease, but are, for example, voluntarily carried out by the lessee, the allowance is not available. If the improvements are carried out in terms of a later, separate agreement, the allowance is again not available.

The improvements must be used or occupied for the production of income: the allowance may not be claimed for the period prior to the improvements being so used.

The allowance is not available for any expenditure incurred on improvements to land or buildings if the value of the improvements or the amount to be expended on the improvements, as contemplated in para *(h)* of the definition of 'gross income' in s 1, does not constitute income of the person to whom the right to have the improvements effected has accrued (proviso (vi) to s 11*(g)*). Improvements to land owned by a tax-exempt public benefit organisation do not qualify for the s 11*(g)* allowance.

7.7.2.2 Calculation of the allowance

The aggregate of the allowances under s 11*(g)* may not exceed the amount stipulated in the agreement as the value of the improvements or as the amount to be expended on the improvements or, if no amount is so stipulated, an amount representing in the opinion of the Commissioner the fair and reasonable value of the improvements (proviso (i) to s 11*(g)*).

The allowance for any one year is the aggregate of the allowances under s 11*(g)* (that is, the stipulated value or amount to be expended or the fair and reasonable value) divided by the number of years for which the taxpayer is entitled to the use or occupation (calculated from the date on which the improvements are completed, but not more than twenty-five years) (proviso (ii) to s 11*(g)*).

If the taxpayer is entitled to the use or occupation of the land or building for an indefinite period or the taxpayer or the person by whom the right of use or occupation was granted holds a right or option to extend or renew the original period of the use or occupation, the taxpayer shall for the purposes of s 11*(g)* be deemed to be entitled to the use or occupation for the period as represents the probable duration of the use or occupation (proviso (iii) to s 11*(g)*).

The aggregate of the s 11*(g)* allowances in respect of any building or improvements referred to in s 13(1) (used in a process of manufacture, for research and development or similar process) or s 27(2)*(b)* (used by an agricultural co-operative) may not exceed the cost (after the deduction of any recoupment which has been set off against the cost) to the taxpayer of the building or improvements less the aggregate of the allowances in respect of the building or improvements made to the taxpayer under s 13(1) or s 27(2)*(b)* (proviso (iv) to s 11*(g)*).

If during any year of assessment the agreement by which the right of use or occupation of the land or buildings is granted is terminated before expiry of the period to which that taxpayer was entitled to the use or occupation, so much of the allowance as has not yet been allowed in that year or any previous year of assessment, shall be allowable as a deduction in that year of assessment (proviso (vii) to s 11*(g)*).

Example

MNO Ltd entered into a lease agreement with a lessor who is a taxpayer, for the use of land from 1 January 2016. In terms of the lease, MNO Ltd is obliged to erect a factory building on the land at a cost of R1 000 000 (excluding VAT). The building was completed and brought into use in a process of manufacture on 1 July 2016, at a total cost of R1 200 000 (excluding VAT). Calculate the s 11*(g)* allowance to which MNO Ltd is entitled in its year of assessment ended 31 December 2016 and 2017 if:

- the period of the lease is twenty years; and
- the period of the lease is thirty years.

Solution

Period of lease is 20 years:

Section 11*(g)* allowance for 2016	R1 000 000 × 1/(20–0,5) × 6/12	R25 641
Section 11*(g)* allowance for 2017	R1 000 000 × 1/(20–0,5)	R51 282

The amount stipulated in the agreement, not the eventual cost, must be used in the calculation of the allowance. That amount is divided by the period of the lease remaining on completion of the improvements, ie 19,5 years. The result must be apportioned for the period that the improvements were used by the taxpayer to produce income (six months in the 2016 year of assessment).

Period of lease is 30 years:

Section 11*(g)* allowance for 2016	R1 000 000 × 1/25 × 6/12	R20 000
Section 11*(g)* allowance for 2017	R1 000 000 × 1/25	R40 000

The amount stipulated in the agreement, not the eventual cost, must be used in the calculation of the allowance. That amount is divided by the period of the lease remaining on completion of the improvements, twenty-nine and a half years but limited to a maximum of twenty-five years. The result must be apportioned for the period that the improvements were used by the taxpayer to produce income (six months in the 2016 year of assessment).

As the building is a factory building used in a process of manufacture, it qualifies for the s 13 allowance on the excess cost of R200 000 that may not be claimed in terms of s 11*(g)*.

7.7.3 Lessor's allowance

If the right to have improvements effected to land and buildings by a lessee accrues to a lessor during a particular year of assessment in terms of an agreement relating to the use of the land and buildings, the amount stipulated as the value of the improvements or the amount to be expended on them or their fair and reasonable value is gross income in the hands of the lessor (para *(h)* of the definition of 'gross income' in s 1).

The gross income inclusion in respect of the right to have improvements effected would result in tax becoming payable by the lessor although the benefit received by him or her is in kind (the improvements), not in cash. This difficulty is lessened by the availability of a special lessor's allowance in s 11*(h)* that is also potentially available for a lessor who has an inclusion in his or her gross income in terms of para *(g)* of the definition (a lease premium).

7.7.3.1 Calculation of the allowance

The s 11*(h)* allowance in respect of amounts included in the taxpayer's gross income under para *(g)* (a lease premium) or para *(h)* (improvements to leasehold property) of the definition of 'gross income' in s 1 is an amount that the Commissioner may 'deem reasonable' having regard to any special circumstances of the case and, in the case of an amount included in respect of improvements, to the original period for which the right of use or occupation was granted or to the number of years taken into account in the determination of the relevant allowance granted to the lessee under the provisions of s 11*(g)* (s 11*(h)*). Although it is not spelt out in s 11*(h)* exactly how the amount of the allowance must be calculated, it is understood that it is the practice of SARS to allow a deduction of the difference between the value of the inclusion in the gross income of the lessor and the present value of that amount discounted at 6% over the period taken into account in calculating the deduction for the improvements in the hands of the lessee. The effect of the inclusion of the value of the improvements in the hands of the lessor and the deduction of the special lessor's allowance is that the net inclusion in his or her hands is the present value of the improvements.

No allowance is available to a lessor in terms of s 11*(h)* if:

- he or the other person (the lessee) is a company and the lessee or the lessor is interested in more than 50% of any class of shares issued by that company, whether directly as a shareholder in that company or indirectly as a shareholder in any other company; or
- both the lessor and the lessee are companies and any third person is interested in more than 50% of any class of shares issued by one of those companies and in more than 50% of any class of shares issued by the other company, whether directly as a shareholder in the company by which the shares in question were issued or indirectly as a shareholder in any other company (proviso to s 11*(h)*).

Example

GHI Ltd owns a vacant plot of land that it rented out with effect from 1 January 2016. In terms of the rental agreement the lessee is obliged to build a mini-factory on the land for a cost of R300 000 (excluding VAT). The period of the lease is ten years.

Calculate the taxable income of GHI Ltd arising from the letting out of its land for its year of assessment ending 30 June 2016 from the above information.

Solution

Gross income inclusion – right to have improvements effected (para *(h)* of the definition of 'gross income')		R300 000
Less: Lessor's allowance (s 11*(h)*)		
Stipulated cost of improvements	R300 000	
Less: Present value of improvements discounted at 6% pa over a period of ten years (R300 000 × 0,5584)	(R167 520)	(R132 480)
Taxable income		R167 520

Note: The effect of the gross income inclusion and the s 11*(h)* deduction is that the taxable income of GHI Ltd for its year of assessment ending 30 June 2016, R167 520, is equal to the present value of the improvements to be effected on its vacant land.

7.7.4 Limitation of allowances for lessors

In certain situations the allowance available to a lessor for an asset let by him or her may be limited by the anti-avoidance provisions of s 23A.

7.7.4.1 Limitation

The sum of the deductions which may be allowed to a taxpayer (the lessor) in a year of assessment under the provisions listed below in respect of any 'affected assets' let by him or her may not exceed his or her taxable income (as determined before making those deductions) derived during that year from rental income (s 23A(2)).

The deductions that are subject to the limitation are the following:

- s 11*(e)* (wear and tear allowance);
- s 11*(o)* (allowance on disposal of an asset);
- s 12B (assets used in farming operations and in generating renewable energy);
- s 12C (assets used by manufacturers; for the storage and packing of agricultural products; by hotel keepers; ships and aircraft; and assets used for research and development);
- s 12DA (rolling stock);
- s 14*bis* (aircraft – a provision that is now obsolete); and
- s 37B(2)*(a)* (environmental expenditure).

The limitation applies currently only to *affected assets*. These are any machinery, plant, implement, utensil, article, aircraft or ship:

- which has been let; and

- in respect of which the lessor is or was entitled to an allowance under s 11*(e)*, s 12B, s 12C, s 12DA or s 37B(2)*(a)*, whether in the current or a previous year of assessment.

(Definition of 'affected asset' in s 23A(1))

In calculating the limitation, it is necessary to refer to the lessor's taxable income derived during the year from rental income. 'Rental income' means income derived by way of rent from the letting of any affected asset in respect of which an allowance has been granted to the lessor under s 11*(e)*, s 12B, s 12C, s 12DA or s 37B(2)*(a)*, whether in the current or any previous year of assessment, and includes any amount:

- which is included in the income of that person in terms of s 8(4) in respect of an amount deducted in any year of assessment in respect of any affected asset; and
- derived from the disposal of any affected asset (definition of 'rental income' in s 23A(1)).

Where the taxpayer is entitled to any deduction which relates to rental income and other income derived by him or her, an appropriate portion of the deduction must be taken into account in the determination of the taxable income derived by him or her from rental income (s 23A(3)).

Any deduction which is disallowed under s 23A(2) must be carried forward to the succeeding year of assessment and shall be deemed to be a deduction to which the taxpayer is entitled in that year, but subject to the provisions of s 23A as it applies in relation to that year (s 23A(4)).

7.7.4.2 Assets excluded from the limitation

Any machinery, plant, implement, utensil, article, aircraft or ship that is let by the lessor under an operating lease (see below) or that was during the year of assessment mainly used by him or her in the course of any trade carried on by him or her, other than the letting of these assets, are excluded from being affected assets (definition of 'affected asset' in s 23A(1)). The limitation in s 23A(2) therefore does not apply to these assets.

An 'operating lease' means a lease of movable property concluded by a lessor in the ordinary course of a business (other than a banking, financial services or insurance business) of letting the property, if:

- the property may be hired by members of the general public directly from that lessor in terms of a lease, for a period of less than one month;
- the cost of maintaining the property and of carrying out repairs to it required in consequence of normal wear and tear is borne by the lessor; and
- subject to any claim that the lessor may have against the lessee by reason of the lessee's failure to take proper care of the property, the risk of destruction or loss of or other disadvantage to the property is not assumed by the lessee (definition of 'operating lease' in s 23A(1)).

Example

On 1 December 2016, LMN Ltd entered into a five-year rental agreement with a manufacturer (the lessee) in terms of which a new and unused machine was rented to him for R25 000 per month with effect from that date. The machine:

- was brought into use in a process of manufacture on 5 December 2016;
- cost LMN Ltd R1 000 000 excluding VAT; and
- had an expected useful life of five years.

Calculate the taxable income of LMN Ltd for its year of assessment ending 31 December 2016 if its income for that year comprises R25 000 of rental income from the machine and R50 000 of other (non-rental) income and it incurred deductible expenditure of R15 000 in producing both streams of its income.

Solution

The taxable income of LMN Ltd for its year of assessment ending 31 December 2016 is calculated as follows:

	Rental income	**Other income**	**Total**
Rental received	R25 000	R0	R25 000
Other income received	R0	R50 000	R50 000
	R25 000	R50 000	R75 000
Less: expenditure incurred	(R5 000)	(R10 000)	(R15 000)
	R20 000	R40 000	R60 000
Less: s 12C allowance – R1 000 000 × 40% = R400 000, but limited to	(R20 000)	R0	(R20 000)
Taxable income	R0	R40 000	R40 000

Note: The balance of the s 12C allowance not claimed in the 2016 year of assessment (R380 000 (R400 000 – R20 000)) is carried forward to the 2017 year of assessment and may, subject to the provisions of s 23A, be claimed in that year. In the absence of s 23A, LMN Ltd would have had an assessed loss of R340 000 for its 2016 year of assessment.

7.7.5 Limitation of allowances granted in respect of certain assets

Section 23D is an anti-avoidance provision aimed at schemes whereby, for example, assets that have increased in value are disposed of to a lessor and then leased back, with deductible lease payments for the lessee that are based on the increased value and that therefore result in increased tax deductions. The provisions of s 23D limit the deduction, in the hands of a lessor (or a grantor of a licence), of allowances on assets that are leased (or licensed) in certain circumstances.

The s 23D limitation applies where a depreciable asset, which is let or licensed by a taxpayer to a lessee or licensee, was held within a period of two years preceding the commencement of the lease or licence:

- by the lessee or licensee, or by any sublessee or sublicensee in relation to the asset; or
- by a person who was at any time during that period a connected person in relation to the lessee, licensee, sublessee or sublicensee (s 23D(2)).

The cost or value of the depreciable asset for the purpose of s 23D and any deduction or allowance claimed by the taxpayer in respect of the asset may not exceed an amount (the limit) determined as shown below (s 23D(2)).

The limit is the sum of:

- the cost of the asset to the most recent lessee, licensee, sublessee, sublicensee or connected person contemplated in s 23D(2) that previously held that asset, less the sum of:
    - all deductions which have been allowed to the lessee, licensee, sublessee, sublicensee or connected person in respect of the asset; and
    - all deductions that are deemed to have been allowed to the lessee, licensee, sublessee, sublicensee or connected person in respect of the asset in terms of certain sections (see below);
- any amount contemplated in para *(n)* of the definition of 'gross income' in s 1 that is required to be included in the income of the lessee, licensee, sublessee, sublicensee or connected person that arises as a result of the disposal of the asset; and
- the applicable percentage in para 10 of the Eighth Schedule (33,3% or 66,6%), of the capital gain of the lessee, licensee, sublessee, sublicensee or connected person that arises as a result of the disposal (s 23D(2A)).

The deemed deductions that must be included in the calculation (see above) are those in terms of the following sections:

- 11*(e)*(ix) (the wear and tear allowance);
- 12B(4B) (assets used in farming operations and in generating renewable energy);
- 12C(4A) (assets used by manufacturers; for the storage and packing of agricultural products; by hotel keepers; ships and aircraft; and assets used for research and development);
- 12D(3A) (pipelines, transmission lines and railway lines);
- 12DA(4) (rolling stock);
- 12F(3A) (airport and port assets);
- 13(1A) (buildings used in a process of manufacture or for research and development);
- 13*bis*(3A) (buildings used by hotel keepers);
- 13*ter*(6A) (residential buildings – this allowance is now obsolete);
- 13*quin*(3) (commercial buildings); and
- 37B(4) (environmental expenditure).

7.7.6 Sale and leaseback arrangements

Section 23G is another anti-avoidance provision aimed at sale and leaseback schemes where, for example, assets that have increased in value are sold to a lessor that is a tax-exempt entity and then leased back with lease payments that are based on the increased value of the asset that would be deductible for the lessee and that therefore would result in increased tax deductions. The provisions of s 23G are aimed at situations where either the lessee or the lessor is a tax-exempt entity.

7.7.6.1 Tax-exempt lessee

Where the receipts or accruals of any person who is a lessee or sublessee in relation to a sale and leaseback arrangement (see below) do not constitute income of that lessee or sublessee:

- any amount which is received by or accrues to any lessor in relation to that sale and leaseback arrangement, is limited to an amount which constitutes interest as contemplated in s 24J; and
- the lessor shall, notwithstanding the provisions of the Act, not be entitled to any deduction in terms of certain provisions (see below) in respect of an asset which is the subject matter of the sale and leaseback arrangement (s 23G(2)).

The effect of s 23G(2) is that the transaction is treated as a financing transaction in the hands of the lessor, the party to the transaction that is a taxpayer.

The deductions to which the lessor will not be entitled in terms of s 23G(2) are those listed in the sections below:

- 11*(e)* (wear and tear or depreciation allowance);
- 11*(f)* (lease premiums);
- 11(*g*A) (intangible assets – an allowance that is now obsolete);
- 11(*g*C) (intangible assets);
- 12B (assets used in farming operations and in generating renewable energy);
- 12C (assets used by manufacturers; for the storage and packing of agricultural products; by hotel keepers; ships and aircraft; and assets used for research and development);
- 12DA (rolling stock);
- 13 (buildings used in a process of manufacture or for research and development); and
- 13*quin* (commercial buildings).

A 'sale and leaseback arrangement' is defined as any arrangement where:

- any person disposes of any asset (whether directly or indirectly) to any other person; and

- that person or any connected person in relation to that person leases (whether directly or indirectly) that asset from that other person (definition of 'sale and leaseback arrangement' in s 23G(1)).

An 'asset' is defined as any asset, whether movable or immovable, or corporeal or incorporeal (definition of 'asset' in s 23G(1)).

The provision in s 23G(2) that limits the amount received or accrued in the hands of the lessor to an amount of interest shall not apply to any person who is both a lessor and a lessee in relation to the same sale and leaseback arrangement during any year of assessment (s 23G(4)).

7.7.6.2 Tax-exempt lessor

Where the receipts or accruals of any person, who is a lessor in relation to a sale and leaseback arrangement, arising from the arrangement, do not constitute income of that person, any deduction to which a lessee or sublessee in relation to that sale and leaseback arrangement is entitled under the provisions of the Act shall, subject to the provisions of s 11*(f)*, be limited to an amount which constitutes interest as contemplated in s 24J (s 23G(3)). Once again, the transaction is treated as a financing transaction, this time in the hands of the lessee or sublessee (the party to the transaction that is a taxpayer).

7.8 INTANGIBLE ASSETS

7.8.1 Patents, designs, copyrights and similar assets

Any expenditure actually incurred by a taxpayer during a year of assessment to acquire any of the following intangible assets may qualify for an allowance in terms of s 11*(gC)*:

- an invention or patent as defined in the Patents Act;
- a design as defined in the Designs Act;
- a copyright as defined in the Copyright Act;
- any other property which is of a similar nature (*other than* trade marks as defined in the Trade Marks Act); and
- any knowledge essential to the use of the patent, design, copyright or other property or the right to have such knowledge imparted.

The expenditure must be actually incurred in *acquiring* the intangible asset: expenditure incurred by way of *devising, developing or creating* an intangible asset does not qualify for the allowance in terms of s 11*(gC)*, but may qualify for an allowance in terms of s 11D (see chapter 6 of this book).

The allowance in terms of s 11*(gC)* is available for expenditure actually incurred during years of assessment commencing on or after 1 January 2004: prior to that date a similar allowance was available in terms of s 11*(gA)*. One noteworthy difference between the provisions of s 11*(gA)* and s 11*(gC)* is that the former permitted an allowance for expenditure incurred in acquiring a trade mark or similar asset, but only if incurred prior to 29 October 1999. The allowance in terms of s 11*(gC)* is specifically not permitted for trade marks and similar assets.

The allowance is granted during the year of assessment in which the invention, patent, design, copyright, other property or knowledge is brought into use for the first time by the taxpayer for the purposes of his or her trade, if it is used by the taxpayer in the production of his or her income (s 11*(gC)*).

Where the expenditure actually incurred by the taxpayer exceeds R5 000, the allowance may not exceed in any year of assessment:

- 5% of the amount of the expenditure in respect of an invention, patent, copyright or other property of a similar nature or any knowledge essential to the use of the invention, patent, copyright or other property or the right to have the knowledge imparted; or
- 10% of the amount of the expenditure in respect of any design or other property of a similar nature or any knowledge essential to the use of the design or other property or the right to have the knowledge imparted (proviso *(aa)* to s 11*(gC)*).

If the expenditure does not exceed R5 000, it is fully deductible in the year of assessment in which it is incurred.

7.8.2 Registration and similar costs incurred in respect of intangible assets

Registration and similar costs incurred in respect of intangible assets may qualify for a deduction in terms of s 11*(gB)*, if they do not qualify in whole or in part for a deduction or allowance under any of the other provisions of s 11.

To qualify for a deduction in terms of s 11*(gB)*, the expenditure must be actually incurred by the taxpayer during the year of assessment in obtaining:

- the grant of any patent or the restoration of any patent, or the extension of the term of any patent under the Patents Act 57 of 1978;
- the registration of any design, or extension of the registration period of any design under the Designs Act 195 of 1993; or
- the registration of any trade mark, or the renewal of the registration of any trade mark under the Trade Marks Act 194 of 1993,

if the patent, design or trade mark is used by the taxpayer in the production of his or her income.

The deduction is also available if the qualifying expenditure is incurred 'under similar laws of any other country' (s 11*(gB)*).

It is important to note that expenditure incurred to *register* or to *renew the registration* of a trade mark is deductible under s 11*(gB)*, even though the expenditure to *acquire* a trade mark does not qualify for the allowance in s 11*(gC)*.

7.8.3 Licences

If a taxpayer's trade constitutes:

- the provision of telecommunication services;
- the exploration, production or distribution of petroleum; or
- the provision of gambling facilities,

he or she will qualify for a deduction for any expenditure incurred to acquire a licence from the government of the Republic in the national, provincial or local sphere, or an institution or entity contemplated in Schedule 1 (certain constitutional institutions) or Part A or C of Schedule 3 (certain public entities) to the Public Finance Management Act 1 of 1999, where that expenditure is incurred in terms of the licence and the licence is required to carry on that trade (s 11*(g*D*)*). The deduction is not available, however, in respect of expenditure on infrastructure.

The deduction for any one year may not exceed the amount of the expenditure divided by the number of years for which the taxpayer has the right to the licence after the date on which the expenditure was incurred, or thirty, whichever is the lesser (s 11*(g*D*)*).

7.8.4 Prohibition of deductions in respect of certain intellectual property

Section 23I is an anti-avoidance provision that prohibits or limits deductions in respect of certain 'tainted' intellectual property. It is aimed, for example, at schemes in terms of which a taxpayer transfers intellectual property (for which it received a deduction for tax purposes, say, when it created the intellectual property) to an entity that is not a taxpayer (possibly a non-resident fellow subsidiary) that then licenses the intellectual property back to the taxpayer, that thereafter pays and claims a deduction for the royalties it pays for the use of the intellectual property. From the perspective of the South African fiscus, there would then be a mismatch: it would allow a deduction for royalty expenditure for one taxpayer with no corresponding inclusion in income in the hands of another taxpayer.

7.8.4.1 Tainted intellectual property

The concept of 'tainted intellectual property', which is key to the application of s 23I, is defined in s 23I(1). To understand the meaning of tainted intellectual property, the meaning of 'intellectual property' for the purposes of s 23I must first be understood.

'Intellectual property' is defined in s 23I(1) as:

- a patent as defined in the Patents Act 8, including any application for a patent in terms of that Act (para *(a)*);
- a design as defined in the Designs Act (para *(b)*);
- a trade mark as defined in the Trade Marks Act (para *(c)*);

- a copyright as defined in the Copyright Act (para *(d)*);
- a patent, design, trade mark or copyright defined or described in any similar law to that in paras *(a)*, *(b)*, *(c)*, or *(d)*, of a country other than the Republic (para *(e)*);
- any property or right of a similar nature to that in paras *(a)*, *(b)*, *(c)*, *(d)*, or *(e)* (para *(f)*); and
- any knowledge connected to the use of the patent, design, trade mark, copyright, property or right (para *(g)*).

When will intellectual property as defined above be tainted intellectual property? The definition of 'tainted intellectual property' in s 23I sets out four situations where intellectual property will be tainted:

- The intellectual property was the property of the end user or of a taxable person that is or was a connected person, as defined in s 31(4), in relation to the end user (para *(a)*). The concepts of 'end user' and 'taxable person' are discussed below. For the purposes of s 23I, the concept of 'connected person' is as defined in s 31(4), not as defined in s 1.
- The intellectual property is the property of a taxable person (para *(b)*).
- A material part of the intellectual property was used by a taxable person in carrying on a business while that property was the property of a taxable person and the end user of that property acquired that business or a material part thereof as a going concern (para *(c)*).
- The intellectual property was discovered, devised, developed, created or produced by the end user of that property, or by a taxable person that is a connected person, as defined in s 31(4), in relation to the end user, if that end user, together with any taxable person that is a connected person in relation to that end user, holds at least 20% of the participation rights, as defined in s 9D, in a person by or to whom an amount is received or accrues:
  - by virtue of the grant of use, right of use or permission to use that property; or
  - where that receipt, accrual or amount is determined directly or indirectly with reference to expenditure incurred for the use, right of use or permission to use that property (para *(d)*).

An 'end user' is defined in s 23I(1) as:

- a taxable person; or
- a person with a permanent establishment within the Republic,

that uses intellectual property or any corresponding invention during a year of assessment to derive income. A person that derives income mainly by virtue of the grant of use, right of use or permission to use intellectual property or any corresponding invention is, however, not an end user.

A 'taxable person' is defined in s 23I(1) as any person *other than* those listed below:

CHAPTER 7

- a person that is not a resident (para *(a)*);
- the government of the Republic in the national, provincial or local sphere contemplated in s 10(1)*(a)* (para *(b)*);
- an institution, board or body contemplated in s 10(1)*(cA)* (for example, an organisation that promotes scientific research) (para *(c)*);
- any public benefit organisation as defined in s 30 that has been approved by the Commissioner in terms of that section (para *(d)*);
- any recreational club as defined in s 30A that has been approved by the Commissioner in terms of that section (para *(e)*);
- any company or trust contemplated in s 37A (a closure rehabilitation company or trust) (para *(f)*);
- any fund contemplated in s 10(1)*(d)*(i) or (ii) (for example, a pension fund) (para *(g)*); and
- any person contemplated in s 10(1)*(t)* (for example, the Council for Scientific and Industrial Research) (para *(h)*).

The persons listed above are not regarded as *taxpayers* as they are either not fully subject to tax in South Africa (for example, non-residents) or are exempt from tax (for example, public benefit organisations).

7.8.4.2 Application of s 23I

The remedy available to the Commissioner to use against tainted intellectual property is the prohibition or limitation of any deduction for certain expenditure in respect of the use of the intellectual property (effectively any royalties paid).

A deduction is not allowed in respect of:

- any amount of expenditure incurred for the use, right of use or permission to use tainted intellectual property; or
- expenditure, the incurral or amount of which is determined directly or indirectly with reference to expenditure incurred for the use, right of use or permission to use tainted intellectual property,

to the extent that the amount of expenditure does not constitute:

- income received by or accrued to any other person; or
- a proportional amount of net income of a controlled foreign company, an amount equal to which is included in the income of any resident in terms of s 9D.

The prohibition or limitation does not apply to a deduction allowed in terms of s 11*(gC)* (expenditure incurred for the acquisition of intellectual property) or a deduction allowed in respect of trading stock. (Section 23I(2))

If, however, tax contemplated in Part IVA (the withholding tax on royalties in s 49A to 49G) is payable in respect of an amount of any expenditure contemplated in s 23I(2) at a rate of:

- 10%, then an amount equal to one-third of the expenditure is allowed to be deducted (s 23I(3)*(a)*); or
- 15%, then an amount equal to one-half of the expenditure is allowed to be deducted (s 23I(3)*(b)*).

The withholding tax rate in Part IVA is currently 15%: if the recipient of the royalty is subject to this rate of withholding tax, then the taxpayer that pays the royalty will qualify for a deduction of one-half of the expenditure. In certain instances, however, a double tax agreement between South Africa and another country may limit the withholding tax: if the reduced rate of withholding tax is 10%, then the deduction of only one-third of the expenditure is permitted.

7.9 ENVIRONMENTAL EXPENDITURE

Section 37B provides for three different allowances for qualifying environmental expenditure that may be deducted from the income of a taxpayer. There are two allowances available for environmental treatment and recycling assets and for environmental waste disposal assets that are brought into use by taxpayers for the first time. There is also an allowance for certain expenditure or losses in respect of decommissioning, remediation or restoration on cessation of trade.

7.9.1 Environmental treatment and recycling assets

An environmental treatment and recycling asset is defined as any air, water and solid waste treatment and recycling plant or pollution control and monitoring equipment (and any improvement to the plant or equipment) if the plant or equipment is:

- utilised in the course of a taxpayer's trade in a process that is ancillary to any process of manufacture or any other process which, in the opinion of the Commissioner, is of a similar nature; and
- required by any law of the Republic for purposes of complying with measures that protect the environment (definition of 'environmental treatment and recycling asset' in s 37B(1)).

7.9.2 Environmental waste disposal assets

An environmental waste disposal asset is defined as any air, water and solid waste disposal site, dam, dump, reservoir, or other structure of a similar nature, or any improvement thereto, if the structure is:

- of a permanent nature;
- utilised in the course of a taxpayer's trade in a process that is ancillary to any process of manufacture or any other process which, in the opinion of the Commissioner, is of a similar nature; and
- required by any law of the Republic for purposes of complying with measures that protect the environment (definition of 'environmental waste disposal asset' in s 37B(1)).

7.9.3 Allowances

In the case of a new and unused environmental treatment and recycling asset, the allowance is 40% of the cost to the taxpayer to acquire the asset in the year of assessment that it is brought into use for the first time by that taxpayer, and 20% in each succeeding year of assessment (s 37B(2)*(a)*). The asset can be owned by the taxpayer or can be acquired by the taxpayer as purchaser in terms of an agreement contemplated in para *(a)* of the definition of an 'instalment credit agreement' in s 1 of the Value-Added Tax Act.

In the case of a new and unused environmental waste disposal asset, the allowance is 5% of the cost to the taxpayer to acquire the asset in the year of assessment that it is brought into use for the first time by that taxpayer, and 5% in each succeeding year of assessment (s 37B(2)*(b)*). The asset can be owned by the taxpayer or can be acquired by the taxpayer as purchaser in terms of an agreement contemplated in para *(a)* of the definition of an 'instalment credit agreement' in s 1 of the Value-Added Tax Act.

The cost to a taxpayer of any asset is deemed to be the lesser of:

- the actual cost to the taxpayer; or
- the cost which a person would, if that person had acquired that asset under a cash transaction concluded at arm's length on the date on which the transaction for the acquisition was in fact concluded, have incurred in respect of the direct cost of the acquisition (s 37B(3)).

The deductions which may be allowed in terms of s 37B in respect of any asset shall not in the aggregate exceed the cost to the taxpayer of the asset (s 37B(9)).

No deduction is allowed in respect of any asset that has been disposed of by the taxpayer during any previous year of assessment (s 37B(5)).

No deduction is allowed under s 11 (for example, a wear and tear or depreciation allowance), s 12C (for example, for plant used directly in a process of manufacture) or s 13 (a building used in a process of manufacture or for research and development) in respect of the cost of an environmental treatment and recycling asset or an environmental waste disposal asset (s 37B(8)).

Where any asset in respect of which any deduction is claimed in terms of this section was during any previous year of assessment used by the taxpayer for the purposes of any trade carried on by it, the receipts and accruals of which were not included in its income during that year, any deduction which could have been allowed in terms of s 37B during that year or any subsequent year in which the asset was used by it shall for the purposes of s 37B be deemed to have been allowed during that previous year or years as if the receipts and accruals of that trade had been included in its income (s 37B(4)).

7.9.4 Decommissioning, remediation or restoration

In determining the taxable income derived during any year of assessment by a taxpayer, a deduction is allowed for any expenditure or loss in respect of decommissioning, remediation or restoration arising from any trade previously carried on by that taxpayer to the extent that the expenditure or loss meets all of the requirements listed below:

- It is incurred for purposes of complying with any law of the Republic that provides for the protection of the environment upon the cessation of trade.
- It would otherwise have been allowed as a deduction in terms of s 11 had that taxpayer still been carrying on that trade.
- It is not otherwise allowed as a deduction. (Section 37B(6))

Any assessed loss of a taxpayer as defined in s 20(2) that is attributable to any decommissioning, remediation or restoration expenditure or loss as contemplated in s 37B(6) may be set off against income derived by that taxpayer during a year of assessment notwithstanding the fact that the taxpayer is not carrying on any trade during that year (s 37B(7)). This is an important provision as it overrides the usual requirement of s 11 that a taxpayer must be carrying on a trade in order to qualify for a deduction.

7.10 CERTAIN PIPELINES, TRANSMISSION LINES AND RAILWAY LINES

Section 12D provides for an allowance in respect of the cost actually incurred by a taxpayer in respect of the acquisition of any new and unused 'affected asset', being the following:

- a pipeline used for the transportation of natural oil;
- a pipeline for the transportation of water used by power stations in the process of generating electricity;
- a line or cable used for the transmission of electricity;
- a line or cable used for the transmission of electronic communications; or
- a railway line used for the transportation of persons, goods or things,

including any earthworks or supporting structures forming part of the pipeline, transmission line or cable or railway line and any improvement to the pipeline, transmission line or cable or railway line (definition of 'affected asset' in s 12D(1)).

To qualify for the allowance the relevant asset must be:

- owned by the taxpayer and brought into use for the first time by that taxpayer; and
- used directly by the taxpayer for the purposes listed above (s 12D(2)).

For any one year, the allowance may not exceed:

- 10% of the cost incurred in respect of a pipeline used for the transportation of natural oil; or
- 5% of the cost incurred in respect of any of the remaining assets listed in the definition of affected asset (s 12D(3)).

Where any affected asset in respect of which any deduction is claimed in terms of s 12D was during any previous year of assessment used by the taxpayer for the purposes of any trade carried on by it, the receipts and accruals of which were not included in its income during that year, any deduction which could have been allowed in terms of s 12D during that previous year or any subsequent year in which that asset was used by it shall for the purposes of s 12D be deemed to have been allowed during that previous year or years as if the receipts and accruals of that trade had been included in its income (s 12D(3A)).

The cost to a taxpayer of any affected asset shall be deemed to be:

- where the asset has been acquired to replace any asset which has been damaged or destroyed, the actual cost of the asset, less any amount which has been recovered or recouped in respect of the damaged or destroyed asset which has been excluded from its income in terms of s 8(4)*(e)*, whether in the current or any previous year of assessment; or
- in any other case, the lesser of:
    - the actual cost of the asset incurred by the taxpayer; or
    - the cost which it would, if it had acquired or improved the asset under a cash transaction concluded at arm's length on the date on which the transaction for the acquisition or improvement of the asset was in fact concluded, have incurred in respect of the direct cost of acquisition or improvement of the asset (including the direct cost of the installation or erection thereof) (s 12D(4)).

No deduction is allowed under s 12D in respect of any affected asset which has been disposed of by a taxpayer during any previous year of assessment (s 12D(5)).

The deductions which may be allowed or deemed to have been allowed in terms of s 12D and any other provision of the Act in respect of the cost of any affected asset shall not in the aggregate exceed the amount of the cost (s 12D(6)).

If a taxpayer completes an improvement as contemplated in s 12N (for example, in terms of a public private partnership), the expenditure incurred by it to complete that improvement shall be deemed to be the cost actually incurred by it in respect of the acquisition of a new and unused affected asset (s 12D(2A)).

7.11 ROLLING STOCK

Section 12DA provides for an allowance in respect of the cost actually incurred by a taxpayer in respect of the acquisition or improvement of any rolling stock which is owned by it, or acquired by it as purchaser in terms of an agreement contemplated in para *(a)* of an 'instalment credit agreement' as defined in s 1 of the Value-Added Tax Act 89 of 1991, and is used directly by it wholly or mainly for the transportation of persons, goods or things to the extent that the rolling stock is used in the production of its income (s 12DA(1)).

The allowance in respect of any one year of assessment is 20% of the cost incurred in respect of any rolling stock (s 12DA(2)).

The cost to a taxpayer of any rolling stock is deemed to be the lesser of:

- the actual cost to the taxpayer; or
- the cost which a person would, if that person had acquired or improved the rolling stock under a cash transaction concluded at arm's length on the date on which the transaction for the acquisition or improvement of the rolling stock was in fact concluded, have incurred in respect of the direct cost of the acquisition or improvement of the rolling stock.

Where any rolling stock in respect of which any deduction is claimed in terms of s 12DA was during any previous year of assessment used by the taxpayer for the purposes of any trade carried on by it, the receipts and accruals of which were not included in its income during that year, any deduction which could have been allowed in terms of s 12DA during that year or any subsequent year in which that asset was used by it shall for the purposes of s 12DA be deemed to have been allowed during that previous year or years as if the receipts and accruals of that trade had been included in its income (s 12DA(4)).

No deduction is allowed under s 12DA in respect of any rolling stock that has been disposed of by a taxpayer during any previous year of assessment (s 12DA(5)).

The deductions which may be allowed or deemed to have been allowed in terms of s 12DA and any other provision of the Act in respect of the cost of any rolling stock shall not in the aggregate exceed the amount of the cost (s 12DA(6)).

7.12 AIRPORT AND PORT ASSETS

Section 12F provides for an allowance in respect of airport and port assets, as defined.

An 'airport asset' means any aircraft hangar, apron, runway or taxiway on any designated airport, and includes any earthworks or supporting structures forming part of the aircraft hangar, apron, runway or taxiway and any improvements to the aircraft hangar, apron, runway or taxiway (definition of 'airport asset' in s 12F(1)).

A 'designated airport' means an airport approved by the Minister of Finance, in consultation with the Minister of Transport, as a designated airport by notice in the *Gazette* for purposes of s 12F (definition of 'designated airport' in s 12F(1)).

A 'port asset' means any port terminal, breakwater, sand trap, berth, quay wall, bollard, graving dock, slipway, single point mooring, dolos, fairway, surfacing, wharf, seawall, channel, basin, sand bypass, road, bridge, jetty or off-dock container depot, and includes any earthworks or supporting structures forming part of the terminal, breakwater, sand trap, berth, quay wall, bollard, graving dock, slipway, single point mooring, dolos, fairway, surfacing, wharf, seawall, channel, basin, sand bypass, road, bridge, jetty or depot and any improvements thereto (definition of 'port asset' in s 12F(1)).

The new and unused airport asset or port asset must be:

- brought into use for the first time by the taxpayer; and
- used directly by it solely for the purposes of carrying on its business as airport, terminal or transport operator or port authority (s 12F(2)).

The allowance is granted in respect of the cost actually incurred by a taxpayer in respect of the acquisition (including the construction, erection or installation) of the asset to the extent that the asset is used in the production of its income (s 12F(2)).

The allowance in respect of a qualifying asset shall, in respect of any one year of assessment, be 5% of the cost incurred in respect of that asset (s 12F(3)).

Where any asset in respect of which any deduction is claimed in terms of s 12F was during any previous year of assessment used by a taxpayer for the purposes of any trade carried on by it, the receipts and accruals of which were not included in its income during that year, any deduction which could have been allowed in terms of s 12F during that year or any subsequent year in which that asset was used by it shall for the purposes of s 12F be deemed to have been allowed during that previous year or years as if the receipts and accruals of that trade had been included in its income (s 12F(3A)).

The cost to a taxpayer of any asset shall be deemed to be the lesser of:

- the actual cost to it; or
- the cost which a person would, if he or she had acquired the asset under a cash transaction concluded at arm's length on the date on which the transaction for the acquisition of the asset was in fact concluded, have incurred in respect of the direct cost of acquisition of the asset,

including the direct cost of the installation or erection thereof (s 12F(4)).

Where the asset has been acquired to replace an asset which has been damaged or destroyed, the cost must be reduced by any amount which has been recovered or recouped in respect of the damaged or destroyed asset and which has been excluded from the taxpayer's income in terms of s 8(4)*(e)*, whether in the current or any previous year of assessment (s 12F(4)).

No deduction is allowed under s 12F in respect of any asset which has been disposed of by a taxpayer during any previous year of assessment (s 12F(5)).

Where a taxpayer completes improvements as contemplated in s 12N (for example, in terms of a public private partnership), the expenditure incurred by it to complete that improvement shall be deemed to be the cost actually incurred by it in respect of the acquisition of a new and unused airport asset or port asset (s 12F(2A)).

The deductions which may be allowed or deemed to have been allowed in terms of s 12F and any other provision of the Act in respect of the cost of any asset shall not in the aggregate exceed the amount of the cost (s 12F(6)).

7.13 ADDITIONAL INVESTMENT AND TRAINING ALLOWANCES IN RESPECT OF INDUSTRIAL POLICY PROJECTS

The objectives of the introduction of the s 12I additional investment and training allowances were to support:

- investment in manufacturing assets that will improve the productivity of the South African manufacturing sector; and
- training of personnel to improve labour productivity and the skills of the labour force.[28]

The allowances provided by s 12I include an additional investment allowance for new and unused manufacturing assets used in qualifying industrial policy projects (s 12I(2)) and an additional training allowance (s 12I(4)). Section 12I also provides for an assessed loss from the granting of the allowances to be increased by an interest factor in certain circumstances (s 12I(6)). The allowances are available for projects for which approval applications are submitted to the Minister of Trade and Industry not later than 31 December 2015 (s 12I(7)*(d)*).

7.13.1 Additional investment allowance

The additional investment allowance is equal to:

- 55% of the cost of any new and unused manufacturing asset used in an industrial policy project with preferred status (s 12I(2)*(a)*(i)); or
- 100% of the cost of any new and unused manufacturing asset used in an industrial policy project with preferred status that is located within an industrial development zone (s 12I(2)*(a)*(ii)); or
- 35% of the cost of any new and unused manufacturing asset used in any industrial policy project other than a project with preferred status (s 12I(2)*(b)*(i)); or

[28] Explanatory Memorandum on the Revenue Laws Amendment Bill 2008 [W.P.2 – '08] 81.

- 75% of the cost of any new and unused manufacturing asset used in any industrial policy project other than a project with preferred status that is located within an industrial development zone (s 12I(2)*(b)*(ii)).

The cost to a taxpayer of any manufacturing asset is deemed to be the lesser of:

- the actual cost to the taxpayer; or
- the cost which a person would, if the person had acquired that manufacturing asset under a cash transaction concluded at arm's length on the date on which the transaction for the acquisition was in fact concluded, have incurred in respect of the direct cost of the acquisition of the manufacturing asset (s 12I(24)).

The allowance is granted in the year of assessment during which the asset is first brought into use by the company that owns the asset for the furtherance of the industrial policy project carried on by it, if that asset was acquired and contracted for on or after the date of approval and was brought into use within four years from the date of approval (s 12I(2)).

If a taxpayer completes an improvement as contemplated in s 12N (for example, in terms of a public private partnership), the improvement shall be deemed to be a new and unused manufacturing asset and the expenditure incurred by it to complete the improvement shall be deemed to be the cost of that new and unused manufacturing asset (s 12I(1A)).

The additional investment allowance may not exceed:

- R900 million in the case of any greenfield project with preferred status, or R550 million in the case of any other greenfield project from the date of approval; or
- R550 million in the case of any brownfield project with preferred status, or R350 million in the case of any other brownfield project from the date of approval (s 12I(3)).

7.13.2 Additional training allowance

In addition to any other deductions allowable in terms of the Act, a company may deduct an additional training allowance equal to the cost of training provided to employees in the year of assessment during which the cost of training is incurred for the furtherance of the industrial policy project carried on by it (s 12I(4)).

The cost of training must, however, be incurred within six years from the date of approval of the project (s 12I(5)*(a)*).

The additional training allowance granted to a company may not exceed R36 000 per employee (s 12I(5)*(a)*). In addition, the additional training allowance granted to a company within the six-year period from the date of approval of the project may not exceed:

- R30 million in the case of an industrial policy project with preferred status; and
- R20 million in the case of any other industrial policy project (s 12I(5)*(b)*).

The cost of training means:

- in the case of training provided by the taxpayer, the cost of remuneration of its employees who are employed exclusively to provide training to its employees and the cost of training materials;
- in the case of training provided by a person that is a connected person in relation to the taxpayer, so much of the cost charged by the connected person as is incurred in respect of the remuneration of employees who are employed to provide training to the taxpayer's employees and the cost of materials used by the connected person to provide the training; and
- in any other case, the cost to the taxpayer of the training charged by the person providing the training (definition of 'cost of training' in s 12I(1)).

7.13.3 Assessed loss adjustment

Where a taxpayer is or was allowed a deduction for an additional investment allowance in the current or any previous year of assessment, any balance of assessed loss carried forward by it during a year of assessment must be increased by the amount by which that balance of assessed loss exceeds an amount equal to any balance of assessed loss that would have been carried forward during that year had that deduction not been allowed, multiplied by the rate contemplated in para *(a)* of the definition of 'prescribed rate' as at the end of the year of assessment (s 12I(6)*(a)*).

The adjustment of an assessed loss by an amount based on the prescribed rate does not apply in respect of any balance of assessed loss incurred by a taxpayer during any year of assessment more than four years after the year during which the approval of the industrial project is granted (s 12I(6)*(b)*).

7.13.4 Definitions

An 'industrial project' means a trade solely or mainly for the manufacture of products, goods, articles or other things within the Republic that:

- is classified under 'Section C: Manufacturing' in version 7 of the Standard Industrial Classification Code (referred to as the 'SIC Code') issued by Statistics South Africa; or
- in the case of products, goods, articles or things which are not yet classified, the adjudication committee is of the view will be classified as above,

but does not include the manufacture of certain products, for example, tobacco products and arms and ammunition (definition of 'industrial project' in s 12I(1)).

An industrial project of a company constitutes an industrial policy project if certain requirements are met, for example, the Minister of Trade and Industry, after taking into account the recommendations of an adjudication committee, is satisfied, inter alia, that the cost of all manufacturing assets to be acquired by the company for the purposes of the project will exceed in the case of:

- greenfield projects, R200 million; and

- brownfield projects, the higher of R30 million or the lesser of R200 million or 25% of the expenditure incurred to acquire assets previously used in the project.

(Section 12I(7))

The Minister of Trade and Industry must, after taking into account the recommendations of an adjudication committee, approve an industrial project as an industrial policy project, either with or without preferred status, where that Minister is satisfied that the industrial policy project will significantly contribute to the Industrial Policy Programme within the Republic, having regard to certain matters, for example, the extent to which the project will upgrade an industry within the Republic by utilising new technology that results in improved energy efficiency and by providing skills development (s 12I(8)).

The Minister of Trade and Industry may not approve any industrial project where the potential additional investment and training allowances in respect of that project and all other approved industrial projects will in the aggregate exceed R20 billion (s 12I(9)).

A 'manufacturing asset' means any building, plant or machinery acquired, contracted for or brought into use by a company, which:

- will mainly be used by it in the Republic for the purposes of carrying on its industrial project within the Republic; and
- will qualify for a deduction in terms of s 12C(1)*(a)* (machinery and plant used directly in a process of manufacture or similar process), s 13 (building in which a process of manufacture or research and development is carried out), or s 13*quat* (buildings in urban development zones),

and includes any improvement to the building, plant or machinery (definition of 'manufacturing asset' in s 12I(1)).

A 'brownfield project' means a project that represents an expansion or upgrade of an existing industrial project (definition of 'brownfield project' in s 12I(1)).

A 'greenfield project' means a project that represents a wholly new industrial project which does not utilise any manufacturing assets other than wholly new and unused manufacturing assets (definition of 'greenfield project' in s 12I(1)).

7.13.5 Administrative provisions

The extensive administrative provisions that are contained in s 12I include the following:

- The Minister of Finance, in consultation with the Minister of Trade and Industry, must make regulations prescribing, for example, the factors to be taken into account in determining the extent to which a project creates direct employment within the Republic (s 12I(10)).
- A company carrying on an industrial policy project must report to the adjudication committee with respect to the progress of the industrial policy project within 12 months after the close of each year of assessment, starting with the year in which approval is granted (s 12I(11)).

7.14 IMPROVEMENTS NOT OWNED BY TAXPAYER

To qualify for certain allowances, a taxpayer is required to own the relevant asset, for example, the allowance for buildings in urban development zones in s 13*quat.* This ownership requirement is problematic when a building is erected or improvements are carried out on land that is not owned by the taxpayer but by a branch of government from which it rents the land, as the taxpayer does not own the building or improvements.

Section 12N provides a solution to the problem of assets not being owned by a taxpayer that wishes to claim an allowance for a building or improvements on land that it does not own but for which it holds a right of use, by deeming the land to be owned by a lessee in certain circumstances. The deemed ownership opens the door for affected taxpayers to claim the allowance on qualifying assets in terms of various allowances. Section 12N also provides for the termination and renewal of the right to use the land.

7.14.1 Deemed ownership

A taxpayer must be deemed to be the owner of an improvement, for the purposes of the deductions in the provisions listed below and for the purposes of the capital gains tax provisions in the Eighth Schedule, if it satisfies all of the following requirements:

- It holds a right of use or occupation of land or a building.
- It incurs an obligation to effect an improvement on the land or to the building in terms of:
  - a public private partnership;
  - an agreement in terms of which the right of use or occupation is granted, if the land or building is owned by:
    - the government of the Republic in the national, provincial or local sphere; or
    - any entity of which the receipts and accruals are exempt from tax in terms of s 10(1)*(c*A*)* (certain tax-exempt institutions) or s 10(1)*(t)* (certain other tax-exempt bodies); or
  - the Independent Power Producer Procurement Programme administered by the Department of Energy.
- It incurs expenditure to effect the improvement contemplated above.
- It completes the improvement contemplated above.
- It uses or occupies the land or building for the production of income or derives income from the land or building.

The deductions contemplated are those in the following sections:

- 11D (scientific research and development);
- 12B (assets used in farming operations and in generating renewable energy);

- 12C manufacturers, hotel keepers, aircraft, ships and agricultural products;
- 12D (certain pipelines, transmission lines and railway lines);
- 12F (airport and port assets);
- 12I (industrial policy projects);
- 12S buildings in special economic zones;
- 13 (buildings in which a process of manufacture, research and development or similar process is carried on);
- 13*bis* (buildings used by hotel keepers);
- 13*ter* (a now obsolete residential building allowance);
- 13*quat* (buildings in urban development zones);
- 13*quin* (commercial buildings);
- 13*sex* (residential units); or
- 36 (mining operations).

(Section 12N(1))

7.14.2 Termination of right of use

When the right of use or occupation terminates, the taxpayer must be deemed to have disposed of the improvement to the owner of the land or building on the later of the date when:

- the right of use or occupation terminated; or
- the use or occupation ended (s 12N(2)*(a)*).

If the right of use or occupation terminates and the taxpayer:

- continues to use or occupy the land or building; or
- renews the right of use or occupation,

the renewed right of use or occupation must be deemed to be the same right of use or occupation as the right of use or occupation previously held by the taxpayer (s 12N(2)*(b)*).

7.14.3 Anti-avoidance provision

The deemed ownership provision of s 12N does *not* apply to taxpayers in two situations.

The first category of disqualified taxpayers is persons carrying on any banking or financial services or insurance business.

The second category of disqualified taxpayers is those that enter into an agreement whereby the right of use or occupation of the land or building is granted to any other person, unless:

- the land or building is occupied by that other person and that other person is a company that is a member of the same group of companies as that taxpayer in terms of the agreement;
- the cost of maintaining the land or building and of carrying out repairs thereto required in consequence of normal wear and tear is borne by the taxpayer; and
- subject to any claim that the taxpayer may have against the other person by reason of the other person's failure to take proper care of the land or building, the risk of destruction or loss of or other disadvantage to the land or building is not assumed by that other person.

(Section 12N(3))

7.15 NATIONAL KEY POINTS

A taxpayer may have to incur capital expenditure in order to comply with its obligations in terms of the National Key Points Act: s 24D provides a deduction for this expenditure.

The deduction from the income of a taxpayer for a year of assessment is so much of any expenditure actually incurred by him or her as the Commissioner is satisfied was so incurred during such year:

- directly in the performance of any act ordered, performed or executed under the provisions of the National Key Points Act 102 of 1980, in respect of any national key point or key point as defined in s 1 of that Act; or
- directly in providing efficient security against loss, damage, disruption or immobilisation of any place or area as defined in s 1 of that Act which, although not declared a national key point under the provisions of that Act, has been evaluated and approved by the Minister of Defence or any person or committee appointed by him or her as such a place or area in respect of which measures for the efficient security thereof ought to be taken by the taxpayer.

The amount of any expenditure allowed to be deducted under s 24D(1) is restricted to expenditure:

- actually incurred by the taxpayer on or after 1 September 1978; and
- which was or is not otherwise allowable as a deduction under the provisions of the Act,

and no claim by the taxpayer for the deduction of any expenditure under the provisions of s 24D shall be admitted by the Commissioner unless confirmation has been received by him or her from the Minister of Defence or any person or committee appointed by that Minister to the effect that it was deemed necessary or expedient that the expenditure in question be incurred by the taxpayer concerned (s 24D(2)).

Where an amount has been paid by the state to a taxpayer in respect of expenditure incurred by him or her prior to 1 July 1983 which has qualified for deduction from his or her income under s 24D(1) and the Minister, person or committee referred to in s 24D(2) confirms that the amount was paid as a supplement to the benefit which the taxpayer has enjoyed or will enjoy by way of the deduction, the recoupment provisions of s 8(4)*(a)* shall not apply in respect of the amount (s 24D(3)).

7.16 ASSETS ACQUIRED IN EXCHANGE FOR SHARES OR DEBT ISSUED

Section 40CA contains provisions that apply when a company acquires an asset in exchange for shares or debt issued. As a transaction such as this is not for a cash consideration, when the company wishes to claim an allowance on the relevant asset, it may be uncertain what the cost of the asset is.

In *CSARS v Labat*,[29] the taxpayer was not successful in its claim that it had incurred expenditure on the acquisition of a trade mark when it issued shares to the seller in settlement of the consideration for the trade mark. Harms JA stated (at [12]) that expenditure requires a diminution of or at very least movement of assets of the person who expends. Harms JA also referred (at [14]) to Goldblatt J's statement in *ITC 1783*[30] that an allotment or issuing of shares does not in any way reduce the assets of a company although it may reduce the value of the shares held by its shareholders.

Section 40CA provides a solution to this problem. The assets to which the provisions of s 40CA apply are assets as defined in para 1 of the Eighth Schedule, other than shares (to which the provisions of s 24B apply). Section 40CA came into effect on 1 January 2013 and applies to any acquisitions of assets other than shares on or after that date. Prior to 1 January 2013, the provisions of s 24B applied to acquisitions of both shares and other assets.

If a company acquires any asset from any person in exchange for shares issued by that company, that company is deemed to have actually incurred an amount of expenditure in respect of the acquisition of that asset which is equal to the market value of the shares immediately after the acquisition (s 40CA(1)*(a)*).

If the asset is acquired for an amount of debt issued by that company, that company is deemed to have actually incurred an amount of expenditure in respect of the acquisition of the asset which is equal to that amount of debt (s 40CA(1)*(b)*).

---

[29] *CSARS v Labat Africa Ltd* 2013 (2) SA 33 (SCA), 74 SATC 1.

[30] (2004) 66 SATC 373.

Chapter 8

Employees' tax and provisional tax

8.1 EMPLOYEES' TAX

8.1.1 Introduction

The Fourth Schedule to the Income Tax Act 58 of 1962 requires every 'employer' (as defined in the Fourth Schedule)[1] to deduct or withhold employees' tax from 'remuneration' paid by that employer to an 'employee' (as defined).[2] This system is commonly called 'PAYE' (pay-as-you-earn), which connotes that the

[1] See para 1 of the Fourth Schedule.
[2] Ibid.

tax is, on a continuous basis, withheld by the employer from each payment of remuneration to an employee and is then paid over to SARS. By contrast, where income is not subject to tax in the form of PAYE or provisional tax, the requisite income tax is generally payable to SARS in a lump sum on the basis of an assessment issued by SARS at the end of each year of assessment.

The provisions of the Income Tax Act in relation to employees' tax are laid down in the Fourth Schedule to the Act, which must be read in conjunction with the Tax Administration Act 28 of 2011. The latter Act deals with the administrative aspects of employees' tax, as distinct from the 'charging' provisions, which impose liability to tax and are located in the Income Tax Act and its schedules. The Fourth Schedule defines 'employees' tax' as the tax required to be deducted or withheld by an employer[3] from 'remuneration' (as defined)[4] that is paid or payable by an 'employer' to an 'employee'.

For this purpose, every employer is required to register with SARS and is then provided with the applicable tax deduction tables, which show the amount of the deduction to be made from the remuneration of employees.

The employer must, within seven days from the end of each month, pay over to the SARS office where he or she is registered, the total amount of the employees' tax deducted by him or her from remuneration paid to employees during the previous month.

Within a stipulated period after the end of each year of assessment, an employer must provide each employee with an employees' IRP 5 tax certificate, showing remuneration earned and the total amount of employees' tax deducted. The employer must also provide each employee who, during the course of that year, had derived a non-monetary taxable benefit (commonly called a 'fringe benefit') from that employer from which employees' tax had not been fully deducted, with a separate certificate showing the nature and the cash equivalent of the value of that taxable benefit. An employer must also make an annual statement as to the fringe benefits provided to employees.

At the end of each year of assessment, an employer must furnish SARS with a statement showing the remuneration that has accrued to each employee in that year, and the employees' tax that has been paid over to SARS.

If an employee is required to submit an income tax return, he or she will submit it in the usual way. If he or she submits the return electronically, he or she does not provide SARS with the hard copy of the employees' tax certificate, but SARS will credit the employee with an amount of tax equal to the employees' tax shown on the certificate as having been deducted from his or her remuneration. If the assessed tax is greater than the employee's tax credit, the employee must pay the shortfall in the tax, and can do so interest-free if it is paid within the period specified on the notice of assessment. On the other hand, if the employee's tax credit exceeds the assessed taxes, the employee will receive a refund of the excess, unless the Act prohibits the making of a refund.

[3] In terms of para 2 of the Fourth Schedule.

[4] See para 1 of the Fourth Schedule.

Amounts that are paid or are payable to a person in the course of a trade carried on by him or her independently of the person by whom the amount is paid or payable are not subject to the deduction of employees' tax, because the recipient taxpayer was not paid those amounts as an 'employee' but as an independent contractor. However, the definition of 'remuneration' in the Fourth Schedule contains far-reaching and complex deeming provisions as to the circumstances in which a person will not be regarded, for purposes of the Schedule, as carrying on a trade independently, in which event amounts payable to the person by the payer constitute 'remuneration' from which employees' tax must be deducted.

8.1.2 'Remuneration'

Central to the operation of the Fourth Schedule is its definition of 'remuneration'.[5]

Remuneration is defined as an amount of income that is paid or is payable to a person by way of any salary, leave pay, wage, overtime pay, bonus, gratuity, commission, fee, emolument, pension, superannuation allowance, retiring allowance or stipend, whether in cash or otherwise and whether or not for services rendered.

The definition of 'remuneration' goes on to expressly include various specific amounts and benefits, of which the following are the most significant:

- an amount referred to in para *(a)* of the definition of the term 'gross income' in s 1, that is to say, an amount received or accrued by way of an annuity and any 'annuity amount' as defined in s 10A(1);
- an amount referred to in para *(c)* of the definition of the term 'gross income', that is to say, an amount, including a voluntary award, received or accrued for services rendered or to be rendered or an amount (other than an amount referred to in s 8(1) which covers travelling, subsistence and certain other allowances) that has been derived from employment or the holding of any office;
- an amount referred to in para *(d)* of the definition of the term 'gross income', that is to say, an amount, including a voluntary award, received or accrued for the relinquishment, termination, loss, repudiation, cancellation or variation of any office or employment or of any appointment to any office or employment, excluding lump sum awards from pension, provident and retirement annuity funds;
- an amount referred to in para *(e)* of the definition of the term 'gross income', that is to say, a lump sum benefit received by or accrued to a person from an approved pension, provident or retirement annuity fund, if that person is or was a member of the fund;
- an amount referred to in para *(eA)* of the definition of the term 'gross income' in s 1, that is to say, in relation to a member or the dependants or nominees of a deceased member, an amount transferred from a

[5] In para 1 of the Fourth Schedule.

'public sector' pension fund to a 'public' or 'private sector' provident fund or, alternatively, an amount transferred on the conversion of a 'public' sector pension fund to a provident fund;

- an amount referred to in para *(f)* of the definition of the term 'gross income', that is to say, any amount received or accrued in commutation of an amount due under a contract of employment or service;
- an amount included in a person's gross income under para *(i)* of the definition of the term 'gross income', as the cash equivalent during the tax year of any fringe benefit taxable under the Seventh Schedule other than the value of a right to the private or domestic use of a motor vehicle (the value of which is, as from years of assessment commencing on or after 1 March 2011, separately provided for in para *(c*B*)* of the definition of 'remuneration'). Where a fringe benefit provided by an employer to an employee falls within the scope of the Seventh Schedule, its value (that is to say, its 'cash equivalent') has to be determined in accordance with that Schedule, and SARS has no discretion to elect to collect the tax or to assign a value to the benefit by any other process;[6]
- an allowance or advance that a person is required to include in his or her taxable income under s 8(1)*(a)*(i). In other words, an allowance or advance that has to be included in taxable income to the extent that it was not, in fact, expended on travelling on business or not expended by reason of the duties attendant upon his or her public office. Certain benefits are specifically exempted from having to be included under this provision;
- 80% of the amount of an allowance or advance for transport expenses referred to in s 8(1)*(b)*, which could take the form either of an allowance or of an advance provided by an employer to an employee for travelling expenses or for the expenditure incurred by the employee on a motor vehicle used by him or her. However, no amount need be included if it is a 'reimbursive motor-vehicle allowance' that is based on the actual distance travelled by the employee.. With effect from the commencement of years of assessment commencing on or after 1 March 2011, where the employer is satisfied that at least 80% of the use of the motor vehicle for a tax year will be for business purposes, only 20% of the allowance must be so included;[7]
- with effect from the commencement of years of assessment commencing on or after 1 March 2011, para *(c*B*)* was added to include in 'remuneration' 80% of a taxable fringe benefit that takes the form of a right to the use, for private purposes, of a motor vehicle. But where the employer is satisfied that at least 80% of the use of the motor vehicle for a tax year will be for business purposes, only 20% of the value of such a benefit must be so included;

[6] *Vacation Exchanges International (Pty) Ltd v CSARS* 2009 JDR 0743 (WCC), (2009) 71 SATC 249.

[7] See para *(c*A*)* of the definition of 'remuneration'.

- 100% of so much of the amount paid or granted as an allowance or advance referred to in s 8(1)*(b)*(iii) as exceeds the amount determined by applying the rate per kilometre for the simplified method in the notice fixing the rate per kilometre under s 8(1)*(b)*(ii) and (iii) to the actual distance travelled;[8]
- a gain determined under s 8B (that is to say, a gain from the disposal of equity shares acquired in terms of a broad-based employee share plan) which must be included in income;[9] and
- a gain determined in terms of s 8C which is required to be included in income. Section 8C provides for the taxation of equity instruments (essentially, shares) in the hands of an employee or director from a right obtained to acquire an equity instrument, the gain or loss of which must be included in or deducted from income if it was acquired by virtue of his or her employment or office of director of a company.[10]

'Remuneration', as defined in the Fourth Schedule, expressly *excludes* (and therefore employees' tax need not be deducted from) the following amounts:

- a pension under the Aged Persons Act 81 of 1967 or the Blind Persons Act 26 of 1968, any disability grant or additional or supplementary allowance under the Disability Grants Act 27 of 1968 or a grant or contribution under the Children's Act 33 of 1960;[11]
- an amount payable to a non-resident or to a person for services rendered as an independent contractor and not as an employee;[12]
- an amount paid or payable to an employee wholly in reimbursement for expenditure actually incurred by him or her in the course of his or her employment;[13]
- an annuity under an order of divorce or decree of judicial separation or under an agreement of separation;[14] and
- an amount paid or payable for services rendered or to be rendered by a person in the course of a trade carried on by him or her independently of the person by whom the amount is paid or payable and of the person to whom the services have been or are to be rendered.

In the context of the last bulleted point, above, a person is regarded as not 'carrying on a trade independently' if the services in question are required to be performed mainly at the premises of the person by whom the amount is paid or payable or of the person to whom such services were or are to be rendered and if the person who rendered or will render the services is

[8] Section 8(1)*(cC)*, applicable to years of assessment commencing on or after 1 March 2018.

[9] See para *(d)* of the definition of the term 'remuneration'.

[10] See para *(e)* of the definition of the term 'remuneration'.

[11] See para (iii) of the exclusions from the definition of the term 'remuneration'.

[12] See para (ii) of the exclusions from the definition of the term 'remuneration'. The question whether a person is an independent contractor in this context must be determined in accordance with the specific criteria laid down in this provision.

[13] See para (vi) of the exclusions from the definition of the term 'remuneration'.

[14] See para (viii) of the exclusions from the definition of the term 'remuneration'.

subject to the control or supervision of any other person as to the manner in which his or her duties are or are to be performed or as to his or her hours of work. (These are obvious hall-marks of an employer–employee relationship, as distinct from the circumstances in which an independent contractor carries out appointed tasks.) However, such a person will be deemed to be carrying on a trade independently if, throughout the year of assessment, he or she employs three or more employees who are engaged on a full-time basis in his or her business of rendering any such service, other than any employee who is a connected person.[15]

8.1.3 Remuneration – allowances

Employees' tax must be deducted from all allowances paid or payable to an employee by an employer, which are included in the definition of 'remuneration' in the Fourth Schedule, and no employees' tax need be deducted from any amounts that do not fall within that definition.

8.1.4 Remuneration – fringe benefits

The 'cash equivalent' of taxable benefits falling under the Seventh Schedule are included in the employee's 'gross income'[16] and are consequently included in 'remuneration' as defined in the Fourth Schedule.[17] Such amounts are therefore subject to the deduction of employees' tax. Conversely, 'fringe benefits' that escape inclusion in the employee's 'gross income' because they fall within exemptions contained in the Seventh Schedule, do not fall within the scope of 'remuneration', as defined, and are therefore not subject to the deduction of employees' tax.

The following are the most common fringe benefits.

8.1.4.1 The acquisition of an asset by an employee at less than its actual value

Employees' tax is deductible from the cash equivalent of a taxable benefit that takes the form of the acquisition of an asset by an employee from his or her employer for no consideration or for a consideration that is less than its value as determined in the Seventh Schedule.[18] The amount of such cash equivalent must be shown on the employee's tax certificate, and employees' tax must be deducted in the month in which the employee acquires the asset.

[15] See para (ii) of the exclusions from the definition of the term 'remuneration'.
[16] In terms of para (i) of the exclusions from the definition of 'gross income' in s 1.
[17] See para 1 of the Fourth Schedule.
[18] See para 5 of the Seventh Schedule.

8.1.4.2 *Right of use of an asset*

This benefit takes the form of the right to use an asset (other than the right to use residential accommodation provided to the employee, which is separately provided for in the Seventh Schedule). The right to use an asset is, of course, distinct from being given the asset itself, that is to say, given ownership in the asset.

Where an employer grants an employee the sole right of use of the asset during its useful life, or for a major portion of its useful life, employees' tax must be deducted from the full value of the benefit during the month in which he or she is first granted the right of use, since the full benefit is deemed to accrue to him or her on that date.[19]

The tax must be reflected on the employee's tax certificate.

8.1.4.3 *The right to use a motor vehicle*

For the purposes of employees' tax, the cash equivalent of the value of the taxable benefit enjoyed by an employee who is granted the right to use a motor vehicle for private purposes (as distinct from being given ownership of the vehicle) is a taxable benefit.[20] The benefit of the right to use the vehicle for private purposes is regarded as accruing monthly, and employees' tax must therefore be deducted monthly from the employee's remuneration. The full amount of the value of the benefit must be reflected on the employee's tax certificate.

8.1.4.4 *Meals, refreshments and vouchers for meals and refreshments*

The full cash equivalent of the taxable benefit derived by an employee who has been provided with a meal, or with a voucher entitling the employee to a meal or refreshment, is subject to the deduction of employees' tax.[21] Such cash equivalent must be reflected on the employee's tax certificate.

8.1.4.5 *Residential accommodation*

For the purposes of employees' tax, a portion of the cash equivalent of the value of the taxable benefit enjoyed by an employee who has been granted the right to occupy residential accommodation must be allocated to each period during the year of assessment for which any cash remuneration is paid or becomes payable by the employer to the employee.[22] The amount of the cash equivalent of such a benefit is a taxable fringe benefit and is therefore subject to the deduction of employees' tax. The value of this benefit must be reflected on the employee's tax certificate.

---

[19] Paragraph 6(2)*(b)* of the Seventh Schedule.
[20] See para 7 of the Seventh Schedule.
[21] See para 8 of the Seventh Schedule.
[22] See para 9 of the Seventh Schedule.

8.1.4.6 Holiday accommodation

For the purposes of employees' tax, the cash equivalent of the value of the taxable benefit enjoyed by an employee who has been granted the temporary occupation of holiday accommodation[23] must be allocated to each period during the year of assessment for which any cash remuneration is paid or becomes payable by the employer to the employee.[24] The amount of the cash equivalent is a taxable fringe benefit and is therefore subject to the deduction of employees' tax, and this amount must be reflected on the employee's tax certificate.

8.1.4.7 Free or cheap services

Employees' tax has to be deducted from the cash equivalent of the value of the taxable benefit derived by an employee in the form of a service that has been rendered.[25] The cash equivalent must be shown on the employee's tax certificate.

8.1.4.8 Interest on loans

For the purposes of employees' tax, the cash equivalent of the value of the benefit derived by an employee as a result of a loan granted to the latter is a taxable fringe benefit.[26]

8.1.4.9 Subsidies in respect of loans

The cash equivalent of a taxable benefit that consists of a subsidy of interest or of capital repayments of a loan[27] owing by an employee where such interest or capital repayments are paid by an employer is subject to the deduction of employees' tax. The deduction of such tax takes place on a monthly basis, and the amount must be reflected on the employee's tax certificate.

8.1.4.10 The payment of an employee's debt or release of the employee from the obligation to repay a debt

Employees' tax must be deducted from the cash equivalent of the benefit enjoyed by an employee where the latter's employer has paid an amount owing by the employee to any lender, without requiring any reimbursement, or where the employer has released the employee from an obligation to pay an amount owing by him or her.[28] The cash equivalent of this benefit must be reflected on the employee's tax certificate.

[23] As determined under para 9 of the Seventh Schedule.

[24] See para 9(8) of the Seventh Schedule.

[25] See para 10 of the Seventh Schedule.

[26] See para 11 of the Seventh Schedule.

[27] Determined under para 12 of the Seventh Schedule.

[28] See para 13 of the Seventh Schedule.

8.1.4.11 Contributions to a medical scheme

Employees' tax must be deducted from the cash equivalent of the benefit derived by an employee whose employer has made a contribution or payment to a medical scheme for the benefit of the employee or his or her dependants.[29]

8.1.4.12 Medical costs of an employee, dependant or relative incurred by employer

Employees' tax must be deducted from the cash equivalent of the benefit derived by an employee where the employer has incurred expenditure on medical, dental and similar services, hospital and nursing services or medicines in respect of the employee, the employee's spouse, child or other relative or dependants.[30]

8.1.4.13 Benefits granted to relatives of employees and others

An employee will be regarded as having derived a taxable benefit where the benefit has been granted, not to the employee, but to a relative of the employee.[31]

The cash equivalent of the benefit will be included in the employee's 'remuneration' and will be subject to the deduction of employees' tax.

8.1.4.14 Bursaries and scholarships

A bona fide bursary or scholarship to enable a person to study at a recognised educational or research institution is exempt from income tax.[32] However, a bursary or scholarship is a taxable fringe benefit where it is granted by an employer or an associated institution to an employee or to a relative of the employee where it would not have been so granted if the employee in question had not been employed by the employer.

In practice, SARS takes the following view as regards what constitutes a taxable fringe benefit in this regard:[33]

- A bursary or scholarship that is granted to an employee subject to the condition that it must be repaid if certain conditions are not fulfilled (for example, on condition that the employee in due course passes an examination) is regarded as a bona fide bursary or scholarship.
- Low-interest or interest-free loans granted by the employer to an employee to enable the latter to further his or her studies are not regarded as bursaries, but as loans on which no value is placed for

[29] See para 12A of the Seventh Schedule.

[30] See para 12B of the Seventh Schedule.

[31] See para 16 of the Seventh Schedule.

[32] See s 10(1)*(q)*.

[33] See SARS *Guide for Employers in respect of Employees' Tax (2018 Tax Year)* 52.

fringe benefits tax purposes, and hence are not taxed as fringe benefits. However, if the employee is not required to repay the loan, he or she is regarded as having derived a taxable fringe benefit[34] and employees' tax must be deducted from that person's remuneration.

- There is no taxable fringe benefit where an employer sends an employee on a training course and pays for the course.
- Where an employer rewards an employee for having obtained a qualification or for successfully completing a course of study or where the employer reimburses the employee for study expenses, the reward or reimbursement is regarded as taxable remuneration.

8.1.4.15 Share-incentive schemes

Where an employee derives a benefit from a share incentive scheme that is exempt from tax,[35] this is not regarded as a taxable fringe benefit and no employees' tax need be deducted.[36]

8.1.4.16 Uniforms and uniform allowances

Where an employee is required, as a condition of his or her employment, to wear a special uniform while on duty, and the uniform is clearly distinguishable from ordinary clothing, the value of the uniform provided to the employee by the employer or an allowance given to the employee to acquire such a uniform is exempt from income tax[37] and no employees' tax need be deducted.

8.1.4.17 Transfer costs

Certain 'relocation benefits' (that is to say, benefits given where an employee has been transferred from one place of employment to another) are exempt from income tax[38] where the employer has borne the expense. Relocation expenses paid by the employer which do not fall within the exemption from income tax in this regard are subject to the deduction of employees' tax and must be reflected on the employee's tax certificate.

8.1.5 Remuneration – directors' fees

There is a distinction between an *executive director* and a *non-executive director* of a company.

A non-executive director's duties are of an intermittent nature. Such a director's duties extend only to attending and participating in meetings of the board of

[34] In terms of para 2*(h)* of the Seventh Schedule.
[35] In terms of s 10(1)*(n*E*)*.
[36] SARS *Guide for Employers in respect of Employees' Tax (2018 Tax Year)* 52.
[37] In terms of s 10(1)*(n*A*)*.
[38] In terms of s 10(1)*(n*B*)*.

directors, however frequently or infrequently they are held. Such a director does not work, so to say, nine to five for the company.

SARS accepts that non-executive directors are not employees of the company but are independent contractors in that the company exercises no control over them in relation to the way in which they perform their duties.

Consequently, a company is not required to withhold employees' tax (PAYE) from amounts paid to its non-executive directors. Non-executive directors are, however, liable for income tax on their directors' fees and must register for provisional tax.

By contrast, an executive director (such as the company's managing director) is a director of the company and, in that capacity, attends and participates in meetings of the board of directors. He or she is also an employee of the company and, in this capacity, works nine to five for the company and is paid a salary. In essence, an executive director is a salaried employee whose remuneration is subject to the withholding of employees' tax on a monthly basis in the same way as any other employee.

Close corporations do not have directors and all members of the corporation are entitled to participate in its management. In relation to a close corporation, the Act defines a 'director' as any person who, in respect of such close corporation, holds any office or performs any functions similar to the office or functions of a director of a company other than a close corporation.

8.1.6 Remuneration – rights to acquire shares

The amount of any gain from the disposal of qualifying equity shares acquired in terms of a broad-based employee share plan[39] or as a result of the vesting of an equity instrument[40] is included in the remuneration of an employee.[41]

The Fourth Schedule deems the amount of such a gain to be 'remuneration' that is payable to the employee by the person by whom the right was granted or from whom the qualifying equity share or equity instrument was acquired,[42] with the result that such 'remuneration' is subject to employees' tax. Also subject to employees' tax is any such gain where the equity instrument was acquired by the taxpayer by virtue of the latter's employment or the holding of office as director.[43]

Unless the Commissioner has given authority to the contrary, employees' tax must be deducted by the employer from any consideration payable by the latter to the employee for the cession or release of the right or from the disposal of the qualifying equity share or equity instrument or from any cash remuneration paid

[39] As envisaged in s 8B.

[40] In terms of s 8C.

[41] By virtue of paras *(b)*, *(d)* and *(e)* of the definition of the term 'remuneration' in para 1 of the Fourth Schedule.

[42] Paragraph 11A(1) of the Fourth Schedule.

[43] Paragraph 11A(1)*(c)* of the Fourth Schedule read with s 8C.

or payable by the employer to the employee after the right has been exercised, ceded or released or the equity instrument has vested or the qualifying equity share has been disposed of.[44]

The amount of employees' tax in question must be deducted during the year of assessment in which the gain arises.

An employee who has made a gain under a transaction to which the employer is not a party or who has disposed of a qualifying equity share must immediately inform his or her employer of the gain or the disposal and of the amount of the gain.[45]

8.1.7 Remuneration – annuities

Annuities are expressly included in the definition of the term 'remuneration'.[46] Consequently, the payer of an annuity is an 'employer' for the purposes of the Fourth Schedule, irrespective of how the annuity arose. For example, the annuity may have been purchased (in other words, where a person outlaid a lump sum, and in return acquired a right to an annual payment of a specified amount) or it may have been created in terms of a will.

In relation to all annuities, the payer must deduct employees' tax before making payments to the recipient of the annuity, except for annuities payable under an order of divorce or decree of judicial separation or under any agreement of separation.[47]

8.1.8 Remuneration – independent contractors, labour brokers and personal service providers

The definition of 'remuneration' in the Fourth Schedule[48] excludes any amount paid or payable for services rendered or to be rendered by a person in the course of a trade carried on independently of the person by whom the amount is paid and of the person to whom the services are rendered.

Essentially, this provision is intended to draw a distinction between 'employees' (whose remuneration will be subject to the deduction of employees' tax) and 'independent contractors' (in respect of whom no employees' tax need be deducted from amounts paid for work done). However, this relatively simple distinction between an employee (in essence, a person who works under instruction and is paid a wage or salary) and an independent contractor (who does not work under instruction but is paid to achieve a particular result) has been considerably complicated by the intrusion of statutory rules and artificial deeming provisions laid down in the Fourth Schedule.

[44] Paragraph 11A(2).
[45] Paragraph 11A(6) of the Fourth Schedule.
[46] See item *(a)* of the definition in para 1 of the Fourth Schedule.
[47] See item (viii) of the definition of the term 'remuneration' in para 1 of the Fourth Schedule.
[48] See para 1 of the Fourth Schedule.

The basic principle of the 'independent-contractor' rule is that an amount paid for services rendered or to be rendered to a person in the course of a trade carried on by him or her independently of the person paying him or her and independently of the person to whom the services have been or are to be rendered, is not 'remuneration'. In this way, independent contractors are excluded from the employees' tax system and no employees' tax need be deducted from payments made to them for work done.

However, the Fourth Schedule contains provisions that deem certain persons[49] not to be independent contractors in this sense, with the result that amounts paid to them constitute 'remuneration' from which employees' tax must be deducted. These deeming provisions state, in essence, that the following persons are not independent contractors:

- a labour broker;
- a declared employee, in other words, a person or a class or category of persons whom the Minister of Finance has declared, by notice in the *Government Gazette*, to be an employee for the purposes of the Fourth Schedule; and
- a 'personal service provider', which is a category comprising what used to be called a 'personal service company' and a 'personal service trust'.

There is, in addition, an over-arching rule, namely that a person will be deemed not to be an independent contractor if the services in question are to be performed mainly at the premises of the person by whom payment for the services is to be made or of the person to whom such services were or are to be rendered and if the person who renders the services is subject to the control or supervision of any other person as to the manner in which his or her duties are performed or as to his or her hours of work. However, despite the aforegoing, a person will be regarded as an independent contractor if, throughout the year of assessment, he or she employs three or more employees on a full-time basis in his or her business of rendering the services, other than an employee who is a shareholder in the company or who is a settlor or beneficiary of the trust. or who is a connected person (as defined)[50] in relation to such person.[51]

Despite the difficulty of drawing the line, for the purposes of the Fourth Schedule, between 'employees' (whose earnings are subject to the deduction of employees' tax) and 'independent contractors' (payments to whom are not subject to the deduction of employees' tax) it is clear that professional fees payable to self-employed professional persons such as medical practitioners, accountants and auditors, architects, quantity surveyors, attorneys and advocates, are not subject to the deduction of employees' tax.

---

[49] See paras *(b)*, *(c)*, *(d)* or *(e)* of the definition of an 'employee' in para 1 of the Fourth Schedule.

[50] See s 1 sv 'connected person'.

[51] See para *(f)*(ii) of the definition of the term 'remuneration' in para 1 of the Fourth Schedule.

8.1.8.1 Labour brokers

A 'labour broker' is a natural person, that is to say, an individual, whose business is to provide clients with persons to render a service or perform work for the client in terms of an arrangement whereby the labour broker, not the client, will pay the person who carries out the work.[52] The client will, in turn, pay the labour broker directly for the services that have been rendered in an amount which secures a profit to the labour broker. In essence, therefore, a labour broker does not, himself, carry out the work required by the client, but provides the client with a person who will do the work.

8.1.9 'Employer'

For the purposes of employees' tax, the term 'employer' is defined in the Fourth Schedule.[53]

A person who pays or is liable to pay to any person an amount by way of 'remuneration' is an 'employer'. In addition, the following persons are specifically included in the definition of 'employer':

- a person acting in a fiduciary capacity;
- a trustee in an insolvent estate;
- an executor; and
- an administrator of a benefit fund, pension fund, pension preservation fund, provident fund, provident preservation fund, retirement annuity fund or any other fund.

8.1.10 Employer – liability of 'representative employer'

The duty to deduct employees' tax and pay it over to SARS is imposed on the 'employer'.

The term 'representative employer' is defined in the Fourth Schedule.[54] The following persons (all of whom who must reside in the Republic in order to come within the system of employees' tax) are representative employers:

- the public officer of a company;
- the liquidator of a company in liquidation;
- the judicial manager of a company under judicial management;
- the manager, secretary, officer or other person responsible for paying remuneration on behalf of a municipality or body, corporate or unincorporated (other than a company or partnership);

52 See the definition of 'labour broker' in para 1 of the Fourth Schedule.
53 See para 1 of the Fourth Schedule.
54 See para 1 of the Fourth Schedule.

- the guardian, curator, administrator or other person having the management or control of the affairs of a person under legal disability; and
- the agent of an employer who is not resident in the Republic if the agent has authority to pay remuneration.

It is expressly provided that nothing in the definition of a 'representative employer' is to be construed as relieving any person from any liability, responsibility or duty imposed upon him or her by the Fourth Schedule.

8.1.11 Employer – registration

Every person who is an 'employer' must, in accordance with chapter 3 of the Tax Administration Act, apply for registration as such, except where he or she has no employees who are liable for normal tax.[55]

The employer will then be registered with the SARS office of the area within which he or she is ordinarily resident or, if a company, within which its registered office is situated.

A person who is registered as an employer must, within fourteen days after ceasing to be an employer, notify the Commissioner in writing accordingly.[56]

8.1.12 Employer – obligation to deduct and pay over tax

Employers are obliged to deduct employees' tax from their employees' remuneration and pay it over to SARS.[57] Employees' tax must be paid in accordance with the provisions of the Fourth Schedule at whatever place is notified by the Commissioner.[58]

Every employer who is a resident or who, in the case of a non-resident, is a representative employer and whether or not he or she is registered as an employer, who pays an amount of 'remuneration' to an employee (including certain types of 'variable remuneration' such as overtime pay)[59] must, unless the Commissioner has granted authority to the contrary, deduct or withhold the relevant amount of employees' tax from such payment.

The amount of employees' tax to be so deducted is determined in accordance with the employees' tax deduction tables provided by SARS[60] or in accordance with a directive given by SARS to the particular employer.

The amount of employees' tax so deducted or withheld must be paid to the Commissioner within seven days after the end of the month during which it was deducted or withheld or, when a person ceases to be an employer before the

55 See the proviso to para 15(1) of the Fourth Schedule.
56 Paragraph 15(3) of the Fourth Schedule.
57 Paragraph 2 of the Fourth Schedule.
58 Section 162(1) of the Tax Administration Act.
59 See para 2(1B) of the Fourth Schedule read with s 7B(1).
60 See para 9 of the Fourth Schedule.

end of the month, for example, on the sale of a business, within seven days after the date of his or her ceasing to be an employer.[61]

However, where a company or trust furnishes an employer with an affidavit or solemn declaration stating that the more-than-80% rule in para *(d)* of the definition of 'personal service provider'[62] does not apply and the recipient relies thereon in good faith, he or she is not required to deduct and pay over employees' tax.[63] In effect, para *(d)* deems an entity to be a personal service provider – and therefore not an independent contractor – where more than 80% of its income from the rendering of services consists of amounts received from any one client or an associated institution. The logic is that where a company or trust receives more than 80% of income from a single client, it seems as though the personal service provider is, in essence, an employee of that client and not a true independent contractor who carries out work for a number of different clients.

A person who, wilfully and without just cause, pays remuneration and fails to deduct or withhold from it the requisite amount of employees' tax or to pay such tax over to SARS[64] is guilty of an offence and liable on conviction to a fine, to imprisonment for a period not exceeding twelve months, or to both a fine and imprisonment.[65]

An employer is not allowed to use employees' tax that he or she has withheld from his or her employees' remuneration for any purpose other than to pay it to SARS. If the employer fails to pay it by the prescribed date, SARS can institute legal proceedings against him or her and can also estimate the amount of employees' tax required to be withheld or paid over and issue a notice of assessment of the unpaid amount, and collect that amount as though it were tax owing by the employer himself or herself.

8.1.13 Employer – declaration

Whenever an employer makes a payment of employees' tax, he or she must render a tax return to SARS.[66]

8.1.14 Employer – late payments of employees' tax

Penalties are payable if payments of employees' tax are late or incorrect.

An employer must pay over to SARS the employees' tax that he or she has deducted and withheld within seven days after the end of the month during which the amount was so deducted or withheld or within fourteen days after the day on

---

61 Paragraph 2(1) of the Fourth Schedule.
62 See para 1 of the Fourth Schedule.
63 Paragraph 2(1A) of the Fourth Schedule.
64 As required by para 2 of the Fourth Schedule.
65 Paragraph 30(1)*(a)* of the Fourth Schedule.
66 Paragraph 14(2)) of the Fourth Schedule.

which he or she ceased to be an employer.[67] If the employer fails to do so, SARS may impose a penalty and levy interest on the amount not paid or paid late.[68]

An employer who fails to pay employees' tax to SARS is also guilty of an offence and liable on conviction to a fine or to imprisonment for a period not exceeding twelve months.[69]

8.1.15 Employer – failure to pay over tax

If an employer fails, within the allowable period, to pay any amount of employees' tax for which he or she is liable, SARS must, in accordance with chapter 15 of the Tax Administration Act, impose a penalty equal to 10% of such amount.

SARS regards the conduct of an employer who collects employees' tax from employees and then fails to pay it over to the fiscus as fraud, and this is an attitude shared by the courts. In *Estate Agency Affairs Board v McLaggan*[70] the Supreme Court of Appeal described such conduct as 'intrinsically dishonest'.

8.1.16 Employer – recovery of tax, penalties and interest

When employees' tax that is payable in terms of the Fourth Schedule, or interest or a penalty payable in terms of the Tax Administration Act, becomes due or is payable it constitutes a debt due to SARS and may be recovered by SARS in the manner laid down in chapter 11 of the Tax Administration Act.

8.1.17 Employer – personal liability for tax

The employees' tax, which must be deducted or withheld from remuneration,[71] is a debt due to SARS and, except to the extent otherwise provided in the Fourth Schedule, the employer is absolutely liable for its due payment to SARS.[72]

The Tax Administration Act provides for an employer to be personally liable to SARS for the payment of employees' tax that he or she has deducted from his or her employees' remuneration but has not paid over to SARS.[73]

8.1.18 Employer – estimated assessments

Where an employer fails to submit a tax return to SARS or submits a return containing information that is incorrect or inadequate, SARS can issue an estimated assessment in which the employer's liability is estimated, based on the available information.[74]

---

67 Paragraph 2(1) of the Fourth Schedule.
68 See s 187(1) of the Tax Administration Act.
69 Paragraph 30(1)*(a)* of the Fourth Schedule.
70 2005 (4) SA 531 (SCA).
71 Under para 2 of the Fourth Schedule.
72 Paragraph 4 of the Fourth Schedule.
73 Section 157 of the Tax Administration Act.
74 Section 95 of the Tax Administration Act.

8.1.19 Employer – records

Every employer must maintain a record showing the amounts of remuneration paid or due by him or her to each employee, the amount of employees' tax deducted or withheld from the amounts of remuneration paid or due, the tax reference number of the employee and such further information as the Commissioner may prescribe. The record must be maintained in the form prescribed by SARS, which may be an electronic form.[75] The record must be retained by the employer and must be available for scrutiny by the Commissioner upon request.[76]

An employer who fails to keep such a record or to retain it for five years from the date of the last entry will be guilty of an offence and liable on conviction to a fine, to imprisonment for a period not exceeding twelve months or to both a fine and imprisonment.[77]

8.1.20 Employer – annual returns

An employer must provide SARS with a tax return in the prescribed form by the date prescribed by him by notice in the *Gazette* or within such longer period the Commissioner may approve.[78]

If an employer fails to render the return within the prescribed period, he or she may be required to pay a penalty not exceeding 10% of the total of the employees' tax deducted or withheld (or which should have been deducted or withheld) from the remuneration of employees, but the Commissioner may remit the penalty or a portion thereof.[79]

Unless the Commissioner directs otherwise, no employees' tax certificate must be delivered by the employer until the return has been properly rendered.[80] If an employer fails to render a return[81] or to do so within the prescribed period, the Commissioner may impose, under chapter 15 of the Tax Administration Act, a percentage-based penalty for each month that the employer fails to submit a complete return, which in total may not exceed 10% of the total amount of employees' tax deducted or withheld (or which should have been deducted or withheld) from the remuneration of employees for the relevant period.

75 Paragraph 14(4) of the Fourth Schedule.
76 Paragraph 14(1) of the Fourth Schedule.
77 Paragraph 30(1)*(i)* of the Fourth Schedule.
78 Paragraph 14(3) of the Fourth Schedule.
79 Paragraph 14(6) of the Fourth Schedule.
80 Paragraph 14(5) of the Fourth Schedule.
81 As provided for in para 14(3) of the Fourth Schedule.

8.1.21 Employer – employees' tax certificates

An 'employees' tax certificate' is defined in the Fourth Schedule[82] as a certificate required to be issued by an employer to each employee.[83]

The certificate must show the employee's total remuneration and the sum of the amounts of employees' tax deducted or withheld by the employer from remuneration during the period.

An employer who fails or neglects to deliver an employees' tax certificate to any employee[84] is guilty of an offence and liable on conviction to a fine, to imprisonment for a period not exceeding twelve months or to both the fine and imprisonment.[85]

An employer must also provide his or her employees with annual certificates of taxable fringe benefits.[86]

An employees' tax certificate is prima facie evidence that the amount of employees' tax it reflects has been deducted by the employer.[87]

8.1.22 Employer – fringe benefits

Employers have duties under the Seventh Schedule where they provide their employees with 'fringe benefits', that is to say, non-monetary benefits given in return for their services. The cash equivalent of such benefits forms part of the employee's gross income[88] and such cash equivalent is included in the employee's 'remuneration'[89] and is therefore subject to the deduction of employees' tax.

8.1.23 'Employee'

The term 'employee' is defined[90] as:

- any person other than a company who receives any 'remuneration', as defined;[91]
- any person (including a company) who receives 'remuneration' by reason of services rendered by that person to or on behalf of a 'labour broker',[92] that is to say, a 'labour broker's worker';
- any natural person who is a 'labour broker';

[82] See para 1 of the Fourth Schedule.
[83] Paragraph 1 of the Fourth Schedule.
[84] As required by para 13 of the Fourth Schedule.
[85] Paragraph 30(1)*(f)* of the Fourth Schedule.
[86] Paragraph 13(4) of the Fourth Schedule and para 17(1) of the Seventh Schedule.
[87] Paragraph 28(2) of the Fourth Schedule.
[88] In terms of para (i) of the definition of 'gross income' in s 1.
[89] As defined in para 1 of the Fourth Schedule.
[90] See para 1 of the Fourth Schedule.
[91] See para 1 of the Fourth Schedule.
[92] See para *(b)* of the definition of an 'employee' in para 1 of the Fourth Schedule.

- any person or a class or category of person whom the Minister of Finance declares to be an employee. This category of employee may conveniently be called a 'declared employee';
- any 'personal service provider' (this category comprises what were previously called 'personal service companies' and 'personal service trusts'); and
- any director of a private company.

'Labour broker' is defined as a natural person (that is to say, an individual) who carries on a business in which, for a fee, he or she provides a client with persons to render services or perform work for the client, and provides remuneration to those persons. The client in turn pays the labour broker an agreed fee. In other words, a labour broker does not provide his or her clients with services, but with persons who will perform those services.

8.1.24 Employees' tax – amount from which deducted

Employees' tax is deducted from an employee's 'remuneration', as defined.[93]

8.1.25 PAYE exemption certificates

The Commissioner has the power to issue 'certificates of exemption', often called 'PAYE exemption certificates'.[94] The significance of such a certificate is that an employer is not required to deduct or withhold employees' tax from remuneration paid by him or her to a person who presents him or her with a valid certificate of exemption.[95]

The Commissioner is authorised to issue such a certificate to an applicant who:

- carries on an independent trade and is registered as a provisional taxpayer;[96]
- in terms of para 15 of the Fourth Schedule; and
- has submitted all the returns required to be submitted by the relevant tax Act, subject to any extension granted by the Commissioner.[97]

However, the Commissioner cannot issue a certificate of exemption if more than 80% of the gross income of the labour broker or the person in question consists of amounts received from any one client or its 'associated institution', unless in the case of a labour broker he or she employs throughout the year of assessment three or more full-time employees who:

- are engaged on a full-time basis in the business of providing or procuring persons for his clients; and
- are not connected persons in relation to him or her.

CHAPTER 8

---

93 See para 1 of the Fourth Schedule.
94 Paragraph 2(5) of the Fourth Schedule.
95 Paragraph 2(5)*(c)* of the Fourth Schedule.
96 In terms of para 17 of the Fourth Schedule.
97 Paragraph 2(5)*(a)* of the Fourth Schedule.

8.1.26 Tax deduction tables

The Commissioner may from time to time prescribe deduction tables that apply to the classes of employees determined by him and prescribe the manner in which the tables will be applied. The amount of employees' tax to be deducted from any amount of remuneration is then determined in accordance with the tables, except in special circumstances.

The tax deduction tables do not take into account:

- any medical and dental expenses incurred (other than contributions to a registered medical scheme), including those incurred by physically disabled persons;
- the fact that an employee (or a member of his or her family) is a physically disabled person, who would be entitled to the deduction of all medical aid contributions; and
- contributions to the Unemployment Insurance Fund (since benefits received from the fund are not subject to tax).

These allowances and others will be taken into account if the employee is assessed for tax on the basis of a return submitted by him or her after the end of the year of assessment in order to correct any overpayment of employees' tax.

8.2 PROVISIONAL TAX

8.2.1 Introduction

The general rule is that a taxpayer does not pay income tax for a given year of assessment until shortly after the end of that year, when SARS issues an assessment, showing the amount of his or her taxable income for the year, and the amount of tax payable.

However, a 'provisional taxpayer' is required to make advance payments, known as provisional tax payments, on the basis of his or her estimated liability for normal tax for a particular year of assessment.

As with employees' tax (usually called 'PAYE' for pay-as-you-earn), provisional tax is dealt with in the Fourth Schedule to the Income Tax Act read with the Tax Administration Act.

The system for provisional tax applies the principle of PAYE to certain taxpayers other than employees, who are referred to as 'provisional taxpayers'.

Subject to a few exceptions, all provisional taxpayers must make two estimates of their taxable income for each year of assessment. The first estimate must be made on or before the last day of the sixth month of the year of assessment, and the second estimate must be made on or before the last day of the year of assessment. The amounts of such estimates are arrived at rather artificially, in that they are based on specific statutory rules, and not on actual predictions of the taxable income for the year of assessment.

The first payment must be equal to half of the tax that is predicted to be payable for the year, based on the estimated taxable income for that year, less any employees' tax already deducted from remuneration derived by the provisional taxpayer. The second payment must be the full amount of tax payable, based on the estimate of taxable income that accompanies the second payment, *less* the first payment and *less* any employees' tax that has already been deducted from the provisional taxpayer's remuneration.

Certain categories of provisional taxpayer – namely persons other than companies whose taxable income for the year of assessment exceeds R50 000 and companies whose taxable income for the year exceeds R20 000 – are permitted to make further, voluntary provisional tax payments in order to avoid or reduce the liability for interest that would otherwise be incurred if their first two obligatory provisional tax payments turn out to be inadequate. These voluntary payments are colloquially referred to as 'topping-up payments' or 'third provisional tax payments'.

In paying provisional tax, provisional taxpayers can either calculate for themselves their liability for normal tax on their estimated taxable income, or use tables specially prepared by SARS for this purpose.

Late or incorrect payments of tax and a failure to submit estimates or adequate estimates may result in a liability for additional tax, penalties and interest.

8.2.2 Liability for provisional tax

Every provisional taxpayer must make payments of provisional tax[98] to SARS in the manner provided for in the Fourth Schedule, and such payments are taken into account in respect of his or her overall liability for so-called 'normal tax' (ie income tax) for every year of assessment.[99]

8.2.3 Who is a provisional taxpayer?

A 'provisional taxpayer' is defined in the Fourth Schedule[100] as a person who falls into one of the following categories:

- a person, other than a company, who derives income that does not constitute 'remuneration'[101] or certain allowances or advances;[102] thus, where all of a person's income takes the form of 'remuneration', he or she is not a provisional taxpayer;
- a company; and
- any person notified by the Commissioner that he or she is a provisional taxpayer.

---

98 See the definition of 'provisional tax' in para 1 of the Fourth Schedule.
99 See para 17(1) of the Fourth Schedule.
100 See para 1 of the Fourth Schedule.
101 As defined in para 1 of the Fourth Schedule.
102 Namely, those referred to in s 8(1).

8.2.4 Who is exempt from paying provisional tax?

The following are the main categories of persons who are excluded from the definition of 'provisional taxpayer' and are therefore exempt from the payment of provisional tax:

- A natural person who does not derive any income from the carrying on of any business, if:
  - his or her taxable income for the relevant year will not exceed the tax threshold[103] (that is to say, the amount of taxable income below which no income tax is payable when the relevant rate of tax is applied[104] and the appropriate tax rebates[105] are applied to his or her taxable income); or
  - his or her taxable income for the year derived from interest, foreign dividends and rental from the letting of fixed property will not exceed R30 000.[106]

8.2.5 Estimates of taxable income

Every provisional taxpayer (with certain exceptions) must submit to the Commissioner an estimate of the total taxable income that he or she will derive in the year of assessment for which provisional tax is or may be payable, but the estimate must exclude any retirement lump sum benefit or withdrawal benefit or any severance benefit.[107] The estimate, except in respect of a company, must not be less than the 'basic amount' (as explained below) unless a lower estimate is justified by the circumstances of the case.[108]

The return must also show the provisional tax for the period *less* any provisional tax previously paid for the year of assessment and any employees' tax deducted by the provisional taxpayer's employer during the period from remuneration that is included in the estimated taxable income.

When estimating his or her taxable income for the year, a provisional taxpayer is entitled to take into account all the deductions that he or she is allowed to claim in terms of the Income Tax Act.

The procedure is similar for corporate provisional taxpayers.

Thus, the obligation to submit estimates of income arises in respect of each period within which provisional tax is or may be payable. The periods may be summarised as follows:

---

[103] See the definition of 'tax threshold' in para 1 of the Fourth Schedule.

[104] As set out in s 5.

[105] See s 6.

[106] Paragraph 18(1)*(c)* of the Fourth Schedule.

[107] Paragraph 19(1)*(a)* and *(b)* of the Fourth Schedule.

[108] Paragraph 19(1)*(c)* of the Fourth Schedule.

8.2.5.1 Persons other than companies

(a) First period

The period of six months reckoned from the commencement of the year of assessment in question.[109]

This period may be reckoned from another date, if it is approved by the Commissioner, where the latter has accepted accounts from a provisional taxpayer drawn to a date falling after the end of the year of assessment in question.[110]

(b) Second period

Not later than the last day of the year of assessment in question.[111]

8.2.5.2 Companies

(a) First period

This is the period ending six months after the commencement of the year of assessment in question.[112]

(b) Second period

This is the period ending on the last day of that year of assessment.[113]

8.2.5.3 The 'basic amount'

The amount of an estimate that is submitted by a provisional taxpayer for his or her first period or by a corporate provisional taxpayer for its 'first period' must ordinarily not be less than the 'basic amount' applicable to that particular estimate. However, with the Commissioner's agreement to accept a lower estimate, a lower estimate may be submitted, and, in giving or withholding his consent, the Commissioner is required to have regard to the particular circumstances.[114]

The purpose of the 'basic amount' applicable to an estimate submitted by a provisional taxpayer, for either his or her first or second period, is to establish the minimum acceptable estimate for the first period, which is then deemed to be the taxpayer's taxable income for the 'latest preceding year of assessment', less any taxable capital gain as envisaged in s 26A.[115]

[109] Paragraph 21(1)*(a)* of the Fourth Schedule.
[110] Paragraph 21(2) of the Fourth Schedule.
[111] Paragraph 21(1)*(b)* of the Fourth Schedule.
[112] Paragraph 23*(a)* of the Fourth Schedule.
[113] Paragraph 23*(b)* of the Fourth Schedule.
[114] Paragraph 19(1)*(c)* of the Fourth Schedule.
[115] Paragraph 19(1)*(d)* of the Fourth Schedule.

8.2.5.4 General

A provisional taxpayer is allowed to use as the 'basic amount' his or her latest taxable income as printed on his or her provisional tax form for the period concerned. This rule applies where the Commissioner has issued a provisional taxpayer with a return for the payment of provisional tax on an estimate required to be made by him or her.[116]

If a provisional taxpayer fails to submit an estimate for any particular period, the Commissioner will estimate the taxable income.[117]

Even where the provisional taxpayer does submit an estimate, the Commissioner may require him or her to justify his or her estimate or to furnish particulars of his or her income and expenditure or any other particulars that may be required. If the Commissioner is dissatisfied with the provisional taxpayer's estimate, he can increase it to whatever amount he considers to be reasonable, and such an increased estimate is not subject to objection and appeal.[118]

If a person fails to furnish the Commissioner with an estimate for a particular period, he or she will be guilty of an offence and liable on conviction to a fine, imprisonment for a period not exceeding twelve months or both a fine and imprisonment.[119]

It follows that a provisional taxpayer who wishes to avoid incurring liability for interest and a penalty and who wants to base his or her first provisional tax payment on an estimate of taxable income that is lower than the previous year's taxable income, for example, because of a lower trading profit, he or she should obtain the prior consent of SARS.

8.2.6 Payments of provisional tax

Payments of provisional tax must be made in accordance with the provisions of the Fourth Schedule. Any such payments will be regarded as having been made against his or her liability for taxes, whether or not that liability has been ascertained or determined at the date of any payment.[120]

The payments for the first and second periods are to be made as follows:

8.2.6.1 Persons other than companies

(a) First period

Within six months from the commencement of the year of assessment, a provisional taxpayer other than a company must pay one-half of an amount

[116] Proviso to para 19(1)*(e)*(ii) of the Fourth Schedule.
[117] Paragraph 19(2) of the Fourth Schedule.
[118] Paragraph 19(3) of the Fourth Schedule.
[119] Paragraph 30(1)*(m)*.
[120] Section 89*bis*(1).

of his or her total estimated liability[121] for normal tax for that year (based on the basic amount or his or her estimated taxable income for the year of assessment) *less* the total amount of employees' tax (if any) deducted by his or her employer from his or her remuneration during the six months.[122]

This period may be reckoned from another date, approved by the Commissioner, in the light of the particular circumstances and upon the application of the taxpayer.[123] The Commissioner's discretionary decision in this regard has been made subject to objection and appeal.[124]

(b) Second period

By no later than the last day of the year of assessment in question, a provisional taxpayer other than a company must pay an amount equal to his or her total estimated liability as finally determined[125] for normal tax (ie income tax) for that year. This payment will be based on the estimate of taxable income accompanying the second payment *less* the sum of the following amounts: firstly, employees' tax (if any) already deducted by his or her employer from his or her remuneration during the year; secondly, the amount of his or her first provisional tax payment for the year.[126]

(c) Additional provisional tax payments

In order to avoid or reduce liability for interest that may become payable by him or her for a particular year of assessment under chapter 12 of the Tax Administration Act, a taxpayer may elect to make one or more additional payments of provisional tax ('topping up payments') for that year.[127] Such a payment may be made at any time.

Overpayments by a taxpayer will be refunded with interest.

8.2.6.2 Companies

(a) First period

Within six months from the commencement of the year of assessment in question a company that is a provisional taxpayer must pay one-half of its total estimated liability[128] for normal tax for that year, *less* the total amount of employees' tax (if any) deducted by the company's employer from its remuneration during the relevant period.[129]

121 Determined under para 17 of the Fourth Schedule.
122 Paragraph 21(1)*(a)* of the Fourth Schedule.
123 Paragraph 21(2) of the Fourth Schedule.
124 See s 3(4).
125 Under para 17 of the Fourth Schedule.
126 Paragraph 21(1)*(b)* of the Fourth Schedule.
127 Paragraph 23A(1) of the Fourth Schedule.
128 Determined under para 17 of the Fourth Schedule.
129 Paragraph 23*(a)* of the Fourth Schedule.

(b) Second period

Within the period ending on the last day of that year, a company must pay an amount equal to its total estimated liability[130] for normal tax for that year less the amount of its first provisional tax payment for that year, *less* the total amount of employees' tax (if any) that has been deducted by the company's employer from its remuneration during the relevant period.[131]

(c) Additional provisional tax payments

The rules governing additional, voluntary payments are the same for companies as for persons other than companies, except that only a company whose taxable income for the year of assessment exceeds R20 000 will be liable to interest or will be eligible for interest on refunds.

8.2.6.3 Increased estimates

The Commissioner may[132] increase the amount of an estimate of taxable income submitted by a provisional taxpayer.

8.2.7 Amount and rate of provisional tax to be paid

As was noted above, a provisional taxpayer is required to estimate his or her total liability for normal tax for a particular year of assessment. For this purpose, his or her liability is deemed to be the amount of normal tax that would be payable by him or her on the amount of taxable income estimated by him or her[133] during the period prescribed for the payment of the provisional tax.

Such normal tax is required to be calculated at the relevant rate applicable.[134]

But as long as a provisional taxpayer uses the latest set of provisional tax tables, he or she need not concern himself or herself with establishing the relevant rate of normal tax in calculating his or her liability for normal tax based on an estimate of his or her taxable income made for provisional tax purposes.

8.2.8 Where taxable income is impossible to estimate

The Commissioner can absolve a provisional taxpayer paying provisional tax for his or her first period[135] if he is satisfied that the taxable income derived by the taxpayer for the year of assessment in question cannot be estimated on the facts available at the time when the provisional tax payment has to be made,[136] for example, where the taxpayer's income is variable and seasonal in nature.

---

[130] Determined under para 17 of the Fourth Schedule.

[131] Paragraph 23*(b)* of the Fourth Schedule.

[132] In terms of para 19(3) of the Fourth Schedule.

[133] In terms of para 19(1) of the Fourth Schedule.

[134] Paragraph 17(3) of the Fourth Schedule.

[135] In terms of paras 21(1)*(a)* or 23*(a)* of the Fourth Schedule.

[136] Paragraph 24 of the Fourth Schedule.

8.2.9 Additional tax – year-end estimate inadequate

An administrative penalty (which is a financial penalty imposed by SARS, and is thus entirely different from a penalty that is imposed by a court for committing a criminal offence) in the form of an understatement penalty is imposed (but may be remitted by the Commissioner, in whole or in part, if satisfied that there was no intent to evade or postpone the payment of tax)[137] where a provisional taxpayer submits an estimate of his or her taxable income during the second period that is less than a prescribed percentage of the actual taxable income and is also less than the applicable 'basic amount'.[138]

8.2.10 Administrative penalty – year-end estimate late

A further administrative penalty is imposed,[139] also at the rate of 20%, where a provisional taxpayer is liable for the payment of normal tax on taxable income derived by him or her in a particular year of assessment, but does not submit his or her year-end estimate of his or her taxable income on time.

The Commissioner has the power to remit the whole or any part of the penalty if satisfied that the provisional taxpayer's failure to submit a year-end estimate timeously was not due to an intent to evade or postpone the payment of provisional tax or normal tax.[140]

8.2.11 Husband and wife

A spouse is responsible for making provisional tax payments on both his or her own income and that of his or her spouse, in circumstances where the Income Tax Act requires the spouse's income to be aggregated with the provisional taxpayer's own income.[141] When furnishing estimates of taxable income a spouse in this position must therefore include the estimated taxable income required to be aggregated in this way.

CHAPTER 8

[137] Paragraph 20(2) of the Fourth Schedule.
[138] By para 20(1)*(a)*–*(b)* of the Fourth Schedule.
[139] By para 20A(1) of the Fourth Schedule.
[140] Paragraph 20A(2) of the Fourth Schedule.
[141] In terms of s 7(2) or (2A) of the Income Tax Act.

Chapter 9

Capital gains tax

9.1 INTRODUCTION

A capital gains tax[1] was introduced into the Republic of South Africa with effect from 1 October 2001. The reason given by the Minister of Finance for the introduction of this new tax was that, hitherto, the absence of a capital gains tax had encouraged taxpayers 'to convert income that would ordinarily be taxable into tax-free capital gains', and that capital gains tax would make the tax system more equitable in that realised capital gains are equivalent to income and can be used in the same way. Capital gains tax thus formed an essential backstop to personal and corporate income tax.

[1] Herein also referred to as 'CGT'.

Another reason for the introduction of capital gains tax was to bring South Africa's tax system more into line with international benchmarks.

The design of the Eighth Schedule to the Income Tax Act[2] ('the Act'), which contains the detail of the capital gains tax, was influenced by the capital gains tax legislation of a number of countries, most notably Australia and the United Kingdom and, to a lesser extent, Canada and the United States of America.

9.2 THE CAPITAL GAINS TAX LEGISLATION

The legislative provisions which impose what is colloquially called 'capital gains tax' (a phrase that does not appear in the legislation itself) are contained in the Eighth Schedule[3] to the Act, read together with s 26A of the Act. Administrative aspects of capital gains tax are contained in the Tax Administration Act.[4]

Capital gains tax is thus an integral part of the income tax system, with taxable capital gains being added to a person's 'taxable income'[5] and taxed, subject to certain relief, at the taxpayer's marginal rate of tax. The 'taxable capital gain' of a natural person or special trust is 40%; that of an insurer's individual policyholder fund, 40%; that of an insurer's untaxed policyholder fund, 0%; company policyholder fund, 80%; risk policy fund, 80% and in any other case, 80% of the person's net capital gain for the year of assessment in question.[6] The administrative aspects of capital gains tax are provided for in the general provisions of the Act read together with the Tax Administration Act of 2011.

Section 26A of the Act states that a person's taxable income for a year of assessment includes the 'taxable capital gain' (in other words, the statutorily stipulated percentage[7] of the person's 'net capital gain') for that year of assessment, as determined under the provisions of the Eighth Schedule. The 'taxable capital gain' is then taxed at the taxpayer's marginal tax rate as laid down in the Income Tax Act. Capital gains tax is therefore not levied or paid separately from income tax. Capital gains and losses are, however, excluded from the computation of provisional tax.

An assessed capital loss cannot be set off against taxable income, nor does it increase a person's assessed loss for income tax purposes. An assessed capital loss is ring-fenced, but may be carried forward to subsequent years and set off against future capital gains. A taxable capital gain will reduce an assessed loss.[8]

---

[2] Act 58 of 1962.

[3] All paragraph numbers in this chapter refer, unless stated otherwise, to paragraphs of the Eighth Schedule.

[4] 28 of 2011.

[5] See s 26A of the Income Tax Act 58 of 1962.

[6] Paragraph 10.

[7] See para 10.

[8] This follows from para *(b)* of the definition of 'taxable income' in s 1 of the Act.

Key definitions, relevant to capital gains tax, that have been added to s 1 of the Act include 'capital gain', 'capital loss' and 'taxable capital gain'. The definition of 'assessment' has been amended to include an assessment for an assessed capital loss. Section 6*quat* has been amended to take account of capital gains tax. The provisions of s 103(2) have been expanded to encompass tax-avoidance schemes in respect of capital gains and losses.

9.3 EFFECTIVE DATE FOR THE COMMENCEMENT OF CAPITAL GAINS TAX

The capital gains tax legislation applies[9] to the 'disposal'[10] of any 'asset'[11] of a 'resident'[12] (and of certain stipulated classes of assets of non-residents)[13] where the disposal occurs on or after 1 October 2001, which the Act calls 'the valuation date'.[14]

Where an asset was disposed of before 1 October 2001, the taxpayer will be taxed in the usual way on receipts and accruals of 'income' (that is to say, amounts which are not of a capital nature), but will not be taxed on 'capital gains' except where the receipt or accrual in question, though in reality of a capital nature, falls within one of the subparagraphs of the statutory definition of 'gross income' and consequently is subject to income tax.[15]

As from 1 October 2001 this changed, and gains of a capital nature arising from the disposal of an asset that would previously have escaped tax under the Act are now subject to capital gains tax in the manner provided for in the Eighth Schedule, unless such gains are specifically excluded. Where the taxpayer acquired the asset prior to 1 October 2001 and did not dispose of it before then (a 'pre-valuation date asset'),[16] only the gain which accrued after that date is potentially subject to capital gains tax.

9.4 THE RESIDENCE BASIS OF CAPITAL GAINS TAX

In colloquial terms it may be said that the Republic's capital gains tax system applies to the worldwide assets of 'residents' (as defined) of the Republic. Persons who are not resident in the Republic, can incur a liability for capital gains tax only in respect of certain limited categories of property held by them, or held indirectly, for example, via equity shares in a company that holds such property.

9 See para 2.
10 As defined in para 11.
11 As defined in para 1 sv 'asset'.
12 As defined in para 1 sv 'resident'.
13 See para 2(1)*(a)* and 2(2).
14 Paragraph 1 sv 'valuation date'.
15 Section 1 sv 'gross income'.
16 Paragraph 1 sv 'pre-valuation date asset'.

Thus, the Eighth Schedule applies to the disposal, on or after valuation date, of:[17]

(a) any 'asset' (as defined)[18] of a 'resident' (as defined);[19]

(b) the following assets of a person who is not a 'resident' (as defined):

(i) immovable property situated in the Republic held by that person or any interest[20] or right of whatever nature to or in immovable property situated in the Republic (in this regard, the meaning of 'an interest in immovable property' is defined to provide for a 'look-through' approach where immovable property is held by a person indirectly via equity shares in a company or ownership or the right to ownership in any other entity or a vested interest in the assets of a trust, if certain further conditions are fulfilled);[21] or

(ii) any asset effectively connected with a permanent establishment of that person in the Republic.

Where a person commences to be a resident or where a foreign company commences to be a controlled foreign company, or where a controlled foreign company ceases to be a controlled foreign company, this event triggers a deemed disposal of all that person's assets other than assets of a non-resident to which the Eighth Schedule applies.[22] Where a person ceases to be a controlled foreign company as a result of becoming a resident, this triggers a similar deemed disposal plus a deemed reacquisition of those self-same assets for a deemed amount of expenditure.[23]

In certain circumstances, a capital gain that has vested in a non-resident, arising from a donation, settlement or other disposition by a resident to that non-resident, can be attributed to (and thus taxed in the hands of) the resident.[24]

Capital gains tax was introduced in the context of, and in harmony with, the (virtually simultaneous) change of the Republic's tax system from being primarily source-based to being primarily residence-based. Thus, liability for capital gains tax will (subject to certain relief for international double taxation)

[17] Paragraph 2(1).

[18] Paragraph 1 sv 'asset'.

[19] As defined in s 1, sv 'resident'.

[20] For this purpose, the Act provides that 'an interest in immovable property situated in the Republic includes any equity shares held by a person in a company or ownership or the right to ownership of a person in any other entity or a vested interest of a person in any assets of any trust' if (a) 80% or more of the market value of the aforementioned shares, ownership, right to ownership or vested interest, at the time of disposal, is attributable directly or indirectly to such immovable property so held; and (b) in the case of a company or other entity, that person (whether alone or together with any connected person) indirectly holds at least 20% of the equity shares in that company or ownership or the right to ownership of that other entity; Schedule 8 para 2(2).

[21] See para 64(2)*(a)*–*(b)*.

[22] See para 12(2) read with para 2(1)*(b)*(i) and (ii).

[23] See para 12(4).

[24] See para 72.

be incurred by persons who are 'residents' (as defined)[25] of the Republic in respect of gains made on the disposal of their worldwide assets. Non-residents will incur liability for capital gains tax only in respect of the particular categories of assets falling under *(b)*(i) and (ii), above.

A juristic person that is resident in the Republic will be subject to the Republic's capital gains tax regime. Even if all its business and investment activities are conducted outside the Republic, such a resident juristic person will not be regarded as a 'controlled foreign entity' for the purposes of s 9D of the Act.

9.5 TAXABLE CAPITAL GAINS AND ASSESSED CAPITAL LOSSES

In terms of s 26A, a person's taxable income for a year of assessment includes the person's 'taxable capital gain' for the year of assessment as determined under the provisions of the Eighth Schedule.

A person's 'taxable capital gain' for a given year of assessment is the prescribed percentage of the person's 'net capital gain' for the particular year of assessment.[26] A person's 'net capital gain' for a year of assessment is the sum of the amount by which that person's 'aggregate capital gain' for that year exceeds that person's 'assessed capital loss' for the previous year of assessment.[27] A special rule applies where the person (other than a headquarter company) has disposed of any equity share in a foreign company.[28]

9.5.1 Determining a person's 'capital gain' or 'capital loss'

The following are the steps involved in the determination of a person's taxable capital gain for a given year of assessment.

A person's 'capital gain'[29] or 'capital loss'[30] is determined separately in respect of each asset disposed of by that person during the year of assessment. Hence, whenever there has been a 'disposal' of an 'asset' during a year of assessment, it is necessary (unless the capital gain falls within one of the statutory exclusions)[31] to determine, in respect of that particular asset, the capital gain or loss arising from that disposal.

A 'capital gain' for a year of assessment in respect of the disposal of an asset during that year is the difference between the 'base cost' of the asset and the 'proceeds' derived from the disposal of the asset.[32] A person's capital loss for

[25] Section 1 sv 'resident'.
[26] Paragraph 10.
[27] Paragraph 8.
[28] As envisaged in s 64B(2), read with s 64B(2A).
[29] As envisaged in para 3.
[30] As envisaged in para 4.
[31] See Parts VII and VIII of the Eighth Schedule.
[32] Paragraph 3*(a)*.

a year of assessment in respect of the disposal of an asset during that year is equal to the amount by which the base cost of that asset exceeds the proceeds received or accrued in respect of that disposal.[33]

9.5.2 Determining the 'aggregate capital gain' or 'aggregate capital loss' for a year of assessment

As has been noted above, a capital gain or loss is determined separately for each asset disposed of by the taxpayer during the year of assessment. A person's 'aggregate capital gain'[34] or 'aggregate capital loss'[35] is thereafter determined by the following two steps:

- First, add all of the person's capital gains (and the capital gains of other persons which are attributed to that person) and subtract capital losses that relate to the disposal of assets during that year of assessment.
- Secondly, where the taxpayer is a natural person or special trust,[36] reduce the total amount of the overall capital gain or loss for the year by the amount of the annual exclusion, namely R40 000, or, where a person dies during a year of assessment, R300 000.[37]

9.5.3 Determining the 'net capital gain' or 'assessed capital loss' for the year of assessment

After a person's aggregate capital gain or loss for a given year of assessment has been determined, as set out above, that person's assessed capital loss (if any) in respect of the previous year of assessment must be deducted from the aggregate capital gain or added to the aggregate capital loss to determine the 'net capital gain'[38] or 'assessed capital loss'[39] for the current year of assessment. A special rule applies in certain circumstances where the person in question has disposed of an equity share in a foreign company.[40]

9.5.4 Determining the 'taxable capital gain' for the year of assessment

Where a person has a net capital gain for the current year of assessment, that figure is subjected to the inclusion rate in order to arrive at that person's 'taxable capital gain' for that year. That 'taxable capital gain' is then included in that person's 'taxable income' for that year of assessment.

33 Paragraph 4*(a)*.
34 As envisaged in para 6.
35 As envisaged in para 7.
36 As defined in s 1 sv 'special trust'.
37 Paragraph 5(1)–(2).
38 As envisaged in para 8.
39 As envisaged in para 9.
40 Paragraph 8*(b)* read with para 64B.

Thus, for example, if a natural person's net capital gain for the year of assessment is R100 000, his or her 'taxable capital gain' is R100 000 multiplied by the inclusion rate of 40%, giving R40 000. The R40 000 is then included in that person's taxable income for the year of assessment, where it is taxed at the ordinary rate applicable to that person as laid down in the Act.

9.5.5 Concession or compromise in respect of a debt

In addition to taxing the gain made on the 'disposal' of an 'asset', the Eighth Schedule contains complex provisions that bring within the scope of CGT the 'debt benefit' arising from a 'concession or compromise' in terms of an arrangement whereby a 'debt' (as widely defined) is cancelled, waived or extinguished.[41]

9.5.6 A taxable capital gain will reduce an assessed loss

SARS takes the view that a taxable capital gain will reduce an assessed loss, on the grounds that this follows from the definition of 'taxable income'[42] and is implicit in s 103(2), which prevents the setting-off of a 'tainted' capital gain against an assessed loss.

9.5.7 Annual exclusion

An 'annual exclusion' is available only to a natural person or special trust[43] or to persons treated as natural persons for the purposes of the Eighth Schedule, namely, deceased and insolvent estates. The amount of such annual exclusion is R40 000 for a natural person or special trust, and R300 000 for the year in which a natural person dies. The latter amount is not subject to apportionment where the person dies during the course of the tax year.

The effect of the annual exclusion is that, for a natural person or special trust, the first R40 000 of a capital gain or a capital loss is ignored in determining the person's aggregate capital gain or capital loss for the year of assessment.

Any unused balance of the annual exclusion cannot be carried forward into the following year.

A natural person or special trust can therefore avoid or reduce liability to capital gains tax by staggering the disposal of assets over a period of years, thereby using the annual exclusion to the full. There is a deemed disposal, at market value, of all a person's assets on death.[44] This can result in a 'bunching' of CGT in the year of death for a person who has not managed to dispose of assets *inter vivos*, but some relief is given by the increase of the annual exclusion to R300 000 in the year of death.[45]

---

[41] Paragraph 12A.
[42] Section 1 sv 'taxable income'.
[43] Paragraph 5(1)–(2).
[44] Paragraph 40(1).
[45] Paragraph 5(2).

The purpose of the annual exclusion is to reduce the compliance cost to taxpayers, and simplify the administration of the capital gains tax system by keeping small gains and losses out of the system.

The following points may be noted regarding the annual exclusion:

- It does not apply to companies, close corporations and trusts other than special trusts.
- It is available only to natural persons and persons who are treated as natural persons for the purposes of the Eighth Schedule, namely deceased and insolvent estates.
- It reduces both gains and losses.
- It is not apportioned where the period of assessment is less than a year, for example where a person dies or is sequestrated mid-way through the tax year.
- It is not cumulative; any unutilised portion cannot be carried forward into the following year; nor does it reduce an assessed loss that has been carried forward from a previous year. It applies only against the sum of the capital gains and losses for the current year.
- The R300 000 annual exclusion in the year of death provides relief from the 'bunching' effect in that year as a result of the deemed disposal of all assets at market value on the date of death.[46] In effect, the deceased is given five years' worth of annual exclusions.

The following table illustrates the annual exclusion for the various classes of person.

Person	Annual exclusion	Comment
natural person	R40 000	
natural person – year of death	R300 000	Not subject to apportionment
special trust	R40 000	Where the beneficiary dies, the exclusion will only remain available until the earlier of: • the date when all the trust's assets have been disposed of; or • two years after the date of the beneficiary's death(see para 82)

[46] Paragraph 40(1).

Person	Annual exclusion	Comment
deceased estate	R40 000	The annual exclusion of R340 000 is available in the year of death and in each year thereafter. It is not subject to apportionment in the year of death (para 40(3))
insolvent estate	R40 000	The annual exclusion of R40 000 is available in the year of death and in each year thereafter. It is not subject to apportionment in the year of death (para 40(3))
companies, close corporations and trusts other than special trusts	nil	

9.6 CAPITAL LOSSES MAY ONLY BE SET OFF AGAINST CAPITAL GAINS, AND NOT AGAINST INCOME

It follows from what has been said, above, that if a person makes a 'taxable capital gain'[47] during a year of assessment, that taxable capital gain is included in that person's 'taxable income'[48] and is taxed at the applicable marginal rate.

If, however, a person makes an 'assessed capital loss'[49] during a year of assessment, that loss cannot be set off against that person's ordinary income, and therefore does not decrease that person's 'taxable income', nor does it increase any assessed loss of a revenue nature.

An assessed capital loss is in this sense 'ring-fenced'; it may, however, be carried forward indefinitely and be set off against capital gains arising in a future year of assessment.[50]

9.7 DISREGARDING, LIMITING AND ROLLING OVER CERTAIN CAPITAL GAINS

Certain capital gains or losses are limited, disregarded, or rolled over when determining a capital gain or loss for the year of assessment.

[47] As contemplated in para 10.
[48] As required by s 26A.
[49] As contemplated in para 9.
[50] As contemplated in para 8.

9.7.1 Disregarding and limiting of certain capital gains

The situations in which certain capital gains are limited or disregarded are set out in Part IV, Part VII and Part VIII of the Eighth Schedule.

Thus, for example:

- The situations in which a loss is limited for capital gains tax purposes are set out in Part IV of the Eighth Schedule; these include the losses on certain personal-use assets (that is to say, non-trading assets) and losses on the disposal of certain shares.
- The situations in which a capital gain or loss is disregarded for capital gains tax purposes are set out in Parts VII and VIII of the Eighth Schedule. Thus, for example, a capital gain or loss sustained by a natural person or special trust from the disposal of a primary residence is disregarded to the extent that such gain or loss does not exceed R2 million.[51]
- Gains or losses in respect of the disposal of most personal-use assets are disregarded for capital gains tax purposes.[52]

9.7.2 The roll-over of certain capital gains

In certain circumstances, set out in Part IX of the Eighth Schedule, a capital gain is 'rolled over', in other words, it is not taken into account for capital gains tax purposes until the occurrence of a future event. Thus, for example, where the 'disposal' of an asset is by way of the operation of law (eg expropriation), theft or destruction of the asset (other than a financial instrument) for which a person receives compensation in excess of the base cost of the asset, and the person expends that compensation on the acquisition of a replacement asset within a specified period, the capital gain that resulted from the initial 'disposal' is not taken into account until the person disposes of the replacement asset.[53]

Roll-over relief is also available where the taxpayer disposes of an asset which qualifies for certain capital allowances or deductions and, within the requisite period, acquires one or more replacement assets.[54]

9.8 THE CONCEPT OF AN 'ASSET'

A key concept in the capital gains tax regime is the 'disposal' of an 'asset', for it is this event, during a year of assessment, which triggers a potential liability for capital gains tax.[55] (The Eighth Schedule also deals (see below) with part-disposals and with events that are treated as disposals.) It follows that if the event in question was not a 'disposal', no liability to capital gains tax can arise; equally, if the subject-matter of the disposal was not an 'asset', there will be no capital gains tax consequences.

---

51 Paragraph 45(1).
52 Paragraph 53(1)–(2).
53 Paragraph 65(5).
54 See para 66.
55 See paras 3–4.

9.8.1 The definition and relevance of an 'asset'

The Eighth Schedule[56] defines an 'asset' as including—

(a) property of whatever nature, whether movable or immovable, corporeal or incorporeal, excluding any currency, but including any coin made mainly from gold or platinum; [57] and

(b) a right or interest of whatever nature to or in such property.

The definition thus consists of two parts, set out in paras *(a)* and *(b)*, respectively. Each of these two parts is self-sufficient; thus an item that falls within either para *(a)* or *(b)* will be an 'asset'. They are, however, inter-related in that para *(b)*, in referring to 'such property', is referring to property which comes within the scope of para *(a)*. Of particular note is that para *(b)* extends the scope of the definition of an asset beyond 'rights' to or in property so as to include certain 'interests' to or in property.

Most 'personal-use assets'[58] are excluded from capital gains tax in terms of para 53.

9.9 THE 'DISPOSAL' OF AN ASSET

The 'disposal' (or deemed disposal)[59] of an asset, during the year of assessment, is the event that triggers a potential liability for capital gains tax.[60] (It is sometimes colloquially called 'a CGT event'.) If there has been such a disposal, the capital gain or loss in respect of the disposal of that particular asset must be determined, as required by para 3 or 4 of the Eighth Schedule, as the first step in quantifying the amount of that person's overall 'taxable capital gain' for the year of assessment. Conversely, if an act or event does not constitute the 'disposal' of an asset, it is irrelevant for CGT purposes and cannot give rise to a CGT liability.

What constitutes the 'disposal' of an asset is defined in para 1,[61] read with para 11(1). The definition in para 11(1)*(a)*–*(g)* must be read together with para 11(2), which provides that certain acts and events (which might otherwise have constituted disposals) are not disposals; the definition must also be read together with para 12(1), which provides that certain events, which would not otherwise constitute a 'disposal', are treated as disposals; and with para 13(1), which defines the time when a disposal occurs.

A number of traps for unwary taxpayers lurk in this wide definition of 'disposal'. Thus, apparently fiscally innocuous acts such as the variation of an agreement or a trust, or the waiver of a debt or the renunciation of a right – which may not

---

[56] Paragraph 1 sv 'asset'.

[57] Such coins are excluded from the definition of 'personal-use asset'; see para 53(3)*(a)*.

[58] As defined in para 53.

[59] As contemplated in para 11(1)–(2).

[60] See paras 3–4.

[61] Paragraph 1 sv 'disposal'.

have put any money into the taxpayer's pocket – may nonetheless constitute a 'disposal' and may result in a CGT liability.

Some of the acts and events listed in para 11(1) and its subparagraphs are bilateral juristic acts, others are unilateral; some result in the acquisition of the asset by other persons, and some do not – for example, there is a 'disposal' of an asset without its being acquired by another person on its 'loss or destruction', where it is scrapped, or where a debt ceases to exist as the result of a release by the creditor.

9.9.1 The creation of an asset

Paragraph 11(1)[62] begins by defining a 'disposal' as 'any event, act, forbearance,[63] or operation of law which results in the creation, variation, transfer or extinction of an asset', other than certain acts that are declared[64] not to constitute the disposal of an asset. (It then goes on to define a 'disposal' as including certain specific events and acts listed in sub-paras *(a)*–*(g)*; these are discussed under the next sub-heading, below.)

The concepts of 'disposal' and 'asset' are of central importance in the CGT regime.

The statutory definition of what constitutes the 'disposal'[65] of an 'asset', read together with the provisions that lay down the events that will *be treated as* a disposal,[66] and the provisions that lay down what will *not be regarded* as a disposal,[67] coupled with the definition of 'asset',[68] make up the statutory framework that determines whether an event has occurred that gives rise to a potential CGT liability.

9.9.2 Conversion of a company to a close corporation or vice versa; co-operative converting to a company

Where a company has converted to a close corporation (and it should be noted that no such conversions are permissible after the date that the Companies Act 71 of 2008 came into effect) or vice versa, the two entities are treated as one and the same for the purposes of the Act.[69] The same applies to a co-operative that converts to a company. The Companies Act and the Close Corporations Act provide that the corporate existence and rights remain unchanged.[70] It follows that conversions of this nature are not disposals (nor are they deemed disposals) and do not trigger a capital gains tax liability in the entities concerned.

CHAPTER 9

62 This provision must be read with the definition of 'disposal' in para 1.

63 Forbearance means 'abstinence from enforcing what is due, esp the payment of a debt' (*Shorter Oxford Dictionary*).

64 See para 11(2).

65 See para 1 sv 'disposal' and para 11(1).

66 See para 12(1)–(4).

67 See para 11(2).

68 See para 1 sv 'asset'.

69 Section 40A.

70 Companies Act 61 of 1973, s 29(1) and 29D; Close Corporations Act 69 of 1984, s 27(5).

9.9.3 Part-disposals

Part-disposals of an asset (in other words, the 'disposal' of something less than the entire asset) are dealt with in para 33(1)–(3).

A part-disposal, as contemplated in para 33(1), covers the situation where 'part of an asset is disposed of', and hence where part of an asset is the subject of one of the acts or events which are defined in para 11(1) as a 'disposal', for example where part of the asset is transferred, extinguished, sold, donated, etc.

If a part-disposal occurs, that event has capital gains tax consequences in the year in which it occurs, rather than in the later year in which the entire asset is disposed of. Where the part-disposal results in a capital loss, the part-disposal brings forward the juncture at which that loss can be claimed, instead of the taxpayer's having to wait until the entire asset is disposed of.

9.10 LIMITATION OF LOSSES

Part IV of the Eighth Schedule provides for a number of situations in which, for CGT purposes, capital losses must be disregarded.

Such disregarding relates to capital losses in respect of:

- personal-use aircraft and boats, fiduciary, usufructuary or similar interests whose value decreases over time, and leases of immovable property;[71] any time-sharing interest or share in a share-block company with a fixed life, the value of which decreases over time, and any right of interest in any of these;
- any 'intangible asset', as defined,[72] acquired prior to 1 October 2001 from a connected person[73] or which was associated with a business taken over by that person or any connected person in relation to that person;[74]
- forfeited deposits in respect of the acquisition of an asset which is not intended wholly and exclusively for business purposes, other than in respect of a coin made mainly from gold or platinum[75] whose market value is mainly attributable to the material from which it is minted or cast, immovable property other than that intended to be the primary residence of the person in question, a financial instrument, or any right or interest in any of the aforegoing assets;[76]

[71] Paragraph 15.
[72] In para 16(2).
[73] As defined in s 1 sv 'connected person'.
[74] Paragraph 16.
[75] Coins made mainly from gold or platinum fall within the definition of 'foreign equity instrument' in s 1 and are taxed on disposal in terms of para 43(4).
[76] Paragraph 17.

- the disposal of options (by way of abandonment, expiry, or any disposal other than by way of exercise of the option) to acquire or dispose of an asset not intended for use wholly and exclusively for business purposes, except options in respect of the types of property covered in the exceptions listed under the immediately preceding point, above;[77] and
- the disposal of certain shares, within two years after acquisition; the capital loss must be disregarded to the extent of any 'extraordinary dividends'[78] received or accrued within that period, save in respect of dividends derived by a company which is a holding company or intermediate company in relation to the distributing company,[79] and in respect of taxable or exempt foreign dividends, and distributions from unit trusts.

9.11 BASE COST

For purposes of income tax, as opposed to capital gains tax, the basic formula for arriving at a person's taxable income is to subtract the expenditure that qualifies as an allowable deduction from that person's gross income. In implementing this formula, all of the amounts falling within the definition of 'gross income'[80] are lumped together into a single amount; similarly, all of a person's deductible expenditure is lumped together into a single amount; and the latter aggregate sum is deducted from the former.

By contrast, under the capital gains tax system, laid down in the Eighth Schedule, it is necessary to determine, separately for each 'asset', the capital gain or the capital loss arising from its disposal.[81] The Eighth Schedule does not refer to 'deductible expenditure' in the determination of a capital gain. Instead, it requires the 'base cost' of each asset to be determined, and this base cost is deducted from the proceeds derived from the disposal of that asset to yield the 'capital gain' or 'capital loss' in respect of the disposal of that particular asset.[82]

Ultimately, the expenditure incurred by the taxpayer, which he or she is entitled to include in the base cost of the asset, is in effect 'deductible' in determining the capital gain or loss arising from the disposal of the asset.

The types of expenditure that qualify for inclusion in the base cost of an asset are tightly defined in Part V of the Eighth Schedule. They include:[83]

[77] Paragraph 18.
[78] As defined in para 19(3)*(c)*.
[79] Paragraph 19.
[80] Section 1 sv 'gross income'.
[81] See paras 3 and 4.
[82] Ibid.
[83] See para 20(1).

- expenditure actually incurred in respect of the cost of acquisition of the asset; this includes the purchase price and transfer duty in the case of immovable property);
- expenditure actually incurred in valuing an asset for purposes of capital gains tax; and
- expenditure actually incurred in effecting an improvement to the property (but not the cost of 'repairs') if that improvement is still reflected in the asset at the time of disposal.

There is an overarching rule that, to the extent that expenditure was deductible for income tax purposes, it is not included in the base cost of an asset,[84] thereby ensuring that there is no double deduction.

9.11.1 Certain expenditure is not included in base cost unless it was wholly and exclusively incurred for business purposes

The following categories of expenditure, directly related to the cost of ownership of the asset, qualify for inclusion in the base cost of an asset only if it is used 'wholly and exclusively' for business purposes or if it is a share listed on a recognised stock exchange[85] or a participatory interest in a portfolio of a collective investment scheme.[86] (Thus, for example, such expenditure would not be included in the base cost of a holiday house which was leased for most of the year but was used occasionally for private purposes.) In other words, there is no apportionment of these types of expenditure where the asset was used partly for business purposes and partly for private or domestic purposes. The categories of expenditure are:

- the cost of maintaining, repairing, protecting or insuring that asset (but a pro rata amount of such expenditure would usually qualify as a deduction for income tax purposes);
- rates or taxes on immovable property (thus, for example, such expenditure would not be included in the base cost of a primary residence); and
- interest, as contemplated in s 24J, on money borrowed to finance directly expenditure on the acquisition, disposal, valuation, establishing, maintaining or defending legal title to the property, or in effecting improvements.

---

84 Paragraph 20(3)*(a)*.

85 As defined in s 1 sv 'recognised exchange'.

86 Paragraph 20(1)*(g)*.

9.11.2 Interest, raising fees, and other borrowing costs, repairs, maintenance, protection, insurance, rates and taxes and similar expenditure

Borrowing costs, including interest and raising fees, repairs, maintenance, protection, insurance, rates and taxes and similar expenditure are included in the base cost of an asset only if they fall within para 20(1)*(g)*, summarised above.[87] Thus, expenditure in these categories is included in the base cost of an asset only if it was incurred in respect of an asset used 'wholly and exclusively for business purposes' or which is a listed share or a participatory interest in a portfolio of a collective investment scheme.

Thus, for example, no part of the expenditure in these categories is included in the base cost of an asset that is not used for business purposes at all (for example, a primary residence) and there is no apportionment where the expenditure is used partly for private purposes and partly for business purposes.

There would, however, normally be an income tax deduction[88] for expenditure in these categories if the asset in question was used for business purposes.

9.11.3 Effect on base cost of income tax deductions and allowances in respect of the asset

The Eighth Schedule provides that the base cost of an asset must be reduced by any amount which was included in that base cost and which is or was allowable as a deduction in determining the taxable income of that person before the inclusion of any capital gain.[89]

This can be more simply, albeit colloquially, expressed by saying that, to the extent that expenditure qualifies as a deduction for income tax purposes, it cannot form part of the base cost of an asset for CGT purposes. This rule was obviously necessary to ensure that the same expenditure is not deducted twice, once for income tax purposes and again for CGT purposes.

CHAPTER 9

9.11.4 Expenditure 'actually incurred'

In relation to expenditure which forms part of the base cost of an asset for capital gains tax purposes, para 20(1) of the Eighth Schedule requires that the various types of qualifying expenditure be 'actually incurred'. The tax treatment of unquantified expenditure is now governed by s 24M.

---

[87] Paragraph 20(2).

[88] In terms of s 11*(d)* in respect of repairs and s 11*(a)* for the other types of expenditure listed in this provision.

[89] Paragraph 20(3)*(a)*.

9.11.5 Donations tax included in base cost

A proportion of the donations tax (determined in accordance with a statutory formula) payable by a person in respect of the disposal of an asset is included in its base cost.[90] This gives relief from the double taxation that would otherwise be incurred on the donation.

9.11.6 Determination of the base cost of a pre-valuation date asset

The capital gains tax regime applies not only to assets which were acquired after 1 October 2001, when capital gains tax took effect, but also to an asset acquired by a person prior to that date which has not been disposed of by that person before valuation date (which the Eighth Schedule calls a 'pre-valuation date asset');[91] but, in the latter event, only the capital gain which accrued after 1 October 2001 in respect of that asset is brought into account for CGT purposes when it is disposed of.

A person's capital gain in respect of a particular asset is equal to the proceeds from the disposal (or deemed disposal) of the asset, less its base cost.[92] Hence, the starting point for determining the amount of the capital gain on disposal of an asset is to establish its 'base cost'. This amount will be instrumental in determining the amount of a capital gain (or loss) in respect of that asset, not only where there has been an actual 'disposal' (as defined in para 11(1)), but also where there has been a deemed disposal of the asset in terms of para 11(2) or para 40(1).

If an asset was acquired after 1 October 2001, the base cost will consist of the expenditure, falling within the scope of para 20, in respect of that asset. *Ex hypothesi*, all of that expenditure will have been incurred after 1 October 2001. An important component of that base cost – the acquisition cost of the asset as envisaged in para 20(1)*(a)* – is a precise, objectively ascertainable figure. To such acquisition cost must be added the other amounts permitted to be taken into account under para 20(1), but excluding the categories of expenditure laid down in para 20(2).

9.11.7 Market-value valuation to determine the base cost of pre-valuation date assets

The taxpayer has an election to choose any of three methods of determining the value of a pre-valuation date asset.[93] One of those methods is for the taxpayer to obtain a market-value valuation of the asset[94] as at 1 October

90 Paragraph 22.
91 Paragraph 1 sv 'pre-valuation date asset'.
92 Paragraph 3*(a)*.
93 Paragraph 25(1).
94 Paragraph 26(1)*(a)*.

2001, within three years of that date.[95] Where the taxpayer's election in this regard is statutorily overridden, as envisaged in para 27(1), market value is again an element in the statutory formula which determines the valuation date value.

The Eighth Schedule makes specific provision for the way in which market value is determined in relation to particular assets:

- a financial instrument;[96]
- South African equity unit trusts and property unit trusts;[97]
- foreign unit trusts;[98] and
- the controlling interest in listed shares.[99]

All other assets are valued at market value as laid down in para 31.[100]

9.11.8 The meaning of 'market value'

The Eighth Schedule defines 'market value' in relation to specific categories of assets:

- financial instruments listed on a recognised stock exchange; for such assets, the market value is an average of buying and selling prices quoted on the last day of trading before disposal of the asset;[101]
- long-term insurance policies;[102]
- unit trusts and property trusts;[103]
- foreign unit trusts;[104]
- fiduciary, usufructuary and other like interests;[105]
- property subject to fiduciary, usufructuary and other like interests;[106]
- immovable farming property;[107] and
- unlisted shares.[108]

In relation to any other asset, 'market value' means the price that could have been obtained on a sale of the asset between a willing buyer and a willing seller dealing at arm's length in an open market.[109]

95 Paragraph 29(4).
96 See paras 28 and 29.
97 Paragraph 29(1)*(b)*(i).
98 Paragraph 29(1)*(b)*(ii).
99 Paragraph 29(2).
100 Paragraph 29(1)*(c)*.
101 Paragraph 31(1)*(a)*.
102 Paragraph 31(1)*(b)*.
103 Paragraph 31(1)*(c)*(i).
104 Paragraph 31(1)*(c)*(ii).
105 Paragraph 31(1)*(d)*.
106 Paragraph 31(1)*(e)*.
107 Paragraph 31(1)*(f)*.
108 Paragraph 31(3).
109 Paragraph 31(1)*(g)*.

9.11.9 Time-apportionment base cost of pre-valuation date assets

One of the three authorised methods[110] by which a person can elect to value a pre-valuation date asset (other than an instrument or an identical asset valued by the weighted-average method), which has been disposed of for more than the aggregate of the expenditure allowable in terms of para 20, is the time-apportionment method.

Essentially, time-apportionment assumes that the value of an asset, acquired prior to 1 October 2001 and disposed of after that date, increased at an even rate (in other words, in a straight line if plotted on a graph) from the date of acquisition to the date of disposal. On the basis of this assumption it is then possible to determine the value of the asset as at 1 October 2001.

The growth or decline in the value of the asset that occurred prior to 1 October 2001 is added to or subtracted from the pre-CGT expenditure (that is to say, the acquisition cost and other expenditure authorised by para 20) to arrive at the time-apportionment base cost (TAB) which constitutes the valuation date value (VDV), that is to say, the value of the asset as at 1 October 2001. To this TAB or VDV is added the expenditure which occurred after 1 October 2001 in order to arrive at the base cost in terms of para 25. Time-apportionment base cost can, of course, only be determined after the asset has been disposed of.

There are two possible variables in determining the value of an asset as at 1 October 2001. The first possibility is that qualifying expenditure (that is to say, expenditure allowable in terms of para 20) was incurred in relation to the asset prior to 1 October 2001, but not thereafter; in this event, the time-apportionment base cost is determined under what may conveniently be called 'the basic formula' laid down in para 30(1), and the period prior to 1 October 2001 is capped at 20 years for the purposes of applying the formula. The second possibility is that there was expenditure in relation to the asset in years of assessment falling both before and after 1 October 2001; in this event, what can usefully be called 'the proceeds formula', laid down in para 30(2), is applied to derive the component 'P' (proceeds on disposal) which forms part of the basic formula in para 30(1).

These formulae must be applied to each asset separately, and it is not permissible to perform the calculation by grouping several assets together.

9.11.10 The base cost of identical assets

Paragraph 32 provides for the method of valuation of identical assets by any of three methods:

- specific identification;
- first-in, first-out; or
- weighted average, determined in the manner laid down in para 32(4).

---

[110] As contemplated in para 26(1)*(a)*–*(c)*.

Identical assets are those that satisfy two tests: first, that if any of the assets in the particular holding were to be sold, the sale would realise the same amount as for any other asset in that group; second, that the assets are not individually distinguishable, apart from any identifying numbers that they may bear.

9.12 PROCEEDS

A person's 'capital gain' (as laid down in in para 3 of the Eighth Schedule) from the disposal of a particular asset is equal to the 'proceeds from the disposal' of the asset (as contemplated in para 35(1)) minus the 'base cost' of the asset (as contemplated in Part V of the Eighth Schedule).

Where the base cost of the asset is greater than such proceeds, the difference is a 'capital loss' as envisaged in para 4.

The Eighth Schedule requires that such capital gain or capital loss be determined separately in respect of each asset disposed of during the year of assessment.[111] It is not permissible to lump several assets together in performing the calculation.

9.12.1 Disposals to and from a deceased estate

A deceased person is treated as having disposed of all his or her assets (other than certain excluded assets)[112] to his or her deceased estate for proceeds equal to the market value of those assets at the time of death. The deceased estate, in turn, is treated as having acquired those assets at that market value.[113] A deceased estate is a person for purposes of the Act and is thus a separate taxable entity in its own right for capital gains tax purposes.

Hence, death has capital gains tax consequences for the deceased person in the tax year of his or her death as a result of the deemed disposal of such assets to the deceased estate. The death also has potential capital gains tax consequences for heirs and legatees.

When an asset is disposed of by a deceased estate to an heir or legatee (other than the surviving spouse), the deceased estate is treated as having disposed of the asset for proceeds equal to the asset's base cost in the hands of the deceased estate – namely, market value at the date of death.[114] The heir or legatee (other than the surviving spouse) is treated as having acquired the asset at that same base cost, that is to say, market value at the date of death.[115]

Hence, the deceased, in his or her last tax year of life, may incur a liability to capital gains tax on the difference between the base cost and the market value

[111] See paras 3*(a)* and 4*(a)*.
[112] See para 40(1)*(a)*–*(d)*.
[113] Paragraph 40(1).
[114] Paragraph 40(2).
[115] Paragraph 40(2)*(a)*–*(b)*.

of the asset at the date of death. (In addition, there may be a liability to estate duty. These are two separate taxes.)

If an heir or legatee in turn disposes of the asset, he or she may incur a liability to capital gains tax on the difference between the base cost of the asset in his or her hands, and the proceeds on disposal.

9.13 EXCLUSIONS

Parts VII and VIII of the Eighth Schedule provide for certain capital gains and losses to be 'disregarded', in other words, to be left out of account in determining the amount of a person's capital gain or loss as contemplated in para 3 or 4 of the Eighth Schedule.

These exclusions are additional to the 'inclusion rate relief' in terms of para 10, whereby the 'taxable capital gain' is only a percentage (and not the full amount) of the 'net capital gain'. The exclusions are also additional to the R40 000 annual exclusion, available to natural persons and special trusts,[116] and the R300 000 annual exclusion that applies in the tax year of a person's death. The inclusion rate relief and the annual exclusion apply only to capital gains which are not excluded.

9.13.1 Primary residence exclusion

This exclusion applies to the first R2 million of the capital gain or loss on the disposal of a 'primary residence' (the terms 'residence' and 'primary residence' are both defined),[117] and is available only to a natural person or special trust.[118]

Only one residence can be a primary residence of a person or special trust at any given time.[119] But a person who changes his or her primary residence several times over his or her lifetime can claim this exclusion on every disposal, unless the circumstances are such that he or she incurs a liability to income tax on any of the sales, in which event the Eighth Schedule will not apply to that disposal.[120]

Specific provision is made for the size of the residential property that qualifies for exclusion.[121] Thus, the exclusion applies only to a disposal of a primary residence and the land on which it is situated in so far as that land, including unconsolidated adjacent land, does not exceed two hectares, is used mainly for private or domestic purposes together with that residence and is disposed of at the same time and to the same person as that residence.[122] The distinction

[116] Paragraph 5(1)–(2).
[117] See para 44 sv 'residence' and 'primary residence'.
[118] Paragraph 45(1).
[119] Paragraph 45(3).
[120] Paragraph 35(3)*(a)*.
[121] Paragraph 46.
[122] Paragraph 46*(a)*–*(c)*.

between 'private' and 'domestic' usage in this regard means that, for example, land used for a tennis court or a parking area is 'private' use but may not necessarily be regarded as 'domestic' use.[123]

9.13.1.1 Apportionment of the capital gain or loss

Specific provision is made for the apportionment of the capital gain or loss that is to be disregarded to take account of:

- periods when the person in question was not ordinarily resident in the residence throughout the relevant period;[124]
- periods when the person in question was not ordinarily resident in the residence in question for up to two years, where such non-residence was due to the residence being offered for sale and vacated due to the acquisition or intended acquisition of a new primary residence, or where the residence was being built on land acquired for that purpose, or the residence had been accidentally rendered uninhabitable, or the death of the person in question;[125]
- periods when the property or a portion thereof was used for purposes of carrying on a trade;[126] and
- periods when the primary residence was being let.[127]

9.13.1.2 Transfer of a primary residence from a company or trust

The primary residence exclusion is available only to natural persons and special trusts.[128] When capital gains tax first came into force, many primary residences were held by companies, close corporations or trusts. To create an extended window period to allow such structures to be unwound, para 51 made provision for the transfer to a natural person, or for a joint transfer to spouses to be deemed to be a disposal at market value as at 1 October 2001 where the acquisition by that natural person from the company (which, as defined, includes a close corporation) or trust took place not later than 30 September 2010.

9.13.2 Exclusion in respect of personal-use assets

A natural person or a special trust must disregard a capital gain or loss in respect of the disposal of a 'personal-use asset', as defined.[129] There is no ceiling on the amount to be disregarded; provided the asset qualifies as a personal-use asset, the full amount of the gain (or loss) is disregarded.

---

[123] Explanatory Memorandum on the Revenue Laws Amendment Bill, 2001 [WP2–'01] para 30.

[124] Paragraph 47.

[125] Paragraph 48.

[126] Paragraph 49*(b)*.

[127] Paragraph 50.

[128] Paragraph 44.

[129] Paragraph 53(1)–(2).

9.13.3 Other exclusions

Part VIII of the Eighth Schedule provides for capital gains or losses to be disregarded in relation to:

- retirement benefits;[130]
- long-term assurance benefits;[131]
- 'debt defeasance', whereby a creditor disposes of a debt owed by debtor who is a connected person in relation to that creditor;[132]
- the disposal of small business assets, subject to stipulated conditions and limitations;[133]
- certain disposals by a micro business of its business assets;[134]
- a capital gain or loss as the result of the termination of an option as a result of its being exercised;[135]
- compensation for personal injury, illness or defamation;[136]
- gambling, games and competitions;[137]
- capital gains or losses made by a holder of a participatory interest in a portfolio of a collective investment scheme in securities on the disposal of that interest;[138]
- the donation or bequest of an asset to a public benefit organisation[139] and other exempt persons;[140]
- the disposal of an asset to a person who is exempt from tax;[141]
- assets used to produce exempt income;[142]
- the situation where substantially the whole use of that asset from the valuation date was by an approved public benefit organisation in carrying on a public benefit activity;[143] and
- the disposal of a restricted equity instrument as envisaged in s 8C(4)*(a)*, 5*(a)* or *(c)*.[144]

130 Paragraph 54.
131 Paragraph 55.
132 Paragraph 56.
133 Paragraph 57.
134 Paragraph 57A.
135 Paragraph 58.
136 Paragraph 59.
137 Paragraph 60.
138 Paragraph 61.
139 See also para 63A.
140 Paragraph 62.
141 Paragraph 63.
142 Paragraph 64.
143 Ibid.
144 Paragraph 64C.

9.14 ROLL-OVERS

Part IX of the Eighth Schedule provides for the 'roll-over' of certain capital gains or losses, which has the result that the recognition of a capital gain or loss, which would normally have occurred on the disposal of the asset in question, is instead deferred until the occurrence of a later act or event.

In overview, the Eighth Schedule provides for a roll-over of the capital gain or loss, subject to provisions in regard to the acquisition of a replacement asset, and subject to certain time stipulations, where:

- a person disposes of an asset other than a financial instrument by way of operation of law, theft or destruction, in return for proceeds equal to or exceeding the base cost;[145]
- an approved recreational club so elects in relation to the disposal of an asset, the whole of which was used mainly to provide social and recreational facilities and amenities for members of the club;[146] and
- a person disposes of an asset which qualifies for a capital allowance or deduction in terms of s 11*(e)*, s11D(2), s 12B, s 12C, s 12DA, s 12E, s 14 or s 14*bis* or 37B for proceeds in excess of the base cost and acquires a replacement asset within 12 months after disposal, all of which are brought into use within three years of the disposal.[147]

There is also a roll-over of the capital gain or loss where a person disposes of an asset to his or her spouse. That spouse is then regarded as having acquired the asset at its base cost to the disposing spouse, and the capital gain or loss on that deemed disposal is then deferred until the recipient spouse disposes of the asset.[148]

9.15 ATTRIBUTION OF CAPITAL GAINS

Part x of the Eighth Schedule lays down 'rules of attribution' whereby a capital gain made by one person is, by a legal fiction, attributed to (and taxable in the hands of) another person.

Rules of attribution apply to:

- a person's capital gain or loss which is attributable, wholly or partly, to a donation, settlement or other disposition, or a transaction, operation or scheme by that person's spouse, entered into for the purpose of tax avoidance;[149]

[145] Paragraph 65(1).
[146] Paragraph 65B.
[147] Paragraph 66.
[148] Paragraph 67(1)–(2).
[149] Paragraph 68(1).

- a gain made by a person from a trade carried on in partnership or association with that person's spouse, or which is connected in any way with any trade carried on by that spouse;[150]
- a gain made by a person which is derived from that person's spouse or any partnership or private company at a time when that spouse was a member of the partnership or the sole, main, or a principal shareholder of that company;[151]
- a minor child's capital gain, or a gain that has vested in that child or has been used for the benefit of that minor child during the year of assessment which can be attributed wholly or partly to a donation, settlement or other disposition made by a parent of that child or by way of a reciprocal donation;[152]
- certain capital gains that are subject to conditional vesting;[153]
- certain capital gains that are subject to revocable vesting;[154] and
- certain capital gains vesting in a non-resident.[155]

Of particular significance in tax planning is para 69, noted above, which attributes the capital gain made by a minor child to the parent, in circumstances where the minor's capital gain can be attributed wholly or partly to any 'donation, settlement or other disposition' made by that parent, or by another person if it was a reciprocal donation. Where the minor's gain can be attributed partly to such donation, settlement, etc, it will be attributed *pro tanto* to the parent.

9.16 COMPANY DISTRIBUTIONS

Part XI of the Eighth Schedule applies where a company distributes cash or assets in respect of previously existing shares, and addresses the impact of such distributions *vis-à-vis* the distributing company and *vis-à-vis* the recipient shareholder.

9.17 TRUSTS AND TRUST BENEFICIARIES

Part XII of the Eighth Schedule deals specifically with trusts, trust beneficiaries and insolvent estates.

For the purposes of the Act, a trust is a legal person in its own right.[156] A capital gain arising from the disposal of an asset by a trust is subject to capital gains tax either in the hands of the trust or, where a rule of attribution applies, in the

[150] Paragraph 68(2)*(a)*.
[151] Paragraph 68(2)*(b)*.
[152] Paragraph 69.
[153] Paragraph 70.
[154] Paragraph 71.
[155] Paragraph 72.
[156] Section 1 sv 'person'.

hands of a beneficiary or of the person who had made a donation, settlement or other disposition to the trust.

In terms of the definition of 'disposal' in para 11(1)*(d)*, the vesting of an interest in an asset of the trust in a beneficiary constitutes a 'disposal' by the trust.[157] It is thus the vesting of the interest, and not the distribution of the asset, that constitutes the 'disposal'.

9.17.1 Incidence of capital gains tax in the context of a trust

A capital gain from the disposal of a trust asset (unless exempted) is subject to capital gains tax either in the hands of the trust or (where the trust is, in essence, a mere conduit) in the hands of a beneficiary or, where a rule of attribution applies,[158] in the hands of some other person.

Trusts are subject to capital gains tax at a higher rate than individuals, except for 'special trusts'[159] which are, in effect, accorded the same tax treatment as natural persons in relation to the annual exclusion,[160] the inclusion rate,[161] the primary residence exclusion,[162] personal-use assets[163] and compensation for personal injury, illness or defamation.[164]

Non-resident beneficiaries of a trust are treated differently from resident beneficiaries. In terms of para 80(1)–(2), the *conduit principle* (in terms of which the trust's capital gain is taxed in the hands of the beneficiary) applies only where the beneficiary in question is a resident.

9.17.2 Time of disposal

The time of disposal of an asset by means of a change of ownership from one person to another:[165]

- in the case of an agreement, is the date of the agreement, but if the agreement is subject to a suspensive condition, then it is the date on which the condition is satisfied;
- in the case of the distribution of a trust asset to a trust beneficiary is the date on which the beneficiary acquires a vested interest in the asset;
- in the case of a donation, is the date of compliance with all the legal requirements for a valid donation;
- in the case of the expropriation of an asset, is the date on which the person receives the full compensation agreed to or determined by a tribunal or court;

157 Paragraph 11(1)*(d)*.
158 See paras 68–73.
159 Section 1 sv 'special trust'.
160 Paragraph 5(1).
161 Paragraph 10.
162 Paragraph 45(1).
163 Paragraph 53(1).
164 Paragraph 59.
165 See para 13(1)*(a)*.

- in the case of the exercise of an option, is the date on which it is exercised; and
- in any other case, is the date of change of ownership.

The time of disposal of an asset by means of the extinction of an asset by way of forfeiture, cancellation, relinquishment, release, waiver, expiry or abandonment, is the date of the extinction of the asset. [166]

The time of disposal of an asset by means of the scrapping, loss or destruction of the asset is the date when full compensation is received in respect thereof or, if no compensation is payable, then the date on which the scrapping, loss or destruction is discovered or the date on which it is discovered that no compensation is payable.[167]

The time of disposal in consequence of the decrease of a person's interest in a trust as a result of a value-shifting arrangement is the date on which the value of that person's interest decreases.[168]

A person to whom an asset is disposed of is treated as having acquired that asset at the time of the disposal of the asset, as envisaged above.[169]

9.18 VALUE-SHIFTING ARRANGEMENTS

A value-shifting arrangement connotes the transfer of value from one entity to another in circumstances where there has, nonetheless, been no 'disposal' for CGT purposes.[170] The value-shifting provisions of the Eighth Schedule apply only to arrangements between 'connected persons'.[171]

A 'value-shifting arrangement' for the purposes of the Eighth Schedule is defined[172] as—

> an arrangement by which a person retains an interest in a trust or partnership, but following a change in the rights or entitlements of the interests in that trust or partnership (other than as a result of a disposal at market value as determined before the application of para 38), the market value of the interest of that person decreases and—
>
> *(a)* the value of the interest of a connected person in relation to that person held directly or indirectly in that trust or partnership increases; or
>
> *(b)* a connected person in relation to that person acquires a direct or indirect interest in that trust or partnership.

[166] See para 13(1)*(b)*.
[167] Paragraph 13(1)*(c)*.
[168] Paragraph 13(1)*(f)*.
[169] Paragraph 13(2).
[170] Explanatory Memorandum on the Taxation Laws Amendment Bill, 2001 [WP1–'01] clause 38.
[171] As defined in s 1 sv 'connected person'.
[172] Paragraph 1 sv 'value-shifting arrangement'.

Value-shifting is typically found between connected persons, for example, between parents and their children. The definition of 'value-shifting arrangement' links with para 11(1)*(g)*, which provides that a 'disposal' includes the decrease in value of a person's interest in a trust or partnership as a result of a value-shifting arrangement.

SARS takes the view that 'value-shifting involves the effective transfer of value from one entity to another without constituting an ordinary disposal for CGT purposes'.[173]

9.18.1 Value-shifting arrangements in the context of a partnership

Where partners agree to a variation of their rights to partnership capital, this falls within the definition of a 'value-shifting arrangement'. (It is a moot point whether a variation of their rights to the future income of the partnership would be a value-shifting arrangement.) Partners are 'connected persons',[174] thus satisfying this element of the definition.

It needs to be borne in mind that unless 'proceeds'[175] are received or accrued by one of the parties as a result of the value-shifting arrangement, no capital gains tax consequences will ensue. (But an anti-avoidance provision in the Eighth Schedule nullifies the tax benefit that would otherwise be gained where a person disposes of an asset on terms whereby the proceeds of the disposal will not accrue to that person in the year of disposal and where he or she subsequently disposes of any right to claim payment in respect of that disposal, thereby seeking to avoid having any amount accrue to him or her from the disposal.)[176] It is significant that entering into a value-shifting arrangement does not result in a deemed accrual;[177] hence only an actual receipt or accrual in this regard will have capital gains tax consequences.

9.19 ANTI-AVOIDANCE

The general anti-avoidance provision of the Income Tax Act, namely part IIA of the Act, applies in relation to capital gains tax, where the elements of that section are present.

[173] Explanatory Memorandum on the Taxation Laws Amendment Bill, 2001 [WP1–'01] clause 38.

[174] See s 1 sv 'connected person' para *(c)*.

[175] As contemplated in para 35.

[176] See para 35A.

[177] As provided for in para 12(2).

9.20 ADMINISTRATIVE PROVISIONS

Most of the administrative aspects of capital gains tax (as distinct from statutory provisions which impose a charge to tax) are regulated by the Tax Administration Act.[178]

9.21 RESTRAINT OF TRADE PAYMENTS

A payment in restraint of trade is inherently of a capital nature, representing a payment for the surrender or sterilisation of a capital asset.[179] However, restraint payments made on or after 23 February 2000 to the following persons must be included in their gross income in terms of para *(c*A*)* of the definition of 'gross income':[180]

- individuals;
- labour brokers without exemption certificates issued in terms of the Seventh Schedule;
- personal service companies; and
- personal service trusts.

As a result, restraint payments to such persons are taxable under the income tax regime, and are not subject to capital gains tax, since para 35(3)*(a)* excludes from proceeds any amount included in the gross income of a person.

However, not all restraint payments are deemed in terms of para *(c*A*)* to be gross income. Such payments to companies and trusts that are not personal service providers are not included in gross income and will therefore be subject to capital gains tax.

[178] 28 of 2011.

[179] *Taeuber and Corssen (Pty) Ltd v SIR* 1975 (3) SA 649 (A), 37 SATC 129.

[180] See s 1 sv 'gross income'.

Chapter 10

Taxable persons

10.1 INTRODUCTION

Normal tax is payable annually by all persons on their 'taxable income'. The term 'taxable income' as defined in s 1 of the Income Tax Act 58 of 1962 ('the Act' or 'the Income Tax Act') means the aggregate of the amount remaining after deducting from the 'income' of any person all amounts allowed to be deducted or set off in terms of the Act, and all amounts to be included or deemed to be included in the taxable income of any person in terms of the Act.

The concept of 'person' and the concept of 'taxpayer' are not defined comprehensively in the Act. The term 'person' is defined in s 1 of the Act to include:

- an insolvent estate;
- the estate of a deceased person;
- any trust; and
- any portfolio of a collective investment scheme.

Section 152 of the Tax Administration Act 28 of 2011 ('Tax Administration Act') defines a 'person chargeable to tax' as 'a person upon whom the liability for tax due under a tax Act is imposed and who is personally liable for the tax'.

The term 'taxpayer' is defined in s 1 of the Income Tax Act to mean 'any person chargeable with any tax leviable under this Act'. For purposes of the Tax Administration Act, a taxpayer is defined in s 151 to mean:

- a person who is or may be chargeable to tax or with a tax offence;
- a representative taxpayer;
- a withholding agent;
- a responsible third party; or
- a person who is the subject of a request to provide assistance under an international tax agreement.

Note that the Income Tax Act distinguishes between the taxation of companies and persons other than companies. It also distinguishes between natural persons and persons other than natural persons. From the above, it can be inferred that the following are 'persons' for purposes of the Act:

- natural persons; and
- persons other than natural persons (trusts, deceased estates, insolvent estates and companies).

The special rules that apply to the taxation of each of these persons will be dealt with below. The taxation of companies is dealt with in chapter 11.

10.2 THE TAXATION OF NATURAL PERSONS

The Act provides for special rules that apply to the taxation of certain categories of natural persons.

The general principles of the Act apply to natural persons. In addition, certain deductions, dealt with in chapter 6, are available to natural persons only. For example, only natural persons can claim deductions in respect of contributions to a retirement annuity fund, a medical aid scheme etc. Thus, taxable income derived by a natural person must be calculated in the normal way.

It must be noted that South Africa has a unitary tax rate applicable to all natural persons, whether they are married or not. The tax payable is determined by taking account of the person's level of taxable income on a progressive scale. Thus, the higher the taxpayer's taxable income, the higher the rate of tax applicable to that taxpayer. Under s 6(2)*(a)* of the Act, natural persons are entitled to a primary rebate which reduces the tax payable. Where the taxpayer is over the age of 65, a secondary rebate is available under s 6(2)*(b)*. If the taxpayer is over the age of 75 on the last day of the tax year, he or she qualifies for a tertiary rebate in terms of s 6(2)*(c)* of the Act. The Minister regularly adjusts the amount of the rebates in his National Budget and they are then enacted into law.

10.2.1 The taxation of minors

In terms of the Children's Act 38 of 2005, a child means a person who is below the age of 18 years. A married person who divorces or is widowed before he or she reaches the age of 18 retains full contractual capacity. The fact that a minor is emancipated does not change his or her status for income tax purposes.

The definition of a child in s 1 of the Income Tax Act includes stepchildren and adopted children of the taxpayer. Tax is payable by a representative taxpayer on the minor's behalf. Section 153 of the Tax Administration Act defines a representative taxpayer as a person who is responsible for paying the tax liability of another person as an agent. In terms of s 1 of the Income Tax Act, the representative taxpayer in respect of the income of any minor is the minor's guardian for purposes of submission of returns and the payment of tax due. Section 154 of the Tax Administration Act sets out the liability of the representative taxpayer in such capacity as regards:

- the income to which the representative taxpayer is entitled;
- moneys to which the representative taxpayer is entitled or has the management or control;

- transactions concluded by the representative taxpayer; and
- anything else done by the representative taxpayer.

Section 155 of the Tax Administration Act provides that a representative taxpayer is personally liable for tax payable in the representative taxpayer's representative capacity, if, while it remains unpaid:

- the representative taxpayer alienates, charges or disposes of amounts in respect of which the tax is chargeable; or
- the representative taxpayer disposes of or parts with funds or moneys, which are in the representative taxpayer's possession or come to the representative taxpayer after the tax is payable, if the tax could legally have been paid from or out of the funds or moneys.

Note, however, that s 153(3) of the Tax Administration Act provides that a taxpayer is not relieved from any liability, responsibility or duty imposed under a tax Act by reason of the fact that the taxpayer's representative failed to perform such responsibilities or duties, or is liable for the tax payable by the taxpayer.

In terms of s 68(3)*(a)*(i) of the Income Tax Act, every parent of a minor child must show in his or her return what income the minor earned, either directly or indirectly, from the parent or his or her spouse. Section 68(3)*(a)*(ii) further stipulates that every parent shall be required to include in his or her return any capital gain or capital loss in respect of any transaction entered into directly or indirectly by that parent, which is taken into account in the determination of the aggregate capital gain or aggregate capital loss of any of that parent's minor children.

Minor children are taxed in their own right on income that is received by or accrues to them. Section 7(1) of the Act provides:

> Income shall be deemed to have accrued to a person notwithstanding that such income has been invested, accumulated or otherwise capitalized by him or that such income has not been actually paid over to him but remains due and payable to him or has been credited in account or reinvested or accumulated or capitalized or otherwise dealt with in his name or on his behalf, and a complete statement of all such income shall be included by any person in the returns rendered by him under this Act.

Where the income arises as a result of the minor child's parent making a donation to, or settling income upon, that child (directly or indirectly) the resultant income is taxed in the parent's and not in the child's hands.[1] This is intended to prevent tax avoidance.

10.2.1.1 Anti-tax avoidance provisions that relate to minors

Section 7(3) is an anti-tax-avoidance provision which provides that if a parent makes a donation, settlement or other disposition to his or her minor child which results in income being received by or accruing in favour of the minor

[1] Section 7(3) of the Act.

or being expended for his or her maintenance, education or benefit, or being accumulated for the child's benefit, that income is deemed to have been received by or accrued to the parent of the child, who will be taxed accordingly.

The words 'donation' and 'settlement' as used in the section were defined in *Ovenstone v SIR*[2] to mean a disposal of property for no consideration, ie a wholly gratuitous disposal, made out of the liberality or generosity of the donor, and the term 'other disposition' excludes any disposition of property that is a wholly commercial or business one. The facts in the *Ovenstone* case were that a father lent his minor children money to enable them to take up shares privately placed with him, which subsequently produced dividends. He charged them the same rate of interest as his bank would have charged him for borrowing the money to enable him to make the loans, which were made without security and without specific terms of repayment. The court held that the loans constituted a disposition that was partly gratuitous and, as such, qualified as a donation, settlement or other disposition under s 7(3).

In *Kohler v CIR*,[3] income was received by the taxpayer's daughter from a re-investment of the income which accrued from a donation made by the father. Briefly, the facts were that a father donated a certain amount of money to each of his daughters. Each daughter purchased shares using the income which accrued to her from the investment of the money. The Commissioner taxed the father on the income which accrued from the shares in terms of s 9(3) (now s 7(3)). Finding in favour of the father, it was held that once income has accrued to or been received by the minor, and has been capitalised, its subsequent earning is attributed not to the source from which the original income was derived but to the advantageous employment of the minor's new capital. The court ruled that such 'income upon income' stands on the same footing as income derived by the minor from the employment of any other capital of his or hers, borrowed, earned or bequeathed.

The circumstances in the *Kohler* case can, however, be distinguished from those in *CIR v Widan*.[4] The facts in this case were that in terms of a deed of trust, a father had donated all the shares in a company to his four children. The company declared a dividend of P21 000, which the trustees distributed to the father in his capacity as guardian of the four children (the beneficiaries). The money was then used to subscribe for shares in another company, and it was the income from the second company that was at issue. It was held that the income from the second company was by reason of the donation, because the original donation was intended to produce income which would be used to acquire the shares in the second company. The court ruled that, in cases of this nature, there were no hard and fast rules, and each case would have to be judged on its merits. In the context of the *Widan* case, Centlivres CJ held:

---

[2] 1980 (2) SA 721 (A) 735.

[3] 1949 (4) SA 1022 (T).

[4] 1955 (1) SA 226 (A) 234.

> There must be some causal relation between the donation and the income in question. Difficult cases may conceivably arise. Where, for instance, a father donates a sum of money to a minor child and the child buys a business to which he contributes his skill and labour and from which he earns an income that may be regarded as being attributable to two causes, viz, the donation and the skill and labour of the child. In such a case it may be impossible to say which part of the income was the result of the donation and which part the result of his skill and labour and it may be that the Commissioner would not be able to apply s 9(3) [now (s 7(3)].

In *Joss v SIR*[5] the taxpayer sold assets to a company on an interest-free loan. The taxpayer's minor daughter was a shareholder in the company and received a dividend. SARS deemed the dividend to be the taxpayer's. The court found that the portion of the dividend that accrued to the minor was attributable to the parent; as it was 'by reason of' the interest-free loan made by the parent, it thus constituted a donation for purposes of s 7(3).

When a minor child receives income in his or her own right and not by reason of any donation, settlement or other disposition made by his or her parents, the income is subject to tax in the child's own hands and not in the hands of his or her parent or parents. Examples of where the minor would be taxed in his or her own right are on income derived by the minor from an inheritance bequeathed in his or her favour, or where the minor appears in an advert and receives an appearance fee for services rendered.

Section 7(4) is another tax avoidance provision which provides that the income of a minor child is deemed to be the parent's income if that parent made a donation, settlement or other disposition, or gave some other consideration to some other person or that other person's family in return for a donation, settlement or other disposition by that person to the parent's minor child.

10.2.2 The taxation of married persons

Each spouse in a marriage is taxed separately on his or her taxable income during the year of assessment. The word 'spouse' is defined in s 1 of the Act to include partners in:

- marriages or customary unions recognised under the laws of the Republic (these marriages are deemed to be in community of property);
- unions recognised according to the tenets of any religion (these marriages are deemed to be in community of property); and
- same-sex or heterosexual unions which the Commissioner is satisfied are intended to be permanent (spouses married under this latter category are deemed to be married out of community of property unless otherwise specified).

The marriage, separation or divorce or death of a spouse during a year of assessment does not affect his or her liability to tax. A spouse who dies during

[5] 1980 (1) SA 674 (T) 683.

the year of assessment will have a period of assessment of less than 12 months and will qualify for a proportional primary and/or secondary rebate only.[6] There are, however, certain deeming, anti-tax avoidance provisions that relate to married persons.

Section 68(1) of the Act provides that:

(a) any income received by or accrued to or in favour of any person married in or out of community of property which in terms of s 7(2) is deemed to be income received by or accrued to such person's spouse; or

(b) capital gain which is in terms of para 68 of the Eighth Schedule taken into account in the determination of the aggregate capital gain or aggregate capital loss of such person's spouse,

shall be included by such spouse in returns of income required to be rendered by that spouse under this Act.

Section 68(2) provides that 'in the event of the death of any person during any year in respect of which such income is chargeable or in which such capital gain is taken into account, the income or capital gain of such person's spouse for the period elapsing between the date of such death and the last day of the year of assessment shall be returned as the separate income of such spouse'.

10.2.2.1 Tax avoidance provisions that relate to married persons

Section 7(2) prevents tax avoidance if married couples reduce their liabilities to normal tax by arranging for taxable income to be split between the spouses:

- Section 7(2)*(a)* provides that if a spouse receives income in consequence of a donation, settlement or other disposition made by, or scheme carried out by his or her spouse, and the sole or main purpose is the reduction, postponement or avoidance of tax, the donor spouse will be taxed on the income of the recipient spouse.
- Section 7(2)*(b)* provides that if a spouse receives income in excess of what he or she would reasonably be entitled to, from a trade connected to that of the donor via a partnership, association or private company of which the donor spouse was the sole or main shareholder or one of the principal shareholders, the donor spouse will be taxed on the excess income and the recipient spouse on the reasonable income he or she would have earned, depending on the nature of the recipient's participation in that trade or his or her services to that trade.[7]

CHAPTER 10

10.2.2.2 Marriage in community of property

Income accruing to spouses married in community of property accrues equally to each spouse, except in certain circumstances:

[6] De Koker AP *South African Income Tax* (August 2013) LexisNexis para 10.49.

[7] De Koker *South African Income Tax* para 10.40.

- Section 7(2A)*(a)* provides that income (other than from letting of fixed property) derived from the carrying on of a trade is deemed to accrue to the spouse who is carrying on the trade. Where the trade is carried on jointly by both spouses in partnership, the income is deemed to have accrued to both spouses in the proportions determined by the partnership agreement. If there is no partnership agreement, then the income accrues in the proportions to which each spouse would reasonably be entitled, taking into consideration the nature of the trade, the extent of each spouse's participation, the services rendered by each spouse and any other relevant factors.
- Section 7(2A)*(b)* provides that income derived from the letting of fixed property and any other income derived other than from carrying on of a trade (eg interest, dividends and annuities other than s 10A annuities) is deemed to accrue in equal shares to both spouses. Income derived by spouses married in community of property from the letting of fixed property is deemed to have accrued in equal shares to both spouses. But if it does not fall into their joint estate, it is deemed to be income that has accrued to the spouse who is entitled to it.
- Section 7(2C) deems certain income to be the income derived by a spouse from a trade carried on by him or her. This includes income from retirement funds or preservation funds, s 10A annuities, patents, designs, trademarks, copyrights and property of a similar nature.[8]

10.2.2.3 The tax treatment of alimony and maintenance as a result of divorce or separation

(a) Pre-1962 divorces and separations

Section 21 of the Income Tax Act provides that where, by virtue of a judicial order, written agreement of separation, or order of divorce, an allowance or maintenance is paid to the spouse, former spouse, or children, that amount may be deducted from the paying spouse's taxable income, provided it is paid out of that taxable income (not exempt income, foreign source income or capital profits). The taxpayer may not create an assessed loss with this deduction; therefore, any excess that is not deductible will fall away. In terms of s 102 of the Tax Administration Act, the onus is on the taxpayer to prove out of which income the amount is paid.

(b) Post-1962 divorces and separations

- Where, by virtue of a judicial order, written agreement of separation, or order of divorce, an allowance or maintenance is paid to the spouse, former spouse, or children, that amount may not be deducted from the paying spouse's taxable income.

[8] Ibid.

- The spouse receiving the payment must include it in his or her gross income in terms of para *(b)* of the gross income definition, if it is from a Republic source. Note, however, that s 10(1)*(u)* exempts from tax any amount received by or accrued to any person from or on behalf of such person's spouse or former spouse by way of alimony or allowance or maintenance of such person under an order of judicial separation or divorce granted in consequence of proceedings instituted after 21 March 1962, or under any agreement of separation entered into after that date.

10.2.3 Determination of taxable incomes of permanently separated spouses

Section 25A of the Act provides that 'where during any period of assessment any taxpayer who is married in community of property has lived apart from his or her spouse in circumstances which indicate that the separation is likely to be permanent, his or her taxable income for such period shall be determined at the amount at which such taxpayer's taxable income would have been determined under the provisions of this Act if such taxpayer had not been married in community of property'.

10.3 THE TAXATION OF DECEASED ESTATES

Upon the death of a person, he or she ceases to be a taxpayer but the tax payable on the income derived by the deceased prior to death is a debt due by his or her estate.[9]

Section 9HA(1) of the Act provides that a deceased person must be treated as having disposed of his or her assets at the date of that person's death for an amount received or accrued equal to the market value, as contemplated in para 1 of the Eighth Schedule, of those assets as at that date. This excludes:

- assets disposed of for the benefit of his or her surviving spouse in terms of s 9HA(2);
- a long-term insurance policy of the deceased, if any capital gain or capital loss that would have been determined in respect of a disposal that resulted in proceeds of that policy being received by or accruing to the deceased would have been disregarded in terms of para 55 of the Eighth Schedule; or
- an interest of the deceased in a pension, pension preservation, provident, provident preservation or retirement annuity fund in the Republic, or outside the Republic if any capital gain or capital loss that would have been determined in respect of a disposal of that interest that resulted in a lump sum benefit being received by or accruing to the deceased would have been disregarded in terms of para 54 of the Eighth Schedule.

[9] De Koker *South African Income Tax* para 12.4.

Section 9HA(2)*(a)* provides that a deceased person must, if his or her surviving spouse is a resident, be treated as having disposed of an asset for the benefit of that surviving spouse if that asset is acquired by that surviving spouse:

- by *ab intestato* or testamentary succession;
- as a result of a redistribution agreement between the heirs and legatees of that person in the course of liquidation or distribution of the deceased estate; or
- in settlement of a claim arising under s 3 of the Matrimonial Property Act 88 of 1984.

Section 9HA(2)*(b)* provides that a deceased person must, if his or her surviving spouse is a resident, be treated as having disposed of an asset for an amount received or accrued that is equal to:

- in the case of trading stock, livestock or produce contemplated in the First Schedule, the amount that was allowed as a deduction in respect of that asset for purposes of determining that person's taxable income, before the inclusion of any taxable capital gain, for the year of assessment ending on the date of that person's death; or
- in the case of any other asset, the base cost of that asset, as contemplated in the Eighth Schedule, as at the date of that person's death.

Under s 9HA(3), if any asset that is treated as having been disposed of by a deceased person is transferred directly to an heir or legatee of that person, that heir or legatee must be treated as having acquired that asset for an amount of expenditure incurred equal to the market value (as contemplated in para 1 of the Eighth Schedule) of that asset as at the date of that deceased person's death.

In terms of the definition of 'person' in s 1 of the Act, the estate of a deceased person is a taxable person.

Section 25(5)*(a)* of the Act provides that a deceased estate must be treated as if that estate were a natural person (this does not apply when determining normal tax rebates – s 6; medical scheme fees tax credit – s 6A; and additional medical expenses tax credit – s 6B). And s 25(5)*(b)* provides that the deceased estate be treated as if that estate were a resident if the deceased person was a resident at the time of his or her death.

The deceased estate consists of all assets and liabilities of the deceased taxpayer. Normally upon death, the deceased's net assets are distributed to the deceased's heirs and legatees in terms of either the will or the laws of intestate succession (if he or she dies leaving no will). If the deceased's assets produce income in the estate before the assets are distributed to the heirs or legatees, the Act contains special provisions for the taxation of this income.

Paragraph *(e)* of the definition of 'representative taxpayer' in s 1 of the Act states that a representative taxpayer in respect of the income received by or accrued to any deceased person during his or her lifetime, and the income received by or accrued to the estate of any deceased person, is the executor or administrator of the estate of the deceased person. Section 1 of the Act defines 'executor' as any person to whom letters of administration have been granted by a Master or an Assistant Master of the High Court appointed under the Administration of Estates Act 66 of 1965 in respect of the estate of a deceased person under any law relating to the administration of estates. The term executor includes a person acting or authorised to act under letters of administration granted outside the Republic but signed and sealed by the Master or Assistant Master for use within the Republic. The term also includes a person administering an estate that is not required to be administered under the supervision of the Master or Assistant Master.

The executor is taxable in a representative capacity in respect of the income received by or accrued to the deceased during his lifetime. The executor must make the return of income up to the date of death, admit the resulting claim for tax against the assets of the estate and generally represent the estate in all matters relating to taxation. Any tax assessed upon the deceased up to the date of death must be paid by the executor out of the assets of the estate.[10]

Section 25(1) of the Act provides for the tax liability of the deceased estate as well as the heirs and legatees of the estate. The section states that:

- Any amount received by or accrued to or in favour of a person in his or her capacity as the executor of an estate, that would have been income in the hands of the deceased person had it been received by or accrued to or in favour of him or her during his or her lifetime, will be taxed in the estate of the deceased person. This includes income received or accrued from the deceased's death up to the date on which the executor ceases to function as such.
- To the extent to which income has been derived for the immediate or future benefit of any ascertained heir or legatee of the deceased person, that income will be deemed to be income received by or accrued to that heir or legatee. To the extent to which it is not so derived, it is deemed to be the income of the estate.

10.3.1 Income taxable in the hands of the executor

In *ITC 1293*[11] the executrix was also an heiress of an estate. In her capacity as executrix, she sold a mealie crop that was harvested from a farm that was included in the assets of the estate in order to discharge the debts of the estate. Then she sold the livestock on the farm and awarded the proceeds to herself in her capacity as heiress. The court ruled that the proceeds of the mealie crop were correctly included in the income of the estate, but that the proceeds of the livestock ought not to have been included in her gross income (as heiress) since proceeds from the sale of livestock are capital in nature.

In terms of s 25(2), where the deceased estate of a person acquires an asset from that deceased person, that deceased estate must, if that asset is an asset:

[10] De Koker *South African Income Tax* para 12.5.

[11] (1979) 41 SATC 166.

- other than an asset contemplated in s 9HA(2), be treated as having acquired that asset for an amount of expenditure incurred equal to the amount contemplated in s 9HA(1); and
- contemplated in s 9HA (2), be treated as having acquired that asset for an amount of expenditure incurred equal to the amount contemplated in s 9HA(2)*(b)*.

10.3.2 Income taxable in the hands of ascertained heirs or legatee

In *Saacks v CIR*[12] the taxpayer was not an ascertained heir in terms of the deceased's will but became an heir after the deceased's widow renounced (repudiated) her rights under the will. The Commissioner sought to tax the taxpayer. It was held that the Commissioner could not tax the taxpayer before the filing of the liquidation and distribution account in the estate and the widow's renouncement of her rights under the will. The erstwhile Supreme Court held:

> Section 25 ... determines the *person* on whom liability for tax on the income dealt with in the section rests, viz an ascertained heir or legatee if there is one, or the estate if there is no ascertained heir or legatee. The section in no way purports to enable the [Commissioner] to include in the assessment of such person's taxable income for a particular tax year, income which was not derived for the benefit of that person during that tax year.[13]

The income apportioned to the heirs or legatees in terms of the deceased's will or the law of intestate succession retains its nature in their hands. Therefore, if the executor has received, say, dividends, rent or interest that must be apportioned to the heirs or legatees, with the result that they are deemed to have received dividends, rent or interest.[14]

Section 25(3) provides:

> Where the deceased estate of a person disposes of an asset to an heir or legatee of that person—
>
> (*a*) that deceased estate must be treated as having disposed of that asset for an amount received or accrued equal to the amount of expenditure incurred by the deceased estate in respect of that asset; and
>
> (*b*) the heir or legatee must be treated as having acquired that asset for an amount of expenditure incurred equal to the expenditure incurred by the deceased estate in respect of that asset.

Section 25(4)*(a)* applies to situations where an asset has been acquired by a surviving spouse of a deceased person as contemplated in s 9HA(2). The section applies when determining the amount of any allowance or deduction to which that spouse may be entitled or that is to be recovered or recouped by or

12 1979 (1) SA 359 (C).
13 (1979) (1) SA 359 (C) 363B.
14 De Koker *South African Income Tax* para 12.5.

included in the income of that spouse in respect of that asset. The section also applies to the amount of any capital gain or capital loss in respect of a disposal of that asset by that spouse. In terms of s 25(4)*(b)* the surviving spouse must be treated as one and the same person as the deceased person and deceased estate with respect to—

(i) the date of acquisition of that asset by that deceased person;

(ii) any valuation of that asset effected by that deceased person as contemplated in paragraph 29 (4) of the Eighth Schedule;

(iii) the amount of any expenditure and the date on which and the currency in which that expenditure was incurred in respect of that asset—

(aa) by that deceased person as contemplated in section 9HA(2)*(b)*; and

(bb) by that deceased estate, other than the expenditure contemplated in section 9HA(2)*(b)*;

(iv) the manner in which that asset had been used by the deceased person and the deceased estate; and

(v) any allowance or deduction allowable in respect of that asset to the deceased person and the deceased estate.

10.3.3 Other amounts that will be taxed in the deceased estate

The amounts taxed in the deceased estate include the following:

- The liability to tax of a deceased taxpayer in relation to amounts derived for services rendered: para *(c)*(ii) of the definition of 'gross income' in s 1 of the Act states that an amount received by or accrued to or for the benefit of any person in respect of services rendered or to be rendered by any other person must, for the purposes of the definition, be deemed to have been received by or to have accrued to that other person.
- Section 8A(1)*(b)* provides for the inclusion in a taxpayer's income – up to the date of death – of gains made by him or her as a director of a company or as an employee on rights to acquire marketable securities.
- Where a business asset for which a wear and tear allowance was previously allowed in the determination of the taxable income of the deceased person is disposed of by the executor, a recoupment of such allowance would have been income in the hands of the deceased if such asset was sold during his or her lifetime (s 8(4)*(a)*). The recoupment will be included in the gross income of the deceased estate or the ascertained heir or legatee that is entitled to the asset.
- Shares received in exchange for fixed property or other shares in the circumstances set out in s 24A are deemed to have been disposed of by the taxpayer on the day preceding the date of his or her death for a consideration equal to the lesser of the market value on that day or the market value on the date of the original exchange (s 24A(5)).
- Lump sum awards from pension, pension preservation, provident, provident preservation and retirement annuity funds payable on the death of a member or past member of such a fund are deemed to accrue prior to the taxpayer's death.

If the period of assessment to the date of death is less than 12 months, the rebates must be reduced proportionately, unless the Commissioner directs otherwise. In an assessment made upon the executor as representative taxpayer of the estate, normal tax is assessed at the rates applicable to persons (other than companies) and special trusts. However, the estate does not qualify for the primary rebate and the 'over-65' rebate applicable to natural persons. The deceased estate also does not qualify for the basic interest exemption provided for in s 10(1)*(i)*.[15]

The fees received by an executor from an estate are regarded as amounts received (in his or her personal capacity) for services rendered and are taxable in his or her hands in terms of para *(c)* of the definition of 'gross income' in s 1 of the Act.

10.4 TAXATION OF INSOLVENT ESTATES

When a natural person becomes insolvent three taxpayers have to be dealt with:

- the insolvent natural person for the period before sequestration;
- the insolvent estate; and
- the insolvent natural person for the period after sequestration.

10.4.1 The insolvent natural person for the period before sequestration

When a natural person becomes insolvent, his or her tax status is terminated on the day before the date of sequestration of his or her estate.

10.4.2 The insolvent estate

On the date of sequestration, a new taxpayer (the insolvent estate) comes into existence. The term 'insolvent estate' means an insolvent estate as defined in s 1 of the Insolvency Act 24 of 1936. Section 2 of the Insolvency Act, in turn, defines an insolvent estate as an estate under sequestration. Section 1 of the Income Tax Act provides that an insolvent estate is a taxable person. For administrative purposes, a new income tax reference number is allocated to the insolvent estate. In the case of the insolvency of a partner in a partnership, the insolvency brings about the dissolution of the partnership and the estate of each insolvent partner constitutes a separate person.

In terms of para *(f)* of the definition of 'representative taxpayer' in s 1 of the Income Tax Act, the trustee of an insolvent estate is the representative taxpayer in respect of the income received by or accrued to an insolvent person prior to the date of sequestration of his or her estate. A 'trustee' is defined in s 1 of the Act to include – in addition to every person appointed or constituted as

[15] De Koker *South African Income Tax* para 12.5.

trustee by the act of the parties, by will, by order or declaration of court or by operation of law – an executor or administrator, tutor or curator, and any person having the administration or control of any property subject to a trust, *usufruct*, *fideicommissum* or other limited interest or acting in any fiduciary capacity or having (either in a private or in an official capacity) the possession, direction, control or management of any property of a person under legal disability.

In terms of the Insolvency Act, any tax payable by the insolvent on income earned prior to the date of insolvency, even if it has become payable only after that date, is a debt due to the government by the estate, and the trustee must admit the claim and accord it the preference to which it is entitled. Section 101 *(a)* of the Insolvency Act confers a preference on 'any tax on persons or the incomes or profits of persons for which the insolvent was liable under any Act of Parliament or Ordinance of the Territory or a Provincial Council in respect of any period prior to the date of sequestration of his estate, whether or not that tax has become payable after that date'.

In terms of s 153 and s 154 of the Tax Administration Act 28 of 2011, any assessment made on the trustee would be deemed to be made upon him or her in his or her representative capacity. The trustee is responsible for the administration and liquidation of an insolvent estate. He or she must make a return of the income derived by the insolvent estate, admit resulting claims for tax against the assets of the estate and generally represent the estate in all matters relating to taxation.

In an assessment made upon the trustee as representative taxpayer of the estate, normal tax is assessed at the rates applicable to persons other than companies. But the estate does not qualify for the primary rebate and the 'over-65' rebate that applies to natural persons. Likewise, it does not qualify for the basic interest exemption provided for in s 10(1)*(i)* of the Act.[16]

The trustee is entitled to claim any deductions for which the estate qualifies in terms of the Act in the determination of the income subject to tax in his or her hands as trustee. For example, administration charges, such as the trustee's remuneration and the premium on a fidelity bond, are deductible under s 11*(a)* of the Act.

Where a provisional sequestration order is set aside by the court, the Commissioner is obliged to withdraw any assessment issued in respect of the estate of an insolvent person for the period prior to the date of sequestration and his or her insolvent estate. The consequence is that the person concerned is placed in the same position as if he or she had never been insolvent, and will have a single year of assessment in the year in which the rescinded provisional order was issued.

[16] De Koker *South African Income Tax* para 12.2.

10.4.3 The insolvent natural person for the period after sequestration

From the date of sequestration, the insolvent person is regarded as a new taxpayer. The 'date of sequestration' is defined in s 1 of the Act as the date of voluntary surrender of an estate if accepted by the court, or the date of provisional sequestration of an estate if a final order of sequestration is granted by the court. In the case of voluntary surrender of an estate by a taxpayer, the date of sequestration is the date on which the estate is surrendered. In the case of compulsory sequestration, the date of sequestration is the date of the provisional order.

An insolvent person whose estate is voluntarily or compulsorily sequestrated during a year of assessment can, with the consent of his trustee, enter into employment, carry on a profession or run a business in his or her own right. In that case, he or she (not the trustee) is liable for tax on all income so derived. He or she is then regarded as a new taxpayer from the date of insolvency and is liable to tax on any income that he or she derives in his or her own right from that date.[17]

The summary of the above is thus: in the year in which insolvency takes place, three assessments are raised: two on the insolvent and one on the insolvent estate:

- The first one on the insolvent covers the period from the beginning of the year of assessment to the date of insolvency.
- The second one on the insolvent covers the period from the date of insolvency until the end of that year of assessment. Since the two periods of assessment on the insolvent are each less than 12 months, in terms of s 66(13)*(a)* and *(b)*(ii) of the Act, the primary and secondary rebates available to the insolvent are apportioned proportionately between the periods before and after sequestration. The first income tax return for the period after sequestration has to be completed for the period from the date of sequestration to the last date of that year of assessment.
- The third assessment is raised on the insolvent estate.

10.4.4 Deeming provisions

Section 25C of the Act provides that, subject to any such adjustments as may be necessary, the estate of the insolvent person prior to his or her sequestration and his or her insolvent estate are deemed to be one and the same person for purposes of determining:

- the amount of any allowance, deduction or set-off to which the insolvent estate may be entitled;

[17] *Matanzima v Minister of Welfare and Pensions and Others* 1990 (4) SA 1 (TkA), 52 SATC 330.

- any amount which is recovered or recouped by, or otherwise required to be included in the income of the insolvent estate; and
- any taxable capital gain or assessed capital loss of the insolvent estate.

In effect, this section ensures continuity between the person prior to insolvency and his or her insolvent estate.[18] The Explanatory Memorandum on the Taxation Laws Amendment Bill, 2001 explains that s 25C 'has the effect of crystallizing all capital gains and capital losses in the hands of the insolvent estate. It also has the effect of permitting an assessed loss or assessed capital loss to be carried forward from the insolvent prior to sequestration into his or her insolvent estate.'

10.4.5 How assessed losses of insolvent are dealt with

In terms of s 20(1)*(a)*(i):

- A person whose estate has been voluntarily or compulsorily sequestrated is not entitled to carry forward any assessed loss incurred prior to the date of sequestration, unless the order of sequestration has been set aside.
- If the order of sequestration has been set aside, the balance of the assessed loss at the date of sequestration to be carried forward must be reduced by the amount thereof that was allowed to be set off against the income of the insolvent estate of such person from the carrying on of any trade. In effect, this ensures that the assessed loss to be carried forward is reduced by any income of the insolvent estate.

10.4.6 The effect of setting aside an order of sequestration

When a person's estate has been voluntarily or compulsorily sequestrated and the sequestration order has not been set aside, any assessed loss incurred prior to the date of sequestration may not be carried forward. Even if he or she is subsequently rehabilitated, he or she is debarred from carrying forward the assessed loss incurred prior to sequestration, since no person whose estate has been sequestrated is entitled to carry forward any assessed loss incurred prior to the date of sequestration, unless the order of sequestration has been set aside.[19]

Fees received by a trustee from the insolvent estate for services rendered are taxable in the trustee's personal capacity in terms of para *(c)* of the definition of 'gross income' in s 1 of the Act.

[18] De Koker *South African Income Tax* para 12.2.

[19] Stiglingh M et al *Silke: South African Income Tax* (LexisNexis 2011) 890.

10.5 THE TAXATION OF PARTNERSHIP INCOME

A partnership has been defined in *Joubert v Tarry & Co*[20] as a legal relationship between two or more persons who carry on a lawful business or undertaking, to which each contributes either money or labour or anything else with the object of making a profit, and of sharing it between them. The *Joubert* case set out the following as the characteristics of a partnership:

- Each partner must bring either money, labour or skills into the partnership.
- The partnership business must be carried on for the joint benefit of its partners.
- The object of the partnership must be to make a profit.
- The partnership agreement or contract between the parties must be legitimate.

Partnerships can be divided into two main categories: 'general partnerships' (ordinary partnerships) and 'limited partnerships' (extra-ordinary partnerships).

In a 'general partnership', all the partners have the ability to actively manage or control the business. Every partner has authority to make decisions about how the business is run and they all have the authority to make legally binding decisions. The partners do not have any limit on their personal responsibility for the debts of the business. Each partner is also 'jointly and severally' liable for the debts and obligations of the partnership business. Joint and several liability means that each partner is equally liable for the debts of the business, but each is also totally liable. So if a creditor can't get what he is owed by one or more of the partners, he can collect it from another partner, even if that partner has already paid his share of the total debt. Thus, an individual partner's personal assets are at risk from claims arising out of actions against the partnership which exceed its own resources.

In 'limited partnerships' an agreement is entered into whereby some partners have limited liability in that they do not bear total responsibility for the debts of the partnership.

The trade-off for this limited liability is a lack of management control, in that a limited partner does not have the authority to run the business but is more or less an investor in the business. It is, however, important that a limited partnership has at least one general partner that is responsible for running the day-to-day management of the business and has the authority to make legally binding business decisions.

South Africa's statutory law and common law (Roman-Dutch law) recognises two types of limited liability partnerships, the 'anonymous' (silent) partnership and the 'partnership *en commandite*'. Section 24H of the Income Tax Act defines a 'limited partner' as 'a member of a partnership *en commandite*,

[20] 1915 TPD 277.

an anonymous partnership, any similar partnership or a foreign partnership if the member's liability toward a creditor of the partnership is limited to the amount which the member has contributed or undertaken to contribute to the partnership or is in any other way limited'.

An anonymous partnership is created where parties agree to share the profits of a business whereby the business is carried on by one or more partners in their names, along with other partners whose names are not disclosed (anonymous partners) to the outside world. The anonymous partner still shares the risk of the undertaking with his co-partners and is liable to them for his or her *pro rata* share of partnership losses.

Under the partnership *en commandite*, business is carried on in the name of one or some of the partners, along with the undisclosed partner(s) called partner *en commandite*. The latter contributes a fixed sum of money on condition that he or she receives a certain share of the profits, if any. In the event of loss, he or she is liable to his or her co-partners to the extent of the fixed amount of his or her agreed capital contribution only.

The similarities between the partnership *en commandite* and the anonymous partnership are as follows: in both cases, the anonymous or the commanditarian partner is undisclosed and their liable is only to the known co-partners, and not to creditors of the partnership. Thus, if the known partner becomes insolvent, the anonymous or the commanditarian partner cannot claim concurrently with the creditors of the partnership against the partnership. In addition, the anonymous or the commanditarian partner may not participate actively in the business of the partnership, and may not, while the partnership is still in existence, claim possession of assets of the business. The only difference between an anonymous and a commanditarian partner is that the anonymous partner is liable for his or her full share of the partnership debts to the known partner. However, a commanditarian partner is liable to the known partner only to the extent of the amount of the capital contributed or agreed to be contributed by him or her.

Section 24(H)(2) provides that where any trade or business is carried on in partnership, each member of such partnership shall, notwithstanding the fact that he or she may be a limited partner, be deemed for the purposes of this Act to be carrying on the trade or business of the partnership.

In South Africa, a partnership is not a separate legal *persona*, with the result that the partnership is not distinct from the partners who are members of the partnership. Thus, any property contributed to the partnership does not vest in their individual capacities. Instead, they hold the property as partners in joint and undivided shares.[21] As the partnership does not exist as a legal entity separate from the partners, the question arises as to how property passes from a partner to the partnership. In the case of *Berman v Brest and Another*[22] it was held that movable property contributed by a partner to the partnership does not

[21] *Sacks v CIR* 1946 AD 31, 13 SATC 343.

[22] 1934 WLD 135.

vest in the partnership due to the act of the partner contributing it, but rather it vests by operation of law. In legal terminology, what takes place is known as a *constitutum possessorium*. This is a transfer of ownership as a result of a contractual change of intention on the part of the partner bringing the property into the partnership. Although that partner retains physical control over his or her assets, once his or her assets are brought into the partnership, he or she effectively controls the property both as a principal, that is, as a partner, and as an agent for his or her partners.[23]

A partnership is not defined as a person for normal tax purposes. It is therefore not a taxable entity. It is the individual partners who are liable for normal tax on their portion of the partnership profits. In *Chipkin (Natal) (Pty) Ltd v CSARS*,[24] it was ruled that what must happen in the ordinary course—

> ... is that for tax purposes at the end of a partner's tax year (which may not coincide with the interval agreed on by the partners in sharing profits), the income of the partnership will be determined; amounts exempt from tax will be deducted; each partner's share of the income will then be calculated; and each partner will then be entitled to that partner's portion of any deduction or allowance in respect of that partner's share to produce that partner's taxable income derived from the partnership.

Thus, it was held in the *Chipkin* case that where a partner sold part of his share in the partnership, he recouped a proportionate share of the allowances on the asset held by the partnership.

Although the Act does not recognise a partnership as a taxable entity, in terms of s 25 of the Tax Administration Act, each partner is separately and individually liable for the rendering of the joint return. Separate tax assessments must be made on each partner. The partners are therefore liable for normal tax in their individual capacities on their proportion of income derived from the partnership.

In practice, the Commissioner first determines the taxable income of a partnership on the basis that it is a separate taxable entity. The Commissioner then proceeds to apportion this taxable income among the partners according to their rights to share in the profits of the partnership. The partners are then individually assessed on their respective shares of the partnership income after account is taken of any income derived from sources outside the partnership. Each partner pays tax according to his or her total income (including his or her share of the partnership income) and the rebates available to him or her.

10.5.1 The date of accrual of partnership income

The position regarding the date of accrual of partnership income was rather unclear until the enactment of s 24H of the Act. This lack of clarity can be

[23] Huxham K & Haupt P *Notes on South African Income Tax* (Hedron Tax Consulting and Publishing CC 2011) 232.

[24] 2005 (5) SA 566 (SCA) 571.

exemplified by the decisions in the cases that follow. In *Sacks v CIR*[25] it was held that profits from a partnership are ascertainable and accrue to the individual partners only on the conclusion of the agreed period for the taking of account of the profits. The erstwhile Appellate Division of the Supreme Court held as follows:

It is clear that during the subsistence of a partnership agreement the partnership property is owned in common in undivided shares. Consequently, save in so far as the partnership agreement may modify the position, the receipts and accruals in the partnership business are acquired by the partners in common and no one partner acquires any several right of ownership in the receipts or accruals of the partnership. Furthermore, a partnership agreement almost invariably provides, either expressly or by implication, for the division of profits after the lapse of fixed periods of time. The effect of such a clause in a partnership agreement is to place an obligation upon the partners to continue to hold the receipts and accruals of the partnership business in common, subject to an obligation to bring them into account at the end of each fixed period for the purpose of ascertaining the profit or loss for the accounting period. When that time arrives, then, for the first time under the partnership agreement, a partner becomes entitled to claim a separate determinable share of the partnership profits and then, for the first time under the partnership agreement, that determinable share accrues to him as gross income. Besides a partner's right to claim such separate share of the partnership profits under the conditions of the partnership agreement, he also acquires such a right when the partnership agreement terminates, eg, by dissolution, and in that case also an accrual of a right to a determinable amount takes place.

However, in *ITC 751*,[26] a partner in a firm of accountants, who was entitled to 25% of the net profits of the firm, arrived at on the basis of fees received during the accounting period of the firm, was held to be correctly assessed on his proportion of certain fees that had accrued to the partnership in the particular year but had not been received. The court held that the fees that had been earned by the partnership but had not been received during the year of assessment had accrued to the partners for tax purposes, notwithstanding the provision in the partnership agreement that only fees received during the accounting period were to be brought into account in the determination of the partnership profits.

To clarify the issues regarding the accrual of partnership income, s 24H(5) of the Act was enacted:

- Section 24H(5)*(a)* provides that income that has been received by a partnership will be deemed to have been received by the partners individually on the same date as receipt by the partnership. The portion of the income deemed to have been received by the individual partners must be determined in accordance with the profit-sharing ratios stated in the partnership agreement.

25 1946 AD 31 at 40, 13 SATC 343 at 349.

26 (1952) 18 SATC 416.

- Section 24H(5)*(b)* applies when a portion of any income is deemed to have been received by a partner. A portion of any deduction or allowance that may be granted under the Act in the determination of the taxable income derived from such income will then be granted. The portion of the deduction or expenditure must be determined in accordance with any agreement between the partners in the ratio to which the profits or losses of the partnership are to be shared.

In *ITC 1819*[27] the appellant was a partner in a firm of attorneys which was registered as a partnership in Lesotho and which did business from a permanent establishment in Lesotho. The firm was registered in Lesotho as a tax entity and was required to file a partnership return, but the profits of the partnership were taxed in Lesotho in the hands of the individual partners. SARS, however, included those profits in the appellant's taxable income for the years 2002 and 2003, but credited him with the amounts of tax paid thereon in Lesotho. The appellant contended that his share of the profits from the Lesotho firm was taxable only in Lesotho and exempt from tax in South Africa in terms of the tax treaty between the two countries. It was held that the appellant's reliance on the provisions of the tax treaty to claim that the profits of the Lesotho firm were taxable only in Lesotho was unacceptable. The court pointed out that the position in respect to the taxation of partnerships in Lesotho appears to be similar to the position of partners in South Africa's Income Tax Act. The court referred to s 24H(2) of South Africa's Income Tax Act, which provides that where any trade or business is carried on in the form of a partnership, each member of such partnership shall be deemed to be carrying on the trade or business of the partnership. When the matter proceeded to the High Court in *Grundlingh v CSARS*,[28] the High Court held that as a partnership is not a separate legal entity, it could not be argued that the Lesotho partnership was a permanent establishment of the South African partnership. The High Court's decision is, however, contrary to s 24H(2) of South Africa's Income Tax Act, which provides that where any trade or business is carried on in partnership, each member of such partnership shall be deemed to be carrying on the trade or business of the partnership.[29]

10.5.2 Assessed losses of partnerships

Should the determination of the taxable income of a partnership result in an assessed loss, the assessed loss is apportioned among the partners according to their rights to participate in profits or losses under the partnership agreement. Each partner is entitled to set off his or her share of the assessed loss against any income derived during the same year from sources outside the partnership. Dividends derived by the partnership must be apportioned among the partners separately.[30]

---

[27] 69 SATC 159.

[28] 72 SATC 1.

[29] Ger B 'International tax: Partnerships, Permanent Establishments and the Problem of Double Taxation' (August 2010) *De Rebus* 41.

[30] De Koker *South African Income Tax* para 11.2.

In determining the taxable income or assessed loss of a partnership, the Commissioner must have regard to the terms of the partnership agreement. If, in terms of the agreement, salaries are payable to the partners or interest is to be credited on capital contributions made by them, the salaries or interest will be allowed as a 'deduction' to the partnership but will be included in the taxable incomes of the partners. It is therefore the practice of the Commissioner to subject a partner to tax on his or her transactions with the partnership as if he or she were a third party. Partnerships and the partners are treated as distinct entities. This practice is in conflict with the principle of law that a partnership is not a legal entity, but whether an amount of salary, interest or rent paid by the firm to a partner is treated as an allowable deduction to the partnership or as an allocation of a share of the profits, the result is the same.[31]

10.5.3 Limited liability partnerships (partnerships *en commandite*)

A limited liability partnership is one that involves an undisclosed partner who contributes a specified amount of capital. In return, he or she receives a percentage of profits. Losses are restricted to the amount of capital contributed by the limited partner. Section 24H(1) defines a 'limited partner' as a member of a partnership *en commandite*, an anonymous partnership or any similar partnership if that member's liability towards a creditor of the partnership is limited to the amount that he or she has contributed or undertaken to contribute to the partnership, or is in any other way limited.

In terms of s 24H(2), limited liability partners are also deemed to be carrying on a trade or business of partnership. To prevent the use of limited partnerships in tax-avoidance schemes, s 24H(3) limits the claimable allowances and deductions by providing that the amount of an allowance or deduction that may be granted to a taxpayer under any provision of the Act in connection with a trade carried on by him or her in a partnership of which he or she is a limited partner may not in the aggregate exceed the sum of:

- the amount for which he or she is or may be held liable to any creditor of the partnership, whether it consists of his or her contribution to the partnership or of any other amount; and
- any income received by or accrued to him or her from that trade or business.

In terms of s 24H(4), the allowance or deduction that has been disallowed under s 24H(3) may be carried forward and will be deemed to be an allowance or deduction to which the taxpayer is entitled in the succeeding year of assessment.

[31] Ibid.

10.6 TAXATION OF TRUSTS

The trust concept was imported into South African law by common usage after the British occupation of the Cape in 1806.[32] The concept was unknown in Roman-Dutch law (ie the South African common law) and South African courts had difficulty explaining the trust concept from Roman-Dutch law principles. In *Estate Kemp v McDonald's Trustee*,[33] the first South African case in which the validity of a trust had to be determined, it was held that the English law of trusts formed no part of our law.[34] It was, however, acknowledged that the trust concept of placing assets under a trustee's custodianship for the benefit of others (whereby the trustee has no beneficial interest in the property) was so firmly rooted in practice that it needed to be given legal recognition, as there was nothing in Roman-Dutch law that was inconsistent with the working of trusts. The trust concept is now part of South African law. The courts have devised distinctive South African rules and principles applicable to trusts, and new rules are constantly being created. These rules are a mixture of English, Roman-Dutch and indigenous South African rules.[35]

In terms of s 1 of the Trust Property Control Act 57 of 1988 the term 'trust' means—

> the arrangement through which the ownership of property of one person is by virtue of a trust instrument made over or bequeathed—
>
> *(a)* to another person, the trustee, in whole or in part, to be administered or disposed of according to the provisions of the trust instrument for the benefit of the person or class of persons designated in the trust instrument or for the achievement of the object stated in the trust instrument; or
>
> *(b)* to the beneficiary designated in the trust instrument, which property is placed under the control of another person, the trustee, to be administered or disposed of according to the provisions of the trust instrument for the benefit of the person or class of persons designated in the trust instrument or for the achievement of the objective stated in the trust instrument;
>
> but does not include the case where the property of another is to be administered by another person as executor, tutor or curator or in terms of the provisions of the Administration of Estates Act 1965.

From the above definition, the parties to a trust are the founder, the trustees and the beneficiaries. The founder is the person who establishes the trust, and he or she is usually the original owner of the property being placed in the trust. The founder appoints the trustees by way of a trust deed and also specifies

[32] Cameron E et al *Honore's South African Law of Trusts* 5 ed (Juta 2002) 2–3; Pace RP *Wills and Administration of Estates* (Butterworths 2006) para B2.

[33] 1915 AD 491 at 494.

[34] See also *CIR v Estate Crewe* 1943 AD 656; *CIR v Smollan's Estate* 1955 (3) SA 266 (A) 269F; *Crookes NO and Another v Watson and Another* 1956 (1) SA 277 (A) 280F.

[35] Cameron et al *Law of Trusts* 82; De Waal MJ 'In search of a model for the introduction of the trust into a civilian context' (2001) *Stell LR* 63.

the beneficiaries to the trust property. The trustees are the 'management' of the trust.[36] They are also the legal owners of the trust property, but they have no beneficial interest in the property. The beneficiaries are the equitable or beneficial owners of the trust property, and all conduct by the trustees and the founder should in principle be for their benefit.

10.6.1 The essentials of a valid trust in South Africa

In South African law, there are five basic essentials for a valid trust:[37]

- The founder must intend to create a trust. He or she must not merely use the trustees as contracting parties and yet retain too much power and control over the way in which the trust is managed.[38]
- The founder must express his or her intention to create a trust in a manner that places a legal obligation on the trustees to manage the trust object. This could be done through a will or a contract. In South African law, a unilateral declaration of intent to create a trust is insufficient.[39]
- The subject matter of the trust must be defined with reasonable certainty. A trust does not come into existence without an asset donated by the founder to the trustees.[40]
- The objective of the trust must be defined with reasonable certainty. For instance, it might be specified in the trust deed that the trust funds will be used for the benefit of named or ascertainable beneficiaries, or that the funds will be donated to charity. Where the trustees have the discretion to choose the beneficiaries, a valid trust would not be created. If a class of beneficiaries is mentioned, that class must be defined with reasonable certainty.[41]
- Lastly, the trust object must not be illegal.[42]

[36] Pace *Wills and Administration* para B2; Du Toit F *South African Trust Law: Principles and Practice* (Butterworths 2002) 6; Soars PC *Trusts and Tax Planning* 3 ed (Butterworths 1987) 7.

[37] *Administrators, Estate Richards v Nichol* 1996 (4) SA 253 (C) 258E–F; Cameron et al *Law of Trusts* 117; Du Toit *Trust Law* 27.

[38] Cameron et al *Law of Trusts* 118; Pace *Wills and Administration* para B8.1.

[39] Pace *Wills and Administration* par B8.2; Cameron et al *Law of Trusts* 117 notes that in terms of the South African law of trusts, a trust cannot be created unintentionally. Thus, the English law mechanisms of resulting and constructive trusts have not been received in South African law. See also Hayton DJ *The Law of Trusts* 4 ed (Sweet & Maxwell 2003) 17.

[40] Cameron et al *Law of Trusts* 146; Pace *Wills and Administration* para B8.3.

[41] *Ex parte Estate Kemp* 1940 WLD 26; Pace *Wills and Administration* para B8.4.

[42] Cameron et al *Law of Trusts* 11; Olivier L & Honiball M *International Tax: A South African Perspective* 5 ed (Siber Ink 2008) 269; Davis DM, Beneke C & Jooste RD *Estate Planning* (Butterworths Service Issue 27) para 5.4.

10.6.2 Classification of trusts

Trusts can be classified and distinguished from each other by considering the way in which they were created.[43] In that regard, trusts could fall into one of two categories, namely the testamentary trust, or the *inter vivos* trust.[44]

10.6.2.1 Testamentary trust

A 'testamentary trust' is a trust created in terms of a will, whereby a deceased person leaves his or her estate to a trustee, who administers the estate assets on behalf of the beneficiaries.[45] A testamentary trust exists from the date of the testator's death, and actual transfer of the property is not essential for the trust to come into existence.[46]

10.6.2.2 Inter vivos *trust*

An *inter vivos* trust is a trust created by a living person, who transfers some of his or her assets to a trustee or trustees, who then deal with the assets on behalf of the beneficiaries.[47] An *inter vivos* trust is created by means of a contract[48] between the founder and the trustee(s), in terms of which contract the founder donates and transfers property to the trustees for the benefit of the beneficiaries.[49]

Irrespective of whether a trust was created as a testamentary or an *inter vivos* trust, the rights of the beneficiaries to the ownership of the income or capital of the trust could be bewind, vested or discretionary.[50]

A trust in which the beneficiaries have bewind rights is one where the real rights of ownership of the trust vest in the trust beneficiaries, but the administration or management and control over these assets vest in the trustee.[51] If the beneficiary dies, ownership is included in his or her estate for estate duty purposes, and the asset itself is transferable to his or her heirs, either conditionally or unconditionally, depending on the terms of the trust deed.[52]

---

43 Du Toit *Trust Law* 3; Pace *Wills and Administration* para B3; King R *Law and Estates Planning Easiguide* (LexisNexis 2009) para 16.

44 Pace *Wills and Administration* para B3.

45 Du Toit *Trust Law* 21; Clegg DJM *Income Tax in South Africa* (LexisNexis 2012) para 17.3 and 17.3.1; De Koker *South African Income Tax* para 24.126.

46 Davis et al *Estate Planning* para 5.5.

47 Clegg *Income Tax* para 17.3; De Koker *South African Income Tax* para 24.126; King *Law and Estates* para 16.3.1.

48 *Crookes NO v Watson* 1956 (1) SA 277 (A). When the beneficiaries of an *inter vivos* trust accept the rights conferred on them by the contract, they acquire a personal right against the trustee. See also King *Law and Estates* para 16.1.2.2.

49 Clegg *Income Tax* para 17.3.2.

50 Du Toit *Trust Law* 3; Oguttu AW *Curbing Offshore Tax Avoidance: The Case of South African Companies and Trusts* (LLD Dissertation, UNISA 2007) 323.

51 Cameron et al *Law of Trusts* 6; Pace *Wills and Administration* para B6.3.2.

52 King *Law and Estates* para 16.3.2; Oguttu *Curbing Offshore Tax Avoidance* 324.

A trust in which the beneficiaries have vested rights is one where ownership and control or administration of the trust assets vest in the trustee in his or her representative capacity, and the beneficiaries have only personal rights to claim their trust benefits from the trustees upon the happening of a certain event (such as the attainment of a certain age or upon marriage) as specified in the trust deed. The right that such a beneficiary has in the income or capital of the trust is termed a 'vested right'. In *ITC 76*,[53] the Special Court defined a vested right as 'something substantial; something which could be measured in money; something which had a present value and could be attached.' Furthermore, in the context of income tax, a vested right is an accrued right. This implies that, upon the happening of the relevant specified event, the income or capital of the trust must be paid to that particular beneficiary and the trustees are merely administering the income or the capital for the beneficiary.[54]

A trust in which the beneficiaries have discretionary rights is one where discretion is conferred by the founder on the trustees to decide (or vary) which member or members of a class of beneficiaries should be entitled to the income or capital of the trust.[55] The beneficiaries are only beneficiaries in name, and what they have is just a 'contingent right', that is, a hope or *spes*, to the income or capital of the trust. The meaning of the term 'contingent right' was described by Watermeyer CJ in *Durban City Council v Association of Building Societies*[56] as being 'the conditional nature of someone's title to the right'.[57] Thus, although the beneficiaries may be eligible to the income or capital of the trust, they are not entitled thereto, unless the trustees in their sole and absolute discretion decide to pay over the benefits.[58] This implies that there is a possibility that a beneficiary may never receive any portion of the income or capital in the trust.[59] In *ITC 76*[60] the Special Court defined the term 'contingent right' as a mere *spes* – an expectation that might never be realised.

10.6.3 The taxation of trusts

Although a trust is not generally recognised by South African courts as a legal person, it is considered a 'person' for income tax purposes. The income tax treatment of trusts was prompted by the decision of the Appellate Division of

[53] (1927) 3 SATC 68 at 69.

[54] Pace *Wills and Administration* para B6.3.1; Meyerowitz *Income Tax* para 16.136; Van der Merwe BA 'Meaning and Relevance of the Phrase "Vested Right" for Income Tax Law' (2000) 3 *SA Merc LJ* 319; Oguttu *Curbing Offshore Tax Avoidance* 325.

[55] Cameron et al *Law of Trusts* 20; Davis et al *Estate Planning* para 5.11; Ginsberg A *International Tax Havens* 2 ed (Butterworths 1997) 28; Oguttu *Curbing Offshore Tax Avoidance* 326.

[56] 1942 AD 27 33.

[57] See also *Jewish Colonial Trust Ltd v Estate Nathan* 1940 AD 163 175; Meyerowitz *Income Tax* para 16.135. Davis et al *Estate Planning* para 6.3.1; Grundy M *Grundy's Tax Havens: Offshore Business Centres – A World Survey* 6 ed (Sweet & Maxwell 1993) 78; Clarke G *Offshore Tax Planning* 9 ed (LexisNexis 2002) 12.

[58] Cameron et al *Law of Trusts* 473; King *Law and Estates* para 16.3.4. See also *Jewish Colonial Trust Ltd v Estate Nathan* 1940 AD 163 175; *Pentz v Gross* 1996 (2) SA 518 (C) 523.

[59] Meyerowitz *Income Tax* para 16.135.

[60] (1927) 3 SATC 68 70.

the Supreme Court (as it then was) in *Friedman and Others NNO v CIR: In Re Phillip Frame Will Trust v CIR*,[61] which ruled that income retained in a trust was not taxable, as a trust was not a legal person and the trustees were not considered to be its representative taxpayers in respect of its undistributed income. The *Friedman* decision prompted the legislator to amend the definition of 'person' in s 1 of the Act to include a trust. This section defines a trust as 'any trust fund consisting of cash or other assets, which are administered and controlled by a person acting in a fiduciary capacity, where such person is appointed under a deed of trust, or by agreement, or under the will of a deceased person'.[62]

If a trust is resident in the Republic it will be taxable on its worldwide income. A non-resident trust is taxed on income that has its source in the Republic.

10.6.4 Determining the residence of a trust

A trust is not a natural person. It thus falls into the category of a person other than a natural person. In terms of s 1 of the Act, a person other than a natural person is deemed to be a resident of the Republic, if it is incorporated, established or formed in the Republic, or if it has its place of effective management in the Republic. Ordinarily, as a trust is not required to be incorporated (as is the case with a company),[63] it can only be deemed a resident of the Republic if it is established or formed, or if it has a place of effective management, in the Republic.[64]

In order to determine where a trust was established or formed, an inquiry has to be made into how the trust was created. As a testamentary trust is created by the will of a testator, by implication such a trust can be deemed a South African resident, if the will under which the trust was created was drawn up in South Africa.[65] Section 4 of the Trust Property Control Act also requires that a trust be registered with the Master of the High Court. As an *inter vivos* trust is a contract,[66] it may be argued that such a trust will be resident in South Africa, if the contract bringing about its existence was concluded in South Africa. According to the South African law of contract, a contract is generally deemed to be concluded at the location where the offeror is informed of the acceptance of his or her offer.[67] By implication, if the contract that brought the trust into existence was concluded in South Africa, such a trust would be resident in the Republic.

---

[61] 1991 (2) SA 340 (W).

[62] Section 1 of the Income Tax Act 58 of 1962 (as amended).

[63] Section 32 of the Companies Act 61 of 1973.

[64] De Koker *South African Income Tax* para 5.21; Oguttu *Curbing Offshore Tax Avoidance* 347.

[65] Oguttu *Curbing Offshore Tax Avoidance* 347.

[66] *Crookes NO and Another v Watson and Others* 1956 (1) SA 277 (A) 258F; *Hofer v Kevitt NO* 1998 (1) SA 382 (SCA) 384F.

[67] Christie RH *The Law of Contract in South Africa* 5 ed (Butterworths 2006) 32; Kerr AJ *The Principles of the Law of Contract* 6 ed (Butterworths 2002) 97; Van der Merwe S *Contract: General Principles* 2 ed (Juta 2003) 43.

If the place of effective management of a trust is in South Africa, the trust will be deemed resident in the Republic. As explained in chapter 3, in South Africa there is no statutory definition of the concept 'place of effective management', nor is there any case law that provides guidance on the interpretation of the term. However, the term 'place of effective management' is used in a tax treaty context as a tie-breaker rule in the case of dual resident entities (for details on the treaty aspects in this regard, see chapter 14).[68] In *SIR v Downing*,[69] the court held that South Africa is bound to take cognisance of the guidelines for interpretation issued by the Organisation for Economic Co-operation and Development (OECD) in its commentaries on the concepts used in the OECD Model Tax Convention. Article 4 of the OECD Model Tax convention defines the place of effective management as—

the place where the key management and commercial decisions that are necessary for the conduct of the entity's business are in substance made. All relevant facts and circumstances must be examined to determine the place of effective management. An entity may have more than one place of management, but it can have only one place of effective management at any one time.

This interpretation of the term can be applied in South Africa. Most of South Africa's treaties largely follow the OECD Model Tax Convention on Income and on Capital,[70] although South Africa is not a member of the OECD.[71] It is also notable that s 231 of the Constitution of the Republic of South Africa, 1996 provides that the courts are bound to apply customary international rules and practices, such as the commentaries on the concepts used in the OECD Model Tax Convention.

As noted in chapter 3, SARS previous Interpretation Note 6 (Issue 1) of 26 March 2002, defined the place of 'effective management' as the place of 'regular, day-to-day management by directors or senior managers of the entity through implementation of the policy and strategic decisions of its board of directors'. This interpretation differed from the OECD's interpretation above. On 3 November 2015, SARS issued a revised Interpretation Note 6 (Issue 2)[72] which reforms its interpretation of the concept of place of effective management. In terms of the Interpretation Note, SARS clarifies that although multiple facts must be considered when determining where the place of effective management of a company is situated, the test it applies is 'where the key management and commercial decisions are regularly and predominantly made'.[73] It should, however, be noted that SARS's Interpretation Notes are not

[68] Article 4(3) of the OECD Model Tax Convention on Income and on Capital (2008).

[69] 1975 (4) SA 518 (A), 37 SATC 249.

[70] Olivier & Honiball *International Tax* 7; Huxham & Haupt *South African Income Tax* 341.

[71] Olivier & Honiball *International Tax* 10; Huxham & Haupt *South African Income Tax* 341.

[72] SARS Interpretation Note 6 (Issue 2): s 1(1) of the Income Tax Act 58 of 1962 'Resident – place of effective management (companies)' 3 November 2015.

[73] SARS Interpretation Note 6 (Issue 2) at 6.

law, and in a number of cases it has been argued that SARS is not bound by its own Practice Notes and Interpretation Notes.

In an endeavour to explain how the place of effective management of a trust can be determined, Olivier and Honiball[74] are of the view that as the trustees are the ones who have the power and duty to manage a trust, the place of effective management of a trust can be determined by considering the place where the substantial or day-to-day management decisions are taken and implemented by the trustees. De Koker[75] is of the view that the place of effective management of the trust can be determined by considering the country of residence of the trustees, the country from which the trust fund is administered, or the country where trustees meet to attend to the affairs of the trust.[76] Each case has to be decided on its own merits in order to understand the business activities of the trust and the activities of the trustees. In the case of active business operations carried on by the trust, it may be easy to determine its place of effective management, as the day-to-day business operations of the trust will normally be located where the active business of the trust takes place. In the case of a passive investment holding trust, the activities of the trustees would be limited to trustees' meetings to manage the investments of the trust on an infrequent basis.[77] In such a case, determining the place of effective management of the trust may be difficult, as it would require knowing the place where the decisions concerning the trust are made and where they are actually carried out. Where the place of effective management is not clear, in that the duties of the trustees are not centralised in one specific country, then the residence status of the trustees may have to be considered to decide the tax residence of the trust.[78] It may also be necessary to consider evidence regarding the trustees' visits to specific countries for the purposes of taking and implementing decisions relating to the trust. The passports of the trustees could then be produced as evidence.[79] In *Nathan's Estate v CIR*[80] the court held a trust to be resident in Natal because the trustees were resident in that province, and the trust fund was administered from that province.

Some non-resident trusts make provision for the appointment of a 'protector',[81] who is generally a person with certain powers over the trustees, such as appointing or removing trustees, whose consent is required before capital distributions are made.[82] The concept of a protector is however not formally recognised in South African law.[83] A question that may arise is whether a trust set up outside South Africa, but with a protector resident in South Africa, can

[74] Honiball M & Olivier L *The Taxation of Trusts in South Africa* (Siber Ink 2009) 69.
[75] De Koker *Silke on South African Income Tax* para 5.21.
[76] De Koker para 5.21.
[77] Ibid.
[78] Olivier & Honiball *International Tax* 153–154.
[79] Olivier & Honiball *International Tax* 153–154; Oguttu *Curbing Offshore Tax Avoidance* 349.
[80] 1948 (3) SA 866 (N).
[81] Roper REW 'Getting to grips with offshore trusts' (December 1998) *Insurance and Tax Journal* 5.
[82] Ibid; Olivier & Honiball *The Taxation of Trusts* 35.
[83] Olivier & Honiball *The Taxation of Trusts* 36.

be deemed to be effectively managed and thus resident in South Africa for tax purposes. This question challenges the validity of the office of the protector in South African law.

Since South African trust law principles are largely contractual in nature, it can be argued that there is no reason why the office of the protector cannot be created in a trust deed in line with international practices.[84] Internationally, a protector would be expected to act in a fiduciary capacity.[85] If the office of a protector interferes with the fiduciary duties of the trustees, demanding that the trustees are accountable to the protector, then the protector can be deemed invalid. Olivier and Honiball[86] are of the view that the fact that another person has the right to appoint a trustee does not necessarily imply that the founder never intended to create a valid trust. Each case should be analysed to determine whether the protector is a mere puppet of the founder, or whether he or she is acting in an advisory capacity in the best interests of the beneficiaries.[87] It can thus be argued that in determining the place of effective management of a trust, it may be necessary to consider the residence status of the protector if he or she acts in a fiduciary capacity and in the best interest of the beneficiaries.

10.6.5 Taxing trust income

Section 25B of the Act[88] provides that income received by, or accrued to or in favour of, any person in his or her capacity as the trustee of a trust shall, subject to the provisions of s 7, to the extent to which such income has been derived for the immediate or future benefit of any ascertained beneficiary with a vested right to such income, be deemed to be income which has accrued to the beneficiary, and to the extent to which such income is not so derived, be deemed to be income of the trust.

Section 25B, read together with s 7 of the Act, sets out three possibilities as regards the incidence of tax on income that is the subject of a trust:

- If income is retained in a trust, it is taxed in the trust.
- Income that accrues to ascertained beneficiaries who have a vested right to the income is taxed in the hands of those beneficiaries.
- Income may be taxed in the hands of the founder of the trust (donor) where certain circumstances as set out in s 7 come into play.

[84] Ibid.

[85] A duty to act impartially in the interests of the principal. See Davis et al *Estate Planning* para 17.2; Olivier & Honiball *The Taxation of Trusts* 35.

[86] Olivier & Honiball *The Taxation of Trusts* 37.

[87] Ibid; in the English case *IRC v Schroder* 57 TC 94 the settlor was one of the members of a protection committee. The trust was held to be valid as on the facts the settlor did not have control of the protection committee.

[88] Act 58 of 1962 (as amended).

10.6.5.1 Liability of the trust

In terms of s 25B(1), if trust income is not distributed to beneficiaries, but is retained in the trust, the trust is liable for tax since it is deemed to be a 'person', and thus a taxpayer, for income tax purposes.[89] Currently trusts (excluding 'special trusts') are taxed at a flat rate of 45% on all retained income of a revenue nature. [90]

10.6.5.2 Liability of the beneficiaries

Section 25B(1) also provides that the income of a trust may be taxed in the hands of an ascertained beneficiary with a vested right to such income, if such income is derived for his or her immediate or future benefit.

Where income is accumulated in a non-resident trust for a period exceeding a year, with the intention that when it is distributed, it will be regarded as capital in nature and therefore not taxable in the hands of the beneficiary,[91] s 25B(2A)[92] comes into play by providing as follows:

> Where during any year of assessment any resident acquires any vested right to any amount representing capital of any trust which is not a resident, that amount must be included in the income of that resident in that year, if—
>
> *(a)* that capital consists of or is derived, directly or indirectly, from any receipts and accruals of such trust which would have constituted income if such trust had been a resident, in any previous year of assessment during which that resident had a contingent right to that amount; and
>
> *(b)* that amount has not been subject to tax in the Republic in terms of the Act.

Section 25B(2A) is limited to receipts or accruals that would have constituted income, if the trust had been resident in any previous year of assessment at the time of the receipt or accrual. This implies that the section cannot apply to receipts or accruals before 1 January 2001 (when the residence basis of taxation was introduced) as those receipts or accruals then had a non-South African source, and so they would not have constituted 'income' at that time.[93] Likewise, if the trust has received income that is exempt from tax under South African law, s 25B(2A) cannot be applied.[94] Where the income or the receipts and accruals have been subjected to tax in the Republic, the section cannot be applied.[95]

[89] See the definition of 'trust' in s 1 of the Income Tax Act. In terms of s 1 of the Income Tax Act, the trustee is the representative taxpayer of the trust.

[90] Section 5 of the Income Tax Act.

[91] Davis et al *Estate Planning* para 6.3.1.

[92] As amended by s 27 of the Revenue Laws Amendment Act 32 of 2004.

[93] Davis et al *Estate Planning* para 6.3.1.

[94] Olivier & Honiball *International Tax* 281–282.

[95] Jooste RD 'Offshore trusts and foreign income – the specific anti-avoidance provisions' (2002) *Acta Juridica* 201; Davis et al *Estate Planning* para 6.3.1 at 6-9; De Koker *South African Income Tax* para 12.15A.

10.6.5.3 Liability of the donor

In terms of s 25B of the Act, income retained in a trust is taxable in the trust, and beneficiaries with vested rights to the income of the trust are liable to tax on any receipt or accrual in their favour. This section is, however, subject to s 7 of the Act, which is an anti-avoidance measure that provides that in certain circumstances the donor is liable to tax on income derived by the trust.

(a) Trusts subject to a condition

In terms of s 7(5):

> If any person has made any donation, settlement or other disposition which is subject to a stipulation or condition, whether made or imposed by such person or anybody else, to the effect that the beneficiaries thereof or some of them shall not receive the income or some portion of the income thereunder until the happening of some event, whether fixed or contingent, so much of any income as would, but for such stipulation or condition, in consequence of the donation, settlement or other disposition be received by or accrue to or in favour of the beneficiaries, shall, until the happening of that event or the death of that person, whichever first takes place, be deemed to be the income of that person.[96]

The general aim of this section is to prevent tax avoidance where and so long as the donor does not permit the beneficiary to enjoy the income derived from the trust, by deeming the income in issue to be that of the donor.[97] There are three factors that have to be in place for this section to apply, namely:

- There must be a deed of donation, settlement or other disposition.
- It must contain a stipulation to the effect that the beneficiaries, or some of them, shall not receive the income, or some portion of it, until the happening of some event, whether fixed or contingent.
- But for that stipulation, income would have been received by or accrued to the beneficiary.

If an affirmative answer is given to each of these questions, then 'the income' must be deemed to be the income of the person who made the stipulation. In *ITC 673*[98] it was held:

> An analysis of the subsection shows that it first of all contemplates a hypothesis, viz. the existence of a stipulation that the beneficiary shall not receive the income under the deed till the happening of an event. Secondly, the subsection provides what is to be deemed to be a devolution of the income until the event takes place. That devolution is back to the donor if apart from the stipulation it would be received by or accrue to the beneficiary concerned.

[96] It important to note that s 7(5) applies irrespective of whether the stipulation or condition withholding income from the beneficiaries was made by the person making the donation, or by some other person. See De Koker *South African Income Tax* para 12.20; Clegg *Income Tax* para 17.3.5.

[97] Meyerowitz *Income Tax* para 16.144; De Koker *South African Income Tax* para 12.20; Clegg *Income Tax* para 17.3.

[98] (1948) 16 SATC 230 at 233; see also *ITC 1033* (1959) 26 SATC 73 at 75.

In *Estate Dempers v SIR*,[99] the trust deed settled monies upon trustees and directed that until the donor's death, the annual income could be used by the trustees in their discretion for the benefit of the donor's grandson and/or his issue, or for making charitable donations. After the donor's death, the annual income was to be used in the trustees' discretion for the benefit of the grandson, and the balance of the income was to accumulate in the trust. One-third of the total fund was to be paid to the grandson when he attained the age of 25, 50% of the remainder when he attained the age of 30, and the balance when he attained the age of 35. If he were to die before reaching any one of these ages, other beneficiaries were substituted for him. It was held that a stipulation in the trust deed, to the effect that the beneficiary should not receive the accumulated income until the happening of an event (viz the termination of the trust by the donee's attainment of the ages stated in the trust deed, or the predecease of the donee, causing a devolution upon his issue) satisfied the requirements of the subsection.

(b) Retaining the power to revoke the right to income

Section 7(6) provides as follows:

> If any deed of donation, settlement or other disposition contains any stipulation that the right to receive any income thereby conferred may, under powers retained by the person by whom that right is conferred, be revoked or conferred upon another, so much of any income as in consequence of the donation, settlement or other disposition is received by or accrues to or in favour of the person on whom that right is conferred, shall be deemed to be the income of the person by whom it is conferred, so long as he retains those powers.

In *ITC 543*[100] the taxpayers were two brothers who carried on a business in which a third brother had been employed. Desiring to provide their brother with a pension in consideration of his services, the taxpayers (two brothers) formed a trust fund, whereby the third brother was to receive a portion of the income from the trust fund during his lifetime. On his death, the trustees had the discretion of paying the income to his widow, or to the donors, or their legal representatives. The taxpayers' brother died, and in the exercise of their discretion, the trustees paid the income to his widow. The Commissioner invoked s 9(6) (as it was then) and taxed the donors on the trust income. The court held that the section was applicable, as the trustees were not bound to pay the trust income to the widow. In terms of the trust deed, the balance not paid to her was to be divided between the two donors.

It is not clear whether s 7(6) is limited to an express provision in the deed, which empowers the donor to revoke a beneficiary's right to income and confer it upon another, or whether it can also be applied where the exercise of this power is implied.[101] If, for instance, the donor has the power to require that

[99] 1977 (3) SA 410 (A); 1977 *The Taxpayer* 150.
[100] (1942) 13 SATC 118.
[101] Meyerowitz *Income Tax* para 16.151.

income be lent to him, it is not clear whether this could amount to a right to revoke the income, since the trustee would have been deprived of the power to distribute it.[102] In *ITC 673*[103] the trust deed provided that the donor had the right to exercise voting powers in respect of the shares donated, to require the trustees to lend him the income of the trust without security and with or without interest, to revoke the appointment of any trustee, and to fill any vacancy. In addition, the trustees were permitted to abandon any claim or debts due to the trust. The Commissioner contended that all these provisions amounted to an implied power to revoke the right to receive income. The court rejected this contention, and held that s 7(6) only contemplates an express provision in the deed, which reserves the right to the donor to revoke the right to any accruing income and to confer it upon another. This judgment has been criticised in that s 7(6) should have been applied as the circumstances of the case show that the donor had retained the power to revoke the right to income.[104]

Section 7(6) could also be applied where the donor retains the right to cancel the trust as he or she would have retained the right to confer or revoke the rights under the trust deed. However, if the trust deed provides for the automatic termination of the trust at the end of a fixed period, even if, on expiry of that period, the income and capital of the trust will revert to the donor, he or she does not retain the power to revoke or confer upon another the right to receive the income of the trust as contemplated in s 7(6).[105]

Section 7(6) can only be invoked where the beneficiary has a vested right to receive the income that is subject to revocation through the exercise of powers retained by the donor.[106] Thus, where a donation confers discretion on trustees to decide whether to distribute the income to a beneficiary, who has only a contingent right to that income, s 7(6) cannot be applied until the trustees exercise their discretion. Section 7(5) would be applicable in such a case.[107]

(c) Donation of the right to income

In terms of s 7(7), if a taxpayer cedes his or her right to receive income generated by his or her asset but still retains the ownership of the asset or retains the right to regain the ownership at a future date, that income is deemed to have been received or accrued to the cedent (donor). Section 7(7) provides:

> If by reason of any donation, settlement or other disposition made, whether before or after the commencement of this act, by any person (hereinafter referred to as the donor) –

CHAPTER 10

[102] Cameron et al *Law of Trusts* 282.

[103] (1948) 16 SATC 230.

[104] Meyerowitz *Income Tax* para 16.151; Cameron et al *Law of Trusts* 282; Oguttu *Curbing Offshore Tax Avoidance* 364.

[105] Davis et al *Estate Planning* para 6.3.5 at 6-19; De Koker *South African Income Tax* para 12.21.

[106] De Koker *South African Income Tax* para 12.21.

[107] Ibid.

> *(a)* the donor's right to receive or have paid to him or for his benefit any amount by way of rent, dividend, foreign dividend, interest, royalty or similar income in respect of any movable or immovable property (including without limiting the foregoing any lease, company share, marketable security, deposit, loan, copyright, design or trade mark) or in respect of the use of, or the granting of permission to use, such property, is ceded or otherwise made over to any other person or to a third party for that other person's benefit in such manner that the donor remains the owner of or retains an interest in the said property or if the said property or interest is transferred, delivered or made over to the said other person or to a third party for the said person's benefit, in such manner that the donor is or will at a fixed or determinable time be entitled to regain ownership of or the interest in the said property; or
>
> *(b)* the donor's right to receive or have paid to him or for his benefit any income that is or may become due to him by any other person acting in a fiduciary capacity is ceded or otherwise made over to any other person or to a third party for that other person's benefit in such manner that the donor is or will at a determinable time be entitled to regain the said right,
>
> any such rent, dividend, foreign dividend, interest, royalty or income (including any amount which, but for this subsection, would have been exempt from tax in the hands of the said other person) as is received by or accrued to or for the benefit of the said other person on or after 1 July 1983 and which would otherwise, but for the said donation, settlement or other disposition, have been received by or have accrued to or for the benefit of the donor, shall be deemed to have been received by or to have accrued to the donor.

In summary, dividends, interest and royalties (and similar income) in respect of movable or immovable property that are received by or accrued to another person as a result of a donation while the donor remains the owner of the property or is entitled to regain ownership, are deemed to have been received by or accrued to the donor.

It appears that s 7(7) was enacted after the successful appeal by the taxpayer in *ITC 1378.*[108] The facts of the case were that the taxpayer, a shareholder in a private company, concluded two donation contracts and in terms of each ceded his rights to receive payment of future dividends to a fund for a period of approximately three years. At the taxpayer's request the company made certain payments to the fund in advance and in anticipation of the declaration of dividends. The Commissioner included the amount of the dividends received by the fund in the taxpayer's gross income. After his objection had been overruled the taxpayer appealed to the Special Court, where the Commissioner resisted the appeal on two grounds: first, that the cession of future dividends amounted to the cession of a *spes* (hope) and as such was bad in law, and second, that since the company had paid the fund on the taxpayer's behalf the dividends in issue must, by virtue of s 7(1), be deemed to have accrued to the taxpayer. The Special Court rejected both contentions and held that the dividend income was not taxable in the taxpayer's hands.

---

[108] (1983) 45 SATC 230.

(d) Donations made to non-residents

Section 7(8) applies in the case of donations made to non-residents. The section provides:

> Where by reason of or in consequence of any donation, settlement or other disposition (other than a donation, settlement or other disposition to an entity which is not a resident and which is similar to a public benefit organisation contemplated in section 30) made by any resident, any amount is received by or accrued to any person who is not a resident (other than a controlled foreign company in relation to such resident), which would have constituted income had that person been a resident, there shall be included in the income of that resident so much of that amount as is attributable to that donation, settlement or other disposition.

For s 7(8) to apply, income must have been received by, or accrued to, a non-resident by 'reason of or in consequence' of a donation, settlement, or other disposition made by a resident. The phrase 'donation, settlement or other disposition' bears the same meaning of a gratuitous disposition.[109] The phrase 'in consequence' is interpreted to carry the same meaning as 'by reason of'. These phrases denote that there must be a certain nexus between the income received by the non-resident and the donation, settlement or other disposition made by the resident.

The phrase by 'reason of' was held In *CIR v Widan*[110] to imply that some causal relation existed between the donation and the income in question, and that, in ascertaining whether such causal relation exists, one must look not necessarily to the cause which is proximate in time, but to the real, effective cause of the income being received. In *Joss v SIR*,[111] the taxpayer sold assets to a company on an interest-free loan. The taxpayer's minor daughter was a shareholder in the company and received a dividend. The court found that the portion of the dividend that accrued to the minor was attributable to the parent, as it was 'by reason of' the interest-free loan made by the parent.

In *CIR v Berold*,[112] it was held that as long as the taxpayer refrained from compelling the company to pay the loan in issue, there was a continuing loan by him of the interest on the loan, which made it subject to tax in terms of s 7(8).

In *CSARS v Woulidge*,[113] the respondent sold shares in some companies to trusts he created for the benefit of his children. It was agreed that the purchase price would be paid in such amounts and at such times as may be mutually agreed upon and that the respondent would be entitled to charge interest, not exceeding the prevailing bank rate, on the balance of the purchase price. The Commissioner taxed the respondent on the basis that notional interest was due to him in respect of the unpaid purchase price of the shares sold by him to the

[109] *Ovenstone v SIR* 1980 (2) SA 721 (A) 735.
[110] 1955 (1) SA 226 (A) 233.
[111] 1980 (1) SA 674 (T); 1980 *The Taxpayer* 192.
[112] 1962 (3) SA 748 (A).
[113] 2002 (1) SA 68 (SCA).

trusts. The Supreme Court of Appeal agreed that the forbearance of interest (in the form of annual donations of the interest not charged) was a gratuitous disposal which was taxable.

In *CSARS v Brummeria Renaissance (Pty) Ltd and Others,*[114] a case that does not specifically deal with trusts but the judgment in which is wide enough to cover trusts, the taxpayers were developers of retirement villages. To finance the construction of the units in a retirement village, the taxpayers obtained interest-free loans from potential occupants of the units in exchange for granting life occupation rights of those units to the potential occupants. The court held that the right to retain and use borrowed funds without paying interest had a monetary value that had to be included in the taxpayer's gross income for the year of assessment in which the rights accrued to the taxpayer. Following the *Brummeria* decision, SARS issued Interpretation Note 58,[115] which states that even though the receipt or accrual of the right is in a form other than money (*in casu,* the benefit of the use of an interest-free loan) and it cannot be alienated or turned into money, it does not mean that the receipt of the right has no money value. The value of such a receipt or accrual constitutes an amount that accrues to the taxpayer and should be included in the gross income of the taxpayer for the year of assessment in which the right is received by or accrued to the taxpayer. This is because of the link between the interest-free loan and the use of the property which resulted in the *quid pro quo* (a consideration for the receipt, or use, of the loan free of interest).

A matter that is worth addressing in the context of trusts is whether SARS would succeed in imputing interest on an interest-free loan made by a person to his or her family trust. The answer to the question would depend on whether there is a *quid pro quo* involved. Where a person makes a loan to a family trust and the use of the loan would result in a *quid pro quo*, the *Brummeria* decision would apply. If, however, the loan is made with the intention of providing long-term working capital to the family trust (which is the case for the majority of interest-free loans made to family trusts) such a loan would not be affected by the *Brummeria* decision since the loan would be capital in nature.[116]

10.6.5.4 Donation of an asset below market value

Section 7(9) provides that where an asset is disposed of for a consideration that is below the market value of the asset, the amount by which the market value exceeds the consideration is deemed to be a donation.

---

[114] 2007 (6) SA 601 (SCA), 69 SATC 205.

[115] Paragraph 4 of SARS Interpretation Note 58 'The *Brummeria* Case and the Right to Use Loan Capital Interest Free' 30 June 2010.

[116] De Koker *South African Income Tax* para 2.9B. See also Editorial 'Gross Income: The *Brummeria* Judgment' *Integritax* (January 2008) Issue 1, available at http://www.saica.co.za/integritax/2008/1591_The_Brummeria_Judgment.htm (accessed 17 October 2012).

10.6.5.5 Disclosure of donations contemplated in s 7

In terms of s 7(10), a resident who, during a year of assessment, makes a donation, settlement or other disposition as contemplated in s 7 is required to disclose this fact to the Commissioner when submitting his or her tax return for that year.

Chapter 11

Taxation of companies

11.1 INTRODUCTION

A company is a legal entity that is separate and distinct from its shareholders. In most countries' legal systems, a company derives its existence from statute.[1] The capital of a company is divided into shares and owned by shareholders. However, the company is the owner of the assets and the shareholders do not have proportionate property rights in the assets of the company. The capital of the company is raised by the issue of shares and the liability of the shareholders of a company is limited to the amount that each shareholder has paid for the shares.[2]

11.2 DEFINITION OF COMPANY

For South African purposes a company obtains its legal existence from legislation. Previously, South African companies were incorporated in terms of the Companies Act 61 of 1973 ('Companies Act 1973'). The companies' legislative regime underwent changes in terms of which companies are

[1] See IBFD *International Tax Glossary* (2005) definition of 'company'.

[2] As to the nature of a company, see further *Salomon v Salomon & Co* 1897 AC 22; *Stellenbosch Farmers' Winery v Distillers Corporation* 1962 (1) SA 458 (A); *S v De Jager* 1965 (2) SA 616 (A); *Dadoo Ltd v Krugersdorp Municipal Council* 1920 AD 530.

now regulated under the provisions of the new Companies Act 71 of 2008 ('Companies Act 2008'), which took effect on 1 May 2011. For tax purposes, the Income Tax Act 58 of 1962 ('the Act') defines a company. As such it is appropriate to discuss the definition of company in terms of these three pieces of legislation.

11.2.1 Companies Act 1973

Section 1 of the Companies Act defined a company as a company incorporated under chapter IV of the Companies Act 1973 and included any body which, immediately prior to the commencement of the Companies Act 1973, was a company in terms of any law repealed by that Act.

Section 32 of the Companies Act 1973 provided for the rules of formation of a company. It provided that:

> Any seven or more persons or, where the company to be formed is a private company, any two or more persons associated for any lawful purpose or, where the company to be formed is to be a private company with a single member, any one person for any lawful purpose, may form a company having a share capital or a company limited by guarantee and secure its incorporation by complying with the requirements of this Act in respect of the registration of the memorandum and articles.[3]

The Act classified companies as private or public companies.[4] The income tax implications facing these companies are the same. The only difference is that donations tax is applicable to private companies but is not applicable to public companies, as defined in the Act, and payments made by public companies to their directors are subject to employees' tax in terms of the normal rules, while payments made by private companies to their directors are subject to special rules (see para 11C of the Fourth Schedule to the Act).

11.2.2 Companies Act 2008

The new Companies Act 2008 defines a company as—

> a juristic person incorporated in terms of this Act, a domesticated company, or a juristic person that, immediately before the effective date—
>
> *(a)* was registered in terms of the—
>
> (i) Companies Act, 1973 (Act 61 of 1973), other than as an external company as defined in that Act; or
>
> (ii) Close Corporations Act, 1984 (Act 69 of 1984), if it has subsequently been converted in terms of Schedule 2;
>
> *(b)* was in existence and recognised as an 'existing company' in terms of the Companies Act, 1973 (Act 61 of 1973); or

CHAPTER 11

[3] Section 32 of the Companies Act 61 of 1973.

[4] Section 38.

(c) was deregistered in terms of the Companies Act, 1973 (Act 61 of 1973), and has subsequently been re-registered in terms of this Act ...;

A juristic person, for purposes of the Companies Act, includes a foreign company[5] and a trust, irrespective of whether or not it was established within or outside the Republic.[6]

11.2.3 Income tax definition

The Act defines a company for tax purposes. The definition in the Act differs from the definition found in the two companies' statutes discussed above, as the Act and the companies' statutes seek to achieve different purposes. The companies' statutes regulate companies and define the relationship that exists between companies and shareholders.[7] The Act, on the other hand, seeks to determine the tax liability of the company.

For income tax purposes a company includes the following six types of entities:

(a) an association, corporation or company (other than a close corporation) incorporated or deemed to be incorporated by or under any law in force or previously in force in South Africa or in any part thereof, or any body corporate formed or established or deemed to be formed or established by or under any such law;

(b) an association, corporation or company incorporated under the law of any country other than the Republic or any body corporate formed or established under such law;

(c) a co-operative;

(d) an association (not being an association referred to in para *(a)* or *(f)*) formed in the Republic to serve a specified purpose, beneficial to the public or a section of the public;

(e) a portfolio comprised in any investment scheme carried on outside the Republic that is comparable to a portfolio of a collective investment scheme in participation bonds or a portfolio of a collective investment scheme in securities in pursuance of any arrangement in terms of which members of the public (as defined in s 1 of the Collective Investment Schemes Control Act) are invited or permitted to contribute to and hold participatory interests in that portfolio through shares, units or any other form of participatory interest; or portfolio of a collective investment scheme in property that qualifies as a real estate investment trust as defined in the JSE Limited Listings Requirements; or

(f) a close corporation.

---

5 A foreign company is in turn defined in s 1 of the Companies Act 2008 as an entity incorporated outside the Republic, irrespective of whether it is a profit, or non-profit, entity; or carrying on business or non-profit activities, as the case may be, within the Republic.

6 See also Dachs P 'New Companies Act – Some Tax Implications' (2010) *The Taxpayer* 166.

7 See preambles to the Companies Act 1973 and the Companies Act 2008.

The Act specifically excludes a foreign partnership from the definition of company.

This definition is wider than the definitions contained in the companies' statutes. This is because the legislature identified entities that have characteristics that are similar to companies and that should be taxed similarly to companies, and defined them as companies for tax purposes. These entities, for example close corporations and co-operatives, are governed by specific legislation, ie the Close Corporations Act[8] and the Co-operatives Act[9] respectively.

11.2.4 Year of assessment of a company

The taxable income of a company is determined in respect of a year of assessment. A company's year of assessment is its financial year for legal and financial reporting.[10] In the first year of formation of the company, the year of assessment of a company may be less or more than twelve months, in line with the company's financial year.[11] Thus, if a company chooses the calendar year as its financial year, its year of assessment will run from 1 January to 31 December of the same year. 'Year of assessment' is also commonly referred to as 'tax year'.

11.2.5 Taxable income of a company

As a general rule, the taxable income of a company is calculated in the same way as that of any other taxpayer. Thus, a company's taxable income is its gross income less exempt income less deductible expenses. A company is allowed to set off assessed losses from its income in the tax year and can also carry forward assessed losses from the previous year of assessment.[12] Subject to exceptions, a company does not pay income tax on capital profits, although it might be subject to capital gains tax on such profits. Resident companies are subject to tax on foreign income including taxable foreign dividends and the proportional amount attributable to it from its controlled foreign company.[13]

11.2.6 Residence of a company

South Africa taxes residents on their worldwide income and non-residents on their South African sourced income.[14] This means that for a company to be taxable in South Africa that company must be resident in South Africa.

8 Act 69 of 1984.

9 Act 14 of 2005.

10 See definition of 'year of assessment' read with s 5(1)*(d)* of the Act.

11 In accordance with s 285 of the Companies Act 1973.

12 See Meyerowitz D, Emslie T & Davis D 'Assessed Losses for Companies' (2005) *The Taxpayer* 164.

13 See para *(k)* of s 1 definition of 'gross income' and s 9D of the Act. See further chapter 14.

14 Section 1 definition of 'gross income'. See also Olivier L & Honiball M *International Tax: A South African Perspective* (Siber Ink CC 2011) 11–30.

For tax purposes a resident in relation to a company is defined in s 1 as 'any person (other than a natural person) which is incorporated, established or formed in the Republic or which has its place of effective management in the Republic'.[15] This basically refers to companies that are registered in South Africa, but can technically be extended to companies that are officially and legally registered elsewhere. However, according to the Companies Act of 1973, a company could only be formed by complying with the requirements of the Companies Act of 1973 in respect of the registration of the memorandum and the articles.[16] A company that is not incorporated, formed or established in South Africa will be resident in South Africa if its place of effective management is in South Africa. Interpretation Note 6 defines the 'place of effective management' as the place where the key management and commercial decisions that are necessary for the conduct of a company's business as a whole are in substance made.[17] The Interpretation Note states as follows:

> A company may have more than one place of management but it can only have one place of *effective* management at any one time. If a company's key management and commercial decisions affecting its business as a whole are made at a single location, that location will be its place of effective management. However, if those decisions are made at more than one location, the company's place of effective management will be the location where those decisions are primarily or predominantly made.[18]

Determining effective management is a factual matter.[19] From the definition of effective management above, it is clear that although shareholders can be said to have final control of a company, it is generally accepted that they do not manage a company.

11.2.7 Foreign companies

Companies which are not resident in South Africa (ie companies that are not incorporated, formed or established in South Africa and which are not effectively managed in South Africa) are not taxable in South Africa unless they earn income from a South African source. Only income that is sourced in South Africa is taxable in South Africa.[20] The tax rate applicable to such income is 28%. For example, if a company operates a branch in South Africa, being a permanent establishment,[21] the income of that branch will be taxable in South Africa at the rate of 28%.[22] Branch profits remitted by a South African branch

---

[15] See s 1.

[16] Section 32 of the Companies Act 61 of 1973.

[17] South African Revenue Service ('SARS') Interpretation Note 6 (Issue 2), issued on 3 November 2015. See also Olivier & Honiball *International Tax* 25–30. Meyerowitz D, Emslie T & Davis D 'Place of Effective Management' (2007) *The Taxpayer* 82.

[18] At 6.

[19] See chapter 14 on aspects of international tax; see also Van der Merwe BA 'Residence of a Company – the Meaning of "Effective Management"' (2002) *SA Merc LJ* 79.

[20] See Part I s 4*(f)* of the Taxation Laws Amendment Act 7 of 2010.

[21] See Olivier L 'The "Permanent Establishment" Requirement in an International and Domestic Taxation Context: An Overview' (2002) *SALJ* 866.

[22] Olivier & Honiball *International Tax* 89–91; Stiglingh et al *Silke: South African Income Tax* 436.

of a foreign company were exempt from the Secondary Tax on Companies and now from the dividends tax.

11.2.8 Holding company and subsidiary

A holding company is a company that owns part, all or a majority of the other companies' outstanding stock or issued shares.[23] It is usually a company that does not produce goods or services itself; rather, its purpose is to own shares in other companies.[24] Thus, in essence, for a company to be a holding company it should own enough voting stock in another company to control management and operations by influencing or electing its board of directors. Such a company is literally a super-corporation which owns or at least controls such a dominant interest in one or more other corporations that it is able to dictate its policies through voting power.[25]

In the South African context, a 'holding company' is not directly defined for purposes of the corporate law. The Act also does not define holding and subsidiary companies. The Companies Act 1973 defined a holding company thus: 'a company shall be deemed to be a holding company of another company if that other company is its subsidiary.'[26] In terms of the new Companies Act 2008 a holding company, 'in relation to a subsidiary, means a juristic person or undertaking that controls that subsidiary'.[27] In terms of both these pieces of legislation, it is, therefore, the definition of subsidiary that determines what constitutes a holding company.

The definitions of 'subsidiary' and 'holding company' are premised on the control that the holding company has over the subsidiary. A holding company is basically 'a company that holds the controlling shares in one or more companies so that they form part of the same group of companies'.[28] The definition of subsidiary in the Companies Act 2008 is largely a replica of the definition in the Companies Act 1973.

A company is a subsidiary of another if that other company satisfies one of the following requirements:

- it is directly able to exercise or control the exercise of a majority of the general voting rights in the company; or
- it has the right to appoint or elect or control the appointment or election of directors who control a majority of the voting rights at meetings of the board.[29]

[23] See Connell L 'Holding Companies to Account: The Expense Apportionment Conundrum' (2004) *SALJ* 117.
[24] IBFD *International Tax Glossary* definition of 'holding company'.
[25] http://www.trueblueauctions.com/Auction_Terms.html accessed on 30 May 2019.
[26] See s 1(4) of the Companies Act.
[27] Section 1 of the Companies Act 2008 definition of 'holding company'.
[28] Olivier & Honiball *International Tax* 689.
[29] See s 1(3)*(a)*(i) of the Companies Act 1973; s 3(1) of the Companies Act 2008.

A subsidiary is an entity controlled by another entity. Control is the power to control the financial and operating policy of an entity in order to benefit from the activities of that other entity.[30] Control is presumed to exist when the other entity owns, directly or indirectly, more than half of the voting power of an entity unless it can be clearly demonstrated that such ownership does not constitute control.[31]

The additional characteristics of 'the power to control the financial and operating policy of an entity in order to benefit from the activities of that other entity' are central to the essence of a holding and subsidiary relationship.[32] In this regard it is noted that 'benefit' is not limited to financial benefit. The holding company may also strategically direct the operations of its subsidiaries or the group.

The impact of control and supplementary relationships between companies might differ based on the amount of the shareholding involved. Often the holding and subsidiary relationship results in the companies forming a group of companies. Conversely, the companies often have to be in a group of companies to have a holding and subsidiary relationship.

11.2.9 Group of companies

There is a distinction between companies which belong to a group of companies and which hold significant shareholdings in other companies, and those which hold a diversified portfolio of shares (or bonds) for a group of investors.[33] The former case is an example of a company group situation. A group of companies consists of at least one subsidiary company and its holding company or at least two subsidiaries of the same (common) holding company.[34]

In some countries the definitions of holding company require that the holding company together with its subsidiary should form a group of companies. South African law does not have such a requirement. However, where companies form a group of companies in terms of the Act, such companies would have a holding-subsidiary relationship.[35]

A group of companies is defined in the Act as follows:[36]

> '[G]roup of companies' means two or more companies in which one company (hereinafter referred to as the 'controlling group company') directly or indirectly holds shares in at least one other company (hereinafter referred to as the 'controlled group company'), to the extent that—

---

[30] Kunst JA, Delport P & Vorster Q *Henochsberg on the Companies Act* (LexisNexis 2008) 14.

[31] See Kunst, Delport & Vorster *Henochsberg on the Companies Act* 14.

[32] See Kunst, Delport & Vorster *Henochsberg on the Companies Act* 14. See also Haydock JD 'The Effect of the Amendments to the Definition of a Subsidiary in the Companies Amendment Act 82 of 1992' (1993) *SA Merc LJ* 166.

[33] IBFD *International Tax Glossary* definition of 'holding company'.

[34] 'Glossary of Terms' http://www.veoliaenvironmentalservices.co.uk/pages/pack_glossary.asp accessed on 9 May 2019.

[35] Section 1 definition of 'group of companies'.

[36] See s 1 definition of 'group of companies'.

(a) at least 70 per cent of the equity shares in each controlled group company are directly held by the controlling group company, one or more other controlled group companies or any combination thereof; and

(b) the controlling group company directly holds at least 70 per cent of the equity shares in at least one controlled group company ...

A distinction has to be made between a holding and subsidiary relationship and a head office and branch relationship. Whereas a subsidiary is a legal person in its own right, a branch is an extension of its parent company and it is a part or division of the parent company. They are one legal entity. When a company does business through a branch, the company is subject to tax on the profits of the branch wherever it is located. The company may also be taxable in the country where the branch is located on the profits of the branch based on the source rule.[37]

11.3 SECONDARY TAX ON COMPANIES

In order for a company to transfer its after-tax profits to its shareholders, the company declares and pays those profits to shareholders as dividends.[38] The ordinary meaning of a dividend is a proportionate payment to shareholders from the profits of a company.[39] A dividend represents the only way in which a return on a share held by a shareholder can be paid by a company.[40]

Dividends constitute gross income in the hands of the shareholders. However, because these dividends arise out of amounts that would have been taxed in full in the hands of the company, they are not fully taxed as income in the hands of the taxpayer. Prior to the implementation of the dividends tax, on 1 April 2012, a company that declared dividends to its shareholders was subject to the secondary tax on companies ('STC') at the rate of 10% of the net amount of dividends declared.[41] STC was levied only on resident companies. It was a tax on the company and not on the shareholder.[42] The connection with dividends was that it was calculated with reference to the amount of the dividend declared. Non-resident companies were not subject to STC on profits distributed.[43] Non-resident companies conducting business in South Africa via a branch office were, prior to the introduction of the dividends tax, subject to a 33% income tax rate, and this theoretically included the amount equivalent to

[37] See Article 5 of the OECD Model Convention, read with Article 7 of the OECD Model Convention and the commentaries in respect thereof.

[38] McLennan JS 'Company dividends: The New Law' (2001) *SALJ* 126.

[39] Van Dorsten JL *The Law of Dividends in South Africa* (Obiter Publishers CC 1993) 26.

[40] Van der Linde K 'The Regulation of Distributions to Shareholders in the Companies Act 2008' (2009) *TSAR* 484 at 487; see also *South African Iron and Steel Industrial Corporation Ltd v Moly Copper Mining and Exploration Co (SWA) Ltd* 1993 (4) SA 705 (Nm) 712.

[41] Section 64B(2) of the Act.

[42] Meyerowitz D, Emslie T & Davis D 'STC: Application of Double Taxation Agreement with Germany (*Volkswagen SA (Pty) Ltd v CSARS*)' (2008) *The Taxpayer* 196.

[43] See Meyerowitz D, Emslie T & Davis D 'STC: Foreign Parents of Resident Subsidiaries' *The Taxpayer* (2005) 223.

STC payable on dividends. Based on a 28% corporate income tax rate and a 10% STC, resident companies were effectively taxed at 34%, assuming they declared all their after-tax profits as dividends. Once taxed in terms of the STC system, dividends were tax exempt in the hands of the shareholders receiving them or to whom the dividends accrued.[44]

11.4 DIVIDENDS TAX

In the 2007 Budget Review, the National Treasury announced the change from the STC system to a new system to be referred to as the dividends tax system.[45] The National Treasury stated as follows:

> While dividend taxes are a familiar feature of taxation worldwide, they are typically imposed at a shareholder level, with treaty relief for foreign investors. Some have argued that South Africa's secondary tax on companies raises the cost of equity financing to the detriment of economic growth. To help lower the cost of doing business, government proposes to phase out the secondary tax on companies and replace it with a dividend tax.[46]

The rationale for government to change from the STC system to the dividends tax system can be summarised as follows:[47] internationally, company dividends are generally taxed at the shareholder level (as opposed to the company level). This difference from the STC gives rise to collateral problems, including the following: First, because the STC reduced the accounting profits of South African resident companies, those companies are at a disadvantage compared to their international counterparts, which do not bear any adverse accounting profit reduction when paying dividends. Secondly, since the STC was levied at company level, tax treaty limits on the rate of tax which could be imposed in respect of dividends generally had no effect unless the relevant treaty made specific provision for STC. Thirdly, foreign investors are generally unfamiliar with STC and its mechanics, thereby creating uncertainty. The Treasury argued that the combined effect of these three problems is that the cost of equity financing is increased. Finally, the Treasury considered that problems existed with the tax base upon which the STC relied in that the STC dividend definition drew its meaning from the term 'profits', but that the term 'profits' itself was never expressly defined in the Act. It was understood that the term 'profits' drew its meaning from company law and accounting principles. The Treasury considered that this mixture of often complex concepts of accounting, company

---

44 Section 10(1)*(k)*(i); Meyerowitz *Income Tax* para 15.1A.

45 National Treasury *Budget Review* (2007) 67. See also Meyerowitz D, Emslie T & Davis D 'Substituting Shareholders 'Tax on Dividends in the Place of STC' (2007) *The Taxpayer* 101; Meyerowitz D, Emslie T & Davis D 'STC: Change from 12.5% to 10% and Other Amendments Taking Effect on 1 October 2007' (2007) *The Taxpayer* 203; Meyerowitz D, Emslie T & Davis 'Removing Secondary Tax on Companies' (2008) *The Taxpayer* 1.

46 National Treasury *Budget Review* (2007) 67.

47 See the Explanatory Memorandum on the Revenue Laws Amendment Bill, 2008 24.

law and tax had complicated the tax system and created opportunities for avoidance.[48]

The dividends tax has been developed since 2007 and came into effect on 1 April 2012.[49]

11.4.1 Definition of dividend under the new dividends tax system

The dividends tax provisions define a dividend specifically for application in Part VIII of the Act. A dividend is defined as any dividend as defined in s 1 that is paid by a company that is a resident or paid by a company that is not a resident if the share in respect of which that dividend is paid is a listed share.[50] A listed share is a share that is listed on a South African Securities Exchange. Thus, the dividends tax is levied on distributions by foreign companies on shares that are listed on the Johannesburg Stock Exchange. A foreign dividend that consists of an asset *in specie* is not a dividend.[51]

A dividend is defined in s 1 as any amount transferred or applied by a company for the benefit of any shareholder in relation to that company by virtue of any share held by that shareholder in that company. An amount will be a dividend whether it is transferred or applied by way of a distribution or as consideration for the acquisition of any share in that company.[52] However, an amount will not constitute a dividend to the extent that the amount so transferred or applied results in a reduction of contributed tax capital of the company transferring or applying the amount[53] or that amount constitutes shares in that company.[54] Furthermore, where a company transfers or applies an amount in order to acquire[55] or redeem its own shares, the transfer or application of the amount will not constitute a dividend.[56]

[48] See further on the change from STC to the dividends tax Mazansky E 'From STC to Dividends Tax' (2007) *Tax Planning* 78; Mitchell L 'Dividends Tax: "New" Second Leg of Company Tax' (2007) *Tax Planning* 47.

[49] National Treasury *Budget Review* (2011) 71.

[50] Section 64D definition of 'dividend'.

[51] Subparagraph *(b)*(ii) of s 64D definition of 'dividend'.

[52] Section 1 definition of 'dividend'.

[53] Subparagraph (i) of s 1 definition of 'dividend'.

[54] Subparagraph (ii) of s 1 definition of 'dividend'. Companies often issue shares, referred to as capitalisation shares, which are basically funded from the already existing capital of the company distributing the shares. Generally these shares do not confer any additional benefits on the shareholders.

[55] This refers to an acquisition by a company of its own securities as contemplated in para 5.67 of s 5 of the JSE Limited Listings Requirements, where that acquisition complies with the requirements prescribed by paras 5.67 to 5.84 of s 5 of the JSE Limited Listings Requirements.

[56] Subparagraphs (iii) and (iv) of s 1 definition of 'dividend'.

11.4.2 Definition of contributed tax capital

Contributed tax capital is defined in relation to a class of shares issued by a company.[57] In relation to a class of shares issued by a company, in the case of a resident company, CTC is an amount equal to the stated capital or share capital and share premium of that company immediately before 1 January 2011 in relation to shares in that company of that class issued by that company before that date, less so much of that stated capital or share capital and share premium as would have constituted a dividend, as defined before that date, had the stated capital or share capital and share premium been distributed by that company immediately before that date.[58] Any consideration received by or accrued to that company for the issue of shares of that class on or after 1 January 2011 is added to the CTC.[59]

In the case of a foreign company that becomes a South African tax resident on or after 1 January 2011, CTC is an amount equal to the sum of the market value of all the shares in that company of that class immediately before the date on which that company becomes a resident[60] and the consideration received by or accrued to that company for the issue of shares of that class on or after the date on which that company becomes a resident.[61]

If the shares of that class include or consist of shares that were converted from another class of shares of that company to that class of shares, CTC would include any consideration received by or accrued to that company in respect of that conversion; and the amount contemplated in subpara *(cc)*[62] of the definition of CTC that was determined in respect of shares of the other class of shares that were so converted.

The amount of CTC is reduced by so much of the CTC amount as:

- the company has transferred on or after the date on which the company becomes a resident for the benefit of any person holding a share in that company of that class in respect of that share;[63]
- has by the date of the transfer been determined by the directors of the company or by some other person or body of persons with comparable authority to be an amount so transferred;[64] and

---

[57] Section 1 definition of 'contributed tax capital'.

[58] Paragraph *(b)*(i) of s 1 definition of 'contributed tax capital'.

[59] Paragraph *(b)*(ii) of s 1 definition of 'contributed tax capital'.

[60] Paragraph *(a)*(i) of s 1 definition of 'contributed tax capital'.

[61] Paragraph *(a)*(ii) of s 1 definition of 'contributed tax capital'.

[62] Paragraph *(cc)* refers to 'so much of the amount contemplated in this paragraph in respect of that convertible class of shares immediately prior to that conversion as bears to that amount the same ratio as the number of shares so converted bears to the total number of that convertible class of shares prior to that conversion.'

[63] Subparagraph *(aa)* of para *(a)* of s 1 definition of 'contributed tax capital' and subpara *(aa)* of para *(b)* of s 1 definition of 'contributed tax capital'.

[64] Subparagraph *(bb)* of para *(a)* of s 1 definition of 'contributed tax capital' and subpara *(bb)* of para *(b)* of s 1 definition of 'contributed tax capital'.

- in the case of a convertible class of shares, some of the shares of which have been converted to another class of shares, so much of the amount contemplated in this paragraph in respect of that convertible class of shares immediately prior to that conversion as bears to that amount the same ratio as the number of shares so converted bears to the total number of that convertible class of shares prior to that conversion.[65]

11.4.3 Beneficial ownership

The determination of the taxability of a dividend in terms of the dividends tax is based on the concept of beneficial ownership, as opposed to the concept of shareholder.

> The term beneficial owner is used in the domestic law of a limited number of countries whose legal systems are based on common law. Its meaning has been developed by the courts in these countries but differences exist as between those countries and even within a particular country as to its exact scope. Factors which have at times been considered by the courts as relevant features include the right to enjoy the economic benefits of the underlying property, as well as control over the disposition of that property.[66]

The Act defines beneficial owner as 'the person entitled to the benefit of the dividend attaching to a share'.[67] Thus, for the purposes of the dividends tax, the term beneficial owner is limited only to the dividend entitlement. Beneficial ownership for purposes of the dividends tax attaches to the dividend and not the share. As a result, a person may be a beneficial owner of a dividend regardless of the fact that such person has no rights over the disposition of the share, or no rights whatsoever to the share. Beneficial ownership of the dividend is detached from the ownership or registration of the share. Based on the concurrence of the definition of shareholder and beneficial owner, most shareholders would be beneficial owners of the dividends.

11.4.4 Levying of tax and timing of dividends

Section 64E levies the dividends tax on the amount of any dividend paid by any resident company. The rate of dividends tax is 15%. A dividend is deemed to be paid on the date that the dividend is paid in relation to a dividend declared by a listed company.[68] A dividend declared by a company that is not a listed company or a dividend that constitutes a distribution of an asset *in specie* is deemed to be paid on the earlier of the date on which the dividend is paid or becomes due and payable. Different valuation rules apply where a dividend *in specie* is distributed or the dividend consists in part of a dividend *in specie*.

CHAPTER 11

[65] Subparagraph *(cc)* of para *(a)* and subpara *(cc)* of para *(b)* of s 1 definition of 'contributed tax capital'.

[66] IBFD *International Tax Glossary* definition of 'beneficial owner'.

[67] Section 64D definition of 'beneficial owner'.

[68] Section 64E(2).

The amount of the dividend *in specie* is determined on a specific day, which is not necessarily the day the asset is transferred to the shareholder. Where a dividend paid by a company consists of a distribution of an asset *in specie* the value of the dividend is deemed to be the market value of the asset on the date that the dividend is deemed to be paid.[69] If the dividend is a listed share the dividend is deemed to be equal to the ruling price of that share on that recognised exchange at close of business of the last business day before the date that the dividend is deemed to be paid.[70]

The dividends tax is levied on the distributions made by a company. Thus, the dividends tax will apply to distributions by the following institutions:

- any South African association, corporation, company, or body corporate;
- any foreign association, corporation, company, or body corporate;
- a co-operative;
- an association formed in the Republic to serve a specified purpose, beneficial to the public or a section of the public;
- a portfolio comprised in any investment scheme carried on outside the Republic that is comparable to a portfolio of a collective investment scheme in participation bonds or a portfolio of a collective investment scheme in securities in pursuance of any arrangement in terms of which members of the public are invited or permitted to contribute to and hold participatory interests in that portfolio through shares, units or any other form of participatory interest;
- a portfolio of a collective investment scheme in property that qualifies as a real estate investment trust; and
- a close corporation.

11.4.5 Liability for tax

The liability for dividends tax falls on the beneficial owner of the dividend.[71] However, if the dividend is a dividend *in specie* paid by a resident company, the liability falls on the company declaring the dividend.[72] *In specie* dividends paid by non-resident JSE listed companies are excluded from the definition of 'dividend' in s 64D and are therefore not subject to the dividends tax. The shareholder receiving a dividend *in specie* from a non-resident JSE listed company is liable to normal tax at a maximum of 20%.[73] Where the liability falls on the beneficial owner of the dividend, the Act provides for an administrative collective mechanism of withholding to collect the tax. Note that the withholding mechanism does not impose a tax, but merely provides a collection facility for the administration of the tax.

[69] Section 64E(3)*(b)*.
[70] Section 64E(3)*(a)*.
[71] Section 64EA*(a)*.
[72] Section 64EA*(b)*.
[73] Section 10B.

11.4.6 Exemptions from dividends tax

As the dividends tax is a tax on the shareholder of the company, the exemptions from dividends tax are granted at the level of the shareholder. Thus, it is the shareholder that is exempt and not the company declaring the dividend. Dividends distributed to the following shareholders are exempt from the dividends tax in terms of s 64F of the Act:

- a company which is a resident;
- the government, a provincial administration or a municipality;
- a public benefit organisation approved by the Commissioner in terms of s 30(3);
- a trust or company contemplated in s 37A. This is a trust or company whose sole purpose is to maintain funds and utilise those funds for purposes of rehabilitation of the environment on the closure of mining activities;
- certain institutions, boards or bodies established by law for specific public interest purposes as contemplated in s 10(1)*(cA)* – this includes the universities and companies wholly owned by the universities;
- a benefit fund as contemplated in s 10(1)*(d)*(i) or (ii) – this generally includes a pension fund, provident fund, retirement annuity fund, friendly society or medical scheme;
- a person contemplated in s 10(1)*(t)* – these include specifically exempt institutions in which the government has an interest such as the Council for Scientific and Industrial Research, the South African Inventions Development Corporation, the Armaments Development and Production Corporation of South Africa Limited, a recognised traditional council or community, a regional electricity distributor, water services providers and the Development Bank of South Africa;
- a shareholder in a registered micro business, as defined in the Sixth Schedule, paying that dividend, to the extent that the aggregate amount of dividends paid by that registered micro business to its shareholders during the year of assessment in which that dividend is paid does not exceed the amount of R200 000;
- a person that is not a resident and the dividend is a dividend that is paid by a company that is not a resident and the share in respect of that dividend is a listed share;
- any person to the extent that the dividend constitutes income of that person;
- any person to the extent that the dividend was subject to the secondary tax on companies;
- any fidelity or indemnity fund contemplated in s 10(1)*(d)*(iii); or
- a natural person or deceased estate or insolvent estate of that person in respect of a dividend paid in respect of a tax-free investment as contemplated in s 12T(1).

CHAPTER 11

Dividends paid by headquarter companies are excluded from the application of s 64E and are therefore not subject to the dividends tax.[74] Furthermore, s 64FA(1)*(c)* provides for an exemption of any distribution of an amount *in specie* if that distribution constitutes a disposal of an interest in a residence as contemplated in para 51A of the Eighth Schedule.

11.4.7 Payment of the tax

As indicated earlier, the liability for the dividends tax is borne by the beneficial owner of the dividends as opposed to the company paying the dividend under the STC regime.[75] In addition to the liability for the tax, the beneficial owner has the liability to pay the dividends tax to SARS.[76] The company paying the dividend, or, if the company pays the dividend to a regulated intermediary, that regulated intermediary has the liability to withhold the dividends tax. Such a company or regulated intermediary is obliged to pay the tax to SARS.[77] These provisions imply that both the beneficial owner of the dividend and the person liable to withhold the dividend tax, be it the company declaring the dividend or the regulated intermediary, must pay the tax to SARS.[78] However, the Act imposes a joint and several liability on the parties by providing that any person who fails to withhold the dividends tax or withholds the dividends tax, but fails to pay the tax to SARS, is liable for the payment of the tax as if that person was liable to the tax, unless the tax is paid by any other person.[79]

If a company or regulated intermediary withheld a reduced amount of tax as a result of the beneficial owner being entitled to a tax treaty reduction, the company or regulated intermediary should justify the withholding of the reduced amount of tax by submitting to SARS the declaration submitted by the beneficial owner.[80] If the Commissioner considers that the amount of dividends tax is not paid in full, he may issue a notice of assessment of the unpaid amount.[81] Interest is levied on any outstanding dividends tax amount.[82]

A person that is liable for any amount of dividends tax in respect of a dividend, must pay that amount to the Commissioner by the last day of the month following the month during which that dividend is paid by the company.[83]

---

[74] Section 64E(1).
[75] Section 64K(1).
[76] Section 64K(1).
[77] Section 64K(2)*(a)*.
[78] Section 64K(2).
[79] Section 64K(3).
[80] Section 64K(4) read with ss 64G(3) and 64H(3).
[81] Section 64K(5).
[82] Section 64K(6); See also Gani G 'Delayed Declarations: Refunds of Dividends Tax' (2010) *Tax Planning* 201.
[83] Section 64K(1)*(b)*.

11.4.8 Dividend withholding

As stated above, STC was a tax on the company declaring the dividend. Conversely, under the dividends tax regime, the tax liability is on the shareholder to whom the dividend accrues. However, for administrative convenience, the company declaring the dividend is obliged to withhold the amount of the dividends tax from the amount paid to the shareholder. Section 64G(1) provides that a company that declares and pays a dividend, to the extent that the dividend does not consist of a distribution of an asset *in specie*, must withhold dividends tax from that payment at a rate of 20% of the amount of that dividend. The rules applicable to withholding for dividends apply *mutatis mutandis* in terms of s 64FA with regards to *in specie* dividends.

In certain specific circumstances, a company may be absolved from the liability to withhold the dividends tax. A company does not have to withhold the dividends tax if the person to whom the dividend is declared is exempt from the dividends tax. However, in order for the company to be absolved from the withholding obligation, the person to whom the dividend accrues must submit to the company a declaration that the dividend is exempt from dividends tax.[84] This declaration must be submitted in a prescribed form on the date determined by the company. If the company did not determine such date, the declaration should be submitted on the date that the dividend is paid. [85] The beneficial owner should also make an undertaking to forthwith inform the company in writing should the circumstances affecting the exemption applicable change or should the beneficial owner cease to be the beneficial owner.[86]

A company declaring dividends does not have to withhold the dividends tax if the beneficial owner forms part of the same group of companies as the company that pays the dividend.[87] There are no additional requirements attached to this scenario because the company declaring the dividend can determine whether the company receiving the dividend is resident in South Africa.

In certain instances a company may be obliged to withhold an amount lower than 15% if the beneficial owner is entitled to a reduction in the tax in terms of a treaty between South Africa and the country of residence of the beneficial owner.[88] In order for the company to withhold a lower rate the person to whom the dividend accrues must submit to the company a declaration that the dividend is subject to a rate lower than 15% as determined by the tax treaty.[89] This declaration must be submitted in a prescribed form on the date determined by the company. If the company did not determine such date, the declaration should be submitted on the date that the dividend is paid.[90] The beneficial owner should also make an undertaking to forthwith inform the company in

[84] Section 64G(2)*(a)*.
[85] Section 64G(2)*(a)*(i) and (ii).
[86] Section 64G(2)*(a)(bb)*.
[87] Section 64G(2)*(b)*.
[88] Section 64G(3).
[89] Section 64G(3)(i).
[90] Section 64G(3)(i).

writing should the circumstances relating to the reduced rate applicable to the beneficial owner change or the beneficial owner cease to be the beneficial owner.[91]

In some cases the obligation to withhold the dividends tax is placed on persons other than the company declaring the dividends, as the circumstances may require. One of these instances is where a dividend is paid to a regulated intermediary.[92] A regulated intermediary is defined as follows:[93]

> 'regulated intermediary' means any—
>
> *(a)* central securities depository participant contemplated in section 32 of the Financial Markets Act;
>
> *(b)* authorised user as defined in section 1 of the Financial Markets Act;
>
> *(c)* approved nominee contemplated in section 76 of the Financial Markets Act;
>
> *(d)* nominee that holds investments on behalf of clients as contemplated in section 9.1 of Chapter 1 and section 8 of Chapter II of the Codes of Conduct for Administrative and Discretionary Financial Service Providers, 2003 (Board Notice 79 of 2003) published in *Government Gazette* 25299 of 8 August 2003;
>
> *(e)* portfolio of a collective investment scheme in securities;
>
> *(f)* transfer secretary that is a person other than a natural person and that has been approved by the Commissioner subject to such conditions and requirements as may be determined by the Commissioner; or
>
> *(g)* a portfolio of a hedge fund collective investment scheme.

A regulated intermediary does not have to withhold the dividends tax if the person to whom the dividend is declared is exempt from the dividends tax.[94] However, in order for the regulated intermediary to be absolved from the withholding obligation, the person to whom the dividend accrues should submit to the regulated intermediary a declaration that the dividend is exempt from dividends tax.[95] This declaration must be submitted in the prescribed form on the date determined by the regulated intermediary.[96] If the regulated intermediary did not determine such date, the declaration should be submitted on the date that the dividend is paid.[97] The beneficial owner should also make an undertaking to forthwith inform the regulated intermediary in writing should the circumstances affecting the exemption applicable change or the beneficial owner cease to be the beneficial owner.[98]

---

91 Section 64G(3)(ii).
92 Section 64G(2)*(c)*.
93 Section 64D.
94 Section 64H(2).
95 Section 64H(2)*(a)(aa)*.
96 Section 64H(2)*(a)*(i).
97 Section 64H(2)*(a)*(ii).
98 Section 64H(2)*(a)(bb)*.

A regulated intermediary paying dividends does not have to withhold the dividends tax if the dividend is paid to another regulated intermediary.[99] There are no additional requirements attached to this scenario as the regulated intermediary paying would know that the dividend is paid to another regulated intermediary.

In certain instances a regulated intermediary may be obliged to withhold an amount lower than 15% if the beneficial owner is entitled to a reduction in the rate of tax in terms of a treaty between South Africa and the country of residence of the beneficial owner.[100] In order for the regulated intermediary to withhold a lower rate, the person to whom the dividend accrues must submit to the regulated intermediary a declaration that the dividend is subject to a rate which is lower than 15% as determined by the tax treaty.[101] This declaration must be submitted in a prescribed form on the date determined by the regulated intermediary. If the regulated intermediary did not determine such date, the declaration should be submitted on the date that the dividend is paid.[102] The beneficial owner should also make an undertaking to forthwith inform the regulated intermediary in writing should the circumstances relating to the reduced rate applicable to the beneficial owner change or the beneficial owner cease to be the beneficial owner.[103]

11.4.9 Refund of the dividends tax

In certain instances dividends tax may be paid to SARS when it is not required to be paid because the beneficial owner of the dividend is exempt from the dividends tax, or the dividend is paid to a regulated intermediary. In other instances a full amount of the dividends tax may be paid to SARS instead of a reduced rate.[104] In both these cases the Act provides for a refund mechanism for the tax incorrectly paid to SARS.[105]

The first provision for refunds applies in cases where the company withheld the dividends tax as a result of a declaration and written undertaking which were not submitted on time but was submitted within three years after the payment of the dividend. In this case the dividends tax that is unduly withheld should be refunded by the company to the person to whom the dividend was paid.[106] The company can set off the amount of the dividend refundable against the subsequent amount of the dividends tax arising out of subsequent dividends declared within one year after the declaration and written undertaking were submitted.[107] If the amount of the refundable dividends tax exceeds the amount of the dividends tax payable in a subsequent declaration (eg because the

CHAPTER 11

[99] Section 64H(2)*(b)*.
[100] Section 64H(3).
[101] Section 64H(3)(i).
[102] Section 64H(3)*(b)*.
[103] Section 64H(3)(ii).
[104] See ss 64G and 64H.
[105] Section 64L.
[106] Section 64L(1).
[107] Section 64L(2).

subsequent dividend is lower than the preceding dividend) the excess amount can be recovered from SARS. Claims from SARS can only be made within five years from the date the dividend was withheld.

The provisions relating to the refund of the dividends tax withheld and paid by regulated intermediaries are similar to the refund provisions discussed above in relation to companies.[108] However, in the case of regulated intermediaries no provision is made for refunds to be made by SARS.[109]

11.4.10 Rebate in respect of foreign taxes on dividends

Dividends paid by non-resident companies on shares that are listed on the JSE are subject to the dividends tax.[110] These dividends may also be subject to tax in the jurisdiction where the company declaring the dividend is resident for tax purposes. This would result in double taxation of the same dividend in the hands of the same shareholder. Section 64N provides for a mechanism to relieve the shareholder of the double tax burden that could arise as a result of the application of the tax laws of the two jurisdictions. This section provides for the credit against the South African tax of the amount of the tax paid in the other jurisdiction.[111] In its basic form this credit system applies *mutatis mutandis* to the rebate on foreign taxes provided for in s 6*quat*. However, this special provision is required for dividends tax as the dividends tax does not constitute normal tax on income.

The credit applies if the beneficial owner of the dividend does not have any right to recover the tax payable in this regard.[112] The amount of the credit cannot exceed the amount of dividends tax payable in South Africa.[113] This ring-fencing provision is to ensure that the South African fiscus is not disadvantaged by tax losses generated by the payment of taxes in other jurisdictions. If this were not the case, the South African tax base would effectively subsidise the payment of tax liabilities in other countries. As the amount of tax paid in other jurisdictions is generally paid in the currency of that particular country, the rebate is calculated by translating the amount into South African rand by applying the exchange rate used to convert the amount of the dividend into rand.[114]

11.4.11 STC credits

STC credits can be used to reduce the amount of the dividends tax payable. If the company declares a dividend out of amounts that it received as a dividend under the STC regime and STC was paid in relation to that dividend, the

[108] See s 64H; see also Gani *Tax Planning* 203.
[109] Section 64M.
[110] Paragraph *(b)* of s 64D definition of 'dividend'.
[111] Section 64N(1).
[112] Section 64N(2).
[113] Section 64N(3).
[114] Section 64N(4).

dividend declared by the company is not subject to the dividends tax.[115] In effect, the tax paid under the STC system is credited against the dividends tax payable. Any excess amount paid as a dividend will be subject to the dividends tax under the general dividends tax rules. In order for the STC credit to be used successfully against the dividends tax the company declaring the dividend must notify the person to whom the dividend is paid of the amount by which the dividend reduces the STC credit of the company.[116] All STC credits of a company will expire on the third anniversary of the coming into effect of the dividends tax, ie 1 April 2015, as a result of a proposal contained in the 2012 Taxation Laws Amendment Bill. Initially, STC credits were scheduled to expire after a period of five years from 1 April 2012.[117]

11.4.12 Dividends tax anti-avoidance measures

Dividends tax can be avoided by the transfer of money or assets in such a manner that the transfer does not constitute a dividend. The erstwhile STC system contained special provisions to combat this form of avoidance by deeming certain transactions to result in deemed dividends.[118] When the new dividends tax was legislated[119] in 2008 an analogous provision was introduced in the form of a value extraction tax ('VET'). This provision imposed a separate tax on amounts that were considered to be disguised dividends that had the effect of extracting value from the company.[120] The objective of the VET was to trigger a tax when any form of value was extracted from a company for the benefit of connected persons in relation to the paying company.[121] The VET covered several forms of disguised dividends, including disguised dividends resulting from the granting of financial assistance (ie discounted loans or advances).

In 2011, the VET was repealed.[122] No general anti-avoidance section was introduced in relation to dividends. The Act also contains a specific anti-avoidance provision in s 64EB that applies to specific cession of dividends paid on shares whereby taxpayers sought to escape the payment of the withholding tax on dividends. The section has the result that the cession and other affected transactions are disregarded and the dividends withholding tax remains payable on the dividends declared by the company.

The effect of a general anti-avoidance provision in relation to dividends was achieved by amendments to several provisions of the Act to ensure that any transfers to shareholders and their connected persons that are intended to

[115] Section 64J(1)*(a)*. See also Mitchell L 'Dividend Tax II: STC Credits and Other Issues' (2009) *Tax Planning* 63.

[116] Section 64J(1)*(b)*.

[117] This provision was repealed by s 63 of Act 23 of 2018 for obsolescence.

[118] Section 64C.

[119] The new dividends tax was legislated in 2008 but the application was deferred to a date determined by the Minister of Finance, which date was subsequently set at 1 April 2012.

[120] Sections 64O–64R.

[121] See Mitchell L 'Hello VET: Bye Deemed Dividends' (2010) *Tax Planning* 164.

[122] Section 85 of the Taxation Laws Amendment Act 24 of 2011.

disguise dividends are subject to tax. Central to this form of anti-avoidance is the wide definition of dividend, which refers to 'any amount transferred or applied by a company that is a resident for the benefit or on behalf of any person in respect of any share in that company'.[123] For example, s 64C(2)*(g)* specifically provided that any loan or advance granted or made available to a shareholder or connected person in relation to a shareholder is deemed to be a dividend. No such specific provision exists in terms of the current law. However, a loan or advance granted to a shareholder or connected person in relation to a shareholder will be a dividend in that it is an amount transferred by a company for the benefit of any person in respect of a share in that company (in terms of the definition of dividend).

11.5 FOREIGN DIVIDENDS

As a general rule, foreign dividends form part of a taxpayer's gross income.[124] A foreign dividend is defined as any amount that is paid or payable by a foreign company in respect of a share in that foreign company where that amount is treated as a dividend or similar payment by that foreign company.[125] The South African determination of the nature of the dividend depends on the tax laws of the country in which that foreign company is resident by virtue of that company being effectively managed in that country. Where that country does not have tax laws, the determining laws will be the company laws of the country in which that company is incorporated, formed or established.

The definition of foreign dividend excludes any amounts that are paid or payable that (i) constitute a redemption of a participatory interest in a collective investment scheme; or (ii) are deductible by that foreign company.

Certain amounts that qualify as foreign dividends are excluded from the taxation of dividends. Furthermore, the tax regime also provides for a partial exemption of other dividends.

11.5.1 Full exemption

The following foreign dividends are fully exempt from tax:

- First, a foreign dividend is exempt if it is received by or accrues to a person that holds at least 10% of the total equity shares and voting rights in the company declaring the foreign dividend. For companies that form a group of companies this requirement is satisfied if such company holds such equity shares or voting rights alone or together with any other company forming part of the same group of companies as the company receiving the dividend or to which the dividend accrues.[126]

---

[123] Section 1 definition of 'dividend'.

[124] Section 1 definition of 'gross income' para *(k)*.

[125] A foreign dividend also includes a dividend paid or declared by a headquarter company. For a discussion of this, see chapter 14 on international tax.

[126] Section 10B(2)*(a)*.

- Secondly, a foreign dividend is exempt if it is received by or accrues to a company and the foreign dividend is paid or declared by another foreign company that is resident in the same country as the company receiving the dividend or to which the dividend accrues.[127]
- Thirdly, dividends that are taxable in terms of the provisions applicable to controlled foreign companies are exempt. This is because such dividends are already taxable in South Africa. These are dividends received by controlled foreign companies and dividends received by shareholders of controlled foreign companies whose income is attributable to such shareholders of the controlled foreign company.[128]
- Fourthly, a foreign dividend is exempt to the extent that the foreign dividend is received by or accrues to a person in respect of a listed share and does not consist of a distribution of an asset *in specie*.[129]

The full exemption provisions do not apply in respect of any foreign dividend received by or accrued to any person if any amount of that foreign dividend is determined directly or indirectly with reference to any amount payable by any person to any other person;[130] or if that foreign dividend arises directly or indirectly from any amount payable by any person to any other person.[131]

Furthermore, the provisions do not apply if the amount of the foreign dividend is deductible by the person declaring the dividend and is not subject to normal tax in the hands of the person receiving the dividend or to whom the dividend accrues.[132]

The exemption is also not applicable where the amount of the foreign dividend received by a controlled foreign company is deductible in the hands of the company declaring the dividend and is not taken into account in determining the net income of that controlled foreign company.[133] Finally, the exemption is not available where the amount is received from a collective investment scheme.[134]

11.5.2 Partial exemption

Section 10B further provides for a partial exemption. The partial exemption applies to dividends that are taxable and that do not qualify for the exemptions listed above.[135] Only a portion of the dividend is exempt. The exempt portion is determined in terms of a formula provided in s 10B(3).

The full and partial exemptions do not extend to any payments out of any foreign dividend received by or accrued to any person.[136]

CHAPTER 11

---

127 Section 10B(2)*(b)*.
128 Section 10B(2)*(c)*.
129 Section 10B(2)*(d)*.
130 Section 10B(4)*(a)*(i)*(aa)*.
131 Section 10B(4)*(a)*(i)*(bb)*.
132 Section 10B(4)*(a)*(ii)*(aa)*.
133 Section 10B(4)*(a)*(ii)*(bb)*.
134 Section 10B(4)*(b)*.
135 Section 10B(3)*(a)*.
136 Section 10B(5).

11.5.3 Deductibility of expenditure incurred in producing foreign dividends

Expenditure incurred in the production of foreign dividends was previously deductible in the determination of the taxable income of a shareholder when foreign dividends were fully taxed, but from 1 April 2012 this is no longer the case.[137] Prior to 1 April 2012 s 11C limited such deduction to interest expenditure.[138] There was no deduction available for other expenditure such as professional fees, brokers' commission, agency fees, etc incurred in the production of dividends.

11.5.4 Rebate in respect of foreign taxes paid

The Act provides for a rebate in respect of foreign taxes on income.[139] This provision applies in addition to many other provisions of the Act, such as CFC income,[140] foreign dividends[141] and foreign capital gains.[142] Basically, this rebate is granted to residents for non-recoverable income taxes payable to a foreign country on income derived from a foreign country or on CFC income. Taxes payable in the foreign country could be paid by any person, for example in the case of taxes on dividends, by the company declaring the dividend. The rebate in respect of foreign taxes is a unilateral form of tax relief aimed at providing relief from double taxation. The rebate is deducted from the income tax payable of a resident in whose taxable income is included the above-mentioned and other specific categories of income.[143]

This provision provides relief on the taxes paid by a foreign company, for example a subsidiary in the foreign country. Thus, where the foreign subsidiary incurs some tax liability in the foreign country, such liability would be offset against the income that the South African company receives from the foreign subsidiary. Without such relief the ultimate income of the South African company would be diluted by taxation, as it would be taxed in the foreign country and

---

[137] See Mitchell L, Stein M, Silke J & Jooste R 'Interest Incurred on Earning Foreign Dividends' (2001) *Income Tax Reporter* 71.

[138] It should be noted that expenditure incurred in the production of South African dividends is not deductible. This is because South African dividends are exempt from tax in the hands of the shareholder. The dividends tax is not a tax on income and thus expenses incurred in generating domestic dividends will not be deductible under s 11*(a)* or under the rules imposing the dividends tax.

[139] The provisions are contained in s 6*quat* of the Act. See Silke & Stretch 'Interpretation Note No 18: Rebate for Foreign Taxes and Natural Persons' (2003) 6 *Taxgram* 5.

[140] See s 6*quat*(1)*(b)* of the Act. See Mitchell L, Stein M & Silke J 'Controlled Foreign Entities' (2001) *Income Tax Reporter* 39.

[141] See s 6*quat*(1)*(d)* of the Act; Mitchell et al *Income Tax Reporter* 39.

[142] See s 6*quat*(1)*(e)* of the Act; Meyerowitz *Income Tax* para 19.3. See also Mitchell L, Stein M, Silke J & Jooste R 'Rebate or Deduction of Foreign Taxes' (2008) *Income Tax Reporter* 137.

[143] See Dachs P 'Foreign Taxes Levied' (2006) *Tax Planning* 138. The rebate applies in relation to foreign-sourced income. In relation to income earned in South Africa taxpayers qualify for a deduction for the expenditure incurred in the production of income in terms of s 11*(a)* read with s 23*(g)*. See also SARS Draft Interpretation Note 18 (2009) para 3.1.

in South Africa. For example, a Congolese subsidiary would be subject to the Congolese corporate tax rate of 40% and when it declares dividends to a South African company such income would be taxed at the corporate income tax rate of 28%, resulting in a net income after tax of 32% of the gross income received by the Congolese company, ie an overall effective rate of 68%.

The rebate is limited to the amount which bears to the total normal tax payable the same ratio as the total taxable income attributed to the specific category of income in respect of which the rebate may be claimed bears to the total taxable income.[144] Where the sum of the foreign taxes proved to be payable exceeds the rebate as determined, the excess amount may be carried forward to the immediately succeeding year of assessment and shall be deemed to be a tax on income paid to the government of any other country in that year. The excess may then be set off against the normal tax payable in that succeeding year.[145]

11.5.5 Foreign-source income

In order to qualify for the rebate, the foreign taxes must be payable in respect of income derived from a foreign source.[146] Foreign-source income is income that is not sourced in South Africa. Source is not defined in the Act but it has been held that source is not a legal concept, but something that an ordinary man would regard as the real source of income.[147] The court in *CIR v Lever Bros and Another*[148] stated as follows regarding the source of income:

> [The source of income] ... is not the quarter whence they come, but the originating cause of their being received as income, and ... this originating cause is the work which the taxpayer does to earn them, the *quid pro quo* which he gives in return for which he receives them. The work which he does may be a business which he carries on, or an enterprise which he undertakes, or an activity in which he engages and it may take the form of personal exertion, mental or physical, or it may take the form of employment of capital by using it to earn income or by letting its use to someone else. Often the work is some combination of these.[149]

Owing to the fact that in certain instances income may have multiple originating causes, the case law requires that the dominant cause be established.[150] For South African tax law purposes there are no apportionment rules for the source of income. Due to the different nature of amounts of income, different rules have been created for specific types of income.

CHAPTER 11

144 See s 6*quat*(1B) of the Act. See also Meyerowitz *Income Tax* para 19.5.2.

145 See s 6*quat*(1B)*(a)*(ii). See also Olivier & Honiball *International Tax* 322–324.

146 See s 6*quat*(1A); SARS Interpretation Note 18 (2003) para 2; SARS Draft Interpretation Note 18 (2009) 3.4.

147 See *Rhodesia Metals Ltd (in Liquidation) v COT* 1938 AD 282.

148 1946 AD 441.

149 At 450.

150 See *CIR v Lever Bros and Another* 1946 AD 441 449–450; *CIR v Black* 1957 (3) SA 536 (A) 542–543.

The source of business income is the place where the business is carried on or where the capital is employed, whichever is dominant. The source of a dividend is the place where the register of the share in respect of which the dividend is paid is located.[151] The source of interest is not the debt but the granting of the credit or the transfer of the lender's right to credit to the borrower, the granting of credit normally being situated where the creditor's business is located.[152] Deeming provisions in relation to interest deem interest to be received or accrued from a South African source where such interest is derived from the utilisation or application in South Africa by any person of funds or credit obtained in terms of an interest-bearing arrangement.[153]

Where the South African resident earns income that is sourced from a foreign country and is not deemed to be sourced from South Africa, the foreign tax credit will be applied in relation to the amount of that income that is included in the taxable income of the resident.[154] If income is deemed to be from a South African source, the rebate cannot be applied in relation to such income.[155] Where the taxable income of a resident includes a foreign dividend in relation to which foreign taxes have been paid, the rebate will be applied to the amount of that dividend in calculating the taxable income of the resident.[156]

11.6 CORPORATE REORGANISATIONS

Ordinarily, the change in ownership of assets gives rise to revenue or capital gains or losses for the person disposing of the asset. A reorganisation is basically any transaction that involves significant changes in the legal or economic structure of one or more companies.

Reorganisations form part of business practices throughout the world. Company groups are often reorganised in order to enable company groups to access some convenience, economy or business activities. Reorganisations can occur as part of a privatisation process or after privatisation as the ownership of companies changes hands. It can happen as part of the fragmentation or consolidation of trades or business activities, or in order to centralise or divide management of the group of companies. This can be pursuant to the group strategy to increase efficiency or it can be in compliance with laws, rules and regulations.[157]

---

[151] See *Boyd v CIR* 1951 (3) SA 525 (A) 528. See also Emslie TS, Davis DM & Hutton SJ *Income Tax Cases and Materials* (Taxpayer 1995) 111.

[152] See *CIR v Lever Bros and Another* 1946 AD 441; *First National Bank of Southern Africa Ltd v CIR* 2002 (3) SA 375 (SCA), 64 SATC 245. See also Silke J & Stretch R 'New Test for Source of Interest?' (2001) 7 *Taxgram* 6.

[153] See Tsatsawane K 'Interest Income from a Source Within, or Deemed to be Within, South Africa' (2000) *Juta's Business Law* 178.

[154] See Dachs (2006) *Tax Planning* 138–139.

[155] Deeming provisions apply in relation to certain specific forms of income including royalties, mining income, pensions and capital gains. See s 9.

[156] Section 6*quat*(1)*(d)*; SARS Draft Interpretation Note 18 (2009) para 3.2.

[157] Vanistendael F 'Taxation of Corporate Reorganizations' in V Thuronyi (ed) *Tax Law Design and Drafting* (International Monetary Fund 1998) 895–897.

Corporate reorganisation rules are intended to neutralise the tax burden where assets are transferred from one company to another where there is no change in ownership of the assets because of the common ownership of the companies that are engaged in the transactions. The tax law contains specific rules for corporate reorganisations which provide for the tax-free treatment of transfers of assets.[158] Without these rules, reorganisations would attract tax and this would make reorganisations costly for the companies.[159] This might also have the effect of discouraging reorganisations and could stifle corporate existence in the particular jurisdiction.

Reorganisations take the following forms: amalgamation, asset-for-share transactions, substitutive share-for-share transactions, intra-group transactions, unbundling transactions and liquidation distributions

11.6.1 Amalgamation

Generally, an amalgamation is a transaction in terms of which a company transfers all of its assets to another company and the former company, the transferor company, legally ceases to exist. Generally, the transfer takes place in exchange for shares in the company to which the assets are transferred. An amalgamation can take the form of a merger or a consolidation. In a merger, pre-existing companies merge to form one new company. All pre-existing companies cease to exist with the exception of one company into which they merge. In a consolidation a new company is formed and pre-existing companies merge into a newly formed company, and as a result all the pre-existing companies cease to exist.[160]

Amalgamations are dealt with in terms of s 44 of the Act. Parties to the amalgamation are the amalgamated company and the amalgamating or resultant company. An amalgamation is defined specifically in the Act as a transaction in terms of which the amalgamated company disposes of all of its assets to the resultant company which is a resident, by means of an amalgamation, conversion or merger as a result of which that amalgamated company's existence will be terminated.[161] The resultant company will then own assets that belonged to the amalgamated company as well as those that belonged to the resultant company prior to the amalgamation. Assets exclude those assets that the amalgamated company elects to use to settle any debts incurred by it in the ordinary course of its trade.[162] The transfer is effected in return for equity shares in the resultant company.[163] These shares are then transferred to the shareholders of the amalgamated company as a dividend *in specie*, with the result that the erstwhile shareholders of the amalgamated

158 Vanistendael in Thuronyi (ed) *Tax Law Design and Drafting* 896.

159 Olivier L 'Tax Implications of the Sale of a Business' (2007) *SALJ* 600.

160 Vanistendael in Thuronyi (ed) *Tax Law Design and Drafting* 899; Meyerowitz *Income Tax* para 17A.24.

161 Section 44(1) definition of 'amalgamation transaction'.

162 Paragraph *(a)* of s 44(1) definition of 'amalgamation transaction'.

163 Section 44(4); Meyerowitz *Income Tax* para 17A.25.

company will then hold equity shares in the resultant company, generally equal to the value they held in the amalgamated company.[164]

The amalgamated company will then be wound up or deregistered, resulting in the termination of the corporate existence of the amalgamated company. Section 44 will apply if the amalgamated company takes steps[165] to liquidate, wind up or deregister within 18 months after the date of the amalgamation. The Commissioner may extend this period upon request.[166]

The roll-over relief does not apply if the resultant company is not resident in South Africa, or if the company is exempt from gross income in terms of s 10, because the roll-over relief would not have any impact on the transaction. Assets which may be transferred in terms of an amalgamation transaction are capital assets,[167] trading stock,[168] allowance assets[169] and any contract as part of the disposal of a business as a going concern.[170] An allowance asset is an asset in terms of which the taxpayer is allowed to claim a deduction of depreciation allowance such as assets dealt with, for example, in terms of s 11*(e)* and 12C.[171] The company should acquire the asset for the same purpose as that for which the person disposing of the asset held it. Thus, if the asset being disposed of is held by the person disposing of it as trading stock, the company acquiring the asset should acquire the asset as trading stock. It is not required that the company should hold that asset as such. The company may change the nature of the asset subsequent to the acquisition, for example from trading stock to an allowance asset.

The effect of s 44 is that no tax (ie normal tax, STC, dividends tax, capital gains tax or securities transfer tax)[172] is payable as a result of the transaction.[173] This is achieved as follows:

- Capital assets: the amalgamated company is deemed to have disposed of any capital asset at its base cost. The amalgamated company and the resultant company are deemed to be one and the same person with respect to the date of acquisition of the asset and all expenses for the determination of the base cost of the asset and the valuation of the asset for capital gains purposes.[174]
- Trading stock: the amalgamated company is deemed to have disposed of the trading stock at tax value.[175] The resultant company and the

[164] Meyerowitz *Income Tax* para 17A.26.
[165] In terms of s 41(4).
[166] Section 44(13); Meyerowitz *Income Tax* para 17A.27.
[167] Section 44(2)*(a)*.
[168] Section 44(2)*(b)*.
[169] Section 44(3)*(a)*.
[170] Section 44(3)*(b)*.
[171] Section 41(1) definition of 'allowance asset'.
[172] See s 8(1) of the Securities Transfer Tax Act 25 of 2007.
[173] See Kolitz M 'Amalgamation Transactions: A Loophole is to be Closed' (2007) *Tax Planning* 94.
[174] Section 44(2)*(a)*.
[175] The tax value is the value of the asset less any amounts of depreciation allowance that the taxpayer has taken into account in determining its taxable income.

amalgamated company are deemed to be the same person in relation to the date of, and the costs and expenses incurred in, the acquisition of the trading stock.[176]

- Allowance assets: an amalgamated company is deemed to have disposed of any allowance asset at its tax value. The amalgamated company and the resultant company are deemed to be the same person in respect of claiming allowances on the asset and recoupments.[177]
- Contracts: in respect of contracts no amount that has been allowed to the amalgamated company in respect of that obligation is included in that amalgamated company's income for the year of that transfer.[178] In addition, the amalgamated company and the resultant company are deemed to be one and the same person for purposes of determining the amount of any allowance or deduction to which that resultant company may be entitled in respect of that obligation or the amount that is to be included in the income of that holding company in respect of that asset.[179]

Anti-avoidance provisions apply in cases where the amalgamation transaction is entered into and as a result tax may be avoided. Specific provisions apply, for example, where shares acquired in terms of the amalgamation are disposed of within 18 months.[180] Broadly, in these cases, the tax neutrality of the transaction is withdrawn and the transaction will be taxable.

11.6.2 Asset-for-share transactions

Asset-for-share transactions occur generally on the formation of a company or when additional assets are acquired by a company by way of share capital or contributed tax capital, as the case may be. In an asset-for-share transaction, a person who may be or may not be a shareholder in a company disposes of an asset to a company. In return for that disposal of an asset, that person acquires equity shares.[181]

In summary, s 42 defines an asset-for-share transaction as a transaction in terms of which a person disposes of an asset to a company which is a resident in exchange for the issue of an equity share or shares of that company and that person at the close of the day on which that asset is disposed of, holds a qualifying interest in that company.[182] The company should acquire the asset with the same purpose as the person disposing of the asset. Thus, if the asset being disposed of is held by the person disposing of it as a capital asset, the company acquiring the asset should acquire the asset as a capital asset. The company is not required to retain that asset as such. The company may

[176] Section 44(2)*(b)*.
[177] Section 44(3)*(a)*.
[178] Section 44(3)*(b)*(i).
[179] Section 44(3)*(b)*(ii).
[180] See s 44(4) and (13).
[181] Meyerowitz *Income Tax* para 17A.3.
[182] Section 42(1) definition of 'asset-for-share transaction'. See Meyerowitz *Income Tax* para 17A.8.

change the nature of the asset subsequent to the acquisition, for example from a capital asset to trading stock.

A 'qualifying interest' is defined[183] as:

(a) an equity share held by a person in a company which is a listed company or will become a listed company within 12 months after the transaction as a result of which that person holds that share;

(b) an equity share held by a person in a portfolio of a collective investment scheme in securities;

(c) equity shares held by a person in a company that constitute at least 10% of the equity shares and voting rights of a company; or

(d) an equity share held by a person in a company which forms part of the same group of companies as that person; or

(e) any equity share held in a portfolio of a hedge fund collective investment scheme.

The roll-over treatment applies automatically to disposals that qualify as asset-for-share transactions unless the transferor and the company agree that the section does not apply.[184] The requirement that the person disposing of an asset must hold a qualifying interest at the close of the day on which the disposal of the asset takes place is important. If this is not satisfied, then the transaction does not qualify as an asset-for-share transaction and therefore would not qualify for the roll-over treatment.

Parties to the asset-for-share transaction are the transferor and the company to which the asset is transferred. Assets which may be transferred in terms of an asset-for-share transaction are capital assets,[185] trading stock,[186] allowance assets[187] and any contract as part of the disposal of a business as a going concern.[188] An allowance asset is an asset in terms of which the taxpayer is allowed to claim a deduction or depreciation allowance, such as assets dealt with in terms of s 11*(e)* and 12C.

The effect of s 42 is that the tax implications attendant upon the transaction are rolled over from the transferor to the transferee until the transferee disposes of the asset. This is achieved as follows:

- Capital assets: the transferor of the asset is deemed to have disposed of any capital asset at its base cost. That person and the company are deemed to be one and the same person with respect to the date of acquisition of the asset and all expenses for the determination of the

[183] Section 42(1) definition of 'qualifying interest'.

[184] Previously, the parties had to jointly elect that the section would not apply, but no election mechanism was provided for by the Act or SARS in any guideline. The Act was therefore amended for administrative ease to provide for the agreement mechanism of turning off the application of the roll-over provisions.

[185] Section 42(3)*(a)*.

[186] Section 42(3)*(b)*.

[187] Section 42(3)*(a)*.

[188] Section 42(3)*(c)*.

base cost of the asset and the valuation of the asset for capital gains purposes.

- Trading stock: the transferor of the trading stock is deemed to have disposed of the trading stock at tax value.[189] The transferor and the company are deemed to be the same person in relation to the date of, and the costs and expenses incurred in, the acquisition of the trading stock.
- Allowance assets: the transferor is deemed to have disposed of the allowance asset at its tax value. The transferor and the company are deemed to be the same person in respect of claiming allowances on the asset and recoupments.

Anti-avoidance provisions apply in cases where the asset-for share transaction is entered into and as a result tax may be avoided. Specific provisions apply, for example, where shares acquired in terms of the asset-for-share transaction are disposed of within 18 months.[190] Broadly, in these cases, the tax neutrality of the transaction is withdrawn and the transaction will be taxable.

11.6.3 Substitutive share-for-share transaction

This form of reorganisation was introduced into the Act in 2013. The rationale for the introduction is that reorganisations do not only involve multiple companies. Companies often enter into share-for-share recapitalisations that involve a single company. The provision is aimed at recapitalisation in which 'shareholders of a company surrender all (or some) of the shares held in exchange for the issue of new shares by the same company'.[191] This action is referred to in s 43 as a 'substitutive share-for-share transaction' and typically entails a share split, share consolidation or share conversion.

A substitutive share-for-share transaction is a transaction between a person and a company in terms of which that person disposes of an equity share interest in that company and acquires another equity share interest in that company or disposes of a non-equity share interest in that company and acquires another non-equity share interest in that company by means of a subdivision or consolidation.[192] In addition, the definition requires that the other equity share interest or the other non-equity share interest, as the case may be, is acquired by that person either as a capital asset or as trading stock, in the case where the equity share interest or non-equity share interest disposed of is disposed of as a capital asset or as trading stock in the case where the

CHAPTER 11

[189] The tax value is the value of the asset less any amounts of depreciation allowance taken into account by the taxpayer in determining its taxable income.

[190] Section 42(7).

[191] See National Treasury 'Explanatory Memorandum on the Taxation Laws Amendment Bill' 2012 at 37.

[192] Paragraph *(a)* of s 43(1)*(a)* definition of 'substitutive share-for-share transaction'.

equity share interest or non-equity share interest disposed of is disposed of as trading stock.[193]

In terms of s 43, a person who disposes of a share interest in a company and acquires another share interest in that company is deemed to have disposed of the share interest for an amount equal to the expenditure incurred in acquiring the share interest disposed of.[194] Furthermore, that person is deemed to have disposed of the share interest disposed of for an amount equal to the expenditure incurred in acquiring that share interest.[195]

11.6.4 Intra-group transaction

An intra-group transaction (also referred to as an asset acquisition) is a transfer of assets or liabilities, or both, by a company to a newly established or pre-existing company in exchange for some or no consideration.[196] Parties to an intra-group transaction are companies in the same group of companies. They are the company transferring the asset, the transferor company, and the company to which the asset is transferred, the transferee company.

The Act defines an intra-group transaction as a transaction in terms of which an asset is disposed of by the transferor company to a transferee company.[197] The residence requirement specifically excludes the application of the roll-over benefit to transfers of assets to non-resident companies, because that would undermine the tax system by divesting the South African tax authority of jurisdiction over the assets or growth that is taxable in South Africa. In order to qualify for s 45 relief, both the transferor company and the transferee company must form part of the same group of companies on the date of the transaction.[198] This implies that both companies should be tax resident in South Africa in order to qualify for the relief.[199] The relief in s 45 cannot apply where the transferor company is not resident because South Africa would not be entitled to tax the profits previously made in the transferor company as it is not resident. Even if the transferor company were to become resident at the time of the transaction, South Africa would not have a justifiable right to tax such profits.

Assets which may be transferred in terms of an intra-group transaction are capital assets,[200] trading stock,[201] allowance assets[202] and any contract as part of the disposal of a business as a going concern.[203] The roll-over relief applies

[193] Paragraph *(b)* of s 43(1)*(a)* definition of 'substitutive share-for-share transaction'.
[194] Section 43(2)*(a)*.
[195] Section 43(2)*(b)*.
[196] Vanistendael in Thuronyi (ed) *Tax Law Design and Drafting* 899.
[197] Section 45(1)*(a)*.
[198] Section 45(1)*(a)*; Meyerowitz D, Emslie T & Davis D 'Company Formations' (2008) *The Taxpayer* 32; Meyerowitz *Income Tax* para 17A.29.
[199] See para (i)*(ee)* of s 41 definition of 'group of companies'.
[200] Section 45(2)*(a)*.
[201] Section 45(2)*(b)*.
[202] Section 45(3)*(a)*.
[203] Section 45(3)*(b)*.

if the transferee acquires the asset and retains the character of the asset as it was held by the transferor; thus if the disposal is a disposal of an allowance asset, the transferee should acquire the asset as an allowance asset. The roll-over relief is achieved in the following manner:[204]

- Capital assets: the transferor company is deemed to have disposed of any capital asset at its base cost. The transferor and the transferee company are deemed to be one and the same person with respect to the date of acquisition of the asset and all expenses for the determination of the base cost of the asset and the valuation of the asset for capital gains purposes.[205]
- Trading stock: the transferor company is deemed to have disposed of the trading stock at tax value.[206] The transferor and the transferee company are deemed to be the same person in relation to the date of, and the costs and expenses incurred in, the acquisition of the trading stock.[207]
- Allowance assets: a transferor company is deemed to have disposed of any allowance asset at its tax value. The transferor and the transferee company are deemed to be the same person in respect of claiming allowances on the asset and recoupments.[208]
- Contracts: in respect of contracts no amount that has been allowed to the transferor company in respect of that obligation is included in that transferor company's income for the year of that transfer.[209] In addition, the transferor and the transferee company are deemed to be one and the same person for purposes of determining the amount of any allowance or deduction to which that transferee company may be entitled in respect of that obligation or the amount that is to be included in the income of that holding company in respect of that asset.[210]

The roll-over provision applies automatically unless the transferor company and the transferee company agree in writing at the time of the disposal of the asset that the roll-over provision does not apply to that disposal.[211] Where assets are disposed of for no consideration or for consideration that is less than market value, the donations tax provisions do not apply if the transfer qualifies for the intra-group roll-over.[212]

Anti-avoidance measures are built into these intra-group transactions. In the main, if the companies that are party to the intra-group transaction cease to be part of the same group, ie if they 'degroup', within six years after the intra-

[204] See a further discussion in Meyerowitz *Income Tax* para 17A.30.
[205] Section 45(2)*(a)*.
[206] The tax value is the value of the asset less any amounts of depreciation allowance taken into account by the taxpayer in determining its taxable income.
[207] Section 45(2)*(b)*.
[208] Section 45(3)*(a)*.
[209] Section 45(3)*(b)*(i).
[210] Section 45(3)*(b)*(ii).
[211] Section 45(6)*(g)*.
[212] Section 56(1)*(r)*.

group transaction, the transferee will be deemed to have disposed of the assets acquired in terms of the intra-group transaction and will therefore be taxable on that deemed disposal.[213] Thus, in effect the transferee would be taxed on the gains made on the sale of the asset that is attributable both at the time the asset was held by the transferor and the period it was held by the transferee. In fact, the Act calculates the taxable income as the higher of the amounts if the disposal occurred at the time of the intra-group transaction or at the time of the degrouping. The amount to be included in taxable income for the transferee following the degrouping varies depending on the nature of the asset.

11.6.5 Unbundling transactions

An unbundling is generally a division of a company, hence it is commonly referred to as a corporate division. In effect, an unbundling transaction is the opposite of an amalgamation. In an unbundling transaction, one company is divided into two or more companies.

> Three types of divisive reorganisations can be identified. In a spin-off, the shares of a subsidiary are distributed to the shareholders of the parent company. In a split-off, the shares of a subsidiary are distributed in exchange for the surrender of shares of the parent company. In a split-up the parent company distributes its shares in two or more subsidiaries in complete liquidation.[214]

An unbundling for South African purposes takes the form of a spin-off.

In general terms an unbundling transaction is a transaction in terms of which all the equity shares of a company (the "unbundled company") which is a resident that are held by a company (the "unbundling company") which is a resident, are distributed by that unbundling company to any shareholder of that unbundling company in accordance with the effective interest of that shareholder in the shares of that unbundling company The transaction qualifies as an unbundling transaction, inter alia, only to the extent to which those equity shares are so distributed in relation to an unbundling company that is a listed company and the equity shares of the unbundled company are listed shares or will become listed shares within 12 months after that distribution to the shareholders of that unbundling company. If the unbundling company is an unlisted company the equity shares must be distributed to any shareholder of that unbundling company that forms part of the same group of companies as that unbundled company.[215]

Parties to the unbundling are the unbundling company, the unbundled company and the shareholder of the unbundling company. In summary, a s 46 unbundling is a transaction in terms of which the shares of an unbundled company are distributed to the shareholders of the unbundling company.[216] The unbundling company must preserve the character of the shares as they were held by the

---

[213] See Morphet A 'Degrouping Developments: More on s 45' (2009) *Tax Planning* 42; Meyerowitz D, Emslie T and Davis D 'Company Formations' (2008) *The Taxpayer* 35.

[214] Vanistendael in Thuronyi (ed) *Tax Law Design and Drafting* 899.

[215] Section 46(1) definition of 'unbundling transaction'.

[216] Meyerowitz *Income Tax* para 17A.36.

unbundled company.[217] This transaction allows shareholders of a company to acquire shares held by that company in any other company. The acquisition is effected through a dividend *in specie*.

The effect of this transaction is that the unbundled company continues to exist after the unbundling. However, its shareholder will no longer be the unbundling company, but the shareholders of the unbundling company. Thus, the unbundled company and the unbundling company will both be subsidiaries of the shareholder of the unbundling company. In a qualifying unbundling transaction, the shares are deemed to be transferred at their base cost to the transferor and are deemed to be the same shares in the hands of the transferee, who is the shareholder of the unbundling company.[218] The acquisition of the shares in the unbundled company is deemed not to be a dividend distributed by the unbundling company.[219] The distribution is also deemed not to be a dividend received in the hands of the shareholder of the unbundled company.[220] The distribution of the shares is deemed to be made first from the share premium account of the unbundling company and then from reserves.[221]

11.6.6 Liquidation distributions

Where a company is liquidated for whatever reason, the assets in that company are returned to the owners of that company. Section 47 provides for the tax-free transfer of such assets upon liquidation of the company. Parties to a liquidating distribution are the liquidating company and its shareholders. A liquidation distribution is a transaction in terms of which a liquidating company which is a resident disposes of all its assets to its shareholders in anticipation of or in the course of the liquidation, winding up or deregistration of that company. In distributing assets the company may keep those assets that it elects to use to settle any debts incurred by it in the ordinary course of its trade.[222] The shareholders to which the distribution is made should be South African tax resident. Furthermore, at the date of the disposal, the shareholder and the liquidating company must constitute part of the same group of companies.[223]

The assets transferred in terms of a liquidation distribution can be a capital asset,[224] trading stock,[225] an allowance asset,[226] and/or a contract as part of a disposal of a business as a going concern.[227] The liquidating company must hold the assets

[217] See Meyerowitz *Income Tax* para 17A.37.
[218] Meyerowitz *Income Tax* para 17A.38.
[219] Section 46(5)*(a)*.
[220] Section 46(5)*(b)*.
[221] Section 46(6).
[222] Section 47(1).
[223] Section 47(1) definition of 'liquidation distribution'. Special qualifying criteria apply where the liquidating company is a controlled foreign company.
[224] Section 47(2)*(a)*.
[225] Section 47(2)*(b)*.
[226] Section 47(3)*(a)*.
[227] Section 47(3)*(b)*.

with the same purposes as the liquidated company held the assets. The disposal or transfer of the assets will not attract tax.[228] This is achieved as follows:

- Capital assets: in the case of a transfer of a capital asset the liquidating company is deemed to have disposed of that asset for an amount equal to the base cost of that asset on the date of the disposal thereof.[229] On the other hand, the liquidating company and that holding company are deemed to be one and the same person for purposes of determining any capital gain or capital loss in respect of a disposal of that asset by that holding company, with respect to the date of acquisition of that asset by that liquidating company and the amount and date of incurral by that liquidating company of the base cost of the assets. The companies are also deemed to be one and the same person in relation to any valuation of that asset affected by that liquidating company.[230]
- Trading stock: in the case of a distribution of trading stock the liquidating company must be deemed to have disposed of the trading stock for an amount equal to the expenditure incurred in acquiring the trading stock or the cost of the trading stock.[231] Furthermore, the liquidating company and that holding company are deemed to be one and the same person for purposes of determining any taxable income derived by that holding company from a trade carried on by it with respect to the date of acquisition of that asset by that liquidating company and the amount and date of incurral by that liquidating company of any cost or expenditure incurred in acquiring the trading stock.[232]
- Allowance asset: in respect of allowance assets, no amount that has been allowed to the liquidating company in respect of that asset is recovered or recouped by that liquidating company or included in that liquidating company's income for the year of that transfer.[233] In addition, the liquidating company and the holding company are deemed to be one and the same person for purposes of determining the amount of any allowance or deduction to which that holding company may be entitled in respect of that asset or the amount that is to be recovered or recouped by or included in the income of that holding company in respect of that asset.[234]
- Contracts: in respect of contracts no amount that has been allowed to the liquidating company in respect of that obligation is included in that liquidating company's income for the year of that transfer.[235] In addition, the liquidating company and the holding company are deemed to be one and the same person for purposes of determining the amount

[228] See Arendse J 'Liquidation Distributions: STC Implications' (2006) *Tax Planning* 104.
[229] Section 47(2)*(a)*(i).
[230] Section 47(2)*(a)*(ii). See also Meyerowitz *Income Tax* para 17A.44.
[231] Section 47(2)*(b)*(i).
[232] Section 47(2)*(b)*(ii). Meyerowitz *Income Tax* para 17A.45.
[233] Section 47(3)*(a)*(i).
[234] Section 47(3)*(a)*(ii). Meyerowitz *Income Tax* para 17A.46.
[235] Section 47(3)*(b)*(i).

of any allowance or deduction to which that holding company may be entitled in respect of that obligation or the amount that is to be included in the income of that holding company in respect of that asset.[236]

11.7 DIVIDENDS DEEMED TO BE INTEREST

11.7.1 Hybrid equity instruments

For income tax purposes, debt and equity are treated differently. A taxpayer incurring interest expenditure is allowed a deduction for that expenditure in accordance with the general deduction formula, provided all other requirements are met.[237] The taxpayer receiving interest includes such interest in gross income and is taxable thereon. On the other hand, a company declaring a dividend based on the equity of the shareholder would have been subject to STC if the dividend was declared before 1 April 2012 and the shareholder receiving the dividend is exempt from tax on the dividend received under the STC regime.[238] Alternatively the shareholder would be subject to dividends tax if the dividend is declared after 1 April 2012. However, a resident corporate shareholder would be exempt from the dividends tax. This state of affairs presents an opportunity for tax avoidance in that taxpayers are able to utilise instruments that have characteristics of both debt and equity to avoid the tax. This could be achieved by, for example, the company paying the dividend treating that dividend as interest expenditure in terms of the debt character of the instrument and the shareholder receiving the amount treating the amount as a dividend that is either exempt or subject to a lower rate of tax in accordance with the equity character of the instrument.

The Act contains a specific anti-avoidance measure in s 8E to combat this form of tax avoidance by usage of instruments that have a dual character such as preference shares.[239] The Act refers to these as hybrid equity instruments.

A hybrid equity share is defined in the Act and can take one of three forms.[240] First it is a share, other than an equity share, if the issuer of that share is obliged to redeem it in whole or in part, or if it may, at the option of the holder, be redeemed in whole or in part within three years from the date of issue of

236 Section 47(3)*(b)*(ii). Meyerowitz *Income Tax* para 17A.47.

237 Section 11*(a)*. See *CIR v Standard Bank of SA (Ltd)* 1985 (4) SA 485 (A); *CIR v G Brollo Properties* (1994) 56 SATC 47; Brincker E *Taxation Principles of Interest* chapter A.

238 See Mitchell L 'Hybrid Arrangements: Dividends Tax Consequences' (2010) *Tax Planning* 141.

239 Preference shares are shares that are afforded preference in terms of payments. They carry a fixed dividend (that usually represents a percentage of the issue price of the shares) which is paid out before ordinary shareholders receive a dividend. In the case of the termination of the existence of a company, such as a liquidation, the fixed dividend on the preference share is paid after prior claims on the company have been met, but before ordinary shareholders. In this regard preference shares possess the character of a debt instrument on which interest is payable.

240 Section 8E(1) definition of 'hybrid equity instrument'.

that share.[241] Secondly, it is any other share (other than the type of share described above) if the issuer of that share is obliged to redeem it in whole or in part, or if it may, at the option of the holder, be redeemed in whole or in part within three years from the date of issue of that share, or if at the time of the issue of the share the existence of the company issuing the share is to be terminated within a period of three years or is likely to be so terminated upon a reasonable consideration of all the facts at the time.[242] This definition has additional requirements relating to the nature of the dividends derived from the share.[243] Thirdly, a hybrid equity share is a preference share if that share is secured by a financial instrument or is subject to an arrangement in terms of which a financial instrument may not be disposed of unless that share was issued for a qualifying purpose.[244]

As Meyerowitz, Emslie and Davis state, '[s]ection 8E was enacted to overcome a situation where a company, usually with a tax loss, issues short term preference shares so that the holder can enjoy the tax exemption on dividends instead of paying tax on interest on a loan to the company'.[245] This anti-avoidance measure deems any dividend or foreign dividend declared by a company on a hybrid equity instrument to be an amount of income accrued to the recipient. This deeming provision applies to a dividend that is received by or accrued to a person during any year of assessment.[246]

11.7.2 Limitation of interest payments

In line with the anti-avoidance purpose of s 8E, s 8F denies a deduction in respect of any amount paid or payable by a company in terms of a hybrid debt instrument which is paid or becomes payable after that instrument becomes a hybrid debt instrument.[247] A hybrid debt instrument is basically an instrument that is convertible into shares or is to be settled by an issue or subscription for shares.[248] These instruments are equity in substance but are treated by the issuing company as debt in order to avoid the imposition of STC or dividends tax, as the case may be. The disallowed interest on the hybrid debt instrument is treated as a deemed dividend and therefore is subject to STC or dividends tax, as the case may be.[249]

---

[241] Paragraph *(a)* of s 8E(1) definition of 'hybrid equity instrument'.

[242] Paragraph *(b)*(i) of s 8E(1) definition of 'hybrid equity instrument'.

[243] Paragraph *(b)*(ii) of s 8E(1) definition of 'hybrid equity instrument'.

[244] Paragraph *(c)* of s 8E(1) definition of 'hybrid equity instrument'.

[245] Meyerowitz D, Emslie T & Davis D 'Dividends Deemed to be Interest: Section 8E of the Income Tax Act' *The Taxpayer* (2008) 179.

[246] Section 8E(2).

[247] Section 8F(2).

[248] Section 8F(1) definition of 'hybrid debt instrument'.

[249] Section 64C(2)*(h)*.

11.7.3 Third-party backed shares

In 2011 the concept of third-party backed shares was introduced into the Act by the insertion of s 8EA.[250] This section prescribes that any dividend declared in respect of a hybrid equity instrument or a third-party backed share will be deemed to be income, which is subject to normal tax, and not a tax-free dividend or a dividend subject to a low rate of tax.[251] A third-party backed share is 'any preference share or equity instrument in respect of which an enforcement right is exercisable by the holder of that preference share or equity instrument or an enforcement obligation is enforceable as a result of any amount of any specified dividend, foreign dividend, return of capital or foreign return of capital attributable to that share or equity instrument not being received by or accruing to any person entitled thereto'.[252]

The third-party backed shares inclusion targets the acquisition of shares that have debt-like features due to third-party backing. There are, however, exceptions. Funding by way of preference shares qualifies for dividend treatment if the preference shares are used directly or indirectly to fund the acquisition of ordinary shares of an operating company. The permissible use of funding can come in various forms, for example, options and guarantees. Impermissible guaranteeing or backing relates only to the nature of the preference share yield and not guarantees of share capital value.

11.8 TRANSACTIONS RELATING TO THE ISSUE OF SHARES BY A COMPANY

11.8.1 Transactions where assets are acquired as consideration for shares issued

Section 24BA of the Act regulates the tax consequences where assets are acquired as consideration for shares issued by a company.

The term asset used in s 24BA(1) of the Act means an asset as defined in para 1 of the Eighth Schedule to the Act.[253] The section applies where as a consequence of any transaction, a company acquires an asset from another person and issues shares to the seller in settlement of the purchase price due for such asset.[254] In addition, the section will apply where the consideration contemplated in s 24BA(2)*(a)* is, before taking account of any other transaction, operation, scheme, agreement or understanding that directly or indirectly affects that consideration, different from the consideration which would have been paid

[250] Section 21(1) of the Taxation Laws Amendment Act 24 of 2011. See also s 12 of the Taxation Laws Amendment Act 22 of 2012.

[251] Section 8EA(2).

[252] Section 8E(1) definition of 'third-party backed share'.

[253] Section 24BA(1).

[254] Section 24BA(2)*(a)*.

if that asset had been acquired in exchange for the issue of those shares in terms of a transaction between independent persons dealing at arm's length.[255]

Where a company acquires an asset from a person in exchange for the issue of shares by that company and the market value of the asset immediately before that disposal exceeds the market value of the shares, that excess will be deemed to be a capital gain arising in respect of a disposal by that company of the shares.[256] This provision applies notwithstanding the provisions of para 11(2)*(b)* of the Eighth Schedule to the Act and subject to s 24B of the Act. Furthermore, where the purchaser acquires the shares as a capital asset, the excess must be applied to reduce any base cost which is allowable in terms of para 20 of the Eighth Schedule to the Act.[257] Where the shares are acquired as trading stock, the excess must go to reduce any amount taken into account by the purchaser in respect of the shares in terms of s 11*(a)* or s 22(1) or (2) of the Act.[258] In addition, where the market value of the shares immediately after the share issue exceeds the market value of the asset before the disposal, the amount of the excess must, for purposes of Part VIII, be deemed to be a dividend as defined in s 64D that consists of a distribution of an asset *in specie*[259] and is paid by the company on the date on which the shares are issued.[260]

The section will not apply where a company acquires an asset from a person referred to s 24BA(2)*(a)* if that company and that person form part of the same group of companies.[261]

Section 24BA was inserted into the Act by way of s 52(1) of the Taxation Laws Amendment Act 22 of 2012 with effect from 1 January 2013 and applies in respect of any transactions entered into on or after that date.

11.8.2 Distribution of shares and issue of shares or options for no consideration

Section 40C of the Act provides that where a company distributes a share in that company or issues a share in that company or an option or other right to the issue of a share in that company, to a person for no consideration, the expenditure actually incurred by the person to acquire the share, option or right is deemed to be nil. Thus, where a company issues capitalisation shares to its shareholders, those shareholders will be deemed to have acquired those shares for no consideration. It must be noted that s 24B(2) of the Act overrides the provisions contained in s 40CA which in certain cases allow for the deduction of expenditure where shares are issued by a company.

---

255 Section 24BA(2)*(b)*.
256 Section 24BA(3)*(a)*.
257 Section 24BA(3)*(a)*(ii)*(aa)*.
258 Section 24BA(3)*(a)*(ii)*(bb)*.
259 Section 24BA(3)*(b)*(i).
260 Section 24BA(3)*(b)*(ii).
261 Section 24BA(4).

This section was inserted into the Act by s 47(1) of the Taxation Laws Amendment Act 22 of 2012 with effect from 1 January 2013 and applies in respect of any distributions and issues made after that date.

11.8.3 Share issues or debt acquisitions in return for asset

If a company acquires any asset from any person in exchange for shares issued by that company, that company must be deemed to have actually incurred an amount of expenditure in respect of the acquisition of that asset which is equal to the market value of the shares immediately after the acquisition.[262] If the company acquires such asset in exchange for any amount represented by a debt instrument issued by that company, the company is deemed to have actually incurred an amount of expenditure in respect of the acquisition of that asset which is equal to that amount of debt.[263]

Section 40CA was inserted by s 71(1) of the Taxation Laws Amendment Act 22 of 2012 with effect from 1 January 2013 and applies in respect of acquisitions made on or after that date.

Provisions applicable to particular types of businesses

11.8.3.1 Farming

Farmers are liable to tax at rates applicable to the type of taxpayer and taxable income is determined in the manner set out in the First Schedule to the Act. Under provisions of the First Schedule farmers must account for the value of livestock and agricultural produce at the beginning and at the end of the year of assessment.[264] The Act requires that livestock be valued using the so-called 'standard values' as promulgated by regulation in the *Government Gazette* from time to time. The standard value is a relatively low value compared to the market value of livestock. The taxable income of a farmer is determined as the growth in the value of the livestock that has been held and not disposed of by the farmer during the year of assessment. Farmers include in income the value of livestock or produce held and not disposed of at the end of the year of assessment.[265] From this amount farmers are allowed a deduction of the livestock and produce held and not disposed of at the beginning of the year of assessment.[266]

The tax treatment for livestock or produce held and not disposed of continues for as long as the taxpayer holds and does not dispose of the livestock or produce, even if the taxpayer discontinues farming operations.[267]

CHAPTER 11

262 Section 40CA(1)*(a)*.
263 Section 40CA(1)*(b)*.
264 Paragraph 2 of the First Schedule.
265 Paragraph 2 of the First Schedule.
266 Paragraph 3(1) of the First Schedule.
267 Paragraph 3(2) of the First Schedule.

Where a farmer has incurred expenditure in respect of the acquisition of livestock or produce, the amount of the deduction is limited to an amount which, together with the value of livestock held and not disposed of by him or her at the beginning of such year, does not exceed the aggregate of the income received by or accrued to him or her from farming during such year and the value of livestock held and not disposed of by him at the end of such year.[268] Any amount that has been disallowed is carried forward and deemed to be expenditure incurred by the farmer in respect of the acquisition of livestock during the succeeding year of assessment.[269]

Farmers are also allowed a special deduction for expenditure incurred in respect of specific farming preparations and maintenance, some of which are of a capital nature such as *(a)* the eradication of noxious plants and alien invasive vegetation; *(b)* the prevention of soil erosion; *(c)* dipping tanks; *(d)* dams, irrigation schemes, boreholes and pumping plants; *(e)* fences; *(f)* the erection of, or extensions, additions or improvements (other than repairs) to, buildings used in connection with farming operations, other than those used for domestic purposes; *(g)* the planting of trees, shrubs or perennial plants for the production of grapes or other fruit, nuts, tea, coffee, hops, sugar, vegetable oils or fibres, and the establishment of any area used for the planting of such trees, shrubs or plants; and *(h)* the building of roads and bridges used in connection with farming operations.[270]

Any amount received by or accrued to a farmer in respect of the disposal of any plantation is deemed not to be a receipt or accrual of a capital nature and forms part of such farmer's gross income.[271] This deeming provision applies whether such plantation is disposed of separately or with the land on which it is growing.

The recoupment provisions of s 8(4)*(e)* do not apply to wear and tear allowances in terms of s 11*(e)* that are subsequently recovered by farmers.[272]

11.8.3.2 Mining

Mining companies are, as a general matter, taxed at the normal corporate tax rate of 28%. However, gold mining companies pay tax at a rate determined using a prescribed formula which takes account, inter alia, of the company's profitability. Dividends declared by mining companies are subject to a dividend withholding tax under general rules. Special allowances apply for mining companies in lieu of the general allowances.[273] Taxpayers undertaking mining operations are allowed to deduct any expenditure incurred on prospecting

---

[268] Paragraph 8(1) of the First Schedule.
[269] Paragraph 8(2) of the First Schedule.
[270] Paragraph 12(1) of the First Schedule.
[271] Paragraph 14(1) of the First Schedule.
[272] Paragraph 12(1B)*(b)*.
[273] General allowances are provided by ss 11*(e)*, *(f)*, *(gA)*, *(gC)*, *(o)*, 12D, 12DA, 12F and 13*quin*.

operations in respect of any area located within South Africa as well as any expenditure that is incidental to such operations.[274]

A special rule also applies in relation to trading stock for mining operations. Trading stock related to mining operations includes anything acquired during the course of mining operations by a taxpayer for the purposes of extraction, processing, separation, refining, beneficiation, manufacture, sale or exchange by the taxpayer or on the taxpayer's behalf.[275]

Revenue expenditure of mining operations is deductible under the general deduction provisions contained in the Act.[276] Capital costs on the other hand are deductible in terms of the special capital expenditure rules. In terms of this provision, capital expenditure incurred is deductible in full in the year in which that expenditure is incurred.[277]

The following constitutes capital expenditure:[278]

- expenditure on shaft sinking and mine equipment (other than interest or finance charges);
- expenditure on development, general administration and management prior to the commencement of production or during any period of non-production. This includes any interest and other charges payable after 31 December 1950, on loans utilised for mining purposes;
- a capital allowance in the case of qualifying gold mines and natural oil mines; and
- expenditure the payment of which has become due on or after 1 July 1989 in respect of the acquisition, erection, construction, improvement or laying out of various assets qualifying for partial annual redemption.

11.8.3.3 Small businesses

The Act provides for the special tax treatment of small businesses.[279] This special treatment is an incentive for small businesses to allow them to flourish by providing a preferential tax treatment for such businesses. Broadly, a small business corporation is a company, which includes a close corporation or a co-operative, which satisfies the following four criteria:[280]

- its gross income for the year of assessment does not exceed R14 million;
- none of its shareholders, at any time during the year of assessment of the company, holds any shares or has any interest in the equity of any other company (subject to specific exclusions);

274 Section 15*(b)*.
275 Section 15A*(a)*.
276 Section 11*(a)* read with s 23*(g)*.
277 Section 15*(a)* read with s 36.
278 Section 36(11) definition of 'capital expenditure'.
279 Section 12E.
280 Section 12E(4)*(a)* definition of 'small business corporation'.

- not more than 20% of the total of all receipts and accruals (other than those of a capital nature) and all the capital gains of the company, close corporation or co-operative consists collectively of investment income and income from the rendering of a personal service; and
- such company is not a 'personal service' provider as defined in the Fourth Schedule.

Qualifying small business corporations are allowed to deduct the full cost of any plant or machinery owned by the small business corporation or acquired in terms of an instalment sale agreement and used in the process of manufacture in the first year that the plant or machinery is brought into use.[281] With regard to all other assets to which s 11*(e)* wear and tear allowance would apply, small corporations can elect to apply s 11*(e)* or deduct 50%, 30% and 20% in the first, second and third years, respectively, in which the asset is used by the small business corporation.[282] In addition, qualifying taxpayers pay a preferential rate of tax.

11.8.3.4 Micro businesses

In order to ease the tax administrative burden for businesses with low income, the Act provides for a presumptive tax system for certain businesses, referred to as micro businesses.[283] Broadly, a micro business is an individual or company that satisfies the following criteria:[284]

- the qualifying turnover of that person for the year of assessment does not exceed R1 million;
- none of the shareholders, at any time during the year of assessment of the company, holds any shares or has any interest in the equity of any other company (subject to specific exclusions);
- where the micro business is a company, all its shareholders are natural persons;
- less than 20% of that person's total receipts during that year of assessment consists of income from the rendering of a professional service for natural persons and the aggregate of income from the rendering of a professional service and investment income in the case of a company;
- the total amount of all its receipts from the disposal of immovable property and capital assets for the tax year and two immediately preceding years do not exceed R1,5 million;
- its year of assessment ends on the last day of February; and
- such company is not a 'personal service' provider or 'labour broker' as defined in the Fourth Schedule.

---

281 Section 12E(1).
282 Section 12E(1A).
283 See Explanatory Memorandum to the Revenue Laws Amendment Bill, 2008 56–67.
284 Part II of the Sixth Schedule.

The taxable turnover of a registered micro business in relation to any year of assessment consists of all amounts not of a capital nature received by that registered micro business during that year of assessment from carrying on business activities in the Republic, less any amounts refunded to any person by that registered micro business in respect of goods or services supplied by that registered micro business to that person during that year of assessment or any previous year of assessment.[285]

Micro businesses are taxed on their taxable turnover at a progressive scale of up to 6%. No deductions are allowed. However, taxpayers can elect to be taxed using the normal accounting system.

11.8.3.5 Co-operatives

A co-operative is defined in the Co-operatives Act as an 'autonomous association of persons united voluntarily to meet their common economic and social needs and aspirations through a jointly owned and democratically controlled enterprise organised and operated on co-operative principles'.[286] Co-operatives are included in the definition of 'company' in the Act and are treated for tax purposes as companies and are subject to the particular provisions contained in s 27 of the Act.[287] Thus, qualifying co-operatives do benefit from the small business corporation incentive outlined above.[288]

11.8.3.6 Insurers

Insurance companies are subject to tax in terms of the general rules at the 28% corporate income tax rate. However, due to the unique nature of the insurance business, special rules apply to the calculation of the taxable income of insurers. Different rules apply to short-term insurers and long-term insurers.

(a) Short-term insurers

Prior to the Taxation Laws Amendment Act 22 of 2012, short-term insurers were allowed a deduction from the sum of all premiums received, the amount of liability incurred on any premiums for reinsurance and the amount of liability incurred in respect of claims during the year of assessment, less the value of any claims recovered or recoverable.[289] In order to avoid the multiple deduction of the same expense, no deduction was allowed in terms of s 11*(a)* in respect of any liability incurred in respect of reinsurance premiums and any claims in respect of the insurance business.[290]

Short-term insurers are required to include premiums in gross income. Advance premium receipts will be ignored for tax purposes and are only included in the

CHAPTER 11

[285] Paragraph 5 of the Sixth Schedule.
[286] Section 1 of the Co-operatives Act 14 of 2005 definition of 'co-operative'.
[287] Section 1 definition of 'company'.
[288] Section 12E.
[289] Section 28(2).
[290] Section 28(6)*(a)*.

insurer's gross income on the date of commencement of the risk cover under the policy.[291] Amounts recoverable by an insurer via rights of subrogation are included in the gross income of the insurer when the amount is received by the insurer.[292] The insurer may deduct expenses under the general deduction formula in respect of claims only when the expenses are actually paid and not when they are merely incurred.[293] Furthermore, amounts of expenditure actually incurred by an insurer in respect of a refund of a premium may only be deducted to the extent that the amount of the premium was included in a short-term insurer's gross income.[294] This new regime comes into effect on 1 January 2014.

(b) Long-term insurers

Long-term insurers are taxable in terms of the general provisions of the Act.[295] In addition, special provisions apply to long-term insurers. Long-term insurers are required to establish and maintain four separate funds for tax purposes.[296] This adheres to the trustee principle, whereby the insurer is taxed on the basis that it is holding the funds owned by it as a trustee for the various types of policyholders. These funds are: 1) untaxed policyholder fund; 2) individual policyholder fund; 3) company policyholder fund; and 4) corporate fund.[297]

Income accrued to or received by a long-term insurer from assets held by the insurer in, or business conducted by it in relation to, its untaxed policyholder fund is exempt from tax.[298] A special formula-based methodology is used to determine the taxable income of a long-term insurer in respect of the insurer's individual policyholder fund, company policyholder fund and corporate fund.[299]

The taxable income derived by an insurer in respect of its individual policyholder fund, its company policyholder fund and its corporate fund is determined separately in accordance with the provisions of the Act as if each such fund had been a separate taxpayer. Furthermore, the individual policyholder fund, company policyholder fund, untaxed policyholder fund and corporate fund are deemed to be separate companies that are connected persons in relation to each other.[300] A long-term insurer is required to recalculate the value of liabilities in relation to each of its policyholder funds as at the end of the tax year within four months after the end of the tax year.[301]

---

291 Section 28(2)*(a)*.
292 Section 28(2)*(e)*.
293 Section 28(2)*(d)*.
294 Section 28(2)*(b)*.
295 Section 29A(2).
296 Section 29A(3).
297 Section 29A(4).
298 Section 29A(9).
299 Section 29A(11).
300 Section 29A(10). The deeming provision with regard to the funds being connected persons applies only for purposes of sub-ss (6), (7) and (8) and ss 9B, 20, 24I, 24J, 24K, 24L and 26A and the Eighth Schedule.
301 Section 29A(7).

Section 29B of the Act required long-term insurers to recognise immediately all unrealised gains and losses arising before 1 March 2012 in respect of policyholder funds. This followed the increase in the capital gains tax rate and ensures that pre-1 March 2012 capital appreciation will only be taxed at the historic 7,5%.[302]

11.8.3.7 Taxation of Real Estate Investment Trusts ('REITs') – s 25BB

The Taxation Laws Amendment Act 22 of 2012 introduced rules regulating the taxation of Real Estate Investment Trusts ('REITs'), a concept which has been in existence in a number of other countries, such as the United States of America, Germany and the United Kingdom.

The rules may apply to qualifying entities in the property sector so that the rental derived is passed from the property company through to the ultimate investor who will pay tax on the distributions received from the REIT.

Section 1 of the Act introduced a definition of a REIT which refers to a company which is a resident and the shares of which are listed on an exchange as defined in s 1 of the Securities Services Act 36 of 2004, and licensed under s 10 of that Act and as shares in a REIT as defined in the JSE Limited Listings Requirements.

The REIT regime is aimed at ensuring that the investors in property unit trusts and variable loan stock companies are treated in the same manner for tax purposes. It was pointed out above that s 11*(s)* of the Act has been repealed and effectively replaced by the rules contained in s 25BB of the Act.

Section 25BB allows for a REIT, or a controlled property company that is a resident, to deduct the qualifying distribution declared or incurred by the REIT or a controlled property company that is a subsidiary, as defined in International Financial Reporting Standards 10 of IFRS, of a REIT. A 'qualifying distribution' is defined in s 25BB(1) as any dividend, excluding a dividend referred to in para *(b)* of the definition of dividend, declared, or interest incurred in respect of a debenture forming part of a property linked unit, during the year of assessment where more than 75% of the gross income derived by the REIT, a controlled property company or an associated company in the preceding year of assessment comprises rental income. Section 25BB defines an associated company as a company in which a REIT or a controlled property company holds 20% or more of the equity shares or linked units.

The deduction is limited to the taxable income of the REIT or controlled property company before the deduction of the qualifying distribution and the amount of taxable capital gain included in taxable income under s 26A of the Act.

[302] This amendment was brought in by s 63 of the Taxation Laws Amendment Act 22 of 2012.

It must be noted that s 25BB prohibits a REIT or a controlled property company from deducting any allowance that would otherwise have been deductible in terms of ss 11*(g)*, 13, 13*bis*, 13*ter*, 13*quat*, 13*quin* and 13*sex*.

The section took effect on 1 April 2013 and applies in respect of years of assessment commencing on or after that date.

Chapter 12

Administration, returns, assessments, dispute resolution and collection of tax

12.1 INTRODUCTION

The purpose of this chapter is to discuss the administration of the Income Tax Act 58 of 1962 ('the Act'), returns, assessments, dispute resolution procedures and the collection of tax. Most of these provisions were previously contained in the Act but are now contained in the Tax Administration Act 28 of 2011 ('the TAA'), which became effective on 1 October 2012. The Rules of the Tax Court were published on 11 July 2014[1] and is effective from that date. These rules were promulgated in terms of s 103 of the TAA.[2] Rule 42(1) provides that if

[1] GN 550 in *GG* 37819 of 11 July 2014.

[2] At the publication of the previous edition of this book, the Rules published in terms of s 107 of the Income Tax Act were still applicable.

the Tax Court Rules do not provide for a procedure in the Tax Court, the most appropriate High Court Rule may be utilised to the extent that it is consistent with the TAA and the Rules of the Tax Court.

12.2 ADMINISTRATION OF THE ACT

The Commissioner for the South African Revenue Service ('the Commissioner') is responsible for carrying out the provisions of the Act.[3] The Commissioner may exercise or perform the powers and the duties imposed upon him by the Act personally or delegate them to an officer or a person under his control, direction or supervision. The South African Revenue Service ('SARS') is responsible for the administration of the TAA, under the control or direction of the Commissioner.[4] If the TAA is silent on the administration of a tax Act and it is specifically provided for in a tax Act, the specific tax Act applies.[5] Should there be any inconsistency between the TAA and a specific tax Act, the specific tax Act prevails.[6] The powers and duties of SARS and SARS officials are set out in ss 6, 9 and 10 of the TAA.

SARS is defined in s 1 of the Act to mean the South African Revenue Service established by s 2 of the South African Revenue Service Act 34 of 1997. SARS deals with the affairs of all taxpayers, resident and non-resident, who fall within the ambit of the Act.

Certain decisions, which are listed in s 3(4) of the Act, are subject to objection and appeal.[7] However, these are not the only decisions of the Commissioner or provisions of the Act which are subject to objection and appeal. In some instances, the provisions of a section itself state that it is subject to objection and appeal.

Administrative action by the Commissioner which is not made subject to objection and appeal may be reviewed by a competent court. In *South Atlantic Jazz Festival v Commissioner for South African Revenue Service*[8] the court held that the position as set out in *Kommissaris van Binnelandse Inkomste v Transvaal Suikerkorporasie*[9] is correct, namely that the Tax Court may, for instance, as part of considering an appeal to the Tax Court, set aside a decision taken by SARS in terms of s 16(2)*(f)* of the Value-Added Tax Act 89 of 1991. The Tax Court will in that instance review the decision of the Commissioner. This power that is exercised by the Tax Court is, however, done as part of considering the appeal to the Tax Court. In *Jazz Festival* the court further held that the Tax Court must be taken to have been invested with all the powers that are inherently necessary for it to fulfill its expressly provided functions.

---

3 Section 2(1) of the Act.
4 Section 3(1) of the Tax Administration Act 28 of 2011 (the 'TAA').
5 Section 4(2) of the TAA.
6 Section 4(3) of the TAA.
7 Section 3(4) of the Act was amended by para 25 of Schedule 1 to the TAA.
8 77 SATC 254.
9 1985 (2) SA 668 (T).

12.3 CONFIDENTIALITY OF INFORMATION

Every person employed or engaged by the Commissioner in carrying out the provisions of the Act must preserve and aid in preserving secrecy with regard to all matters that may come to his or her knowledge in the performance of his or her duties.[10] Such person may not communicate any matter to any person whatsoever other than the taxpayer concerned or his or her lawful representative, nor give any other person, apart from the taxpayer or his or her duly authorised representative, access to any records of the taxpayer. There are, however, certain exceptions to these secrecy provisions in order, *inter alia*, to combat tax evasion and/or criminal activity.[11] It is for this reason that the Commissioner insists on a written power of attorney when a representative acts on behalf of a taxpayer, for instance, when he or she requests reasons for an assessment or lodges an objection on behalf of a taxpayer. The secrecy provisions are also applicable to the Tax Ombud.[12]

12.4 RETURNS

Returns are governed by chapter 4 of the TAA. A person who is required under a tax Act to submit a return, or voluntarily submits a return, must do so in the prescribed form and manner and by the date specified in the relevant tax Act. In the absence of a specified date, it must be submitted by the date specified by the Commissioner in the public notice requiring the submission.[13] SARS may extend the time period for filing a return in a particular case, in accordance with the procedures and criteria in policies published by the Commissioner. However, such an extension does not affect the deadline for paying the tax.[14]

A return must be signed by the taxpayer or by the taxpayer's duly authorised representative. A person's not receiving a return form does not affect the obligation of the taxpayer to submit a return. Returns and payments required to be made in terms of the TAA must be submitted in a form and manner (including electronically) and at such place as the Commissioner may prescribe.[15]

The Commissioner must annually give public notice that all persons who are personally or in a representative capacity liable to taxation under a tax Act are required by the Commissioner to submit returns within the period prescribed in that notice, or a longer period as the Commissioner may allow.[16]

[10] Section 67 of the TAA; s 68 defines 'confidential information'.

[11] Sections 69, 70 and 71 of the TAA.

[12] The Office of the Tax Ombud is created and governed by the provisions of Part F of the TAA. The confidentiality provisions applicable to the Office of the Tax Ombud are contained in s 21 of the TAA.

[13] Section 25 of the TAA.

[14] Section 25(6) and (8) of the TAA.

[15] Section 25(3) and (4) of the TAA.

[16] Section 25 of the TAA.

A person who is required to render a return or has rendered a return must retain all records relevant to that return for a period of five years from the date upon which the Commissioner received the return. However, if a person lodges an objection or appeal against an assessment, he or she must retain all relevant records until that assessment becomes final.[17]

Persons that must render returns include companies and other persons, for instance persons who administer a collective investment scheme, and employers.[18]

In most instances, returns are submitted electronically via the SARS electronic filing system ('eFiling'). The eFiling system provides inter alia for submission of value-added tax (VAT) returns, PAYE returns and income tax returns.

12.5 ASSESSMENTS

Assessments are governed by chapter 8 of the TAA. Income tax is assessed on an annual basis in respect of the taxable income received by or accrued to any person during the period of assessment and is determined in accordance with the provisions of the Act. It is only at the end of the year of assessment that it is possible to determine the amounts received or accrued and the expenditure actually incurred during that year of assessment.[19]

12.5.1 Definition

'Assessment' is defined to have the meaning assigned to it under s 1 of the TAA[20] and includes a determination by the Commissioner of:

- any loss ranking for set-off;
- any assessed capital loss determined in terms of para 9 of the Eighth Schedule; or
- any amounts to be taken into account in the determination of tax payable on income in future years.

'Assessment' is defined in the TAA to mean 'the determination of the amount of a tax liability of refund, by way of self-assessment by the taxpayer or assessment by SARS'.[21]

Where the Commissioner issues an assessment as opposed to self-assessment, there must be a determination. In *Irvin & Johnson SA Ltd v CIR*[22] it was held that to constitute a 'determination', a mental act or process is required. What is required is at least a purposeful act, one whereby the document embodying

[17] Sections 29 and 32 of the TAA.
[18] Section 26 of the TAA.
[19] *Caltex Oil (SA) Ltd v SIR* 1975 (1) SA 665 (A), 37 SATC 1 at 11.
[20] Section 1 of the Act.
[21] Section 1 of the TAA.
[22] 1946 AD 483 at 486–7 and 494; 14 SATC 24 at 27–29 and 35–36.

the mental act is intended to be an assessment.[23] A 'simulated assessment' probably does not constitute an assessment.[24] The onus is on the Commissioner to prove that an assessment has been issued.[25] A letter issued by SARS could, in appropriate circumstances, constitute an assessment, even if it states in the letter that 'tax assessments will be issued to you in due course'.[26]

12.5.2 Date of assessment

'Date of assessment'[27] is defined to mean—

(a) in the case of an assessment by SARS, the date of the issue of the notice of assessment; or

(b) in the case of self-assessment by the taxpayer—

(i) if a return is required, the date that the return is submitted; or

(ii) if no return is required, the date of the last payment of the tax for the tax period or, if no payment was made in respect of the tax for the tax period, the effective date.

12.5.3 Original assessments

An original assessment is an assessment where a taxpayer is required to submit a return that does not incorporate a determination of the amount of a tax liability. SARS must issue an original assessment based on the return submitted by the taxpayer or other information available or obtained in respect of the taxpayer.[28] If a taxpayer is required to submit a return that incorporates a determination of the amount, the submission of the return is an original self-assessment of the tax liability.[29] If a tax Act requires a taxpayer to make a determination of an amount of tax liability but no return is required, the payment of the amount of tax due constitutes an original assessment.[30]

12.5.4 Return

'Return' is defined to mean 'a form, declaration, document or other manner of submitting information to SARS that incorporates a self-assessment or is the basis on which an assessment is to be made by SARS'.[31]

---

[23] *ITC 1740* 65 SATC 98 at 104.

[24] Ibid 105.

[25] Ibid 105.

[26] *CSARS v South African Custodial Services (Pty) Ltd* 2012 (1) SA 522 (SCA), 74 SATC 61 at 70 (paras 29–33).

[27] Section 1 of the TAA: 'effective date' is defined to have the meaning described in s 187(3), (4) and (5) of the TAA.

[28] Section 91(1) of the TAA.,

[29] Section 91(2) of the TAA.

[30] Section 91(3) of the TAA.

[31] Section 1 of the TAA.

12.5.5 Estimated assessments

The Commissioner is entitled to raise an estimated assessment if a person is in default in furnishing a required return or information about his or her taxable income or if the return or information furnished is incorrect or inadequate.[32] If a taxpayer is unable to submit an accurate return, the Commissioner and the taxpayer may agree, in writing, to the amount of taxable income and issue an assessment accordingly. Such assessment is not subject to objection and appeal.[33] The onus is on SARS, in terms of s 102(2) of the TAA, to prove that an estimated assessment is reasonable.

In *CIR v Taylor*[34] the Appellate Division (as it then was) held that when the Commissioner makes an estimated assessment he or she:

- cannot make an assessment 'on a purely imaginative estimate of the person's income';
- may have to justify his assessment before the special or other superior court; and
- must not act in an irresponsible manner in making his estimate.

In *Nondabula v Commissioner for South African Revenue Service and Another*[35] the court held that if an estimated assessment is issued in terms of s 95 of the TAA, there must also be compliance with s 96(1), which is couched in peremptory terms. Section 96(2) of the TAA states that SARS must give the person assessed 'a statement of the grounds for the assessment'.

The taxpayer must therefore be informed of the grounds for issuing the estimated assessment. If SARS fails to do this, any collection steps taken, for instance, appointing a third-party agent in terms of s 179 of the TAA, will be unlawful.[36]

12.5.6 Jeopardy assessments

In terms of s 94 of the TAA, SARS may make a jeopardy assessment in advance of the date on which the return is normally due. This may be done if the Commissioner is satisfied that it is necessary in order to secure the collection of tax that would otherwise be in jeopardy.

Section 94(2) of the TAA states that a review application may be made to the High Court on the grounds that:

- the amount of the jeopardy assessment is excessive; or
- there are no circumstances to justify the issuing of a jeopardy assessment.

If review proceedings are instituted, SARS bears the onus of proving that the making of the jeopardy assessment is reasonable under the circumstances.[37]

---

32 Section 95 of the TAA.
33 Section 95(3) of the TAA.
34 1936 AD 100, 8 SATC 19.
35 79 SATC 333.
36 *Nondabula v Commissioner for SARS* 79 SATC 333 para 22.
37 Section 94(3) of the TAA.

12.5.7 Additional assessments

The Commissioner is empowered and obliged to issue an additional assessment if SARS at any time is satisfied that an assessment does not reflect the correct application of a tax Act to the prejudice of SARS or the fiscus.[38]

12.5.8 Periods of limitation for issuance of assessments

In terms of s 99 of the TAA, SARS may not make an assessment:

- three years after the date of assessment of the original assessment;
- in the case of a self-assessment for which a return is required, five years after the date of assessment of the original assessment;
- in case of a self-assessment for which no return is required after the expiry of five years from the date of the last payment of the tax for the tax period or the effective date, if no payment was made in respect of the tax for the tax period;
- in the case of an additional assessment, if the:
  - amount which should have been assessed to tax was not so assessed, in accordance with a practice generally prevailing at the date of the assessment; or
  - full amount which should have been assessed was not assessed, in terms of a practice generally prevailing;
- in the case of a reduced assessment if the preceding assessment was made in accordance with the practice generally prevailing at the date of that assessment;
- in the case of a tax for which no return is required, if payment was made in accordance with the practice generally prevailing at the date of that payment; or
- in respect of a dispute that has been resolved, in terms of chapter 9 of the TAA.

The above periods do not apply if:

- in respect of assessments issued by SARS, the fact that the amount that should have been assessed to tax, was not so assessed is due to:
  - fraud;
  - misrepresentation; or
  - non-disclosure of material facts;
- in case of self-assessment, the fact that the full amount of tax chargeable was not so assessed, was due to:
  - fraud;
  - intentional or negligent misrepresentation;
  - intentional or negligent non-disclosure of material facts; or

CHAPTER 12

[38] Section 92 of the TAA.

    - the failure to submit a return or, if no return is required, the failure to make the required payment of tax; or
- the Commissioner and the taxpayer agree otherwise prior to the expiry of the three-year period.[39]

Holmes JA in *Natal Estates v SIR*[40] held that the Commissioner's satisfaction that the above factors or some of them are present is a substantive and far-reaching determination and has to be communicated to the taxpayer, at the latest at the hearing before the Tax Court.

In *SIR v Trow*[41] it was held that an additional assessment may only be raised if the Commissioner was satisfied that:

- there had been non-disclosure of material facts by the taxpayer; and
- the fact that the profit in question was not assessed to tax prior to the expiration of the relevant period of three years was due to non-disclosure, ie that the non-assessment was causally related to the non-disclosure of material facts.

Section 99 of the TAA does not require that the Commissioner be satisfied in respect of certain factors, which was the case with the now repealed s 79 of the Act, being the relevant section pronounced on by the *Natal Estates* case. The test in s 99 of the TAA is therefore objective and a question of law, which must be decided on the available facts.

The non-issuing of the assessment must have been caused by the fraud, misrepresentation or non-disclosure of material facts. If the Commissioner had the necessary information to be able to issue an assessment within the three-year period, but failed to do so, he cannot rely on the taxpayer's fraud, misrepresentation or non-disclosure.[42]

12.5.9 Reduced assessments

The Commissioner may issue a reduced assessment if:

- the taxpayer successfully disputed an assessment in terms of chapter 9 of the TAA;
- it is necessary to give effect to a settlement in terms of s 149 of the TAA;
- it is necessary to give effect to a judgment pursuant to an appeal and there is no further appeal or right to appeal;
- SARS is satisfied that there is an error in the assessment as a result of an undisputed error by:
    - SARS; or
    - the taxpayer in a return; or

---

39 Section 99(2) of the TAA.
40 1975 (4) SA 177 (A), 37 SATC 193.
41 1981 (4) SA 821 (A), 43 SATC 189 at 194.
42 *ITC 1776* 66 SATC 296 at 301.

- a senior SARS official is satisfied that an assessment was based on:
  - the failure to submit a return or submission of an incorrect return by a third party under s 26 or by an employer under a tax Act;
  - a processing error by SARS; or
  - a return fraudulently submitted by a person not authorised by the taxpayer.

SARS may issue a reduced assessment despite the fact that no objection has been lodged or appeal noted.[43]

12.5.10 Finality of assessments

In terms of s 100 of the TAA, an assessment is final if:

(a) an estimated assessment was issued in terms of s 95 and no return was submitted by the taxpayer or an agreed assessment was issued in terms of s 95(3) of the TAA;

(b) no objection has been made or an objection has been withdrawn;

(c) after a decision has been made on an objection, no notice of appeal has been filed;

(d) the dispute has been settled;

(e) an appeal has been determined by the Tax Board and there is no referral to the Tax Court;

(f) an appeal has been determined by a Tax Court and there is no further right of appeal; or

(g) an appeal has been determined by a higher court and there is no right of further appeal.

In respect of *(d)*, *(e)* and *(f)* described above, SARS may only issue additional assessments if there has been fraud, misrepresentation or non-disclosure of material facts, as envisaged in s 99 of the TAA.

12.5.11 Reasons for an assessment

A taxpayer who is aggrieved by an assessment may request reasons for the assessment.[44] Although a taxpayer is entitled to reasons for the assessment under the Promotion of Administrative Justice Act 3 of 2000 ('PAJA') the procedure provided for in the Rules of the Tax Court, promulgated under s 103 of the TAA, entitles the taxpayer to obtain reasons before he or she lodges an objection.

[43] Section 93 of the TAA.

[44] Rule 6 of the Rules promulgated under s 103 of the TAA.

12.5.12 Adequate reasons

The Commissioner must furnish the taxpayer with adequate reasons for the assessment. Adequate reasons have been held to mean:[45]

- The decision-maker is required to explain his or her decision in a way that will enable a person aggrieved to say, in effect, 'even though I do not agree with it, I now understand why the decision went against me; I am now in a position to decide whether that decision has involved any unwarranted finding of fact, or an error of law, which is worth challenging'.
- The decision-maker should set out his or her understanding of the relevant law, any findings of fact on which his or her conclusions depend (especially if those facts have been in dispute) and the reasoning process which led him or her to those conclusions.
- It must be done in clear and unambiguous language, not in vague generalities or the formal language of legislation.
- The appropriate length of the statement covering such matters will depend upon considerations such as the nature and importance of the decision, its complexity and the time available to formulate the statement.

12.5.13 Period within which reasons may be requested

The taxpayer may request reasons for the assessment within 30 days from the date of the assessment.[46] 'Day' is defined in the Rules of the Tax Court to mean 'business day' as defined in s 1 of the TAA. Section 1 of the TAA defines 'business day' to mean any day other than a Saturday, Sunday or public holiday and excludes the days between 16 December of a year and 15 January of the following year, both inclusive.[47] The 30-day period may be extended by the Commissioner for a period of not more than 45 days if the Commissioner is satisfied that reasonable grounds exist for the delay in complying with the 30-day period.[48]

If the Commissioner is of the opinion that adequate reasons have already been provided, the Commissioner must, within 30 days after receipt of the request for reasons, notify the taxpayer in writing that he is of this opinion and must also refer to the documents in which such reasons were provided.

Where the Commissioner is of the opinion that adequate reasons have not yet been provided, the Commissioner must provide written reasons for the assessment within 45 days after receipt of the request for reasons. Should the

[45] *Minister of Environmental Affairs and Tourism v Phambili Fisheries* 2003 (6) SA 407 (SCA) para 40 (which passage is taken from an Australian decision, *Ansett Transport Industries (Operations) (Pty) Ltd v Wraith* 1983 (48) ALR 500 507).

[46] Definition of 'date of assessment' in s 1 of the TAA.

[47] Section 1 of the TAA.

[48] Rule 6(3) of the Rules of the Tax Court.

Commissioner be of the opinion that more time is required due to exceptional circumstances, the complexity of the matter or the principle or the amount involved, the Commissioner must, before expiry of that 45-day period, inform the taxpayer that written reasons will be provided not later than 45 days after the date of expiry of the first 45-day period.[49]

The terms 'if the Commissioner is of the opinion' or 'if the Commissioner is satisfied', are often used in the Act and other tax Acts, for instance the Customs and Excise Act. It has been held that the Commissioner's satisfaction in respect of a certain issue is measured against an objective standard, ie what a reasonable person would have done in the same circumstances with the same relevant facts at his or her disposal.[50]

12.6 OBJECTION AGAINST AN ASSESSMENT

A taxpayer who is aggrieved by an assessment may object to the assessment.[51] The following decisions may be objected to and appealed against, in the same manner as an objection against an assessment:[52]

- a decision in terms of s 104(4) of the TAA – if extension of the time period within which an objection must be lodged is not granted by SARS;
- a decision under s 107(2) of the TAA not to extend the period for lodging an appeal; and
- any other decision that may be objected to or appealed against under a tax Act. Section 3(4) of the Income Tax Act, for example, contains a list of decisions against which objection may be made.

The objection must be lodged in the required manner in terms of rule 7 of the Rules of the Tax Court.

12.6.1 Time period for the lodging of an objection

A taxpayer who wants to object to an assessment must deliver his or her objection within 30 days after:

- in the case where the taxpayer requested reasons, the date of notice by the Commissioner that adequate reasons have been provided or the date that reasons were furnished by the Commissioner, as the case may be; or
- where no reasons were requested, the date of the assessment.[53]

CHAPTER 12

[49] Rule 6(5) – rule 6(7) of the Rules of the Tax Court.

[50] *Commissioner of Customs and Excise v Container Logistics (Pty) Ltd; Commissioner of Customs and Excise v Rennies Group Ltd t/a Renfreight* 1999 (3) SA 771 (SCA) 782G–784B.

[51] Section 104(1) of the TAA.

[52] Section 104(2) of the TAA.

[53] Rule 7(1) of the Rules of the Tax Court.

12.6.2 Extension of the time period

The Commissioner may extend the period within which objection must be made if the Commissioner is satisfied that reasonable grounds exist for the delay in lodging the objection. A senior SARS official may extend the period for the lodging of an objection for a period not exceeding 30 business days.[54] If exceptional circumstances exist which gave rise to the delay in lodging the objection, SARS may extend the period beyond the 30 days.[55]

The Commissioner may not extend the time period for the lodging of an objection where more than three years have lapsed from the date of assessment, or if the ground of objection is based on a change in a practice generally prevailing, which applied on the date of the assessment or decision.[56]

The relevant factors that the Commissioner should consider when deciding whether to extend the period for lodging of the objection include:[57]

- the prospects of success on the merits;
- the reasons for the delay;
- the period of the delay; and
- the balance of prejudice.

An application for extension of time should be well motivated, with sufficient information to enable the Commissioner to exercise his discretion. The prescribed form (form ADR1 or NOO) which is used when an objection is lodged normally does not have sufficient space for this and a taxpayer should rather attach to the form an annexure, setting out the reasons for requesting an extension of time.

Should the Commissioner not be willing to extend the time period for the lodging of the objection, the taxpayer may lodge an objection and appeal against such decision.[58] The court, considering such objection, will consider it afresh and will substitute its own decision for that of the Commissioner by taking into account all relevant factors.[59] In considering whether condonation should be granted or not, a court will try to do justice between the parties.[60]

12.6.3 The format of the objection

The objection must be in such form as may be prescribed by the Commissioner.[61] If a taxpayer is not signing the form himself or herself, but makes use of a

[54] Section 104(4) of the TAA.

[55] Section 104(5)*(a)* of the TAA.

[56] Section 104(5)*(b)* and *(c)* of the TAA.

[57] SARS Interpretation Note 15 of 8 November 2004; *General Accident Insurance Co SA Ltd v Zampelli* 1988 (4) SA 407 (C) 410.

[58] Section 104(2)*(a)* of the TAA.

[59] *Rand Ropes (Pty) Ltd v CIR* 1944 AD 142, 13 SATC 1; *CIR v Da Costa* 1985 (3) SA 768 (A), 47 SATC 87 at 94–95.

[60] *S v Yusuf* 1968 (2) SA 52 (A) 53G–54B.

[61] Section 104(3) of the TAA.

representative, that representative must attach to the objection a duly completed and signed power of attorney. An objection may also be lodged using the SARS eFiling system. The prescribed document is a notice of objection (NOO). Rule 7(2)*(c)* of the Rules of the Tax Court states that if SARS's eFiling service is not used, then the taxpayer must specify an address where he or she will accept delivery of SARS's decision.

12.6.4 The content of an objection

Rule 7(2) of the Rules of the Tax Court states that a taxpayer who lodges an objection must:

- complete the prescribed form in full; and
- specify the grounds of the objection in detail, including:
  - the part or specific amount of the disputed assessment objected to;
  - which of the grounds of assessment are disputed; and
  - delivery of the documents required to substantiate the grounds of objection that the taxpayer has not previously delivered to SARS for purposes of the disputed assessment.

12.7 THE COMMISSIONER'S DECISION IN RESPECT OF THE OBJECTION

If the taxpayer delivers an objection that does not comply with the requirements of the TAA and the Rules of the Tax Court, the Commissioner may inform the taxpayer by notice, within 30 days, that he does not accept the objection. The taxpayer may then within 20 days submit an amended objection.[62]

If the Commissioner is satisfied that the taxpayer has not furnished all the information, documents or things required to decide on the taxpayer's objection, the Commissioner may, not later than 30 days after receipt of the objection, notify the taxpayer accordingly and request him or her in writing to deliver the information, documents or things specified in that notice.[63] The taxpayer must, within 30 days after the date of the notice referred to above, deliver the information, documents or things requested. The 30-day period which the taxpayer has to deliver the additional information, documents or things may be extended by another 20 days by the Commissioner if there are reasonable grounds.[64]

The Commissioner must, on receipt of the objection, within 60 days:

- disallow the objection or allow the objection either in whole or in part;[65]

[62] Rule 7(4) and 7(5) of the Rules of the Tax Court.
[63] Rule 8 of the Rules of the Tax Court.
[64] Rule 8(3) of the Rules of the Tax Court.
[65] Section 106(2) of the TAA.

- if the objection is allowed either in whole or in part, the assessment must be altered accordingly; and
- notify the taxpayer of the decision of the Commissioner.[66]

If the Commissioner requested further documents and information in terms of rule 8, the Commissioner's decision in respect of the objection must be delivered to the taxpayer within 45 days. In terms of rule 9(2), SARS may extend the 60-day period with a further 45 days.

The notice informing the taxpayer of the Commissioner's decision in respect of his or her objection must state the basis for the decision and a summary of the procedures for appeal.[67]

12.7.1 Test cases

If a senior SARS official considers that the determination of the objection or appeal is likely to be determinative of a substantial number of other similar matters, the official may:

- designate that objection or appeal as a test case; and
- stay the other objections or appeals by reason of the taking of a test case on a similar objection or appeal before the Tax Court.[68]

12.8 APPEAL AGAINST AN ASSESSMENT OR DECISION

A taxpayer that is entitled to object to an assessment and who is dissatisfied with the decision of the Commissioner, ie when the objection is disallowed, may appeal against that decision.[69]

In the notice of appeal the taxpayer must specify in detail:

- in respect of which grounds of objection referred to in rule 7 the taxpayer is appealing;
- the grounds for disputing the basis of the decision to disallow the objection; and
- any new ground on which the taxpayer is appealing.

In terms of rule 10(3), the taxpayer may not appeal on a ground that constitutes a new objection against a part or amount of the disputed assessment not objected to under rule 7.

---

66 Section 106(40 of the TAA.
67 Section 106(5) of the TAA.
68 Section 106(6) of the TAA.
69 Section 107(1) of the TAA.

12.8.1 Time period

The taxpayer must lodge a notice of appeal within 30 days after the date of the notice informing him or her that his or her objection has not been allowed or has been partly allowed.[70] A senior SARS official may extend the period within which an appeal may be lodged for 21 days if he or she is satisfied that reasonable grounds exist for the delay, or up to 45 days if exceptional circumstances exist that justify an extension beyond 21 days.[71]

If SARS decides not to extend the time period for lodging the appeal, the taxpayer may lodge an objection against that decision not to extend the time period.[72] If that objection is also disallowed by SARS, then the taxpayer may approach the Tax Court for an extension of the period to lodge a notice of appeal. The taxpayer may bring an application to the Tax Court for an order extending the time period for lodging the notice of appeal.[73]

12.9 ALTERNATIVE DISPUTE RESOLUTION

Where the taxpayer has indicated in his or her notice of appeal that he or she wishes to make use of the Alternative Dispute Resolution process ('ADR'), the Commissioner must inform the taxpayer within twenty days of receipt of the notice of appeal whether he is of the opinion that the matter is appropriate for ADR. The ADR process may only be used if there is mutual agreement between the taxpayer and SARS.[74]

12.9.1 Facilitator

If the ADR process is followed, the Commissioner may appoint a facilitator if the parties agree thereto.[75] The person may be employed by SARS or may be an outside party, for instance a retired judge. The taxpayer, the Commissioner and the facilitator may agree, at the commencement of the proceedings, that if no agreement or settlement is ultimately reached between the parties, the facilitator may make a written recommendation at the conclusion of the proceedings.[76] The facilitator must deliver his or her recommendation within 30 days after the termination of the proceedings. A recommendation by a facilitator is not admissible during any subsequent proceedings unless it is required by the Tax Court for purposes of deciding whether a costs order should be granted in terms of s 130 of the TAA.[77]

[70] Rule 10 (1) of the Rules of the Tax Court.
[71] Section 107(2) of the TAA.
[72] Section 104(2)*(b)* of the TAA.
[73] Rule 52(2)*(e)* of the Rules of the Tax Court.
[74] Section 107(5) of the TAA.
[75] Rule 16(2) of the Rules of the Tax Court.
[76] Rule 21(1) of the Rules of the Tax Court.
[77] Rule 21(2) and (3) of the Rules of the Tax Court.

12.9.2 Representation

The taxpayer may be represented by a representative if SARS so agrees. The taxpayer must, however, be personally present or participate by telephone or video conference.[78]

12.9.3 Confidentiality of proceedings

Representations made or documents tendered to the facilitator in confidence by a party during the ADR process must be kept by the facilitator in confidence and not be disclosed to the other party except with the consent of the party that disclosed the information.[79] ADR proceedings are not recorded and any representation made or document tendered in the course of the proceedings is made or tendered without prejudice and may not be tendered in subsequent proceedings as evidence, except:

- with knowledge and consent of the party who made the representation or tendered the document;
- where such representation or document is already known to or in possession of that party;
- where such representation or document is obtained by that party otherwise than in terms of the ADR proceedings;[80] or
- where a senior SARS official is satisfied that the representation or document is fraudulent.

12.9.4 Nature of the process

The ADR process is one of mediation in which the facilitator assists the parties to try to reach a settlement. The facilitator, however, does not have the authority to make an award. If a settlement is reached, SARS will make such settlement subject to approval by its Tax Appeals Committee (TAC). The taxpayer is not entitled to be present when the matter is presented to the TAC, which creates the impression that the ADR process is not a transparent one. The taxpayer may, however, request that he or she be allowed to be present at the presentation to the TAC.

12.9.5 Resolution of dispute by agreement

If a dispute is resolved during the ADR proceedings, either in whole or in part, such agreement must be reduced to writing.[81] Both parties must sign this agreement. If not all the issues in dispute are resolved, the written agreement must state which issues are resolved and which issues remain in dispute. The settlement agreement may also be made an order of court.[82]

---

[78] Rule 20(3) of the Rules of the Tax Court.
[79] Rule 22(1) of the Rules of the Tax Court.
[80] Rule 22(3) of the Rules of the Tax Court.
[81] Rule 23(1) and (2) of the Rules of the Tax Court.
[82] Rule 23(2)*(d)* of the Rules of the Tax Court.

Where such a settlement agreement is concluded, SARS must issue an assessment to give effect to the agreement within 45 days after the date of the last party signing the agreement.

If the appellant wishes to pursue the appeal on the unresolved issues to the Tax Board or the Tax Court, the appellant must give notice to that effect to the clerk or registrar of the Tax Court within 15 days of the date of the settlement agreement.[83]

12.10 APPEALS TO THE TAX BOARD

12.10.1 Jurisdiction

An appeal may be heard by the Tax Board where:

- the amount of tax in dispute does not exceed the amount fixed by the Minister from time to time in the *Government Gazette*, currently an amount of R1 million;[84] and
- a senior SARS official and the appellant (taxpayer) so agree.[85]

12.10.2 Constitution of the Tax Board

The Tax Board consists of an advocate or attorney who is the chairperson. If the chairperson, after considering any representations by a senior SARS official or the taxpayer, considers it necessary, an accountant and a representative of the commercial community may also be appointed.[86] Chairpersons are appointed by the Minister in conjunction with the Judge President of the relevant High Court division to a panel and a chairperson is selected from that panel.[87]

12.10.3 Location

The Commissioner determines the places for hearing of appeals by the Tax Board. An appeal is heard at a place closest to the taxpayer's residence, unless a senior SARS official and the taxpayer agree that the appeal be heard at another place.[88]

12.10.4 Procedure

Subject to the procedure provided for in the Rules of the Tax Court, the procedure followed before the Tax Board is determined by the chairperson.[89]

83 Rule 23(4) of the Rules of the Tax Court.
84 GN 1196 in *GG* 39490 of 17 December 2015.
85 Section 109(1) of the TAA.
86 Section 110(1)*(b)* of the TAA.
87 Section 111(1) of the TAA.
88 Section 109(3) of the TAA.
89 The procedure provided for by the Rules are contained in rule 27 and 28 of the Rules of the Tax Court.

The procedure is normally the same as that followed in the High Court or magistrate's court. The Tax Board is not a forum of record and the proceedings may not be recorded in any way.[90]

12.10.5 Representation

A senior SARS official must appear at the hearing for SARS. The taxpayer, if a natural person, must appear in person and, if a non-natural person, must be represented by the representative taxpayer. If a third party prepared the taxpayer's return which relates to the assessment or decision before the Tax Board, the third party may appear on behalf of the taxpayer.[91] The appellant (taxpayer) may, together with the notice of appeal or within a further period as determined by the chairperson, request permission to be represented at the hearing otherwise than by himself or by the representative taxpayer. This representation may be in the form of a legal practitioner, such as an advocate or an attorney.[92]

12.10.6 Failure to appear

If the taxpayer fails to appear at the hearing of the matter, the Tax Board may confirm the assessment on proof that the appellant was furnished with a notice of the sitting of the Tax Board.[93] The taxpayer may thereafter not request that the matter be referred to the Tax Court.[94] Similarly, if the senior SARS official fails to appear before the Tax Board at the time and place set for the hearing, the Tax Board may allow the appellant's appeal.[95] SARS may thereafter not refer the appeal to the Tax Court.[96]

12.10.7 Decision

The chairperson must deliver a written judgment within 60 business days after the conclusion of the hearing.[97] The decision of the Board is final and conclusive unless the taxpayer or the Commissioner is not satisfied with the decision of the Board, in which event either party may refer the appeal to the Tax Court.[98] If an appeal is referred from the Tax Board to the Tax Court, the Tax Court will hear the appeal *de novo*.[99]

---

[90] Section 113 of the TAA.
[91] Section 113(5)–(7) of the TAA.
[92] Section 113(8) of the TAA.
[93] Section 113(9) of the TAA.
[94] Section 113(10) of the TAA.
[95] Section 113(11) of the TAA.
[96] Section 113(12) of the TAA.
[97] Section 114 of the TAA.
[98] Section 115(1) of the TAA.
[99] Section 115(2) of the TAA.

12.11 APPEALS TO THE TAX COURT

Appeals to the Tax Court are governed by ss 116–132 of the TAA and the Rules of the Tax Court. Although the proceedings are referred to as an appeal, it is a misnomer, as the proceedings actually constitute a trial. In this regard Kriegler J observed in *Metcash Trading Ltd v CSARS*:[100]

> The Commissioner is not a judicial officer and assessments and concomitant decisions by the Commissioner are administrative, not judicial, actions; from which it follows that challenges to such actions before the special court or board are not appeals in the forensic sense of the word. They are proceedings in terms of a statutory mechanism specifically created for the reconsideration of this particular category of administrative decision – and appropriate corrective action – by a specialist tribunal.

12.11.1 Not a public hearing

The Tax Court sittings are not public. The President of the Tax Court may, in exceptional circumstances, allow a person to attend, but only after considering representations by SARS and the taxpayer in this regard.[101]

12.11.2 Representation

A senior SARS official may appear at a hearing of an appeal before the Tax Court and a taxpayer may be represented by his or her authorised representative.[102]

12.11.3 Constitution of Tax Court

A Tax Court consists of a judge of the High Court, an accountant and a representative of the commercial community.[103] A special Tax Court may be constituted in terms of s 118(5) of the TAA. A special court consists of three judges or acting judges of the High Court and the two assessors. This may be done if the amount in dispute exceeds R50 million or SARS and the appellant jointly apply to the Judge President.[104] If an appeal to the Tax Court involves a matter of law or is an interlocutory application or an application in a procedural matter, the President of the court, sitting alone, must decide the appeal without the assessors.[105] The President of the court alone decides whether a matter for decision involves a matter of fact or a matter of law.[106]

CHAPTER 12

[100] 2001 (1) SA 1109 (CC) 1130.
[101] Section 124 of the TAA.
[102] Section 125 of the TAA.
[103] Section 118 of the TAA.
[104] Section 118(5) of the TAA.
[105] Section 118(3) of the TAA.
[106] Section 118(4) of the TAA.

12.11.4 Pleadings

The proceedings in the Tax Court are facilitated by pleadings, which consist of the statement of grounds of assessment and opposing appeal,[107] which is filed by the Commissioner, and the statement of grounds of appeal,[108] which is filed by the taxpayer. SARS may, after delivery of the statement of grounds of appeal, deliver a reply.[109] The issues in any appeal to the Tax Court will be those defined in the statement of grounds of assessment and opposing appeal, read with the statement of grounds of appeal, and the reply, if any is filed.[110]

12.11.5 Statement of grounds of assessment

12.11.5.1 Time period

The Commissioner must deliver his or her statement of grounds of assessment and opposing appeal within 45 days after delivery of:

- the documents required by SARS under rule 10(4);
- if ADR proceedings were followed, the notice by the appellant in terms of rule 24(4) or 25(3) that the matter be referred to the Tax Court;
- if the matter was decided by the Tax Court, the notice of the *de novo* referral to the Tax Court; or
- in any other case, the notice of appeal under rule 10.[111]

12.11.5.2 Content

The statement of grounds of assessment and opposing appeal must be in writing and signed by the Commissioner. It must set out in clear and concise terms:

- the consolidated grounds of the disputed assessment;
- which of the facts or legal grounds in the notice of appeal under rule 10 are admitted and which of those facts or legal grounds are opposed; and
- the material facts and legal grounds upon which SARS relies in opposing the appeal.[112]

SARS may not include in the statement of grounds of assessment and opposing appeal a ground that constitutes a novation of the whole of the factual or legal basis of the disputed assessment or which requires the issue of a revised assessment.[113]

---

[107] Rule 31 of the Rules of the Tax Court.
[108] Rule 32 of the Rules of the Tax Court.
[109] Rule 33 of the Rules of the Tax Court.
[110] Rule 34 of the Rules of the Tax Court.
[111] Rule 31(1) of the Rules of the Tax Court.
[112] Rule 31(2) of the Rules of the Tax Court.
[113] Rule 31(3) of the Rules of the Tax Court.

12.11.6 Statement of grounds of appeal

12.11.6.1 Time period

The taxpayer must, within 45 days after delivery by the Commissioner of the statement of grounds of assessment, deliver his or her statement of grounds of appeal.[114]

12.11.6.2 Content

The statement of grounds of appeal must be in writing and signed by the appellant or his or her representative and must set out clearly and concisely:[115]

- the grounds upon which the appellant appeals;
- which of the facts or the legal grounds in the statement under rule 31 are admitted and which of those facts or legal grounds are opposed; and
- the material facts and legal grounds upon which the appellant relies for the appeal and opposing the facts or legal grounds in the statement under rule 31.

The statement of grounds of appeal is a combination of a particulars of claim and a plea, as the taxpayer must set out his or her grounds of appeal and plead to the Commissioner's statement of grounds of assessment in the same document.

The appellant (taxpayer) may not include in the statement of grounds of appeal a statement that constitutes a new ground of objection against a part or amount of the disputed assessment not objected to under rule 7.[116]

In *ITC 1912*[117] the court held that an appellant (taxpayer) may raise a new ground of objection in its statement of grounds of appeal, provided that it relates to a part or an amount in the assessment that was placed in dispute by the objections in terms of rule 7.[118]

12.11.7 Reply

SARS may within 20 days after delivery of the statement of grounds of appeal reply to any new grounds, material facts or applicable law set out in the grounds of appeal.[119]

CHAPTER 12

[114] Rule 32(1) of the Rules of the Tax Court.
[115] Rule 32(2) of the Rules of the Tax Court.
[116] Rule 32(3) of the Rules of the Tax Court.
[117] 80 SATC 417 paras 29–31.
[118] *ITC 1912* 80 SATC 417 para 30.
[119] Rule 33 of the Rules of the Tax Court.

12.12 OTHER PROCEDURAL RULES OF THE TAX COURT

12.12.1 Amendments

The Commissioner and the taxpayer are entitled to amend their pleadings if they agree in writing to the amendment thereof.[120] If the parties cannot agree on an amendment, the party that wishes to amend his or her pleading may apply on notice for leave to amend his or her pleading.[121] A judge sitting alone will hear such application. In general, a court will lean towards granting an amendment and will only refuse an amendment if the prejudice caused to the other party cannot be addressed by a cost order.

12.12.2 Discovery

The appellant (taxpayer) may, within 10 days after delivery of the rule 31 statement (grounds of assessment), request SARS to make discovery of any documents material to the grounds of assessment to the extent that such document is required by the appellant (taxpayer) to formulate his or her statement of grounds of appeal (rule 32 statement).[122]

SARS may, within 10 days after delivery of the statement of grounds of appeal (rule 32 statement), deliver a notice to the taxpayer to make discovery of a document which is required by SARS to formulate its grounds of reply under rule 33.

The provision in the Rules of the Tax Court to request discovery – by the appellant before he or she submits his or her statement of grounds of appeal and by SARS before it delivers its reply – is different from the position in the High Court, where discovery is only made after the close of pleadings (after all the pleadings have been filed).

The Commissioner and the appellant may, within 15 days after delivery of the grounds of appeal, request the other party to make discovery.[123] This discovery is over and above the discovery referred to above.

Discovery is a process where a party makes available, to the other party, all relevant documents in respect of the dispute which are in his or her agent's possession. The purpose of discovery is to prevent either party to the dispute being taken by surprise in the proceedings before the Tax Court.

A party that has been requested to discover must do so within 20 days by delivery of an affidavit in which the following is stated:[124]

120 Rule 35(1) of the Rules of the Tax Court.
121 Rule 35(2) and rule 52 of the Rules of the Tax Court.
122 Rule 36(1) of the Rules of the Tax Court.
123 Rule 36(3) of the Rules of the Tax Court.
124 Rule 36(4) of the Rules of the Tax Court.

- the documents, information or things in his or her possession or control or that of his or her agent;
- the documents, information or things which he or she previously had in his or her possession or control, or that of his or her agent, which are no longer in his or her control or possession or that of his or her agent; and
- the documents, information or things to the production of which he or she has a valid objection, for instance, privileged documents.

12.12.3 Further discovery

If either party believes that there are, in addition to the documents so discovered, other documents, information or things, he or she may deliver a document to the other party requesting the party to discover such specific document, information or things. The party so requested must, within ten days, make available the documents, information or things requested or state under oath that these documents, information or things are not in his or her possession and also state their whereabouts, if known to him or her.[125]

Any document, information or thing not disclosed may not, save with leave of the court, be used for purposes of the trial by the party that is obliged but failed to disclose it – provided, however, that the other party may use such document, information or thing.[126]

12.12.4 Expert witnesses

A party who intends to call an expert witness at the trial must:[127]

- give notice of his or her intention to do so at least 30 days before the hearing; and
- not less than 20 days before the hearing deliver to the other party and the registrar of the Tax Court a summary of the expert's opinions and the relevance thereof.

'Expert evidence' means the evidence of a person that expresses an opinion. If a person is merely tendering factual evidence, it is not regarded as expert evidence and no notice need be given. Expert evidence may in certain instances not be tendered, for instance the interpretation of a contract, the meaning of a word (except if it is a technical word), and questions of law belong to the court exclusively. No expert evidence may be tendered in respect of these issues.[128]

If both parties have given notice to call an expert(s), the court will normally require that the expert(s) of the taxpayer and SARS meet before the trial in order to try and agree on certain issues pertaining to their expert evidence. In

CHAPTER 12

---

[125] Rule 36(6) of the Rules of the Tax Court.

[126] Rule 36(7) of the Rules of the Tax Court.

[127] Rule 37 of the Rules of the Tax Court.

[128] *International Business Machines SA (Pty) Ltd v Commissioner for Customs and Excise* 1985 (4) SA 852 (A) 874A–C.

practice, the experts will often compile a minute of their meeting wherein they will set out which issues they agree on and in respect of which issues they disagree. The experts are called to assist the court and should be independent.

12.12.5 Pre-trial conference

A pre-trial conference must be arranged by the Commissioner. During the pre-trial conference the Commissioner and the appellant must reach consensus on certain prescribed issues, namely:[129]

- what facts are common cause and what facts are in dispute;
- the resolution of preliminary points;
- the sufficiency of the discovery process;
- the preparation of a paginated bundle of documents;
- the manner in which evidence is to be dealt with, including an agreement on the status of documents and if a document or a part thereof will serve as evidence of what it purports to be;
- whether evidence on affidavit will be admitted;
- expert witnesses and the evidence to be given in an expert capacity;
- the necessity for an inspection *in loco*;
- an estimate of the time required for the hearing and any means by which the proceedings may be shortened; and
- if the dispute could be resolved or settled in whole or in part.

12.12.6 Pre-trial minute

The Commissioner must, within ten days of conclusion of the pre-trial conference, prepare a minute and deliver it to the taxpayer. If the taxpayer does not agree with the content of the minute, he or she must deliver his or her own minute to the Commissioner within ten days after receiving the Commissioner's minute.[130]

12.13 THE DATE OF THE HEARING

The appellant must apply to the registrar to allocate a date for the hearing within 30 days after delivery of the appellant's statement of grounds of appeal or SARS's reply, if applicable.[131]

[129] Rule 38(2) of the Rules of the Tax Court.
[130] Rule 38(4) and (5) of the Rules of the Tax Court.
[131] Rule 39(1) of the Rules of the Tax Court.

If the appellant fails to apply, SARS must apply for a date of hearing within 30 days after the expiry of the period within which the appellant (taxpayer) should have applied.[132]

The registrar, in his or her sole discretion, may allocate a date for hearing and must deliver written notice to the parties of the time and place appointed at least 80 days before the hearing of the appeal.[133]

12.14 THE DOSSIER

The Commissioner must, at least 30 days before the hearing, deliver to the taxpayer and the registrar a dossier containing the following:[134]

- all returns by the taxpayer relevant to the year of assessment in issue;
- all assessments issued by the Commissioner;
- the taxpayer's objection;
- SARS's notice of disallowance of objection;
- the notice of appeal;
- the statement of grounds of assessment and opposing appeal;
- the statement of grounds of appeal;
- SARS's reply, if any;
- SARS's minute of the pre-trial conference and, if any, the appellant's differentiating minute;
- any request for referral from the Tax Board to the Tax Court; and
- any order by the Tax Court or a higher court in an interlocutory application on a procedural matter relating to the objection or the appeal.

The registrar must deliver copies of the dossier to the court at least twenty days before the hearing. This means the judge and assessors that will hear the matter must be furnished with the dossier.

12.15 THE PLACES WHERE THE TAX COURT SITS

The Judge President of the divisions of the High Court having jurisdiction in the area in which the Tax Court will sit must determine the place and times of sitting of the court by arrangement with the registrar of the Tax Court.[135] The Tax Court normally sits at the High Court building, but in some instances, for example in the Gauteng South Division, the Tax Courts sits at a different venue.

[132] Rule 39(2) of the Rules of the Tax Court.
[133] Rule 39(3) and (4) of the Rules of the Tax Court.
[134] Rule 40 of the Rules of the Tax Court.
[135] Rule 41 of the Rules of the Tax Court.

A tax appeal must be heard by the court in the area which is nearest to the residence or principal place of business of the taxpayer. The taxpayer may, however, agree that the matter be heard at another place. If a taxpayer is therefore desirous to have a matter resolved speedily, he or she may agree that the matter be heard in the division where there is place available on the court roll.

12.16 PROCEDURES NOT COVERED BY THE INCOME TAX ACT AND THE RULES OF THE TAX COURT

The Rules of Court in terms of the Superior Courts Act 10 of 2013 ('Uniform Rules of Court') apply insofar as the Rules of the Tax Court do not provide for a specific issue.[136] For instance, rule 33(4) of the Uniform Rules of Court provides for a separation of issues. The Tax Court does not have a similar rule and therefore the parties may utilise rule 33(4) of the Uniform Rules of Court. Another example is rule 37(4) of the Uniform Rules of Court, which entitles a party to request certain information and admissions at a pre-trial conference.

12.17 SUBPOENAS

The purpose of issuing a subpoena is to ensure that a witness is present at the hearing of the matter. If a person who received a subpoena fails to be present at court, he or she may be found to be in contempt of court and may be imprisoned for such contempt. Any party or the President of the Tax Court may subpoena a witness.[137] The subpoenas are issued by the registrar of the Tax Court. Should it be necessary, a subpoena may require the person summoned to produce a book, document, information or thing in his or her possession or under his or her control. The Uniform Rules of Court governing the service of subpoenas in civil matters in the High Court are *mutatis mutandis* applicable in respect of subpoenas issued in the Tax Court.[138]

A person who has been subpoenaed and fails to give evidence at the hearing or to remain in attendance throughout the proceedings, unless excused by the President of the Tax Court, or to produce a document or thing in that person's possession or control, is liable to a fine or imprisonment.[139] The President of the Tax Court may impose a fine or, in default of payment, imprisonment for a period not exceeding three months. The President of the Tax Court may also issue a warrant for the person to be apprehended and brought to give evidence or to produce a document or thing in accordance with the subpoena.[140]

---

136 Rule 42 of the Rules of the Tax Court.
137 Section 126 of the TAA.
138 Rule 43 of the Rules of the Tax Court.
139 Section 127(1) of the TAA.
140 Section 127(2) of the TAA.

12.18 PROCEDURES IN THE TAX COURT

The procedures followed in the Tax Court are similar to those in the High Court. Unless the taxpayer takes a point *in limine*, the proceedings are commenced by the taxpayer. An example of a point *in limine* is where the taxpayer denies that an assessment has been issued, in which instance the Commissioner must first prove this and must therefore start.

The party who starts is afforded the opportunity to address the court, called an 'opening address', wherein he or she briefly sets out the issues in dispute and how he or she intends to deal therewith. The other party is not afforded an opportunity to respond.

After the opening address, the party who starts calls his or her witnesses. Each witness is examined in chief by the party calling the witness, after which the witness is cross-examined by the other party, followed by re-examination (by the party calling the witness). After the party starting has called all his or her witnesses, he or she closes his or her case. The other party may then call his or her witnesses, if any. Once that party has closed his or her case, both parties have the opportunity to address the court in argument. It is practice that written heads of argument are prepared for this purpose.[141]

12.18.1 Contempt of court

If, during the sitting of a Tax Court, a person wilfully insults a judge or member of the Tax Court, wilfully interrupts the Tax Court proceedings, or otherwise misbehaves, the President of the Tax Court may impose upon that person a fine or, in default of payment, imprisonment for a period not exceeding three months.[142]

12.18.2 Orders that the Tax Court may make

The court may:

- in the case of any assessment under appeal:[143]
  - confirm the assessment or decision;
  - order the assessment or decision to be altered;
  - if it considers it appropriate, refer the assessment back to the Commissioner for further investigation and assessment; or
  - make any appropriate order in a procedural matter; or
- in the case of any appeal against the amount of understatement penalty, reduce, confirm or increase the amount of understatement penalty.[144]

CHAPTER 12

141 Rule 44 of the Rules of the Tax Court.
142 Section 128 of the TAA.
143 Section 129(2) of the TAA.
144 Section 129(3) of the TAA.

If the court makes an order to refer the assessment back to SARS in terms of s 129(2)*(c)* and SARS alters the assessment as a result of that referral, that assessment so altered is subject to objection and appeal.[145]

12.19 COST ORDERS

The Tax Court may make an order as to costs if:[146]

- the grounds of assessment or decision of the Commissioner is held to be unreasonable;
- the taxpayer's grounds of appeal are held to be unreasonable;
- the decision of the Tax Board is substantially confirmed;
- the hearing of the appeal is postponed at the request of one of the parties; or
- the appeal is withdrawn or conceded by one of the parties after the registrar has allocated a date of hearing.

The Tax Court is deemed to be aware of the different scales of costs and may make a punitive cost order, for instance an order on the scale as between attorney and client.[147]

12.20 CONDONATION OF THE RULES OF THE TAX COURT

In terms of rule 4, any time period prescribed by the Rules, except where the extension is prescribed under the TAA or the Rules of the Tax Court, may be extended by agreement between:

- the parties;
- a party or the parties and the clerk (of the Tax Board); or
- a party or parties and the registrar (of the Tax Court).[148]

A request for extension must be delivered before expiry of the period prescribed under the Rules, unless the parties agree that the request may be delivered after the expiry of the period.[149]

If a party requests an extension of time in terms of rule 4 and the other party refuses, that party may bring an application to the Tax Court for condoning the non-compliance with the period and extend the period for such further period as the Tax Court deems appropriate.[150]

145 Section 129(4) of the TAA.
146 Section 130 of the TAA.
147 *ITC 1806* 68 SATC 117.
148 Rule 4(1) of the Rules of the Tax Court.
149 Rule 4(2) of the Rules of the Tax Court.
150 Rule 52(1) of the Rules of the Tax Court.

Rule 4 applies only to situations where the TAA or the Rules of the Tax Court do not deal with the extension of a time period; for instance, the extension of the time period to lodge an objection and an appeal are governed by the Rules of the Tax Court and the TAA and rule 4 will not apply in those instances.

12.21 ORDERS TO COMPEL A PARTY TO COMPLY WITH THE RULES OF THE COURT

If a party has failed to comply with a period or obligation prescribed under the Rules of the Tax Court, the other party may:

(a) deliver a notice to the defaulting party informing that party of the intention to apply to the Tax Court for a final order in terms of s 129 in the event that the default is not remedied within 15 days of delivery of the notice; and

(b) if the defaulting party fails to remedy the default within 15 days, the other party may apply to the court for a final order in terms of s 129(2).[151]

On application the Tax Court may, on the hearing of this application, make one of the following orders:

(a) in the absence of good cause shown by the defaulting party for the default issue, an order under s 129(2) confirming the assessment if the defaulting party is the taxpayer, or upholding the appeal if the defaulting party is SARS; or

(b) make an order compelling the defaulting party to comply with the relevant requirements within such time as the court deems appropriate, and if the defaulting party fails to abide, to then make an order in terms of s 129(2) without any further notice to the defaulting party.

In *ITC 1904*[152] the Tax Court granted a final order in terms of s 129(2) of the TAA, confirming the appeal lodged by the taxpayer, in circumstances where SARS failed to deliver its statement of grounds of assessment and opposing appeal within the prescribed time period. Although SARS eventually delivered its statement of grounds of assessment, after an application was brought to compel it to deliver the same, the court nevertheless granted default judgment. The court held that SARS did not provide any reasonable explanation for the delay in its non-compliance with the Rules of the Tax Court.

12.22 APPLICATIONS TO THE TAX COURT

12.22.1 Types of applications provided for

Part F of the Rules of the Tax Court (rules 50–64) makes provision for applications to the Tax Court.

151 Rule 56(1)*(a)* and *(b)*.

152 80 SATC 159.

Rule 52(1) states that the following applications may be brought to the court:

- applications to condone the non-compliance with the periods prescribed by the Rules; and
- applications to extend the period for a further period that the Tax Court deems appropriate.

Rule 52(2) also makes provision for the following applications by the taxpayer:

- to compel SARS to provide reasons;
- for an order that an objection that SARS treated as invalid, is valid;
- if the period of time to lodge an objection to an assessment has not been extended by SARS under s104(4), for an order extending the period within which an objection must be lodged by a taxpayer;
- to extend the period within which to provide documents to substantiate an objection; and
- to extend the period within which to lodge an appeal under s 107(2).

Rule 52(3) provides for certain instances where SARS may apply in the form of an application for an order, including an order that an objection and appeal be treated as a test case.

Other applications that may be brought to the Tax Court include:

- an application for amendment (rule 52(7));
- an interlocutory application (rule 51(2)); and
- an application for default judgment (rule 56).

12.22.2 Procedure

The applications in the Tax Court are similar to those in the superior courts. The Rules of the Tax Court provide for the following:

- a notice of motion supported by a founding affidavit that contains the facts on which the applicant relies for the relief sought;[153]
- a notice of intention to oppose and answering affidavit,[154] and the notice to oppose must be delivered within 10 days after delivery of the notice of motion and founding affidavit;[155]
- an answering affidavit, which must be delivered within 15 days after delivery of the notice of intention to oppose; and[156]
- a replying affidavit, which may be filed by the applicant within 10 days after delivery of the answering affidavit.[157]

The applications are set down by the Registrar of the Tax Court, who informs the parties by delivery of a written notice indicating the date when the matter is set down.[158]

[153] Rule 57(1).
[154] Rule 60.
[155] Rule 58.
[156] Rule 60*(c)*.
[157] Rule 61.
[158] Rule 62 and rule 63 of the Rules of the Tax Court.

12.23 APPEALS AGAINST DECISIONS OF THE TAX COURT

Appeals against decisions of the Tax Court are governed by ss 133 to 141 of the TAA. Either party before the Tax Court has a right to appeal against the decision of the Tax Court and leave to appeal is not required. The appeal lies to the Full Bench of the provincial division of the High Court or to the Supreme Court of Appeal.[159] A Full Bench means a court consisting of three judges. An appeal directly to the Supreme Court of Appeal is only possible if the President of the Tax Court grants leave[160] or if the Tax Court is one as contemplated in s 118(5) of the TAA, ie a court consisting of three judges.

12.23.1 Notice of intention to appeal

A party who intends to appeal must, within 21 business days after the date of the notice issued by the registrar of the Tax Court notifying the party of the decision of the Tax Court, lodge a notice of intention to appeal with the registrar of the Tax Court as well as with the opposing party or his or her attorney. The notice of intention to appeal must:

- state whether the party wishes to appeal to the Full Bench of the High Court or to the Supreme Court of Appeal; and
- set out the contemplated grounds of appeal.[161]

If a party wants to appeal directly to the Supreme Court of Appeal, leave must be requested. Reasons for such a request should include the amount involved, the importance of the matter to the party appealing, and if an important legal principle is at issue. In terms of s 135 of the TAA, the President of the Tax Court who presided in the matter decides whether the appeal lies to the Full Bench of the High Court or directly to the Supreme Court of Appeal, and his or her decision is final.

12.23.2 Notice to appeal

Once the registrar of the Tax Court has notified a party wishing to appeal of the court to which the appeal lies, a notice of appeal must be lodged within twenty-one days or such longer period as the rules of the court of appeal provide for.[162] Attached to the notice of appeal must be the order of the President of the Tax Court which indicates to which court the appeal lies.

159 Section 133 of the TAA.
160 Section 133 of the TAA.
161 Section 134 of the TAA.
162 Section 137 read with s 138 of the TAA.

12.23.3 Cross-appeal

If a party files a notice of appeal, the other party may lodge a cross-appeal. A cross-appeal is also an appeal but by the other party (not the party lodging the notice of appeal). A cross-appeal will be in respect of a part of the order or judgment of the Tax Court with which the party lodging the cross-appeal does not agree.

If a notice of appeal as well as a notice of cross-appeal is lodged, the court of appeal will consider both the appeal by the appellant and the cross-appeal by the respondent when hearing the matter.

A notice of cross-appeal shall state:

- whether the whole or only part of the judgment is appealed against and, if only a part, what part; and
- the grounds of cross-appeal specifying the findings of facts or ruling of law appealed against.[163]

A party who wishes to lodge a cross-appeal must, in terms of s 139(1) of the TAA, lodge the notice of cross-appeal within 21 days after the date of noting of the appeal.

12.23.4 What is appealable?

An appeal or cross-appeal lies against the Tax Court's 'judgment' or 'order'. Not every decision or ruling of a court constitutes an order. A party can only appeal or cross-appeal if the Tax Court found against it on an issue; for instance, if the Tax Court confirms an assessment, the taxpayer may appeal. The reasons for the court's finding is not appealable, ie if the court finds, for instance, in favour of the taxpayer but for a reason different to what the taxpayer relied on, no appeal lies against the order or judgment of the court.[164]

12.23.5 Record

The record which is before the court of appeal generally consists of:

- the dossier;
- the trial bundles; and
- a transcript of the proceedings, except the arguments.

The record to be used in an appeal before the Supreme Court of Appeal must be lodged within three months after the notice of appeal has been lodged. The appellant must then lodge his or her heads of argument within six weeks after the record has been lodged and the respondent must lodge his or her heads of argument within four weeks after the lodging of the appellant's heads of argument. The Rules of the Supreme Court of Appeal and the practice

[163] Section 139(3)*(b)* of the TAA.
[164] *Dickinson and Another v Fisher's Executors* 1914 AD 424 at 427.

directives issued by that court must be carefully considered in this regard. For instance, the Supreme Court of Appeal Rules and/or directives require that if the record exceeds five volumes (500 pages) a core bundle must be prepared, which may not exceed 200 pages. The documents contained in the core bundle are not repeated in the record. The core bundle contains the documents that a party wishes to refer to in argument and may not contain the transcript of the evidence tendered during the Tax Court trial.

12.23.6 Appeal from Full Bench to Supreme Court of Appeal

If the President of the Tax Court who adjudicated on the matter directs that the appeal lies to the Full Bench of the Provincial Division ('Full Bench'), a party not satisfied with the decision of the Full Bench may appeal to the Supreme Court of Appeal. However, such a party does not have a right to appeal but must request leave from the Supreme Court of Appeal.[165]

It is noteworthy that the notice of appeal required to be lodged under s 134 of the TAA differs from the notice of appeal that is lodged in an appeal from the Full Bench to the Supreme Court of Appeal. In the latter instance there is no requirement that the grounds of appeal be set out. The reason for this is that an appeal from the High Court to the Full Bench of the High Court requires leave and in the application for leave to appeal the party sets out his or her intended grounds of appeal. It is therefore not necessary to repeat it in the notice of appeal.

12.24 PAYMENT OF TAX PENDING APPEAL

The obligation to pay any tax chargeable under the Act is not, unless a senior SARS official so directs, suspended by any appeal or pending appeal.[166] In terms of s 164 of the TAA the Commissioner has a discretion to suspend the payment of tax pending an appeal. This discretion is not made subject to objection and appeal and if the Commissioner refuses to exercise his or her discretion in favour of a taxpayer, the taxpayer's remedy is to seek a review of the Commissioner's decision. This review lies with the High Court.

The senior SARS official, in considering whether to suspend the obligation to pay, pending appeal, will consider inter alia the following:[167]

- the compliance history of the taxpayer;
- the risk of dissipation of assets by the taxpayer;
- the amount of tax involved;
- whether, if the taxpayer is forced to pay, it will cause irreparable hardship to the taxpayer, for instance, will have the result that it will have to close its business and could possibly lead to job losses;

[165] Section 16(1)*(b)* of the Superior Courts Act 10 of 2013.
[166] Section 164 of the TAA.
[167] Section 164(3) of the TAA.

- whether there is any fraud involved;
- whether sequestration or liquidation proceedings are imminent; and
- whether the taxpayer furnished information requested by SARS.

When a taxpayer requests the Commissioner to suspend the obligation to pay tax, such request should be supported with reasons. The Commissioner is obliged to exercise his discretion judicially. Whilst the Commissioner is considering the taxpayer's application, the payment of the tax is effectively postponed as SARS cannot recover the tax until a decision is made on the application for postponement, unless SARS has a reasonable belief that there is a risk of dissipation of assets. Should a senior SARS official refuse to suspend payment, the taxpayer's remedy is that of review. If SARS is not prepared to hold over collection steps pending the institution of a review application, the taxpayer's remedy is to bring an application (urgent if necessary) to the High Court for an interim interdict preventing SARS from collecting the alleged tax liability, pending the institution of the review.

The 'pay now argue later' rule has been considered by the Constitutional Court and has been found not to be unconstitutional.[168]

12.25 RECOVERY OF TAX

12.25.1 Section 172 civil judgment

The TAA enables the Commissioner to recover tax in extraordinary ways. The Commissioner may file with the clerk or registrar of any competent court a statement certified by him as correct, setting out the amount of tax or interest due and payable by a person, and such statement has the effect of a civil judgment. SARS must give a taxpayer ten business days' notice, before taking judgment, unless it would prejudice the collection of tax.[169] These provisions are far-reaching in that the taxpayer is not given the opportunity to be heard before the judgment is taken against him or her. It is not a judgment in the ordinary sense, which is granted in an open court after the papers have been served on all the parties concerned.

The Commissioner may follow this procedure notwithstanding that objection and appeal may have been lodged against that assessment.[170] In the *Metcash* case[171] it was pointed out that that does not mean that the taxpayer may not attack the judgment on other grounds, for instance if the judgment was taken without an assessment being issued or before the taxpayer had been notified of the assessment. The taxpayer may therefore still attack the procedural deficiencies of the judgment.

---

168 *Metcash Trading Ltd v CSARS and Another* 2001 (1) SA 1109 (CC) 1130.

169 Section 172 and s 174 of the TAA.

170 Section 172(2) of the TAA.

171 *Metcash Trading Ltd v CSARS and Another* 2001 (1) SA 1109 (CC).

In *Nondabula v Commissioner for South African Revenue Service and Another*[172] the court held that if SARS appoints a third-party agent, based on an estimated assessment issued in terms of s 95, such an appointment is unlawful if the notice in terms of s 96(2) of the TAA does not contain a statement of the grounds for the estimated assessment.

The Commissioner may withdraw the statement lodged in terms of s 172 of the TAA by filing a notice with the clerk or registrar of the court which granted the judgment.[173]

12.26 APPOINTMENT OF AGENTS

The Commissioner may, if he thinks necessary, declare any person to be an agent of any other person. A person so declared an agent by the Commissioner may be required to pay any tax, interest or penalty due, from any monies including pensions, salaries or wages, which he or she may hold for or owe to the person whose agent he or she has been declared to be.[174]

Generally, the Commissioner appoints a taxpayer's bank or other financial institution which holds funds on its behalf. The courts have held that this procedure, previously provided for in s 99 of the Act, is to facilitate and enhance the Commissioner's ability to recover promptly taxes that are due and to avoid assets of taxpayers being put beyond his reach. As there are no equally effective methods which could be used in the circumstances to achieve the desired result, it has been held that any limitation of constitutional rights is reasonable and necessary in an open and democratic society is therefore not unconstitutional.[175] The agent so appointed is obliged to pay over to the Commissioner any monies that the agent owes, to the taxpayer. The Commissioner has the same remedies against all property of any kind vested or under control or management of any agent as he would have against the property of any person liable to pay the tax.[176] Therefore if an agent fails to pay over to the Commissioner the funds he or she holds on behalf of a taxpayer, the Commissioner may claim the same amount from the agent.

12.26.1 Personal liability of financial management for tax debts

A person is personally liable for any tax debt of the taxpayer to the extent that the person's negligence or fraud resulted in failure to pay the tax debt, if:

- the person controls or is regularly involved in the management of the overall financial affairs of the taxpayer; and
- a senior SARS official is satisfied that the person is or was negligent or fraudulent in respect of the payment of the taxpayer's tax debt.[177]

CHAPTER 12

[172] 79 SATC 333 para 23
[173] Section 176 of the TAA.
[174] Section 179 of the TAA.
[175] *Hindry v Nedcor Bank Ltd and Another* 1999 (2) SA 757 (W) 781J–782B, 61 SATC 163.
[176] Section 179(3) of the TAA.
[177] Section 180 of the TAA.

12.26.2 Personal liability of shareholders for tax debts

Where a company is wound up by means of an involuntary liquidation without having satisfied its tax debt, the shareholders of the company, within one year prior to its winding-up, are jointly and severally liable to pay the unpaid tax to the extent that:

- they received assets of the company in their capacity as shareholders within one year prior to its winding-up; and
- the tax debt existed at the time of the receipt of the assets or would have existed had the company complied with its obligations under a tax Act.[178]

This section does not apply in respect of listed companies or in respect of a shareholder of a listed company.[179]

12.26.3 Personal liability of persons assisting in dissipation of assets

If a person knowingly assists a taxpayer in dissipating his or her assets in order to obstruct the collection of tax, that person is jointly and severally liable with the taxpayer for the tax debt, to the extent that the person's assistance reduced the assets available to pay the taxpayer's tax debt.[180]

12.26.4 Personal liability of a representative taxpayer

A representative taxpayer is personally liable for the tax payable in their representative capacity if, while the tax remains unpaid, the representative taxpayer alienates, charges or disposes of amounts in respect of which the tax is chargeable or the representative taxpayer disposes of funds or monies which are in the their possession after the tax is payable, if the tax could legally have been paid from those funds or monies.[181] A representative taxpayer means a person who is responsible for paying the tax liability of another person as an agent and include:

- a representative taxpayer in terms of the Act;
- a representative employer in terms of the Fourth Schedule to the Act; and
- a representative vendor in terms of s 46 of the Value-added Tax Act.

In terms of the Income Tax Act, a representative taxpayer in respect of a company is the public officer of that company, or in the event that such company is placed under business rescue, the business rescue practitioner, or if liquidated, the liquidator.[182]

---

[178] Section 181(2) of the TAA.
[179] Section 181(5) of the TAA.
[180] Section 183 of the TAA.
[181] Section 155 of the TAA.
[182] Definition of 'representative taxpayer' in s 1 of the Income Tax Act.

The Fourth Schedule to the Income Tax Act states that a representative employer means, in the case of a company, its public officer, or if the company is placed under business rescue, the business rescue practitioner, or if liquidated, the liquidator.[183]

12.26.5 Personal liability of withholding agent

A withholding agent means a person who must, under a tax Act, withhold an amount of tax and pay it to SARS.[184] A withholding agent is personally liable for an amount of tax withheld but not paid over to SARS or which should have been withheld but was not so withheld.[185]

12.26.6 Recovery of tax debt from other persons

SARS has the same powers for recovery against the assets of a person who is personally liable in terms of ss 155, 157 and 180–183 of the TAA as SARS has against the assets of the taxpayer. The person who SARS holds personally liable also has the same rights and remedies as the taxpayer against such powers of recovery.

In terms of s 184(2) of the TAA, SARS must provide a person who it wants to hold personally liable with an opportunity to make representations before the person is held personally liable. This is normally done by SARS in the form of a notice informing the taxpayer that SARS intends to hold him or her personally liable and then afford the taxpayer 10 days to state reasons why he or she should not be held personally liable.

12.27 SETTLEMENT OF DISPUTES

Apart from the ADR procedure[186] the TAA also provides, in ss 142 to 150, for the settlement of disputes.[187] 'Dispute' is defined as a disagreement of either the fact or the law applicable to it, which arises pursuant to the issue of an assessment or the making of a decision.[188] 'Settle' is defined to mean 'to resolve a dispute' after an appeal has been lodged with the Tax Court.

12.27.1 When appropriate to settle

It will be appropriate for the Commissioner to settle under the following circumstances:[189]

183 Paragraph 1 of the Fourth Schedule to the Income Tax Act.
184 Section 156 of the TAA.
185 Section 157 of the TAA.
186 Rules 13–25 of the Rules of the Tax Court; s 107(5) of the TAA.
187 Part F of chapter 9 of the TAA.
188 Section 142 of the TAA.
189 Section 146 of the TAA.

- where it would be in the interest of good management of the tax system, overall fairness and the best use of the Commissioner's resources;
- where the cost of litigation in comparison to the possible benefits with reference to the prospects of success justifies it;
- where there are complex factual or quantum issues or evidentiary difficulties;
- where a participant or a group of participants in a tax avoidance scheme or arrangement has accepted the Commissioner's position in the dispute; or
- where the settlement will promote compliance with the tax law by the person concerned or the group of taxpayers concerned.

12.27.2 When not appropriate to settle

The circumstances under which it will be inappropriate to settle are:[190]

- where there is tax evasion or fraud;
- where the settlement would be contrary to the law or a clearly established practice of the Commissioner;
- where it is in the public interest to have judicial clarification of the issue;
- where the pursuit of the matter through the courts will significantly promote tax compliance (the Commissioner wants an example to be made of a person); and
- where the person concerned has not complied with the provisions of any Act administered by the Commissioner (ie the person is not tax compliant and the non-compliance is, in the Commissioner's opinion, of a serious nature).

12.27.3 Procedure for settlement

All disputes settled[191] must be evidenced by a written agreement and must include details on:

- how each particular issue was settled;
- relevant undertakings by the parties;
- treatment of that issue in future years;
- withdrawal of objections and appeals; and
- arrangements for payment.

The written agreement will represent the final agreed position between the parties and will be in full and final settlement of all or the specified aspects of

[190] Section 145 of the TAA.
[191] Section 147 of the TAA.

the dispute in question between the parties.[192] The settlement must be signed by a senior SARS official.

Any settlement entered into under this section will be conditional upon full disclosure of material facts known to the person concerned.[193]

12.28 WRITE OFF OF A TAX DEBT

Sections 192–207 of the TAA determine the circumstances under which the Commissioner may write off, or compromise, in whole or in part, any amount of tax, duty, levy, charge, interest, penalty or any other amount payable by a person.

In circumstances where a taxpayer does not dispute his or her liability to pay a tax debt, but the taxpayer is not in a financial position to pay the full amount of the tax debt, he or she may request the Commissioner to compromise the tax debt. If a taxpayer has already lodged an objection against an assessment, he or she must first withdraw that objection before he or she can apply for a compromise of his or her tax debt.[194]

The TAA makes provision for the temporary write off of a tax debt as well as the permanent write off of a tax debt.[195] There is a difference between 'write off', which means to reverse a tax debt either in whole or in part, and 'compromise', which means an agreement between SARS and the taxpayer in terms of which the taxpayer undertakes to pay less than the full amount of the tax debt, in full satisfaction of that tax debt, and SARS undertakes to write off permanently the remaining portion of the debt.[196]

12.29 COMPROMISE OF A TAX DEBT

12.29.1 Factors that will be considered in a request for a compromise of the tax debt

In considering the request for a compromise, the Commissioner will have regard to inter alia the following:[197]

- savings in the costs of collection;
- collection at an earlier date than would otherwise be the case without the compromise;
- collection of a greater sum than would otherwise have been recovered;
- the value of the debtor's present assets;

CHAPTER 12

192 Section 148 of the TAA.
193 Section 148(2) of the TAA.
194 Section 194 of the TAA.
195 Section 195 and s 196 (temporary write off) and ss 197–199 (permanent write off).
196 Section 192 of the TAA.
197 Section 202 of the TAA.

- the future prospects of the debtor, including any arrangements which have been implemented or proposed, which may have the effect of diverting income or assets that may otherwise accrue to the taxpayer or a connected person in relation to the taxpayer;
- past transactions of the taxpayer; and
- the position of any connected person in relation to the taxpayer.

12.29.2 Circumstances where it is not appropriate to compromise a tax debt

The Commissioner may not compromise any amount of tax debt if:[198]

- the compromise will prejudice other creditors – unless the affected creditors consent to the compromise or where the other creditors will be placed in a position of advantage relative to the Commissioner;
- any other creditor has communicated its intention to initiate or has initiated liquidation or sequestration proceedings;
- the tax affairs of the debtor (other than the outstanding tax debt) are not up to date;
- it may adversely affect broader taxpayer compliance;
- the taxpayer, within a period of three years immediately prior to the request for the compromise, was a party to an earlier agreement with the Commissioner to compromise a tax debt; or
- the 'debtor' is a company or a trust and SARS has not first explored action against or recovery from the personal assets of the persons who may be liable for the debt under part D of chapter 11.

12.29.3 Content of a request for a compromise

A taxpayer's request for a debt to be compromised by the Commissioner must be signed by the taxpayer and supported by a detailed statement setting out:[199]

(a) the assets and liabilities of the debtor, reflecting fair market value of those assets;

(b) all amounts received by or accrued to and expenditure incurred by the debtor during the 12 months immediately preceding the request;

(c) all assets which have been disposed of in the preceding three years, the value of all assets disposed of, the consideration received or accrued, the identity of the persons who acquired the assets and the relationship between the debtor and the person who acquired the assets (if any);

(d) the debtor's future interest in any asset, whether certain or contingent or subject to the exercise of a discretionary power by any other person;

---

198 Section 203 of the TAA.

199 Section 201 of the TAA.

(e) all assets over which the debtor, either alone or with other persons, has any direct or indirect power of appointment or disposal, whether as trustee or otherwise;

(f) details of any connected persons in relation to the debtor;

(g) debtor's present sources and level of income and anticipated sources and level of income for the next three years, the outline of the debtor's financial plans for the future; and

(h) debtor's reason for seeking a compromise.

12.29.4 Procedure for considering a request for a compromise

Once a taxpayer has submitted a compromise request, such request is considered by the debt collector concerned. The information contained in the request for a compromise is verified by SARS. Once the official is satisfied with the correctness thereof, the request is submitted to a committee. The committee takes the decision whether to agree to a compromise or not. Unfortunately, the taxpayer has no right to be present or to make recommendations to this committee. This creates the impression that the procedure is not a transparent one.

In some instances, the committee will request further information before making a decision in respect of the request for a compromise. In the event of the committee declining the request for a compromise, there is nothing in the TAA that prohibits a taxpayer from submitting a further request. In these circumstances, however, it would be advisable to first establish from the relevant SARS officials what the reasons were for not approving the initial request. In terms of PAJA, the taxpayer is entitled to be supplied with the reasons for the decision of the relevant committee. A taxpayer that is not satisfied with the Commissioner's decision not to approve a request is entitled to a review of the Commissioner's decision in terms of the provisions of PAJA. The review application must be made to the High Court.

12.29.5 Procedure for the compromise of a debt

If the Commissioner compromises a tax debt, a senior SARS official and the taxpayer must sign a written agreement which sets out:[200]

- the amount payable by the debtor in full satisfaction of the debt;
- the undertaking by SARS not to pursue recovery of the balance of the tax debt; and
- all other conditions subject to which the tax debt is compromised by SARS.

CHAPTER 12

[200] Section 204 of the TAA.

12.29.6 Circumstances under which SARS is not bound by a compromise

SARS will not be bound by a compromise if:[201]

- the debtor failed to make full disclosure of all material facts to which the compromise relates;
- the debtor supplied materially incorrect information;
- the debtor fails to comply with any provision in the compromise agreement; and
- the debtor is liquidated or his or her estate is sequestrated before he or she has complied with the provisions of the compromise agreement.

12.30 DEFERRAL OF PAYMENT

The TAA makes provision for a taxpayer to enter into an instalment payment agreement in respect of a tax debt. A senior SARS official may enter into such agreement with a taxpayer if he or she is satisfied that:

- the criteria or risks that may be prescribed by the Commissioner by public notice have been taken into consideration; and
- the agreement facilitates the collection of the debt.[202]

The instalment payment agreement may contain provisions regarding security for the collection of tax. SARS may for instance require that a taxpayer furnish security in the form of a bank guarantee or other acceptable form of security for the period in which the taxpayer will make payments in terms of the instalment payment agreement.[203]

12.30.1 Criteria for instalment payment agreement

A senior SARS official may only enter into an instalment payment agreement if:[204]

- the taxpayer suffers from a deficiency of assets or liquidity which is reasonably certain to be remedied in future;
- the taxpayer anticipates earning income or other receipts that can be used to satisfy the tax debt;
- the prospect of immediate collection, if such agreement is not entered into, is poor or uneconomical but is likely to improve in future;
- collection activity would be harsh in the particular case and the deferral arrangement is unlikely to prejudice the collection of the tax debt; or
- the taxpayer provides such security as may be required by the senior SARS official.

---

[201] Section 205 of the TAA.
[202] Section 167(1) of the TAA.
[203] Section 167(2) of the TAA.
[204] Section 168 of the TAA.

12.30.2 Amendment or termination of an instalment payment agreement

SARS may terminate an instalment payment agreement if the taxpayer fails to pay an instalment or otherwise fails to comply with the terms of the agreement.[205] A SARS official may also modify or terminate an instalment payment agreement if he is satisfied that:[206]

- the collection of tax is in jeopardy;
- the taxpayer has furnished materially incorrect information when entering into the agreement; or
- the financial position of the taxpayer has materially changed since entering into the agreement.

205 Section 167(4) of the TAA.
206 Section 167(5) of the TAA.

Chapter 13

Avoidance and evasion

13.1 INTRODUCTION

Tax avoidance is the reduction of a taxpayer's tax liability using the provisions of the fiscal legislation to his or her advantage and is legal, despite being unpopular with the revenue authorities. Tax evasion, in contrast, is the reduction of a taxpayer's tax liability by illegal means, for example, by the non-declaration of income that is properly subject to tax or by claiming deductions to which the taxpayer is not entitled. Tax evasion simply constitutes a fraud against the fiscus and appropriate remedies are available to SARS in s 235 of the Tax Administration Act 28 of 2011 (TAA) to use against taxpayers guilty of tax evasion.

The courts, in both South Africa and other countries, have often supported the right of taxpayers to avoid tax. Viscount Sumner in *Levene v IRC*[1] said that taxpayers—

> are free, if they can, to make their own arrangements so that their cases may fall outside the scope of the taxing Acts. They incur no legal penalties and, strictly, speaking, no moral censure if, having considered the lines drawn by the Legislature for the imposition of taxes, they make it their business to walk outside them.

In his judgment in *IRC v Duke of Westminster*, Lord Tomlin stated the following:[2]

> Every man is entitled, if he can, to order his affairs so that the tax attaching under the appropriate Acts is less than it would otherwise be. If he succeeds in ordering them so as to secure this result, then, however unappreciative the Commissioners of Inland Revenue or his fellow taxpayers may be of his ingenuity, he cannot be compelled to pay an increased tax.

This principle has been accepted by the courts in South Africa. Kroon J referred in *ITC 1636*[3] to—

> the recognised legal principle that any person is entitled, if he can, so to order his affairs that the tax attracted under the relevant legislation is less than it otherwise would be.

Tax avoidance has, however, also been the subject of harsh words and has been referred to as a mischief that needs to be suppressed (in *Glen Anil Development Corporation Ltd v SIR*[4] and more recently in *CIR v Ocean Manufacturing Ltd*).[5] In *Vestey's (Lord) Executors v IRC* Lord Normand went so far as to state that[6] '[t]ax avoidance is an evil'.

Tax avoidance, although legal, draws criticism because, when successful, it reduces the flow of tax revenues to the fiscus. In certain instances, aggressive tax avoidance schemes may verge on tax evasion. It is therefore necessary for tax legislation to provide anti-avoidance provisions that can be used by the revenue authorities to counter tax avoidance.

Anti-avoidance provisions may be aimed at specific types of tax avoidance. An example of such a provision in the South African Income Tax Act 58 of 1962 ('the Act') is s 103(2) that limits the set-off of an assessed loss in certain circumstances.

---

1 (1928) AC 217 at 227.
2 (1936) AC 1 at 19.
3 (1998) 60 SATC 267 at 302.
4 1975 (4) SA 715 (A), 37 SATC 319 at 334.
5 1990 (3) SA 610 (A), 52 SATC 151 at 162.
6 (1949) 1 All ER 1108 (HL) 1120.

As well as specific anti-avoidance provisions, tax legislation may contain general anti-avoidance provisions that can be used against any type of tax avoidance. Sections 80A to 80L of the Act make up the general anti-avoidance rule (commonly referred to as the GAAR) that the Commissioner may use against any type of income tax avoidance.

In this chapter, the general anti-avoidance rule is examined in detail and also the specific anti-avoidance provisions that are aimed at reportable arrangements, assessed losses and dividend/income swops. Other specific anti-avoidance provisions are examined in other chapters; for example, the so-called attribution rules in s 7 are examined in chapter 10 (Taxable persons) under the heading 'Taxation of trusts' and various connected person provisions are examined in chapter 7 (Deductions and capital allowances).

13.1.1 Substance versus form

The questions of substance versus form and simulated or disguised transactions can be pertinent when a tax avoidance transaction or scheme is being examined by a court. In *Erf 3183/1 Ladysmith (Pty) Ltd and Another v CIR*[7] Hefer JA, after considering[8] the principle from the *Duke of Westminster's* case[9] that every man is entitled, if he can, to order his affairs so that the tax attaching under the appropriate Acts is less than it otherwise would be, considered[10] the following principle that was succinctly stated by Wessels ACJ in *Kilburn v Estate Kilburn*:[11] 'Courts of law will not be deceived by the form of a transaction: it will rend aside the veil in which the transaction is wrapped and examine its true nature and substance.'

When considering, in the *Ladysmith* case, how the rights under an agreement should be interpreted by a court, Hefer JA quoted[12] from the judgment of Innes J in *Zandberg v Van Zyl* in which Innes J stated the following:[13]

> And when a court is asked to decide any rights under such an agreement, it can only do so by giving effect to what the transaction really is; not what in form it purports to be ... But the words of the rule indicate its limitations. The court must be satisfied that there is a real intention, definitely ascertainable, which differs from the simulated intention. For if the parties in fact mean that a contract shall have effect in accordance with its tenor, the circumstances that the same object might have been attained in another way will not necessarily make the arrangement other than it purports to be.

[7] 1996 (3) SA 942 (A), 58 SATC 229.
[8] 1996 (3) SA 942 (A) 950, 58 SATC 229 at 237–8.
[9] *IRC v Duke of Westminster* 19.
[10] 1996 (3) SA 942 (A) 951, 58 SATC 229 at 238.
[11] 1931 AD 501 at 507.
[12] 1996 (3) SA 942 (A) 952, 58 SATC 229 at 239.
[13] 1910 AD 302 at 309.

In determining whether a transaction is simulated or not, it is therefore necessary for a court to establish the actual intention of the contracting parties, but this is not sufficient.

The question of disguised transactions was also considered in *Commissioner of Customs and Excise v Randles Brothers & Hudson Ltd*, where it was held:[14]

> A disguised transaction ... is a dishonest transaction: dishonest, inasmuch as the parties to it do not really intend it to have, *inter partes*, the legal effect which its terms convey to the outside world. The purpose of the disguise is to deceive by concealing what is the real agreement or transaction between the parties. The parties wish to hide the fact that their real agreement or transaction falls within the prohibition or is subject to the tax, and so they dress it up in a guise which conveys the impression that it is outside the prohibition or not subject to the tax. Such a transaction is said to be in *fraudem legis*, and is interpreted by the courts in accordance with what is found to be the real agreement or transaction between the parties.

Of course, before the court can find that a transaction is in *fraudem legis* in the above sense, it must be satisfied that there is some unexpressed agreement or tacit understanding between the parties.

The parties in *Commissioner for the South African Revenue Service v NWK Ltd*[15] concluded a loan agreement with additional features that were intended to inflate the amount of the loan so as to increase the deductible interest in the hands of the borrower. The Commissioner argued that the agreements concluded between NWK and FNB and its subsidiary, Slab, did not reflect the substance of the real transaction. In reply, NWK contended that the contracts concluded between the parties were performed in accordance with their terms. In line with the decision in Ladysmith, The Tax Court found in favour of NWK on the basis that it was clear that NWK and FNB at all times intended to fulfil all the contractual terms agreed upon.

On appeal by the SARS Commissioner, the Supreme Court of Appeal found that the loan amount was obviously calculated with reference to a factor that did not relate to the amount needed by NWK. The SCA held that the loan sum was established by taking the interest payable and calculating what capital sum was needed to generate that interest at the rate agreed.[16] Lewis JA expressed the crux of the SCA's decision as follows:[17]

> In my view the test to determine simulation cannot simply be whether there is an intention to give effect to a contract in accordance with its terms. Invariably where parties structure a transaction to achieve an objective other than the one ostensibly achieved they will intend to give effect to the transaction on the terms agreed. The test should thus go further, and require an examination of the commercial sense of the transaction: of its real substance and purpose. If the purpose of the transaction is only to achieve an object that allows the evasion of tax, or of a peremptory law,

14 1941 AD 369, 33 SATC 48 at 66–7.
15 2011 (2) SA 67 (SCA), 73 SATC 55.
16 At para 65.
17 At para 55.

then it will be regarded as simulated. And the mere fact that parties do perform in terms of the contract does not show that it is not simulated: the charade of performance is generally meant to give credence to their simulation.

The SCA decision in *NWK* focused on the transaction, regardless of what the parties intended to do. This is in contrast with prior cases that focused on the form that the taxpayers projected the transaction to be vis-à-vis the substance that was the real object of the transaction.[18]

The taxpayers in *Commissioner: SARS v Bosch and Another*[19] were offered an employee share incentive scheme with suspensive conditions that deferred the imposition of income tax on the options until a future period. The commissioner assessed the taxpayers and in court argued that while the parties were honest in their contracts, dishonesty was not a requirement for simulation, and that because the transaction was formulated to avoid tax liability imposed by the Act, the transaction was simulated. The court found that this submission involved a misunderstanding of the judgment in *NWK*.[20]

Wallis JA held that simulation is a question of genuineness, that a transaction that is genuine is not simulated and that a simulated transaction is a dishonest transaction. He went further to clarify that if a transaction is simulated it may amount to tax evasion, but there is nothing impermissible about a taxpayer arranging its affairs to minimise its tax liability, and, as a result, that there is nothing wrong with tax avoidance. If the tax authority did not like the particular form of avoidance, they were free to close such tax loophole.[21]

The case of *Roshcon (Pty) Ltd v Anchor Auto Body Builders CC and Others*[22] concerned the issue of whether supplier and floor plan agreements reserving ownership of trucks to a finance house as security over the trucks before they were fully paid resulted in a simulated or disguised transaction. The court stated that whether a particular transaction is a simulated transaction is a question of its genuineness. The court held that if a transaction is genuine, the court will give effect to it. Accordingly, if the transaction is not genuine, the court will give effect to the underlying transaction that it conceals, and whether it is genuine will depend on a consideration of all the facts and circumstances surrounding that particular transaction.[23]

---

[18] For further discussion of the *NWK* case, see Legwaila T 'Modernising the 'Substance over Form' Doctrine: *CSARS v NWK Ltd*' (2012) *SA Merc LJ* 116 at 121 ; Emslie T 'Simulated Transactions – *NWK* Revisited' (2011) 60(2) *The Taxpayer* 83; Moosa F '*C:SARS v NWK Ltd* – A Tax Planning Sham(e)?' (2012) 27 *ITJ* 8; Vorster H '*NWK* and Purpose as a Test for Simulation' (2011) 60(5) *The Taxpayer* 83.

[19] 2015 (2) SA 174 (SCA).

[20] At para 40.

[21] Ibid.

[22] 2014 (4) SA 319 (SCA).

[23] At para 27.

13.2 GENERAL ANTI-AVOIDANCE RULE

The general anti-avoidance rule (the GAAR) is contained in s 80A to s 80L of the Act and was introduced in 2006 to replace the previous general anti-avoidance rule in s 103(1), which was then deleted. The general anti-avoidance rule sets out the requirements that must be met in order for the rule to be applied and the possible consequences of its application. Certain of the concepts on which the rule is based were also found in the previous s 103(1) rule and have been examined by the courts in various cases. Other concepts are new in South Africa: while there is as yet no South African case law to assist with their interpretation, foreign case law can sometimes assist.

13.2.1 Impermissible tax avoidance arrangements

In order for the Commissioner to invoke the general anti-avoidance rule, there must be an impermissible tax avoidance arrangement:

- First, there must be an *arrangement* as defined in s 80L.
- Secondly, the arrangement must be an *avoidance arrangement* as defined in s 80L, that is, the arrangement must result in a tax benefit.
- Thirdly, the avoidance arrangement must be an impermissible tax avoidance arrangement, as described in s 80A, that is, the sole or main purpose of the arrangement must be to obtain a tax benefit and there must be a tainted or abnormal element present in the arrangement.

13.2.1.1 An arrangement

An arrangement is defined in s 80L for the purposes of the general anti-avoidance rule as any transaction, operation or scheme, agreement or understanding (whether enforceable or not), including all steps therein or parts thereof, and it also includes any of these involving the alienation of property.

The term 'transaction, operation or scheme' was used in s 103(1) and its predecessor section (s 90 of the Income Tax Act 31 of 1941). In *Meyerowitz v CIR*[24] a series of transactions was entered into as a result of which the income that the appellant would have received for his work and labour was transferred to his children. The effect of the transactions was to avoid liability by the appellant for tax on that income. Beyers JA agreed[25] with the lower court that the word 'scheme' was a wide term and that there was little doubt that it was sufficiently wide to cover a series of transactions.

The words 'agreement' and 'understanding' were not contained in the previous general anti-avoidance rule and there is no case law that clarifies their meaning. In its *Draft Comprehensive Guide to the General Anti-Avoidance*

[24] 1963 (3) SA 863 (A), 25 SATC 287.
[25] 1963 (3) SA 863 (A) 873, 25 SATC 287 at 299–300.

Rule (the *Draft Guide*),[26] SARS indicates that an agreement may be in writing, an oral agreement, merely an oral understanding or a tacit agreement.[27] The *Draft Guide* gives as examples of agreements that are not legally enforceable, but which are nevertheless agreements for the purposes of the general anti-avoidance rule, so-called gentlemen's agreements and heads of agreement between parties which set out the intended result the parties wish to achieve but which are not necessarily legally binding at the time.[28]

A letter of wishes, which is also not legally enforceable, but which informs a different implementation in practice to agreements reduced to writing between the parties, is given by the *Draft Guide* as an example of an understanding.[29]

The use of the words 'including all the steps therein or parts thereof' is important, as they enable the Commissioner to apply the rule to either an arrangement as a whole or to only certain parts of it, depending on which is most appropriate.

13.2.1.2 An avoidance arrangement

An avoidance arrangement is defined in s 80L simply as 'any arrangement that, but for the general anti-avoidance rule, results in a tax benefit'. The term 'tax benefit' is in turn defined in s 1 as including 'any avoidance, postponement or reduction of any liability for tax'.

Once it has been established that there is an arrangement that would result in a tax benefit if the general anti-avoidance rule were not applied, it is necessary to determine whether this arrangement meets the requirements of an impermissible avoidance arrangement as set out in s 80A.

13.2.1.3 An impermissible avoidance arrangement

The first requirement for an avoidance arrangement to be an impermissible avoidance arrangement is that its sole or main purpose must have been to obtain a tax benefit.

The second requirement is the presence of one or more tainted elements that depend on the context in which the arrangement was entered into.

If the arrangement was entered into in the *context of business*, it will be an impermissible avoidance arrangement if:

- it was entered into or carried out by means or in a manner which would not normally be employed for bona fide business purposes, other than obtaining a tax benefit;[30] or
- it lacks commercial substance, in whole or in part, taking into account the provisions of s 80C (s 80A*(a)*(ii)).

---

[26] Available on www.sars.gov.za.
[27] SARS *Draft Guide* 14.
[28] Ibid.
[29] Ibid.
[30] Section 80A*(a)*(i).

If the arrangement was entered into in a *context other than business*, it will be an impermissible avoidance arrangement if it was entered into or carried out by means or in a manner which would not normally be employed for a bona fide purpose, other than obtaining a tax benefit.[31]

If the arrangement was entered into in *any context*, it will be an impermissible avoidance arrangement if:

- it has created rights or obligations that would not normally be created between persons dealing at arm's length;[32] or
- it would result directly or indirectly in the misuse or abuse of the provisions of the Act (including the provisions of the general anti-avoidance rule) (s 80A*(c)*(ii)).

To summarise, to determine whether an avoidance arrangement in a business context is an impermissible avoidance arrangement, the four tests that need to be applied are:

- the business purpose test;
- the commercial substance test;
- the abnormal rights and obligations test; and
- the misuse or abuse test.

For an avoidance arrangement in a context other than business, there are three tests to be applied:

- the abnormality of manner and means test;
- the abnormal rights and obligations test; and
- the misuse or abuse test.

The important concepts embodied in these requirements and the tests listed above will be examined before the tax consequences of impermissible tax avoidance are considered.

13.2.1.4 Sole or main purpose

In order for the general anti-avoidance rule to be applied, the obtaining of a tax benefit must have been the sole or main purpose of the arrangement. It is not enough for the obtaining of a tax benefit to have been one of the purposes of the arrangement: it must have been its sole or main purpose. The meaning of the word 'mainly' has been examined by the courts: in *SBI v Lourens Erasmus (Edms) Bpk*[33] it was held to be a purely quantitative measure of more than 50%.

The sole or main purpose test is an objective test: it is the sole or main purpose of the arrangement that must be considered, not the subjective purpose of the taxpayer.

[31] Section 80A*(b)*.
[32] Section 80A*(c)*(i).
[33] 1966 (4) SA 434 (A), 28 SATC 233 at 245.

Section 80G(1) provides that there is a rebuttable presumption that the entering into of an avoidance arrangement was for the sole or main purpose of obtaining a tax benefit. The presumption can be rebutted by the party that obtained the benefit by proving, reasonably considered in the light of the relevant facts and circumstances, that obtaining the benefit was not the sole or main purpose.

The purpose of a step or part of an avoidance arrangement may differ from the purpose of the arrangement as a whole.[34] If a particular step in an avoidance arrangement has the sole or main purpose of obtaining a tax benefit, this is sufficient for the general anti-avoidance rule to be applied (provided that the other requirements have been met), as the Commissioner can apply the rule to the arrangement as a whole or to or any of its steps or parts.[35]

13.2.1.5 Tax benefit

A 'tax benefit' is defined in s 1 as 'any avoidance, postponement or reduction of any liability for tax'. The term appeared in s 103(1) and has been considered by the courts. In *CIR v King*[36] it was held that the tax liability avoided, postponed or reduced is not an existing liability but an anticipated liability.

When determining whether or not a tax benefit exists, the Commissioner may treat parties that are connected persons as one and the same person or may disregard any accommodating or tax-indifferent party or treat any accommodating or tax-indifferent party and any other party as one and the same person.[37]

13.2.1.6 Business purpose test or business abnormality test

What is commonly referred to as the business purpose test (or alternately, and possibly more accurately, it is also referred to as the business abnormality test) considers whether an avoidance arrangement was entered into in a manner or by means that would not normally be employed for bona fide business purposes, other than the obtaining of a tax benefit. It is an abnormality test and it is not a test of whether or not the avoidance arrangement was entered into for business purposes, but rather whether it was entered into in a manner or by means that would not normally be employed for bona fide business purposes other than obtaining a tax benefit.

13.2.1.7 Commercial substance test

If an avoidance arrangement in a context of business lacks commercial substance, in whole or in part, then it could potentially meet the requirements of the general anti-avoidance rule. In a composite transaction, the commercial

[34] Section 80G(2).
[35] Section 80H.
[36] 1947 (2) SA 196 (A), 14 SATC 184 at 190.
[37] Section 80F.

substance test must be applied to the whole transaction and to its individual steps. If a single step is tainted by the lack of commercial substance, the general anti-avoidance rule can potentially be applied.[38]

In determining whether or not the avoidance arrangement lacks commercial substance the provisions of s 80C must be taken into account. For the purposes of applying s 80C, the Commissioner may treat parties that are connected persons as one and the same person or may disregard any accommodating or tax-indifferent party or treat any accommodating or tax-indifferent party and any other party as one and the same person.[39]

Section 80C provides guidance on when an avoidance arrangement will lack commercial substance.

Firstly, an avoidance arrangement will lack commercial substance if, but for the provisions of the general anti-avoidance rule, it would result in a significant tax benefit for a party but does not have a significant effect on either the business risks or net cash flows of that party, apart from the effect of the tax benefit.[40] What is noteworthy in this provision is that the tax benefit must be significant.

The SARS *Draft Guide* states that the terms 'business risk' and 'net cash flows' are not statutorily defined and must be given their ordinary meaning.[41] The *Draft Guide* gives the following examples:

- business risk: market risk, credit risk, operational risk and foreign exchange risk; and
- net cash flows: cash flows from operational, investment and financing activities.[42]

Secondly, s 80C(2) lists the following characteristics that are indicative of a lack of commercial substance:

- the legal substance or effect of the avoidance arrangement as a whole is inconsistent with or differs significantly from the legal form of its individual steps; and
- the inclusion or presence of:
  - round trip financing as described in s 80D;
  - an accommodating or tax-indifferent party as described in s 80E; and
  - elements that have the effect of offsetting or cancelling each other.

13.2.1.8 Legal substance and effect

The question of the legal substance and effect of an avoidance arrangement being inconsistent with or different from the legal form of its individual steps has

[38] SARS *Draft Guide* 25.
[39] Section 80F.
[40] Section 80C(1).
[41] SARS *Draft Guide* 28.
[42] Ibid.

been the subject of much debate. The *Draft Guide* states[43] that 'the intention is that the word "effect" is given a wide interpretation, and includes economic, commercial or practical effect'. The *Draft Guide* then goes on to state[44] that the test consists of the following two sub-tests:

- First, the legal substance of the arrangement must be compared to the legal form of the individual steps. Any inconsistencies are indicative of lack of commercial substance.
- Secondly, the commercial, economic or practical effect of the arrangement must be compared to the individual steps. Again, any inconsistencies are indicative of lack of commercial substance.

13.2.1.9 Round trip financing

The concept of 'round trip financing' is described in s 80D as including any avoidance arrangement in which all of the following requirements are met:

- Funds are transferred between or among the parties (round tripped amounts).
- The transfer of the funds would result, directly or indirectly, in a tax benefit but for the general anti-avoidance rule.
- The transfer of the funds would significantly reduce, offset or eliminate any business risk incurred by any party in connection with the avoidance arrangement.

For the purposes of s 80D, the term 'funds' includes any cash, cash equivalents or any right or obligation to receive or pay the same.[45]

Section 80D applies to any round tripped amounts without regard to:

- whether or not the round tripped amounts can be traced to funds transferred to or received by any party in connection with the avoidance arrangement;
- the timing or sequence in which round tripped amounts are transferred or received; or
- the means by or manner in which round tripped amounts are transferred or received.[46]

The *Draft Guide* points out that the description of round trip financing in s 80D(1) is not an exhaustive definition and that these provisions must not be restrictively interpreted. It gives as an example of round trip financing a loan arrangement where the original loan finds its way back to the lender by way of a security deposit.[47]

43 SARS *Draft Guide* 29.
44 Ibid.
45 Section 80D(3).
46 Section 80D(2).
47 SARS *Draft Guide* 30.

13.2.1.10 Accommodating or tax-indifferent parties

Section 80E(1) sets out the circumstances in which a party to an avoidance arrangement is an accommodating or tax-indifferent party.

There are two requirements that must both be met for a party to an avoidance arrangement to be an accommodating or tax-indifferent party.

The first requirement is that any amount derived by a party to an avoidance arrangement in connection with the avoidance arrangement is either:

- not subject to normal tax; or
- significantly offset either by any expenditure or loss incurred by the party in connection with that avoidance arrangement or by any assessed loss of that party.[48]

The second requirement is that either of the following applies:

- as a direct or indirect result of the participation of a party to an avoidance arrangement an amount that would have:
  - been included in the gross income (including the recoupment of any amount) or receipts or accruals of a capital nature of another party, would be included in the gross income or receipts or accruals of a capital nature of that party; or
  - constituted a non-deductible expenditure or loss in the hands of another party, would be treated as a deductible expenditure by that other party; or
  - constituted revenue in the hands of another party, would be treated as capital by that other party; or
  - given rise to taxable income to another party, would either not be included in gross income or be exempt from normal tax; or
- the participation of a party to an avoidance arrangement directly or indirectly involves a prepayment by any other party.[49]

It is not necessary for a connected person relationship to exist in order for a party to be an accommodating or tax-indifferent party: a person may be an accommodating or tax-indifferent party whether or not that person is a connected person in relation to any party.[50]

The accommodating or tax-indifferent party provisions do not apply in the following two so-called 'safe harbour' situations: where a party is subject to foreign tax comparable to that in South Africa or where a party is engaged in active trading activities.

[48] Section 80E(1)*(a)*.
[49] Section 80E(1)*(b)*.
[50] Section 80E(2).

(a) Comparable foreign tax

The first situation where the accommodating or tax-indifferent party provisions do not apply is where the amounts derived by the party in question are cumulatively subject to income tax by one or more spheres of government of countries other than the Republic which is equal to at least two-thirds of the amount of normal tax which would have been payable in connection with those amounts, had they been subject to tax under the Act.[51] The amount of tax imposed by another country must be determined after taking into account any applicable agreements for the prevention of double taxation and any assessed loss, credit or rebate to which the party in question may be entitled, or any other right of recovery to which that party or any connected person in relation to that party may be entitled.[52]

(b) Active trading activities

The second situation where the accommodating or tax-indifferent party provisions do not apply is where the party in question continues to engage directly in substantive active trading activities in connection with the avoidance arrangement for a period of at least 18 months.[53]. These activities must be attributable to a place of business, place, site, agricultural land, vessel, vehicle, rolling stock or aircraft that would constitute a foreign business establishment as defined in s 9D(1) if it were located outside the Republic and the party in question were a controlled foreign company.[54]

These safe harbour provisions are of limited application: they are merely an indication that an arrangement does not lack commercial substance. They are not an overall safe harbour from the application of the general anti-avoidance rule itself.[55]

13.2.1.11 Offsetting or cancelling elements

The Act does not provide any clarification of what is meant by elements that have the effect of offsetting or cancelling each other. The SARS *Draft Guide* points out that these elements 'may take any form and need not only be amounts, but could also be rights and obligations which offset each other' and gives as an example two agreements forming part of a composite transaction, which create rights and obligations that cancel each other.[56]

Whilst the existence of round trip financing, accommodating or tax-indifferent parties or elements that offset or cancel each other are all indicative of a lack of commercial substance, it is important to note that the scenarios that are listed

[51] Section 80E(3)*(a)*.
[52] Section 80E(4).
[53] Section 80E(3)*(b)*.
[54] Proviso to s 80E(3)*(b)*.
[55] SARS *Draft Guide* 33.
[56] SARS *Draft Guide* 35.

in s 80C(2) are not exhaustive. The *Draft Guide* identifies[57] other scenarios that may also be indicative of a lack of commercial substance, for example an anticipated pre-tax profit being insignificant in comparison to an anticipated tax benefit; significant accounting and tax differences; unnecessary steps and complexity; and high transaction costs.

13.2.1.12 Abnormality tests

There are two abnormality tests that are used to determine whether an avoidance arrangement is an impermissible avoidance arrangement.

Firstly, an avoidance arrangement in a context other than business, for example, an arrangement involving a family investment trust, will potentially be an impermissible avoidance arrangement if it was entered into or carried out *by means or in a manner* that would not normally be employed for a bona fide purpose other than obtaining a tax benefit.

Secondly, an avoidance arrangement in any context that has created *rights and obligations* that would not normally be created between persons dealing at arm's length will potentially be an impermissible avoidance arrangement.

These abnormality tests are not new: there were similar provisions in s 103(1) that have been considered by the courts in numerous cases.

Features of transactions that were found by the courts to be abnormal include:

- no security having been demanded by a taxpayer from a foreign company to which it had transferred valuable rights, for the performance of the company's obligations;[58]
- the granting of loans to the directors of a company free of interest and without any definite repayment plans (this was found to be abnormal both as to the means and manner of granting the loans, and as to the rights and obligations created);[59]
- the transfer of a business from an existing company to a new company without any agreement, either written or verbal, having been entered into;[60] and
- a lease that provided for an unrealistically low rental of R10 a year.[61]

Prior to the introduction of the new general anti-avoidance rule, the Commissioner was often unsuccessful in showing that there was the required element of abnormality in transactions, because s 103(1) required the question of abnormality to be considered for a transaction 'of the nature of the transaction ... in question' and 'having regard to the circumstances under

57 SARS *Draft Guide* 35–7.
58 *ITC 1113* (1967) 30 SATC 8 (C) 12.
59 *CIR v Louw* 1983 (3) SA 551 (A), 45 SATC 113 at 138.
60 *ITC 1178* (1972) 35 SATC 29 (C) 33.
61 *ITC 1496* (1990) 53 SATC 229 (T) 251–2.

which the transaction ... was entered into or carried out'. Importantly, these words have been omitted from the new general anti-avoidance rule.

The question of whether the parties to an arrangement are dealing at arm's length is an important one. Agreements involving parties who are dealing at arm's length are more likely to create rights and obligations that are normal and to employ normal means and manner in entering into or carrying out the transaction.[62]

13.2.1.13 Misuse or abuse test

The misuse or abuse test is one of the tainted elements tests that are used to determine whether an avoidance arrangement is an impermissible avoidance arrangement. It applies to an avoidance arrangement in any context. An avoidance arrangement will potentially be an impermissible avoidance arrangement if it will result directly or indirectly in the misuse or abuse of the provisions of the Act, including the general anti-avoidance rule provisions.

The concept of the misuse or abuse of the provisions contained in s 80A*(c)*(ii) of the Act is new in South African law and was inspired by a similar, but different, provision in Canadian law. Because it is a new concept in South African law, there is no direct South African judicial precedent to aid in its interpretation, but there are South African cases that have considered the questions of purposive and literal interpretation that can assist in its interpretation. Assistance can also be sought from decisions in other jurisdictions. The *Draft Guide* published by SARS provides useful insight into its interpretation of the concept.[63]

The Canadian misuse or abuse test was considered by that country's Supreme Court in *Canada Trustco Mortgage Co v Canada*[64] where it was held that the test involves a two-part enquiry:

> The first is 'to interpret the provisions giving rise to the tax benefit to determine their object, spirit and purpose'. The second is to examine the factual context of a case in order to determine whether the avoidance arrangement defeated the object, spirit or purpose of the provisions in issue.[65]

The *Draft Guide*[66] also refers to the purposive approach to the interpretation of legislation that has been used in the United Kingdom and the so-called 'Ramsay doctrine' expressed by Lord Wilberforce in *WT Ramsay Ltd v IRC*[67] that requires the court to consider 'the context and scheme of the relevant Act as a whole, and its purpose'.

---

62 *Hicklin v SIR* 1980 (1) SA 481 (A), 41 SATC 179 at 195.
63 SARS *Draft Guide* 39.
64 2005 SCC 54.
65 SARS *Draft Guide* 39.
66 SARS *Draft Guide* 41.
67 [1982] AC 300.

CHAPTER 13

How will the South African courts interpret the misuse or abuse test? The *Draft Guide* states[68] that a tax benefit will be denied if it would 'misuse or abuse the object, spirit or purpose of the provisions of the Income Tax Act that are relied upon for the tax benefit'.

Clearly this will require the courts to apply a purposive approach to the interpretation of the relevant legislation in a particular instance of tax avoidance, as was done in *Glen Anil Development Corporation Ltd v SIR,*[69] where Botha JA stated[70] that the anti-avoidance provision being considered (s 103(2)) should not be construed as a taxing measure but rather in a way that will advance the remedy provided by the section and suppress the mischief against which the section is directed. This requires that a court applies a purposive approach.

The *Draft Guide* warns taxpayers that 'a mere literal interpretation of the provisions will no longer safeguard' them if they apply the provisions in a context or manner not intended by the Act.[71]

13.2.1.14 Onus of proof

Before the general anti-avoidance rule can be applied by the Commissioner, he must be satisfied that certain requirements in the legislation are met and the onus of proving these therefore appears to rest on him, although this is not specifically spelt out in the Act. The onus of proof rests on the Commissioner in respect of the following requirements:

- the existence of a tax benefit;[72]
- the existence of any of the tainted elements, for example, a lack of commercial substance[73] or abnormal rights and obligations;[74] and[75]
- the existence of a misuse or abuse of the provisions of the Act.[76]

The onus of proof rests on the taxpayer in respect of the following requirements:

- The sole or main purpose of an arrangement was not to obtain a tax benefit.[77]
- The facts and circumstances that must be reasonably considered in proving that a tax benefit was not the sole or main purpose of an arrangement.[78]

---

68 SARS *Draft Guide* 40.
69 1975 (4) SA 715 (A), 37 SATC 319.
70 37 SATC 319 at 334.
71 At 40.
72 Definition of an 'avoidance arrangement' in s 80L; SARS *Draft Guide* 18.
73 Section 80A*(a)*(ii).
74 Section 80A*(c)*(i).
75 SARS *Draft Guide* 24.
76 Section 80A*(c)*(ii). See also SARS *Draft Guide* 44.
77 Section 80G(1); SARS *Draft Guide* 22.
78 Section 80G(1); SARS *Draft Guide* 22.

- The arrangement does have commercial substance, indicated for example, by showing the existence of a significant effect on the business risks of the taxpayer.[79]

13.2.2 Tax consequences of impermissible tax avoidance arrangements

Once the Commissioner has identified the existence of an impermissible avoidance arrangement, he may determine the tax consequences under the Act of the arrangement for any party by applying any of the following remedies:

- disregarding, combining, or re-characterising any steps in or parts of the impermissible avoidance arrangement (s 80B(1)*(a)*);
- disregarding any accommodating or tax-indifferent party or treating any accommodating or tax-indifferent party and any other party as one and the same person (s 80B(1)*(b)*);
- deeming persons who are connected persons in relation to each other to be one and the same person for purposes of determining the tax treatment of any amount (s 80B(1)*(c)*);
- reallocating any gross income, receipt or accrual of a capital nature, expenditure or rebate amongst the parties (s 80B(1)*(d)*);
- re-characterising any gross income, receipt or accrual of a capital nature or expenditure (s 80B(1)*(e)*); and
- treating the impermissible avoidance arrangement as if it had not been entered into or carried out, or in such other manner as in the circumstances of the case the Commissioner deems appropriate for the prevention or diminution of the relevant tax benefit (s 80B(1)*(f)*).

The Commissioner must make compensating adjustments that he is satisfied are necessary and appropriate to ensure the consistent treatment of all parties to the impermissible avoidance arrangement. This is subject to the time limits imposed by ss 99, 100 and 104(5)*(b)* of the TAA. (Section 80B(2))

The Commissioner may apply the general anti-avoidance rule provisions in the alternative, or in addition to, any other basis for raising an assessment (s 80I).

The Commissioner must, prior to determining any liability of a party for tax by applying the remedies available to him in s 80B, give the party notice that he believes that the provisions of the general anti-avoidance rule may apply in respect of an arrangement, and must set out in the notice his reasons therefor (s 80J(1)).

A party who receives notice in terms of s 80J(1) may, within 60 days after the date of that notice or such longer period as the Commissioner may allow, submit reasons to the Commissioner why the provisions of the general anti-avoidance rule should not be applied (s 80J(2)).

[79] Section 80C; SARS *Draft Guide* 28.

The Commissioner must within 180 days of receipt of the reasons or the expiry of the 60-day period contemplated in s 80J(2):

- request additional information in order to determine whether or not the general anti-avoidance rule applies in respect of an arrangement (s 80J(3)*(a)*);
- give notice to the party that the notice in terms of s 80J(1) has been withdrawn (s 80J(3)*(b)*); or
- determine the liability of that party for tax in terms of the general anti-avoidance rule (s 80J(3)*(c)*).

If at any stage after giving notice to the party in terms of s 80J(1), additional information comes to the knowledge of the Commissioner, he may revise or modify his reasons for applying the general anti-avoidance rule or, if the notice has been withdrawn, give notice in terms of s 80J(1) (s 80J(4)).

Section 80K provided that where the Commissioner has applied the general anti-avoidance rule in determining a party's liability for tax, the Commissioner may not exercise his discretion in terms of s 89*quat*(3) or (3A) to direct that interest is not payable in respect of that portion of any tax which is attributable to the application of the general anti-avoidance rule. (Section 80K was repealed by s 271 of the TAA with effect from a date that is still to be determined. Section 89*quat* was also repealed by s 271 of the Tax Administration Act 28 of 2011, with effect from a date that is still to be determined. It must be noted that all provisions of the TAA, except those dealing with interest, took effect on 1 October 2012. Thus, the old rules dealing with interest will remain in force until the new rules take effect. Once the new provisions dealing with interest take effect, interest will be calculated on the daily balance owing by taxpayers and compounded monthly. Similarly, interest paid by SARS to taxpayers will also be compounded monthly.)

13.3 SPECIFIC ANTI-AVOIDANCE PROVISIONS

13.3.1 Reportable arrangements

The reportable arrangement provisions in ss 34 to 39 of the TAA enable the Commissioner to be given advance warning of tax avoidance arrangements against which he could potentially apply the general anti-avoidance rule in s 80A to 80L or any of the specific anti-avoidance provisions.

Section 35 sets out the general requirements for an arrangement to be a reportable arrangement (s 35(1)) and also provides that the Commissioner may list an arrangement by public notice if satisfied that the arrangement may lead to an undue tax benefit (s 35(2)). An arrangement is a reportable arrangement in terms of s 35(1) either if it meets the requirements set out in s 35(1) or if it is listed in a public notice in terms of s 35(2) . An arrangement meets the requirements of s 35(1) and is therefore a reportable arrangement in terms of that section if any tax benefit is or will be derived or is assumed to be derived by any participant by virtue of that arrangement and the arrangement:

- contains provisions in terms of which the calculation of 'interest' as defined in s 24J of the Act, finance costs, fees or any other charges is wholly or partly dependent on the assumptions relating to the tax treatment of that arrangement (otherwise than by reason of any change in the provisions of a tax Act) (s 35(1)*(a)*);
- has any of the characteristics, or characteristics which are substantially similar to those, contemplated in s 80C(2)*(b)* of the Act (round trip financing; an accommodating or tax-indifferent party; or elements that offset or cancel each other) (s 35(1)*(b)*);
- gives rise to an amount that is or will be disclosed by any participant in any year of assessment or over the term of the arrangement as:
  - a deduction for purposes of the Act but not as an expense for purposes of financial reporting standards; or
  - revenue for purposes of financial reporting standards but not as gross income for purposes of the Act (s 35(1)*(c)*);
- does not result in a reasonable expectation of a pre-tax profit for any participant (s 35(1)*(d)*); or
- results in a reasonable expectation of a pre-tax profit for any participant that is less than the value of that tax benefit to that participant, if both are discounted to a present value at the end of the first year of assessment when that tax benefit is or will be derived or is assumed to be derived, using consistent assumptions and a reasonable discount rate for that participant (s 35(1)*(e)*).

The following terms are defined for the purposes of the reportable arrangement provisions:

- An 'arrangement' is any transaction, operation, scheme, agreement or understanding (whether enforceable or not).
- 'Financial reporting standards' means, in the case of a company required to submit financial statements in terms of the Companies Act 71 of 2008, financial reporting standards prescribed by that Act, or, in any other case, the International Financial Reporting Standards or appropriate financial reporting standards that provide a fair presentation of the financial results and position of the taxpayer.
- Participant, in relation to an 'arrangement', means *(a)* a 'promoter'; *(b)* a person who directly or indirectly will derive or assumes that the person will derive a 'tax benefit' or 'financial benefit' by virtue of an 'arrangement'; or *(c)* any other person who is party to an 'arrangement' listed in a public notice referred to in s 35(2).
- 'Pre-tax profit', in relation to an arrangement, means the profit of a participant resulting from that arrangement before deducting normal tax. The profit must be determined in accordance with financial reporting standards after taking into account all costs and expenditure incurred by the participant in connection with the arrangement and deducting any foreign tax paid or payable by the participant in connection with the arrangement.

- 'Promoter', in relation to an 'arrangement', means a person who is principally responsible for organising, designing, selling, financing or managing the 'arrangement'.
- A 'tax benefit' includes avoidance, postponement or reduction of a liability for tax (s 34).

On 3 February 2016 SARS issued a public notice[80] which adds the listed reportable arrangements above. It identifies the following as reportable arrangements:

- an arrangement that would have qualified as a 'hybrid equity instrument' in terms of s 8E of the Act if the prescribed period in that section had been 10 years, but does not include any instrument listed on an exchange regulated in terms of the Financial Markets Act 19 of 2012;
- an arrangement in terms of which a company buys back shares – on or after the date of publication of the SARS public notice – from one or more shareholders for an aggregate amount exceeding R10 million, and that company issued or is required to issue any shares within 12 months of entering into that arrangement or of the date of any buy-back in terms of that arrangement;
- an arrangement in terms of which a person that is a resident makes any contribution or payment on or after 16 March 2015 to a trust that is not a resident and has or acquires a beneficial interest in that trust, and the amount of all contributions or payments – whether made before or after 16 March 2015 – or the value of that interest exceeds or is reasonably expected to exceed R10 million;[81]
- an arrangement in terms of which one or more persons acquire the controlling interest in a company – on or after the date of publication of the SARS public notice – including by means of acquiring shares, voting rights or a combination of both that:
  - has carried forward or reasonably expects to carry forward a balance of assessed loss exceeding R50 million from the year of assessment immediately preceding the year of assessment in which the controlling interest is acquired, or has or reasonably expects to have an assessed loss exceeding R50 million in respect of the year of assessment during which the controlling interest is acquired; or
  - directly or indirectly holds a controlling interest in a company referred to above;[82]

---

[80] GN 140 in *GG* 39650 of 3 February 2016.

[81] The contributions exclude any contributions or payments made to or beneficial interest acquired in any: *(a)* portfolio comprised in any investment scheme contemplated in para *(e)*(ii) of the definition of 'company' in s 1(1) of the Act, or *(b)* foreign investment entity as defined in s 1(1) of the Act.

[82] See the bullet point directly above.

- an arrangement between a person that is a resident and a person that qualifies as an insurer in terms of any law of any country other than the Republic (hereinafter referred to as the 'foreign insurer') in terms of which:
  - an aggregate amount that exceeds or is reasonably expected to exceed R5 million has been paid or becomes payable by the resident to the foreign insurer; and
  - any amount payable on or after 16 March 2016, in cash or otherwise, to any beneficiary in terms of that arrangement is to be determined mainly by reference to the value of particular assets or categories of assets that are held by or on behalf of the foreign insurer or by another person for purposes of that arrangement; and
- an arrangement for the rendering to a person – which either *(a)* is a resident, or *(b)* is not a resident that has a permanent establishment in the Republic to which that arrangement relates – of consultancy, construction, engineering, installation, logistical, managerial, supervisory, technical or training services, in terms of which:
  - a person that is not a resident or an employee, agent or representative of that person was or is physically present in the Republic, or is anticipated to be physically present in the Republic, in connection with or for purposes of rendering those services; and
  - the expenditure in respect of those services under that arrangement incurred or to be incurred, on or after the date of publication of the notice, exceeds or is anticipated to exceed R10 million in aggregate, and does not qualify as remuneration for purposes of the Fourth Schedule to the Act.

13.3.1.1 Excluded arrangements

An arrangement is an excluded arrangement (that is, the reportable arrangement provisions do not apply to it) if the aggregate tax benefit which is or may be derived from that arrangement by all participants to that arrangement does not exceed R5 million, or if the tax benefit which is or will be derived or is assumed to be derived from that arrangement is not the main or one of the main benefits of that arrangement.

13.3.1.2 Disclosure obligation

The information referred to in s 38 in respect of a 'reportable arrangement' must be disclosed by a person who is a participant in an arrangement on the date on which it qualifies as a reportable arrangement or becomes a participant in an arrangement after the date on which it qualifies as a reportable arrangement.

Participant is defined as: *(a)* a 'promoter'; *(b)* a person who directly or indirectly will derive, or assumes that the person will derive, a 'tax benefit' or 'financial benefit' by virtue of an 'arrangement'; or *(c)* any other person who is party to an 'arrangement' listed in a public notice referred to in s 35(2).[83] A promoter is in turn defined as a person who is principally responsible for organising, designing, selling, financing or managing the arrangement.[84] A 'participant' need not report a transaction if that participant has obtained a written statement from any other 'participant' that the other 'participant' has disclosed the 'reportable arrangement'.[85] SARS may grant an extension for disclosure for a further 45 business days, if reasonable grounds exist for the extension.[86]

13.3.1.3 Information to be submitted

The participant must submit in relation to a reportable arrangement, in the prescribed form and manner and by the date specified:

- a detailed description of all its steps and key features, including, in the case of an arrangement that is a step in or part of a larger arrangement, all the steps and key features of the larger arrangement;
- a detailed description of the assumed tax benefits for all participants, including, but not limited to, tax deductions and deferred income;
- the names, registration numbers and registered addresses of all participants;
- a list of all its agreements; and
- any financial model that embodies its projected tax treatment.[87]

After receipt of the information listed above, SARS must issue a reportable arrangement reference number to each participant for administrative purposes only[88]

13.3.1.4 Penalties

Any participant who fails to disclose the information in respect of a reportable arrangement, as required, shall be liable to a penalty for each month that the failure continues (up to 12 months) of:

- R50 000 in the case of a participant other than the promoter; or
- R100 000 in the case of the promoter.[89]

The amount of the penalty is doubled if the amount of the anticipated tax benefit for the participant by reason of the arrangement exceeds R5 million and is tripled if the benefit exceeds R10 million.[90]

---

[83] Section 34 of the TAA definition of 'participant'.
[84] Section 34 of the TAA definition of 'promoter'.
[85] Section 37(3) of the TAA.
[86] Section 37(5) of the TAA.
[87] Section 39 of the TAA.
[88] Section 39 of the TAA.
[89] Section 212(1) of the TAA.
[90] Section 212(2) of the TAA.

A participant who is a participant in a transaction that is a reportable arrangement as published in the SARS public notice of 3 February 2016,[91] and who fails to disclose the information as required, is liable to a penalty in the amount of R50 000.

13.3.2 Assessed losses

The provisions of s 103(2) are aimed specifically at the so-called trafficking of assessed losses and enable the Commissioner to disallow the set-off of an assessed loss in certain circumstances.

In order to apply the provisions of s 103(2) the Commissioner must be satisfied that the following requirements are met. First, there must be:

- an agreement affecting a company or trust;[92]
- a change in:
  - the shareholding in a company;[93]
  - the members' interests in a company that is a close corporation;[94] or
  - the trustees or beneficiaries of any trust.[95]

Secondly, as a direct or indirect result of the agreement or change referred to above:

- income must have been received by or have accrued to that company or trust during any year of assessment;[96] or
- any proceeds received by or accrued to or deemed to have been received by or to have accrued to that company or trust in consequence of the disposal of any asset, as contemplated in the Eighth Schedule, must have resulted in a capital gain during any year of assessment.[97]

Thirdly, the agreement or change must have, at any time, been entered into or effected by any person solely or mainly for the purpose of utilising:

- any assessed loss;
- any balance of assessed loss;
- any capital loss; or
- any assessed capital loss,

incurred by the company or trust, in order to avoid liability on the part of that company or trust or any other person for the payment of any tax, duty or levy on income, or to reduce the amount thereof.[98]

---

[91] GN 140 in *GG* 39650 of 3 February 2016.
[92] Section 103(2)*(a)*.
[93] Section 103(2)*(b)*(i).
[94] Section 103(2)*(b)*(ii).
[95] Section 103(2)*(b)*(iii).
[96] Section 103(2)(A).
[97] Section 103(2)(B).
[98] Section 103(2).

CHAPTER 13

Once the Commissioner is satisfied that the requirements listed above have been met:

- the set-off of the assessed loss or balance of assessed loss against the income received or accrued as a result of the agreement or change must be disallowed;[99]
- the set-off of the assessed loss or balance of assessed loss against any taxable capital gain, to the extent that the taxable capital gain takes into account the capital gain resulting from the agreement or change, must be disallowed;[100] or
- the set-off of the capital loss or assessed capital loss against the capital gain resulting from the agreement or change must be disallowed.[101]

Any decision of the Commissioner under s 103(2) is subject to objection and appeal.[102] If it is proved in any objection and appeal proceedings that:

- the agreement; or
- change in:
  - shareholding;
  - members' interests; or
  - trustees or beneficiaries of the trust in question,

would result in the avoidance or the postponement of liability for payment of any tax, duty or levy imposed by:

- the Act;
- any previous Income Tax Act; or
- any other law administered by the Commissioner,

or in the reduction of the amount thereof, it shall be presumed, until the contrary is proved, that it has been entered into or effected solely or mainly for the purpose of utilising the:

- assessed loss;
- balance of assessed loss;
- capital loss; or
- assessed capital loss,

in question in order to avoid or postpone the liability or to reduce the amount thereof (s 103(4)).

Where the Commissioner has applied the provisions of s 103(2) in determining a party's liability for any tax, duty or levy imposed in terms of the Act, he may not exercise his discretion in terms of s 89*quat*(3) or (3A) to direct that interest is not payable in respect of that portion of any tax which is attributable to the

99 Section 103(2)*(aa)*.
100 Section 103(2)*(bb)*.
101 Section 103(2)*(cc)*.
102 Section 3(4)*(b)*.

application of the provisions.[103] Section 103(6) was repealed by s 271 of the TAA with effect from a date that is still to be determined. Section 89*quat* was also repealed by s 271 of the TAA with effect from a date that is still to be determined.

CIR v Ocean Manufacturing Ltd[104] involved a reconstruction in terms of which a merger agreement and a transfer agreement (for the subsequent transfer of business assets as a going concern) were concluded. Nicholas AJA held[105] that the expression 'any agreement affecting any company' in s 103(2) is not restricted to an agreement which affects the control of the company or one which affects any person's right to participate in the profits or dividends of the company. The provisions of s 103(2) could therefore be applied to the transfer agreement. Nicholas AJA also held[106] that s 103(2) should be construed in such a way as to advance the remedy provided and to suppress the mischief against which it is directed.

Conshu (Pty) Ltd v CIR[107] concerned the question of the timing of the disallowance of the set-off by the Commissioner in terms of s 103(2). The taxpayer had entered into an agreement and had effected a change in shareholding in its 1985 year of assessment, but had claimed the set-off of an assessed loss only in its 1986 year of assessment, as it had no taxable income in the 1985 year of assessment. It was held[108] that it 'was competent for' the Commissioner to apply s 103(2) for the first time in the 1986 year of assessment.

When the new general anti-avoidance rule in ss 80A to 80L was introduced in the Act and s 103(1) was deleted, s 103(2) was not deleted. An interesting question that then arises is whether the provisions of s 103(2) are still required: it may well be that agreements or changes to which the provisions of s 103(2) can be applied by the Commissioner would also come within the provisions of the new general anti-avoidance rule.

13.3.3 Dividend/income amount swops

The provisions of s 103(5) are aimed specifically at tax avoidance schemes in terms of which a taxpayer swops an amount (for example, interest that would be taxable in his or her hands) for dividends (that would be exempt from tax in terms of s 10(1)*(k)*).

In order for the provisions of s 103(5) to be applied by the Commissioner, all of the following requirements must be met:

- There must be a 'transaction, operation or scheme'.
- A taxpayer must have ceded the right to receive any amount in exchange for an amount of dividends under the transaction, operation or scheme.

[103] Section 103(6).
[104] 1990 (3) SA 610 (A), 52 SATC 151.
[105] At 161.
[106] At 162.
[107] 1994 (4) SA 603 (A), 57 SATC 1.
[108] At 11.

- In consequence of that cession, the liability for normal tax of the taxpayer or any other party to the transaction, operation or scheme, as determined before applying the provisions of s 103(5), must have been reduced or extinguished.

If these requirements are met, the Commissioner must determine the liability for normal tax of the taxpayer and any other party to the transaction, operation or scheme as if the cession in question had not been effected.[109]

For a discussion of the meaning of the term 'transaction, operation or scheme', see para 13.2.1 above.

The cession envisaged in s 103(5) is of a 'right to an amount'. The Act contains no definition of a 'right to an amount': it is submitted that this means a right to an amount in the nature of a future income flow, not an amount from the disposal of an underlying asset.[110] The provisions of s 103(5) are not aimed at cessions of amounts that have already accrued to or been received by a taxpayer: these amounts are gross income in that taxpayer's hands in terms of the definition of 'gross income' in s 1 when they accrue or are received and any subsequent cession of the amounts by that taxpayer will not reduce his or her liability to tax on the amounts.

Where the Commissioner has applied the provisions of s 103(5) in determining a party's liability for any tax, duty or levy imposed in terms of the Act, he may not exercise his discretion in terms of s 89*quat*(3) or (3A) to direct that interest is not payable in respect of that portion of any tax which is attributable to the application of the provisions.[111] Section 103(6) was repealed by s 271 of the TAA with effect from a date that is still to be determined. Section 89*quat* was also repealed by s 271 of the TAA with effect from a date that is still to be determined.

---

[109] Section 103(5).

[110] De Koker AP & Williams RC *Silke on South African Income Tax* (LexisNexis 2011) para 19.48.

[111] Section 103(6).

Chapter 14

International tax aspects

14.1 INTRODUCTION

The term 'international tax law' is often misunderstood. What is referred to as international tax law generally refers to the international aspects of the income tax laws of particular countries. In general, tax laws are not 'international' in nature. Tax laws are the creations of sovereign states. The most obvious international aspect of a country's income tax system is its tax treaties.[1] The scope of what is normally referred to as international tax law is very broad. It encompasses all tax issues in a country's income tax laws that include some foreign element. These include:

- the income tax aspects of cross-border trade in goods and services;
- cross-border manufacturing by multinational enterprises;
- cross-border investment by individuals or by investment funds; and
- the taxation of individuals who work or do business outside their countries of residence.

[1] Arnold B & McIntyre J *International Tax Primer* (Kluwer Law International 2002) 2.

In general, the international tax law aspects of any given country fall under two broad dimensions:

- Out-bound transactions: these are transactions that involve the export of capital or other resources from one country to another country. The relevant tax laws ensure the taxation of individuals, entities and corporations on income arising in foreign countries.
- In-bound transactions: these are transactions that involve the import of capital or other resources from a foreign country.[2] The relevant tax laws ensure the taxation of non-residents on income arising domestically.

Taking the above into consideration, in this book the study of the international tax law aspects in South Africa's income tax laws considers:

- the provisions in the Income Tax Act 58 of 1962 ('the Act') that regulate the taxation of international transactions; and
- the impact of double taxation agreements on the taxation of international transactions in South Africa.

14.2 PROVISIONS IN THE ACT THAT REGULATE THE TAXATION OF INTERNATIONAL TRANSACTIONS

14.2.1 Jurisdiction to tax international transactions

If a person is involved in any international transaction in South Africa, South Africa has the jurisdiction to tax the income derived by a person from those transactions if there is a nexus or connection between South Africa and that person's transaction. As discussed in chapter 3 of this book, the Act sets out two bases of taxation that can be applied to determine a person's gross income. In terms of the definition of 'gross income' in s 1 of the Act, the basis of taxation is whether a person is a resident or a non-resident. Residents are taxed on a residence basis, implying that a resident's worldwide income is subject to tax in South Africa. In the case of non-residents, 'gross income' comprises only that income that has its source in the Republic. See chapter 3 on details regarding jurisdiction to tax.

14.2.2 International transactions that are exempt from tax in South Africa

As explained in chapter 3, after a person's gross income has been determined, the next step is to exclude exempt income from it in order to arrive at income. Chapter 5 of this book dealt with the exemptions provided for in the Act. For purposes of this chapter, the following exemptions apply with regard to taxpayers that are involved in international transactions.

[2] Arnold & McIntyre *International Tax* 4.

14.2.2.1 Foreign governments and assistance agreements

Section 10(1)*(b*A*)* exempts from tax receipts and accruals of:

- the government of any other country;[3]
- any foreign government agency appointed by that government to administer its responsibilities and functions in terms of an official development assistance agreement;[4] and
- any multinational organisation providing foreign donor funding in terms of an official development assistance agreement (s 231(3) of the Constitution of the Republic of South Africa, 1996). The Minister must announce the exemption in terms of a notice in the *Government Gazette*.

14.2.2.2 Salaries of foreign government officials and their staff

Section 10(1)*(c)*(iii) exempts from tax the salary or remuneration paid to foreign state officials (such as diplomats, consuls and ambassadors) if they are not ordinarily resident in the Republic.

Section 10(1)*(c)*(iv) exempts from tax amounts paid to a domestic or private servant of a foreign diplomat, for domestic or private services rendered to the foreign diplomat, if the servant is not a South African citizen and if the servant is not ordinarily resident in the Republic.

14.2.2.3 Special inter-government agreements

Section 10(1)*(c)*(v) exempts from tax the salary of a foreign subject temporarily employed in the Republic, provided the exemption is authorised by an agreement entered into by the government of the foreign state in South Africa.

14.2.2.4 Foreign social security and pension payments

Section 10(1)*(g*C*)*(i) provides an exemption for any amount received by or accrued to any resident under the social security system of any other country.

Section 10(1)*(g*C*)*(ii) (amended by the Taxation Laws Amendment Act 17 of 2017) provides an exemption for a lump sum, pension or annuity received by or accrued to any resident from a source outside the Republic as consideration for past employment outside the Republic. This excludes amounts from any pension fund, pension preservation fund, provident fund, provident preservation fund or retirement annuity fund as defined in s 1(1), or a company that is a resident and that is registered in terms of the Long-term Insurance Act 52 of 1998 by a person carrying on long-term insurance business (excluding any amount transferred to that fund or that insurer from a source outside the Republic in respect of that member). The commencement date for this provision was 1 March 2018.

---

[3] Section 10(1)*(b*A*)*(i).

[4] Section 10(1)*(b*A*)*(ii).

14.2.2.5 Foreign banks

In terms of s 10(1)*(j)*, the receipts and accruals of foreign banks are exempt from tax if all the following requirements are met:

- The bank is not resident in South Africa.
- The bank is entrusted by the government of a territory outside the Republic with the custody of the principle foreign exchange reserves of that territory.
- The Minister of Finance must have granted this exemption to the specific bank for the particular year of assessment. The exemption is granted annually.

14.2.2.6 Ship crews

Section 10(1)*(o)*(i) exempts from tax any remuneration (as defined in the Fourth Schedule to the Act) derived by any person as an officer or crew member of a ship engaged in international transportation of passengers or goods if:

- such person was outside the Republic for a period exceeding 183 full days in aggregate during the year of assessment; or
- the crew of the ship is used in the prospecting, exploration, mining or production (including surveys and other work of a similar nature) for any minerals (including natural oils) from the seabed outside the Republic. Such officer or crew members may also have their remuneration exempted under this provision where such officer or crew member is employed on board such ship solely for purposes of the 'passage' of such ship, as defined in the Marine Traffic Act 2 of 1981, and the 'days' requirement is met. A full day runs from 00h00 to 24h00.

According to SARS Interpretation Note 34 of 12 January 2006, s 10(1)*(o)*(i) was inserted into the Act in 1993 in order to bring the provisions of the Act in line with those of the major maritime nations, which exempt their seamen from income tax if they are absent from their home countries for a period exceeding 183 days in aggregate during the tax year. For the purpose of this exemption, weekends, public holidays, vacation and sick leave spent outside South Africa are considered to form part of the 183-day period.

Section 10(1)*(o)*(i) applies to any person, whether a South African tax resident or not, as long as such person is engaged in the international transportation for reward of passengers or goods. This will include passenger lines and cargo ships travelling in international waters. The transportation must be for reward, which means there must be a *quo pro quo* for the conveyance of passengers or goods. According to SARS Interpretation Note 34, the requirement that the ship must be engaged in the business of transportation means that the transport of fish from the fishing ground to the port by a fishing trawler will not constitute transportation. Applying the same reasoning, the crew of a luxury yacht owned by a wealthy businessman for private use would not be able to utilise this exemption.

14.2.2.7 Foreign dividends and dividends paid or declared by a headquarter may qualify for the following exemptions

Paragraph *(k)* of the definition of the term 'gross income' in s 1 includes in gross income any amount received or accrued by way of local dividends or foreign dividends. A foreign dividend is defined in s 1 as an amount paid by a foreign company in respect of a share in that foreign dividend. However, s 10B exempts certain foreign dividends totally from tax, such as where the participation exemption or country-to-country exemptions apply. Other foreign dividends, such as from CFCs and those declared on JSE-listed shares, are partially exempt.

14.2.2.8 Exemption for royalties (as defined in s 49A) received by or accrued to a non-resident subject to certain conditions (s 10(1)(l)*)*

Section 49A of the Act defines 'royalty' to mean any amount that is received or accrues in respect of—

(a) the use or right of use of or permission to use any intellectual property as defined in section 23I; or

(b) the imparting of or the undertaking to impart any scientific, technical, industrial or commercial knowledge or information, or the rendering of or the undertaking to render any assistance or service in connection with the application or utilisation of such knowledge or information.

Section 10(1)*(l)* exempts the amount of any royalty as defined in s 49A which is received by or accrues to any person that is not a resident, unless—

(i) that person is a natural person who was physically present in the Republic for a period exceeding 183 days in aggregate during the twelve-month period preceding the date on which the amount is received by or accrues to that person; or

(ii) the intellectual property or the knowledge or information in respect of which that royalty is paid is effectively connected with a permanent establishment of that person in the Republic ...

14.2.2.9 Section 10(1)(lA) exempts amounts received by or accrued to foreign entertainers or sportsmen if those amounts are subject to withholding tax on foreign entertainers or sportsmen under ss 47A–47K

Section 10(1)*(lA)* exempts an amount received by or accrued to a non-resident if that amount is subject to tax on a foreign entertainer or sportsperson in terms of ss 47A–47K. In terms of ss 47A–47K, a final withholding tax at a flat rate of 15% is levied on the amount received by or accrued to a non-resident entertainer or sportsperson.

14.2.2.10 Exemption of foreign employment income

Section 10(1)*(o)*(ii) exempts from tax any remuneration received or accrued by an employee:

- for a period or periods exceeding 183 full days in aggregate during any 12-month period commencing or ending during that or any other year of assessment;
- for a continuous period of 60 days during the 12-month period; and
- if such services were rendered during such periods worked outside the Republic, provided that days in transit in the Republic are deemed to be outside the Republic. Days on holiday outside the Republic count towards the days required.

For the calculation of the number of days during which a person is outside of South Africa, SARS Interpretation Note 16[5] provides that weekends, public holidays, vacation leave and sick leave spent outside South Africa are considered to be part of the days during which services are rendered and should therefore be included in the calculation of the 183-day and 60-day periods of absence.

Note that an amendment will be effected to this provision commencing in 2020. In terms of the Explanatory Memorandum to Taxation Laws Amendment Bill 2017, the purpose of introducing the exemption was to prevent double taxation of an individual's income between South Africa and the host country. Unfortunately, the exemption instead creates opportunities for double non-taxation in instances where the host country imposes little or no tax on employment income. This is contrary to the policy intent expressed when the exemption for foreign employment income tax was introduced. The explanatory memorandum on the Revenue Laws Amendment Act, 2000 cautioned against the undue exploitation of this exemption by stating that 'the effect of this relief measure will be monitored to determine whether certain categories of employees abuse it to earn foreign employment income without foreign taxation'.

It is required of policy-makers to continuously ensure that the tax system espouses the principle of fairness and progressivity. Therefore, considerable attention should be given to the principle of equity, which ensures that taxpayers in an equal position should be taxed in an equal manner as they have the same ability to bear the tax burden (horizontal equity) and that taxpayers with better circumstances should bear a larger part of the tax burden as a proportion of their income (vertical equity). For this reason, it was proposed that foreign employment income earned by a resident should no longer be fully exempt as is currently provided. Tax residents who spend more than 183 days outside of South Africa rendering employment services will now only be exempted up to the first R1 million of their employment income earned abroad. The R1 million exemption will provide relief for lower to middle income South Africans working abroad. Any foreign employment income earned over and above this amount

[5] 'Exemption from income tax: Foreign employment income' (27 March 2003).

will be taxed in South Africa, applying the normal tax tables for that particular year of assessment. Residents will still be required to have spent a continuous period of at least 60 full days, rendering employment services outside South Africa, during any 12-month period in order to qualify for the exemption. The proposed amendment will come into effect on 1 March 2020 and applies in respect of years of assessment commencing on or after that date.

14.2.2.11 International shipping income (s 12Q)

International shipping income received by an international shipping company in respect of years of assessment that commence on or after 1 April 2014 will be exempt from normal tax. The purpose of this exemption is for this industry to remain competitive internationally. The international trend has been to reduce the taxation of international shipping transport due to the highly mobile nature of this activity. In order to qualify for this exemption, the international shipping company must be a South African resident that holds a share or shares in one or more South African ships that are used in international shipping. International shipping is defined in s 12Q as the conveyance for compensation of passenger or goods by means of the operation of a South African ship mainly engaged in international traffic. A South African ship is a ship which is registered in the Republic in accordance with s 15 of the Ship Registration Act 58 of 1998. The tax regime for qualifying international shipping companies includes exemptions from normal tax, capital gains, dividends tax as well as cross-border withholding tax on interest.

14.2.2.12 Ships and aircraft: Foreign owners or characters (s 10 (1)(cG))

Section 33 imposes what is known as a 'liftings tax' on owners or characters of ships or aircraft who are not residents but embark passengers or load livestock, mail or goods in South Africa. However, s 10(1)*(cG)* provides that receipts and accruals of non-resident ship or aircraft owners or charterers are exempt if 'a similar exemption or equivalent relief' is granted to SA residents by the country in which that person is resident.

14.2.2.13 Exemption of interest – residents

Section 10(1)*(i)* (as amended by the Taxation Laws Amendment Act 24 of 2011) exempts from tax, in the case of any taxpayer who is a natural person, so much of the aggregate of any interest received by or accrued to him or her from a source in the Republic as does not during the year of assessment exceed:

- in the case of any person who was or, had he or she lived, would have been at least 65 years of age on the last day of the year of assessment, the amount of R34 500; or
- in any other case, the amount of R23 800.

14.2.2.14 Exemptions for foreign interest – non-residents

Section 10(1)*(h)* exempts from tax, interest received by or accrued to a non-resident during any year of assessment, unless:

- in the case of a natural person, he or she was physically present in the Republic for a period exceeding 183 days in aggregate during that year; or
- in the case of a company, it carried on business at any time during that year through a permanent establishment in the Republic.

14.2.3 Allowable deductions

After exempt income has been deducted from a person's gross income, allowable deductions are subtracted in terms of ss 11 and 23 in order to arrive at taxable income. In the case of international transactions, the following provisions that relate to allowable deductions are also relevant.

Section 6*quat*(1C) provides that a resident may claim certain foreign taxes that do not qualify for the rebate under s 6*quat*(1) as a deduction in determining taxable income, that is, essentially, foreign taxes payable on South African-sourced amounts. SARS Interpretation Note 18[6] provides guidance on this deduction.

Section 64N provides for relief from foreign taxes paid on foreign cash dividends paid by a foreign company in respect of its listed shares. Section 64N(1) provides for the deduction of certain foreign taxes against dividends tax on such a dividend.

14.2.3.1 Ring-fencing of losses from foreign trade income (s 20(1))

Foreign trade income, such as income derived from sales in foreign countries and a resident's share of profit derived from a foreign partnership, are included in the gross income of a resident. Any allowances and deductions incurred in the production of this foreign income will be granted in terms of the Act. It must be noted that proviso *(b)* to s 20(1) ring-fences losses from a foreign trade. The proviso states that an assessed loss which was incurred in the same year of assessment, or any balance of assessed loss which was incurred in a previous year of assessment, from the carrying on of any trade outside South Africa, may not be set off against any amounts derived from the carrying on of any trade in South Africa.

---

[6] 'Rebate or deduction for foreign taxes on income'.

14.3 THE TAX TREATMENT OF INCOME DERIVED BY DIFFERENT TYPES OF TAXPAYERS INVOLVED IN INTERNATIONAL TRANSACTIONS

14.3.1 Income from foreign companies

In terms of the definition of the term 'resident' in s 1 of the Act, a company, being a legal entity, is taxable in the Republic if it is incorporated, registered or has its place of effective management in the Republic. If a company that is resident in South Africa sets up a subsidiary company in another country, the foreign-sourced income of the subsidiary company is not subject to tax in South Africa, since the subsidiary is a foreign company incorporated and recognised as a separate juridical entity in that other country. Thus, South Africa cannot apply the 'residence basis of taxation' to tax income of such a subsidiary company incorporated in another country until such income is distributed to the shareholders as dividends. This, however, has the potential of encouraging the deferral of taxes.[7]

In order to bring into the taxing net the income earned by South African-owned foreign subsidiaries and to counter the deferral of taxes, the worldwide taxation of South African residents is extended in the Act, in order to deem income of a foreign company to be that of South African residents, notwithstanding the fact that the actual income is received by or accrues to a foreign company.[8] This is effected through the use of controlled foreign company ('CFC') legislation, which ensures that the undistributed income of a CFC is not deferred, but is taxed in the hands of its domestic shareholders as and when it is derived. Basically, this legislation ensures that South African owners of foreign companies are taxed on the income earned by those foreign companies, as if they had repatriated their foreign income as soon as it was earned.[9]

14.3.1.1 The workings of the CFC legislation

The CFC legislation is set out in s 9D of the Act. In order to apply s 9D successfully, the following issues have to be determined:

- whether the entity qualifies as a foreign company;
- whether the foreign company qualifies as a CFC;
- the net income of the CFC as determined in accordance with the Act; and
- what may be excluded in the determination of the net income of the CFC.

[7] Oguttu AW *International Tax Law: Offshore Tax Avoidance in South Africa* (2015) 135; Arnold & McIntyre *International Tax* 87.

[8] Jooste RD 'The Imputation of Income of Controlled Foreign Entities' (2001) 118 *SALJ* 473; Oguttu *International Tax Law* 136.

[9] Olivier L & Honiball M *International Tax: A South African Perspective* 5 ed (Siber Ink 2011) 558.

14.3.1.2 There must be a 'foreign company'

In terms of s 1 of the Act (as amended by the Taxation Laws Amendment Act 7 of 2010) a 'foreign company' means any company which is not a resident. The following companies qualify as foreign companies, provided that they are not resident in South Africa:

- associations, corporations, bodies corporate or companies incorporated or deemed to be incorporated under South African law;
- associations, corporations, companies or bodies corporate incorporated under foreign law;
- ·certain local and offshore collective investment schemes in securities (previously known as unit trusts);
- a co-operative as defined in s 1 of the Act; and
- a close corporation as defined in s 1 of the Act.[10]

Foreign partnerships are excluded from the definition of 'company' and consequently cannot constitute a foreign company as defined.[11] Since the foreign company has to be a body corporate under the laws of the relevant foreign jurisdiction, CFC legislation does not apply where the foreign entity is a trust or other unincorporated entity (such as a limited liability partnership) even if it has limited liability, unless such an entity is a body corporate.[12]

14.3.1.3 The foreign company must be a controlled foreign company

The next step is to determine whether a foreign company is a 'controlled foreign company'. In terms of s 9D(1) of the Act:

> '[C]ontrolled foreign company' means any foreign company where more than 50 per cent of the total participation rights in that foreign company are directly or indirectly held, or more than 50 per cent of the voting rights in that foreign company are directly or indirectly exercisable, by one or more persons that are residents other than persons that are headquarter companies ...

The term 'participation rights' refers to the right to participate in the share capital, share premium, current or accumulated profits or reserves of the foreign company. Voting rights will only be taken into account where a company has no shares and has only voting rights.

The definition of a CFC excludes residents who are connected persons who, in aggregate, hold more than 50% of the participation rights or voting rights in a foreign listed company[13] or a foreign collective investment scheme or

---

[10] Olivier & Honiball *International Tax* 562.

[11] Ibid.

[12] Olivier & Honiball *International Tax* 563.

[13] In terms of the definition of 'listed company' contained in s 1 of the Income Tax Act, a listed company is defined as a company whose shares or depository receipts for its shares are listed on a stock exchange or a stock exchange in another country recognised by the Minister. See De Koker AP *South African Income Tax* (LexisNexis) para 5.44.

arrangement, but individually hold less than 5% of the participation rights or voting rights in the listed company or 'foreign collective investment scheme' or arrangement (or a so-called 'equity unit trust' as contemplated in para *(e)* (ii) of the definition of a company in s 1). In relation to a CFC, the country of residence means the country where the company has its place of effective management.

The definition of a CFC excludes headquarter companies in the determination of the participation rights and voting rights of South African residents in a foreign company. In terms of s 1 of the Act, as amended by the Taxation Laws Amendment Act 24 of 2011, a 'headquarter company' in respect of any year of assessment means a company contemplated in s 9I(1) in respect of which an election has been made in terms of that section. Section 9I(1), as amended by the Taxation Laws Amendment Act 22 of 2012, provides that a headquarter company has to be a resident company that complies with the requirements set out in s 9I(2) (these requirements are discussed in para 14.3.5 of this chapter). A resident company may elect, in the form and manner determined by the Commissioner, to be a headquarter company for a year of assessment of that company.

If a resident company meets the requirements in s 9I(2) of the Act, it is not caught by the CFC legislation. In effect, this tax relief ensures that foreign subsidiaries of companies that qualify as headquarter companies are not treated as CFCs if the headquarter company has significant equity interests in those foreign subsidiaries.[14]

14.3.1.4 The net income of the CFC has to be determined

When it has been established that a CFC exists, the net income of the CFC is attributed to the affected South African resident. 'Net income' is defined in s 9D(2) in relation to a CFC to mean an amount equal to the taxable income of the company determined in accordance with the provisions of the South African Act as if the company had been a South African resident taxpayer. For example:

- 'Gross income' in s 1 requires the CFC to include its worldwide receipts and accruals in its gross income.
- In terms of s 7(8), if the CFC makes a disposition and that disposition causes income to accrue to a non-resident, that income is deemed to accrue to the CFC.
- In terms of s 10(1)*(h)*, the CFC will not enjoy the exemption for interest earned on ESKOM (and similar) bonds.
- In terms of s 25B, the CFC will be treated as a resident 'donor' or as a resident beneficiary in relevant circumstances.
- In terms of para 2(1)*(a)* of the Eighth Schedule, all of the assets of a CFC will be subject to capital gains tax.
- In terms of para 12 of the Eighth Schedule, the deemed disposal and deemed re-acquisition provisions will apply.

[14] Explanatory Memorandum on the Taxation Laws Amendment Bill, 2010 para 5.4, part III.

- In terms of para 24 of the Eighth Schedule, if a foreign company becomes a CFC after valuation date (1 October 2001), the base cost of its assets will be determined under the provisions of para 24.
- In terms of paras 70, 71, 72 and 80 of the Eighth Schedule, the CFC will be treated as a resident beneficiary or as a resident donor in the relevant circumstances.

However, the above provisions of the Act are applied to the CFC's taxable income, subject to the following limitations:

- In terms of s 9D(2A)*(a)*, any deductions and allowances that may be claimed or any amount that may be set off against a CFC's income in terms of the Act are limited to the amount of that income.
- In terms of s 9D(2A)*(b)*, where the deductions of the CFC exceed its income and the result would be an assessed loss, the assessed loss may not be set off against income received by the South African resident from other trades outside the Republic, but must instead be carried forward to the immediately succeeding foreign tax year to be offset against future income of the CFC.[15]
- In terms of s 9D(2A)*(c)*, no deduction is allowed for interest, royalties, rental or income of a similar nature paid or payable by the company to another CFC. This would include amounts adjusted for transfer pricing purposes (s 31) or any exchange difference determined under s 24I. These amounts are deemed not to be attributed to the South African resident in terms of s 9D(9)*(f*A*)*.
- There are certain capital gains tax (CGT) implications. In terms of s 9D(2A)*(e)*, where a foreign company becomes a CFC after 1 October 2001 (when CGT was introduced) the valuation date for CGT purposes is the date the company became a CFC. The Income Tax Act includes capital gains in taxable income; therefore, the tax rate is 28% for companies, and 18% to 40% for natural persons. However, the amount of the capital gain so included varies depending on the profile of the taxpayer. Thus, only 25% of a capital gain is included in the taxable income of natural persons, special trusts and the individual policyholder fund of long-term insurers, whilst 50% is included in the taxable income of companies and trusts. This principle is followed in the determination of the net income of a CFC. Hence, only 25% of capital gains will be included in the net income of a CFC to the extent that the imputation is to a natural person, special trust or the individual policyholder fund of a long-term insurer.
- In terms of s 9D(2A)*(f)* where the resident is a natural person, special trust or an insurer in respect of its individual policyholder fund, the taxable capital gain of the CFC shall, for the purposes of para 10 of the Eighth Schedule, be 40% of that company's net capital gain for the relevant foreign tax year.

---

[15] See Meyerowitz D *Meyerowitz on Income Tax* (Taxpayer CC 2008) para 9.115.

- For the purposes of para 43 of the Eighth Schedule, 'local currency' of a CFC, other than in relation to a permanent establishment of the CFC, means the currency used by it for the purposes of its financial reporting (s 9D(2A)*(k)*).
- In terms of s 9D(2A)*(l)* where the functional currency of a CFC (1) was in a foreign country which abandoned its currency and which had an official rate of inflation of 100% or more for the foreign tax year preceding the abandonment of the currency, and (2) the CFC adopted a new functional currency, the CFC must, for the purposes of determining the cost of an asset, be deemed to have acquired the asset in the new currency on the first day of the foreign tax year of the CFC for an amount equal to the market value of the asset on the date on which the new currency was adopted.

A further proviso was added and this relates to the 75% foreign tax threshold. In terms of this proviso, the net income of a CFC in respect of a foreign tax year shall be deemed to be nil if its aggregate amount of taxes on income payable to all spheres of government of any country is at least 75% of the amount of normal tax that would have been payable by that CFC if it had been a resident for that foreign tax year. The net income of a CFC in respect of a foreign tax year shall also be deemed to be nil.

The aggregate foreign tax payable by the CFC (as contemplated above) must be determined after taking into account any applicable double taxation agreement and any credit, rebate or any right of recovery of the foreign tax from any sphere of foreign government. One must also disregard any balance of assessed loss brought forward from earlier tax years or any losses taken into account from other companies.[16]

The normal tax that would have been payable by the CFC if it had been a resident (as contemplated above) must be determined before taking into account the amount that would have been included in the income of that CFC in terms of s 9D(2) (had that CFC been a resident for that foreign tax year).

14.3.1.5 Exemptions to the CFC provisions

The net income of a CFC is excluded from the ambit of s 9D and will not be attributed to the residents who hold voting or participation rights in the entity concerned under the following circumstances.

(a) Foreign business establishment exemption

A 'foreign business establishment' in relation to a CFC is defined in s 9D as a fixed place of business located in a country other than the Republic that is used or will continue to be used for the carrying on of the business of that CFC for a period of not less than one year. The OECD Model Tax Convention refers to the phrase 'fixed place of business' to connote a link between the place

[16] De Koker and Brincker (2010) *Silke on International Tax* (LexisNexis) par 3.5.4.7

of business and a specific geographical point.[17] Evidence of a fixed place of business could be places where:

- that business is conducted through one or more offices, shops, factories, warehouses or other structures;
- that fixed place of business is suitably staffed with on-site managerial and operational employees of that CFC who conduct the primary operations of that business;
- that fixed place of business is suitably equipped for conducting the primary operations of that business;
- that fixed place of business has suitable facilities for conducting the primary operations of that business; and
- that fixed place of business is located outside the Republic solely or mainly for a purpose other than the postponement or reduction of any tax imposed by any sphere of government in the Republic.

In order to determine whether there is a fixed place of business, a CFC may take into account the utilisation of physical structures, employees, equipment and facilities belonging to any other company, provided that:

- that other company is subject to tax in the country in which the fixed place of business of the CFC is located by virtue of residence, place of effective management or other criteria of a similar nature;
- that other company forms part of the same group of companies as the CFC; and
- to the extent that the structures, employees, equipment and facilities are located in the same country as the fixed place of business of the CFC.

The legislation acknowledges that circumstances may exist where business activities are legitimately conducted in one or more locations for reasons wholly unrelated to South African tax, but the nature of those activities may be such that the criteria for a fixed foreign business establishment may not necessarily be met. In this regard, the Act provides specific examples of foreign business establishments that would be recognised.[18] These are:

- any place outside the Republic where prospecting or exploration operations for natural resources are carried on, or any place outside the Republic where mining or production operations of natural resources are carried on, where that CFC carries on those prospecting, exploration, mining or production operations;
- a site outside the Republic for the construction or installation of buildings, bridges, roads, pipelines, heavy machinery or other projects of a comparable magnitude which lasts for a period of not less than six months, where that CFC carries on those construction or installation activities;

---

[17] Article 5(1) of the OECD Model Tax Convention.

[18] *Silke on International Tax* para 3.6.1.2

- agricultural land in any country other than the Republic used for *bona fide* farming activities directly carried on by that CFC;
- a vessel, vehicle, rolling stock or aircraft used for the purposes of transportation or fishing, or prospecting or exploration for natural resources, or mining or production of natural resources, where that vessel, vehicle, rolling stock or aircraft is used solely outside the Republic for such purposes and is operated directly by that CFC or by any other company that has the same country of residence as that CFC and that forms part of the same group of companies as that CFC;
- a South African ship as defined in section 12Q engaged in international shipping as defined in that section; or
- a ship engaged in international traffic used mainly outside the Republic.

From the above, it appears that for a place of business to qualify as a 'foreign business establishment' there must be an 'economic substance' and 'a business purpose'. For there to be 'economic substance' the foreign business must not exist merely on paper. The foreign business must maintain a presence consisting of persons who make the day-to-day management decisions. In *SIR v Downing*[19] it was pointed out that the use of independent agents does not qualify a business as a business establishment. The 'business purpose' requirement ensures that there must be permanence and economic substance; the exemption will not be granted if the business activities are conducted not for *bona fide* business purposes but to obtain a tax benefit.[20]

Even though a CFC may have a foreign business establishment, this will not automatically protect all of the CFC's income from potential inclusion in the taxable income of the CFC's South African shareholder or shareholders. Certain types of income are excluded from the foreign business establishment exemption.

Non-arm's length transactions with connected persons who are South African residents: The foreign business exemption will not be granted if a CFC supplies goods or services to a connected person (as defined in s 1 of the Act) who is a South African tax resident if the income derived does not reflect an arm's length price in terms of the transfer pricing provisions in s 31 of the Act. Section 9D(9)*(b)*(i) of the Act provides that in determining the amount that is attributable to a foreign business establishment, it must be treated as if it were a distinct and separate enterprise engaged in the same or similar activities under the same or similar conditions and dealing wholly independently with the CFC of which it is a foreign business establishment. The amount must be determined as if it arose in the context of a transaction, operation, scheme, agreement or understanding that was entered into on the terms and conditions that would have existed had the parties been independent persons dealing at arm's length.

[19] 1975 (4) SA 518 (A) 525.

[20] Olivier & Honiball *International Tax* 582.

Sale of goods to connected South African resident: In terms of s 9D(9A)*(a)*(i) any amount derived from a sale of goods by a CFC to a connected person who is South African resident will be excluded from the foreign business establishment exemption unless:

- that CFC purchased those goods within its country of residence from any person who is not a connected person in relation to that CFC;
- the creation, extraction, production, assembly, repair or improvement of goods undertaken by that CFC amount to more than minor assembly or adjustment, packaging, repackaging and labelling;
- that CFC sells a significant quantity of goods of the same or a similar nature to persons who are not connected persons in relation to that CFC at comparable prices (after accounting for the level of the market, volume discounts and costs of delivery); or
- that CFC purchases the same or similar goods mainly within the country of residence of that CFC from persons who are not connected persons in relation to that CFC.

Sale of goods acquired by the CFC from connected South African residents: In terms of s 9D(9A)*(a)*(iA) any amount derived from a sale of goods by a CFC, where those goods or any tangible intermediary inputs into the goods were purchased by the CFC from a connected person who is South African resident will be excluded from the foreign business establishment exemption unless:

- those goods or tangible intermediary inputs amount to an insignificant portion of the total goods or tangible intermediary inputs acquired by the CFC overall.
- the CFC undertakes the creation, extraction, production, assembly, repair or improvement of goods which amounts to more than minor assembly or adjustment, packaging, repackaging and labelling;
- the CFC sells products to a person who is not a connected to that CFC, for physical delivery to a customer's premises situated within the country of residence of that CFC; or
- products of the same or similar nature are sold by that CFC mainly to persons who are not connected persons in relation to that CFC for physical delivery to customers' premises situated within the country of residence of that CFC.

Services performed by CFC for connected South African resident: In terms of section 9D(9A)*(a)*(ii) amounts derived by a CFC from services performed for a connected person who is South African tax resident will not benefit from the foreign establishment exemption unless the service is performed outside South Africa and:

- the service relates directly to the creation, extraction, production, assembly, repair or improvement of goods utilised within one or more countries other than the Republic;
- the service relates directly to the sale or marketing of goods of a connected person (in relation to that CFC) who is a resident and those goods are sold to persons who are not connected persons in relation

to that CFC for physical delivery to customers' premises situated within the country of residence of that CFC;

- the service is rendered mainly in the country of residence of that CFC for the benefit of customers that have premises situated in that country; or
- to the extent that no deduction is allowed of any amount paid by that connected person to that CFC in respect of the service.

In terms of s 9D(9A)*(a)*(iii) an amount that arises in respect of a financial instrument will not benefit from the foreign establishment exemption unless:

- that financial instrument is attributable to the principal trading activities of the foreign business establishment and those activities constitute the activities of a bank, financial service provider or insurer, and do not constitute the activities of a treasury operation or captive insurer; and
- that amount is attributable to any exchange difference determined in terms of s 24I in respect of that financial instrument, and exchange difference arises in the ordinary course of business of the principal trading activities of that foreign business establishment, and those the principal trading activities do not constitute the activities of a treasury operation or captive insurer.

In terms of s 9D(9A)*(a)*(iv) any amount that arises by way of rental in respect of any movable property will not benefit from the foreign establishment exemption, *unless* that movable property is leased by the CFC in terms of an operating lease that constitutes a financial instrument.

In terms of s 9D(9A)*(a)*(v) any amount that arises in respect of the use or right of use of, or permission to use, any intellectual property as defined in s 23I will not benefit from the foreign establishment exemption, unless:

- that CFC directly and regularly creates, develops or substantially upgrades any intellectual property as defined in s 23I which gives rise to that amount; and
- that intellectual property does not constitute property which constitutes tainted intellectual property as defined in s 23I.

In terms of s 9D(9A)*(a)*(vi) any amount of capital gain determined in respect of the disposal or deemed disposal of any intellectual property as defined in s 23I will not benefit from the foreign establishment exemption, unless that CFC directly and regularly creates, develops or substantially upgrades any intellectual property as defined in s 23I which gives rise to that amount.

In terms of s 9D(9A)*(a)*(vii) any amount that is in the form of an insurance premium will not benefit from the foreign establishment exemption, unless that amount is attributable to the principal trading activities of the foreign business establishment and those principal trading activities constitute the activities of an insurer (and not those of a captive insurer).[21]

[21] A captive insurance company is a foreign insurance subsidiary company established by a group of companies for the purpose of insuring the risks of the group as an alternative to the use of external insurance markets. See Oguttu *International Tax Law* 131.

(b) The insurance policy exemption

In terms of s 9D(9)*(c)* a CFC that issues long-term insurance policies can exclude from its net income the calculation, for s 9D purposes, of any amounts that it derives that relate to policyholders that are neither South African tax resident nor CFCs.

(c) Withholding tax on interest and royalties

Section 9D(9)*(d)* provides that in determining the net income of a CFC any amount which is subject to the withholding tax on interest (Part IVB of the Act) and the withholding tax on royalties (Part IVA of the Act) must not be taken into account; after taking into account any applicable agreement for the prevention of double taxation.

(d) Exemption of amounts included in the taxable income of a company

Section 9D recognises that a CFC may earn income from a South African source that is taxable in South Africa under provisions of the Act other than the CFC rules. Section 9D(9)*(e)* provides that in determining the net income of a CFC, there must not be taken into account any amount which is included in the taxable income of the company provided that it is not exempt from tax or liable to a reduced rate of tax in South Africa as a result of the application of tax treaty provisions.

(e) Exemption of foreign dividends

Where profits of a CFC have been imputed to South Africa under the CFC rules, the legislation requires these profits should again be subject to South African tax under the CFC rules when distributed to another CFC in the form of a foreign dividend. Section 9D(9)*(f)* provides that any foreign dividend declared to a CFC by any other CFC in relation to the resident must be excluded from the net income calculation, to the extent that the foreign dividend does not exceed the aggregate of all amounts included in the income of the resident in any year of assessment.

(f) Exemption for Intra group interest, royalties, rentals, or income of a similar nature

In terms of s 9D(9)*(f*A*)* the CFC rules do not apply to interest, royalties, rentals 'or income of a similar nature' paid or payable to the CFC by any other CFC in the same group of companies, where it is attributable to:

- any interest, royalties, rental or income of a similar nature which is paid or payable to that company by any other CFC (including any similar amount adjusted in terms of s 31);
- any exchange difference determined in terms of s 24I in respect of any exchange item to which that company and any other CFC are parties;
- any exchange difference in respect of any forward exchange contract or foreign currency option contract entered into to hedge the exchange item; or

- the reduction or discharge by any other CFC of a debt owed by that company to that other CFC for no consideration or for consideration that is less than the face value of the debt so reduced or discharged.

14.3.1.6 Tax credit

In terms of the s 6*quat*(1), in calculating the taxable income of a resident taxpayer, a rebate or unilateral tax credit is granted in respect of foreign taxes levied on their income. The rebate is deductible from the normal tax payable of a resident in whose taxable income there is included the certain categories of income, which includes any proportional amount calculated under the CFC rules. In a treaty context, the s 6*quat* rebate may be granted in substitution and not in addition to any relief to which a resident may be entitled under a tax treaty. Thus, a taxpayer may elect not to claim the rebate but rather claim relief under a tax treaty if the tax treaty relief is more beneficial.[22]

14.3.1.7 CFC disclosure requirements

Section 72A(1) of the Act provides that every resident who on the last day of the foreign tax year of a CFC, or immediately before a foreign company ceases to be a CFC, directly or indirectly, together with any connected person in relation to that resident, holds at least 10% of the participation rights in any CFC (otherwise than indirectly through a company which is a resident) must submit a return to the Commissioner.

14.3.2 Income from foreign trusts

Chapter 10 of this book discusses the provisions in the Act that relate to the taxation of trusts in general. The chapter also covers provisions that deal with foreign (non-resident) trusts. Refer to chapter 10 in this regard, taking note of the following points.

In terms of the definition of 'resident' in s 1 of the Act, a trust is deemed resident in South Africa if it is established or formed or it has its 'place of effective management' in the Republic.[23] This implies that income derived by a resident trust is taxable on a worldwide basis. Non-resident trusts are taxed only on income derived from a South African source.

If a South African resident forms a non-resident trust that is subject to a condition, s 7(5) of the Act can be applied to tax the resident trust founder. The application of this section to non-resident trusts is limited, however, since in order to apply the section, the trust deed has to be accessed to prove the presence of a condition. The applicable laws in some jurisdictions may contain

[22] Olivier & Honiball *International Tax* 455.

[23] De Koker *South African Income Tax* para 5.21; Du Plessis I 'The Residence of a Trust for South African Income Tax Purposes' (2009) 21 *SA Merc LJ* 322.

secrecy provisions that could prevent access to the relevant trust deed.[24] It should also be noted that if the income is retained in the non-resident trust, s 7(5) cannot apply to such a trust if it receives income only from a non-South African source.[25]

If a South African resident forms a non-resident trust but he or she retains powers to revoke or confer the income of the trust upon another, s 7(6), which applies generally to discretionary trusts, can be applied to tax the resident donor. Just like s 7(5), the application of this section to non-resident trusts is also limited, since in order to apply the section, the trust deed has to be accessed to prove the presence of retained powers. The applicable laws in some jurisdictions may contain secrecy provisions that could prevent access to the relevant trust deed.[26]

Chapter 10 also discusses s 7(8), which provides that any amount which is received by a non-resident (including a non-resident trust) due to donation made by a resident has to be included in the income of a resident donor.

Also refer to chapter 10 for a discussion of s 25B(2A), which provides that if a resident obtains a vested right to any capital (retained or accumulated income) of a non-resident trust during the year of assessment, the resident has to include that amount in his or her income for that year of assessment. This inclusion applies in respect of capital that arose from receipts or accruals that would have constituted income of the trust if it had been a resident during any previous year of assessment in which the resident had a contingent right to that amount.

14.3.3 Income from foreign partnership structures

The Commentary on Article 1 of the OECD Model Convention states:

> The domestic laws of the various OECD Member countries differ in the treatment of partnerships. The main issue of such differences is founded on the fact that some countries treat partnerships as taxable units (sometimes as companies) whereas other countries disregard the partnership and tax only the individual partners on their share of the partnership income. [27]

For example, one country may treat the entity as a partnership while the other country may treat the entity as a company.[28] The differences in classification may

[24] Oguttu *International Tax Law* 448.

[25] Clegg DJM *Income Tax in South Africa* (LexisNexis 2012) para 17.3.5; Huxham K & Haupt P *Notes on South African Income Tax* (Hedron Tax Consulting and Publishing CC 2011) para 27.3.10.

[26] Oguttu *International Tax Law* 448.

[27] Paragraph 2 of the Commentary on Article 1 of the OECD Model Tax Convention.

[28] OECD 'Issues in International Taxation No 6: The Application of the OECD Model Tax Convention to Partnerships' (OECD Publications 1999) 10; Lassard P, Kyres C & Gagnon C 'Treaty Benefit Entitlements of Trusts, Partnerships and Hybrid Entities' (1997) 49 *Tax Conference Report of the Canadian Tax Foundation* chapter 33; Tremlay R & Wharram K 'Partnerships, Trusts, and Other Entities: Treaty Benefits' in Arnold B & Sasseville J *Special*

lead to completely different tax results in the countries involved.[29] In countries where an entity is classified as a partnership, it is treated as a transparent (pass-through) entity for tax purposes, with the result that it is not taxable.[30] In those countries where the entity is classified as a company, it is normally treated as non-transparent for tax purposes, with the result that it is treated as a taxable entity.[31] Internationally, there is no uniform global treatment of foreign partnerships for tax purposes.[32]

Where two countries have entered into a tax treaty based on the OECD Model Tax Convention,[33] article 1 thereof provides that this Convention applies only to persons who are residents of one or both of the contracting states. In terms of article 3(1)*(a)* of the OECD Model Convention, the term 'person' is said to include an individual, a company, and any other body of persons.[34] Thus, a partnership (being an association of persons for the purpose of sharing benefits from a joint undertaking) can be designated as a body of persons. In terms of this article, the term 'company' is defined as a body corporate or any entity that is treated as a body corporate for tax purposes. Paragraph 2 of the

Seminar on Canadian Tax Treaties: Policy and Practice (2000) chapter 11; Easson A 'Entity Entitlement to Treaty Benefits: A Conceptual Approach to Some Practical Problems' in Arnold & Sasseville *Canadian Tax Treaties* chapter 12; Critchfield R, Honson N & Mendelowitz M 'Pass-through Entities, Income Tax Treaties and Treaty Overrides' (1999) *Tax Notes International* 587; Ault HJ & Arnold BJ *Comparative Income Taxation: A Structural Analysis* 2 ed (Kluwer Law International 2004) 336.

[29] Essers P & Meussen GTK 'The Taxation of Partnership/Hybrid Entities' in McCahery JA, Raaijmakers T & Vermeulen EPM (eds) *The Governance of Close Corporations and Partnerships: US and European Perspectives* (OUP 2004) 416.

[30] Paragraph 3 of the Commentary on Article 1 of the OECD Model Tax Convention. See also Arnold & Mclyntre *International Tax* 144; OECD *Report on Partnerships* para 24.

[31] Paragraph 3 of the Commentary on Article 1 of the OECD Model Tax Convention. See also Arnold & McIntyre *International Tax* 144; Engelen F 'International Double Taxation Resulting from Differences in Entity Characterization: A Dutch Perspective' (1998) *Intertax* 38–43; OECD *Report on Partnerships* para 24.

[32] Essers & Meussen in McCahery et al *Close Corporations and Partnerships* 415; Oguttu AW 'The Challenges of Taxing Investments in Offshore Hybrid Entities: A South African Perspective' (2009) *SA Merc LJ* 51 at 53.

[33] Although different countries use various models for drafting their double tax agreements, there are three commonly used models for drafting such agreements. First, there is the Model Tax Convention on Income and Capital, published by the Organisation for Economic Co-operation and Development ('OECD'). This model was prepared by developed countries of the world and embodies rules proposed by capital-exporting countries. Then there is the United Nations Model Double Taxation Convention. This Model has been drafted between developed and developing countries and it attempts to reflect the interests of developing countries. Lastly, there is the United States Model, which is followed by most treaties that the United States has signed with other countries, including South Africa.

[34] Schaffner J 'The OECD Report on the Application of Tax Treaties to Partnerships' (2001) *Bulletin for International Fiscal Documentation* 218–226; Clayson M 'OECD Partnerships Report: Reshaping Treaty Interpretation?' (2000) *British Tax Review* 71–83; Tillinghast D 'Tax Treaty Issues' (1996) 50 *University of Miami Law Review* 455 at 483, 467–474; Loengard R 'Tax Treaties, Partnerships and Partners: Exploration of a Relationship' (1975) 29 *Tax Lawyer* 31–67. See also Baker P 'The Application of the Convention to Partnerships, Trusts and Other, Non-corporate Entities', available at http://www.taxbar.com/documents/application_convention_pb_000.pdf (last accessed 25 July 2013).

Commentary on Article 1 provides that 'partnerships will also be considered to be "persons" either because they fall within the definition of "company" or because they constitute other bodies of persons'.

It should be noted that in a treaty context, a person will only be liable to tax if it is a 'resident' of one of the contracting states. Article 4(1) of the OECD Model Tax Convention provides that the term 'resident of a contracting state' means any person who, under the law of that state, is liable for tax therein by reason of his or her domicile, residence, place of effective management, or any other criterion of a similar nature. From the above, it can be concluded that although the inclusion of a partnership as a 'body of persons' makes it a 'person' for treaty purposes,[35] this inclusion does not necessarily make a partnership a 'resident of a contracting state'.[36] A partnership can only be considered a resident of a contracting state if it is liable to tax in that state.[37] Generally, a partnership is liable to tax in a contracting state if it is treated as a legal person (a company) that is a resident of that state. Where, however, a partnership is treated as fiscally transparent in a state, the partnership is not 'liable to tax' in that state within the meaning of article 4(1) and so it cannot be treated as a resident of that state for purposes of the Convention.

Examples of partnership and company structures (often referred to as hybrid entities) are the limited liability partnership ('LLP') and the limited liability company ('LLC'). These entities generally have a flow-through tax status in their home jurisdictions, similar to a South African limited partnership.[38] This flow-through tax status means that the profits of an LLC or LLP are taxed in the hands of the members and not the entity. In relation to other commercial activities, the entities provide limited liability to their members similar to that of a company.[39] The United Kingdom LLP[40] is a body corporate (with legal personality separate from that of its members). The LLP combines the organisational flexibility and taxation treatment of a partnership but with limited liability for its members.[41] For purposes of taxation, the UK LLP is not treated as a corporation but as a partnership.[42] The United States LLC is recognised as a corporate entity in the United States but it is treated as a partnership for

[35] Easson A 'Taxation of Partnerships in Canada' (2000) 54 *Bulletin for International Fiscal Documentation* 169.

[36] Ibid; Oguttu (2009) *SA Merc LJ* 51 at 56.

[37] Article 2 of the OECD Model Tax Convention.

[38] Oguttu (2009) *SA Merc LJ* 51 at 56.

[39] Explanatory Memorandum para 5.7, part I.

[40] Freedman J 'Limited Liability Partnerships in the United Kingdom: Do They Have a Role for Small Firms?' in McCahery et al *Close Corporations and Partnerships* 293; Morse G 'Limited Liability Partnerships Law Reform in the United Kingdom' in McCahery et al *Close Corporations and Partnerships* 317, 325.

[41] Armour D *Tolley's Limited Liability Partnerships: The New Legislation* (Reed Elsevier 2001) 295.

[42] Section 10 of the LLPA 2000, which inserts ss 118ZA–118ZD in the Income and Corporation Taxes Act 1988 (ICTA), and ss 59A and 156A in the Taxation of Chargeable Gains Act 1992 (TCGA), which provides that an LLP is treated as if it were a partnership for purposes of these two Acts.

tax purposes.[43] This tax treatment implies that the taxable income of the LLC passes to its owners, thereby avoiding corporate tax.[44]

Until the Taxation Laws Amendment Act 7 of 2010, South Africa did not have legislation to deal with the taxation in LLPs or LLCs. Uncertainty about the tax treatment of foreign LLPs and LLCs has existed for a long time in South Africa, even though there has been growing use of these entities by South Africans investing offshore and foreigners investing in South Africa. The treatment of these entities as companies is one of the factors that perpetuate the uncertainty of their tax treatment.[45]

Regarding the taxation of income from partnerships per se, in South African law, a partnership is not a legal person distinct from the individual partners who comprise the partnership.[46] A partnership is also not a taxable person for the purposes of the Income Tax Act.[47] The general rule regarding the taxation of partnerships (whether local or foreign) is that where a South African resident has an interest in a tax transparent foreign partnership, he or she is taxed in South Africa on his or her share of the partnership income. Section 24H(5) of the Income Tax Act provides that the income of the partnership is taxed in the hands of the individual partners at the time it accrues to or is received by the partnership. In terms of s 25 of the Tax Administration Act 28 of 2011, each of the partners has to submit a tax return.

Where the partners in a partnership are from different countries and a tax treaty has been signed between those two countries, a partner's business activity in the other treaty country is considered an enterprise that is conducted through a permanent establishment in that other country. Consequently, the partner is taxed on the source basis like any other foreign investor.[48] In *ITC 1819*,[49] the appellant was a partner in a firm of attorneys which was registered as a partnership in Lesotho and it did business from a permanent establishment in Lesotho. Article 7.1 of the tax treaty between the two countries provides:

The profits of an enterprise of a contracting state shall be taxable only in that state unless the enterprise carries on business in the other contracting state through a permanent establishment situated therein. If the enterprise carries on business as aforesaid, the profits of the enterprise may be taxed in the other state but only so much of them as is attributed to that permanent establishment.

The court ruled that in terms of article 7.1 of the tax treaty, the appellant carried on an enterprise in respect of a firm in Lesotho, together with others. When the matter proceeded to the High Court in *Grundlingh v CSARS*[50] the High Court held

---

[43] Whittenburg G & Altus-Buller M *Income Tax Fundamentals* (Thomson West Eagan 2007) para 10.8.

[44] Ibid.

[45] Explanatory Memorandum para 5.7, part II.

[46] *R v Levy* 1929 AD 312; *Muller en 'n Ander v Pienaar* 1968 (3) SA 195 (A).

[47] Meyerowitz *Income Tax* para 16.61.

[48] Explanatory Memorandum para 5.5, part I(A).

[49] 69 SATC 159.

[50] 72 SATC 1.

that as a partnership is not a separate legal entity, it could not be argued that the Lesotho partnership constituted a permanent establishment of the South African partnership. The High Court's decision is, however, contrary to s 24H(2) of South Africa's Income Tax Act, which provides that where any trade or business is carried on in partnership, each member of such partnership shall be deemed to be carrying on the trade or business of the partnership.[51] As such it is arguable that the Lesotho partnership was a permanent establishment of the South African partner.[52] Since the appellant was a resident of South Africa, his involvement in the firm was considered as an enterprise of South Africa that carried on business in Lesotho through a permanent establishment therein. Therefore, in terms of article 7.1, the profits of the enterprise carried on by the appellant may be taxed in Lesotho, but taxes so paid should be deducted from taxes due by the appellant in South Africa, in terms of article 23 of the tax treaty.[53]

Before the 2010 amendments to the Income Tax Act, the definition of 'company' in s 1 caused certain anomalies with respect to the taxation of foreign incorporated partnerships. This definition covered both companies incorporated in South Africa and those incorporated outside South Africa. The then s 1 of the Income Tax Act defined a company at para *(b)* of the definition to include 'any association, corporation or company incorporated under the law of any country other than the Republic or any body corporate formed or established under such law'. This implied that foreign partnership or corporate structures would be recognised as corporate entities under South African law if they were recognised as separate legal personalities under foreign law. Such entities included the United Kingdom LLP (described above).[54] The statutory recognition of these entities as companies perpetuated the uncertainty surrounding their tax treatment. For example, it was not clear, if a South African resident and a United Kingdom resident decided to incorporate an LLP in the United Kingdom, whether South African CFC rules would be applied to tax the South African shareholder.[55] A further uncertainty that arose was when an entity such as a United Kingdom LLP was considered a company in terms of para *(b)* of the definition of 'company' in s 1 of the Income Tax Act, it was not clear whether the LLP was considered a South African resident if it was effectively managed in South Africa.[56]

Consequently, s 1 of the Income Tax Act was amended by the Taxation Laws Amendment Act 7 of 2010 to provide that the definition of 'company' in s 1 of the Act does not include a foreign partnership.[57] A 'foreign partnership' is defined in s 1 of the Act as follows:

[51] Ger B 'International Tax: Partnerships, Permanent Establishments and the Problem of Double Taxation' 2010 *The Taxpayer* 97–98.

[52] Olivier & Honiball *International Tax* 187.

[53] Oguttu (2009) *SA Merc LJ* 51 at 72.

[54] Oguttu (2009) *SA Merc LJ* 51 at 70.

[55] Ibid.

[56] Oguttu (2009) *SA Merc LJ* 51 at 71.

[57] Olivier & Honiball *International Tax* 78.

'[F]oreign partnership', in respect of any year of assessment, means any partnership, association, body of persons or entity formed or established under the laws of any country other than the Republic if—

(a) for the purposes of the laws relating to tax on income of the country in which that partnership, association, body of persons or entity is formed or established—

(i) each member of the partnership, association, body of persons or entity is required to take into account the member's interest in any amount received by or accrued to that partnership, association, body of persons or entity when that amount is received by or accrued to the partnership, association, body of persons or entity; and

(ii) the partnership, association, body of persons or entity is not liable for or subject to any tax on income, other than a tax levied by a municipality, local authority or a comparable authority, in that country; or

(b) where the country in which that partnership, association, body of persons or entity is formed or established does not have any applicable laws relating to tax on income—

(i) any amount—

(aa) that is received by or accrued to; or

(bb) of expenditure that is incurred by,the partnership, association, body of persons or entity is allocated concurrently with the receipt, accrual or incurral to the members of that partnership, association, body of persons or entity in terms of an agreement between those members; and

(ii) no amount distributed to a member of a partnership, association, body of persons or entity may exceed the allocation contemplated in subparagraph (i) after taking into account any prior distributions made by the partnership, association, body of persons or entity.

From the above definition, since LLPs or LLCs and similar hybrid entities have been included in the definition of a 'foreign partnership', this synchronises the South African tax treatment with foreign tax practice.

14.3.4 Transfer pricing and thin capitalisation rules

14.3.4.1 The meaning of transfer pricing

The term 'transfer pricing' describes the process whereby related entities set prices at which they transfer goods or services between each other. It entails the systematic manipulation of prices in order to reduce or increase profits artificially or cause losses and avoid taxes in a specific country. [58] A transfer

[58] Commission of Inquiry into Certain Aspects of the Tax Structure of South Africa 'Second Interim Report of the Commission of Inquiry into Certain Aspects of the Tax Structure of South Africa: Thin Capitalisation Rules' (1995) para 1.3b. See also Arnold & McIntyre *International Tax* 53; Stroud A & Masters C *Transfer Pricing* (Butterworths 1991) 10; Ware J & Roper P *Offshore Insight* (Butterworths 2001) 178.

price is a price set by a taxpayer when selling to, buying from, or sharing resources with a related or connected person. It is usually contrasted with a market price, which is the price set in the marketplace for transfers of goods and services between unrelated persons[59] where each party strives to get the utmost possible benefit from the transaction.[60]

Transfer pricing is most problematic when it comes to multinational corporations trading in various jurisdictions.[61] Since related companies operate in different countries, they are not subject to the same laws and regulations, especially in tax matters.[62] Related companies in a multinational group may thus resort to fictitious transfer pricing in order to manipulate profits so that they appear lower in a country with higher tax rates and higher in a country with lower tax rates.[63] Multinationals are able to manipulate transfer prices due to the network of internal payments that result from the goods they supply to each other.

14.3.4.2 Methods used to arrive at an arm's length price

The Commissioner for the South African Revenue Service determines an arm's length price by using one of the methods set out in Practice Note 7,[64] which have been developed internationally in determining and appraising a taxpayer's transfer prices (note that these methods are still applicable even under the new rules discussed below). These methods are recognised by the OECD guidelines.[65] The transfer pricing methods that are recommended by the OECD and also used in South Africa fall into two categories: the 'traditional transactional' methods and the 'profit based' methods.[66] Under the 'traditional transactional' methods fall methods such as the 'comparable uncontrolled price'

---

59 Arnold & McIntyre *International Tax* 55.

60 South African Revenue Service's ('SARS') 'Practice Note No 7: Determination of Taxable Income of Certain Persons from International Taxation: Transfer Pricing (s 31 of the Income Tax Act 58 of 1962)' 6 August 1999 para 7.1; article 9 of the OECD Model Tax Convention on Income and on Capital (2003 condensed version). See also Hay D, Horner F & Owens J 'Past and Present Work in the OECD on Transfer Pricing and Selected Issues' (1994) 10 *Intertax* 424; OECD Report of the Committee on Fiscal Affairs 'Issues in International Taxation No 2: Thin Capitalisation: Taxation of Entertainers, Artistes and Sportsmen' (1987) 17; Miesel VH, Higinbotham HH & Yi CW 'International Transfer Pricing: Practical Solutions for Inter-Company Pricing – Part II' (2003) 29 *International Tax Journal* 1.

61 OECD Report of the Committee on Fiscal Affairs 'Transfer Pricing Guidelines for Multinational Enterprises and Tax Administrators' (1994) 172 *Intertax* 318 para 12; Tanzi V 'Globalization, Tax Competition and the Future of Tax Systems' (International Monetary Fund Working Paper 1996) 6.

62 Plasschaert SRF *Transfer Pricing and Multinational Corporations: An Overview of Concepts, Mechanisms and Regulations* (Saxon House 1979) 1; Arnold & McIntyre *International Tax* 54; Bischel JE & Feinschreiber R *Fundamentals of International Taxation* 2 ed (Practising Law Institute 1985) 27.

63 Plasschaert *Transfer Pricing* 1; Stroud & Masters *Transfer Pricing* 10; Ginsberg A *International Tax Havens* 2 ed (Butterworths 1997) 20; Tanzi 'Globalization, Tax Competition' 7.

64 SARS Practice Note No 7 paras 9.1.2 to 9.1.3; see also De Koker *South African Income Tax* 17.59.

65 OECD 'Transfer Pricing Guidelines' 336 para 87.

66 Ibid; Bischel & Feinschreiber *International Taxation* 231.

method (CUP), the 'resale price' method (RP) and the 'cost plus' method (CP). Under the 'profit based' methods fall the 'transactional net margin' method (TNMM) and the 'profit split' method.

The 'comparable uncontrolled price' (CUP) method is the primary pricing method. This method requires a direct comparison to be drawn between the price charged for a specific product in a controlled transaction and the price charged for a closely comparable product in an uncontrolled transaction in comparable circumstances.[67] The CUP method is the most preferred method because it is the most direct and reliable way to apply the arm's length principle.[68]

Where there are no comparable sales, the 'resale price' method is used. This method is based on the price at which a product, which has been purchased from a connected enterprise, is resold to an independent enterprise. The resale price is then reduced by an appropriate gross margin, to cover the reseller's operating costs. This is intended to provide an appropriate profit, having taken into consideration the functions performed, assets used and risks assumed by the reseller. The balance is then regarded as the arm's length price.[69]

The 'cost plus' method requires an estimation of an arm's length consideration by adding an appropriate mark-up to the costs incurred by the supplier of goods or services in a controlled transaction. This mark-up should provide for an appropriate profit to the supplier, in light of the functions performed, assets used and risks assumed.[70]

In general, a flexible approach is used when applying the above transaction-based methods in that where there are any differences between the controlled and the uncontrolled transactions that have a material effect on the final price, these differences can be accounted for through reasonable adjustments.[71] However, even with such flexibility there are cases where the degree of comparability is not satisfactory. In response to the constraints of the transaction-based methods, the OECD developed other, profit-based methods that are presumed to be less adversely affected.[72] Examples of these methods are the 'transactional net margin' method and the 'profit split' method.

The 'transactional net margin' method (TNMM) examines the net profit margin that a taxpayer realises from a controlled transaction, relative to an appropriate base of, for example, costs, sales or assets. The profit level indicator of

[67] OECD 'Transfer Pricing Guidelines' 337 para 92; see also Campos G 'Transfer Pricing of Major Trading Nations' (1996) *Bulletin for International Fiscal Documentation* 217.

[68] Hay et al (1994) 10 *Intertax* 432 para 64.

[69] SARS Practice Note No 7 para 9.5.1; see also OECD 'Transfer Pricing Guidelines' 338 para 65; Campos (1996) *Bulletin for International Fiscal Documentation* 217; Hay et al (1994) 10 *Intertax* 432 para 66.

[70] SARS Practice Note No 7 para 9.6.1; see also OECD 'Transfer Pricing Guidelines' 342 para 115; Campos (1996) *Bulletin for International Fiscal Documentation* 217.

[71] Hay et al (1994) 10 *Intertax* 433 para 71.

[72] Ibid.

the tested party is compared with the profit level indicators of comparable independent parties.[73]

Under the 'profit split' method, first the combined profit is identified and split between the connected parties in a controlled transaction. The profit is split by economically approximating the division of profits that would have been anticipated and reflected in an agreement made at arm's length.[74] The profit split method is usually applied where transactions are so interrelated that they cannot be evaluated separately.[75]

Generally, all the above methods are based on measuring a multinational's pricing strategies against a benchmark of the pricing strategies of independent entities in uncontrolled transactions.[76] The Commissioner uses the most appropriate of these methods depending on the particular situation and the extent of reliable data. The suitability and reliability of a method thus depend on the facts and circumstances of each business and the market realities applicable to each individual case.[77] As a general rule, however, the 'traditional transaction' methods are preferred. The Commissioner recommends the use of a four-step approach developed by the Australian Tax Office in order to arrive at an arm's length price.[78] The four steps are:

- understanding the cross-border dealings between connected persons in the context of the taxpayer's business and assessing the risk;
- selecting the appropriate transfer pricing method;
- applying the selected method; and
- calculating the arm's length price in accordance with the selected method.

14.3.4.3 Curbing transfer pricing in South Africa

In South Africa transfer pricing was previously dealt with under the old s 31(1) of the Act. However, from years of assessment commencing on or after 1 January 2011, South Africa's transfer pricing provisions were amended as discussed below.[79] The previous transfer pricing rules applied to a supply of goods or services effected between connected parties at a price that is not at arm's length if:

- one party is a resident and the other is a foreign resident;

---

73 SARS Practice Note No 7 para 9.7.1. See also Campos (1996) *Bulletin for International Fiscal Documentation* 218.

74 SARS Practice Note No 7 para 9.8.1; OECD 'Transfer Pricing Guidelines' 346 para 131; Campos (1996) *Bulletin for International Fiscal Documentation* 217; Hay et al (1994) 10 *Intertax* 435 para 82.

75 SARS Practice Note No 7 para 9.8.3; Hay et al (1994) 10 *Intertax* 435 para 84.

76 SARS Practice Note No 7 paras 9.2.1–9.2.3.

77 SARS Practice Note No 7 para 7.6.

78 See Annexure A of the SARS Practice Note No 7.

79 Section 31(1) of the Income Tax Act as amended by the Taxation Laws Amendment Act 7 of 2010.

- one party is a foreign resident and the other is a South African permanent establishment of a foreign resident; or
- one party is a resident and the other is a foreign permanent establishment of a resident.

A price was considered a non-arm's length price if that price differed from the price that the goods or services would have been expected to fetch if the parties had been independent. When these conditions applied, SARS was empowered to adjust the consideration for the transaction to reflect an arm's length price for those goods or services[80]

The wording of the previous transfer pricing rules under the then s 31(2) caused structural problems and uncertainty for taxpayers. The interpretation of these rules was narrow as it focused on separate transactions, as opposed to overall arrangements that drove the profit objective. As a result, taxpayers came up with artificial arguments that placed emphasis on the literal terms of the transaction, instead of the overall economic substance and commercial objective of the arrangement. It was also argued that although the transfer pricing provisions permitted the use of all methods recognised by the OECD in order to arrive at an arm's length price, the provision emphasised the use of the comparable uncontrolled price method over other transfer pricing methodologies (these are discussed below) which may be more reliable under the particular circumstances of a case. Lastly, the provision placed emphasis on the 'price' as opposed to the 'profits' of a given transaction. This emphasis was presumed not to be in line with model tax treaties, thus creating potential difficulties in the mutual agreement procedures available under tax treaties.[81]

Thus, from years of assessment commencing on or after 1 January 2011 South Africa's transfer pricing provisions were amended by merging them with the thin capitalisation rules which were previously contained in s 31(3) of the Act. Bearing in mind the working of the merged transfer pricing and thin capitalisation rules, the meaning of thin capitalisation and how the curbing of thin capitalisation was effected before the amendments are dealt with below.

14.3.4.4 The meaning of thin capitalisation

'Thin capitalisation' is described as the use of unusual proportions of loan to equity capital in order to gain a tax advantage.[82] It has also been described as the funding of a business with a disproportionate degree of debt, as opposed to equity.[83] If a company requires capital to finance its operations, the finance can be provided either as equity capital or debt capital.[84] It can also be financed

[80] Explanatory Memorandum on the Taxation Laws Amendment Bill, 2010 para 5.3, part I(A).

[81] Explanatory Memorandum on the Taxation Laws Amendment Bill, 2010 para 5.3, part II.

[82] United Nations Ad Hoc Group of Experts on International Co-operation in Tax Matters 18.

[83] Commission of Inquiry 'Second Interim Report: Thin Capitalisation Rules' para 1.1.

[84] Van Blerck M 'Transfer Pricing and Thin Capitalisation' (1995) 8 *SA Tax Review* 44; Sommerhalder RA 'Approaches to Thin Capitalisation' (March 1996) *Bulletin for International Fiscal Documentation* 44.

by a combination of debt and equity capital. A company is said to be 'thinly capitalised' when its equity capital is small in comparison to its debt capital.[85] The tax treatment of a company and those that contribute to its capital differs fundamentally according to whether the capital is debt or equity capital. If a company is financed by debt capital, the interest incurred on the debt is usually a deductible expense, in most jurisdictions (unless there are special rules to the contrary).[86] If a company is financed by equity capital (ie by subscribing for the shares of the company) dividends will have to be distributed to those persons that contribute to its capital. In most jurisdictions, dividends are generally not deductible in arriving at the taxable profit of the company. Accordingly, income earned by the company and distributed to its shareholders will be subject to two levels of tax: the corporation tax when the income is earned by the corporation and shareholder tax when the income is distributed to the shareholders as a dividend.[87]

The above illustrates that when a company is funded by debt capital it can repay the loan at any time without triggering tax; whereas a company funded by equity capital may not be able to repay equity investments without triggering a taxable dividend. The effect of these two different tax treatments is that it may sometimes, from a tax point of view, be more advantageous to a particular company and contributor of capital to arrange the financing of the company by way of loans rather than by way of equity contributions.[88]

In order to curb thin capitalisation, most developed countries have debt/equity or thin capitalisation provisions.[89] These provisions are enacted to limit the deductibility of interest on the excessive debt funds[90] that could result in tax advantages if an investor's business is financed by loan capital rather than equity capital.[91] Generally, these provisions may allow debt to be re-characterised as equity or vice versa, or interest and dividends may be reclassified where it appears that capital has been arranged as either debt or equity when, in economic reality, it should be the opposite.[92] The effect of the application of thin capitalisation rules is generally that excessive interest is not deductible. In some countries, this excessive interest is treated as a dividend. In other countries the excessive interest can be carried forward and deducted in subsequent years.[93]

---

[85] Ibid.

[86] Tomsett E 'Treaty Shopping and Debt/equity Ratios in the United Kingdom' (March 1990) *Bulletin for International Fiscal Documentation* 140; OECD 'Issues in International Taxation No 1' 8–9; Commission of Inquiry 'Second Interim Report: Thin Capitalisation Rules' para 1.1; Ware J & Roper P *Offshore Insight* (Butterworths 2001) 178.

[87] Ware & Roper *Offshore Insight* 178.

[88] Tomsett 'Treaty Shopping' 141; Arnold & McIntyre *International Tax* 72–73.

[89] Ibid.

[90] De Koker *South African Income Tax* 17.54.

[91] Arnold & McIntyre *International Tax* 72–73.

[92] Ibid.

[93] Ibid.

Taxpayers can, however, avoid the thin capitalisation rules by channelling inter-company loans through international banks and other financial intermediaries. This is normally referred to as 'back-to-back loans', a term used to describe a situation where funds are deposited by a subsidiary incorporated in a tax haven as collateral for a loan to another foreign subsidiary.[94] Interest earned on the time deposit accumulates free of tax, while in many locations the interest expense of the borrower qualifies as a tax deduction.

14.3.4.5 Curbing thin capitalisation in South Africa

In South Africa, thin capitalisation was (before the 2010 amendments to the Income Tax Act) regulated under the former s 31(3) of the Income Tax Act. The section, in summary, applied where a non-resident directly or indirectly granted financial assistance to any resident that was connected to that non-resident, and the non-resident was entitled to participate in 25% or more of the dividends, profits, capital or voting rights of the resident. The thin capitalisation rules empowered SARS to deny the resident a deduction of any interest or other finance charges to the extent that it was considered excessive in relation to the fixed capital[95] of the resident.[96] The total amount of the excessive interest was deemed to be a dividend. In terms of SARS Practice Note 2 the rules did not apply where the financial assistance to fixed capital ratio did not exceed 3:1.[97] The thin capitalisation rules covered back-to-back arrangements with independent third parties or co-investors.[98]

The legislature sought to amend these rules for the following reasons. The rules applied only to financial assistance granted by a foreign resident investor to certain residents. The rules did not apply to financial assistance by a foreign resident to another foreign resident, even if the latter had a South African permanent establishment. As a result, some taxpayers sought to exploit this loophole by having a foreign company utilise a wholly owned foreign subsidiary with most or all of its operations conducted in South Africa through a permanent establishment. The foreign company would then capitalise the foreign subsidiary with excessive debt, thereby using the interest deductions associated with the excessive debt to offset income attributable to the South African permanent establishment. [99]

The old thin capitalisation rules also paralleled the transfer pricing rules (explained above), which were not in line with international practice, as the OECD and UN Model Tax Conventions deal with thin capitalisation as part

[94] Diamond W & Diamond D *Tax Havens of the World* (Matthew Bender & Co) glossary 1.

[95] This is the share capital, share premium, accumulated profits, whether of a capital nature or not, or any other permanent owner's capital, other than permanent capital in the form of financial assistance as so contemplated.

[96] Explanatory Memorandum para 5.3, part I(C).

[97] Ibid.

[98] Paragraph 8 of SARS Practice Note No 2.

[99] Explanatory Memorandum on the Taxation Laws Amendment Bill, 2010 para 5.3, part II(C).

of the transfer pricing rules.[100] The merging of transfer pricing and thin capitalisation provisions in line with international trends offers greater certainty and minimises the scope for interpretational difficulties, both domestically and under mutual agreement procedures as contained in the tax treaties.[101]

14.3.4.6 The new transfer pricing and thin capitalisation rules

As mentioned above, the transfer pricing and thin capitalisation rules have now been merged. Section 31(1) of the Act, as amended by the Taxation Laws Amendment Act 22 of 2012, defines the term 'financial assistance' to include the provision of any debt, or security or guarantee.

Section 31(2) as amended by the Taxation Laws Amendment Act 24 of 2011 provides:

> Where—
>
> *(a)* any transaction, operation, scheme, agreement or understanding constitutes an affected transaction; and
>
> *(b)* any term or condition of that transaction, operation, scheme, agreement or understanding—
>
> (i) is a term or condition contemplated in paragraph *(b)* of the definition of 'affected transaction'; and
>
> (ii) results or will result in any tax benefit being derived by a person that is a party to that transaction, operation, scheme, agreement or understanding,
>
> the taxable income or tax payable by any person contemplated in paragraph *(b)*(ii) that derives a tax benefit contemplated in that paragraph must be calculated as if that transaction, operation, scheme, agreement or understanding had been entered into on the terms and conditions that would have existed had those persons been independent persons dealing at arm's length.

In summary, the section implies that where any transaction, operation, scheme, agreement or understanding constitutes an affected transaction, and any term or condition thereof results or will result in a tax benefit for a party to that transaction, the taxable income of that person must be calculated as if that transaction had been entered into in an arm's length dealing.

An explanation of the terms used in s 31 is important in understanding how the section operates. The terms are explained below.

An 'affected transaction' is defined in s 31(1)*(a)* to cover any transaction, operation, scheme, agreement or understanding which has been directly or indirectly entered into or effected between or for the benefit of either or both:

- a resident and a non-resident;

[100] Article 9 of the OECD Model Tax Convention.

[101] Explanatory Memorandum on the Taxation Laws Amendment Bill, 2010 para 5.3, part II(C).

- a non-resident and another non-resident that has a permanent establishment in SA to which the transaction, operation, scheme, agreement or understanding relates;
- a resident and another resident that has a PE outside SA to which the transaction, operation, scheme, agreement or understanding relates; or
- a non-resident and a CFC in relation to any resident and the persons are connected persons.

The phrase 'direct or indirect' used in the definition of affected transaction is wide enough to cover transactions, operations, schemes, agreements and understandings that have been directly or indirectly entered into or effected between or for the benefit of either or both of the parties specified in the definition. The section is therefore far wider than a loan between two of the parties specified in the definition of an 'affected transaction'.

The meaning of the term 'connected person' is defined in s 31(1) to carry the meaning it has in s 1 of the Act. In terms of the section:

A connected person in relation to a natural person is:

- any relative; and
- any trust (other than a portfolio of a collective investment scheme in securities or in property) of which such natural person or such relative is a beneficiary.

A connected person in relation to a trust (other than portfolio of a collective investment scheme in securities or in property) is:

- any beneficiary of such trust; and
- any connected person in relation to such beneficiary.

A connected person in relation to a company is:

- any other company that would be part of the same group of companies (if the expression 'at least 70% of the equity the definition of "group of companies"[102] were replaced by the expression "more than 50 per cent of the equity shares or voting rights in"');
- any person, other than a company as defined in s 1 of the Companies Act 71 of 2008 that individually or jointly with any connected person in relation to that person, holds, directly or indirectly, at least 20% of the equity shares or voting rights in the company;

[102] 'Group of companies' is defined in s 1 of the ITA to means two or more companies in which one company (the controlling group company) directly or indirectly holds shares in at least one other company (controlled group company) to the extent that:

'*(a)* at least 70 percent of the equity shares in each controlled group company are directly held by the controlling group company, one or more other controlled group companies or any combination thereof; and

(b) the controlling group company directly holds at least 70% of the equity shares in at least one controlled group company.'

- any other company if at least 20% of the equity shares or voting rights in the company are held by that other company, and no holder of shares holds the majority voting rights in the company;
- any other company that is managed or controlled by any person who or which is a connected person in relation to such company, or any person who or which is a connected person in relation to a person; and
- where such person is close corporation:
  - any member;
  - any relative of such member or any trust other than a portfolio of a collective investment scheme in securities or in property which is a connected person in relation to such member; and
  - any other close corporation or company which is a connected person in relation to any member of the close corporation, or the relative or trust as contemplated above.

A 'tax benefit' is defined in s 1 as including any tax avoidance, postponement or reduction of any liability for tax.

Basically, the focus of the new provision is on cross-border transactions, operations, schemes, agreements or understandings that have been effected between, or undertaken for the benefit of, connected persons. If the terms or conditions made or imposed by the connected persons differ from the terms and conditions that would otherwise have existed between independent persons acting at arm's length, and the difference confers a South African tax benefit on one of the parties, the taxable income of the parties that have benefited must be calculated as if the terms and conditions had been concluded at arm's length.

Taxpayers are thus expected to account for transfer pricing on an arm's length basis without SARS intervention, which is an important change from the previous regime that required SARS to make the transfer pricing adjustments if necessary. SARS also has the power to adjust the terms and conditions of a transaction, operation, scheme, arrangement or understanding to reflect the terms and conditions that would have existed at arm's length. The new transfer pricing rules are closely aligned with the wording of the OECD and UN model tax conventions and are in line with tax treaties and other international tax principles.[103]

Since transfer pricing provisions are merged with the thin capitalisation rules, this implies that transfer pricing rules can also be used to deny deductions for interest that would not have existed had the South African entity not been thinly capitalised with excessive debt. Accordingly, if the terms and conditions of an affected transaction involve loans and other debt that would not have been agreed if the lender and borrower had been transacting at arm's length, and if there is a difference in results in a tax benefit to any of the parties, then that taxpayer is required to calculate its taxable income based on the arm's length terms and conditions.

[103] Explanatory Memorandum on the Taxation Laws Amendment Bill, 2010 para 5.3, part III(A).

The new s 31(1) defines financial assistance as including any loan, advance or debt or any security or guarantee. Thus, any lending (ie foreign financial assistance) from a foreign person to a foreign person with a South African business establishment is subject to the thin capitalisation rules.[104]

The ambit of the term 'affected transactions' is broad. Thus, if a non-resident subsidiary of an multinational enterprise (MNE) provides a loan to another non-resident subsidiary of that MNE and that subsidiary channels the funds through to its South African permanent establishment, the transaction potentially falls within the ambit of an affected transaction.

The phrase 'directly or indirectly' as used in the definition of 'affected transaction' can also cover direct and indirect funding. For example, itcovers back-to-back transactions with banks or other financial institutions (ie where a non-resident member of an MNE places funds on deposit with a bank then the bank loans funds to a South African resident member). It can also cover the provision of guarantees by a non-resident member to a bank or other financial institution in connection with funding given by that bank or financial institution to a resident member, or any other arrangements in which funding provided by a foreign connected person is routed through one or more special purpose entities or an accommodating or tax-indifferent party.

The application of s 31 to thin capitalisation implies that any interest, finance charges and other considerations relating to the excessive portion of the debt are not allowed as a deduction in computing the taxpayer's taxable income. Taxpayers are required to file a return which has been prepared on an arm's length basis. Taxpayers must be able to demonstrate that debt which meets the definition of an affected transaction is at arm's length or that a tax deduction has not been claimed for the expenditure on the portion of the debt that is not arm's length.

Where a taxpayer fails to comply with the transfer pricing and thin capitalisation rules, s 31(2) provides for primary adjustment. In effect, SARS has the power to adjust the terms and conditions of a transaction, operation, scheme, arrangement or understanding to reflect the terms and conditions that would have existed at arm's length.

However, internationally, primary adjustments tend not place the financial position of the parties on an arm's length basis, as it accounts for taxable income, not actual income. So, some countries require secondary adjustments – excess profits from primary adjustment are treated as having been transferred in some other form and taxed accordingly.

In South Africa, s 31(3) provides for a secondary adjustment that arises from the transfer pricing primary adjustment in s 31(2). In terms of s 31(3)(i), if the resident is a company, the difference between taxable income and the arm's length amount is deemed to be a dividend *in specie* (a dividend consisting of a distribution of an asset) declared and paid by that resident to the non-resident.

104 Explanatory Memorandum on the Taxation Laws Amendment Bill, 2010 para 5.3, part III(B).

This implies that the resident company will be liable for dividends tax on the deemed dividend *in specie* at a rate of 20%. The dividend *in specie* is deemed to have been declared and paid on the last day of the period of six months following the end of the year of assessment in respect of which that transfer pricing primary adjustment is made. In terms of s 31(3)(ii), if the resident is a person other than a company, the difference between taxable income and the arm's length amount is deemed to be a donation made by the resident to the non-resident person. This implies that the resident will be liable for donations tax on the deemed donation at a rate of 20%. The donation is deemed to have been made on the last day of the period of six months following the end of the year of assessment in respect of which that transfer pricing primary adjustment is made.

14.3.5 Headquarter companies

South Africa's National Treasury has stated that 'South Africa is the economic powerhouse of Africa. South Africa's location, sizable economy, political stability and overall strength in financial services make South Africa an ideal location for the establishment of regional holding companies by foreign multinationals. South Africa's network of tax treaties provides ready access to other countries in the region which makes it a natural holding company gateway into the region.'[105] In this regard, the National Treasury has embarked on a headquarter company regime in South Africa. However, South Africa's high tax costs and strict exchange controls have prevented foreign multinational companies from establishing headquarter companies in South Africa. To rectify the relevant hindrances and their impact on international transactions, certain provisions in the Act have been amended and new provisions relating to the headquarter company regime have been introduced.[106]

In terms of s 1 of the Act, as amended by the Taxation Laws Amendment Act 24 of 2011, a 'headquarter company' is defined as any company which has made an election in terms of s 9I.

In terms of s 9I(1), introduced by Taxation Laws Amendment Act 24 of 2011 and amended by the Taxation Laws Amendment Act 22 of 2012, a headquarter company has to be a resident company that complies with the requirements set out in s 9I(2).

Below is a summary of the requirements for a headquarter company as set out in s 9I(2).

Minimum participation by shareholders: Each shareholder of the holding company (whether alone or together with any other company forming part of the same group of companies as that shareholder) must hold 10% or more of the equity shares and voting rights in that company.

---

[105] Explanatory Memorandum on the Taxation Laws Amendment Bill, 2010 para 5.4, part II.

[106] Oguttu AW 'Developing South Africa as a Gateway for Foreign Investment in Africa: A Critique of South Africa's Headquarter Company Regime' (2011) 36 *South African Year Book of International Law* 61.

The 80–10 asset test: At the end of that year of assessment and of all previous years of assessment, 80% of the total cost of the assets of the headquarter company (in the form of debt, equity or licensed intellectual property) must be attributed to any foreign company in which that company (whether alone or together with any other company forming part of the same group of companies as that company) held at least 10% of the equity shares and voting rights. In determining the total assets of the company, any amount in cash or in the form of a bank deposit payable on demand must not be taken into account.

Gross income test: The gross income of the company (excluding exchange differences determined in terms of s 24I) for the year of assessment must exceed R5 million and 50% or more of this gross income must consist of amounts in the form of one or both of the following:

- any rental, dividends, interest, royalties or service fees received from a foreign company in which the company holds at least 10% of the equity shares and voting rights; or
- any proceeds of any interest in equity shares in the foreign company or the disposal of any intellectual property as defined in s 23I(1) which was licensed by the company to a foreign company in respect of which the company holds at least 10% of the equity shares and voting rights.

These requirements must be measured at the end of the year of assessment.

If a company's gross income is less than R5 million, it can still elect to be classified as a headquarter company even if 50% or more of its gross income does not consist of rentals, dividends, interest, management fees etc. Provided that it complies with the minimum participation shareholding and the 80% asset requirements as set out above, such company can still elect to be a headquarter company.

Where a company elects to be headquarter company, in terms of s 9I(4), it has to submit to the Minister of Finance an annual report containing certain prescribed information, within such a time as the Minister may specify.

Section 9I makes it clear that the headquarter company regime is voluntary and any company that is resident in South Africa and complies with the criteria set out in the section can elect to be a headquarter company for a year of assessment. In terms of s 9I(1), the election has to be made annually in the form and manner prescribed by the Commissioner. Furthermore, in terms of s 9I(3) the election is only valid from the beginning of the year for which the election is made. In terms of s 9I(4), a headquarter company must submit to the Minister an annual report providing the Minister with the information that the Minister may prescribe within such time and containing such information as the Minister may prescribe.

Section 9H provides that once a company becomes a headquarter company, it is deemed to have disposed of all its assets at their respective market values and to have immediately reacquired those assets at the respective market values. Section 9H came into effect on 1 April 2012.

Where a South African resident company elects to be a headquarter company and it qualifies in terms of the above criteria, it qualifies for specific income tax relief as discussed below.

14.3.5.1 Relief from CFC provisions

With effect from the years of assessment commencing on or after 1 January 2011, the definition of a CFC (discussed above) has been amended by the Taxation Laws Amendment Act 7 of 2010 to provide:

> '[C]ontrolled foreign company' means any foreign company where more than 50 per cent of the total participation rights in that foreign company are directly or indirectly held, or more than 50 per cent of the voting rights in that foreign company are directly or indirectly exercisable, by one or more persons that are residents other than persons that are headquarter companies.[107]

This definition excludes headquarter companies in the determination of the participation rights and voting rights of South African residents in a foreign company. If a resident company meets the criteria of a headquarter company, it is not caught by the CFC legislation. For purposes of determining whether a foreign company is a CFC in relation to a qualifying headquarter company, the qualifying headquarter company is deemed to be a foreign resident. In effect, its interest in the participation rights and voting rights of a foreign company are taken into account in determining whether the foreign company is a CFC.[108]

This means that the CFC status of a foreign subsidiary of a qualifying headquarter company is determined based on the indirect ownership of the qualifying headquarter company's shareholders. If the indirect owners are more than 50% South African, then the foreign subsidiary will qualify as a CFC. Then, the net income of the CFC that is attributable to the resident company will be included in the income of the shareholders of the headquarter company and not in the income of the headquarter company itself.[109]

14.3.5.2 Relief from dividends tax

Dividends declared by headquarter companies are in terms of s 10B(1) and 10B(2) exempt from normal tax.

14.3.5.3 Relief from capital gains tax

For the purposes of the capital gains tax participation exemption in para 64B(2) of the Eighth Schedule to the Act, a headquarter company is deemed to be a foreign company.[110] Since a headquarter company is deemed to be a foreign

[107] Section 16 of the Taxation Laws Amendment Act 7 of 2010.

[108] Oguttu (2011) *South African Year Book of International Law* 75.

[109] Section 9D(2) of the Income Tax Act. See also the Explanatory Memorandum on the Taxation Laws Amendment Bill, 2010 para 5.4, part III(C).

[110] Paragraph 64B as amended by s 108(1)*(b)* of the Taxation Laws Amendment Act 7 of 2010.

company, CGT would not be levied on the disposal of a shareholder's interest in terms of para 64B.[111] Paragraph 64B(2), as amended by the Taxation Law Amendment Act 22 of 2012, provides:

> A headquarter company must disregard any capital gain or capital loss determined in respect of the disposal of any equity share in any foreign company (other than an interest contemplated in paragraph 2(2)) if that headquarter company (whether alone or together with any other person forming part of the same group of companies as that headquarter company) immediately before that disposal held at least 10 per cent of the equity shares and voting rights in that foreign company.

This implies that headquarter companies can dispose of their foreign interests to any person without incurring capital gains tax. Because of this advantageous tax position for headquarter companies, the shares held in headquarter companies by South African residents are not eligible for the participation exemption. However, foreign residents holding shares in headquarter companies are exempt if the shares are not attributable to a permanent establishment in South Africa.[112]

14.3.5.4 CGT implications on change of residence or becoming a headquarter company

Section 9H(3)*(a)* provides that where a company that is a resident company ceases to be resident during any year of assessment, or where a resident company becomes a headquarter company in a year of assessment, that company must be treated as having disposed of its assets to a resident person on the date immediately before the day it ceased to be a resident or became a headquarter company, and it is presumed to have reacquired those assets on the day it ceased to be a resident or became a headquarter company, for an amount equal to the market value of those assets.

Section 9H(3)*(b)* provides that where a CFC ceases to be one (otherwise than by way of becoming a resident) during any foreign tax year of that CFC, it must be treated as having disposed of its assets to a resident person, on the date immediately before the day it ceased to be a CFC, and it is presumed to have reacquired those assets on the day it ceased to be a CFC for an amount equal to the market value of each of those assets.

In terms s 9H(3)*(c)*, where a resident company ceases to be a resident or becomes a headquarter company during any year of assessment, that year of assessment is deemed to have ended on the date immediately before the day on which that company ceased to be a resident or became a headquarter company. It's the next succeeding year of assessment is deemed to have commenced on the day on which that company ceased to be a resident or

[111] Olivier & Honiball *International Tax* 708; Oguttu (2011) *South African Year Book of International Law* 82–83.

[112] Explanatory Memorandum on the Taxation Laws Amendment Bill, 2011 54; Oguttu (2011) *South African Year Book of International Law* 82–83.

became a headquarter company. In addition, that company must, on the date immediately before the day on which it ceased to be a resident or became a headquarter company, be deemed to have declared and paid a dividend of an asset *in specie* (consists solely of a distribution of an asset). The amount of the dividend *in specie* must be deemed to be equal to the sum of the market values of all the shares in that company on that date less the sum of the contributed tax capital of all the classes of shares in the company as at that date. The said distribution is deemed to be made to the person or persons holding shares in that company in accordance with the effective interest of that person or those persons in the shares in the company as at that date.

Section 9H(4) provides that s 9H(3) above do not apply if the asset of a person constitutes of:

- immovable property situated in the Republic that is held by that person;
- any asset of the person that ceases to be a resident or a CFC which is attributable to a permanent establishment of that person in the Republic;
- any qualifying equity share in terms of s 8B that was granted to that person less than five years before the date on which that person ceases to be a resident;
- any equity instrument in terms of s 8C that had not yet vested at the time that the person ceases to be a resident; or
- any right of that person to acquire any marketable security in terms of s 8A.

14.3.5.5 Relief from transfer pricing and thin capitalisation provisions

For years of assessment commencing on or after 1 April 2012,[113] the thin capitalisation rules have been amended with respect to headquarter companies.

In general, headquarter companies will be subject to the transfer pricing rules (which include the thin capitalisation rules) if any foreign financial assistance that is granted to that headquarter company is regarded as excessive or is granted at a rate that is not regarded as an arm's length rate. The headquarter company will not be granted a deduction for the portion of the interest that it incurs in respect of the foreign financial assistance. However, in terms of s 31(5) of the Act, as amended by the Taxation Laws Amendment Act 22 of 2012, the transfer pricing and thin capitalisation rules will not apply to any transaction, operation, scheme, agreement or understanding:

- where a non-resident grants financial assistance to a headquarter company directly or indirectly (whether alone or together with any other company forming part of the same group of companies as that headquarter company) holds at least 10% of the equity shares and voting rights;

[113] Section 57 of Taxation Laws Amendment Act 24 of 2011.

- where financial assistance is granted by a headquarter company to a foreign company in which the headquarter company directly or indirectly (whether alone or together with any other company forming part of the same group of companies as that headquarter company) holds at least 10% of the equity shares and voting rights;
- where a non-resident grants the use, right of use or permission to use any intellectual property as defined in s 23I(1) to a headquarter company, if that headquarter company grants that right of use or permission to use that intellectual property to any foreign company in which the headquarter company directly or indirectly (whether alone or together with any other company forming part of the same group of companies as that headquarter company) holds at least 10% of the equity shares and voting rights; or
- where a headquarter company grants the use, right of use or permission to use any intellectual property as defined in s 23I(1) to that foreign company, in which the headquarter company directly or indirectly (whether alone or together with any other company forming part of the same group of companies as that headquarter company) holds at least 10% of the equity shares and voting rights.

Section 31(5) became effective on 1 April 2012 and applies in respect of years of assessment commencing on or after that date. [114]

The effect of this provision is that interest-free loans to foreign companies (in which a headquarter company holds an interest of at least 10%) will be excluded from the transfer pricing provisions. The headquarter company will not be deemed to violate the thin capitalisation rules merely because of the existence of back-to-back cross-border loans involving the headquarter company, and foreign creditors of the qualifying headquarter company will be exempt from the pending withholding tax on interest in respect of back-to-back loans.[115]

Although the exclusions from the provisions of the thin capitalisation rules, as discussed above, constitute tax relief for a headquarter company, this tax relief is limited in terms of s 20C of the Act, which provides for the ring-fencing of interest and royalties incurred by headquarter companies.

Section 20C(2) provides that where a headquarter company has, during any year of assessment, incurred any interest in respect of financial assistance granted to it by a non-resident company that directly or indirectly (and whether alone or together with any other company forming part of the same group of companies as that person) holds at least 10% of the equity shares and voting rights in that headquarter company, the allowable interest deduction for that headquarter company in that year of assessment is limited to the portion of the financial assistance that is directly applied.

[114] Section 31(5) of the Income Tax Act as amended by the Taxation Laws Amendment Act 24 of 2011.

[115] Explanatory Memorandum on the Taxation Laws Amendment Bill, 2010 para 5.4, part III; Oguttu (2011) *South African Year Book of International Law* 78–79.

Section 20C(2A) ring-fences royalties incurred by headquarter companies. The section provides that if a headquarter company has during a year of assessment incurred any royalty payable to a non-resident company that directly or indirectly (and whether alone or together with any other company forming part of the same group of companies as that person) holds at least 10% of the equity shares and voting rights in that headquarter company, the allowable royalty deduction for that headquarter company in that year of assessment is limited to the amounts received by or accrued to the headquarter company in respect of the use of the intellectual property from that foreign company.

In terms of s 20C(3), the amount that is disallowed as a deduction for headquarter company in a year of assessment, in terms of s 20C(2) (which ring-fences interest incurred by headquarter companies) or s 20C(2A) (which ring-fences royalties incurred by headquarter companies), must be carried forward to the immediate succeeding year of assessment. If an amount of interest is disallowed as a deduction it is deemed to be actually incurred by the headquarter company during that succeeding year in respect of financial assistance granted to that headquarter company by the non-resident company. Likewise, if a royalty amount is disallowed as a deduction, it is deemed to be actually incurred by the headquarter company during that succeeding year that it constitutes a royalty payable to the non-resident company.

In terms of s 31(6) of the Act, where a resident (other than a headquarter company) grants financial assistance, or the use, right of use or permission to use any intellectual property as defined in s 23I, to that resident's CFC, s 31(6) shall not apply in calculating the taxable income of that resident in respect of any amount received by or accrued if:

- that resident (whether alone or together with any other company forming part of the same group of companies as that resident) owns at least 10% of the equity shares and voting rights in that CFC; or
- that CFC has a foreign business establishment as defined in s 9D(1), and the aggregate amount of tax payable to any foreign country by that CFC is at least 75% of the amount of normal tax that would have been payable had that CFC been a resident (taking into consideration any double tax treaty, any credit, rebate or other right of recovery of tax from any foreign country and after disregarding any losses incurred in the Republic).

14.3.6 Translation of foreign currency amounts

Where income is earned in foreign currency, the Act provides two rules regarding the translation of foreign currency amounts:

- general translation rules; and
- the specific translation rules.

14.3.6.1 General translation rules

Section 25D provides for the translation of amounts expressed in foreign currency generally into South African currency. The following definitions in s 1 of the Act are important to the application of these rules:

- Average exchange rate: this is the rate of exchange in relation to a year of assessment that is determined by using the closing spot rate at the end of daily or monthly intervals during the year of assessment. This average exchange rate must be applied consistently during the year of assessment.
- Spot rate: the appropriate quoted exchange rate at a specific time by any authorised dealer in foreign exchange for the delivery of currency.

Section 25D was amended by the Taxation Laws Amendment Act 7 of 2010, which added 25D(4) to the Act from years of assessment commencing on or after 1 January 2011.[116] This section provides:

> Where, during any year of assessment—
>
> *(a)* any amount—
>
> (i) is received by or accrued to; or
>
> (ii) of expenditure is incurred by, a headquarter company in any currency other than the functional currency of the headquarter company; and
>
> *(b)* the functional currency of that headquarter company is a currency other than the currency of the Republic,
>
> that amount must be determined in the functional currency of the headquarter company and must be translated to the currency of the Republic by applying the average exchange rate for that year of assessment.

The purpose of this provision is to provide flexibility to the headquarter company in South Africa when determining its taxable income in respect of the translation of foreign currency amounts. In summary, any amount received by or accrued to a headquarter company, or any amount of expenditure which is incurred by a headquarter company during a year of assessment, must be determined in the functional currency of the headquarter company (if the functional currency of the headquarter company is not the South African rand). Thus, dollar-based headquarter companies can rely on the dollar as their base currency for tax purposes. The taxable income must then be translated into rands using the average exchange rate for the year of assessment.[117] The term 'functional currency', added to s 1 of the Act by the Taxation Laws Amendment Act 7 of 2010, is defined as follows:

---

116 Explanatory Memorandum on the Taxation Laws Amendment Bill, 2010 para 5.8 part IV.

117 Explanatory Memorandum on the Taxation Laws Amendment Bill, 2010 para 5.8 part III.

'[F]unctional currency', in relation to—

(a) a person, means the currency of the primary economic environment in which the business operations of that person are conducted; and

(b) a permanent establishment of any person, means the currency of the primary economic environment in which the business operations of that permanent establishment are conducted.

Consequently, the functional currency is determined with reference to the currency of the economic environment in which a significant part of the activities are conducted.

14.3.6.2 Specific translation rules

(a) Gains or losses from foreign exchange transactions

Section 24I deals with the tax treatment of foreign exchange gains and losses that arise from 'exchange items', for example, foreign currency loans owing by a taxpayer. The gains and losses on foreign exchange transactions mainly comprise finance charges. Section 24I requires the inclusion of gains and losses on foreign exchange transactions in the determination of a taxpayer's taxable income at the end of a year of assessment, irrespective of whether they have been realised or not and irrespective of whether the gains or losses are of a capital nature.[118] The section applies to the following persons and transactions:

- Companies: the section covers all exchange items, including 'non-trade' exchange items, of a company.
- Trusts: for the section to apply to trusts, the trust must be carrying on a trade or it must hold a forward exchange contract or currency option contract, irrespective of whether or not it is held for trade purposes.
- A natural person: the section applies to natural persons who hold a unit of currency or loan, advance or debt as trading stock or any forward exchange contract or currency option contract irrespective of whether or not it is held for purposes of trade.

With respect to non-residents' exchange items, s 24I(2) applies only to gains or losses which are attributable to a non-resident's permanent establishment in the Republic. If, however, a non-resident is a CFC, s 24I applies to it as if it were a resident.

As s 24I applies to a trust only if it carries on a trade, and to natural persons only if they hold the items listed above as trading stock, there is a distinction between the types of transactions covered by s 24I and those covered by the Eighth Schedule to the Act. Thus, the Eighth Schedule applies only when s 24I does not apply.

[118] Olivier & Honiball *International Tax* 200.

(b) Translation rules that govern capital assets acquired or disposed of in foreign currency

Paragraph 43 of the Eighth Schedule deals with gains and losses on capital assets acquired and disposed of in foreign currency, or acquired in local currency and disposed of in foreign currency, or acquired in foreign currency and disposed of in local currency. Paragraph 43(4) establishes a set of rules for the determination of currency gains or losses in respect of foreign equity instruments.

(c) Translation rules that govern gains and losses from holding foreign currency assets and settling foreign currency liabilities

Part XIII of the Eighth Schedule (paras 84 to 96) established a set of capital gains tax rules for 'foreign currency assets' of individuals and certain trusts that are not regulated by s 24I. A 'foreign currency asset' was defined in para 84, in relation to a person, as any amount in foreign currency that constitutes a unit of foreign currency of that person or owing to him in respect of any loan, advance or debt payable to him.[119] These rules were repealed with effect from years of assessment commencing on or after 1 April 2011.

(d) Translation rules that govern the translation of a CFC's net income or loss

In terms of s 9D(6) of the Act, as amended by the Taxation Laws Amendment Act 24 of 2011, from years of assessment commencing 1 January 2012:

> The net income of a controlled foreign company in respect of a foreign tax year shall be determined in the functional currency of that controlled foreign company and shall, for purposes of determining the amount to be included in the income of any resident during any year of assessment under the provisions of this section, be translated to the currency of the Republic by applying the average exchange rate for that foreign tax year.

(e) Translation rules that relate to headquarter companies

Section 25D(4) of the Act provides some flexibility in determining the taxable income that arises from the translation of foreign currency amounts for headquarter companies. The section provides that where, during a year of assessment, any amount is received by or accrues to a headquarter company, or any amount of expenditure is incurred by a headquarter company in any currency other than the functional currency of that headquarter company, the amount must be determined in the functional currency of the headquarter company (if that functional currency is not South African rand). The amount that is determined must then be translated to rand using the average exchange rate for the specific year of assessment.

---

119 Olivier & Honiball *International Tax* 195 and 207.

14.4 DOUBLE TAXATION AGREEMENTS AND INTERNATIONAL TRANSACTIONS

A double taxation treaty/agreement is an agreement between two countries that sets out rules for the taxation for transactions and relationships between persons resident in the two countries.[120] Article 2(1)*(a)* of the Vienna Law of Treaties defines a 'treaty' as 'an international agreement concluded between states in written form and governed by international law, whether embodied in a single instrument or in two or more related instruments and whatever its particular designation'. Specific provisions in a treaty may be clarified by an exchange of notes or a protocol. These become part of the treaty.[121]

Tax treaties are usually signed on the basis of a particular model and they generally follow the provisions in the prescriptive articles of such models. There are three main models for drafting double taxation agreements:

- the OECD Model Tax Convention on Income and on Capital, which embodies rules and proposals by developed capital exporting countries;
- the United Nations Model Double Taxation Convention, which attempts to reflect the interests of developing countries; and
- the United States Model, which the United States uses when signing treaties with other countries.[122]

Most of South Africa's treaties largely follow the OECD Model Tax Convention. Although South Africa is not a member of the OECD, it was awarded observer status of the OECD in 2004.

Although tax treaties are binding agreements between sovereign states, they generally do not have any effect on taxpayers unless they are specifically incorporated into a country's tax laws by domestic statute.[123] Where there is a conflict between the treaty provisions and the provisions of domestic law, the treaty should prevail, since it is in essence a contract between the contracting states.[124]

14.4.1 Objectives of tax treaties

The main objective of tax treaties is to facilitate cross-border trade and investment by eliminating the tax impediments to cross-border flows.[125] Thus, the most important objective of tax treaties is the elimination of double taxation, and it is reflected in the preamble to most treaties, which usually mentions 'the avoidance of double taxation and the prevention of fiscal evasion'. How

---

[120] Reinhold RL 'What is Tax Treaty Abuse? (Is Treaty Shopping an Outdated Concept?)' (2000) 53 *Tax Lawyer* 673.

[121] Olivier & Honiball *International Tax* 10.

[122] Arnold & McIntyre *International Tax* 106.

[123] Arnold & McIntyre *International Tax* 3.

[124] Arnold & McIntyre *International Tax* 104.

[125] Arnold & McIntyre *International Tax* 105.

treaties eliminate double taxation is dealt with below. In addition to this main objective, tax treaties also help in:

- countering of tax evasion by encouraging co-operation and the sharing of tax information;
- facilitation of international trade and investment;
- elimination of discrimination based on nationality;
- simplification and harmonisation of laws governing international taxation;
- removal of administrative obstacles to international trade and investment;
- allocation of taxing rights between the states;
- adjustment of prices in transactions between associated enterprises where they do not reflect an arm's length price;
- collection of taxes through exchange of information;
- settlement of disputes through mutual agreement procedure;
- curtailing of abuse of tax treaties through treaty shopping; and
- reduction of withholding taxes.[126]

Some tax treaties provide for the promotion and strengthening of economic development.

14.4.2 Persons covered by a treaty

In terms of article 1 of the OECD Model Tax Convention, the persons covered by the double tax treaty must be resident in one of the contracting states. In terms of article 4(1) of the OECD Model Tax Convention, a person is a resident of a state if the person is liable in that state for tax by reason of: domicile, residence, place of management or some other similar criterion. Note that:

- A permanent establishment is not considered a resident, since it merely creates a taxable presence in a source state.
- A partnership can be resident if it is considered a corporate legal entity (eg the UK limited liability company).

14.4.2.1 Abuse of tax treaties

Tax treaties often contain anti-treaty shopping provisions which are designed to prevent residents of a non-treaty country from obtaining treaty benefits that are not intended to be available to them.[127] Not all states maintain treaty relationships with each other. An investor whose country of residence does not have a treaty with the country in which the investor wants to do business can become involved in treaty shopping schemes whereby he or she uses that

[126] Olivier & Honiball *International Tax* 14.

[127] Oguttu AW 'Curbing "Treaty Shopping": The "Beneficial Ownership Provision" Analysed from a South African Perspective' (2007) XL *CILSA* 238; Becker H & Wurm FJ *Treaty Shopping: An Emerging Tax Issue and its Present Status in Various Countries* (Kluwer 1988) 1.

other country's treaties in order to reduce the rate of tax payable.[128] Treaty shopping is often achieved by interposing or organising a corporation or other legal entity in one of the contracting states.[129]

There are basically two means by which treaty shopping can be achieved: the 'direct conduit' method and the 'stepping stone' method.[130] Under the 'direct conduit' method, income is shifted through a conduit company[131] interposed in a country that has an advantageous tax treaty.[132] Basically, in the 'direct conduit' method treaty shopping is achieved by making use of the treaty concessions (such as exemptions from tax) granted to the intermediary entity by the host and home jurisdictions.[133] Under the 'stepping stone' method the tax liability is reduced by counter-balancing expenses. This can be achieved by setting up conduit companies in tax-haven jurisdictions which are used to extract income from the high-tax countries by changing the nature of the income to appear as tax-deductible expenses.[134]

Treaty shopping is undesirable because it frustrates the spirit of the treaty.[135] When treaties are concluded, the assumption is that a certain amount of income will accrue to both countries concluding the treaty. The anticipated capital flows are distorted if the treaty is used by taxpayers resident in a third country.[136] Furthermore, when unintended beneficiaries are free to choose the location of their businesses, then treaties designed to eliminate double taxation are used to eliminate taxation altogether.[137]

The Commentary on Article 1 of the OECD Model Tax Convention has historically suggested measures that can be inserted in tax treaties to curb different forms and cases of conduit company treaty shopping.

---

[128] Haug SM 'The United States Policy of Stringent Anti-Treaty Shopping Provisions: A Comparative Analysis' (1996) 29 *Vanderbilt Journal of Transnational Law* 191 at 201, 204; Tomsett E *Tax Planning for Multinational Companies* (Prentice Hall 1989) 149; Diamond & Diamond *Tax Havens* 10; Ginsberg *Tax Havens* 15.

[129] Wurm FJ 'Treaty Shopping in the 1992 OECD Model Convention' (1992) *Intertax* 658; Haug (1996) *Vanderbilt Journal of Transnational Law* 196; Tomsett *Tax Planning* 149; Arnold & McIntyre *International Tax* 114–115; Van Weeghel S *The Improper Use of Tax Treaties with Particular Reference to the Netherlands and the United States* (Kluwer 1998) 119; Doggart D 'Tax Havens and Their Uses' *The Economist Publication* (1990) Special Report No 1191 at 91.

[130] Ginsberg *Tax Havens* 39.

[131] Van Weeghel *Improper Use of Tax Treaties* 72–73 defines a conduit company as an intermediary company with very narrow powers, its function being to hold assets or rights as an agent or nominee would on behalf of another company.

[132] Wurm (1992) *Intertax* 658; Rappako A *Base Company Taxation* (1989) 16.

[133] OECD 'Double Taxation Conventions and the Use of Conduit Companies' (OECD Publications 1987) paras 4(2) and 5*(d)*; Haug (1996) *Vanderbilt Journal of Transnational Law* 206; Ginsberg *Tax Havens* 40; Rohatgi R *Basic International Taxation* (Kluwer 2002) 230.

[134] OECD 'Use of Conduit Companies' paras 4(2) and 5*(d)*. See also Haug (1996) *Vanderbilt Journal of Transnational Law* 206; Ginsberg *Tax Havens* 40; Rohatgi *International Taxation* 230.

[135] OECD 'Use of Conduit Companies' para 4(2).

[136] Oguttu (2007) XL *CILSA* 241; Haug (1996) *Vanderbilt Journal of Transnational Law* 216; Van Weeghel *Improper Use of Tax Treaties* 121.

[137] Van Weeghel *Improper Use of Tax Treaties* 121; Haug (1996) *Vanderbilt Journal of Transnational Law* 218.

14.4.2.2 Use of domestic anti-abuse rules

The Commentary on Article 1 of the OECD Model Tax Convention makes it clear that where taxpayers are tempted to abuse the tax laws of a state by exploiting the differences between various countries' laws, such attempts may be countered by jurisprudential rules that are part of the domestic law of the state concerned (for example, general anti-abuse rules and judicial anti-abuse doctrines like the substance over form doctrine) as well as the use of specific treaty anti-avoidance provisions. South Africa may, for instance, apply the general anti-avoidance provisions in ss 80A–80L of the Act and the substance over form common-law doctrine.

Although the commentaries on both the OECD and the UN Model Tax Conventions contend that there is no conflict between double tax treaty provisions and domestic anti-avoidance rules since the latter merely establish the facts to which treaties apply,[138] double tax treaty provisions are generally considered to prevail over domestic law since a double tax treaty is a contract between the contracting states. To prevent arguments about treaty override, it is necessary that countries enact domestic anti-abuse rules that mirror the anti-abuse rules in their double tax treaties.[139]

14.4.2.3 Use of specific anti- abuse rules: The beneficial ownership provision

This provision has historically been applied to prevent treaty shopping with regard to specific types of income (dividends, interest and royalties) often contained in articles 10, 11 and 12 of the OECD Model. Although the term 'beneficial ownership' is not explicitly defined in the Commentary, the OECD Commentary makes it clear that a nominee or agent who is a treaty country resident may not claim benefits if the person who has all the economic interest in, and all the control over, property (the beneficial owner) is not also a resident. The OECD report on conduit companies further explains that a conduit company cannot normally be regarded as a beneficial owner if, through the formal owner, it has, as a practical matter, very narrow powers which render it, in relation to the income concerned, a mere fiduciary or administrator acting on account of the interested parties (who will most likely be the shareholders of the conduit company). Thus, a holding company that simply owns investment assets on behalf of its shareholders may not be the beneficial owner of the income received by it.

South Africa has made use of 'beneficial ownership' clauses in some of its treaties to curb treaty shopping. Such a clause usually provides that the withholding tax exemptions pertaining to interest, royalties and dividends will apply only to the extent that the recipient in the other country is in fact the 'beneficial owner' thereof. For instance, article 11(1) of the South Africa–United

[138] Paragraph 22 of the Commentary on Article 1 of the OECD Model Tax Convention.
[139] Oliver & Honiball *International Tax* 306

States double tax treaty provides that interest derived and beneficially owned by a resident of a contracting state shall only be taxed in that state. The South Africa–United Kingdom double tax treaty also refers to the payment of interest to a resident of the other contacting state if he or she is the beneficial owner of the interest.

However, over the years, the beneficial ownership provision has not been very effective in preventing treaty abuse as is evidenced by the outcomes of international cases such as the Canadian case of *Prevost Car Inc v Her Majesty the Queen*[140] and *Velcro Canada Inc v The Queen*,[141] which were ruled in favour of the taxpayers. OECD acknowledged the limits of using that beneficial concept as a tool to address various treaty-shopping situations. Paragraph 12.5 of the Commentary on Article 10 provides that 'whilst the concept of "beneficial ownership" deals with some forms of tax avoidance (i.e. those involving the interposition of a recipient who is obliged to pass on the dividend to someone else), it does not deal with other cases of treaty shopping and must not, therefore, be considered as restricting in any way the application of other approaches to addressing such cases'.

14.4.2.4 Recommendations in light of OECD BEPS Measures

In light of the recommendations in Action 6[142] of the OECD base erosion and profit shifting project ('BEPS') (explained below) changes were made to the OECD Model to effectively deal with treaty abuse matters.

Action 6 recommends that in cases where a person tries to circumvent the provisions of domestic tax law to gain treaty benefits, treaty shopping must be addressed through domestic anti-abuse rules.[143] Such a provision will ensure that source countries are able to apply their domestic anti-avoidance provisions unconstrained by treaty rules.

For cases where a person tries to circumvent limitations provided by the treaty itself, the OECD recommends that this should be addressed through treaty anti-abuse rules using a three-pronged approach.

- The title and preamble of treaties should clearly state that the treaty is not intended to create opportunities for non-taxation or reduced taxation through treaty shopping.[144] Such a provision augments the treaty interpretation approach of preventing treaty abuse in article 31 of the Vienna Convention on the Law of Treaties, which provides that treaties are to be interpreted in good faith and in the light of the object and purpose of the treaty.[145]

---

[140] 2008 TCC 231.

[141] 2012 TCC 57.

[142] OECD/G20 BEPS Project 'Preventing the Granting of Treaty Benefits in Inappropriate Circumstances' Action 6 (2015) para 15.

[143] OECD/G20 2015 Report on Action Plan 6 para 15.

[144] OECD/G20 2015 Report on Action Plan 6 para 19.

[145] Vienna Convention on the Law of Treaties of 23 May 1969.

- A specific limitation of benefits provision (LOB rule), such as the one normally included in treaties concluded by the United States and a few other countries, should be included. Generally, this provision restricts entitlement to treaty benefits where a person is technically a treaty resident but lacks substantial connection with the residence jurisdiction. To be entitled to treaty benefits, a resident has to pass the test of a 'qualified person'. The OECD is of the view that such a specific rule will address a large number of treaty shopping situations based on the legal nature, ownership in, and general activities of residents of a contracting state. [146]
- To address other forms of treaty abuse not covered by the LOB rule (such as certain conduit financing arrangements) tax treaties should include a more general anti-abuse rule based on the principal purpose test. This rule is intended to provide a clear statement that the contracting states intend to deny the application of the provisions of their treaties when transactions or arrangements are entered into in order to obtain the benefits of these provisions in inappropriate circumstances.[147]

The OECD acknowledges that each rule has strengths and weaknesses and may not be appropriate for all countries.[148] It thus advises that the rules may be adapted to the specificities of individual states and the circumstances of the negotiation of DTAs. [149]

14.4.3 Taxes covered in a treaty

In terms of article 2 of the OECD Model Tax Convention, treaties do not cover all taxes but only those mentioned in the treaty itself. Article 2(2) refers to—

> taxes imposed on total income, total capital, or on elements of income or capital, including taxes on gains from the alienation of movable or immovable property, taxes on the total amounts of wages or salaries paid by enterprises, as well as taxes on capital appreciation.

It is immaterial whether the taxes are levied by central government or a sphere of government. The method of levying tax is also immaterial. Article 2(4) provides that the treaty shall apply to any identical or substantially similar taxes that are imposed after the date of signature of the convention. However, states should undertake to inform each other of significant changes in their taxation laws.

14.4.4 Double taxation

Because different countries use different bases of taxing income, double taxation of income may occur. Thus, double taxation may arise internationally when there is a coincidence of:

---

[146] OECD/G20 2015 Report on Action Plan 6 para 19.
[147] OECD/G20 2015 Report on Action Plan 6 para 19.
[148] OECD/G20 2015 Report on Action Plan 6 para 20.
[149] Ibid.

- source–source bases of taxation: two countries seek to tax the same income of a taxpayer because they both claim that the income is sourced in their country;
- residence–residence bases of taxation: two countries tax the same income of the taxpayer because they both claim that the taxpayer is resident in their country (dual residence); or
- residence–source bases of taxation: one country taxes the foreign source income of a taxpayer because he or she is resident in that country and another country taxes the same income because it claims that the income has its source in that country.

Double taxation could either be 'juridical' or 'economic' double taxation:

- Juridical double taxation occurs when two states impose the same or comparable taxes on the same taxpayer, in respect of the same subject matter and for identical periods. This can be as a result of the coincidence of source and residence bases of taxation imposed on a taxpayer by two different countries, but it may also be caused by the coincidence of two states' residence bases of taxation.
- Economic double taxation occurs when tax is charged by two countries on the same income in the hands of different persons.

14.4.5 Relieving double taxation: Residence–residence conflicts

When the two states treat the same person as 'a resident' for tax purposes under their domestic law, that person is said to be a 'dual resident' and thus fully liable to tax in both states. In terms of article 4(1) of the OECD Model Tax Convention, a person is a resident of a state if liable in that state for tax by reason of domicile, residence, place of management or some other similar criterion.

In order to alleviate the ensuing double taxation, if the two states have entered into a double taxation agreement, the treaty would contain tie-breaker rules to resolve residence–residence conflicts, by allocating the residence of the 'dual resident' person to one of those states so that the person is treated as a resident solely of that state for the purposes of the treaty. Treaties usually provide for tie-breaker rules for both individuals and other persons.

14.4.5.1 Tie-breaker rules for individuals

In terms of article 4(2) of the OECD Model Tax Convention, the tie-breaker rules for individuals consist of a series of questions:

- In which country does the individual have a permanent home? A permanent home is one arranged and retained for permanent use and not merely for stays of short duration.

- If the individual has a permanent home in both countries, he or she is regarded as a resident only of the state in which his or her personal and economic relations are closer (centre of vital interests). This is a question of fact that takes into account family and social relations, occupation, political and other activities, place of business etc.
- If the centre of vital interests cannot be determined, the state in which he or she has a habitual abode is considered. This is the state in which he or she stays more frequently over a reasonable period.
- If the habitual abode cannot be established, he or she is resident in the state in which he or she is a national.
- If he or she is a national of both states, or neither, then residency is settled by the competent authorities of both states by mutual agreement.

14.4.5.2 Tie-breaker rules for persons other than individuals

A person other than an individual (for example a company or a trust) is considered dual resident if it is incorporated or formed in one state and yet it has a 'place of effective management' in another. In order to ensure that only one of the contracting states has jurisdiction to tax the dual resident company (for example), article 4(3) of the OECD Model Tax Convention provides that the dual resident company will only be considered to be a resident of the state in which its 'place of effective management' is situated. Paragraph 24 of the Commentary on Article 4 of the OECD Model Tax Convention defines the 'place of effective management' as follows:

The place of effective management is the place where the key management and commercial decisions that are necessary for the conduct of the entity's business are in substance made. All relevant facts and circumstances must be examined to determine the place of effective management. An entity may have more than one place of management, but it can have only one place of effective management at any one time.

Paragraph 24(1) of the Commentary on Article 4 further provides that where there are difficulties in determining the place of effective management, for instance in the case of new communication technologies, a case-by-case approach may be considered. In such situations, the question concerning the place of effective management of a legal person may be settled by the competent authorities of the contracting states, who may take into account factors such as:

- where the meetings of the board of directors of the legal person are usually held;
- where the chief executive officer and other senior executives usually carry on their activities;
- where the senior day-to-day management of the person is carried on;
- where the person's headquarters are located;
- which country's laws govern the legal status of the person;
- where its accounting records are kept; and

- whether determining that the legal person is resident of one of the contracting states but not of the other for the purposes of the convention would carry the risk of an improper use of the provisions of the convention, etc.

It should be noted that due to the difficulties of proving the place of effective management, which over years created opportunities for base erosion and profit shifting using dual resident entities, Action 6 of the OECD BEPS project came up with a recommendation that resulted in the revision of article 4(3) of the OECD Model which now provides that double taxation as a result of dual resident entities will now be resolved through mutual agreement by the competent authorities having regard to the place of effective management, place of incorporation and other relevant factors. If no agreement is reached, treaty benefits would be denied and the dual resident entity would be subject to double taxation.

14.4.6 Double taxation relief: Residence–source conflicts

For most treaties based on the OECD Model Tax Convention, relief from double taxation resulting from the conflict of residence and source bases of taxation by two countries on the same income is normally granted by the residence country. In other words, the source country's right to tax has priority over the residence country's right.

Internationally, three main methods are used to relieve the ensuing double taxation:

- *The deduction method:* the residence country allows its taxpayers to claim a deduction for taxes, including income taxes, paid to foreign governments in respect of foreign-sourced income.
- *Exemption method:* the residence country provides its taxpayers with an exemption for foreign-sourced income.
- *Credit method:* the residence country provides its taxpayers with a credit against taxes otherwise payable for taxes paid to a foreign country.

Relief from double taxation as a result of residence–source conflicts can be obtained either unilaterally in terms of domestic law, or bilaterally, in terms of tax treaty law.

14.4.7 South Africa's unilateral double tax relief methods

In South African domestic law, double taxation can be relieved by using the exemption method or the deduction method.

14.4.7.1 The exemption method

As discussed in 14.2.2 above, the Act contains certain provisions that exempt certain international transactions from taxation.

14.4.7.2 The credit method

The Act makes provision for a rebate with respect to foreign taxes. Section 6*quat*(1) provides for rebate against normal South African tax of a resident for any foreign taxes paid on any income from foreign sources. Section 6*quat*(1) is a rebate against tax and not against income. This means that it is only after the resident's taxable income has been calculated that the rebate can be utilised against the tax liability. The rebate is available only to residents and cannot be claimed by non-residents who are taxable on a source basis.

The amounts that can be covered by the rebate apply when the taxable income of the resident, during a year of assessment, includes:

- any income received by or accrued to such resident from any source outside South Africa (s 6*quat*(1)*(a)*);
- any proportional amount calculated under the CFC rules (s 9D) (s 6*quat*(1)*(b)*)
- any taxable capital gain contemplated in s 26 from a source within South Africa (s 6*quat*(1)*(e)*);
- any amount which is deemed to have been received by or accrued to a resident in terms of the so-called tax-back or attribution provisions contained in s 7 (s 6*quat*(1)*(f)*(i)); and
- any capital gain of any person from a source outside South Africa which is attributed to a resident in terms of the so-called CGT tax-back provisions – paras 68, 69, 70, 71, 72 or 80 of the Eighth Schedule to the Act (s 6*quat*(1)*(f)*(ii)).

Section 6*quat*(1A) provides for calculation of the rebate. The section states that the the foreign taxes must be taxes on income proved to be payable to any sphere of government of a foreign country without any right of recovery (ie any refund, a credit or a deduction). However, a right of recovery in terms of any entitlement to carry losses during any year of assessment before such year of assessment may still qualify for the rebate.

Proviso (i) to s 6*quat*(1A) states that where the resident is a member of a partnership or a beneficiary of a trust that is liable for tax as a separate entity in the foreign country, a proportional amount of any tax payable by the partnership or trust that is attributable to the interest of the resident in the partnership or trust is deemed to have been payable by the resident. The result is that even though the member did not actually pay the tax, he or she will still qualify for the tax credit.

Proviso (ii) to s 6*quat*(1A) clarifies the interaction between s 6*quat* and the taxation of foreign dividends. If a South African resident receives a foreign dividend (which is income from a source outside South African as per s 6*quat*(1)*(a)*) and foreign taxes were levied on that foreign dividend, the full amount of foreign dividend will qualify for the s 6*quat* rebate, irrespective of whether the foreign dividend qualified for the partial foreign dividend exemption in terms of s 10B(3).

Section s 6*quat*(1B) sets out the following provisos, which put in place limitations to the rebate:

- In determining the taxable income attributable to the income, proportional amount or taxable capital gain, any allowance deductions in terms of s 18A (donations to certain organisations) are deemed to have been incurred proportionally in respect of income derived from sources within and outside South Africa.
- The foreign taxes attributable to any proportional amount of a CFC are in aggregate limited to the amount of normal tax on those proportional amounts if the proportional amount is an amount attributable to a foreign business establishment that is not excluded from the application of s 9D(2) in terms of s 9D(9A)*(a)*, for example, certain passive income of a business establishment. This limitation of the foreign tax to the amount of normal tax in this situation prevents the creation of an 'excess amount' that could otherwise be carried and offset against normal tax in the succeeding year (proviso (iA) to s 6*quat*(1B)*(a)*).
- Any foreign taxes on a taxable capital gain attributable to an asset that is not attributable to a foreign business establishment of a resident is also in aggregate limited to the amount of normal tax ascribable to that taxable capital gain (proviso (iB) to s 6*quat(1B)(a)*).
- Where the sum of the foreign taxes payable exceeds the rebate, the excess amount is carried forward to the immediately succeeding year of assessment (s 6*quat*(1B)(ii)*(aa)*). It is deemed to be an amount of foreign tax paid in that year. It may then be set off against the normal tax payable by the resident in that year on foreign amounts that are proportional amounts included in the taxable income of a resident. However, the excess amount may not be carried forward for more than seven years, reckoned from the year of assessment when the excess amount was for the first time carried forward.

Section 6*quat* provides for its own translation method in terms of s 6*quat*(4) and s 6*quat*(4A). These sections require that the foreign taxes be translated into rand on the last day of the year of assessment of the resident, using the average exchange rate for the year of assessment (s 6*quat*(4)). For the purposes of s 6*quat*, if the amount of the foreign taxes translated into rand includes a number of cents (ie less than R1) then the amount of the translated foreign taxes must be rounded off to the nearest rand (s 6*quat*(4A)).

In terms of s 6*quat*(5), the Commissioner may issue a reduced or additional assessment reflecting the correct amount of the s 6*quat* rebate not more than six years from the date of the original assessment when the rebate was allowed, this notwithstanding ss 93, 99 or 100 of the Tax Administration Act 28 of 2011.

Note: In a treaty context, the s 6*quat* rebate may be granted in substitution for, and not in addition to, any relief to which a resident may be entitled under a tax treaty. Thus, a taxpayer may elect not to claim the rebate but rather to claim relief under a tax treaty if the tax treaty relief is more beneficial.

14.4.7.3 The deduction method

Section 6*quat*(1C)*(a)* provides for a deduction from the income of a resident the sum of any taxes on income paid or proved to be payable by that resident to any sphere of government of any country, without any right of recovery other than in terms of a 'mutual agreement procedure' of an international tax agreement or a right of recovery in terms of any entitlement to carry back losses arising during a year of assessment to any year of assessment prior to such year of assessment.

Section s 6*quat*(1C) also provides for how the amount of the deduction is calculated. When calculating the taxable income of a resident, the deduction that is allowed against the income must be equal to the sum of any taxes on such income paid or proved to be payable by the taxpayer to a foreign country. The foreign taxes must be taxes on income (excluding taxes as intended in s 6*quat*(1A)) proved to be payable to any sphere of government of a foreign country without any right of recovery. According to SARS, the 'right of recovery' is interpreted very broadly and includes any form of relief against a foreign tax liability, for example a refund, a credit or a deduction. However, a right of recovery in terms of a mutual agreement procedure in terms of an international tax agreement or any entitlement to carry back losses during any year of assessment to any year of assessment before such year of assessment, may still qualify for the deduction (s 6*quat*(1C)).

There are, however, certain limitations to the deduction in s 6*quat*(1C) (as amended by Taxation Law Amendment Act 17 of 2017). Section 6*quat*(1D) provides that the deduction of any tax paid or proved to be payable as contemplated in s 6*quat*(1C) shall not in aggregate exceed the total taxable income (before taking into account any such deduction) attributable to income which is subject to taxes as contemplated in that section. This is provided that in determining the amount of the taxable income that is attributable to that income, any allowable deductions contemplated in s 11*(n)* (retirement annuity fund contributions), s 18 (retirement annuity fund contributions) and s 18A (donations to certain organisations) must be deemed to have been incurred proportionately in the ratio that that income bears to total income.

Section 6*quat*(1C) sets out the applicable rules for translation of foreign taxes. In terms of s 6*quat*(4), foreign taxes paid (for which a deduction in terms of s 6*quat*(1C) is claimed) must be translated into rand on the last day of the year of assessment of the resident, using the average exchange rate for that year of assessment.

14.4.7.4 Income blocked in a foreign country

The Act contains a delay mechanism in s 9A which indirectly prevents international double taxation, but it is not an exemption, deduction or credit mechanism. The section applies if a resident received any foreign income during a year of assessment which is blocked in a foreign country.

- Section 9A(1) states that if an amount or part of an amount is received by a person during a year of assessment and is included in that person's income and that amount, due to currency or other restrictions in a foreign country, may not be remitted to South Africa during that specific year of assessment, then the person will be allowed, as a deduction against his or her income, so much of the income as could not be remitted to South Africa.
- Section 9A(2) provides that the amount or part of the amount that may not be remitted during the year of assessment is deemed to have been received by that person in the following year of assessment and has to be included in his or her gross income at that stage.
- Section 9A(3) provides that if the net income or portion of the net income of a CFC may not be remitted to South Africa due to currency or other restrictions in a foreign country, then the amount which could not be remitted to South Africa shall be allowed as a deduction against the income of the CFC.
- Section 9A(4) provides that the amount or part of the amount of net income remitted in the year of assessment has to be included in the CFC's gross income at that stage.

14.4.8 Double tax relief under the OECD Model Tax Convention

14.4.8.1 Exemption method

In terms of article 23A of the OECD Model Tax Convention, where a resident of a contracting state derives income or owns capital which may be taxed in the other contracting state in terms of the tax treaty, the first-mentioned state must exempt such income or capital from tax. This rule does not apply where a resident of a contracting state derives dividends or interest which may be taxed in the other contracting state under articles 10 and 11.

14.4.8.2 Credit method

In terms of article 23B of the OECD Model Tax Convention, where a resident of a contracting state derives income or owns capital which may be taxed in the other contracting state, the resident state must allow as a deduction from its own tax an amount equal to the tax paid in that other state. The deduction may not exceed that part of the income tax or capital tax – as computed before the deduction is given – which is attributable to the income or capital which may be taxed in that other state.

It must be noted that South Africa uses the credit method when negotiating tax treaties with its trading partners.

14.4.9 Treaty distributive rules

Generally, treaties do not impose tax; rather they limit the taxes that can be imposed by the contracting states. In effect, tax treaties are primarily relieving in nature. Thus, in an endeavour to prevent double taxation that arises as a result of residence–source conflicts, the treaty allocates taxing rights between the residence and source states. In effect, tax treaties 'create an independent voice to avoid double taxation through the restriction of contracting states' tax claims where there could be an overlapping of these claims'. The independent voice is created by either one of the contracting parties' undertaking not to levy tax or to levy tax only to a limited extent or, when it does levy tax, to give credit for foreign taxes paid. Thus, a tax treaty lays down the boundaries within which domestic tax provisions are enforceable. A treaty cannot impose tax where the income is not subject to tax under domestic legislation. A country's right to tax depends on the nature of the income derived or to whom the income is paid. This is referred to as the 'distributive' or 'limitation' rules.

14.4.9.1 Distribution rules and the problems and challenges of characterising income

Although a country's right to tax depends on the nature of the income derived, in practice it is not easy to characterise income in a specific manner. For example, income derived by an entertainer who renders services through a company does not fall under the OECD category of 'artistes and sportsmen' but rather under business income.

Income may also be differently classified under the domestic law from that which is set out in tax treaties. For example, a severance package may be classified under the domestic law of one state as compensation for services rendered (article 15) but it may be classified as a pension in the other state (article 18).

When double taxation arises, due to the different classification, this is eliminated by the residence state giving credit for foreign taxes paid or payable. If the residence state refuses to give the credit on the basis that the source state did not levy tax in accordance with the treaty, the Commentary on Article 23 clarifies that the residence state must accept the classification adopted by the source state and must provide relief from double taxation.

In certain instances, exclusive rights to tax are not allocated to either of the contracting states but the primary right to tax is allocated to one country and the residual right to tax is allocated to the other country. Thus, where the source state has the primary right to tax, the residence state is obliged to confer relief for foreign taxes paid. Exclusive rights to tax are awarded by the use of words 'shall be taxed only' and the secondary right to tax is awarded by the use of words 'may be taxed in'. The OECD Model Tax Convention generally awards primary taxing rights to the source state. If the residence state exercises its residual right to tax (and the source state has the primary right to tax) the residence state is obliged to give relief for foreign taxes paid on the source basis, by either the credit method (credit for foreign taxes paid) or the exemption method (exempting foreign taxes paid).

The OECD Model Tax Convention has distributive rules for the following types of income:

(a) Immovable property

In terms of article 6, immovable property includes the following:

- property accessory to immovable property;
- livestock and equipment used in agriculture and forestry;
- rights to which the provisions of general law respecting landed property apply;
- usufruct of immovable property; and
- rights to variable or fixed payments as consideration for the working of, or the right to work, mineral deposits, sources and other natural resources.

Article 6 provides that income from immovable property may be taxed in the state in which it is situated. Income for this purpose means income derived from the direct use, letting or use in any other form of immovable property. This rule applies also to income derived from immovable property of an enterprise, and to income earned from immovable property used for the performance of professional services.

(b) Business profits

Article 7(1) of the OECD Model Tax Convention provides:

> The profits of an enterprise of a contracting state shall be taxable only in that state unless the enterprise carries on business in the other contracting state through a permanent establishment situated therein. If the enterprise carries on business as aforesaid, the profits of the enterprise may be taxed in the state but only so much of them as is attributable to that permanent establishment.

In summary, the business profits of an enterprise of one state cannot be subjected to tax in the other state unless that enterprise carries on a business in the other state through a permanent establishment established in that other state. If the enterprise does carry on a trade or business in this way, the state in which the permanent establishment is situated may tax only those profits that are attributable to the permanent establishment.

Article 5 defines a 'permanent establishment' as a fixed place of business through which the business of an enterprise is wholly or partly carried on. In terms of article 5(2), this definition includes: a place of management; a branch; an office; a factory; a workshop; and a mine, an oil or gas well, a quarry or any place of extraction of natural resources. Article 5(5) deems a permanent establishment to exist where a dependent agent has authority to conclude contracts on behalf of the enterprise and habitually exercises this authority in the source country. Article 5(4) excludes from the definition of a permanent establishment activities of a preparatory or auxiliary nature.

Once a permanent establishment has been established, article 7(2) of the OECD Model Tax Convention provides that only the profits attributable to the permanent establishment are taxable. Article 7(2) states:

> [W]here an enterprise of a contracting state carries on business in the other contracting state through a permanent establishment situated therein, there shall in each contacting state be attributed to the permanent establishment the profits which it might be expected to make if it were a distinct and separate enterprise engaged in the same or similar activities under the same or similar conditions and dealing wholly independently with the enterprise of which it is a permanent establishment.

In effect, the profits to be attributed to a permanent establishment are those that the permanent establishment would have earned if, instead of dealing with its head office, it had had dealings with an entirely separate enterprise under conditions and at prices prevailing in the ordinary market. The OECD recommends that 'transfer pricing' rules applicable to transfers between related persons be used to attribute income to a permanent establishment. This requires that the 'arm's length' principle be applied in determining the profits attributable to the permanent establishment. The 'arm's length' principle, as set out in article 9(1) of OECD Model Tax Convention, provides that when conditions are imposed between two associated enterprises in their commercial or financial relations which differ from those that would have been concluded between independent enterprises, then any profits which would, but for those conditions, have accrued to one of the enterprises, but, by reason of those conditions, have not so accrued, may be included in the profits of that enterprise and taxed accordingly.

(c) Shipping, inland waterways transport, air transport

Article 8 provides that the profits of an enterprise of a contracting state generated from the operation of ships or aircraft in international traffic are taxable only in that state. Such profits would include profits from the rental of ships or aircraft and profits from the use or rental of containers used for the transport of goods or merchandise which is incidental to the operation of such ship or aircraft in international traffic, such as interest on current account deposits of airfare revenues.

(d) Dividends

In terms of article 10, dividends are defined as meaning:

- income from shares participating in profits;
- income from other rights (excluding debt claims) participating in profits;
- income from other corporate rights which is similar to income derived from shares in terms of the tax laws of the state in which the company making the distribution is resident; and
- any other item of income (other than royalties exempt from tax) in terms of the agreement which is treated as a dividend or distribution of a company under the law of the state in which the company concerned is a resident.

Article 10 restricts the taxation of dividends to the state in which the company paying the dividends is a resident.

(e) Interest

In terms of article 11, interest is defined as meaning income from the following:

- government securities;
- bonds or debentures; and
- other debt claims of every kind (whether or not secured by mortgage, and whether or not carrying a right to participate in the debtor's profits).

Interest arising in one state and paid to a resident of the other state shall be taxed only in that other state, if such resident is the beneficial owner of the interest.

(f) Royalties

Article 12 defines royalties as meaning payments of any kind received as consideration for the use of, or the right to use, the following:

- any copyright of literary, artistic or scientific work, including cinematograph films and films, tapes, or discs for radio or television broadcasting;
- any patent, trade mark, or design;
- any model, plan, secret formula or process; or
- information concerning industrial, commercial or scientific experience.

(g) Capital gains

In terms of article 13:

- Gains derived by a resident from the alienation of immovable property situated in the other state may be taxed in the other state.
- Gains derived by a resident from the alienation of shares deriving their value or the greater part of their value directly or indirectly from immovable property situated in the other state or excluding shares quoted on an approved stock exchange may be taxed in that other state.
- Gains derived by a resident from the alienation of an interest in a partnership or trust, the assets of which consist principally of immovable property situated in the other state, or of shares referred to above, may be taxed in that other state.
- Gains from the alienation of movable property forming part of the business property of a permanent establishment which an enterprise of a state has in the other state, including such gains from the alienation of such a permanent establishment (alone or with the whole enterprise), may be taxed in that other state.
- Gains derived by a resident from the alienation of any property not referred to above is taxable only in the state of which the alienator is a resident. However, where any such property was held by an individual (or spouse) prior to becoming a resident of the state in which he or she

is now resident, and such individual had within six years immediately preceding the alienation of the property been a resident of the other state, then the other state may tax such capital gain.

(h) Income from employment

In terms of article 15:

- Salaries, wages and other similar remuneration derived by a resident of one state in respect of employment are subject to tax in that state only, unless the employment is exercised in the other state, in which case the remuneration derived from the other state may be taxed in that state.
- Notwithstanding the general rule described above, remuneration derived by a resident of one state in respect of an employment exercised in the other state may be taxed in the state of residence only if three conditions are met:
    - The recipient is present in the state in which he or she is not resident for a period or periods not exceeding in the aggregate 183 days in any 12-month period commencing or ending in the fiscal year concerned.
    - The remuneration is paid by or on behalf of an employer who is not a resident of the state in which the recipient is not resident.
    - The remuneration is not borne by a permanent establishment which the employer has in the state in which the recipient is not resident.

(i) Directors' fees

Article 16 provides that directors' fees and other similar payments derived by a resident of a contracting state in that person's capacity as a member of the board of directors of a company which is a resident of the other contracting state may be taxed in that other state.

(j) Artistes and sportspersons

Article 17 provides that income derived by a resident of a contracting state as an entertainer – such as a theatre, motion picture, radio or television artiste and musician – or as a sportsperson, from his or her personal activities as such, may be taxed in the state in which these activities are exercised.

Where such income accrues not to the entertainer or sportsperson but to another person, such activities may be taxed in the state where the activities are exercised (notwithstanding the business profits and income from employment articles).

(k) Pensions

Article 18 provides that any pension paid by or out of funds created by a contracting state, or a political subdivision or a local authority, to an individual in respect of services rendered to that state, subdivision or authority is taxable only in that state. However, if the individual is a resident and a national of that state, the pension is taxable only in that state.

Pensions and other similar remuneration paid in consideration of past employment, and any amounts (other than those referred to above) derived by a person who is a resident of a contracting state, shall be taxable only in that state.

(l) Government services

In terms of article 19, remuneration (other than pensions) paid by one state to an individual for services rendered to that state, subdivision or authority in respect of services rendered to the state is exempt from tax in the other state. However, if the individual is not resident in that other state, and either is a national of such state or did not become a resident of that state solely for the purposes of rendering services, the income is only taxable where the services are rendered.

(m) Students

In terms of article 20, payments received by a student or business apprentice from one state, who is present in the other state solely for the purposes of his or her education or training, for the purpose of his or her maintenance, education or training, and who is or immediately before being so present was a resident of the other contracting state, are exempt from tax.

(n) Other income

In terms of article 21 any income not otherwise dealt with in the agreement, which is derived by a resident of one state who is subject to tax on that income in the state of residence, may be subjected to tax only in that state. However, where the income arises in the other contracting state, it may also be taxed in the state in which the income arises.

14.4.10 Tax havens and harmful tax competition

In 1998 the OECD published a report[150] which noted that tax-haven jurisdictions and harmful preferential tax regimes have harmful tax practices that may lead to the depletion of other countries' tax bases. [151]

According to the OECD a tax haven is described as a jurisdiction actively making itself available for the avoidance of tax that would have been paid in high-tax countries.[152] Tax-haven jurisdictions are characterised by high levels of secrecy in the banking and commercial sectors. People who transact business

---

[150] OECD 'Harmful Tax Competition: An Emerging Global Issue' (OECD Publications 1998); Diamond & Diamond *Tax Havens* 13.

[151] OECD 'Harmful Tax Competition' para 75; Oguttu AW 'A Critique on the OECD Campaign Against Tax Havens: Has It Been Successful? A South African Perspective' (2010) 21 *Stell LR* 172–174; Spitz B & Clarke G *Offshore Service* (Butterworths 2002) OECD/3.

[152] OECD 'Issues in International Taxation No 1: International Tax Avoidance and Evasion' (1987) 20; Ginsberg *Tax Havens* 5–6.

in or through tax-haven jurisdictions are therefore assured of confidentiality.[153] This makes it difficult for foreign tax authorities to ascertain the identity of the relevant investors for the purposes of collecting taxes. Tax-haven jurisdictions also lack transparency and effective exchange of information with other governments concerning the benefits taxpayers receive from the tax haven.[154]

Harmful preferential tax regimes can occur in both tax haven and high-tax jurisdictions. Harmful tax regimes are characterised by having no or low effective tax rates on income, the regimes are ring-fenced,[155] and there is a general lack of transparency and effective exchange of information with other countries.[156]

The 1998 OECD report pointed out that tax-haven jurisdictions and harmful preferential tax regimes distort financial and investment flows among countries.[157] The harmful tax practices of these havens undermine the integrity and fairness of tax structures; they discourage compliance by all taxpayers; they cause undesirable shifts of part of the tax burden to less mobile tax bases such as labour, property and consumption; and they increase the administrative costs and compliance burdens on tax authorities and taxpayers respectively.[158] In order to counter those harmful tax practices, the OECD made certain recommendations that countries may adopt in order to enhance the effectiveness of their domestic legislation in curbing offshore tax avoidance.[159]

The OECD recommended that countries should have rules concerning the reporting of international transactions and foreign operations of resident taxpayers and should exchange any information obtained under such rules. Further, that countries should adopt effective legislation to curb offshore tax avoidance. Such legislation includes 'controlled foreign company' legislation, 'transfer pricing' legislation (such as that recommended in the OECD Guidelines on Transfer Pricing) and 'thin capitalisation' legislation.[160] The OECD also recommended that in order to counter harmful tax competition, countries should review their laws, regulations and practices which govern access to banking information with a view to removing impediments to the access to such information by tax authorities.[161] Furthermore, OECD member countries are required to refrain from adopting new measures or strengthening existing measures (legislation and administrative practices) that constitute harmful tax practices. OECD member countries were called upon to produce

[153] Spitz & Clarke *Offshore Service* INT/7.

[154] OECD 'Harmful Tax Competition' para 79.

[155] The term 'ring-fencing' refers to the artificial demarcation or limitation of profits or losses for tax purposes, ignoring the corporate form of the taxable entity or restricting the application of particular provisions to transactions inside the ring fence. See Olivier & Honiball *International Tax* 579.

[156] Olivier & Honiball *International Tax* 562.

[157] OECD 'Harmful Tax Competition' para 75; Spitz & Clarke *Offshore Service* OECD/3.

[158] Ware & Roper *Offshore Insight* 27; Oguttu *Curbing Offshore Tax Avoidance* 33.

[159] OECD 'Harmful Tax Competition' 67–71.

[160] Oguttu *Curbing Offshore Tax Avoidance* 34.

[161] Spitz & Clarke *Offshore Service* OECD/12.

a list of tax-haven jurisdictions. It was also recommended that non-member countries like South Africa be associated with these recommendations. As a follow-up to the 1998 report, the OECD released another report in June 2000 in which it identified and listed jurisdictions with harmful preferential tax regimes.[162] The report called on the listed jurisdictions to commit themselves to principles of transparency and effective exchange of information or they would be regarded as uncooperative tax havens that present a threat not only to the tax systems of developed and developing countries but also to the integrity of international financial systems. The OECD published a document entitled 'Framework for a Collective Memorandum of Understanding on Eliminating Harmful Tax Practices',[163] which provides the jurisdictions identified as tax havens with guidelines required by the OECD to demonstrate their commitment to transparency, non-discrimination and effective co-operation. Since then the OECD has issued a number of progress reports regarding its onslaught on tax havens.

Although the OECD's recommendations are not binding in nature and apply only to member states, its project has shown the world that countries cannot encourage harmful tax practices without repercussions from the international community. Although South Africa is not a member country of the OECD, it was awarded OECD observer status in 2004.[164] It is important for South Africa to adhere to the OECD recommendations, since its recommendations and guidelines have become a globally accepted standard.[165] Indeed, as a result of the OECD initiatives on harmful tax competition, a number of OECD member countries have done away with their harmful preferential tax regimes. Furthermore, a large number of tax-haven jurisdictions have agreed to co-operate with the OECD and implement transparency and exchange of information standards. The OECD developed a 'Model Agreement on Exchange of Information on Tax Matters' (TIEAs) which is now being used by a number of countries and it forms the basis for several tax information exchange agreements between countries.[166] The Model Agreement seeks to promote international co-operation in tax matters through the exchange of information by making use of international standards on transparency and the effective exchange of information. In this regard South Africa signed TIEAs with a number of tax haven jurisdictions such as the Bahamas, Bermuda, Cayman Islands, Jersey and San Marino. The limitation though was that the standard of

[162] OECD 'Towards Global Tax Co-operation: Report of the 2000 Ministerial Council Meeting and Recommendations by the Committee on Fiscal Affairs: Progress in Identifying and Eliminating Harmful Tax Practices' (2000), available at http//www.oecd.org/dataoecd/9/61/2090192.pdf (last accessed 17 July 2009).

[163] OECD 'Framework for a Collective Memorandum of Understanding on Eliminating Harmful Tax Practices', available at http://www.olis.oecd.org/olis/2000doc.nsf/ c707a7b4806fa95c125685d005300b6/c125692700623b74c12569a100492e0c/$FILE/JT00100664.PDF (last accessed 10 July 2009).

[164] Olivier & Honiball *International Tax* 9; Oguttu (2010) 21 *Stell LR* 172 at 187.

[165] SARS Practice Note No 7 para 3.2.1.

[166] OECD 2004 Progress Report para 24; Oguttu (2010) 21 *Stell LR* 172 at 185.

exchange of information in TIEAs was upon request and required a country to first exhaust internal procedures before requesting information.[167]

The world has, however, become increasingly globalised, making it easier for all taxpayers to make, hold and manage investments through financial institutions outside of their country of residence. Countries realised that more co-operation between tax administrations was critical in the fight against tax evasion and avoidance in order to protect the integrity of tax systems. In 2013 the OECD approved automatic exchange of information as the new standard of exchanging information with respect to financial account information.[168] This standard was legislated in South Africa's Tax Administration Act. Section 1 of this Act defines 'international tax standard' as including the OECD Standard for Automatic Exchange of Financial Account Information in Tax Matters. In terms of s 3 of the of the Tax Administration Act, SARS is obliged to exchange information spontaneously to a competent authority of another state that complies with the requirements of the OECD standard.

14.4.11 The OECD BEPS project

Despite the above measures, over the years there arose public concern engineered by non-governmental organisations about multinational enterprises ('MNEs') paying little or no corporation tax in the countries they do business in. Examples cited, for instance, in a 2013 Report by UK House of Lords Committee on fiscal affairs include: Google, Amazon, Starbucks, Thames Water, Vodafone and Cadbury (before takeover by Kraft).[169]

In light of these developments, at the 2012 G20 leaders' summit in Mexico, the national leaders explicitly referred to 'the need to prevent base erosion and profit shifting'.[170] Responding to these concerns, in February 2013 the OECD released a Report entitled 'Addressing Base Erosion and Profit Shifting'.[171] The OECD noted that 'base erosion and profit shifting constitute a serious risk to tax revenues, tax sovereignty and tax fairness for OECD member countries and non-members alike'.[172] Subsequently, an action plan with 15 comprehensive actions was released by the OECD in July 2013.[173] The OECD explains that the gradual removal of trade barriers, and technological and telecommunication developments have encouraged MNEs to exploit the legal arbitrage opportunities due to asymmetries in the tax laws of different countries

[167] Paragraph 9(a) of the Commentary on Article 26(1).

[168] OECD 'Standard for Automatic Exchange of Financial Account Information: Common Reporting Standard' (2013) para 2, available at http://www.oecd.org/ctp/exchange-of-tax-information/automatic-exchange-financial-account-information-common-reporting-standard.pdf (last accessed 22 February 2018).

[169] UK House of Lords Committee on Fiscal Affairs 'Tackling Corporate Tax Avoidance in a Global Economy: Is a New Approach Needed?' (July 2013) – see summary.

[170] G20 Leaders Declaration (Los Cabos, Mexico 2012), available at http://g20mexico.org/images/stories/temp/G20_Leaders_Declaration_2012.pdf (last accessed on 3 August 2018).

[171] Ibid.

[172] Ibid.

[173] OECD 'Action Plan on Base Erosion and Profit Shifting' (2013) 13.

so as to minimise their global tax burdens.[174] The aggressive tax positions taken by these MNEs impact on countries' corporate income tax regimes since MNEs now represent a large proportion of global GDP.[175] Essentially, what is at stake is the integrity of corporate income tax.[176] The OECD further explains that BEPS is caused by the development of modern business models whereby MNEs have shifted from country-specific operating models to global models based on matrix management organisations and integrated supply chains that centralise several functions at a regional or global level.[177]

BEPS is also encouraged by the fact that the rules on the taxation of profits from cross-border activities have remained fairly unchanged, with the principles developed in the past still finding application in domestic and international tax rules. Domestic and international rules on the taxation of cross-border profits have not kept pace with those changes.[178] MNEs engaged in BEPS comply with the legal requirements of the countries involved, in that they use legal methods to circumvent the application of countries' tax law. As businesses increasingly integrate across borders, the tax rules often remain uncoordinated so businesses come up with structures which are technically legal but they take advantage of asymmetries in domestic and international tax rules.[179]

Governments have recognised this and also recognise that a change in this legal framework can only be achieved through international co-operation. For long, governments have acknowledged that the interaction of domestic tax systems can lead to overlaps in the exercise of taxing rights which can result in double taxation. So principles to address double taxation, domestic and international, were developed by the League of Nations in the 1920s, and are applied in double tax treaties.[180] However, the interaction of domestic tax systems can lead to double non-taxation of income. Many international tax concepts 'were built on the assumption that one country would forgo taxation because another country would be imposing tax. In the modern global economy, this assumption is not always correct, as planning opportunities may result in profits ending up untaxed anywhere.'[181]

The sources of the BEPS problem are not to be found in tax-haven jurisdictions alone. The activities that escape taxation take place in the high-tax countries. Thus, countries agreed that the correct starting point is the flawed structure and implementation of corporation tax in the high-tax countries themselves. It is primarily for governments to correct the flaws in the country's corporation tax regime and to pursue measures to make the international tax framework more rigorous.

174 Ibid.
175 Ibid.
176 OECD 'Action Plan on Base Erosion and Profit Shifting' (2013) 8.
177 OECD 'Action Plan on Base Erosion and Profit Shifting' (2013) 25.
178 OECD 'Action Plan on Base Erosion and Profit Shifting' (2013) 27–28.
179 OECD 'Action Plan on Base Erosion and Profit Shifting' (2013) 49.
180 OECD 'Addressing Base Erosion and Profit Shifting' (2013) 6.
181 Ibid.

The OECD noted that because many BEPS strategies take advantage of the interface between the tax rules of different countries, it may be difficult for any single country, acting alone, to fully address the issue. Unilateral and uncoordinated actions by governments responding in isolation could result in the risk of double – and possibly multiple – taxation for business. A comprehensive action plan had to be developed to provide countries with domestic and international instruments aimed at better aligning of the rights to tax with real economic activity. Though governments may have to provide unilateral solutions, there is value and necessity in providing an internationally co-ordinated approach. Collaboration and co-ordination will not only facilitate and reinforce domestic actions to protect tax bases, but it will also be key to providing comprehensive international solutions that may satisfactorily respond to the issue.[182] A holistic approach has to be adopted in order to properly address the issue of BEPS, and government actions should be comprehensive and deal with all the different aspects of the issue.[183]

The OECD's 15 action measures to curtail BEPS are the following:

- address the challenges of base erosion as a result of the digital economy;
- neutralise the effects of hybrid mismatch arrangements; this covers:
  - hybrid instruments; and
  - hybrid entities;
- strengthen CFC rules and develop recommendations regarding the design of CFC rules;
- limit base erosion via interest deductions and other financial payments;
- counter harmful tax practices of preferential regimes taking into account transparency and substance;
- prevent treaty abuse (treaty shopping) as a result of conduit company arrangements;
- prevent the artificial avoidance of PE status;
- ensure transfer pricing outcomes are in line with value creation with regard to moving intangibles among group members;
- ensure transfer pricing outcomes are in line with value creation with regard to transferring risks and allocating excessive capital to group members;
- ensure transfer pricing outcomes are in line with value creation with regard to other high-risk transactions;
- ensure transparency by establishing methodologies to collect and analyse data on BEPS and the actions to address it;
- require taxpayers to disclose their aggressive tax-planning arrangements;
- re-examine transfer pricing documentation;

---

182 Ibid.

183 OECD 'Addressing Base Erosion and Profit Shifting' (2013) 7–8.

- make dispute resolution mechanisms more effective by improving the effectiveness of the Mutual Agreement Procedure; and
- develop a multilateral instrument.

The aim of the 15-point action measures is to ensure that profits are taxed where economic activities generating the profits are performed and where value is created. The results of the OECD work are ultimately expected to be reflected in a variety of forms, including:

- changes in the OECD Model Tax Convention;
- changes in the OECD transfer pricing guidelines;
- amendments to bilateral and multilateral agreements to be considered by countries; and
- changes in domestic tax laws and administration policies by individual countries.

At this stage, it is not known the extent to which the action points will result in realistic action by each country's tax authorities.

However, internationally, there is ongoing political debate in many countries on how to implement these measures. South Africa is a member[184] of the OECD inclusive framework for monitoring BEPS implementation with interested countries, participating on an equal footing.[185] In South Africa, in July 2013, the then Minister of Finance appointed a tax review committee, namely the Davis Tax Committee ('DTC'),[186] to inquire into the role of South Africa's tax system in the promotion of inclusive economic growth, employment creation, development and fiscal sustainability. The DTC was expected to take into account recent domestic and international developments and, in particular, the long-term objectives of the National Development Plan. On the international front, the DTC was required to address concerns about 'base erosion and profit shifting' (BEPS), especially in the context of corporate income tax, as identified by the OECD and G20. [187] In this regard, the DTC set up a BEPS sub-committee, which issued its first interim report on 30 September 2014.[188] On 2 September 2016, the DTC submitted its final recommendations on BEPS to the Minister of Finance. A number of the DTC's recommendations regarding preventing BEPS in South Africa have been enacted into law. For example, legislation regarding Action 13, on country-by-country reporting, has been enacted in South Africa. Section 3*(b)* of the Tax Administration Act[189] provides for the country-by-country reporting standard and s 257 provides for the relevant regulations. In 2016, country-by-country reporting regulations were enacted.[190]

---

[184] OECD 'Members of the Inclusive Framework on BEPS'.

[185] OECD/20 BEPS Project 'Addressing the Tax Challenges of the Digital Economy' Action 1 (2015) 3.

[186] The DTC 'About us – Our Terms of Reference', available at http://www.taxcom.org.za/termsofreference.html (last accessed 17 May 2016).

[187] Ibid.

[188] The DTC 'Library', available at http://www.taxcom.org.za/ (last accessed 12 May 2015).

[189] Tax Administration Act 28 of 2011 as amended by Tax Administration Laws Amendment Act 16 of 2016.

[190] *GG* 40516 of 23 December 2016.

Index

D

F

N

www.ingramcontent.com/pod-product-compliance
Lightning Source LLC
Chambersburg PA
CBHW081210220326
41598CB00037B/6737

* 9 7 8 1 4 8 5 1 2 8 0 8 3 *